ASP.NET 2.0 Website Pi
Problem - Design - So

Marco Bellinaso

WILEY

Wiley Publishing, Inc.

ASP.NET 2.0 Website Programming
Problem - Design - Solution

Published by
Wiley Publishing, Inc.
10475 Crosspoint Boulevard
Indianapolis, IN 46256
www.wiley.com

Copyright © 2006 by Wiley Publishing, Inc., Indianapolis, Indiana

ISBN-13: 978-0-7645-8464-0
ISBN-10: 0-7645-8464-2

Manufactured in the United States of America

10 9 8 7 6 5 4

1B/RW/RR/QW/IN

For general information on our other products and services please contact our Customer Care Department within the United States at (800) 762-2974, outside the United States at (317) 572-3993 or fax (317) 572-4002.

Library of Congress Cataloging-in-Publication Data
Bellinaso, Marco.
  ASP.NET 2.0 Website programming : problem-design-solution / Marco Bellinaso.
    p. cm.
  ISBN-13: 978-0-7645-8464-0 (paper/website)
  ISBN-10: 0-7645-8464-2 (paper/website)
 1. Active server pages. 2. Microsoft .NET. 3. Web sites—Design. 4. Internet programming. I. Title: ASP.NET 2.0 Web site programming. II. Title.
  TK5105.8885.A26B465 2006
  005.2'76—dc22

                    2006007382

Credits

Senior Acquisitions Editor
Jim Minatel

Development Editor
Rosanne Koneval

Technical Editor
Eric Engler

Production Editor
William A. Barton

Copy Editor
Luann Rouff

Editorial Manager
Mary Beth Wakefield

Production Manager
Tim Tate

Vice President and Executive Group Publisher
Richard Swadley

Vice President and Executive Publisher
Joseph B. Wikert

Graphics and Production Specialists
Carrie A. Foster
Lynsey Osborn
Alicia B. South

Quality Control Technicians
John Greenough
Joe Niesen
Brian H. Walls

Project Coordinator
Ryan Steffen

Media Development Specialists
Angela Denny
Kit Malone
Travis Silvers

Proofreading and Indexing
Techbooks

About the Author

Marco Bellinaso is a partner of Code Architects Srl, an Italian company that specializes in consulting, mentoring, development, and training for the Microsoft platform. He works as a senior consultant and developer, and has a particular interest in all "web-things." He focuses on designing and implementing large web sites with a variety of Microsoft products and technologies, including SharePoint 2003, MCMS, and, of course, ASP.NET 2.0 and SQL Server 2005. He's been working with the .NET Framework since the Beta 1 on applications of all types, including Web Services, Windows Forms, and Windows Services. He is also author or co-author of a number of commercial tools for developers, such as the award-winning VBMaximizer add-in, CodeBox for .NET, and FormMaximizer for .NET. Before the .NET era, Marco was a hardcode VB developer who specialized in Windows programming with advanced, low-level API techniques, as well as a COM and ASP developer.

Prior to this book, Marco co-authored a number of other Wrox Press books, including *Fast Track ASP.NET, Visual C# .NET: A Guide for VB6 Developers, Beginning C#*, and the previous edition of this book for ASP.NET 1.1. He also frequently writes for programming magazines such as *MSDN Magazine, MSDN Online, Visual Studio Magazine*, and other Italian magazines such as Computer Programming and Visual Basic & .NET Journal. He is one of the principal developers and editors behind www.dotnet2themax.com, a popular web site for .NET developers that was sired by the even more famous www.vb2themax.com site for VB6. Besides writing, he also does a lot of public speaking (both in English and Italian) at some of the most important Italian conferences organized by Microsoft Italy and other big companies.

If you want to contact Marco to talk about the book, about beer and pubs, or about work-related questions, please use the form on his site (www.dotnet2themax.com) or his blog (www.dotnet2the max.com/blogs/mbellinaso).

Acknowledgments

Wow, I can't believe I'm writing the acknowledgments for this book . . . it means I'm actually done! It has been several years since my last book, and at first it was very difficult to again start writing a book this long in English. Quite a few people deserve credit for helping me complete this book, and it's my great pleasure to say thank you to them. First of all, the two people that I constantly kept in touch with throughout the entire development of the book, which lasted seven months: Eric Engler and Rosanne Koneval. Eric was my technical reviewer, but he did much more than verify the accuracy of the technical details and the code; he actually added more information where required and polished a lot of my prose. I consider him more as a co-author than a tech reviewer. Rosanne was the development editor, who improved my writing even further, making it much more readable and clear. She also tried to ensure I kept the book on schedule. Unfortunately, I wasn't very good at that, but I sincerely thank Rosanne for always being understating and supportive, even when I didn't deserve it. Jim Minatel, the acquisitions editor, was also great in helping to define the overall structure and content of the book, and often provided suggestions to improve it in various ways. What I appreciated most in all three of these people is the fact that they always gave me the impression that they really believed in the project and liked it. I can assure you that this means a lot, especially in moments when you aren't really in the mood for writing.

Besides Wrox, there are two people to whom I owe so many thanks for a lot of things: Francesco Balena and Giuseppe Dimauro. Francesco is probably the greatest author and speaker I can think of, and also the smartest programmer. He always surprises me with the beauty, elegance, and effectiveness of the algorithms and programs he writes to solve very complex problems. Giuseppe is equally impressive for many reasons, but above all for his unique ability to master any technology or product in no time; he can then use his endless knowledge to quickly produce incredibly scalable and robust enterprise applications that integrate many systems and technologies. All of this regularly impresses the clients and colleagues who work with them. Together, they make the best pair of developers, consultants, authors, and speakers I could desire to know. Having the luck to not only know them personally, but also to be a partner in the company they founded (Code Architects) is something I wouldn't have even dreamed about until a short time ago. Guys, you're impressive, and you are the examples I follow to learn and do something good every day in my professional life.

I can't forget Maria Teresa D'Alessandro, a manager and partner in Code Architects, for allowing me to work on the book when there was so much to be done on a multitude of big projects, and for putting me back into great projects now that I'm done with it.

Other people I must say thank you to are all the consultants who work with or around Code Architects, or have some relationship with us, for providing so many useful suggestions, tips, and insights on every technology, product, and issue I face during my work. In particular, Alberto Falossi is the one I consult about Visio and UML, Enrico Sabbadin is the Enterprise Architecture guru, and Eugenio La Mesa is the one with all the marketing- and business-related answers. As for ASP.NET itself, I had the help of the best among the best: Dino Esposito. He always (and promptly) replied to all my questions, even to the strangest ones, and even when I contacted him at 3:00 A.M. and expected some nasty curse in return.

Finally, I want to thank my readers for taking this book in your hands and using it. I hope it will be as useful and enjoyable to you as it was for me to develop and write.

Contents

Contents

Contents

Contents

Contents

Foreword

The opportunity to write a foreword is always a great honor, and when the author is someone you have worked elbow-to-elbow with, it's more than an honor; it's a great pleasure! As readers, you are probably eager to get into the following chapters, and aren't particularly interested in when and how I met Marco, but I believe this story is worth telling.

In late 1990s I started www.vb2themax.com, a web site that quickly became popular among VB6 aficionados. After a few months, Marco began to e-mail me his articles, and it was soon clear to me that he was a smart developer who also had the rare gift of being able to put his experience down in words.

After a couple of years, I decided to write a commercial VB6 add-in and asked Marco to give me a hand. Marco accepted, and in a few months we would launch VBMaximizer, a product that was later voted among the best productivity tools by the readers of *Visual Basic Programmer's Journal* (now *Visual Studio Magazine*). The noteworthy detail of this story is that Marco and I worked on this project exclusively via e-mail, without even talking to each other on the phone. I never needed to explain to him what I needed, and, unbelievably, the code I got from him was virtually defect-free at the first attempt! At the time I didn't know that Marco was only about 20 years old; otherwise, I would have been *far* more impressed!

I physically met Marco a few years later, and since then we have worked together on many other software projects. I continue to be pleasantly surprised by the professionalism he exhibits in everything he does, be it a program, a conference session, an article, or an entire book. Marco is among the few people I know who doesn't really care how long it takes to complete a task, provided that the result is something he can be proud of. Well, the book you're reading is surely something he can be proud of!

As the author explains in his own introduction, this book is different from most others you can find in bookstores. Most are reference books that dissect every little detail of version 2.0 of ASP.NET or the .NET Framework and—in the best cases—provide a short listing to illustrate each feature. (I am well acquainted with these books, having written many reference guides myself.)

Marco's book has a radically different approach: He explains how you can assemble all ASP.NET 2.0's features and leverage its power to design, develop, and deploy a full-featured web site. Don't be fooled by the TheBeerHouse being a fictitious site for a fictitious customer: If the main differences between a sample application and a real-world web site are the performance, security, robustness, scalability, and care for details that you expect from a commercial site, then Marco's TheBeerHouse is *more* real-world than most real-world sites I have seen recently.

In fact, unlike most real site authors, Marco was able to take all the time he needed to implement an impressive list of features and fix all the bugs he encountered. And unlike most sample application authors, he never took a shortcut and never ignored the problems that developers have to solve every day in the real world. Chapters 5 and 9, on articles/news management and the e-commerce module, took him longer than any other portion of the book. As a result of his scrupulous efforts, the overall quality exceeds what you might expect from a mere "book sample," and it's currently the best demonstration of ASP.NET 2.0's new features, including Microsoft's own starter kits.

Foreword

From a teaching perspective, the great value of this book is the rationale underlying all the design and implementation decisions taken in the development phase. Marco does more than just describe what he did; he lists the pros and cons of all the alternatives he tried out and explains how he found the perfect solution (or the best compromise) to each problem. It's like having an expert sitting beside you, able to read your mind, and ready to fix your mistakes before you have a chance to make them. Can you ask for more?

Francesco Balena
Code Architects Srl, co-founder
Blog: www.dotnet2themax.com/blogs/fbalena

Introduction

Dear reader, thanks for picking up this book, and welcome to the new edition of *ASP.NET Website Programming Problem – Design – Solution,* fully updated to ASP.NET version 2.0! The idea for this book was born in 2001, with ASP.NET 1.0, from the desire to have a book that teaches how to create real-world web sites. The first edition was published in 2002, and fortunately it was a success. I believe that this was due to the fact that most ASP.NET books on the market were (and still are) reference-type books, which describe every single control of the framework, and all their methods and properties, but the examples they provide are single-page demos showing how to use a control of a feature. However, typically these references don't show how to integrate all ASP.NET features and controls into a single site with rich functionality, which is what readers have to do at work. Designing and implementing a real-world site is very different from creating simple examples, and that's why I think a book like this is helpful for developers facing real problems in their everyday work.

This new edition of the book was rewritten completely from scratch, to use all the new features of ASP.NET 2.0 as much as possible, and it is hoped that it is better in a number of ways: The project developed is much more complete (there's an e-commerce module, for example) and professional, and each chapter provides enough background information on ASP.NET 2.0 to comfortably read the chapter even if you haven't already had experience with ASP.NET 2.0 (this is something the first edition didn't provide).

First of all, this book is aimed at describing, designing, and implementing a site much like the ones you're probably working on or will be soon, while taking the opportunity to introduce and explain many of the new features that the new great ASP.NET 2.0 Framework offers. I don't hide difficult problems so that the solution can be simpler and shorter to develop; rather, I try to explain most of the problems you'll typically face when writing a modern web site, and provide one or more solutions for them. The result is a web site that features a layout with user-selectable themes, a membership system, a content management system for publishing and syndicating articles and photos, polls, mailing lists, forums, an e-commerce store with support for real-time credit card processing, home page personalization, and localization (refer to Chapter 1 for a more detailed list of features to be implemented). I hope you enjoy reading this book, and that it offers guidance that speeds up the development of your next project and makes it more solid, extensible, and well organized.

> **You can browse the web site online at** www.dotnet2themax.com/thebeerhouse.
>
> **The author's blog is available at** http://www.dotnet2themax.com/blogs/ mbellinaso. **Please keep an eye on it to read about further development and expansion of the sample project.**

What This Book Covers

This book is basically a large case study that starts from the foundation and works its way through to completion with a series of designs and solutions for each incremental step along the way. What sets the Problem-Design-Solution series apart from other Wrox series is the structure of the book and the start-to-finish approach to one completed project. Specifically, this book leads the reader through the development of a complete ASP.NET 2.0 web site that has most of the features users expect to find in a modern content-related and e-commerce site:

❑ Account registration, personalization, and themes

❑ News and events, organized into categories

❑ Opinion polls

❑ Newsletter

❑ Forums

❑ E-commerce store with shopping cart and order management

❑ Localization

From an administrative point of view, the following features and problems are also covered:

❑ Full online back-end administrative section, to manage practically all data from an intuitive user interface

❑ Site deployment

The implementation of each of these features provides the opportunity to teach various new features introduced by ASP.NET 2.0, such as the following:

❑ Master pages

❑ Themes

❑ Personalization and Web Parts

❑ Membership and profile modules

❑ Personalization

❑ The new server-side UI controls such as `GridView`, `DetailsView`, `FormView`, `Wizard`, `MultiView`, the new `xxxDataSource` and navigation controls, among others

❑ The new compilation and deployment modes

❑ The new framework for instrumenting the site, as well as handling and logging exceptions

❑ The new ADO.NET 2.0 features (e.g., caching with database dependency)

❑ The new classes for easy distributed transactions management

Not only does this book cover the new features of ASP.NET 2.0, it also demonstrates how to integrate all of them together, for the development of a single full-featured site. All the design options are explained and discussed (including the database design, the data access and business logic components design, and the overall site architecture); at the end of the book you will have learned many of the best practices for web development, based on a solid, scalable, and extensible architecture.

How This Book Is Structured

The book builds a complete project from start to finish. All the chapters (other than the first one) are self-contained modules within the larger project, and are structured in three sections:

❑ **Problem:** This defines the problem or problems to be addressed in the chapter: What do you want to do in this chapter? What features do you want to add to the site and why are they important? What restrictions or other factors need to be taken into account?

❑ **Design:** After the problem is defined adequately, this section describes what features are needed to solve the problem. This will give you a broad idea of how the solution will work or what will be entailed in solving the problem.

❑ **Solution:** After setting up what you are going to accomplish and why (and how that solves the problem defined earlier), we will produce and discuss the code and any other material that will realize the design and solve the problem laid out at the beginning of the chapter. Just as the coverage of the book as a whole is weighted toward solution, so is each chapter. This is where you will get hands-on practice and create the code.

The book is intended to be read from cover to cover, so that you start with nothing and finish with a complete and deployed web site ready to be launched. However, the book follows a modular structure, so every chapter is quite self-contained and implements a module that, if necessary, can be taken out of the proposed sample project and re-used in some other web site.

Who This Book Is For

Let me state up front that this isn't a book for completely novice programmers, or for experienced developers that have never touched ASP.NET and the .NET Framework in general. This book teaches how to write a real-world web site from scratch to deployment, and as such it can't explain every single detail of the technology, but must concentrate on designing and writing actual solutions. To comfortably read this book, you should already have had some experience with ASP.NET 1.x, even if not advanced solutions. You're not required to know ASP.NET 2.0, as each chapter will introduce the new controls and features that you'll use in that chapter, providing enough background information to implement the solution. If you then want to go deeper and learn everything you can about a control, you can refer to the MSDN official documentation or to another reference-type book such as Wrox's *Professional ASP.NET 2.0*.

What You Need to Use This Book

To follow the book by building the project on your own computer, or to run the downloadable and ready-to-use project, you'll need the following:

- ❏ Windows XP Professional, Windows Server 2003, or Windows 2000 Professional or Server

- ❏ Any edition of Visual Studio 2005 for the C# language, including the freely available Visual Web Developer 2005 Expression Edition. However, Visual Studio 2005 Standard is suggested. You'll be able to follow the book, and run the sample project, even if you don't use a Microsoft editor at all (if, for example, you prefer using Macromedia Dreamweaver MX or some other text editor), because Visual Studio's designers are described and demonstrated in the "Design" section of some chapters, but are not used to write the code in the "Solution" section.

- ❏ The freely available SQL Server 2005 Express Edition, and possibly SQL Server 2005 Standard Edition (in addition to the Express Edition, which is used until the last chapter)

Conventions

To help you get the most from the text and keep track of what's happening, we've used a number of conventions throughout the book.

> **Boxes like this one hold important, not-to-be-forgotten information that is directly relevant to the surrounding text.**

Tips, hints, tricks, and asides to the current discussion are offset and placed in italics like this.

As for styles in the text:

- ❏ We *highlight* new terms and important words when we introduce them.
- ❏ We show keyboard strokes like this: Ctrl+A.
- ❏ We show filenames, URLs, and code within the text like so: `persistence.properties`.
- ❏ We present code in two different ways:

```
In code examples we highlight new and important code with a gray background.
The gray highlighting is not used for code that's less important in the present
context, or has been shown before.
```

Source Code

As you work through the examples in this book, you may choose either to type in all the code manually or to use the source code files that accompany the book. All of the source code used in this book is available for download at `www.wrox.com`. Once at the site, simply locate the book's title (either by using the Search box or by using one of the title lists) and click the Download Code link on the book's details page to obtain all the source code for the book.

Because many books have similar titles, you may find it easiest to search by ISBN; this book's ISBN is 0-7645-8464-2 (changing to 978-0-7645-8464-0 as the new industrywide 13-digit ISBN numbering system is phased in by January 2007).

Once you download the code, just decompress it with your favorite compression tool. Alternately, you can go to the main Wrox code download page at www.wrox.com/dynamic/books/download.aspx to see the code available for this book and all other Wrox books.

Errata

We make every effort to ensure that there are no errors in the text or in the code. However, no one is perfect, and mistakes do occur. If you find an error in one of our books, such as a spelling mistake or faulty piece of code, we would be very grateful for your feedback. By sending in errata you may save another reader hours of frustration, and at the same time you will be helping us provide even higher quality information.

To find the errata page for this book, go to www.wrox.com and locate the title using the Search box or one of the title lists. Then, on the book details page, click the Book Errata link. On this page you can view all errata that has been submitted for this book and posted by Wrox editors. A complete book list including links to each book's errata is also available at www.wrox.com/misc-pages/booklist.shtml.

If you don't spot "your" error on the Book Errata page, go to www.wrox.com/contact/tech support.shtml and complete the form there to send us the error you have found. We'll check the information and, if appropriate, post a message to the book's errata page and fix the problem in subsequent editions of the book.

p2p.wrox.com

For author and peer discussion, join the P2P forums at p2p.wrox.com. The forums are a web-based system for you to post messages relating to Wrox books and related technologies and to interact with other readers and technology users. The forums offer a subscription feature to e-mail you topics of interest of your choosing when new posts are made to the forums. Wrox authors, editors, other industry experts, and your fellow readers are present on these forums.

At http://p2p.wrox.com you will find a number of different forums that will help you not only as you read this book, but also as you develop your own applications. To join the forums, just follow these steps:

1. Go to p2p.wrox.com and click the Register link.
2. Read the terms of use and click Agree.
3. Complete the required information to join as well as any optional information you wish to provide and click Submit.
4. You will receive an e-mail with information describing how to verify your account and complete the joining process.

You can read messages in the forums without joining P2P but in order to post your own messages, you must join.

Once you join, you can post new messages and respond to messages other users post. You can read messages at any time on the Web. If you would like to have new messages from a particular forum e-mailed to you, click the Subscribe to this Forum icon by the forum name in the forum listing.

For more information about how to use the Wrox P2P, be sure to read the P2P FAQs for answers to questions about how the forum software works as well as many common questions specific to P2P and Wrox books. To read the FAQs, click the FAQ link on any P2P page.

Introducing the Project: TheBeerHouse

This chapter introduces the project that we're going to develop in this book. I'll explain the concept behind the sample web site that is the subject of this book, but as you read along you should keep in mind that this is a general-purpose, data-driven, content-based style of web site that can easily be modified to meet the needs of a myriad of real-world web site requirements. Although we'll use many of the older features of ASP.NET, the clear focus of this book is directed at showing you how to leverage the powerful new features of ASP.NET 2.0 in a real-world, non-trivial web site.

This book follows a "Problem–Design–Solution" approach in each chapter: The Problem section explains the business requirements for the module designed in that chapter, the Design section is used to develop our roadmap for meeting those requirements, and the Solution section is where we write the code to implement our design. This is unlike traditional computer books because the focus is not on teaching basic concepts, but rather showing you how to apply your knowledge to solve real-world business requirements. If you are new to ASP.NET, then this is perhaps not the best book to start with, but if you're generally familiar with the basic concepts of web development and ASP.NET (any version of ASP.NET), you're ready to put that knowledge to use, and perhaps you want to learn about the new features in ASP.NET 2.0, then fasten your seat belt!

Problem

In Bologna (the city where I live in Italy) almost half the population consists of students, including many foreigners. With all these young people around here, it goes without saying that there are a lot of pubs and places to spend the evenings and weekends with friends. Concerts, parties, shows, and other special events are commonplace. However, with all this competition, every pub must find something that the others don't have, something that's somehow appealing to their potential customers. Marketing plays a significant role, and our pub owner wants to be stronger in that area. She has always used traditional, printed marketing ads for her pub *TheBeerHouse* (a fictitious name), but she wants to expand into new media possibilities, starting with having her own exciting web site. She thinks that this would be useful, because once customers become familiar with the site they can go there to read about new specials and events, and possibly receive a newsletter right in their e-mail inbox, as well as browse photos of past events, rate them, and share messages with other web site visitors, creating virtual relationships that they can later continue face-to-face right in the pub! The general idea is appealing, especially considering that the target audience is well accustomed to using computers and browsing the web to find out information about news and events. A pub is typically a fun place full of life, and it's perhaps more appropriate for this type of project, rather than, say, a classic restaurant. However, even classic restaurants may like to consider this type of web site, also.

Design

The Design section of each chapter is devoted to discussing the problem and designing a solution. This usually means writing down a list of business requirements and desired features to implement, as well as the design of the necessary database objects for the data storage, and the structure of the classes to retrieve, manipulate, and present the data to the user. At the beginning of a project you start out by thinking about your client's needs, and how you might meet those needs, and possibly even expand on them to give your client more functionality than the minimum needed, while still staying within your time limits and budgetary guidelines. As stated in the problem section, your client in this scenario is a pub owner who wants to have a web site to promote her pub, providing online information about upcoming events, reports about past events, and more. This initial idea can be expanded in many ways, to create a site that has a lot more interesting things, good for its users (who are also potential customers for the physical pub) and for the store owner. We can begin by writing down a list of features that a modern content-based site should have, and a few reasons why they are useful:

❑ An appealing user interface. Appearance is important, since it's the first thing users will notice — well before appreciating the site's functionality and services. But the graphics are not all that matters regarding the UI. The information on the site must be well organized and easily reachable. The site must be usable and provide a good (and possibly great) user experience, which means that users must find it easy to browse and interact with. Some attention should also be given to cross-browser compatibility, i.e., ensuring that the site looks and behaves fine from different platforms and browsers. This is especially true for sites like this one, where you can't know in advance which browser your customers will use, as you might know in the case of an intranet site for a corporation, for example.

❑ A successful content-based site owes its popularity to its users. Loyal users who regularly visit the site, help write content, and participate in polls and special events are those who guarantee that the site will keep growing. To build a vibrant community of active members, users must have some sort of *identity*, something that describes and distinguishes them among other members. Because of this, the site needs a registration feature, as part of a larger authentication/authorization infrastructure. This will also be used to grant and restrict access to some areas of the site.

❑ The site needs a constant supply of fresh content to stay alive and vibrant. If the content becomes stale, visitors will lose interest in the site and won't visit it anymore. A pub's site can't be very good unless it has regular updates about upcoming events, parties, and concerts. What's the point in visiting the site if it doesn't display photos that were shot at the last party? To facilitate a constant stream of new content, the site needs some mechanism that enables the editor to easily update it with dynamic content. Furthermore, the editor who will be in charge of the content updates will probably not be a technical person, so you must build some simple administration pages that make updates easy, even for nontechnical people.

❑ Once the site has new content ready to be read, the site's manager must have some way to inform its users about this. Not all users visit the site every day, so the site manager must be proactive and notify the customers about recent updates. If customers have registered on the site, providing their e-mail address, they might also have requested to receive a newsletter notifying them about recent changes and additions to the site. Of course, there are also other ways to syndicate news, such as exposing Really Simple Syndication (RSS) feeds to which a user can register and then control from their favorite RSS reader, and get automatic notifications about news without having to visit the site daily to get the information.

❑ A site like this can also be a good opportunity to get feedback from customers about a variety of issues: What do they like most in a pub? What brand of beer do they prefer? Do they want to listen to live music while drinking with friends, or perhaps they don't like all that noise? Establishing some kind of user-to-site communication is important, and if you get a good number of responses it can even lead to strategic decisions and changes that may improve the business.

❑ If the presence of some sort of user-to-site communication is important, user-to-user communication may be even more so, because that's the central point of creating a community of loyal users, who come to the site frequently to chat, discuss the news posted on the site, ask suggestions to the others about upcoming events, and more. This translates into more traffic on the site, and a feeling of membership that will pay off in both the short and long run.

❑ Once the store has a discreet user base, the store's owner may decide to expand it so that it supports an online store. In fact, the pub already offers a catalog of products for beer enthusiasts, such as glasses, T-shirts, key chains, and more. If the site has a lot of traffic, it may be a good way to promote these products so people can place orders without even visiting the pub in person. And once users see a product and like it, they can rate that product to tell other people how much they like it. The online store must be easy to manage by nontechnical people, because it might possibly be the pub's owner who adds and edits products, and manages the orders, so there must be a module with a simple and intuitive UI that automates as many operations as possible, and guides the user through the tasks.

❑ With the site offering news and articles, lists of products, user-to-user discussions, and other dynamic content, it's easy to imagine that the home page could easily become crowded, and possibly more difficult to read and understand because of too much information. It would be good if the user herself could build her own home page, according to what she is interested in. Maybe she wants to read about upcoming events, but doesn't care about shopping online for gadgets? Great, we want to give her the capability to do that, by adding and deleting content to and from the home page, or maybe just moving around the existing content so that it's placed and organized in a way that she finds more comfortable and useful for her. This type of customization is done on some large sites such as Windows Live and My MSN, for example, and is a great example of personalization, which helps encourage users to decide to register on the site.

❑ As mentioned previously, the pub is typically visited by a lot of customers coming from many different countries, and the pub's owner expects the same to happen for the web site. Because of this, the site must be partially or fully translated into multiple languages, making it easy for most users to understand it. Not only text must be translated; information such as dates and numbers should also be displayed according to the user's preferred locale settings, so that nobody will misunderstand an announcement about an upcoming party or event.

To recap everything in a few words, the TheBeerHouse site will have everything a modern content-based site will have, including dynamic articles and news, polls for user-to-site communication, forums for user-to-user communication, newsletters and RSS feeds to notify members about new content on the site, an e-commerce store for selling products online, home page personalization, and content localization.

Although the sample project is built around a fictitious pub, you'll recognize in this list of requirements the common features of the majority of content- and commerce-based sites you find online now, and sites that you're likely to develop in the near future, or maybe even sites you're developing right now.

Solution

The Solution section of each chapter will contain the instructions and actual code for implementing all the features and requirements outlined and designed in the previous sections. For this first chapter, however, I'll give you a more detailed description of exactly what the following chapters will cover, so that you can get a good idea of what the final result will be like.

In Chapter 2 you'll build the site's design, the graphics, and the layout that's shared among all pages of the site, through the use of master pages, new in ASP.NET 2.0. You will also use themes — another new feature introduced by ASP.NET 2.0 — to create a couple of different visual appearances for the same master page, and create a mechanism to enable users to select their own favorite theme from a dropdown list, so that they can change the colors and overall appearance of the site according to their taste and possible visual impediments. Finally, a flexible and easy to maintain navigation system will be built by means of the new `Web.sitemap` file and the `Menu` and `SiteMapPath` controls.

In Chapter 3 you'll lay down the foundations for building a flexible, easily configurable, and instrumented site. First of all, there will be a pluggable data access layer (DAL) that can support any type of data store, and scalable to offer the best performance even under high usage. Then a business logic layer will be built on the top of the DAL to expose the data in an object-oriented way, with the required validation logic, transaction management, event logging, and caching. Finally, you'll look at the UI and presentation layer, which takes advantage of the new `GridView`, `DetailsView`, and `FormView` controls and the companion `ObjectDataSource` to quickly generate complex and feature-rich, data-driven pages.

In Chapter 4 you'll integrate ASP.NET 2.0's new membership infrastructure into the site, to create user registration forms and supporting logic to authenticate/authorize users. You'll also discover the new `Profile` module, which allows you to declaratively define user-level properties that are automatically persisted to a durable medium, quite different from the well-known traditional `Session` state variables that only last as long as the user browses the site on one occasion. A complete management console will be built to enable administrators to see the list of members, disable members that behave badly on the site, and view and edit each user's profile.

In Chapter 5 you'll build a sort of Content Management System, a module that enables administrators to completely manage the site's articles from an intuitive UI, accessible also by nontechnical users. The module will integrate with the built-in membership system to secure the module and track the authors of the articles, and will have a syndication service that publishes an RSS feed of recent content for a specific category, or for every category, and will support ratings and comments, among many other features. The result will be quite powerful, enabling the editor to prepare richly formatted content in advance, and schedule it for automatic publication and retirement, so that the site's content updates are as simple as possible, and require the least effort and time. At the end of the chapter, you will have experienced almost everything you can do with the new `GridView`, `DetailsView`, and `ObjectDataSource` controls, which are used to bind the UI to data coming from real object-oriented business classes, which themselves obtain data from a data access layer.

In Chapter 6 you'll implement a solution for creating and managing multiple dynamic polls on the web site. It will feature an administration console for managing the polls through a web browser, a user control that enables you to plug different polls into any page you want with just a couple of lines of code, as well as a history page for viewing archived polls.

In Chapter 7 the site will be enriched with a complete module for sending out newsletters to members who registered for them in their profile page. The module will enable you to send out the e-mail newsletters from a background thread, instead of the main thread that processes the page request, so that the page won't risk timeouts, and more important, so that the editor will not be left with a blank page for minutes at a time. AJAX (Asynchronous JavaScript and XML Programming) will be used to implement partial-page updates that provide real-time feedback about the newsletter being sent in the background. Finally, end users will be able to look at past newsletters listed on an archive page. To implement all this, you'll use advanced features such as multi-threaded programming, the new script callback feature, and new classes for sending e-mails.

In Chapter 8 you'll create a forums system from scratch, which supports multiple subforums with optional moderation, lists threads and replies through custom pagination and with different sorting options, has wide support for standard RSS feeds, configurable user rating, signatures and quoting, and other features typical of most recent forum software. Complete administration features (deleting, editing, approving, moving, and closing threads and posts) will also be provided.

In Chapter 9 you'll add a working e-commerce store with most of the essential features, including a complete catalog and order management system, a persistent shopping cart, integrated online payment via credit cards, product ratings, product stock availability, rich formatting of a product's descriptions, including text and images, configurable shipping methods and order statuses, and much more. All this will be implemented in relatively few pages, since it will leverage the good foundations built in previous chapters, and of course the ASP.NET 2.0 built-in membership and profile systems, and other new features and controls, such as the ubiquitous `GridView`, `DetailsView`, and `ObjectDataSource`, plus the `Wizard` and `MultiView` controls.

In Chapter 10 you'll explore the Web Part Framework, one of the coolest and most striking new features of ASP.NET 2.0, and use it to easily add support for home page personalization. You'll promote some user controls developed earlier in the book into Web Parts, which are boxes of content that can be dragged around the page by the user, and whose properties can be customized at runtime by means of a simple and dynamically built UI, and which can be added and removed to/from pages according to the user's interests and preferences. You'll be impressed by the small amount of code needed to achieve a result that only advanced sites and portal framework (such as Windows SharePoint Services) have typically offered in the past.

In Chapter 11 you'll make the site's home page fully localizable to an additional language and will support the user's preferred locale settings when displaying dates and numbers. All this can now be done easily with ASP.NET 2.0, thanks to its automatic resource generation, implicit and explicit localization expressions, strongly typed and dynamically compiled global resources, and good Visual Studio designer support.

Finally, in Chapter 12 you'll look the different ways to deploy an ASP.NET 2.0 site, either on a local IIS server or to a remote production site, or to an inexpensive shared hosting server. The new ASP.NET compilation model enables you do use a simple `XCOPY` deployment that includes everything, but lacks protection of source code, and takes a little time to compile on first requests. If that's a problem for you, you will see how you can use the new command-line tools and Visual Studio's wizards to pre-compile the site and generate one or more compiled assemblies to deploy. You'll also learn how to deploy the local SQL Server Express database to a remote full-featured SQL Server 2005 instance, and how you can create installer packages for distributing the application to automate as many installation tasks as possible.

Summary

In this first chapter you were given an overview of an aggressive plan to develop a highly functional content-based web site that shows you how to use ASP.NET to its full capacity. I gave you a broad idea about what we're going to discuss, design, and implement throughout the rest of the book. In each chapter, you'll learn something new about ASP.NET 2.0, and at the end of the book you will also have created a real-world site with most of the features required by modern content-centric sites and e-commerce stores. Furthermore, the site you develop in this book may provide a good deal more functionality than any site you've designed in the past, and the relatively small development effort will enable you to do more than you thought possible in a small amount of time. Microsoft has stated that one of their key goals in the 2.0 release is to make a developer's job easier: to reduce the amount of effort required to implement common functionality, thereby giving them more time to focus on business needs, and enabling them to offer more advanced functionality to empower users and site administrators, while keeping the site maintainable and scalable. This book will help you judge whether Microsoft has met this goal. Let this adventure begin!

Developing the Site Design

The first step in developing a new site is to develop the visual site design consisting of the site's overall layout and use of graphics. This visual architecture defines the "look and feel" from the user's perspective. You start by establishing the user experience you want people to have, and then you design the plumbing behind the scenes that will provide that user experience. Some basic considerations that affect the user's experience are the menu and navigation, use of images, and the organization of elements on the page. The menu must be intuitive and should be augmented by navigation hints such as a site map or *breadcrumbs* that can remind users where they are, relative to the site as a whole. Breadcrumbs in this context refer to a set of small links on the page that form a trail that enables users to back up to a previous page by clicking on the link segment for a page higher in the page hierarchy.

You should consider the specific features included in ASP.NET 2.0 before writing any code, so you can take advantage of the work that's already been done by Microsoft. By laying a good foundation for the technical architecture, you can improve code reusability and enhance maintainability. This chapter looks at the overall visual layout of the site and explains how you can take advantage of powerful features such as master pages and themes. Master pages are used to group functionality into templates that provide the common elements shared by many pages, and themes enable users to customize certain aspects of the site to give them a unique look and feel that appeals to them (also called *skinning*).

Problem

Many developers start out writing source code without paying attention to the primary goal of the site: to provide a simple but highly functional graphical application for users to interact with. Developing the user interface seems like a very basic task, but if not done properly, you may have to revisit it several times during development. Every time you go back and change fundamental features it will require a certain amount of rework, not to mention a whole new round of unit and integration testing. Even worse, if you take the user interface too lightly, you will likely end up regretting it because users may choose not to visit your site. There are various elements to consider when creating the site design. First, you must convince yourself of one simple fact: appearance *is* important! You should repeat this out loud a couple of times. If your site doesn't look good, people may regret being there. It's easy for a developer to get caught up with the difficult tasks of organizing source code into classes and coding the business logic — the cosmetics of the site just don't seem so important, right? Wrong! The user interface is the first thing presented to the end user: If it is ugly, unclear, and basically unusable, chances are good the user will be left with a bad impression of the site and the company behind it. And, sadly, this will happen regardless of how fast and scalable the site is. In addition, you need to consider that not all users have the same opinion about a site template. Some users may find it difficult to read text in a site with a specific color scheme and prefer a different color scheme that might be unclear to many others. It's very difficult to make everybody happy with a single template and color scheme. That's why some sites have multiple color schemes and possible layouts available from which users can choose, enabling them to customize their own user experience according to their personal taste — and possibly physical impediments such as color blindness. Studies have shown that a surprising number of people suffer from partial color blindness that makes it hard for them to distinguish certain colors, so they must be able to select colors they can distinguish, but that still appear somewhat pleasant.

After you choose the layout and colors to use, you need to ensure that the site will look the same on different browsers. A couple of years ago, Internet Explorer (IE) was the absolute dominant browser among Windows users, and if you were developing a technical site targeted to Windows developers, you could assume that the majority of your user base would use IE to browse the site, and thus develop and test it only against IE. However, Mozilla Firefox is now gaining popularity among the Internetians and it is available to other operating systems, such as Linux and Mac OS. You are not targeting just a small niche of users (i.e., not just Windows developers, but all people that go to your client's pub), and because there are other popular browsers besides Windows, it is absolutely necessary to ensure that your site works well for the most popular browsers. If you ignore this and just target IE, Firefox users may come to the site and find a layout much different from what they would expect, with wrong alignments, sizes, and colors, with panels and text over others — in other words, a complete mess. As you can guess, a user who is presented such an ugly page would typically leave it, which means losing a potential client or customer for the online store. At the very least, this person's visit would have generated page views and thus banner impressions. Since you don't want to lose visitors, we'll consider both Internet Explorer and Firefox.

Designing the user interface layer doesn't mean just writing the HTML for a page; it also involves the navigation system, and the ability of the webmaster or site administrator (if not the end user) to easily change the appearance of the site without requiring them to edit the actual content pages (which are numerous). It is helpful to develop a system that enables people to easily change the menus of the site, and modify the site appearance (the fonts, the colors, and the size of the various parts that compose the page) because this minimizes the work of administrators and makes users happy. Once you're done with the site's home page, developing all the other pages will take much less time because the home page establishes layout and navigation elements that will apply throughout the site. And if you need to modify something in the site's layout (for example, adding a new poll box to be displayed on the right-hand side of any page) you will be able to do this easily if you've developed a common user interface shared among many pages. This is why it's definitely worth spending some additional time thinking about a well-designed UI foundation layer instead of firing up Visual Studio .NET and starting to code right away. This is really a strategic decision that can save you hours or even days of work later. Remember that fundamental changes applied later in the development phase will require more time and effort to implement.

Design

In this section I'll take the problems described in the first section and discuss how to solve them by devising a technical system design. In practice, you will design and implement the following:

❑ A good-looking graphical template (layout) that appears the same with Internet Explorer and Firefox, and a mechanism to dynamically apply different color schemes and other appearance attributes to it.

❑ A way to easily share the created template to all pages of the site, without physically copying and pasting the entire code to each page.

❑ A navigation system that enables you to easily edit the links shown in the site's menu, and clearly tells users where they currently are in the site map, enabling them to navigate backward.

❑ A way to apply not only a common design to all pages of the site, but also a common behavior, such as counting page views or applying the user's favorite style to the page.

I'll describe how you can utilize some of the new features in ASP.NET 2.0 when implementing your reusability, menu, navigation, and customization requirements. Later, in the "Solution," section, you'll put these powerful new features into action!

Designing the Site Layout

When you develop a site design you typically create a mock-up with a graphics application such as Adobe Photoshop or Jasc Paint Shop Pro to show you what the final site may look like before you do any specific layout or coding in HTML. Once you have a mock-up, you can show this around to the various model users, testers, and managers, who can then make a decision to proceed with coding. You might create a simple picture like the one shown in Figure 2-1, in which you show how the content will be laid out in the various areas of the page.

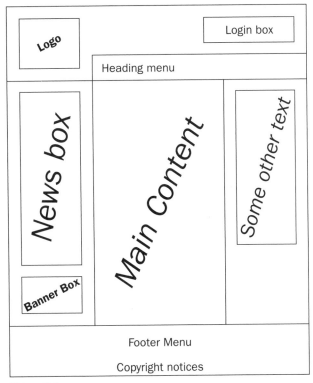

Figure 2-1

This is a typical three-column layout, with a header and footer. When the layout gets approved, you must recreate it with real graphics and HTML. Do this in the graphics program because, on average, it takes much less time for a web designer to produce these mock-ups as images, rather than real HTML pages. Once the client approves the final mock-up, the web designer can cut the mock-up image into small pieces and use them in an HTML page.

Creating a mock-up is not always easy for those of us who aren't very artistic by nature. I must admit that I'm one of the worst graphic artists I know. For a medium or large-size company, this is not a problem because there is usually someone else, a professional web designer, to create the graphical design, and then the developers (people like you and me) will build the application around it. Sometimes it can be helpful to enlist the assistance of a third-party company if you're faced with creating the graphical design by yourself — you can, in effect, subcontract that one aspect of the site to someone more artistically talented, and they can make you a site template. For the purpose of creating the web site discussed in this book, I used TemplateMonster (www.templatemonster.com) to create a good-looking site design that I could use as a starting point. They provided the design as PSD files (to be opened with Photoshop or Paint Shop Pro), JPEG files, and some HTML pages with the images already cut in slices and positioned using HTML tables. I found that it was not possible to use their pre-built HTML pages verbatim because I wanted to create my own styles and customize my HTML markup, but it was very helpful to have a visual template to start with. This can give your site a professional feel early in the game, which can help you sell your design to the appropriate people.

Technologies Used to Implement the Design

ASP.NET 2.0 is the overriding technology that makes the site work. This runs on the web server and takes advantage of the functionality provided by the .NET Framework. However, ASP.NET does not run on the user's computer; instead, it dynamically generates the elements a browser uses to render a page. These elements that are sent down to the browser consist of HTML, images, and Cascading Style Sheets (CSS), which provide colors, sizes, and alignments for various items in the HTML. ASP.NET also generates some JavaScript procedural code that is also sent down to the browser to handle data validation and to tell the browser how to interact with the web server.

HTML is defined in several ways. You can use the visual form designer in Visual Studio to drop controls onto the form, and this automatically creates HTML code. Or, you can hand-edit or author your own HTML code in the .aspx files to give it features that aren't easily specified in the form designer. Lastly, HTML can be dynamically generated by your C# code, or by classes in the .NET Framework.

ASP.NET 1.x used a "code behind" model: HTML (and some presentation-oriented C# code) was put in an .aspx file, and implementation C# code would go into a separate file that would be inherited by the .aspx file. We call the .aspx file "the page" because that's where the visual web page is defined. This provided some separation between presentation code and the related implementation code. One problem with this model is that the auto-generated code created by the form designer would be placed in the same files that the developer uses for his code.

ASP.NET 2.0 modifies the code-behind model and uses a new 2.0 feature of the .NET Framework called *partial classes*. The idea is simple: Allow one class to span more than one file. Visual Studio will auto-generate at runtime the code for declaring the controls and registering events, and then it will combine that with the user-written code; the result is a single class that is inherited by the .aspx page. The @Page directive declared in the .aspx page uses the CodeFile attribute to reference the .cs code-behind file with the user-written code.

Another change in .ASP.NET 2.0 is the elimination of project files. Projects are now determined based on folders on your hard disk. Also, code for all pages of a project was generated into one .dll by ASP.NET 1.x, but now ASP.NET 2.0 generates code separately for each page. Why does this matter? You don't have to re-deploy large amounts of code when changes are made to one page only. You only need to re-deploy the code for the individual page(s) that changed, which gives you more granular control over change management.

Using CSS to Define Styles in Stylesheet Files

It is not possible to give an exhaustive explanation of CSS in this book, but I'll cover some of the general concepts. You should consult other sources for complete details about CSS. The purpose of CSS is to specify how visual HTML tags are to be rendered by specifying various stylistic elements such as font size, color, alignment, and so on. These styles can be included as attributes of HTML tags, or they can be stored separately and referred to by name or ID.

Sometimes HTML files have the styles hard-coded into the HTML tags themselves, such as the following example:

```
<div style="align: justify; color: red; background-color: yellow; font-size:
12px;">some text</div>
```

This is bad because it is difficult to modify these stylistic elements without going into all the HTML files and hunting for the CSS attributes. Instead, you should always put the style definitions in a separate stylesheet file with an extension of .css; or if you insist on including styles inside an HTML file, you should at least define them in a <style> section at the top of the HTML file.

When you group CSS styles together, you can create small classes, which syntactically resemble classes or functions in C#. You can assign them a class name, or ID, to allow them to be referenced in the class= attribute of HTML tags.

If you use stylesheet classes and you want to change the font size of all HTML tags that use that class, you only need to find that class's declaration and change that single occurrence in order to change many visual HTML elements of that given type. If the stylesheet is defined in a separate file you will benefit even more from this approach, because you will change a single file and n pages will change their appearance accordingly.

The primary benefits of using CSS are to minimize the administrative effort required to maintain styles and to enforce a common look and feel among many pages. Beyond this, however, CSS also ensures safety for your HTML code and overall site. Let's assume that the client wants to change some styles of a site that's already in production. If you've hard-coded styles into the HTML elements of the page, then you'd have to look in many files to locate the styles to change, and you might not find them all, or you might change something else by mistake — this could break something! However, if you've used style classes stored separately in CSS files, then it's easier to locate the classes that need to be changed, and your HTML code will be untouched and safe.

Furthermore, CSS files can make a site more efficient. The browser will download it once and then cache it. The pages will just link to that cached instance of the .css file and not contain all the styles again, so they will be much smaller, and therefore faster to download. In some cases this can dramatically speed up the loading of web pages in a user's browser.

Here is an example of how you can redefine the style of the DIV object shown above by storing it in a separate file named styles.css:

```css
.mystyle
{
    align: justify;
    color: red;
    background-color: yellow;
    font-size: 12px;
}
```

Then, in the .aspx or .htm page, you will link the CSS file to the HTML as follows:

```html
<head>
    <link href="/styles.css" text="text/css" rel="stylesheet" />
    <!-- other metatags... -->
</head>
```

Finally, you write the HTML division tag and specify which CSS class you want it to use:

```html
<div class="mystyle">some text</div>
```

Note that when the style was declared, I used the dot (.) prefix for the class name. You have to do this for all of your custom style classes.

If you want to define a style to be applied to all HTML objects of a certain kind (for example, to all <p> paragraphs, or even the page's <body> tag) that don't have another explicit class associated with them, you can write the following specification in the stylesheet file:

```css
body
{
    margin: 0px;
    font-family: Verdana;
    font-size: 12px;
}


p
{
    align: justify;
    text-size: 10px;
}
```

This sets the default style of all body tags and all <p> (paragraph) tags in one place. However, you could specify a different style for some paragraphs by stating an explicit class name in those tags.

Yet another way to associate a style class to a HTML object is by ID. You define the class name with a # prefix, as follows:

```css
#header
{
    padding: 0px;
    margin: 0px;
    width: 100%;
```

```
    height: 184px;
    background-image: url(images/HeaderSlice.gif);
}
```

Then you could use the id attribute of the HTML tag to link the CSS to the HTML. For example, this is how you could define an HTML division tag and specify that you want it to use the #header style:

```
<div id="header">some text</div>
```

You typically use this approach for single objects, such as the header, the footer, the container for the left, right, center column, and so on.

Finally, you can mix the various approaches. Suppose that you want to give a certain style to all links into a container with the sectiontitle class, and some other styles to links into a container with the sectionbody class. You could do it this way:

In the .css file

```
.sectiontitle a
{
    color: yellow;
}

.sectionbody a
{
    color: red;
}
```

In the .aspx/.htm file

```
<div class="sectiontitle">
some text
<a href="http://www.wrox.com">Wrox</a>
some text
</div>

<div class="sectionbody">
some other text
<a href="http://www.wiley.com">Wiley</a>
some other text
</div>
```

Avoid Using HTML Tables to Control Layout

Sometimes developers will use HTML tables to control the positioning of other items on a web page. This was considered the standard practice before CSS was developed, but many developers still use this methodology today. Although this is a very common practice, the W3C officially discourages it (www.w3.org/tr/wai-webcontent), saying "Tables should be used to mark up truly tabular information ("data tables"). Content developers should avoid using them to lay out pages ("layout tables"). Tables for any use also present special problems to users of screen readers." In other words, HTML tables should be used for displaying tabular data on the page, not to build the entire layout of the page. For that, you should use container controls (such as DIVs) and their style attribute, possibly through the use of a separate <style> section or a separate file. This is ideal for a number of reasons:

❑ If you use DIVs and a separate stylesheet file to define appearance and position, you won't need to repeat this definition again and again, for each and every page of your site. This leads to a site that is both faster to develop and easier to maintain.

❑ The site will load much faster for end users! Remember that the stylesheet file will be downloaded by the client only once, and then loaded from the cache for subsequent requests of pages until it changes on the server. If you define the layout inside the HTML file using tables, the client instead will download the table's layout for every page, and thus it will download more bytes, with the result that downloading the whole page will require a longer time. Typically, a CSS-driven layout can trim the downloaded bytes by up to 50%, and the advantage of this approach becomes immediately evident. Furthermore, this savings has a greater impact on a heavily loaded web server — sending fewer bytes to each user can be multiplied by the number of simultaneous users to determine the total savings on the web server side of the communications.

❑ Screen readers, software that can read the text and other content of the page for blind and visually impaired users, have a much more difficult job when tables are used for layout on the page. Therefore, by using a table-free layout, you can increase the accessibility of the site. This is a very important requisite for certain categories of sites, such as those for public administration and government agencies. Few companies are willing to write off entire groups of users over simple matters like this.

❑ CSS styles and DIVs provide greater flexibility than tables. You can, for example, have different stylesheet files that define different appearances and positions for the various objects on the page. By switching the linked stylesheet, you can completely change the appearance of the page, without changing anything in the content pages themselves. With dynamic ASP.NET pages, you can even change the stylesheet at runtime, and thus easily implement a mechanism that enables end users to choose the styles they prefer. And it's not just a matter of colors and fonts — you can also specify positions for objects in CSS files, and thus have a file that places the menu box on the upper-left corner of the page, and another one that puts it on the bottom-right corner. Because we want to allow users to pick their favorite styles from a list of available themes, this is a particularly important point.

❑ CSS enables you to target different classes of devices in some cases without requiring new HTML markup, such as mobile devices like PDAs or smartphones. Due to their constrained screen size, it is necessary to adapt the output for them, so that the content fits the small screen well and is easily readable. You can do this with a specific stylesheet that changes the size and position of some containers (placing them one under the other, rather than in vertical columns), or hide them completely. For example, you might hide the container for the banners, polls, and the header with a big logo. Try to do this if you use tables — it will be much more difficult. You'll have to think about a custom skinning mechanism, and you'll need to write separate pages that define the different layouts available. This is much more work than just writing a new CSS file.

Note that the discussion above referred to the use of tables for the site's overall layout. However, using tables is acceptable to create input forms with a tabular structure, because otherwise too much CSS code would be required in that case to be easy writeable and maintainable. It's also not very likely that you'll need to dynamically change the layout of the input form, so you don't need all the flexibility of CSS for that, and using HTML tables is more immediate.

Sharing the Common Design Among Multiple Pages

Once you finish creating your beautiful site design, you need to find a way to quickly apply it to *n* pages, where *n* could be dozens or even hundreds of pages. In the previous edition of this book for ASP.NET 1.x, we followed the classic approach of isolating common parts of the design into user controls files, to be imported into all pages that needed them. Specifically, we had a user control for the header, and another for the footer. Although this is immensely better than actually replicating all code in all pages, and much better than including files of classic ASP (because of their object-oriented nature), that still wasn't ideal. The problem with this approach was that for each and every page, you would still need to write some lines in .aspx files to import the controls, and other lines to place the controls where you wanted them to appear on the page. Thus, if you place them somewhere on the first page, and somewhere else on the second page, the two pages would appear differently at runtime. You don't want to pay attention to these details every time you create a new content page; instead, you want to focus on the content for that particular page, and have the common layout be applied to all pages consistently and automatically. What you really want is some sort of visual inheritance in practice, where you define a "base" page and have other pages inherit its layout. With ASP.NET 1.x, however, you could apply inheritance just at the code-behind level, and thus affect the behavior of the page (e.g., what to do when the page loads, unloads, or renders), not its appearance. There were partial workarounds for this issue, but I personally didn't find any that really satisfied me with regard to functionally and design-time support. At last, the problem is solved in ASP.NET 2.0.

Enter the Master Page Model

ASP.NET 2.0 introduces a new "master page" feature that enables you to define common areas that every page will share, such as headers, footers, menus, and so on. A master page enables you to put the common layout code in a single file and have it visually inherited in all the content pages. A master page contains the overall layout for your site. Content pages can inherit the appearance of a master page, and place their own content where the master page has defined a `ContentPlaceHolder` control. Although this has the effect of providing a form of visual inheritance, it's not really implemented with inheritance in an OOP sense—instead, the underlying implementation of master pages is based on a template model.

An example is worth a thousand words, so let's see how this concept turns into practice. A master page has a .master extension and is similar to a user control under the covers. Following is some code for a master page that contains some text, a header, a footer, and defines a `ContentPlaceHolder` control between the two:

```
<%@ Master Language="C#" AutoEventWireup="true" CodeFile="MasterPage.master.cs"
Inherits="MasterPage" %>

<html>
<head id="Head1" runat="server">
   <title>TheBeerHouse</title>
</head>

<body>
<form id="Main" runat="server">
   <div id="header">The Beer House</div>
   <asp:ContentPlaceHolder ID="MainContent" runat="server" />
   <div id="footer">Copyright 2005 Marco Bellinaso</div>
</form>
</body>
</html>
```

As you see, it is extremely similar to a standard page, except that it has a `@Master` directive at the top of the page instead of a `@Page` directive, and it declares one or more `ContentPlaceHolder` controls where the .aspx pages will add their own content. The master page and the content page will merge together at runtime — therefore, because the master page defines the `<html>`, `<head>`, `<body>` and `<form>` tags, you can easily guess that the content pages must not define them again. Content pages will only define the content for the master's `ContentPlaceHolder` controls, and nothing else. The following extract shows an example of a content page:

```
<%@ Page Language="C#" MasterPageFile="~/MasterPage.master" AutoEventWireup="true"
CodeFile="MyPage.aspx.cs" Inherits="MyPage" Title="The Beer House - My Page" %>

<asp:Content ID="MainContent" ContentPlaceHolderID="MainContent" Runat="Server">
   My page content goes here...
</asp:Content>
```

The first key point is that the `@Page` directive sets the `MasterPageFile` attribute to the virtual path of the master page to use. The content is placed into `Content` controls whose `ContentPlaceHolderID` must match the ID of one of the `ContentPlaceHolder` controls of the master page. In a content page, you can't place anything but `Content` controls, and other ASP controls that actually define the visual features must be grouped under the outermost `Content` controls. Another point to note is that the `@Page` directive has a new attribute, `Title`, that allows you to override the value specified in the master page's `<title>` metatag. If you fail to specify a `Title` attribute for a given content page, then the title specified on the master page will be used instead.

Figure 2-2 provides a graphical representation of the master page feature.

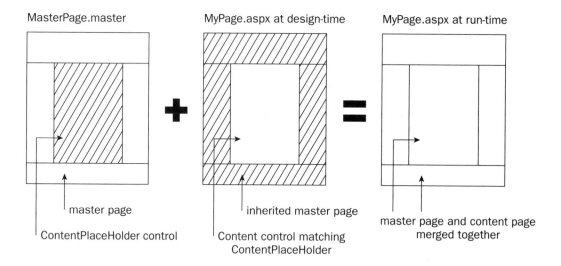

MasterPage.master   MyPage.aspx at design-time   MyPage.aspx at run-time

master page
ContentPlaceHolder control

inherited master page
Content control matching
ContentPlaceHolder

master page and content page
merged together

Figure 2-2

When you edit a content page in Visual Studio, it properly renders both the master page and the content page in the form designer, but the master page content appears to be "grayed out." This is done on purpose as a reminder to you that you can't modify the content provided by the master page when you're editing a content page.

I'd like to point out that your master page also has a code-beside file that could be used to write some C# properties and functions that could be accessed in the .aspx or code-beside files of content pages.

When you define the ContentPlaceHolder in a master page, you can also specify the default content for it, which will be used in the event that a particular content page doesn't have a Content control for that ContentPlaceHolder. Here is a snippet that shows how to provide some default content:

```
<asp:ContentPlaceHolder ID="MainContent" runat="server">
    The default content goes here...
</asp:ContentPlaceHolder>
```

Default content is helpful to handle situations in which you want to add a new section to a number of content pages, but you can't change them all at once. You can set up a new ContentPlaceHolder in the master page, give it some default content, and then take your time in adding the new information to the content pages — the content pages that haven't been modified yet will simply show the default content provided by the master.

The MasterPageFile attribute at the page level may be useful if you want to use different master pages for different sets of content pages. If, however, all pages of the site use the same master page, it's easier to set it once for all pages from the web.config file, by means of the <pages> element, as shown here:

```
<pages masterPageFile="~/Template.master" />
```

If you still specify the MasterPageFile attribute at the page level however, that attribute will override the value in web.config for that single page.

Nested Master Pages

You can take this a step forward and have a master page be the content for another master page. In other words, you can have nested master pages, whereby a master page inherits the visual appearance of another master page, and the .aspx content pages inherit from this second master page. The second-level master page can look something like the following:

```
<%@ Master Language="C#" MasterPageFile="~/MasterPage.master"
AutoEventWireup="true" CodeFile="MasterPage2.master.cs" Inherits="MasterPage2" %>

<asp:Content ID="Content1" ContentPlaceHolderID="MainContent" Runat="Server">
    Some other content...
    <hr style="width: 100%;" />
    <asp:ContentPlaceHolder ID="MainContent" runat="server" />
</asp:Content>
```

Because you can use the same ID for a ContentPlaceHolder control in the base master page and for another ContentPlaceHolder in the inherited master page, you wouldn't need to change anything in the content page but its MasterPageFile attribute, so that it uses the second-level master page.

This possibility has great promise because you can have an outer master page that defines the very common layout (often the companywide layout), and then other master pages that specify the layout for specific areas of the site, such as the online store section, the administration section, and so on. The only problem with nested master pages is that you don't have design-time support from within the Visual Studio IDE (as you do for the first-level master page). When editing content pages, you must code everything from the Source View in the editor, and you can only see the result from the browser when you view the page. This is not much of a problem for developers, like me, who prefer to write most of the code themselves in the Source View, but having the option of using nested master pages is a good thing!

Accessing the Master Page from the Content Page

You also have the capability to access the master page from a content page, through the Page's `Master` property. The returned object is of type `MasterPage`, which inherits directly from `UserControl` (remember that I said master pages are similar to user controls) and adds a couple of properties. It exposes a Controls collection, which allows you to access the master page's controls from the content page. This may be necessary if, for example, in a specific page you want to programmatically hide some controls of the master page, such as the login or banner boxes. Accessing the Controls collection directly would work, but would require you to do a manual cast from the generic `Control` object returned to the right control type, and you would be using the weakly typed approach. A much better and objected-oriented approach is to add custom properties to the master page's code-beside class — in our example, wrap the `Visible` property of some control. This is what you could write:

```
public bool LoginBoxIsVisible
{
    get { return LoginBox.Visible; }
    set { LoginBox.Visible = value; }
}
```

Now in the content page you can add the following line after the `@Page` directive:

```
<%@ MasterType VirtualPath="~/MasterPage.master" %>
```

With this line you specify the path of the master page used by the ASP.NET runtime to dynamically create a strongly typed `MasterPage` class that exposes the custom properties added to its code-beside class. I know that it seems a duplicate for the `MasterPageFile` attribute of the `@Page` directive, but that's how you make the master page properties visible in the content page. You can specify the master type not just by virtual path (as in the example above), but also by name of the master page's class, by means of the `TypeName` attribute. Once you've added this directive, in the content page's code-beside file (or in a `<script runat="server">` section of the .aspx file itself), you can easily access the master page's `LoginBoxIsVisible` property in a strongly typed fashion, as shown below:

```
protected void Test_OnClick(object sender, EventArgs e)
{
    this.Master.LoginBoxIsVisible = false;
}
```

When I say "strongly typed" I am implying that you'll have Visual Studio Intellisense on this property, and that's true: Type "**this.Master.**" and when you press that second period, you'll see your new property in the Intellisense list!

This methodology of accessing master objects from content pages is also particularly useful when you want to put common methods in the master page, to be used by all the pages that use it. If we didn't have access to a strongly typed `MasterPage` object built at runtime by ASP.NET, you'd need to use reflection to access those methods, which is slower and certainly much less immediate to use (in this case, it would have been easier to put the shared methods in a separate class that every page can access).

For those of you who read the first edition of this book, I'd like to point out a difference between using an OOP base page and using a Master Page. In the first edition, we defined a base class called `ThePhile` that was inherited by all of the "content" pages. This was true OOP inheritance at work, but it was of limited usefulness because we couldn't inherit any kind of visual appearance from it. We still had to create user controls to achieve common visual elements. However, in ASP.NET 2.0, when we define a master page, we are able to get full visual inheritance (but not OOP code inheritance). The lack of code inheritance is not a serious limitation because we can access the code in the master page through a `MasterType` reference, as explained above.

Switching Master Pages at Runtime

The last thing I want to describe in this introduction to master pages is the capability to dynamically change the master page used by a content page at runtime! That's right, you can have multiple master pages and pick which one to use after the site is already running. You do this by setting the page's `MasterPageFile` property from within the page's `PreInit` event handler, as follows:

```
protected void Page_PreInit(object sender, EventArgs e)
{
    this.MasterPageFile = "~/OtherMasterPage.master";
}
```

The `PreInit` event is new in ASP.NET 2.0, and you can only set the `MasterPageFile` property in this event handler because the merging of the two pages must happen very early in the page's life cycle (the `Load` or `Init` event would be too late).

When changing the master page dynamically, you must make sure that all master pages have the same ID for the `ContentPlaceHolder` controls, so that the content page's `Content` controls will always match them, regardless of which master page is being used. This exciting possibility enables you to build multiple master pages that specify completely different layouts, allowing users to pick their favorite one. The downside of this approach is that if you write custom code in the master page's code-beside file, then you will need to replicate it in the code-beside class of any page; otherwise, the content page will not always find it. In addition, you won't be able to use the strongly typed `Master` property, because you can't dynamically change the master page's type at runtime; you can only set it with the `@MasterType` directive. For these reasons we will not use different master pages to provide different layouts to the user. We will instead have just one of them, to which we can apply different stylesheet files. Because we've decided to use a table-free layout, we can completely change the appearance of the page (fonts, colors, images, and positions) by applying different styles to it.

Creating a Set of User-selectable Themes

Themes are a new feature in ASP.NET 2.0 that enable users to have more control over the look and feel of a web page. A theme can be used to define color schemes, font names, sizes and styles, and even images (square corners vs. round corners, or images with different colors or shades). The new "skin" support in ASP.NET 2.0 is an extension of the idea behind CSS. Individual users can select a theme from various options available to them, and the specific theme they choose determines a "skin" that specifies which visual stylistic settings will be used for their user session. Skins are a server-side relative of a CSS stylesheet. A skin file is similar to a CSS file but, unlike CSS, a skin can override various visual properties that were explicitly set on server controls within a page (a global CSS specification can never override a style set on a particular control). You can store special versions of images with themes, which might be useful if you want several sets of images that use a different color scheme based on the current skin. However, themes do not displace the need to use CSS; you can use both CSS files and skin files to achieve a great deal of flexibility and control. Speaking of stylesheet files, there's nothing new with them in ASP.NET 2.0 other than a few more controls that allow you to specify a `CssClass` property; and a few more controls have visual designer support to enable you to select a "canned" CSS specification.

A theme is a group of related files stored in a subfolder under the site's /App_Themes folder, which can contain the following items:

❑   Stylesheet .css files that define the appearance of HTML objects.

❑   Skin files — These are files that define the appearance of server-side ASP.NET controls. You can think of them as server-side stylesheet files.

❑   Other resources, such as images.

One cool thing about the way ASP.NET 2.0 implements themes is that when you apply a theme to the page (you'll learn how to do this shortly), ASP.NET automatically creates a <link> metatag in each page for every .css file located in the theme's folder at runtime! This is good because you can rename an existing CSS file or add a new one, and all your pages will still automatically link to all of them. This is especially important because, as you will see, you can dynamically change the theme at runtime (as you can do with the master page) and ASP.NET will link the files in the new theme's folder, thus changing the site's appearance to suit the preferences of individual users. Without this mechanism you would need to manually create all the <link> metatags at runtime according to the theme selected by the user, which would be a pain.

The best new feature in the category of themes is the new server-side stylesheets, called *skin* files. These are files with a .skin extension that contain a declaration of ASP.NET controls, such as the following one:

```
<asp:TextBox runat="server" BorderStyle="Dashed" BorderWidth="1px" />
```

Everything is the same as a normal declaration you would put into an .aspx page, except that in the skin file you don't specify the controls' ID. Once you apply the theme to your page(s), their controls will take the appearance of the definitions written in the skin file(s). For a `TextBox` control it may not seem such a great thing, because you could do the same by writing a style class for the <input> HTML element in a .css stylesheet file. However, as soon as you realize that you can do the same for more complex controls such as the `Calendar` or the `DataGrid` (or the new `GridView` control), you will see that it makes much more sense, because those controls don't have a one-to-one relationship with an HTML element, and thus you could not easily define their style with a single class in the classic stylesheet file.

You can have a single .skin file in which you place the definition for controls of any type, or you can create a separate .skin file for every control type, such as TextBox.skin, DataGrid.skin, Calendar.skin, etc. At runtime, these files will be merged together in memory, so it's just a matter of organizing things the way you prefer.

To apply a theme to a single page, you use the `Theme` attribute in the @Page directive:

```
<%@ Page Language="C#" Theme="NiceTheme" MasterPageFile="~/MasterPage.master" ... %>
```

To apply it to all pages, you can set the `theme` attribute of the <pages> element in web.config, as follows:

```
<pages theme="NiceTheme" masterPageFile="~/MasterPage.master" />
```

As for master pages, you can also change the theme programmatically, from inside the `PreInit` event of the `Page` class. For example, this is how you apply the theme whose name is stored in a `Session` variable:

```
protected void Page_PreInit(object sender, EventArgs e)
{
    if (this.Session["CurrentTheme"] != null)
        this.Theme = this.Session["CurrentTheme"];
}
```

In Chapter 4, we will improve this mechanism by replacing the use of Session variables with the new Profile properties.

> **When you use the** `Theme` **attribute of the** `@Page` **directive (or the** `theme` **attribute in** `web.config`**), the appearance attributes you specify in the skin file(s) override the same attributes that you may have specified in the** `.aspx` **files. If you want themes to work like** `.css` **stylesheets — whereby you define the styles in the** `.skin` **files but you can override them in the** `.aspx` **pages for specific controls — you can do that by linking to a theme with the** `StylesheetTheme` **attribute of the** `@Page` **directive, or the** `styleSheetTheme` **attribute of the** `<pages>` **element in** `web.config`**. Try not to confuse the** `Theme` **attribute with the** `StylesheetTheme` **attribute.**

So far, I've described *unnamed* skins — namely, skins that define the appearance of all the controls of a specific type. However, in some cases you will need to have a control with an appearance that differs from what you've defined in the skin file. You can do this in three different ways:

1. As described above, you can apply a theme with the `StylesheetTheme` property (instead of the `Theme` property), so that the visual properties you write in the `.aspx` files override what you write in the skin file. However, the default behavior of the theming mechanism ensures that all controls of some type have the same appearance, which was intended for situations in which you have many page developers and you can't ensure that everyone uses attributes in the `.aspx` pages only when strictly required.

2. Disable theming for that control only, and apply the appearance attributes as normal, such as in the following code:

```
<asp:TextBox runat="server" ID="btnSubmit" EnableTheming="False"
    BorderStyle="Dotted" BorderWidth="2px" />
```

3. Use a named skin for a control, which is a skin definition with the addition of the `SkinID` attribute, as shown below:

```
<asp:Label runat="server" SkinID="FeedbackOK" ForeColor="green" />
<asp:Label runat="server" SkinID="FeedbackKO" ForeColor="red" />
```

When you declare the control, you'll need to use a matching value for its `SkinID` property, such as the following:

```
<asp:Label runat="server" ID="lblFeedbackOK"
    Text="Your message has been successfully sent."
```

```
        SkinID="FeedbackOK" Visible="false" />

    <asp:Label runat="server" ID="lblFeedbackKO"
       Text="Sorry, there was a problem sending your message."
       SkinID="FeedbackKO" Visible="false" />
```

> In my opinion, this is the best way to go, because it enables you to define multiple appearances for the same control type, all in a single file, and then apply them in any page. Additionally, if you keep all style definitions in the skin files instead of in the pages themselves, you'll be able to completely change the look and feel of the site by switching the current theme (which is the intended purpose behind themes). Otherwise, with hard-coded styles, this is only partially possible.

In the "Solution" section of this chapter, you'll use themes to create a few different visual representations for the same master page.

Creating a Navigation System

As I said in the "Problem" section, you need to find some way to create a menu system that's easy to maintain and easy for users to understand. You might think that you can just hard-code the menu as HTML, but that's not a great choice because you'd need to copy and paste the code if you want to have the menu in more than one place (in this case, in the header and in the footer), or when you want to add or modify some link. In the first edition of this book, we developed a custom control that took an XML file containing the site map (i.e., the name and URL of the links to display on the menu) and built the HTML to render on the page by applying a XSL file to it. ASP.NET 2.0 introduces some new built-in controls and features that enable you to do more or less the same, but with more functionality that makes things easier for the developer.

Defining a Site Map File

The menu options are specified in an XML site map file. The main site map for the whole site is named `web.sitemap`, with a hierarchical structure of `<siteMapPath>` nodes that have the `title` and `url` attributes. The following extract provides an example:

```
<?xml version="1.0" encoding="utf-8" ?>
<siteMap xmlns="http://schemas.microsoft.com/AspNet/SiteMap-File-1.0" >
   <siteMapNode title="Home" url="~/Default.aspx" />
   <siteMapNode title="About" url="~/About.aspx" />
   <siteMapNode title="Contact" url="~/Contact.aspx" />
</siteMap>
```

In our case we'll have first-level nodes, such as Home, Contacts and About, and also second- and maybe third-level nodes such as Store/Shopping Cart. Here is a more complex example showing some second-level entries; it also refers to another child sitemap file that provides the menu entries for the Store:

```
<?xml version="1.0" encoding="utf-8" ?>
<siteMap xmlns="http://schemas.microsoft.com/AspNet/SiteMap-File-1.0" >
  <siteMapNode title="Books" url="~/Books/Books.aspx>
     <siteMapNode title="Authors" url="~/Books/Authors.aspx" />
     <siteMapNode title="Publishers" url="~/Books/Publishers.aspx" />
  </siteMapNode>
```

```
    <siteMapNode title="DVDs" url="~/DVDs/DVDs.aspx">
      <siteMapNode title="Movies" url="~/DVDs/Movies.aspx" />
      <siteMapNode title="Songs" url="~/DVDs/Songs.aspx" />
    </siteMapNode>
    <siteMapNode siteMapFile="~/StoreMenu.sitemap" />
  </siteMap>
```

The child `siteMap` (`StoreMenu.sitemap`) has the same format as the `web.sitemap`, and it has an outer `siteMap` node.

Binding the SiteMap to Menu Controls

Once you've defined the `sitemap` file, you can use it as a data source for new ASP.NET 2.0 controls such as `Menu` and `TreeView`. ASP.NET 2.0 also introduces new nonvisual controls called `DataSource` controls that can link to a database, XML file, or component class. These controls will be used by graphical controls to retrieve the data to be bound and displayed onscreen. In practice, they serve as a bridge between the actual data store and the visual control. The `SiteMapDataSource` is one of these `DataSource` controls, specifically designed for the site's `web.sitemap` file, and defined like this:

```
<asp:SiteMapDataSource ID="SiteMapDataSource1" runat="server" />
```

Note that you don't define the path for the `web.sitemap` file, as there can be only one site map for the whole site and it is named `~/web.sitemap`. When creating child site maps for limited subfolders within your site, the binding is handled transparently because they are linked from the `web.sitemap`.

> *If you don't like the way the default SiteMapDataSource control works (because you may want to support multiple sitemap files, or you may want to store the site map in the database rather than in XML files), you need to either write a new DataSource control or create a new provider class that transparently provides content for SiteMapDataSource.*

The menu control creates popular DHTML fly-out menus, with vertical or horizontal orientation. In ASP.NET 1.1 there were no decent standard `Menu` controls and it seemed like every web component developer company offered their own component to create these menus. However, with ASP.NET 2.0 we have a standard menu control built in for free and it has the capacity to integrate with the various data source controls. To create a `Menu` control bound to the `SiteMapDataSource` defined above, you simply need the following line:

```
<asp:Menu ID="mnuHeader" runat="server" DataSourceID="SiteMapDataSource1" />
```

Of course, the `Menu` control exposes many properties that allow you to specify its orientation (the `Orientation` property), the `CSS` class to use (`CssClass`) or the appearance of its various parts, the number of inner map levels that will be displayed in the fly-outs (`StaticDisplayLevels`), and much more. However, complete coverage of these properties is beyond the scope of this book; you should refer to the official MSDN documentation for details.

Displaying the sitemap with a tree view representation instead of the fly-out menus involves a replacement of the `Menu` declaration with the new `TreeView` control, as shown below:

```
<asp:TreeView runat="server" ID="tvwMenu" DataSourceID="SiteMapDataSource1" />
```

Breadcrumbs

Besides showing the menu, you also want to provide users with a visual clue as to where they are, and some way to allow them to navigate backward from their current location to the home page. This is usually done through the use of *breadcrumbs,* i.e., a navigation bar that shows links to all pages or sections, starting from the home page, that the user visited to arrive on the current page, such as the following:

```
Home > Store > Shopping cart
```

With this navigation system, the user can go back two pages without pressing the browser's Back button (which may not be visible for a number of reasons) and without starting over from the home page and trying to remember the path previously followed. With ASP.NET 2.0, you can add a breadcrumb bar with a single line of code by declaring an instance of the new `SiteMapPath` control on the page:

```
<asp:SiteMapPath ID="SiteMapPath1" runat="server" />
```

As usual, this control has a number of properties that enable you to fully customize its look and feel, as you'll see in practice in the section "Solution."

Creating Accessible Sites

All ASP.NET 2.0 built-in standard controls render well-formatted XHTML 1.0 Transitional code by default. XHTML code is basically HTML written as XML, and as such it must comply with much stricter syntax rules. For example, all attribute values must be enclosed within double quotes, all tags must have a closing tag or must be explicitly self-closing (e.g., no more `<br>` and `<img src="...">`, but `<br />` and `<img src="..." />`), and nested tags must be closed in the right order (e.g., no more `<b><p> hello</b> Marco</p>` but `<p><b>Hello</b> Marco</p>`). In addition, many HTML tags meant to format the text, such as `<font>`, `<center>`, `<s>`, etc., are now deprecated and should be replaced by CSS styles (such as `font-family: Verdana; text-align: center`). The same is true for some attributes of other tags, such as `width` and `align`, among others. The reasoning behind this new standard is to attain a greater separation of presentation and content (something I've already explained earlier), and to create cleaner code — code that can be read by programs that work with XML data. The fact that ASP.NET 2.0 automatically renders XHTML code, as long as you use its controls, is a great time saver for the developer, and makes the process of getting used to XHTML smoother. The official W3C documentation about XHTML 1.0 can be found at `http://www.w3.org/TR/xhtml1/`.

As for accessibility, the W3C defines a set of rules meant to ease the use of the site by users with disabilities. The official page of the Web Content Accessibility Guidelines 1.0 (commonly referred as WCAG) can be found at `www.w3.org/TR/WCAG10/`. Section 508 guidelines were born from WCAG, and must be followed by U.S. federal agencies' sites. You can read more at `www.section508.gov/`. For example, you must use the `alt` attribute in `<img>` tags to provide an alternate text for visually impaired users, so that screen readers can describe the image, and you must use the `<label>` tag to associate a label to an input field. Other guidelines are more difficult to implement and are not specifically related to ASP.NET, so you can check out the official documentation for more information. ASP.NET 2.0 makes it easier to follow some of the simpler rules, such as those mentioned above. For example, the `Image` control has a new `GenerateEmptyAlternateText` that, when set to true, generates `alt=""` (setting `AlternateText=""` would generate nothing instead), and the `Label` control has the new `AssociatedControlID` property that is set to the name of an input control, and at runtime generates the `<label>` control for it (this should be used together with the `AccessKey` property, to create shortcuts to the input field).

If you want to read more about XHTML, accessibility, and the new ASP.NET 2.0 features that pertain to this subject, you can refer to the following free online articles: Alex Homer's "Accessibility Improvements in ASP.NET 2.0 – Part 1" (www.15seconds.com/issue/040727.htm) and "Accessibility Improvements in ASP.NET 2.0 – Part 2" (www.15seconds.com/issue/040804.htm), or Stephen Walther's "Building ASP.NET 2.0 Web Sites Using Web Standards" (http://msdn.microsoft.com/asp.net/default .aspx?pull=/library/en-us/dnaspp/html/aspnetusstan.asp).

Sharing a Common Behavior Among All Pages

Master pages and themes do a great job of sharing the same design and look and feel among all pages of the site. However, you may also want the pages to share some common behavior, i.e., code to run at a certain point of their life cycle. For example, if you want to log access to all pages so that you can build and show statistics for your site, you have to execute some code when the page loads. Another case where you need to run some code for every page is when you need to set the page's Theme property in the PreInit event handler. It's true that you can isolate the common code in an external function and just add a line of code to execute it from within each page, but this approach has two drawbacks:

- ❑ You must never forget to insert that line to call the external function when you design a new page. If multiple developers are creating .aspx pages — which is often the case — you will need to make sure that nobody forgets it.

- ❑ You may want to run some initialization from inside the PreInit event and some other code from the Load event. In this case, you have to write two separate xxxInitialize methods, and add more lines to each page to call the proper method from inside the proper event handler. Therefore, don't rely on the fact that adding a single line to each page is easy, because later you may need to add more and more. When you have hundreds of pages, I'm sure you'll agree that going back and modifying all the pages to add these lines is not a workable solution.

These two disadvantages are enough to make me discard that option. Another option is to write the common code in the master page's code-behind. This may be a very good choice in many situations. Not in our case, however, because we must handle the PreInit event, and the MasterPage class (and its base classes) do not have such an event. You can handle the Init or Load events, for example, but not PreInit, so we must think about something else.

In the previous edition of this book there was a BasePage class from which all the content pages would inherit, instead of inheriting directly from the standard System.Web.UI.Page class. I believe this is still the best option, because you can handle any page event from inside this class by overriding the OnXXX methods, where XXX is the event name.

The snippet that follows is a basic skeleton for such a custom base class that inherits from Page and overrides the OnPreInit and OnLoad methods:

```
public class BasePage : System.Web.UI.Page
{
    protected override void OnPreInit(EventArgs e)
    {
        // add custom code here...

        base.OnPreInit(e);
    }

    protected override void OnLoad(EventArgs e)
```

```
    {
        // add custom code here...

        base.OnLoad(e);
    }
}
```

The classes in the pages' code-beside files will then inherit from your custom `BasePage`, rather than the standard `Page`, as shown below:

```
public partial class Contact : BasePage
{
    // normal page code here...
}
```

You still need to change some code in the code-beside class of every page, but once that's done you can later go back to `BasePage`, add code to the exiting methods or overload new methods, and you will not need to modify any additional lines in the code-beside classes. If you take this approach initially, you'll modify the code-beside classes one by one as you create them, so this will be easy and it gives you a future-proof design.

Solution

At this point you should have a clear idea of what you have to build and how to do it, so let's start developing the solution! Earlier in this chapter I explained how you can create a mock-up of your site using a graphics application such as Photoshop or Paint Shop Pro, and this mock-up could be saved in a PSD file. Once you have been given the go ahead to start coding, you need to break out the individual images from the PSD file into `.gif` and `.jpg` files that can be referenced directly in a web page. Regardless of the method you used to create your images, you can now take those images and use them to create the web site. The first step is to create a new web site project, and then create a master page, home page, and default theme. Later you can develop a second theme for the site, and implement the mechanism to switch themes at runtime.

First, create a new web site project in Visual Studio .NET 2005 (File ➪ New ➪ Web Site ➪ ASP.NET Web Site). Here's another new feature in Visual Studio 2005: You can create a project by specifying a folder on the file system (instead of specify a web location) if you select File System in the Location drop-down list, as shown in Figure 2-3.

This enables you to create an ASP.NET project without creating a related virtual application or virtual directory in the IIS metabase (the metabase is where IIS stores its configuration data), and the project is loaded from a real hard disk folder, and executed by an integrated lightweight web server (called ASP.NET Development Server) that handles requests on a TCP/IP port other than the one used by IIS (IIS uses port 80). The actual port number used is determined randomly every time you press F5 to run the web site in debug mode. For example, it handles requests such as `http://localhost:1168/ProjName/Default.aspx`. This makes it much easier to move and back up projects, because you can just copy the project's folder and you're done — there's no need to set up anything from the IIS Management console. In fact, Visual Studio 2005 does not even require IIS unless you choose to deploy to an IIS web server, or you specify a web URL instead of a local path when you create the web site project.

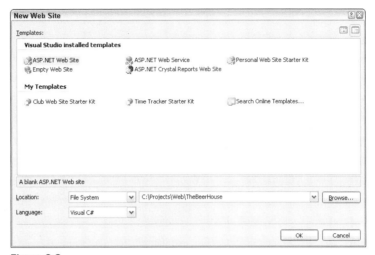

Figure 2-3

If you've developed with any previous version of ASP.NET or VS2005, I'm sure you will welcome this new option. I say this is an option because you can still create the project by using a URL as project path—creating and running the site under IIS—by selecting HTTP in the Location drop-down list. I suggest you create and develop the site by using the File System location, with the integrated web server, and then switch to the full-featured IIS web server for the test phase. VS2005 includes a new deployment wizard that makes it easier to deploy a complete solution to a local or remote IIS web server. For now, however, just create a new ASP.NET web site in a folder you want, and call it TheBeerHouse.

> **The integrated web server was developed for making development and quick testing easier. However, you should never use it for final Quality Assurance or Integration testing. You should use IIS for that. IIS has more features, such as caching, HTTP compression, and many security options that can make your site run very differently from what you see in the new integrated ASP.NET Development Server.**

After creating the new web site, right-click on `Default.aspx` and delete it. We'll make our own default page soon.

Creating the Site Design

Creating the master page with the shared site design is not that difficult once you have a mock-up image (or a set of images if you made them separately). Basically, you cut the logo and the other graphics and put them in the HTML page. The other parts of the layout, such as the menu bar, the columns, and the footer, can easily be reproduced with HTML elements such as DIVs. The template provided by TemplateMonster (and just slightly modified and expanded by me) is shown in Figure 2-4.

Figure 2-4

From this picture you can cut out the header bar altogether and place some DIV containers over it, one for the menu links, one for the login box, and another one for the theme selector (a drop-down list containing the names of the available themes). These DIVs will use the absolute positioning so that you can place them right where you want them. It's easy to determine the correct top-left or top-right coordinates for them — you just hover the mouse cursor on the image opened in the graphics editor and then use the same *x* and *y* values you read from there.

The footer is created with a DIV that uses a slice of image with a width of 1 pixel, repeated horizontally as a background. It also contains a couple of sub-DIVs: one for the menu's links (the same shown in the header's menu) and a second for some copyright notices.

Finally, there is the content area of the page, divided into three columns. The center column has the right and left margins set to 200 pixels, and the margins are filled by two other DIVs docked on the page borders with an absolute positioning. Figure 2-5 provides a visual representation of this work, applied on the previous image

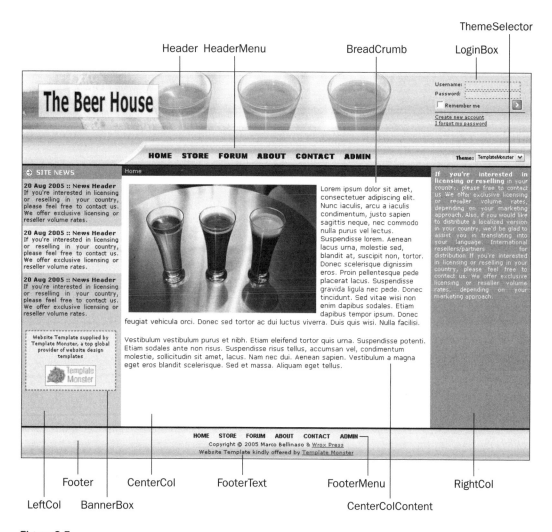

Figure 2-5

Creating the Master Page

In this book I am assuming a certain amount of familiarity with ASP.NET and Visual Studio .NET. More specifically, I assume you have a working knowledge of the basic operation of any previous version of Visual Studio .NET. Therefore, the steps I explain here focus on the new changes in version 2.0, but do not otherwise cover every small detail. If you are not comfortable following the steps presented here, you should consult a beginner's book on ASP.NET before following the steps in this book.

After creating the web site as explained above, create a new master page file (select Website ⇨ Add New Item ⇨ Master Page, and name it `Template.master`), and then use the visual designer to add the ASP.NET server-side controls and static HTML elements to its surface. However, when working with DIV containers and separate stylesheet files, I've found that the visual designer is not able to give me the flexibility I desire. I find it easier to work directly in the Source view, and write the code by hand. As I said earlier, creating the master page is not much different than creating a normal page; the most notable differences are just the `@Master` directive at the top of the file and the presence of `ContentPlaceHolder` controls where the .aspx pages will plug in their own content. What follows is the code that defines the standard HTML metatags, and the site's header for the file `Template.master`:

```
<%@ Master Language="C#" AutoEventWireup="true" CodeFile="Template.master.cs"
Inherits="TemplateMaster" %>
<!DOCTYPE html PUBLIC "-//W3C//DTD XHTML 1.1//EN"
"http://www.w3.org/TR/xhtml11/DTD/xhtml11.dtd">

<html xmlns="http://www.w3.org/1999/xhtml" >
<head id="Head1" runat="server">
    <meta http-equiv="Content-Type" content="text/html; charset=windows-1252">
    <title>TheBeerHouse</title>
</head>

<body>
<form id="Main" runat="server">
    <div id="header">
        <div id="header2">
            <div id="headermenu">
                <asp:SiteMapDataSource ID="SiteMapDataSource1"
                    runat="server" StartingNodeOffset="0" />
                <asp:Menu ID="mnuHeader" runat="server"
                    CssClass="headermenulink"
                    DataSourceID="SiteMapDataSource1"
                    Orientation="Horizontal"
                    MaximumDynamicDisplayLevels="0"
                    SkipLinkText=""
                    StaticDisplayLevels="2" />
            </div>
        </div>
        <div id="loginbox">Login box here...</div>
        <div id="themeselector">Theme selector here...</div>
    </div>
```

As you can see, there is nothing in this first snippet of code that relates to the actual appearance of the header. That's because the appearance of the containers, text, and other objects will be specified in the stylesheet and skin files. The `"loginbox"` container will be left empty for now; we'll fill it in when we get to Chapter 4, which covers security and membership. The `"themeselector"` box will be filled in later in this chapter, as soon as we develop a control that displays the available styles from which users can select. The `"headermenu"` DIV contains a `SiteMapPathDataSource`, which loads the content of the `Web.sitemap` file that you'll create shortly. It also contains a `Menu` control, which uses the `SiteMapPathDataSource` as data source for the items to create.

Proceed by writing the DIVs for the central part of the page, with the three columns:

```
<div id="container">
    <div id="container2">
        <div id="rightcol">
            <div class="text">Some text...</div>
            <asp:ContentPlaceHolder ID="RightContent" runat="server" />
        </div>
        <div id="centercol">
            <div id="breadcrumb">
                <asp:SiteMapPath ID="SiteMapPath1" runat="server" />
            </div>
            <div id="centercolcontent">
                <asp:ContentPlaceHolder ID="MainContent" runat="server">
                    <p> </p><p> </p><p> </p><p> </p>
                    <p> </p><p> </p><p> </p><p> </p>
                </asp:ContentPlaceHolder>
            </div>
        </div>
    </div>
    <div id="leftcol">
        <div class="sectiontitle">
            <asp:Image ID="imgArrow1" runat="server"
                ImageUrl="~/images/arrowr.gif"
                ImageAlign="left" hspace="6" />Site News
        </div>
        <div class="text"><b>20 Aug 2005 :: News Header</b><br />
            News text...
        </div>
        <div class="alternatetext"><b>20 Aug 2005 :: News Header</b><br />
            Other news text...
        </div>
        <asp:ContentPlaceHolder ID="LeftContent" runat="server" />
        <div id="bannerbox">
            <a href="http://www.templatemonster.com" target="_blank">
            Website Template supplied by Template Monster,
            a top global provider of website design templates<br /><br />
            <asp:Image runat="server" ID="TemplateMonsterBanner"
                ImageUrl="~/images/templatemonster.jpg" Width="100px" />
            </a>
        </div>
    </div>
</div>
```

Note that three `ContentPlaceHolder` controls are defined in the preceding code, one for each column. This way, a content page will be able to add text in different positions. Also remember that filling a `ContentPlaceHolder` with some content is optional, and in some cases we'll have pages that just add content to the central column, using the default content defined in the master page for the other two columns. The central column also contains a sub-DIV with a `SiteMapPath` control for the breadcrumb navigation system.

The remaining part of the master page defines the container for the footer, with its subcontainers for the footer's menu (which exactly replicates the header's menu, except for the style applied to it) and the copyright notices:

```
<div id="footer">
    <div id="footermenu">
        <asp:Menu ID="mnuFooter" runat="server"
            style="margin-left:auto; margin-right:auto;"
            CssClass="footermenulink"
            DataSourceID="SiteMapDataSource1"
            Orientation="Horizontal"
            MaximumDynamicDisplayLevels="0"
            SkipLinkText=""
            StaticDisplayLevels="2" />
    </div>
    <div id="footertext">
        <small>Copyright &copy; 2005 Marco Bellinaso &amp
        <a href="http://www.wrox.com" target="_blank">Wrox Press</a><br />
        Website Template kindly offered by
        <a href="http://www.templatemonster.com" target="_blank">
            Template Monster</a></small>
    </div>
</div>
</form>
</body>
</html>
```

A note on cross-browser portability: The footertext DIV declared in the preceding code will have the text aligned in the center. However, the Menu control declared inside it is rendered as an HTML table at runtime, and tables are not considered as text by browsers such as Firefox, and therefore are not aligned as text. Because we're targeting both browsers, we must ensure that the table is aligned on the center on both of them, and so I've added the style attribute to the Menu declaration to put an equal margin on the left and on the right of the menu table, as large as possible. The result will be a table centered horizontally. The style attribute does not map to a server-side property exposed by the control; it appears that there is no such property or a similar one that is transformed to "align" at runtime, so I used the HTML attribute. Since it is not mapped to a control's property, it will be attached "as is" to the HTML table generated when the control is rendered.

Creating the Site Map File

Given how easy it is to add, remove, and modify links in the site's menus when employing the sitemap file and the SiteMapPath control, at this point you don't have to worry about what links you'll need. You can fill in the link information later. You can add a few preliminary links to use as a sample for now, and then come back and modify the file when you need it. Therefore, add a Web.sitemap file to the project (select Website ➪ Add New Item... ➪ Site Map) and add the following XML nodes inside it:

```
<?xml version="1.0" encoding="utf-8" ?>
<siteMap xmlns="http://schemas.microsoft.com/AspNet/SiteMap-File-1.0" >
    <siteMapNode title="Home" url="~/Default.aspx">
        <siteMapNode title="Store" url="~/Store/Default.aspx">
            <siteMapNode title="Shopping cart" url="~/Store/ShoppingCart.aspx" />
        </siteMapNode>
        <siteMapNode title="Forum" url="~/Forum/Default.aspx" />
        <siteMapNode title="About" url="~/About.aspx" />
        <siteMapNode title="Contact" url="~/Contact.aspx" />
        <siteMapNode title="Admin" url="~/Admin/Default.aspx" />
    </siteMapNode>
</siteMap>
```

You may be wondering why the Home node serves as root node for the others, and is not at the same level as the others. That would actually be an option, but I want the SiteMapPath control to always show the Home link, before the rest of the path that leads to the current page, so it must be the root node. In fact, the SiteMapPath does not work by remembering the previous pages — it just looks in the site map for an XML node that describes the current page, and displays the links of all parent nodes.

> **If you deploy the project to the root folder of an IIS site, you could identify the root folder with "/". However, if you deploy the site on a sub virtual folder, that will not work anymore. In the sitemap above, you see that "~/" is used to identify the root folder. These URLs will be resolved at runtime, according to where the pages are located, and it works fine if you deploy the pages to either the site's root folder or to a sub virtual folder.**
>
> **When you use the integrated web server, it always runs the website as if it were deployed on a virtual folder, and in fact the URL includes the project name. This forces you to use "~/" in your URLs, to minimize problems during deployment.**

Creating the First Theme

It's time to create the first theme for the master page: TemplateMonster. There are two ways to do this that are functionally equivalent. You could add a new folder to the project named App_Themes, and then a new subfolder under it called TemplateMonster. Alternately, you could let VS2005 assist you: Select Website ⇨ Add Folder ⇨ Theme Folder, and name it TemplateMonster (the App_Themes folder is created for you in this case). The App_Themes folder is special because it uses a reserved name, and appears in gray in the Solution Explorer. Select the App_Themes \ TemplateMonster folder, and add a stylesheet file to this folder (select Website ⇨ Add New Item ⇨ Stylesheet, and name it Default.css). The name you give to the CSS file is not important, as all CSS files found in the current theme's folder will automatically be linked by the .aspx page at runtime.

For your reference, the code that follows includes part of the style classes defined in this file (refer to the downloadable code for the entire stylesheet):

```
body
{
    margin: 0px; font-family: Verdana; font-size: 12px;
}


#container
{
    background-color: #818689;
}


#container2
{
    background-color: #bcbfc0; margin-right: 200px;
}


#header
{
    padding: 0px; margin: 0px; width: 100%; height: 184px;
```

```
    background-image: url(images/HeaderSlice.gif);
}

#header2
{
    padding: 0px; margin: 0px; width: 780px; height: 184px;
    background-image: url(images/Header.gif);
}

#headermenu
{
    position: relative; top: 153px; left: 250px; width: 500px;
    padding: 2px 2px 2px 2px;
}

#breadcrumb
{
    background-color: #202020; color: White; padding: 3px; font-size: 10px;
}

#footermenu
{
    text-align: center; padding-top: 10px;
}

#loginbox
{
    position: absolute; top: 16px; right: 10px; width: 180px; height: 80px;
    padding: 2px 2px 2px 2px; font-size: 9px;
}

#themeselector
{
    position: absolute; text-align: right; top: 153px; right: 10px; width: 180px;
    height: 80px; padding: 2px 2px 2px 2px; font-size: 9px;
}

#footer
{
    padding: 0px; margin: 0px; width: 100%; height: 62px;
    background-image: url(images/FooterSlice.gif);
}

#leftcol
{
    position: absolute; top: 184px; left: 0px; width: 200px;
    background-color: #bcbfc0; font-size: 10px;
}

#centercol
{
    position: relative inherit; margin-left: 200px; padding: 0px;
```

```
    background-color: white; height: 500px;
}

#centercolcontent
{
    padding: 15px 6px 15px 6px;
}

#rightcol
{
    position: absolute; top: 184px; right: 0px; width: 198px; font-size: 10px;
    color: White; background-color: #818689;
}

.footermenulink
{
    font-family: Arial; font-size: 10px; font-weight: bold;
    text-transform: uppercase;
}

.headermenulink
{
    font-family: Arial Black; font-size: 12px; font-weight: bold;
    text-transform: uppercase;
}

/* other styles omitted for brevity's sake */
```

Note how certain elements (such as `"loginbox"`, `"themeselector"`, `"leftcol"`, and `"rightcol"`) use absolute positioning. Also note that there are two containers with two different styles for the header. The former, header, is as large as the page (if you don't specify an explicit width and don't use absolute positioning, a DIV will always have an implicit width of 100%), has a background image that is 1 pixel large, and is (implicitly, by default) repeated horizontally. The latter, header2, is as large as the `Header.gif` image it uses as a background, and is placed over the first container. The result is that the first container serves to continue the background for the second container, which has a fixed width. This is required only because we want to have a dynamic layout that fills the whole width of the page. If we had used a fixed-width layout, we could have used just a single container.

All images pointed to in this stylesheet file are located in an Images folder under App_Themes/ TemplateMonster. This way, you keep together all related objects that make up the theme.

Now add a skin file named `Controls.skin` (Select the TemplateMonster folder and then select Website ➪ Add New Item ➪ Skin File). You will place all the server-side styles into this file to apply to controls of all types. Alternatively, you could create a different file for every control, but I find it easier to manage styles in a single file. The code that follows contains two unnamed skins for the `TextBox` and `SiteMapPath` controls, and two named (`SkinID`) skins for the `Label` control:

```
<asp:TextBox runat="server" BorderStyle="dashed" BorderWidth="1px" />

<asp:Label runat="server" SkinID="FeedbackOK" ForeColor="green" />

<asp:Label runat="server" SkinID="FeedbackKO" ForeColor="red" />

<asp:SiteMapPath runat="server">
```

```
        <PathSeparatorTemplate>
            <asp:Image runat="server" ImageUrl="images/sepwhite.gif"
                hspace="4" align="middle" />
        </PathSeparatorTemplate>
    </asp:SiteMapPath>
```

The first three skins are mainly for demonstrative purposes, because you can get the same results by defining normal CSS styles. The skin for the `SiteMapPath` control is something that you can't easily replicate with CSS styles, because this control does not map to a single HTML element. In the preceding code, this skin declares what to use as a separator for the links that lead to the current page—namely, an image representing an arrow.

Creating a Sample Default.aspx Page

Now that you have a complete master page and a theme, you can test it by creating a sample content page. To begin, add a new web page named `Default.aspx` to the project (select the project in Solution Explorer and choose Website ➪ Add New Item ➪ Web Form), select the checkbox called Select Master Page in the Add New Item dialog box, and you'll be presented with a second dialog window from which you can choose the master page to use—namely, `Template.master`. When you select this option the page will just contain `Content` controls that match the master page's `ContentPlaceHolder` controls, and not the `<html>`, `<body>`, `<head>`, and `<form>` tags that would be present otherwise. You can put some content in the central `ContentPlaceHolder`, as shown here:

```
<%@ Page Language="C#" AutoEventWireup="true" MasterPageFile="~/Template.master"
    CodeFile="Default.aspx.cs" Inherits="_Default" Title="The Beer House" %>

<asp:Content ID="Content1" ContentPlaceHolderID="RightContent" Runat="Server">
</asp:Content>

<asp:Content ID="MainContent" runat="server" ContentPlaceHolderID="MainContent">
    <asp:Image ID="imgBeers" runat="server"
        ImageUrl="~/Images/3beers.jpg" ImageAlign="left" hspace="8" />
    Lorem ipsum dolor sit amet, consectetuer adipiscing elit...
</asp:Content>

<asp:Content ID="Content3" ContentPlaceHolderID="LeftContent" Runat="Server">
</asp:Content>
```

You could have also added the `Theme` attribute to the `@Page` directive, setting it equal to `"Template Monster"`. However, instead of doing this here, you can do it in the `web.config` file, once, and have it apply to all pages. Select the project ➪ Website ➪ Add New Item ➪ Web Configuration File. Remove the `MasterPageFile` attribute from the code of the `Default.aspx` page, because you'll also put that in `web.config`, as follows:

```
<?xml version="1.0"?>
<configuration xmlns="http://schemas.microsoft.com/.NetConfiguration/v2.0">
    <system.web>
        <pages theme="TemplateMonster" masterPageFile="~/Template.master" />
        <!-- other settings here... -->
    </system.web>
</configuration>
```

Why select a master page from the New Item dialog box when creating Default.aspx, just to remove the master page attribute immediately afterwards? Because this way, VS2005 will create the proper Content controls, and not the HTML code of a normal page.

Creating the Second Theme

To test the user-selectable theming feature described earlier in the chapter, we must have more than one theme. Thus, under the App_Themes folder, create another folder named PlainHtmlYellow (select the project, right-click Add Folder ➪ Theme Folder, and name it PlainHtmlYellow), and then copy and paste the whole Default.css file from the TemplateMonster folder, modifying it to make it look different. In the provided example I've changed most of the containers so that no background image is used, and the header and footer are filled with simple solid colors, like the left- and right-hand columns. Not only is the size for some elements different, but also the position. For the left- and right-hand columns in particular (which use absolute positioning), their position is completely switched, so that the container named leftcol gets docked on the right border, and the rightcol container gets docked on the left. This is done by changing just a couple of style classes, as shown below:

```
#leftcol
{
    position: absolute;
    top: 150px;
    right: 0px;
    width: 200px;
    background-color: #ffb487;
    font-size: 10px;
}

#rightcol
{
    position: absolute;
    top: 150px;
    left: 0px;
    width: 198px;
    color: White;
    background-color: #8d2d23;
    font-size: 10px;
}
```

This is the power of DIVs and stylesheets: Change a few styles, and content that used to be on the left of the page will be moved to the right. This was a pretty simple example, but you can push this much further and create completely different layouts, with some parts hidden and others made bigger, and so on.

As for the skin file, just copy and paste the whole controls.skin file defined under TemplateMonster and remove the definition for the TextBox and SiteMapPath controls so that they will have the default appearance. You'll see a difference when we change the theme at runtime. If you later want to apply a non-default appearance to them, just go back and add a new style definition to this file, without modifying anything else.

Creating the ThemeSelector User Control

You now have a master page, with a couple of themes for it, so now you can develop a user control that will display the list of available themes and allow the user to pick one. Once you have this control, you will plug it into the master page, in the "themeselector" DIV container. Before creating the user control, create a new folder named "Controls", inside of which you'll put all your user controls so that they are separate from pages, for better organization (select the project, right-click Add Folder ⇨ Regular folder, and name it Controls). To create a new user control, right-click on the Controls folder, select Add New Item ⇨ Web User Control, and name it ThemeSelector.ascx. The content of this .ascx file is very simple and includes just a string and a DropDownList:

```
<%@ Control Language="C#" AutoEventWireup="true" CodeFile="ThemeSelector.ascx.cs"
Inherits="ThemeSelector" %>
<b>Theme:</b>
<asp:DropDownList runat="server" ID="ddlThemes" AutoPostBack="true" />
```

Note that the drop-down list has the AutoPostBack property set to true, so that the page is automatically submitted to the server as soon as the user changes the selected value. The real work of filling the drop-down list with the names of the available themes, and loading the selected theme, will be done in this control's code-beside file, and in a base page class that you'll see shortly. In the code-beside file, you need to fill the drop-down list with an array of strings returned by a helper method, and then select the item that has the same value of the current page Theme:

```
public partial class ThemeSelector : System.Web.UI.UserControl
{
    protected void Page_Load(object sender, EventArgs e)
    {
        ddlThemes.DataSource = Helpers.GetThemes();
        ddlThemes.DataBind();

        ddlThemes.SelectedValue = this.Page.Theme;
    }
}
```

The GetThemes method is defined in a Helpers.cs file that is located under another special folder named App_Code. Files in this folder are automatically compiled at runtime by the ASP.NET engine, so you don't need to compile them before running the project. You can even modify the C# source code files while the application is running, hit refresh, and the new request will recompile the modified file in a new temporary assembly, and load it. You'll read more about the new compilation model later in the book, and especially in Chapter 12 about deployment.

The GetThemes method uses the GetDirectories method of the System.IO.Directory class to retrieve an array with the paths of all folders contained in the ~/App_Themes folder (this method expects a physical path and not a URL — you can, however, get the physical path pointed to by a URL through the Server.MapPath method). The returned array of strings contains the entire path, not just the folder name, so you must loop through this array and overwrite each item with that item's folder name part (returned by the System.IO.Path.GetFileName static method). Once the array is filled for the first time it is stored in the ASP.NET cache, so that subsequent requests will retrieve it from there, more quickly. The following code shows the entire content of the Helpers class (App_Code\Helpers.cs):

```
namespace MB.TheBeerHouse.UI
{
    public static class Helpers
    {
        /// <summary>
        /// Returns an array with the names of all local Themes
        /// </summary>
        public static string[] GetThemes()
        {
            if (HttpContext.Current.Cache["SiteThemes"] != null)
            {
                return (string[])HttpContext.Current.Cache["SiteThemes"];
            }
            else
            {
                string themesDirPath =
                    HttpContext.Current.Server.MapPath("~/App_Themes");
                // get the array of themes folders under /app_themes
                string[] themes = Directory.GetDirectories(themesDirPath);
                for (int i = 0; i <= themes.Length - 1; i++)
                themes[i] = Path.GetFileName(themes[i]);
                // cache the array with a dependency to the folder
                CacheDependency dep = new CacheDependency(themesDirPath);
                HttpContext.Current.Cache.Insert("SiteThemes", themes, dep);
                return themes;
            }
        }
    }
}
```

Now that you have the control, go back to the master page and add the following line at the top of the file in the Source view to reference the external user control:

```
<%@ Register Src="Controls/ThemeSelector.ascx" TagName="ThemeSelector"
TagPrefix="mb" %>
```

Then declare an instance of the control where you want it to appear—namely, within the "themeselector" container:

```
<div id="themeselector">
    <mb:ThemeSelector id="ThemeSelector1" runat="server" />
</div>
```

The code that handles the switch to a new theme can't be placed in the DropDownList's SelectedIndexChanged event, because that happens too late in the page's life cycle. As I said in the "Design" section, the new theme must be applied in the page's PreInit event. Also, instead of recoding it for every page, we'll just write that code once in a custom base page. Our objective is to read the value of the DropDownList's selected index from within our custom base class, and then we want to apply the theme specified by the DropDownList. However, you can't access the controls and their values from the PreInit event handler because it's still too early in the page's life cycle. Therefore, you need to read the value of this control in a server event that occurs later: The Load event is a good place to read it.

However, when you're in the Load event handler you won't know the specific ID of the DropDownList control, so you'll need a way to identify this control, and then you can read its value by accessing the row data that was posted back to the server, via the Request.Form collection. But there is still a remaining problem: You must know the ID of the control to retrieve its value from the collection, but the ID may vary according to the container in which you place it, and it's not a good idea to hard-code it because you might decide to change its location in the future. Instead, when the control is first created, you can save its client-side ID in a static field of a class, so that it will be maintained for the entire life of the application, between different requests (post backs), until the application shuts down (more precisely, until the application domain of the application's assemblies is unloaded). Therefore, add a Globals.cs file to the App_Code folder, and write the following code inside it:

```
namespace MB.TheBeerHouse
{
    public static class Globals
    {
        public static string ThemesSelectorID = "";
    }
}
```

Then, go back to the ThemeSelector's code-beside file and add the code to save its ID in that static field:

```
public partial class ThemeSelector : System.Web.UI.UserControl
{
    protected void Page_Load(object sender, EventArgs e)
    {
        if (Globals.ThemesSelectorID.Length == 0)
            Globals.ThemesSelectorID = ddlThemes.UniqueID;

        ddlThemes.DataSource = Helpers.GetThemes();
        ddlThemes.DataBind();

        ddlThemes.SelectedValue = this.Page.Theme;
    }
}
```

You're ready to create the custom base class for your pages, and this will just be another regular class you place under App_Code, and which inherits from System.Web.UI.Page. You override its OnPreInit method to do the following:

1. Check whether the current request is a postback. If it is, check whether it was caused by the ThemeSelector drop-down list. As in ASP.NET 1.x, all pages with a server-side form have a hidden field named "__EVENTTARGET", which will be set with the ID of the HTML control that causes the postback (if it is not a Submit button). To verify this condition, you can just check whether the "__EVENTTARGET" element of the Form collection contains the ID of the drop-down list, based on the ID read from the Globals class.

2. If the conditions of point 1 are all verified, you retrieve the name of the selected theme from the Form collection's element with an Id equal to the ID saved in Globals, and use it for setting the page's Theme property. Then, you also store that value in a Session variable. This is done so that subsequent requests made by the same user will correctly load the newly selected theme, and will not reset it to the default theme.

3. If the current request is not a postback, check whether the `Session` variable used in point 2 is empty (null) or not. If it is not, retrieve that value and use it for the page's `Theme` property.

The following snippet translates this description to real code:

```
namespace MB.TheBeerHouse.UI
{
    public class BasePage : System.Web.UI.Page
    {
        protected override void OnPreInit(EventArgs e)
        {
            string id = Globals.ThemesSelectorID;
            if (id.Length > 0)
            {
                // if this is a postback caused by the theme selector's dropdownlist,
                // retrieve the selected theme and use it for the current page request
                if (this.Request.Form["__EVENTTARGET"] == id &&
                    !string.IsNullOrEmpty(this.Request.Form[id]))
                {
                    this.Theme = this.Request.Form[id];
                    this.Session["CurrentTheme"] = this.Theme;
                }
                else
                {
                    // if not a postback, or a postback caused by controls other then
                    // the theme selector, set the page's theme with the value found
                    // in Session, if present
                    if (this.Session["CurrentTheme"] != null)
                        this.Theme = this.Session["CurrentTheme"].ToString();
                }
            }

            base.OnPreInit(e);
        }
    }
}
```

The downside of the approach used here is that the selected theme is stored in a session variable, which is cleared when the session ends — namely, when the user closes the browser, or when the user does not make a page request for 20 minutes (the duration can be customized). A much better solution would be to use Profile properties, which among other advantages are also persistent between sessions. You'll examine this new feature of ASP.NET 2.0 — and modify this code to use it — in Chapter 4.

The last thing you have to do is change the default code-beside class for the `Default.aspx` page so that it uses your own `BasePage` class instead of the default `Page` class. Your custom base class, in turn, will call the original `Page` class. You only need to change one word, as shown below (change `Page` to `BasePage`):

```
public partial class _Default : MB.TheBeerHouse.UI.BasePage
{
    protected void Page_Load(object sender, EventArgs e)
    { }
}
```

You're done! If you now run the project, by default you'll see the home page shown in Figure 2-4 (except for the login box, which doesn't contain anything so far — it will be filled in Chapter 5), with the `TemplateMonster` theme applied to it. If you pick the `PlainHtmlYellow` item from the `ThemeSelector` drop-down list, the home page should change to something very similar to what is shown in Figure 2-6.

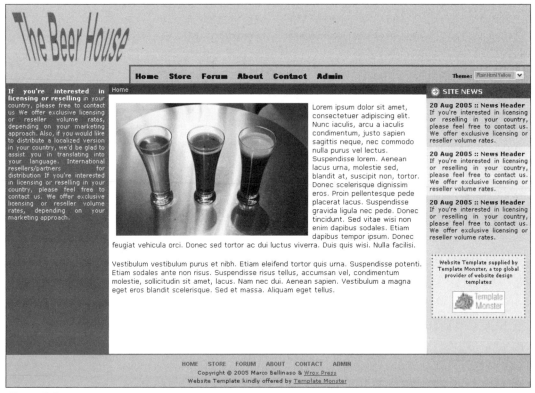

Figure 2-6

Another Small Touch of Style

A single page (`Default.aspx`) is not enough to test everything we've discussed and implemented in this chapter. For example, we haven't really seen the `SiteMapPath` control in practice, because it doesn't show any link until we move away from the home page, of course. You can easily implement the `Contact.aspx` and `About.aspx` pages if you want to test it. I'll take the `Contact.aspx` page as an example for this chapter because I want to add an additional little bit of style to the `TemplateMonster` theme to further differentiate it from `PlainHtmlYellow`. The final page is represented in Figure 2-7.

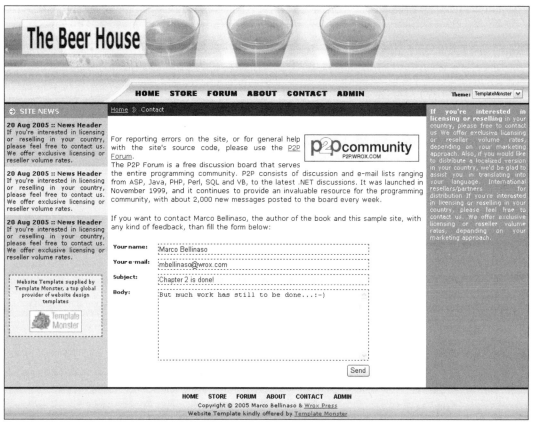

Figure 2-7

I won't show you the code that drives the page and sends the mail in this chapter, because that's covered in the next chapter. I also will not show you the content of the .aspx file, because it is as simple as a Content control inside of which are some paragraphs of text and some TextBox controls with their accompanying validators. Instead, I want to direct your attention to the fact that the Subject textbox has a yellow background color, and that's because it is the input control with the focus. Highlighting the active control can facilitate users in quickly seeing which control they are in, something that may not have otherwise been immediately obvious if they were tabbing through controls displayed in multiple columns and rows. Implementing this effect is pretty easy: You just need to handle the onfocus and onblur client-side events of the input controls, and respectively apply or remove a CSS style to the control by setting its className attribute. The style class in the example sets the background color to yellow and the text color to blue. The class, shown below, should be added to the Default.css file of the TemplateMonster folder:

```
.highlight
{
    background-color: #fefbd2;
    color: #000080;
}
```

To add handlers for the `onfocus` and `onblur` JavaScript client-side event handlers, you just add a couple of `attribute_name/value` pairs to the control's `Attributes` collection, so that they will be rendered "as is" during runtime, in addition to the other attributes rendered by default by the control. You can add a new static method to the `Helpers` class created above, to wrap all the required code, and call it more easily when you need it. The new `SetInputControlsHighlight` method takes the following parameters: a reference to a control, the name of the style class to be applied to the active control, and a Boolean value indicating whether only textboxes should be affected by this routine or also `DropDown List`, `ListBox`, `RadioButton`, `CheckBox`, `RadioButtonList` and `CheckBoxList` controls. If the control passed in is of the right type, this method adds the `onfocus` and `onblur` attributes to it. Otherwise, if it has child controls, it recursively calls itself. This way, you can pass a reference to a `Page` (which is itself a control, since it inherits from the base `System.Web.UI.Control` class), a `Panel`, or some other type of container control, and have all child controls passed indirectly to this method as well. Following is the complete code for this method:

```
public static class Helpers
{
    public static string[] GetThemes() { ... }

    public static void SetInputControlsHighlight(Control container,
        string className, bool onlyTextBoxes)
    {
        foreach (Control ctl in container.Controls)
        {
            if ((onlyTextBoxes && ctl is TextBox) ||
            (!onlyTextBoxes && (ctl is TextBox || ctl is DropDownList ||
            ctl is ListBox || ctl is CheckBox || ctl is RadioButton ||
            ctl is RadioButtonList || ctl is CheckBoxList)))
            {
                WebControl wctl = ctl as WebControl;
                wctl.Attributes.Add("onfocus", string.Format(
                    "this.className = '{0}';", className));
                wctl.Attributes.Add("onblur", "this.className = '';");
            }
            else
            {
                if (ctl.Controls.Count > 0)
                    SetInputControlsHighlight(ctl, className, onlyTextBoxes);
            }
        }
    }
}
```

To run this code in the `Load` event of any page, override the `OnLoad` method in the `BasePage` class created earlier, as shown below:

```
namespace MB.TheBeerHouse.UI
{
    public class BasePage : System.Web.UI.Page
    {
        protected override void OnPreInit(EventArgs e) { ... }

        protected override void OnLoad(EventArgs e)
        {
            // add onfocus and onblur javascripts to all input controls on the forum,
```

```
        // so that the active control has a difference appearance
        Helpers.SetInputControlsHighlight(this, "highlight", false);

        base.OnLoad(e);
    }
   }
 }
```

This code will always run, regardless of the fact that the `PlainHtmlYellow` theme does not define a `"highlight"` style class in its `Default.css` file. For this theme, the active control will not have any particular style.

Little tricks like this one are easy and quick to implement, but they can really improve the user experience, and positively impress them. Furthermore, the simplicity afforded by the use of a custom base class for content pages greatly simplifies the implementation of future requirements.

Summary

In this chapter, you've built the foundations for the site's user interface layer. You've designed and implemented a master page with common HTML and graphics, making it easy to change the layout and the graphics of the site by modifying a single file. You've also used themes—another new feature introduced by ASP.NET 2.0 together with master pages—to create a couple of different visual appearances for the same master page. You've created a mechanism to enable users to dynamically pick their own favorite theme from a drop-down list, so that they can change the appearance of your site to meet their needs and desires. You've also used the new `Web.sitemap` file, and the `Menu` and `SiteMapPath` controls to implement a flexible and easy to maintain navigation system, also new in ASP.NET 2.0. Finally, we've used a custom `BasePage` class to have not just a common look and feel among the pages, but also some common behavior. All in all, you've already developed some significant new features, but with comparatively few lines of code. If you tried to do all we did in this chapter with ASP.NET 1.x or maybe even with an older technology, it may take hundreds of lines of code, maybe even more than 1,000. In the next chapter, we'll continue to talk about foundations, but for the business layer.

3

Planning an Architecture

This chapter lays the groundwork for the rest of the book by creating a number of basic services that will be shared among all future modules: configuration classes to process custom sections and elements in `web.config`, base business and data access classes, caching strategies, and more. I'll also introduce some new UI controls introduced in ASP.NET 2.0, namely the `GridView` control and the `SqlDataSource`/`ObjectDataSource` controls, which give you a data binding solution that's flexible and easy to use. Our job has never been this much fun before!

Problem

Our web site is made up of a number of separate modules for managing dynamic content such as articles, forums and polls, and sending out newsletters. However, all our modules have a number of common "design problems" that we must solve:

❑   Separate the data access code from the business logic code and from the presentation code (user interface) so that the site is much more maintainable and scalable. This is called a *multi-tier design*.

❑   Isolate the data access architecture so that it can allow the support of different underlying data stores — without requiring changes to the business object layer when the underlying data store. Similarly, changes to the business object or presentation layers should also be possible without changing another tier. This is called *decoupling* the tiers.

❑   Design the business object architecture to expose the data retrieved by the data access layer in an object-oriented format. This is the process of mapping relational data to OOP classes.

❑   Support caching of business objects to save the data we've already fetched from the data store so we don't have to make unnecessary fetches to retrieve the same data again. This results in less CPU usage, database resources, and network traffic, and thus results in better general performance.

❏ Handle and log exceptions, and other important events such as the deletion of a record, to help diagnose problems in the event of a system failure, and to provide an audit trail.

❏ Store the site and modules' configuration settings in a place that is easy to read from and write to, and provide helper classes to simplify access to these settings.

❏ Bind many UI controls to the data retrieved by the business logic layer to minimize the amount of work needed in the UI layer, and to put the role of managing data in the business logic layer instead of the UI layer. Ideally, the UI should focus mostly on data presentation; the business logic layer should manipulate the data and apply business rules; and the data layer should only provide persistence (data storage).

The task in this chapter is to devise a common set of classes to address these problems so that the common classes can be utilized by the various modules to be covered in later chapters. Once you finish this chapter you'll have a foundation upon which to build, and you can even distribute the development of future modules to various other developers, who can leverage the same common code to build each module. ASP.NET 2.0 adds new features to help us implement (and in some cases completely implement) a solution for many of the problems mentioned previously.

Design

As explained in the "Problem," there are many issues to solve and a few critical design decisions that must be taken before proceeding with the rest of the site, as they create the underpinnings used for all further development. It would be too late to design architecture to support multiple data stores once you've already developed half the site. Similarly, you couldn't decide on a strategy for handling configuration settings, such as database connection strings, after you wrote an entire module that uses the database. If you ignored these issues and started coding main modules first, you would end up with a poor design that will be difficult to correct later. As with this entire book, many of the new ASP.NET 2.0 classes and controls are utilized, as they apply to each section of code we develop, and sometimes these new features will provide a complete and ready-to-go solution to a particular problem.

Designing a Layered Infrastructure

If you've been doing any software development in recent years you should be familiar with the multi-tier software design (also called *n-tier design*). To recap it in a few words, it divides the functionality, components, and code for a project (not just a web-based project, but also WinForm and other types of projects) into separate tiers. There are generally four of them:

❏ **Data Store:** Where the data resides. This can be a relational database, an XML file, a text file, or some other proprietary storage system.

❏ **Data Access Layer:** The code that takes care of retrieving and manipulating the raw data saved in the data store.

❏ **Business Logic Layer:** The code that takes the data retrieved by the Data Access tier and exposes it to the client in a more abstracted and intuitive way, hiding low-level details such as the data store's schema, and adding all the validation logic that ensures that the input is safe and consistent.

❑ **Presentation Layer (User Interface):** The code that defines what a user should see on the screen, including formatted data and system navigation menus. This layer will be designed to operate inside a web browser in the case of ASP.NET, but some applications might use Windows Forms at this layer.

Depending on the size of the projects, you might have additional tiers, or some tiers may be merged together. For example, in the case of very small projects, the Data Access and Business tiers may be merged together so that a single component takes care of retrieving the data and exposing it in the UI in a more accessible way.

When discussing multi-tier architecture and design, the terms *tier* and *layer* are frequently used interchangeably, but there's actually a subtle difference between them: Tiers indicate a physical separation of components, which may mean different assemblies (DLL, EXE or other file types if the project is not all based on .NET) on the same computer or on multiple computers; but layers refer to a logical separation of components, such as having distinct classes and namespaces for the DAL, BLL, and UI code. Therefore, tier is about physical separation and units of deployment, but layers are about logical separation and units of design.

In the first edition of this book we created many separate assemblies for the site, and each assembly was compiled by a separate Visual Studio project added to the main solution. While that's fine for large enterprise sites, it is often overkill for small and mid-size sites, because it's more difficult to handle many Visual Studio projects (we had dozens!) and the relationships and dependencies between them. In many small to mid-sized sites, a good multi-layered design is usually all you need. ASP.NET 2.0 adds another incentive to use a simplified deployment model: Any code file you put into a special `App_Code` folder (and its subfolders) under your main application folder will be automatically compiled at runtime and referenced by the rest of the application. This automatic and on-demand compilation makes it easier and faster to test and debug your pages, because you can change something in a source code file while the site is running (even if the debugger is attached) and the changes will be automatically compiled on the next request. This process is called *edit and continue.*

While all the older options for compiling assemblies are still supported, this new option makes it easier to work with ASP.NET 2.0 sites at development time, and makes deployment easier as well. The web site we're developing in this book will have the DAL, BLL, and UI code together in a single project. If you prefer to have greater separation (for example, because you want to put the DAL code into a dedicated server separate from the web server, for security reasons), you can still create separate projects, move the DAL files into those projects, and compile them to produce separate deployable assemblies, but I won't cover that option in this book.

Although we'll use only one project, we'll use different folders to organize the different layers' files on the file system (`App_Code/DAL`, `App_Code/BLL`, and the root folder with its subfolders), and we'll use different namespaces to help organize the classes logically in the site's object model (`MB.TheBeerHouse.DAL`, `MB.TheBeerHouse.BLL`, and `MB.TheBeerHouse.UI`). In other words, we'll have various kinds of separation despite the fact that it will all be part of the same project.

Choosing a Data Store

In this book you'll learn how to develop a flexible data access layer that enables you to support different data stores and quickly switch between them without any change on other layers. However, it will only be easy to switch between different data stores after you've developed the low-level data storage structures and a corresponding DAL for each data store you want to support. Therefore, it will still involve a considerable development effort if you want to support more than one data store, but the multi-tier design we're using should ease the pain if that's the route you take.

What kinds of data stores would be possible for this kind of application? We could use only XML files if we expect a fairly static site that doesn't change often, or we might use an Access database format. Access is better than XML files in many ways, but Access is mostly a desktop database and would not be appropriate for situations where we might have even a few concurrent users, or a large database. It doesn't scale at all, and because of this its use for web sites is strongly discouraged. Moving up from there we could consider any of the modern RDBMSs (Relational Database Management Systems), such as SQL Server, Oracle, DB2, MySQL, Postgress, and so on. Any of these would be great choices for our needs, but for the purposes of this book we'll choose only one data store as a target for our sample site.

In the real world your customer may want you to use a specific RDBMS, or they may want you to change to a different RDBMS after the site has been deployed. Your customer may have reasons to use a specific RDBMS because they may already have corporate knowledge of a given platform/engine that would be necessary to maintain the site after you've sold it to them, or maybe they already have an installed/licensed copy of a particular RDBMS and want to use it instead of purchasing a license for different software, or maybe they just have a preference for a specific RDBMS. In this case you might try to explain your reasons for choosing something else, if you think that would be best for them (this is what a consultant is supposed to do, after all), but the customer may insist that their choice be honored.

Most .NET software developers chose Microsoft's SQL Server as their RDBMS for many reasons. These might include the excellent integration of SQL Server tools in Visual Studio, or the fact that it's easier to buy your IDE and RDBMS from the same company (you may have a MSDN software subscription that includes everything), but the reasons I personally favor are the relatively low cost and the high performance of SQL Server running on Windows, coupled together with easy administration. Having decided to use SQL Server as our data store, we now have to select one particular version. This edition of the book revolves around Visual Studio 2005, so it makes a lot of sense to couple this with the newest version of SQL Server, which is named SQL Server 2005. Microsoft has released a free variation of SQL Server 2005 that can be used on developers' computers, and on production servers, called Microsoft SQL Server 2005 Express Edition. This is the 2005 replacement of their older free RDBMS called the Microsoft Data Engine (MSDE), but this one has fewer constraints (no worker threads limit) and a new GUI administration tool, and many new features inside the engine.

I will make the assumption that you will use either SQL Server 2005 Express Edition or one of the full editions of SQL Server 2005 (Workgroup, Standard or Enterprise) for this sample web site. For our purposes, these editions are functionally equivalent, with the main differences relating to the GUI administration tools, and not to the underlying RDBMS engine. All editions of SQL Server 2005 have great integration with Visual Studio 2005, whose Server Explorer tool enables developers to browse registered servers and databases, retrieve all details about a database's schema, add, delete and modify tables, records, stored procedures, functions, triggers, views, types, and relationship. In fact, you can develop the entire database for this web site from inside Visual Studio 2005, without using any of the SQL Server administration tools! The new Diagramming tool in Visual Studio 2005 even enables us to visually relate tables and set constraints and foreign key relationships without leaving the diagram.

Some of the new features of the 2005 version include tight integration with the .NET runtime (SQL Server acts as a host for the CLR), which enables you to write UDFs (user defined functions) and UDTs (user defined types) in C# or VB.NET code; the introduction of XML as a native data type (which means you can chose XML as the type for a column, and you can use special functions and operations to run very fast queries and filters on this column and its index); new functions (such as ROW_NUMBER, which makes it very easy to implement custom pagination, as you will see in Chapter 5); the Service Broker technology, which enables building message-based asynchronous database applications; much finer security permissions; and much more. The limitations of the Express version are that it supports only one CPU, only 1GB of RAM, and the maximum database size is 4GB. Advanced features such as database partitioning, database mirroring, notification services and full text search are also not supported. However, for most small to mid-size sites, SQL Server 2005 Express is an acceptable choice. You can start with it, and should you need more performance on high-end servers, you can upgrade to one of the other editions (Workgroup, Standard, or Enterprise) with no code changes required.

A final advantage of the Express edition that I want to highlight (and one that I'm sure will make many developers happy) is the new `XCopy` deployment: You can just put the `.mdf` database file on a local subfolder (there's a special `/App_Data` folder for web sites) and attach it dynamically by specifying the file path in the connection string by using a new attribute named `AttachDBFilename`. This makes it possible to `XCopy` the site's whole folder structure to the remote server, and you're ready to run without having to do any configuration work to the database server!

Designing the Data Access Layer

The Data Access Layer (DAL) is the code that executes queries to the database to retrieve data, and to update, insert, and delete data. It is the code that's closest to the database, and it must know all the database details, i.e., the schema of the tables, the name of the fields, stored procedures, views, etc. You should keep database-specific code separated from your site's pages for a number of reasons:

- ❑ The developer who builds the user interfaces (i.e., the pages and user controls) may not be the same developer who writes the data access code. In fact, for mid- to large-size sites, they are usually different people. The UI developer may ignore most things about the database, but still provide the user interface for it, because all the details are wrapped into separate objects that provide a high-level abstraction of the table, stored procedure and field names, and the SQL to work with them.

- ❑ Some queries that retrieve data will be typically used from different pages. If you put them directly into the pages themselves, and later you have to change a query to add some fields or change the sorting, you'd have to review all your code and find every place where it's used. If, instead, the data access code is contained in some common DAL classes, then you'd just need to modify those, and the pages calling them will remain untouched.

- ❑ Hard-coded queries inside web pages would makes it extremely difficult to migrate to a new RDBMS, or to support more than one RDBMS.

Using the Provider Model Design Pattern to Support Multiple Data Stores

One thing that's important to consider for your site is that you may need to support different data stores. Our sample site is pretty generic, and as such could easily be adapted for different pubs, bars, and other places. However, as I said before, different clients may have different constraints about which data store to use, and may force you to install and configure the site to work with Oracle or MySQL instead of the SQL Server 2005 database you initially chose. If you don't plan for this possibility up front, you'll have a great deal of trouble trying to retrofit your code later. Different RDBMSs support different functionality and SQL dialects, stored procedures and the parameters for SQL statements are passed in with a different syntax, the data types are different, and so on. For a real-world site of medium complexity, it is impossible to have common data access code that works the same for all possible RDBMSs.

If you tried to write a common code base using the OleDb provider, you would soon start filling your code with an endless number of "if I'm using this database do this, else if I'm targeting this other database do something else"-style blocks. Even if you could put up with the mess in your code, that approach may not be workable in some cases. Say, for example, that you're developing a web site that will be sold by other software companies, which would then integrate your code into a larger solution. You don't know what they'll be using as a data store, because you're developing a commercial product that could be sold to thousands of clients. As such, you can't implement support for all possible data stores. You can't even give them your source code so that they can customize it to add support for their own database because you want to protect your investment. This is exactly the situation with many of the new ASP.NET 2.0 modules, such as membership, profile, personalization, session storage, and more (you'll be introduced to some of these in the next chapter). Microsoft provided a built-in DAL for the SQL Server RDBMS and a few other data stores, but not all possible storage media; however, they wanted you to be able to add this support through the use of the provider model design.

Instead of writing the DAL class directly, you should first write a base abstract class that defines the public interface of the class (the signature of the data access CRUD methods), and the implementation of some helper methods if necessary. The real data access code is inside secondary classes that inherit from the base class, and provide the concrete implementation for its abstract methods. These classes are called *providers,* and are usually specific for one type of data store; when you implement one of them you don't have to worry about compatibility with any other data store.

Different providers are placed in different folders (e.g., App_Code/DAL/SqlClient) and namespaces (e.g., MB.TheBeerHouse.DAL.SqlClient) for organizational purposes. The base class has an Instance static property (or a GetInstance method, if you prefer) that creates and returns an instance of the provider class according to what's specified in the configuration file. This property/method is used by the business classes to get a reference to the concrete DAL object to use to retrieve/modify data. The business classes, in turn, are used by the user interface layer, which never accesses the lower-level DAL classes directly. This pattern enables the developer to write superfast code, because you can take advantage of all optimizations available for the specific data store. The code is also much cleaner, because you don't have to write confusing IF...ELSE blocks to manage all the differences of various RDBMSs. It also allows you to compile the whole site and give your customer the compiled assemblies: If they need to target a different data store from those you have implemented, then they can create their own providers that inherit from your base abstract DAL classes, and they can point to them in the configuration file.

You may argue that if you implement this pattern then you'll have to re-implement the whole DAL code for each data store. That's mostly true, of course. The question becomes whether you want to re-implement one DAL module or all the modules of your site. Also consider that you may only need this pattern for those methods that really must be implemented differently for different data stores. Simpler methods that would work fine on all data stores without any modification could use the OleDb provider with common code in the DAL base class so that all the providers inherit from it so they don't need to re-implement those simple methods. You can make them virtual to allow new providers to override this functionality if they need to. Figure 3-1 provides a graphical representation of the relationship between the user interface, BLL, and DAL layers and the data stores.

We'll talk about this pattern further in subsequent chapters. In Chapter 4 you'll see how the ASP.NET 2.0 team implemented this pattern for the new authentication, membership, and profiling modules. In Chapter 5 you'll design and implement a DAL based on this pattern from scratch, to support the article management module.

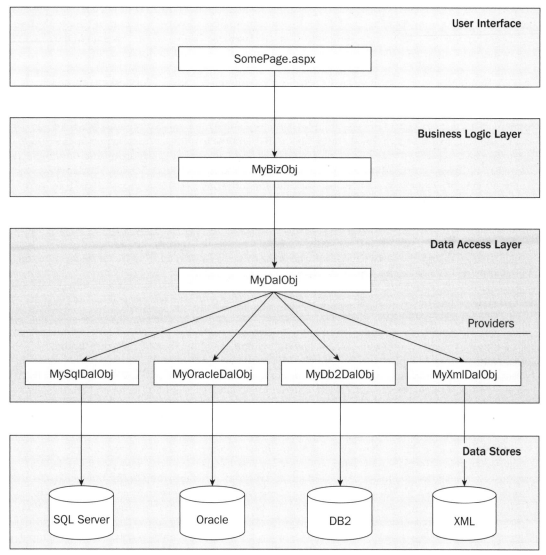

Figure 3-1

The Eternal Question: DataSet or Custom Entities?

When the BLL classes call some methods from the DAL to retrieve some data, how do you think they should receive this data? Perhaps as a `DataSet/DataTable`, or as a collection of custom entity class objects that wrap the fields read from the data store? If there were an award for the most lengthy and hotly contested debate among .NET architects and developers, this question would doubtlessly win first prize. Just search on Google for something like "DataSet vs. custom entities", "DataSet vs. custom collections" or "DataSet vs. domain objects", and you will see a lot of opinions on this subject! Both approaches have their pros and cons, and both have their place in different architectures.

If you choose `DataSets`/`DataTables` for passing data between the DAL and BLL layers, you will need to access the data in the BLL using ADO.NET methods. But if you choose custom entities, all the data will be wrapped in custom classes and collections of classes, so you would access data in the BLL in a more natural manner that has been customized for the particular data in question.

Most people agree that `DataSets`/`DataTables` are clearly the best choice for desktop-based smart-client applications, but the case is not as strong when it comes to scalable high-performance web sites. When I say `DataSet`, in reality I mean a typed `DataSet`, because the plain untyped `DataSet` has many disadvantages: It's just too easy to mistype a table, field or relationship name, or the type of a field when you set it, and thus spend a lot of time debugging and fixing these insidious errors. Typed `DataSets` are easier to use because you get IntelliSense on field names, they provide built-in sorting and filtering facilities, they fully support data-binding for both WinForms and ASP.NET applications, and they have great integration with Visual Studio's IDE. The `DataSets` and the `DataTables` are serializable (`DataTables` did not support serialization in .NET 1.x; you had to add them to a `DataSet` in order to serialize them), and .NET 2.0 now supports true binary serialization, unlike .NET 1.x in which they were always serialized in XML format even when you used a binary formatter (it only gave you a binary header, but the real serialized content was in XML). Finally, `DataSets` can easily support different strategies for handing concurrency, as the `DataTable`'s rows store both the original value read from the data store, and the current value (which the user may have modified).

The disadvantages of `DataSets`/`DataTables` fall into three categories: performance and scalability limitations, representation of data, and business rule validation. If you just need to pass a single row of data, you still need to create and pass an entire `DataTable`/`DataSet` (which is a lot of overhead); and since it's an in-memory mini-database, it can be a fair amount of overhead. It is tightly bound to the relational tabular model of the RDBMS metaphor, without having a clear and customizable object-oriented representation of the data. Despite the nice integration with the IDE, every time the database schema changes a little (a field is renamed, added, or deleted), you have to rebuild the typed `DataSet`, which is harder than modifying a custom collection class. But the thing .NET developers lament the most is the fact that you can't easily add your custom business and validation logic to a `DataSet`, so you have a lot of ugly code to write to enforce all those business rules for both new and current records' values before they are persisted on the database, or before some other statement is run. I've seen some libraries that allow you to add information to the `DataSet`'s `ExtendedProperties` collection, or the `DataSet`'s XSD schema, which allows you to associate simple validation rules to tables and fields: things like ensuring that a string is at least 10 characters long or must match a given pattern, an integer or a date value is inside a given range, and the like. This is all useful, but in the real world there is much more to do than just input validation. You also have to write code for constraint checks and validation that must be performed to ensure that a value, or a record, is valid and meaningful within its context — for example, you can't approve an order if the ordered item is out of stock, and you can't complete the transaction if the credit card information wasn't validated by an external payment gateway or if the customer is marked in your database as a bad risk. These *domain validations* require some custom business logic, which can't be automated by a generic framework or library.

Having made the case against using `DataSets` to pass data from the BLL to the UI, this doesn't mean the `DataSet` will be totally useless in our design. In fact, we'll occasionally pass data from the DAL to the BLL using a `DataSet`, but not from the BLL to the UI. We need to use ADO.NET's classes within the DAL because that's where we interact with the database, so sometimes it makes sense to utilize a `DataSet`/`DataTable` within the DAL layer, and once we have a populated `DataSet`/`DataTable` there would be no additional overhead to pass it up to the BLL. However, it's the BLL that will add all the validation logic, and the BLL can translate data from the general-purpose `DataSet`/`DataTable` into a customized collection of business objects as it does the validation; and these custom collections can be passed up to the UI, where they will present a powerful set of data-specific OOP classes that will be data-bindable and simple for the UI developer to use.

The approach of using custom collections of business entity objects is not new to .NET; it has been around for many years, and long before .NET was even developed. A *custom entity object* is a class that wraps the data retrieved from the database in an object-oriented way, so that it abstracts the data store's schema and other details. If the DAL and BLL are two separate layers (which is usually the case for mid- to large-size projects), there are two levels where these custom collections can be used: between the DAL and BLL, and between the BLL and UI. In the first case the entity classes are very simple, as they typically just wrap the data retrieved from the DB, with a one-to-one relationship with the DB tables (or the DB views, which may join multiple tables), and without methods for inserting, updating, deleting, and retrieving the data. In this context they are just utilized as a container to hold data that is transported between layers. In the second case the classes are more complex: They wrap the data, but also have other properties that reference parent or child objects, and instance methods to manipulate the data. These classes are often called *domain objects* and are not merely entity classes, and one instance should completely represent an element of the domain (an order, an employee, a product, a news article, etc.). Creating entity classes and domain objects is definitely more complex and requires more work than just using a typed `DataSet` automatically created by the designer, which can sort and filter right out of the box, but they're better able to abstract the database's schema, and they're more elegant, easier to use, and more intuitive for use by the UI developer. Domain objects are also easier to maintain by their developer, faster to load from a database and lighter in memory usage, because you can load only the records you really need by utilizing patterns such as the *lazy-load*, which loads data only when it's actually needed by the user, instead of loading everything at the same time from a single query. A custom serialization mechanism can also be implemented, so that only the data you want to save is saved with the exact schema you want it to use. It's also feasible to add custom validation logic to domain objects, because the data is wrapped in properties that you can extend with as much custom logic as you need.

My personal conclusion is that, even though I've seen `DataSets` used in some scalable enterprise applications (even having tens of thousands of users), custom objects are still more flexible and elegant, and I generally prefer them over `DataSets` in web applications, especially between the BLL and UI layers. But the use of custom objects will require you to spend a little extra time and effort to design and code the BLL layer in order to get these advantages. One of the main goals of this book is to teach you how to do these kinds of things, and to show you many best practices in the process. Therefore, this book will present a complete layered project with a separate DAL and BLL, and using custom entity classes and collections to pass data from the DAL to the BLL, utilizing custom domain objects to return data from the BLL and to support data retrieval and modification that can easily be used in the UI layer.

> Some people have developed tools called ORM (Object Relational Mappers) utilities, which can make it easier to map database tables, views, and other relational objects to an OOP class. They can dynamically explore the database's schema and create the wrapper custom entity and domain object classes for you. Some of them work at design time to automatically produce C# classes you can compile into your application, and others work at runtime to perform this mapping function on-the-fly. But sometimes they don't work as well as we'd like them to, and there can be a considerable learning curve to set up these tools to work with your particular database and usage requirements. Some of the most popular tools for .NET developers are NHibernate (`nhibernate.sourceforge.net` [open source]), EntityBroker (`www.thona-consulting.com/content/products/entitybroker.aspx` [free community version and commercial versions available]), and LLBLGen Pro (`www.llblgen.com` [commercial]). A simpler tool for small to mid-size systems is Paul Wilson's ORMapper (`www.ormapper.net`). I decided not to use these tools in this book because I generally prefer a custom-designed mapping solution specific to each application, but I can see that these tools may be your best alternative in some cases. If you have been contracted to develop a new system that will later be maintained by corporate developers, you'll have to get their buy-in before selecting any third-party tools because some companies have policies that prohibit the use of "unapproved" tools they haven't officially sanctioned.

Stored Procedures or SQL Text Queries?

There are two different design models for database access. One is to store all your SQL statements inside stored procedures, and only use the `SqlCommand` object to execute those stored procedures by name. The other model is to store your SQL statements as text to be executed with `SqlCommand` objects. Which methodology is best has been strongly debated for years. We already looked at the question of `DataSets` vs. `Entity` objects, which I suggested was perhaps the most widely debated question. The second most widely debated question is likely: "Should I use user-stored procedures or SQL text queries inside my DAL layer?" As with the first question, different people will give you different answers and opinions, and both of these options have their pros and cons.

If you read a lot, you'll find many sources saying that stored procedures provide better performance than SQL text queries because they are "pre-compiled" (I don't mean compiled to a binary program, but parsed and used to generate an execution plan) and cached in-memory by SQL Server. However, many articles and books miss the fact that this happens for SQL text queries as well (one of the enhancements that was added to SQL Server some years ago), as long as you use parameterized SQL statements (which you should definitely do in all cases, to avoid SQL-injection security attacks). Therefore, the performance of stored procedures and SQL text queries is similar in most cases. However, the name of a stored procedure is shorter and invariant compared to a SQL statement, so it may be easier for the SQL Server engine to find the cached execution plan, but this shouldn't make a significant difference in most cases.

Stored procedures allow finer-grained security access control of the data because you can give your web SQL user account the permission to execute only certain procedures, while not giving full control over the entire underlying tables. Without stored procedures, you can choose to give a user the INSERT permission (for example) on one table but not on another table, and you can limit access to some table fields by creating a view that doesn't include them. Still, stored procedures are better than this because they enable you to add row-level security: If the user account doesn't have any access to the underlying table but only to a stored procedure that only retrieves rows matching a specific filter, then there's no way the user can retrieve/work with the other rows. However, row-level security is admittedly a pretty rare requirement.

Another argument in favor of stored procedures is that they usually include a batch of statements, not just one. If you had to execute them with SQL text queries, you would have to execute multiple separate commands, which would mean much more network traffic for sending data back and forth. When you call a stored procedure, the network traffic is minimized because you call a single procedure with a short name, not dozens of SQL statements, each of which may be hundreds of characters long.

Still another advantage of stored procedures is that they provide a further layering of code. By using them, the DAL code is merely connecting to the database, creating a command that references a stored procedure, sets its parameters, and then executes the procedure. There's no SQL code in the DAL layer. This is often desirable because it allows us to deploy the compiled DAL, and later adjust something in the stored procedures' SQL code without any impact to the DAL; you don't have to recompile or redistribute the DAL. Because I'm not a DBA, I'm not familiar with all the rules, tricks, and best practices of writing the most optimum queries against certain specific tables, so sometimes I like to have a DBA review my SQL code before deploying it in a final release. If I use stored procedures, it's easy to have a DBA check them, reviewing and fine-tuning them without requiring me to change my DAL code. She may not even know what C# is (many DBAs are not programmers), and if that's the case it's better if she only focuses on the T-SQL code and doesn't try to edit the DAL's C# code.

However, stored procedures are not always the best solution. The biggest advantage to using SQL text queries with `SqlCommands`, instead of stored procedures, is that they are more flexible. Sometimes you want to implement advanced search and filtering forms in the UI, whereby the user can partially fill in some data in text boxes to filter the content against some database fields and order the results by other fields. Often, the results must also be paginable. If you have many rows in your results, you don't want to kill performance and scalability, or bore the user by making her wait a long time to download hundreds of records. The query to support all these features would be different according to the fields the user filled in and the sorting option she chose in the UI. If you had to build the query from inside a stored procedure, you would need to write a lot of IF...ELSE statements, which could become unmanageable if you have a lot of optional fields. By using a dynamic type of query in which SQL text is generated at runtime based on UI selections, and then executed in a SqlCommand as SQL text, the overall code is far more elegant and maintainable than any attempt to do this with stored procedures would be.

One concern about using stored procedures instead of SQL text is that they make your code tightly bound to the SQL Server RDBMS, so that if you ever need to support another data store you would need to rewrite most of the SQL stored procedure code. This would be needed because various RDBMSs have a much different stored procedure language, even though their SQL dialect is usually pretty close to the standard ANSI SQL specifications (there are no widely accepted standards for stored procedure languages — they are always highly proprietary). However, this concern only affects the developer who is trying to build a single DAL using only standard SQL, and other portable features that can target with all data stores. I've already explained in the previous section why I don't like this approach: The code will end up being very complex anyway, with a lot of IF...ELSE blocks at the C# level to handle all the differences in data types and other SQL constructs; and even with this huge effort you won't be achieving the best performance possible because portable code can't take advantage of advanced RDBMS-specific features or functions because those aren't portable. Instead of this "one size fits all" approach to portability, I prefer using the provider model design pattern and the creation of different RDBMS-specific DAL classes that will make your application run faster and ease maintenance. The provider model design is not necessarily the easiest option to develop if you have many RDBMSs to support, but its advantages outweigh its disadvantages, even in that case.

The result of all these arguments is that I often use stored procedures for retrieving and working with database data, except for those cases where the query would be too dynamic and complex for a stored procedure; and in that situation I use dynamically built SQL text queries (using SqlCommand and SqlParameters, of course).

A Base Class for All Data Access Classes

For those of you not familiar with the concept of an abstract base class, this is an OOP class that provides common functionality needed by other classes. Because it's abstract you do not need to provide an implementation for each method, but you can provide some method implementations — and if you make them virtual, then they can be overridden in your subclasses (subclasses are child classes that descend from this class). An alternative to using an abstract base class is to use a C# interface to specify the common signature required for a provider class, but this method doesn't allow you to provide any method implementations at this level. C# interfaces are the best choice if you want to allow the DAL class to be coded to the interface, by using only the properties and methods exposed by the interface, which would allow various DAL implementations to be used at runtime (you may have heard the term "plug-in" to refer to this kind of functionality).

In our case we'll use the abstract class, which gives us reusability vertically in the inheritance tree, while the use of interfaces would have given us lateral replaceable functionality across the tree (called *polymorphism*). If you're not familiar with these OOP terms, I urge you to consult a good book on C# because these are powerful concepts you need to master in order to create the best architectures for particular systems.

Each site module will have its own abstract DAL base class, and one or more provider classes that provide the concrete RDBMS-specific implementation. However, all abstract base providers will inherit from a base class themselves. This class, generally called `DataAccess`, provides a few properties that wrap settings read from the `web.config`'s custom settings, and wrappers for the basic methods of a `DbCommand` object (`SqlCommand`, `OleDbCommand`, `OracleCommand`, etc.): `ExecuteNonQuery`, `ExecuteReader`, and `ExecuteScalar`. You may prefer to add helper methods that simplify the creation of parameters and the construction of command objects (the Enterprise Library mentioned before does such things), but I find it simple enough to do it the standard way, and I believe that having the code in the methods that use the command makes it more readable. Figure 3-2 represents the inheritance relationship between this `DataAccess` base class, the abstract provider class and its concrete implementation, and how these wrapper commands work.

The first abstract class, `DataAccess`, is the overall base of all DAL classes, and it contains helper methods that apply to various DAL implementations. The main DAL interface is defined by another abstract class that descends from that one: `MyDalObj`, which defines the functionality (properties and methods) required by all specific DAL implementations. As mentioned before, for this book we'll only have one DAL implementation for SQL Server, so our SQL Server-specific DAL is shown above as `MySqlDalObj`.

The `ExecuteNonQuery` function in the `DataAccess` base class is a special helper method that can be used to translate the name of a stored procedure, or table names in a SQL text query, into the proper naming convention for a particular database used by one site (but in our case we're not going to take it this far, in order to keep things simple). To explain the reason for having this helper method I'd like to relate an experience I had recently that resulted in the need for this kind of helper method. I had developed a web-based Content Management System, or CMS (for the record, it's the one I use behind `www.dotnet2themax.com`, a web site for .NET developers), whose DAL code used hard-coded references at the C# level to the database's table names and stored procedure names. One day I needed to expand the architecture to support other similar sites on the same shared hosting provider using the same shared SQL Server database (a separate hosting account and database for each site would have made my job easy, but would have cost much more on a monthly basis). The DAL and BLL of these new sites would be the same as that used for my first site, and the only differences would be in the UI layer (the pages), and, of course, the content stored in the tables would be different. My idea was basically to clone the existing site to create a couple of new copies of the site, and then I'd go in and modify them as needed. The problem I encountered was that the database structure was not designed to support multiple sites: there wasn't a `SiteID` column in each table that would let me keep the data separate for each site, and there was no easy way to leverage the existing DAL code with only minimal changes.

I debated adding a `SiteID` column to every table to allow existing tables to hold data for different sites, or just developing a new naming convention that would use separate tables for each site. In the end I decided that separate tables gave me a cleaner solution and it would easily allow data for different sites to be backed-up separately, and possibly migrated to a different database or web hosting provider in the future. I decided to use a small prefix on all the table names and stored procedure names to identify the site to which they pertained. To accomplish this change in a simple way at the DAL level, I decided to use a replaceable parameter in the SQL code and stored procedure names that could be changed in one place to customize it for a given site. Therefore, instead of having `usp_DoSomething` for stored procedures, and `Table1` for tables, I should have had something like `usp_Site1_DoSomething` and `usp_Site2_DoSomething` for user stored procedures, and `Site1_Table1` and `Site2_Table1` for tables (*usp* is the system prefix that identifies the overall CMS that uses the tables, so it's the same for all the sites). To simplify the coding changes to the DAL, I added a replaceable parameter placeholder that could be changed by a helper function to swap out the placeholder name with the site name. However, this meant reviewing and modifying the whole DAL code (several thousand lines of code) to find all occurrences of table names and stored procedure names, adding a placeholder prefix to their name (such as usp_{InstanceName}_DoSomething), and then modifying the code that executes SQL text and stored procedures to have them call a helper method that would replace all occurrences of the placeholder with a value for a specific site as identified in a configuration setting. I wished that I started out using helper methods such as ExecuteNonQuery, ExecuteReader, and ExecuteScalar in a base class from the beginning, so now I do create this type of architecture at the outset!

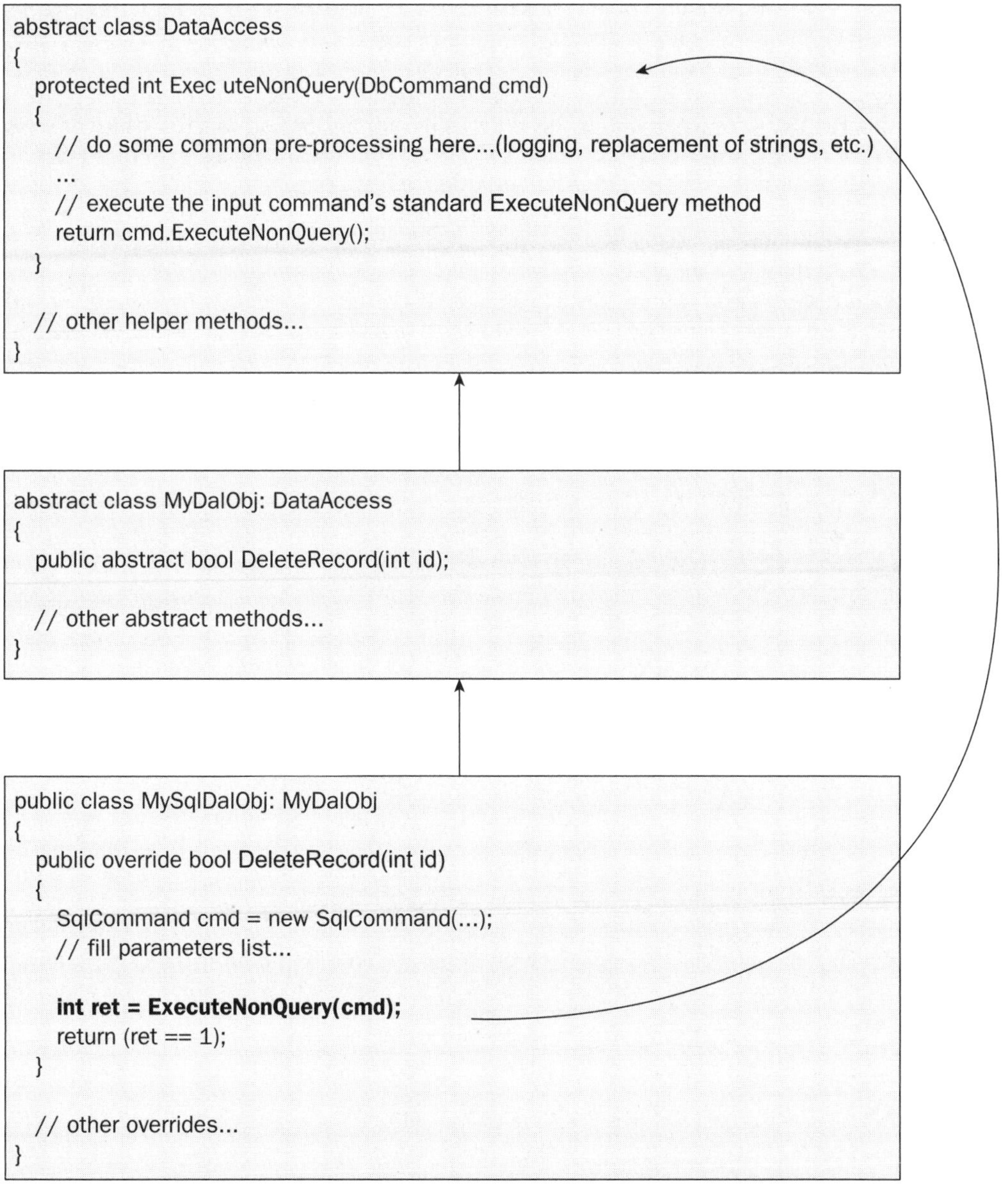

```
abstract class DataAccess
{
    protected int Exec uteNonQuery(DbCommand cmd)
    {
        // do some common pre-processing here...(logging, replacement of strings, etc.)
        ...
        // execute the input command's standard ExecuteNonQuery method
        return cmd.ExecuteNonQuery();
    }

    // other helper methods...
}
```

```
abstract class MyDalObj: DataAccess
{
    public abstract bool DeleteRecord(int id);

    // other abstract methods...
}
```

```
public class MySqlDalObj: MyDalObj
{
    public override bool DeleteRecord(int id)
    {
        SqlCommand cmd = new SqlCommand(...);
        // fill parameters list...

        int ret = ExecuteNonQuery(cmd);
        return (ret == 1);
    }

    // other overrides...
}
```

Figure 3-2

As mentioned earlier, we won't fully implement the replaceable table name and stored procedure name substitution in this book in order to keep the SQL statements and stored procedures easier to understand and work with. If you need to deploy many similar sites and you want to use the same database (which may be the case if you're an application service provider, and you will install sites for different clients on the same web server and database), then you would be better off designing the data store to support this architecture from the beginning. However, the site we're developing in this book will not encounter that situation, and there's no reason to make the design overly complex.

There's another real-world example of why this base class architecture is a good idea. As I was testing an early version of the sample site for this book, it occurred to me that it might be a good idea to put this site online on the Internet to enable people to see how it works. This might help someone decide whether they want to buy the book, and it might help them follow along in the book if they can view a real site as they read it. A large part of this site involves the administration console, which enables users to add, delete, and edit any dynamic content present on the site: articles, pictures, forums posts, newsletter, polls, etc. Therefore, it would be important for a reader to explore that part as well, and not only the end-user interface. However, I didn't want people to modify the sample content I prepared. In my situation, the administration user interface should be completely browsable, but clicking the buttons to edit/delete/insert content should have no effect, and I certainly didn't want to create a separate version of the UI to disable those buttons. Since I had already created the `DataAccess` base class with those methods, and all provider classes use it, it sufficed for me to add some code to the `ExecuteNonQuery` method (which executes all the `insert`, `update`, and `delete` statements), which could avoid executing the command if the site's current user were named `"SampleEditor"` (an account created for these demonstration purposes). It took only one minute, and the result is exactly what I wanted! Later in the chapter you'll see how this is actually implemented, and in the next chapter I'll cover the membership system, which is used to handle user accounts and member registration.

Designing the Business Logic Layer

The DAL discussed in the previous section is made up of a number of classes that retrieve data from the database by running stored procedures and returning as a collection of custom entity classes that wrap the fields of the retrieved data. The data returned by the DAL is still raw data, even though it's wrapped in classes, because these entity classes do not add anything; they are just a strongly typed container used to move data around. The BLL consumes this data and exposes it to the UI layer, but the BLL also adds validation logic and calculated properties, making some properties private or read-only (while they are all public and writeable in the custom entity classes used between the DAL and the BLL), and adds instance and static methods to delete, edit, insert, and retrieve data. For a domain object named `Employee` that represents an employee, there may be a property named `Boss` that returns a reference to another object of type `Employee` that represents the first object's boss. In middle- to large-size projects there are usually dozens, hundreds, or maybe even thousands of such objects, with relationships between them. This object-oriented and strongly typed representation of any data provides an extremely strong abstraction from the database, which merely stores the data, and it provides a simple and powerful set of classes for the UI developer to work with, without needing to know any details about how and where the raw data will be stored, how many tables are in the database, or which relationships exist between them. This makes the UI developer's job easier, and makes it possible for us to change low-level database structures without breaking any of the UI code (which is one of the primary reasons for using a multi-tier design). This definitely requires more development time initially, and more talented and experienced developers to create this design (which is why you're reading this book) than would be required if we just used a `DataSet` to pass data around, but in the long run it pays off in the form of easier maintainability and increased reliability.

Once you have a well-designed, completed BLL using domain objects, developing the user interface will be very easy, and could be done by less experienced developers in less time, so some of the up-front time you spend early in the project can be recovered later when you develop the UI. The diagram in Figure 3-3 represents the relationship between the DAL's providers and entity class, and the BLL's domain objects. As you can see, the `Customer` business class has the same instance properties of the `CustomerDetails` DAL's entity class, plus a `CompleteName` calculated read-only property that returns the concatenation of `FirstName` and `LastName`. Additionally, it has a couple of instance methods to delete and update the data represented by a specific object, and a number of static methods to retrieve a list of `Customer` objects, or a single `Customer` with a specific ID, or to create, update or delete a customer. The following snippet of code shows how a UI developer could retrieve a `Customer` object filled with some data from the database, update some fields, and then save the changes back to the database:

```
Customer cust = Customer.GetCustomerByID(3);
cust.FirstName = "Marco";
cust.LastName = "Bellinaso";
cust.Update();
```

Alternately, in this case it would be simpler to use the `UpdateCustomer` static method because you wouldn't need to create a class instance:

```
Customer.UpdateCustomer(3, "Marco", "Bellinaso");
```

Which method you use depends on the situation, of course. If you just need to update an existing record but don't need to fill a `Customer` object with the current data in the database, use the static method. If, instead, you need to read and display the current data, and then update the data, then the first example using the instance method is best.

When you design the BLL of your application, the layering and class design are not the only things you need to think about. There are a number of other questions you need to consider:

❑ Can I, and how would I, avoid querying for the same, unchanged data every few seconds in order to increase performance and boost the user's experience?

❑ How can I handle transactions for methods made up of multiple sub-operations that must be executed atomically yielding consistent results, so that either all sub-actions complete successfully or they are all rolled back?

❑ How can I log any unhandled exception thrown by the application, so that an administrator can later review it and correct the problem, and also log other events of particular interest, either standard ASP.NET events (application started or shut-down) or custom events (record deleted)?

The following sections consider these questions and suggest a possible solution for them.

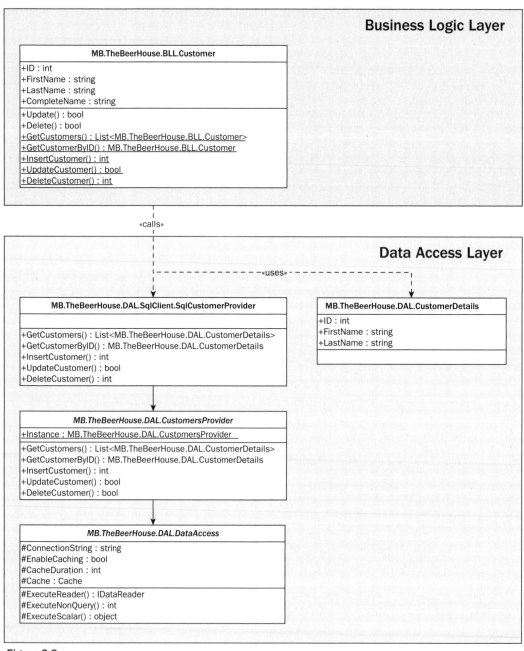

Business Logic Layer

MB.TheBeerHouse.BLL.Customer
+ID : int +FirstName : string +LastName : string +CompleteName : string
+Update() : bool +Delete() : bool +GetCustomers() : List<MB.TheBeerHouse.BLL.Customer> +GetCustomerByID() : MB.TheBeerHouse.BLL.Customer +InsertCustomer() : int +UpdateCustomer() : bool +DeleteCustomer() : int

«calls»

Data Access Layer

«uses»

MB.TheBeerHouse.DAL.SqlClient.SqlCustomerProvider
+GetCustomers() : List<MB.TheBeerHouse.DAL.CustomerDetails> +GetCustomerByID() : MB.TheBeerHouse.DAL.CustomerDetails +InsertCustomer() : int +UpdateCustomer() : bool +DeleteCustomer() : int

MB.TheBeerHouse.DAL.CustomerDetails
+ID : int +FirstName : string +LastName : string

MB.TheBeerHouse.DAL.CustomersProvider
+Instance : MB.TheBeerHouse.DAL.CustomersProvider
+GetCustomers() : List<MB.TheBeerHouse.DAL.CustomerDetails> +GetCustomerByID() : MB.TheBeerHouse.DAL.CustomerDetails +InsertCustomer() : int +UpdateCustomer() : bool +DeleteCustomer() : bool

MB.TheBeerHouse.DAL.DataAccess
#ConnectionString : string #EnableCaching : bool #CacheDuration : int #Cache : Cache
#ExecuteReader() : IDataReader #ExecuteNonQuery() : int #ExecuteScalar() : object

Figure 3-3

Caching Data for Better Performance

In every site or web-based application there is some data that doesn't change very often, which is requested very frequently by a lot of end users. Examples are the list of article categories, or the e-store's product categories and product items, the list of countries and states, and so on. The most common solution to increase the performance of your site is to implement a caching system for that type of data, so that once the data is retrieved from the data store once, it will be kept in memory for some interval, and subsequent requests for the same data will retrieve it from the memory cache, avoiding a round-trip to the database server and running another query. This will save processing time and network traffic, and thus produce a faster output to the user. In ASP.NET 1.x, the `System.Web.Caching.Cache` class was commonly used to cache data. The cache works as an extended dictionary collection, whereby each entry has a key and a related value. You can store an item in cache by writing `Cache.Insert("key", data)`, and you retrieve it by writing `data = Cache["key"]`. The `Insert` method of the `Cache` class has a number of other overloads through which you can specify either the cached data's expiration time or how long the data will be kept in the cache, and whether it is a sliding interval (a sliding interval is reset every time the cached data is accessed), plus a dependency to a file or other cached items. When the dependent file is changed, the expiration time is reached, or the interval passes, the data will be purged from the cache, and at the next request you will need to query the data directly from the database, storing it into the cache again.

The New Caching with SQL Dependency Support

One limitation of the ASP.NET 1.x cache is that when the expiration time or caching interval is reached, the data is removed from the cache and you have to read it again from the DB even if it hasn't actually changed in the database. Conversely, if you cache the data for 30 minutes, and the data changes the second after you cache it, you'll be displaying stale and out-of-sync data for almost 30 minutes. This could be unacceptable for some types of information, such as the price of a product or the number of items in stock. The `Cache` class has been enhanced for ASP.NET 2.0; it now supports dependencies to database tables, in addition to files and other cached items. In practice, you can cache the data for an indeterminate period, until the data in the source database's table actually changes. This cache invalidation mechanism works for all versions of SQL Server (version 7 and later), where it is based on polling and triggers. SQL Server 2005 adds another type of cache invalidation based on receiving events from the database, so it's more efficient if you know you'll be deploying to SQL Server 2005. In addition, the polling method only watches for table-level changes, but the SQL Server 2005 event method enables you to watch individual rows to see if they've been changed.

SQL Server 7+ Support for Table-level SQL Dependencies

When using the polling style of cache invalidation, ASP.NET 2.0 checks a counter in a support table every so often (the interval being configurable), and if the retrieved value is greater than the value read on the last check, then the data was changed, and thus it removes it from cache. There is one counter (and therefore one record in the `AspNet_CacheTablesForChangeNotification` support table) for each table for which you want to add SQL-dependency support. The counter is incremented by a table-specific trigger. You create the required table, trigger, and stored procedure needed to support the SQL dependency system by executing the `aspnet_regsql.exe` command-line tool from Visual Studio's command prompt. Run it once to add the support at the database level to create the `AspNet_Cache TablesForChangeNotification` table and the supporting stored procedure, as follows (this assumes your database is a local SQL Server Express instance named `SqlExpress`):

```
aspnet_regsql.exe -E -S .\SqlExpress -d aspnetdb -ed
```

The -E option specifies that you're using Windows integrated security and thus don't need to pass username and password credentials (you would need to use the -U and -P parameters, respectively, otherwise). The -S option specifies the SQL Server instance name (specifying localhost\SqlExpress is the same). SqlExpress is the default instance name you get when you install SQL Server 2005 Express. The -d option specifies the database name (aspnetdb), and the -ed tells it to "enable database."

The next step is to add support for a specific table, which means you must create a record in the AspNet_CacheTablesForChangeNotification table, and a trigger for the table to which you're adding support:

```
aspnet_regsql.exe -E -S .\SqlExpress -d aspnetdb -t Customers -et
```

In addition to the first command description given earlier, the -t parameter specifies the table name, and the -et parameter stands for "enable table." For the preceding commands to work, the aspnetdb database must be already attached to a SQL Server instance. This is already the case for SQL Server 7/2000 and for the fully featured editions of SQL Server 2005; however, with SQL Server 2005 Express, you typically have the database attach dynamically at runtime, so that you can do the XCopy deployment for the database as well as for the rest of the site's files. If that's your situation, you must first temporarily attach the database file, run aspnet_regsql.exe, and then detach the database. The attachment/detachment can be done by running the sp_attach_db and sp_detach_db system stored procedures. You can execute them from SQL Server Management Studio Express (downloadable from Microsoft if it didn't come with your SQL Express installation), or from the sqlcmd.exe command-line program, run from the VS 2005's command prompt. Many of the SQL commands used as examples in this book use the sqlcmd program because everyone should have this program. It is started from a Visual Studio command prompt as follows (the command-line options are similar to those of aspnet_regsql as explained above):

```
sqlcmd -E -S .\SqlExpress
```

Once you are in the sqlcmd program, you run the following command to attach the database:

```
sp_attach_db "aspnetdb", "c:\Websites\TheBeerHouse\App_Data\AspNetDB.mdf"
go
```

Then run the two aspnet_regsql commands listed above followed by "go" on a separate line to end the batch, and finally detach the database as follows:

```
sp_detach_db "aspnetdb"
go
```

*To close the sqlcmd shell, just type **quit** or **exit** and press Enter. Note that if you were running the stored procedures from SQL Server Management Studio, you would need to replace the double quotes with single quotes, and the GO command would not be needed.*

The last thing to do to complete the SQL dependency configuration is to write the polling settings in the web.config file. You can configure different polling profiles for the same database, or different settings for different databases. This is done by adding entries under the system.web/caching/sqlCache Dependency/databases section, as shown below:

```
<configuration>
  <connectionStrings>
```

```
        <add name="SiteDB" connectionString="Data Source=.\SQLExpress;Integrated
            Security=True;User Instance=True;AttachDBFilename=|DataDirectory|
            AspNetDB.mdf" />
    </connectionStrings>

    <system.web>
        <caching>
            <sqlCacheDependency enabled="true" pollTime="10000">
                <databases>
                    <add name="SiteDB-Cache" connectionStringName="SiteDB"
                        pollTime="2000" />
                </databases>
            </sqlCacheDependency>
        </caching>

        <!-- other settings here... -->
    </system.web>
</configuration>
```

As you see, there is an entry named `SiteDB-cache` that refers to the databases pointed to by the connection string called `SiteDB` (more about this later) and that defines a polling interval of 2 seconds (2,000 milliseconds). If the `pollTime` attribute is not specified, the default value of 10 seconds (in the sample above) would be used.

Now that everything is configured, you can finally write the code to actually cache the data. To create a dependency to a `Customers` table, you create an instance of the `System.Web.Caching.SqlCache Dependency` class, whose constructor takes the caching profile name defined above, and the table name. Then, when you insert the data into the `Cache` class, you pass the `SqlCacheDependency` object as a third parameter to the `Cache.Insert` method, as shown below:

```
SqlCacheDependency dep = new SqlCacheDependency("SiteDB-cache", "Customers");
Cache.Insert("Customers", customers, dep);
```

Let's assume that you have a `GetCustomers` method in your DAL that returns a list of `CustomerDetails` objects filled with data from the `Customers` table. You could implement caching as follows:

```
public List<CustomerDetails> GetCustomers()
{
    List<CustomerDetails> customers = null;

    if (Cache["Customers"] != null)
    {
        customers = (List<CustomerDetails>)Cache["Customers"];
    }
    else
    {
        using (SqlConnection cn = new SqlConnection(_connString))
        {
            SqlCommand cmd = new SqlCommand("SELECT * FROM Customers", cn);
            customers = FillCustomerListFromReader(cmd.ExecuteReader());

            SqlCacheDependency dep = new SqlCacheDependency(
                "SiteDB-cache", "Customers");
```

```
            Cache.Insert("Customers", customers, dep);
        }
    }

    return customers;
}
```

The method first checks whether the data is already in cache: If it is, then it retrieves the data from there; otherwise, it first retrieves it from the database, and then caches it for later use.

Not only can you use this caching expiration mechanism for storing data to be accessed from code, you can also use it for the ASP.NET's Output Caching feature, i.e., caching the HTML produced by page rendering, so that pages don't have to be re-rendered every time, even when the page's output would not change. To add output caching to a page, add the @OutputCache page directive at the top of the .aspx file (or the .ascx file if you want to use *fragment caching* in user controls):

```
<%@ OutputCache Duration="3600" VaryByParam="None"
    SqlDependency="SiteDB-cache:Customers" %>
```

With this directive, the page's output will be cached for a maximum of one hour, or less if the data in the Customers table is modified.

The problem with this implementation of the SQL dependency caching is that the dependency is to the entire table; it invalidates the cache regardless of which data in the table is changed. If you retrieved and cached just a few records from a table of thousands of records, why should you purge them when some other records are modified? With SQL Server 7 and 2000 whole-table monitoring for cache dependencies is your only choice, but SQL Server 2005 adds row-specific cache dependency tracking.

SQL Server 2005-specific SQL Dependency Support

The counter- and polling-based SQL dependency implementation just described is fully supported by SQL Server 2005, but this latest version of SQL Server also has some new features and technology built into it that further extend the capabilities of the Cache class. The new engine is able to create an indexed view (a view with a physical copy of the rows) when a query for which the client wants to create a dependency is executed. If after an insert, delete or update statement the results returned by a query would change, SQL Server 2005 can detect this situation and send a message to the client that registered for the dependency, by means of the Service Broker. These Query Notification events sent from SQL Server back to an application program enable a client to be notified when some data it previously retrieved was changed in the DB since it was originally retrieved, so that the client can re-request that data for the latest changes. A new class, System.Data.SqlClient.SqlDependency, can create a dependency tied to a specific SqlCommand, and thus create a logical subscription for change notifications that are received by its OnChange event handler. The following snippet shows how to create such a dependency:

```
using (SqlConnection cn = new SqlConnection(_connString))
{
    cn.Open();
    SqlCommand cmd = new SqlCommand(
        "SELECT ID, CustomerName FROM dbo.Customers", cn);
    SqlDependency dep = new SqlDependency(cmd);
    dep.OnChange += new OnChangeEventHandler(CustomersData_OnChange);
```

```
    SqlDataReader reader = cmd.ExecuteReader();

    while (reader.Read())
    {
        Trace.Write(reader["CustomerName"].ToString());
    }

}
```

Below is the specified event handler for OnChange, raised when the underlying data returned by the preceding query changes in the database:

```
void CustomersData_OnChange(object sender, SqlNotificationEventArgs e)
{
    Trace.Warn("Customers data has changed. Reload it from the DB.");
}
```

> **Note that in order for this code to work, you must first enable the Query Notifications support in your client by calling the** SqlDependency.Start **method once, somewhere in the application. If you're using it from within a web-based application, the right place to put this call would be in the** Application_Start **global event handler in** global.asax. **For a WinForms application, it may be the Main entry-point method, or the main form's** Form_Load **event.**

The preceding code just shows that we're being notified when the underlying data in the database has changed, but we normally want to go one step further and purge data from the cache when changes are detected in the database. The ASP.NET's SqlCacheDependency has other overloaded versions of its constructor, and one of them takes a SqlCommand instance. It creates a SqlDependency object internally behind the scenes, and handles its OnChange event to automatically remove the data from the cache when data for the specific SELECT query would change. Here's all you have to do to cache some data with a dependency to a SqlCommand:

```
SqlCommand cmd = new SqlCommand("SELECT ID, CustomerName FROM dbo.Customers", cn);
SqlCacheDependency dep = new SqlCacheDependency(cmd);
Cache.Insert("keyname", data, dep);
```

The sample GetCustomers method shown above would then become the following:

```
public List<CustomerDetails> GetCustomers()
{
    List<CustomerDetails> customers = null;

    if (Cache["Customers"] != null)
    {
        customers = (List<CustomerDetails>)Cache["Customers"];
    }
    else
    {
        using (SqlConnection cn = new SqlConnection(_connString))
        {
```

```
        SqlCommand cmd = new SqlCommand(
            "SELECT ID, CustomerName FROM dbo.Customers", cn);
        SqlCacheDependency dep = new SqlCacheDependency(cmd);

        customers = FillCustomerListFromReader(cmd.ExecuteReader());
        Cache.Insert("Customers", customers, dep);
    }
}

    return customers;
}
```

This technology has the obvious advantage that the dependency is at the query level, and not at the entire table level like the implementation for SQL Server 7/2000, and the event method is much more efficient than using a polling mechanism. However, it has a number of serious limitations that drastically reduce the number of occasions when it can be used, so sometimes the whole-table polling method is your only choice. Here are the most important constraints:

❑   You can't use the * wildcard in the SELECT query; instead, you must explicitly list all the fields. This is a good practice anyway, because you should only request fields that you actually need and not necessarily all of them. Listing them explicitly also puts you in control of their order in the returned DataReader or DataTable, something that can be important if you access fields by index and not by name (although access by index is not itself a good practice).

❑   You must reference any table with the full name, e.g., dbo.Customers. Just Customers wouldn't be enough. This is a significant issue because most of us aren't used to fully qualifying table names, but it's a simple matter to handle if you remember that you need to do it.

❑   The query can't use aggregation functions such as COUNT, SUM, AVG, MIN, MAX, etc.

❑   The query can't use ranking and windowing functions, such as the new ROW_NUMBER() function, which is tremendously useful for implementing high-performance results pagination to be used, for example, in the DataGrid, GridView, or other ASP.NET server-side controls. (This function will be explained in Chapter 5.)

❑   You can't reference views or temporary tables in the query.

❑   The query can't return fields of type text, ntext, or image (blob types). Consider that many tables will have such columns, for containing the description of a product, the content of an article or a newsletter, etc.

❑   You can't use DISTINCT, HAVING, CONTAINS and FREETEXT.

❑   The query can't include subqueries, outer-joins or self-joins. This is one of the biggest limitations, as subqueries are commonly used.

❑   All of the preceding limitations exist regardless of whether the query is run directly from the client as a SQL text command, or from inside a stored procedure. For stored procedures, however, there's a further limitation: You can't use the SET NOCOUNT ON statement, which is often used (and suggested) to reduce the quantity of information sent across the network, for cases where you don't need counts.

If you consider that most of the modules developed in the following chapters will need to implement custom pagination to be fast (and thus windowing functions or temporary tables, COUNT, subqueries and other prohibited features), and that many columns will be of type ntext, you can easily understand why you may not be able to use to this form of SQL dependency often.

If you want to know more about the Service Broker and Query Notifications, the technology behind Sql Dependencies, I recommend a whitepaper written by Bob Beauchemin, titled "Query Notifications in ADO.NET 2.0" and available on MSDN Online at `http://msdn.microsoft.com/library/ default.asp?url=/library/en-us/dnvs05/html/querynotification.asp`.

Choosing a Caching Strategy That Fits Your Needs

The `Cache` class has been greatly improved in its latest implementation. However, more is less sometimes, and using your own code to handle the expiration of data and manual purging may be better than using some form of automated SQL dependency. The polling-based approach is done at the table level, so it will often invalidate your data when unrelated data in the same table has been changed. The SQL Server 2005's Service Broker/Query Notification technology is very intriguing, and will be very handy in some situations, but as I said earlier it suffers from too many limitations to be used often. Additionally, both approaches are bound to SQL Server, and should only be used in the DAL provider specific to SQL Server. Therefore, if we used the SQL dependencies, different providers (for different RDBMSs) should implement a different caching strategy, rewritten from scratch. This is something I don't like, because I want my caching code in the BLL (not in the DAL), so that it's executed the same way regardless of which DAL provider is being used. For all these reasons I won't be using any form of built-in SQL dependency for the modules developed in the rest of the book. Instead, I use the good old ASP.NET 1.x caching features based on time/interval expiration. To avoid displaying stale data, we'll implement some simple methods that purge data from cache when it actually changes in the database. To call the methods you won't need to implement triggers at the database level, or use some other connection and notification service between the data store and the application's code. You'll just call them from the BLL methods that add, edit and delete data. Because the site contents will be managed by a web-based custom administration console and your own BLL classes, there won't be a need to intercept the changes at the database level. Instead, you just add some code to the BLL methods themselves. This gives you complete control of what data you need to purge, and when you must actually purge it (e.g., when you remove data if a specific row field changes, but not if another field changes).

Transaction Management

A very important issue you must tackle when designing a business layer is how you plan to manage transactions. Many business methods call multiple DAL methods internally to update, insert, or delete multiple records, potentially in multiple tables. You must ensure that multiple calls run within a transaction, so that if one fails, all actions performed by previous methods are rolled back. If you don't do this, you'll end up having inconsistent, and wrong, data. Managing transactions would be complicated if you had to do everything yourself, but fortunately there are several technologies and frameworks that can do the plumbing for you.

ADO.NET Transactions

In the simplest case you can use explicit ADO.NET client-side transactions. You should already be familiar with them, but here's some sample code that runs a couple of commands inside a transaction to refresh your memory:

```
using (SqlConnection cn = new SqlConnection(connString))
{
    cn.Open();
    SqlTransaction tran = cn.BeginTransaction();

    try
    {
```

```
        SqlCommand cmd1 = new SqlCommand(cmdText1, cn, tran);
        cmd1.ExecuteNonQuery();

        SqlCommand cmd2 = new SqlCommand(cmdText2, cn, tran);
        cmd2.ExecuteNonQuery();

        tran.Commit();
    }
    catch(Exception e)
    {
        tran.Rollback();
    }
}
```

The preceding code is simple and works fine in many situations. However, the transactions managed by ADO.NET are connection-bound, which implies the following limitations:

❑ You have to use them from the DAL, where you have the connection objects, and not from the BLL where you'll typically (but not necessarily) want to manage transactions. This is not a problem if you're employing a lighter architecture with the DAL and BLL mixed together in a single layer, which may actually be a valid choice for small sites, but it does pose a problem for multi-tier systems.

❑ The transaction is bound to a single connection, which means it can't span multiple databases. This may be required if, for example, you store all data for the forums module in one database and the articles data on some other database, and you need some business method that updates some records in both systems within one logical transaction.

❑ All commands you execute must use the same connection. If these commands are executed from different methods, wrapping them into a single transaction means that you must find some way to pass the connection object through all the methods. This could be done with an additional method parameter, but this leads to an ugly and inflexible design.

COM+ and SWC Transactions

All of the problems presented can be solved by using COM+ as the application server for your components. COM+ can handle transactions that include multiple commands and multiple connections (also to different data stores), and generally any action that the DTC (Distributed Transaction Coordinator) can manage, such as sending a MSMQ message. By using COM+ you can easily write atomic and isolated procedures; once you start the transaction in a method, you can have all submethods enlist into the transaction automatically, and have the transaction be committed if no exception is thrown or otherwise rolled back. If your class inherits from `System.EnterpriseServices.ServicedComponent`, the transaction handling is configurable by means of .NET attributes (e.g., `AutoCompleteAttribute`, for the automatic transaction completion just outlined) that you apply at the assembly, class, and method level. Here's a sample transactional class that uses attributes to configure automatic transactions:

```
[Transaction(TransactionOption.RequiresNew)]
public class SampleBO : ServicedComponent
{
    [AutoComplete]
    public void UpdateDate()
    {
        MyBizObject1 obj1 = new MyBizObject1();
```

```
        obj1.DoSomething();

        MyBizObject2 obj2 = new MyBizObject2();
        obj2.DoSomethingElse();
    }
}
```

If you don't like declarative transactions, you can still handle them imperatively in code through the ContextUtil helper class, and its EnableCommit, DisableCommit, SetAbout, and SetComplete methods.

COM+ transactions add a lot of overhead to simple ADO.NET transactions, and as a result they are much slower (even 50%). However, COM+ doesn't just mean transactions, but also object polling, just-in-time activation, queued components and much more—all features that can make your application more reliable and scalable, which is often more important than plain performance statistics. And, after all, if your application shuts down after a high load, how useful is it to know that it was extremely fast with a few users, when it was started? The problem with using COM+ in .NET is that your business objects must inherit from `System.EnterpriseServices.ServicedComponents` and must respect a number of rules (for example, you can't define static methods), and you must make this decision early on; otherwise, adding transaction support later will require a lot of additional work. Another problem is that deploying .NET Enterprise Services is not as easy as deploying a normal assembly, as you must generate a COM type library from the assembly, and register it into the Windows registry and the COM+ catalog. These are operations that only a system administrator for the remote server can do, so you won't be able to do this if you're planning to deploy your site using an inexpensive shared hosting provider service.

Fortunately, though, if you're hosting the site on Windows Server 2003, you can take advantage of a new feature of COM+ 1.5 called Services Without Components (SWC). This should also work on Windows XP, but you should never deploy a production web application to a client version of Windows for performance and reliability reasons. This feature allows you to configure, start, and manage a distributed transaction without actually writing a typical COM+ component that must be registered in the COM+ catalog. With the .NET Framework 1.1, you can do everything with the `ServiceConfig`, `ServiceDomain`, and `ContextUtil` classes that you find in the `System.EnterpriseServices.dll` assembly, under the `System.EnterpriseServices` namespace. You can configure the transaction on-the-fly by creating an instance of `ServiceConfig` and setting the transaction type (`Transaction` and `IsolationLevel` properties), specifying whether tracking is enabled (`TrackingEnabled` property), the application and component name (`TrackingAppName` and `TrackingComponentName` properties), and other options. Finally, you start the transaction by calling the `Enter` static method of the `ServiceDomain` class, which takes the `ServiceConfig` object that specifies the configuration. You use the `SetComplete` and `SetAbort` static methods of the `ContextUtil` class to commit or roll back the transaction, respectively. Here's an example:

```
// configure and start the transaction
ServiceConfig svcConfig = new ServiceConfig();
svcConfig.TrackingEnabled = true;
svcConfig.TrackingAppName = "TheBeerHouse";
svcConfig.TrackingComponentName = "MB.TheBeerHouse.BLL.SampleBO";
svcConfig.Transaction = TransactionOption.RequiresNew;
svcConfig.IsolationLevel = TransactionIsolationLevel.ReadCommitted;
ServiceDomain.Enter(svcConfig);

try
{
```

```
    MyBizObject1 obj1 = new MyBizObject1();
    obj1.DoSomething();

    MyBizObject2 obj2 = new MyBizObject2();
    obj2.DoSomethingElse();

    ContextUtil.SetComplete();
}
catch (Exception e)
{
    // rollback the transaction
    ContextUtil.SetAbort();
}
finally
{
    ServiceDomain.Leave();
}
```

This code wraps the calls to two different business objects into a single distributed transaction controlled by the DTC. You only have to start the transaction, catch exceptions that may be thrown, and commit or roll back the transaction. You don't have any special deployment needs: a simple XCopy is enough. Also, SWC is good because you can easily add transactions to business objects that weren't originally designed to handle distributed transactions — namely, objects that don't inherit from ServicedComponent, and that call DAL methods that are not ADO.NET transaction-aware (that don't pass Transaction objects as parameters). SWC, however, doesn't completely replace traditional Enterprise Services components, as they don't allow you to use other features such as object pooling, just-in-time activation, queued components, and all other COM+ functionality; you can use them just to add transaction support with the least development and deployment effort. All in all, this is a very welcome facility that should be used thoughtfully.

The New System.Transactions Namespace

SWC transactions are definitely good, but version 2.0 of the .NET Framework introduces something even better: a new System.Transactions namespace that provides a modern, managed interface to handle transactions that can not be handled by ADO.NET's SqlTransaction class. Two new transaction managers were introduced: Lightweight Transaction Manager and OleTx Transaction Manager. The former manages transactions bound to a single durable resource (i.e., a single connection to a single data store), while the latter can manage distributed transactions, whereby multiple connections to different data stores come into play. You don't have to choose between the two yourself; a proper transaction manager will be automatically chosen according to the type and number of resources that you wish to use in a transaction scope.

The basic class that you'll be using is System.Transactions.TransactionScope. When an object of this type is created, it starts a lightweight transaction. Then you start creating your connections and other transaction-aware resources (such as MSMQ queues and messages). As long as you use a single resource that supports lightweight transactions, the transaction will be handled by the resource manager itself. SQL Server 2005 (including the Express Edition) has this capability, so if you create a single connection to one of its databases, it will take care of everything internally, consuming as little resources as possible, and with very good performance. As soon as you introduce a second connection/resource into the transaction scope, however, the transaction manager will automatically be *promoted* to an OleTx Transaction Manager, which can handle distributed transactions by means of the COM+ DTC technology under the covers (it dynamically configures a temporary Enterprise Service through SWC). This also happens when you have a single connection to a resource manager that doesn't support lightweight transactions, such as SQL Server 7/2000, Oracle, and other RDBMSs.

Here's an example that starts a transaction and runs a couple of different commands within it:

```
using(TransactionScope scope = new TransactionScope())
{
    using (SqlConnection cn = new SqlConnection(connString))
    {
        cn.Open();
        SqlCommand cmd1 = new SqlCommand(cmdText1, cn);
        cmd1.ExecuteNonQuery();

        SqlCommand cmd2 = new SqlCommand(cmdText2, cn);
        cmd2.ExecuteNonQuery();
    }
    scope.Complete();
}
```

Because the two commands share the same connection, a lightweight transaction will be created if connString points to a SQL Server 2005 database. As I mentioned before, though, transactions are often run from the BLL, and must wrap calls to several other methods, which internally may create separate connections and target different databases. The code is still as simple as the preceding code, though:

```
using(TransactionScope scope = new TransactionScope())
{
    MyBizObject1 obj1 = new MyBizObject1();
    obj1.DoSomething();

    MyBizObject2 obj2 = new MyBizObject2();
    obj2.DoSomethingElse();

    scope.Complete();
}
```

When this code is run, a distributed COM+ transaction will probably be created under the covers (it depends on whether the two methods use two connections or share a single one), but the developer doesn't need to know this, and doesn't have to do anything special at design time or deployment time. Another advantage of using System.Transactions is that you can create transactions only in methods where you really need them, and you don't have to make a whole class transactional. Given how simple it is to work with TransactionScope and related classes, you don't even need to build a framework or some sort to base service to simplify things; it's all already there! However, I would not recommend COM+, SWC, or System.Transactions for use with shared web hosting because the servers are out of your control and it's not clear whether this could be used reliably in an environment where server reconfiguration is commonplace. Also, in the sample web site for this book, we won't make use of these advanced technologies.

> *If you want to know more about System.Transactions, refer to Juval Lowy's whitepaper entitled "Introducing System.Transactions in the Microsoft .NET Framework version 2.0," downloadable from* www.microsoft.com/downloads/details.aspx?FamilyId=AAC3D722-444C-4E27-8B2E-C6157ED16B15&displaylang=en.

Health Monitoring and Exception Handling

Runtime exceptions and errors happen sometimes, but your end user doesn't need to know it. Or if there is such an important error that prevents the site from working, then a simplified error should be shown to the user — you should never display technical info in an error message (for security reasons). Every site should catch exceptions, log them for future review by an administrator, and output a friendly error page to the user. In the "old" days of ASP.NET 1.1, you had to take care of just about everything, including implementing your own logging system that would save exception information to a database, a text file, the Event Viewer, or some other data store, writing and managing some sort of custom configuration to allow administrators to enable or disable the logging, etc.

> *Exception handling, logging, and configuration management can be implemented quite easily using the framework provided in the Enterprise Library, which includes some of the building blocks developed in recent years by the Microsoft Patterns & Practices Team. However, it's an external library and there's a fair amount of work involved to set it up and integrate it into a site. My experience is that it seems like overkill in many situations, and the heavy architecture may lead to new opportunities for a site to fail, but it's quite helpful to study their code, and you can learn a lot from their efforts. You can read more about Enterprise Library and the building blocks that compose it from* http://msdn.microsoft.com/ library/default.asp?url=/library/en-us/dnpag2/html/entlib.asp.

ASP.NET has always had events and configuration settings that allow you to easily implement custom error pages, so that the user doesn't see those yellow pages with raw details about the exception (something that not only was ugly to see, but if you had left debug information in the assemblies uploaded to the server, could even be dangerous, as it could expose small but potentially critical pieces of your source code, SQL table names, etc.). Instead of going to the IIS administration console to specify the path for the custom error pages for different error codes (something you often can't do if you're on a shared hosting site), just use the `customErrors` section in `the web.config` file, as follows:

```
<customErrors mode="RemoteOnly" defaultRedirect="~/FriendlyError.aspx">
   <error statusCode="404" redirect="~/PageNotFound.aspx" />
</customErrors>
```

As you see, you can have error pages for a specific error code, and a default error page that covers all other cases. `mode="RemoteOnly"` means that the custom error page will only be shown to remote clients; if you browse the site from the local machine (i.e., if you have an in-house server and work directly from there, or if you can do it through a Remote Desktop connection), you will still see the raw error information and stack trace.

Besides simply showing the user a friendlier message for errors, you could also log all details about an exception by writing some custom code in the page's `Error` event handler. Even better, you could just override the `OnError` method of a custom page base class (if you had it) so that you write the code only once and the logging behavior would be inherited by all other pages:

```
public class BasePage : System.Web.UI.Page
{
    protected override void OnError(EventArgs e)
    {
        // log last exception, retrieved by Server.GetLastError()
    }
    ...
}
```

Alternatively, if you didn't have a custom base page class, you could do the same from the `Application_Error` event handler, in the `Global.asax.cs` code-behind file:

```
void Application_Error(Object sender, EventArgs e)
{
    // log last exception, retrieved by Server.GetLastError()
}
```

These logging techniques still work, of course, but now with ASP.NET 2.0 there's something much better, and it saves us a lot of time and effort: the *instrumentation and health monitoring system*. This system takes care of logging a number of things: unhandled application exceptions, lifetime events (application started, application stopped, etc.), audit events (failed or successful logins, failed request validation, etc.) and more. In some ways this is similar to the Enterprise Library, but it's built in to ASP.NET. You can also create your own custom events, which you can then raise to log particular actions, such as the deletion of a record. This framework is extensively customizable through the new `<healthMonitoring>` section in `web.config`, where you can define rules for logging events (such as the maximum number of times the same event can be logged in a specified interval), register custom events, and register and select the provider class you want to use to log events. In fact, the health monitoring system — like many other ASP.NET 2.0 parts (such as the Membership system, described in the next chapter) — is based on the provider model design pattern: This means that several classes inherit from a common abstract base class, and provide different concrete implementations. The various providers allow to us save the logged data on different media: The built-in providers can log to a SQL Server database, the Windows Event Log, the WMI Log, or to e-mails. You can also create your own logging providers by inheriting from the `System.Web.Management.WebEventProvider` base provider class, but the built-in providers cover most of the logging needs I can think of (unless you want to log to Oracle, or something like that). I'm not fond of logging onto a database as the only logging mechanism because you might be trying to log an error regarding a database problem, and you may not be able to log the message because the database may be down. However, if you're in a shared-hosting scenario, you probably won't have access to the Event Viewer, and using text files is not good because of potential locking and concurrency issues, so using a database is still the best option.

As an example of what information is logged, here's a case where a `DivideByZero` exception is thrown and not caught, and the following text is logged by the health monitoring framework, if is properly configured:

```
Event code: 3005
Event message: An unhandled exception has occurred.
Event time: 10/10/2005 3:52:47 PM
Event time (UTC): 10/10/2005 10:52:47 PM
Event ID: 82cfbe7544f54a10abfb31fcabc1d466
Event sequence: 221
Event occurrence: 1
Event detail code: 0

Application information:
    Application domain: 71f34b0a-1-127734569896956416
    Trust level: Full
    Application Virtual Path: /TheBeerHouse
    Application Path: C:\Websites\TheBeerHouse\
    Machine name: VSNETBETA2

Process information:
    Process ID: 5064
```

```
        Process name: WebDev.WebServer.EXE
        Account name: VSNETBETA2\Marco

    Exception information:
        Exception type: DivideByZeroException
        Exception message: Attempted to divide by zero.

    Request information:
        Request URL: http://localhost:14376/TheBeerHouse/Default.aspx
        Request path: /TheBeerHouse/Default.aspx
        User host address: 127.0.0.1
        User: SampleEditor
        Is authenticated: True
        Authentication Type: Forms
        Thread account name: VSNETBETA2\Marco

    Thread information:
        Thread ID: 4
        Thread account name: VSNETBETA2\Marco
        Is impersonating: False
        Stack trace:    at _Default.Page_Load(Object sender, EventArgs e) in
    c:\Websites\TheBeerHouse\Default.aspx.cs:line 17
        at System.Web.Util.CalliHelper.EventArgFunctionCaller(IntPtr fp, Object o,
    Object t, EventArgs e)
        at System.Web.Util.CalliEventHandlerDelegateProxy.Callback(Object sender,
    EventArgs e)
        at System.Web.UI.Control.OnLoad(EventArgs e)
        at MB.TheBeerHouse.UI.BasePage.OnLoad(EventArgs e) in
    c:\Websites\TheBeerHouse\App_Code\BasePage.cs:line 46
        at System.Web.UI.Control.LoadRecursive()
        at System.Web.UI.Page.ProcessRequestMain(Boolean includeStagesBeforeAsyncPoint,
    Boolean includeStagesAfterAsyncPoint)


    Custom event details:

    For more information, see Help and Support Center at
    http://go.microsoft.com/fwlink/events.asp.
```

As you see, in addition to the exception error message, a lot of other information is included in the logged message, such as the URL and physical path of the page that threw the exception, the server name and IP address, the application's trust level, the current date and time, the current thread's and current process' username, the name of the site's user if they are currently logged in, the exception's stack trace, and more.

Configuring the Health Monitoring System

Looking at the framework in more details, the events raised and logged are instances of some classes you find under the System.Web.Management namespace, or custom classes:

❑   **WebBaseEvent:** A generic base event class from which all other events inherit

❑   **WebManagementEvent:** A base class for all the application events, including request errors, lifetime events (application start and end) and audit events

- ❑ **WebHeartbeatEvent:** An event raised periodically by the ASP.NET engine, containing information representing the health of the application at that time: number of active threads, queued and executing requests, and memory usage

- ❑ **WebRequestEvent:** The base class for all events related to web requests, such as failed cross-site scripting validation, exceeded maximum post length, or anything else that stops the current request from completing

- ❑ **WebAuditEvent:** This event is raised on failed or successful authentications, and failed decryption and validation of the page's ViewState, cookies, etc.

- ❑ **WebBaseErrorEvent:** The base class for all error events, including exceptions and request/infrastructure errors

- ❑ **WebErrorEvent:** The event for infrastructure errors, such as compilation, parsing and configuration errors

These are the built-in provider classes (all located under the `System.Web.Management`):

- ❑ **EventLogWebEventProvider:** Logs events to the Windows Event Log

- ❑ **SqlWebEventProvider:** Logs events to a SQL Server (7, 2000 or 2005) database, as long as they have the expected tables and stored procedures (explained below)

- ❑ **TraceWebEventProvider:** Sends events to the current trace listener collection (typically the tracing is saved in memory to be displayed by `trace.axd`, or on the page's output itself, but additional listeners can be added to save information on a file or other media)

- ❑ **WmiWebEventProvider:** Forwards the web events to the Windows Management Instrumentation (WMI) subsystems

- ❑ **SimpleMailWebEventProvider:** Sends the web event's information by e-mail to the specified administrator

- ❑ **TemplatedMailWebEventProvider:** Like `SimpleMailWebEventProvider`, but with an additional property that points to a text file to be used as template for the mail, so that it can be completely customized and translated.

The configuration settings stored in the `web.config` file have the following format:

```
<healthMonitoring>
    <eventMappings>...</eventMappings>
    <providers>...</providers>
    <rules>...</rules>
    <profiles>...</profiles>
    <bufferModes>...</bufferModes>
</healthMonitoring>
```

The `eventMapping` subsection registers the event classes by specifying their full type. You must manually register both built-in and custom classes that you want to be logged. You assign a name to the event class you register, and you'll use it in other sections to identify the event type you want to configure. Following is an excerpt from the `default web.config` that registers all built-in events:

```
<eventMappings>
    <add name="All Events" type="System.Web.Management.WebBaseEvent,System.Web, ⤶
        Version=2.0.0.0,Culture=neutral,PublicKeyToken=b03f5f7f11d50a3a"
```

```
                    startEventCode="0" endEventCode="2147483647" />
        <add name="Heartbeats" type="System.Web.Management.WebHeartbeatEvent,System.Web, ⟳
            Version=2.0.0.0,Culture=neutral,PublicKeyToken=b03f5f7f11d50a3a"
                    startEventCode="0" endEventCode="2147483647" />
        <add name="Application Lifetime Events" type="System.Web.Management          ⟳
            .WebApplicationLifetimeEvent,System.Web,Version=2.0.0.0,Culture=neutral,
            PublicKeyToken=b03f5f7f11d50a3a"
                    startEventCode="0" endEventCode="2147483647" />
        <add name="Request Processing Events" type="System.Web.Management            ⟳
            .WebRequestEvent,System.Web,Version=2.0.0.0,Culture=neutral,
            PublicKeyToken=b03f5f7f11d50a3a"
                    startEventCode="0" endEventCode="2147483647" />
        <add name="All Errors" type="System.Web.Management.WebBaseErrorEvent,System   ⟳
            .Web,Version=2.0.0.0,Culture=neutral,PublicKeyToken=b03f5f7f11d50a3a"
                    startEventCode="0" endEventCode="2147483647" />
        <add name="Infrastructure Errors" type="System.Web.Management.WebErrorEvent,  ⟳
            System.Web,Version=2.0.0.0,Culture=neutral,PublicKeyToken=b03f5f7f11d50a3a"
                    startEventCode="0" endEventCode="2147483647" />
        <add name="Request Processing Errors" type="System.Web.Management            ⟳
            .WebRequestErrorEvent,System.Web,Version=2.0.0.0,Culture=neutral,
            PublicKeyToken=b03f5f7f11d50a3a"
                    startEventCode="0" endEventCode="2147483647" />
        <add name="All Audits" type="System.Web.Management.WebAuditEvent,System.Web,  ⟳
            Version=2.0.0.0,Culture=neutral,PublicKeyToken=b03f5f7f11d50a3a"
                    startEventCode="0" endEventCode="2147483647" />
        <add name="Failure Audits" type="System.Web.Management.WebFailureAuditEvent,  ⟳
            System.Web,Version=2.0.0.0,Culture=neutral,PublicKeyToken=b03f5f7f11d50a3a"
                    startEventCode="0" endEventCode="2147483647" />
        <add name="Success Audits" type="System.Web.Management.WebSuccessAuditEvent,  ⟳
System.Web,Version=2.0.0.0,Culture=neutral,PublicKeyToken=b03f5f7f11d50a3a"
                    startEventCode="0" endEventCode="2147483647" />
    </eventMappings>
```

The `providers` subsection registers the providers. If you register multiple providers, then you'll be able to use different providers for different types of events. Here's an example of how to register the providers for SQL Server, the Event Log, and the WMI subsystem:

```
<providers>
    <add name="EventLogProvider" type="System.Web.Management              ⟳
        .EventLogWebEventProvider,System.Web,Version=2.0.0.0,Culture=neutral,
        PublicKeyToken=b03f5f7f11d50a3a" />
    <add name="SqlWebEventProvider" type="System.Web.Management           ⟳
        .SqlWebEventProvider,System.Web,Version=2.0.0.0,Culture=neutral,
        PublicKeyToken=b03f5f7f11d50a3a" connectionStringName="LocalSqlServer"
        maxEventDetailsLength="1073741823"
        buffer="false" bufferMode="Notification" />
    <add name="WmiWebEventProvider" type="System.Web.Management           ⟳
        .WmiWebEventProvider,System.Web,Version=2.0.0.0,Culture=neutral,
        PublicKeyToken=b03f5f7f11d50a3a" />
</providers>
```

Note that the element for registering the SQL Server provider has an additional attribute, `connectionStringName`, that refers to an element of the `<connectionStrings>` section with the connection string for the database that will store the logging information (more about this shortly). The `rules` section is where you actually define which events you want to log, which registered provider, and how often (if a program may get stuck in a loop that generates thousands of exceptions, then you don't want to log them all). Here's an example that configures all errors to be logged to the Windows Event Log, while the failed audit events will be logged to a SQL database:

```
<rules>
    <add name="All Errors Default" eventName="All Errors"
        provider="EventLogProvider" minInstances="1" maxLimit="Infinite"
        minInterval="00:01:00" />
    <add name="Failure Audits Default" eventName="Failure Audits"
            provider="EventLogProvider" profile="Critical" />
</rules>
```

Note that in the first element, the `minInstances`, `maxLimit`, and `minInterval` attributes specify, respectively, how many times the event must occur before it is logged, how many times it can be logged, and the minimum interval of time that must elapse before the next logged event. In my second rule element I'm not setting these values directly, but showing you how to reference to a registered profile to get these settings. An entry of the `profiles` subsection defined below contains this configuration data and allows you to apply it to multiple rules instead of repeating these items for all rules individually:

```
<profiles>
    <add name="Default" minInstances="1" maxLimit="Infinite"
        minInterval="00:01:00" />
    <add name="Critical" minInstances="1" maxLimit="Infinite"
        minInterval="00:00:00" />
</profiles>
```

The last section, `bufferModes`, contains a list of possible buffering profiles that can be applied to providers:

```
<bufferModes>
    <add name="Critical Notification" maxBufferSize="100" maxFlushSize="20"
        urgentFlushThreshold="1" regularFlushInterval="Infinite"
        urgentFlushInterval="00:01:00" maxBufferThreads="1" />
    <add name="Notification" maxBufferSize="300" maxFlushSize="20"
        urgentFlushThreshold="1" regularFlushInterval="Infinite"
        urgentFlushInterval="00:01:00" maxBufferThreads="1" />
    <add name="Logging" maxBufferSize="1000" maxFlushSize="200"
        urgentFlushThreshold="800" regularFlushInterval="00:30:00"
        urgentFlushInterval="00:05:00" maxBufferThreads="1" />
</bufferModes>
```

The only attributes (shown at the end of this chapter) for the parent `<healthMonitoring>` section are `enabled` (true by default, so it only has to be specified if you want it to be false) and `heartbeat Interval`, which is the interval in seconds that specifies how often the heartbeat event is to be raised (zero by default; set it to a positive number to activate this useful feature).

Our site will use a configuration section that specifies that generic and failed audit errors are logged to the SQL Server database used for the rest of the site's data. The Windows Event Log would be a good storage medium for this information, but this cannot be used if you deploy your site to a shared hosting environment. Logging audit failures (e.g., invalid logon attempts, etc.) to SQL Server is a viable plan because we can assume the database will be up.

In the "Solution" section we'll also create a custom event that will be raised every time a record is deleted by someone. The ID of the record and the name of the editor who deleted the record will be stored, so that if some important record is deleted by mistake the administrator can retrieve its ID and restore it from a backup copy, and know who to talk to concerning this error.

Setting Up the Database for the SQL Server Provider

The database used by the SQL Server Web Event Provider must have a particular schema (i.e., a certain table and stored procedure). The data is stored into a table named `aspnet_WebEvent_Events`, by the `aspnet_WebEvent_LogEvent` stored procedure. To create these objects, you should execute the `aspnet_regsql.exe` command-line tool from the VS2005 command prompt. If executed with no parameters, the tool will open a Windows wizard that will guide you through the configuration of an attached SQL Server database for the health monitoring system, and for other systems such as membership, role management, profiles, and personalization. However, if you just want to create the objects needed for the event logging, and not all the other tables and procedures, you can just run the tool with the following parameters (this assumes your database is a local SQL Server Express instance named `SqlExpress`):

```
aspnet_regsql.exe -E -S .\SqlExpress -d aspnetdb -A w
```

If you're using a detached SQL Server 2005 Express database, refer to the section above about caching to see how to temporarily attach to the database to run `aspnet_regsql`.

A Base Class for All Business Classes

Many business objects need access to a lot of shared information, such as the name of the current user, the IP address, and a reference to the current context's `Cache` object. This information can be placed into a `BizObject` base class that all other domain objects will inherit from. This base class also has helper methods to do things like encoding the HTML input by escaping special characters (such as < and >), and purging items from the cache. This cache purging method will be very useful for implementing our custom caching system. This is shared among all business classes, and it removes items from the shared Cache store whose key begins with a specific prefix. By choosing the proper key when entering data into the cache, you can later purge exactly those items that you want to refresh. For example, in Chapter 5 we will be building an Article Management module that handles categories of articles and article comments. You can retrieve the article and comments with an ID equal to 4 and cache them with a key equal to `Articles_Article_4`. When a new comment is inserted, or a parent article is deleted, you can just purge the `Articles_Comments_4`.

The base class written in this chapter is not big and complex — quite the opposite, actually. It's a good design practice to keep base classes small by including only the functionality that will be common to all child classes you will write that will descend from them. Even if you don't have any particular code you want to put in a base class initially, it's always a good idea to make the class anyway. Later you might decide that you need a common property or method, and you'll be glad that you already have a base class in your architecture.

Storing Connection Strings and Other Settings

So far, while discussing the DAL and the BLL, I've mentioned that the site will have a number of config-urable settings, such as the name of the DAL provider to be used, whether the caching is active, the cache duration, and the connection string to the database. Managing the configuration is something that doesn't exactly fit into any of the other three layers, but rather something that all layers will use. For example, the DAL layer will need the name of the concrete database provider to instantiate, and the connections string; the BLL will need the caching settings; and the user interface will need other settings, such as the recipient e-mail address for e-mail sent from the site's Contact Us form, the prefix for their subject lines (so that it's easy to spot them among all the other e-mails, and to set up a rule to move them to a dedicated folder in your favorite e-mail client program). All these settings are saved into the web.config file, so it's easy for an administrator to change them using only a text editor. Anytime the web.config file is changed, ASP.NET will automatically reload it, and its modified settings will be used for new users, and will not require you to restart the IIS application (which would have terminated any users already online).

In the days of ASP.NET 1.x, the connection string was typically stored into the <appSettings> section. Now this setting has its own dedicated section: <connectionStrings>. Here's an example that shows how to store a connection string and give it a shorter and friendlier name that will be used to retrieve it later from code, or from other configuration elements of web.config:

```
<configuration xmlns="http://schemas.microsoft.com/.NetConfiguration/v2.0">
    <connectionStrings>
        <add name="TheBeerHouse" providerName="System.Data.SqlClient"
            connectionString="Data Source=.\SQLExpress;
            Integrated Security=True;User Instance=True;
            AttachDBFilename=|DataDirectory|TheBeerHouse.mdf" />
    </connectionStrings>

    <system.web>
        <!-- some settings here... -->
    </system.net>
</configuration>
```

Notice that the connection string does not specify the typical *Initial Catalog* attribute, which would have been set to the database name. Instead, there is an AttachDBFilename parameter, which points to the path of the SQL Server 2005 MDF file that contains the database. This database will be dynamically attached to a SQL Server instance at runtime. This is what permits the database XCopy deployment men-tioned earlier. To further simplify deployment, we're using a |DataDirectory| placeholder in front of the filename that will be replaced at runtime with the path of the site's App_Data folder in which the database files reside.

These connection strings settings are referenced by many other configuration elements—for example, the element that configures the SqlWebEventProvider of the health monitoring system, or the SQL-dependency caching settings. By default, all these elements have a connectionStringName attribute set to LocalSqlServer, which refers to a connection string pointing to a local SQL Server 2005 database called ASPNETDB.MDF—for convenience we'll use that same filename for our database. If you choose to rename the file, you can create a new connection string element under <connectionStrings>, and change all elements' `connectionStringName` attribute to your new connection string name. A more drastic option would be to remove the `LocalSqlServer` entry from `machine.config`, and then register it again with the new connection string. Here is what you would need to write (in `machine.config`):

```
<connectionStrings>
    <remove name="LocalSqlServer"/>
    <add name="LocalSqlServer" providerName="System.Data.SqlClient"
        connectionString="Data Source=.\SQLExpress;
        Integrated Security=True;User Instance=True;
        AttachDBFilename=|DataDirectory|TheBeerHouse.mdf" />
</connectionStrings>
```

By doing this, all modules pointing to the `LocalSqlServer` setting will take the new connection string, and you won't have to change their individual `connectionStringName` attribute. However, I generally don't recommend changing `machine.config` because it creates deployment issues, and any syntax error in that file can render the whole web server (not just that site) inoperable. And, of course, a web hosting provider company is not going to let you make this change. I mention it only for completeness, and because it might be the right solution on a tightly controlled corporate intranet web server, for example.

To retrieve the connection strings from code, there's a new class called `System.Web.Configuration` `.WebConfigurationManager`, which has a `ConnectionStrings` dictionary property to retrieve the connection string by name, as follows (note the square brackets used to index into the dictionary):

```
string connString = WebConfigurationManager.ConnectionStrings[
    "LocalSqlServer"].ConnectionString;
```

This class also has an `AppSettings` dictionary property that lets you read the values stored in the `<appSettings>` section, like ASP.NET 1.x's `ConfigurationSettings` class does. In ASP.NET 1.x, it was common to store all site settings in that section because it was easy to read. However, if you had pages or sub-applications developed by other developers, and you had to share the `<appSettings>` section with them, there was always a chance for a conflict whereby two different settings may have the same name. A better option would be to create a class that reads from a custom section in `web.config`, so each sub-application would have its settings isolated from one another. Now with ASP.NET 2.0, it's much easier to use custom configuration sections, and this is now the preferred method. You just write a class that inherits from the `System.Configuration.ConfigurationSection` class, and decorate its public properties with the `ConfigurationProperty` attribute to indicate that they need to be filled with settings read from the `web.config` file, and the actual reading will be done for you when your getter reads that setting from your base class! For elements nested under a parent custom section, you need to create a new class that inherits from `ConfigurationElement` (instead of `ConfigurationProperty`), and again define your properties with the `ConfigurationProperty` attribute. Here's an example:

```
public class SiteSection : ConfigurationSection
{
    [ConfigurationProperty("title", DefaultValue="Sample Title")]
    public string Title
    {
        get { return (string)base["title"]; }
        set { base["title"] = value; }
    }

    [ConfigurationProperty("homePage", IsRequired=true)]
```

```
    public HomePageElement HomePage
    {
        get { return (HomePageElement)base["homePage"]; }
    }
}

public class HomePageElement : ConfigurationElement
{
    [ConfigurationProperty("showAdBanners", DefaultValue="true")]
    public bool ShowAdBanners
    {
        get { return (bool)base["showAdBanners "]; }
        set { base["showAdBanners "] = value; }
    }
}
```

This `SiteSection` class will be mapped to a custom configuration section. It has a property named `Title` that maps a `"title"` attribute, which has a default value of `"Sample Title"`. It also has the `HomePage` property of type `HomePageElement`, which maps to a sub-element named `homePage` with the `showAdBanners` Boolean attribute. Note that the `ConfigurationProperty` attribute of the `HomePage` property has the `IsRequired` option set to true, meaning the element is required to be present in the `web.config` file. The other properties do not have this constraint because they have a default value.

Once the class is ready you must register it in the `web.config` file and define the mapping to a section named `"site"`, as follows:

```
<configuration xmlns="http://schemas.microsoft.com/.NetConfiguration/v2.0">
    <configSections>
        <section name="site"
            type="Company.Project.SiteSection, __code"/>
    </configSections>

    <site title="Some nice title for the site">
        <homePage showAdBanners="false" />
    </site>

    <!-- other configuration sections... -->
</configuration>
```

To read the settings from code, you use the `WebConfigurationManager`'s `GetSection` to get a reference to the `"site"` section, and cast it to the `SiteSection` type. Then, you can use its properties and subproperties:

```
SiteSection site = (SiteSection)WebConfigurationManager.GetSection("site");
string title = site.Title;
bool showAdBanners = site.HomePage.ShowAdBanners;
```

This book's sample site requires a number of settings for each module, so there will be a single custom configuration section with one sub-element for each module. Each module will have its own connection string, caching, and provider settings. However, it's useful to provide some default values for these settings at the section level, so that if you want to use the same connection string for all modules, you don't have to specify it separately for each module, but just once for the entire site. In the "Solution" section of this chapter you'll see the custom section class, while the module-specific elements will be added in their specific chapters later in the book. Also in this chapter, we'll develop a class to map a sub-element named `contactForm` with settings for sending the e-mails from the Contact Us page (the subject line's prefix, and the To and CC fields).

User Interface

With the data access and the business logic layers covered, it's now time to examine the user interface layer. ASP.NET 1.x already had some highly functional server-side controls, such as the `DataGrid`, `DataList` and `Repeater`, and it could databind almost any visual control to a back-end data source such as a `DataSet`, `DataReader`, `DataTable`, `DataView`, custom collection classes, and any object implementing the `IList` interface. However, if you've used those controls a lot, you probably ended up writing some dozens of lines to load the data and bind it to the control, handle the `UpdateCommand` event to update the data in the database with the new value entered in the grid, handle the `DeleteCommand` event to delete a record, handle `SortCommand` to change the sorting, handle `PageIndexChanged` to move forward or backward between the pages of results, and more. The structure of this code is almost always the same, with the changes mostly pertaining to SQL statements or the BLL methods you call, and the field names you work with.

New Binding Features and Data-bound Controls

All the controls from ASP.NET 1.x are still there, sometimes with a few changes and improvements, but ASP.NET 2.0 adds some new and powerful bindable controls that can make all this much easier, and enables you to create the same pages you had before, but with a lot less code! These controls are as follows:

❑ **GridView:** This greatly extends the `DataGrid` control, with new types of columns that can automatically display and handle images and checkboxes, in addition to displaying simple textual data, command buttons, hyperlinks, and template-based data that was already available. It also supports pagination, two-way sorting, editing, and deletion by writing very little code, or no code at all!

❑ **DetailsView:** This shows the details of a single record in a tabular layout (a list, as opposed to a grid) using two columns: a name and a value. The control also supports editing and the addition of new records (in these cases the data of the second column is replaced by some input controls). It also supports paging, by means of links that enable users to move forward or backward to other records.

❑ **FormView:** This is similar to the `DetailsView`, but it is completely template-based, which gives it a lot more formatting flexibility. It supports editing, insertion, and paging as well.

Of all the new controls introduced in ASP.NET 2.0, the `GridView` is the single best one, but in order to use it effectively you sometimes have to also use `DetailsView` or `FormView`—these controls can work together to provide the type of UI functionality often needed in a typical site. The nonvisual `DataSource` controls provide the necessary back-end plumbing to make these controls work.

These new controls don't really do any magic. Instead they incorporate a lot of the same code you had to write yourself in ASP.NET 1.x, and they leverage the new `DataSource` controls to assist them in working with the underlying data store. The `DataSource` controls act as a bridge between the data and the data-bound controls, providing all the information necessary to access and work with the data directly in the UI mark-up code. There are various kinds of `DataSource` controls that are named with a different prefix: a `SqlDataSource`, `ObjectDataSource`, `XmlDataSource`, and a `SiteMapDataSource`. As their name suggests, the `SqlDataSource` control specifies a SELECT statement used to retrieve the data to be shown, and the `INSERT`, `UPDATE` and `DELETE` statements to insert or modify it; it can also reference stored procedures instead of using SQL text in command objects (in this case, the Sql prefix does not refer specifically to SQL Server; this control also works with other RDBMSs such as Oracle). The `ObjectDataSource` calls methods in a business class to retrieve data and manipulate it. The `XmlDataSource` refers to a XML file and allows you to specify XPath queries to retrieve the data; and the `SiteMapDataSource` was already used in the previous chapter to retrieve the content of the `Web.sitemap` file and bind it to the `SiteMapPath` and `Menu` controls on the site's master page. Instead of providing a detailed reference to all the properties and methods of these controls, in this section I'll provide a quick example-driven overview of these controls, as they will be used heavily in most of the upcoming chapters.

The SqlDataSource and the GridView Controls

The Data tab of Visual Studio's Toolbox panel contains all data-bound controls and the data source non-visual components. Create a simple test ASP.NET application by selecting File ⇨ New ⇨ Website ⇨ ASP.NET Template and C# language. Click OK and then make sure you have the Design button pressed under the editor for `default.aspx`. Go to the Toolbox, find the Data tab, select the `GridView` control, and drag it over to the form for `default.aspx`. As soon as you drop it, a Smart Tasks pop-up window appears, listing the common actions and customizations you can make. This is a new feature of Visual Studio .NET 2005, and it makes it easier to work with controls by helping you configure the control quickly and easily. The IDE should appear as represented in Figure 3-4.

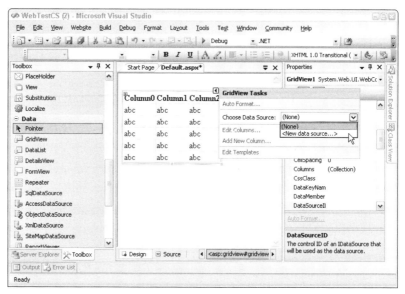

Figure 3-4

If the Smart Tasks pop-up closes and you want to re-open it, just select the control and click the arrow that usually appears near the upper-right corner of the control's area. The first step in configuring the control is to set up data binding. In the list of options for Choose Data Source, select New Data Source, and you will be presented with a dialog (see Figure 3-5) that asks you which type of data source control you want to create.

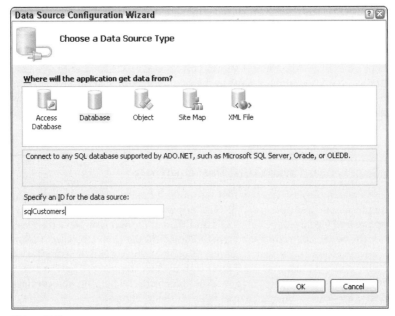

Figure 3-5

In this example, we'll use a `SqlDataSource` (the Database option in Figure 3-5), but later in this chapter and in the rest of the book we'll normally use an object data source. After selecting Database, give it the ID of `sqlCustomers` and press OK. Once you've created the `SqlDataSource`, its configuration wizard starts automatically (but you can start it manually again later from its Smart Tasks window). You are then asked whether you want to select an existing database or connection string to use, or create a new one, as shown in Figure 3-6.

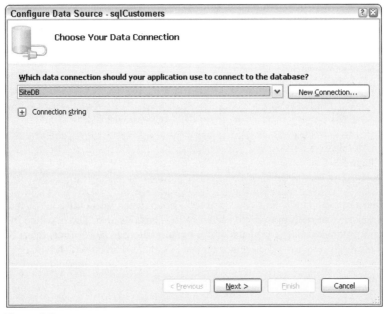

Figure 3-6

The first time you use this database, you'll have to click the New Connection button and set up a connection for your database — after this has been done once you can just select that connection in the dialog in Figure 3-6. After creating the connection (if necessary) and selecting it, click Next twice.

Now you can specify a query or stored procedure, or you can select columns from a table to let it build a SQL statement for you. From this step's Advanced Options window, you can also decide to have the wizard automatically generate the INSERT, UPDATE and DELETE statements according to the table and fields you selected. In this example I'm selecting the Customers table and checking all the columns, and using the Advanced dialog to have it make INSERT, UPDATE and DELETE statements for me. Figure 3-7 shows a screenshot of this step.

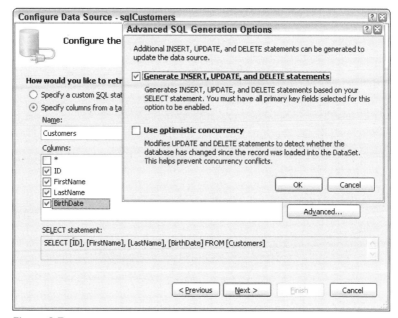

Figure 3-7

Once the wizard is completed, the SqlDataSource control is visible on the form, below the grid. The grid already shows the structure it will have at runtime, with the ID, FirstName, LastName, and BirthDate columns that were selected from the previous wizard (it does not show actual data from the table at this time). Now re-open the GridView's Smart Tasks editor, and select the options to enable sorting, editing, deletion, and selection. While you do this, the new command links are added in a column, as shown in Figure 3-8.

To make the GridView look better, select the Auto Format command from the Smart Tasks panel, and then select one of the color schemes from the dialog that pops up, as shown in Figure 3-9.

Figure 3-8

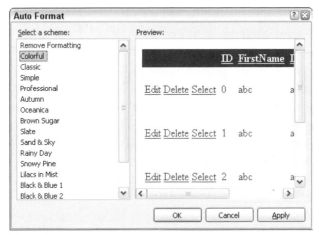

Figure 3-9

Finally, to customize the order and type of the grid's columns, click the Edit Columns link from the Smart Tasks. From the dialog shown in Figure 3-10, you need to click on each field in the Available Fields section and press Add. Then you can move columns up and down in the Selected Fields section, add or remove commands (and thus enable or disable the automatic editing, deletion, and selection), add or remove columns to show links, images, or checkboxes, convert a simple BoundField column to a TemplatedColumn, and, of course, change the column's properties. For example, the grid has a column bound to a field named BirthDate or type DateTime. By default it shows the date/time, but if you want to show just the date, select the column and set its HtmlEncode to False and DataFormatString to {0:d}.

After setting up the fields, press OK. Then go to the Properties for the GridView, and set the DataKeyNames to ID. You can finally run the page by pressing F5, and you'll see your fully functional, editable, sortable, and selectable grid on the browser, without a single line of code written in the C# file. The result is visible in Figure 3-11.

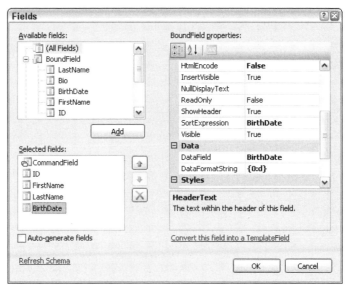

Figure 3-10

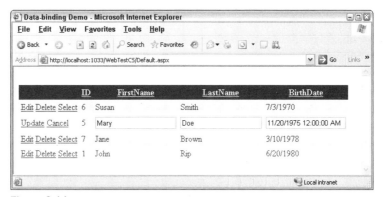

Figure 3-11

Even for this simple example, a few dozen lines of code would have been required to do the same things with the old `DataGrid` and no `SqlDataSource` control. If you now go back to the IDE and switch the editor to the Source View, this is the markup code you will find in `default.aspx` to define the `SqlDataSource` control:

```
<asp:SqlDataSource ID="sqlCustomers" runat="server"
    ConnectionString="<%$ ConnectionStrings:SiteDB %>"
    SelectCommand="SELECT [ID], [FirstName], [LastName], [BirthDate] FROM [Customers]"
    DeleteCommand="DELETE FROM [Customers] WHERE [ID] = @ID"
    InsertCommand="INSERT INTO [Customers] ([FirstName], [LastName], [BirthDate])
        VALUES (@FirstName, @LastName, @BirthDate)"
```

```
    UpdateCommand="UPDATE [Customers] SET [FirstName] = @FirstName, [LastName] =
      @LastName, [BirthDate] = @BirthDate WHERE [ID] = @ID">
    <DeleteParameters>
        <asp:Parameter Name="ID" Type="Int32" />
    </DeleteParameters>
    <UpdateParameters>
        <asp:Parameter Name="FirstName" Type="String" />
        <asp:Parameter Name="LastName" Type="String" />
        <asp:Parameter Name="BirthDate" Type="DateTime" />
        <asp:Parameter Name="ID" Type="Int32" />
    </UpdateParameters>
    <InsertParameters>
        <asp:Parameter Name="FirstName" Type="String" />
        <asp:Parameter Name="LastName" Type="String" />
        <asp:Parameter Name="BirthDate" Type="DateTime" />
    </InsertParameters>
  </asp:SqlDataSource>
```

Note that the ConnectionString property is set to a special binding expression (often called a dollar
expression, because of the $ char in place of the # char used in the other binding expressions) that will
return the connection string pointed to by the SiteDB entry registered under the <connectionStrings>
section of the web.config file. The SelectCommand, InsertCommand, UpdateCommand, and Delete
Command are set to the SQL statements required to retrieve the data and modify it. Note that the DELETE
statements are parameterized, and will dynamically set the value for the @ID parameter to the key of the
GridView's row where the Delete link was clicked. The Update statement is similar and defines parameters for the new values of the record. The <DeleteParameters> and <UpdateParameters> sections list
the parameters expected by the statement, and their type. They don't, however, include the value for the
parameter, as it will be automatically retrieved from the row's key or the row's input controls if the grid is
not in display mode.

Here's the markup code for the GridView control:

```
<asp:GridView ID="GridView1" runat="server" AutoGenerateColumns="False"
    CellPadding="4" DataKeyNames="ID" DataSourceID="sqlCustomers"
    ForeColor="#333333" GridLines="None" AllowSorting="True">
    <FooterStyle BackColor="#990000" Font-Bold="True" ForeColor="White" />
    <RowStyle BackColor="#FFFBD6" ForeColor="#333333" />
    <SelectedRowStyle BackColor="#FFCC66" Font-Bold="True" ForeColor="Navy" />
    <PagerStyle BackColor="#FFCC66" ForeColor="#333333" HorizontalAlign="Center" />
    <HeaderStyle BackColor="#990000" Font-Bold="True" ForeColor="White" />
    <AlternatingRowStyle BackColor="White" />

    <Columns>
        <asp:CommandField ShowDeleteButton="True" ShowEditButton="True"
            ShowSelectButton="True" />
        <asp:BoundField DataField="ID" HeaderText="ID" InsertVisible="False"
            ReadOnly="True" SortExpression="ID" />
        <asp:BoundField DataField="FirstName" HeaderText="FirstName"
            SortExpression="FirstName" />
        <asp:BoundField DataField="LastName" HeaderText="LastName"
            SortExpression="LastName" />
        <asp:BoundField DataField="BirthDate" DataFormatString="{0:d}"
            HeaderText="BirthDate" SortExpression="BirthDate" HtmlEncode="False" />
    </Columns>
</asp:GridView>
```

The first part defines the visual appearance of the control. Recall from the previous chapter: Style definition should not be on the pages themselves, but in the external CSS files or the server-side skin files. Here we used the `AutoFormat` option for demo purposes, but in a real project you should remove the column declarations, the `ID`, and the `DataKeyNames` and `DataSourceID` properties, and copy and paste them into a .skin file under a theme folder, so that it is applied on all grids and is easier to modify and maintain.

The rest of the markup declares a number of `BoundField` columns that can display and edit the data of the specified data source's field, and a `CommandField` column that creates the link commands to edit, delete, or select a row.

Master-Detail Forms with the DetailsView Control

Grids are usually not well suited for showing all the information of a record. Think, for example, of a grid listing products or articles: You certainly can't show the product's description or the article's content in the grid because you don't have room. What you need is a secondary control that shows the details of the first control's selected record. When you do this, you're creating a *Master-Detail form*. ASP.NET 2.0's new `DetailsView` control can be used as this second control to display or edit an existing record, to delete it, or to create new records. To demonstrate this I'll modify the current page by adding a `DetailsView` control to show the biography of the selected customer, which will also support editing. Drag and drop a `DetailsView` control from the Data tab in the Toolbox to the form, and run the Smart Tasks editor (upper-right corner) to create a new `SqlDataSource` named `sqlCustomerDetails`. Select the same DB and table you chose before for the `GridView`'s Data Source, and make sure that the Advanced option of creating the `INSERT`, `DELETE` and `UPDATE` statements is selected. Then, in the same step where you define the `SELECT` statement, click the `WHERE` button and fill the dialog as shown in Figure 3-12.

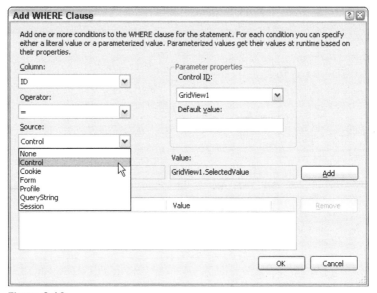

Figure 3-12

After you've selected all the options for Column, Operator, and Source, go over to Parameter Properties and select `GridView1`, click the Add button, and press OK. This adds a filter on the `ID` field, and specifies that the source for its value is a control on the same form — namely, the `GridView` control, which acts as the Master control. The value will actually be retrieved from the `GridView`'s `SelectedValue` property. As you may guess from the screenshot, you could also have selected `QueryString` or some other source for the parameter value — which would have been useful if the `DetailsView` were on a separate page that's called with the ID of the customer record to show what passed on the querystring.

Once this second `SqlDataSource` is created and fully configured, you can set the `DetailsView` control's visual appearance, and enable editing, pagination, and the insertion of new records. All this can be done from the control's Smart Tasks editor, as shown in Figure 3-13.

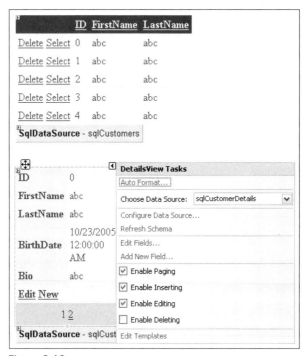

Figure 3-13

Again without writing any C# code, you can run the page, with the output and behavior shown in Figure 3-14. Once you select a row in the grid, you see all customer details in the `DetailsView`.

When the user clicks the Edit button, the `DetailsView`'s UI will display the input controls that enable you to edit the values, as shown in Figure 3-15.

Note that because the `ID` field was recognized as the key field, it was set as a value for the control's `DataKeyNames` property, and is read-only at runtime. When the control switches to Insert mode, the `ID` field is completely hidden, as shown in Figure 3-16.

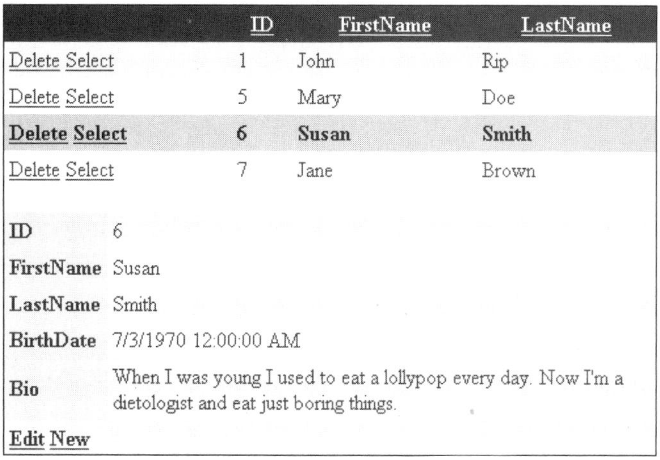

		ID	FirstName	LastName
Delete	Select	1	John	Rip
Delete	Select	5	Mary	Doe
Delete	**Select**	**6**	**Susan**	**Smith**
Delete	Select	7	Jane	Brown

ID	6
FirstName	Susan
LastName	Smith
BirthDate	7/3/1970 12:00:00 AM
Bio	When I was young I used to eat a lollypop every day. Now I'm a dietologist and eat just boring things.
Edit New	

Figure 3-14

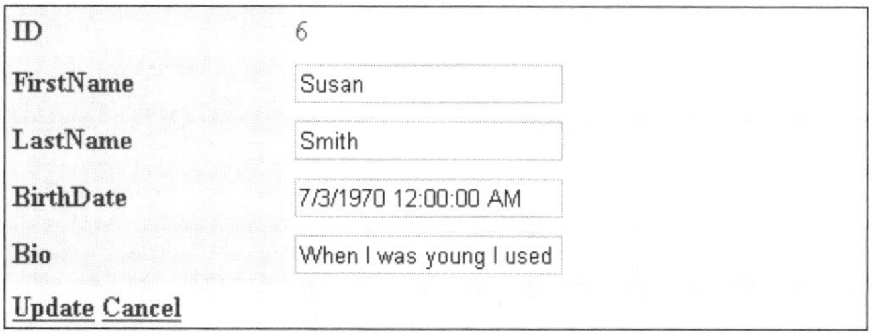

ID	6
FirstName	Susan
LastName	Smith
BirthDate	7/3/1970 12:00:00 AM
Bio	When I was young I used
Update Cancel	

Figure 3-15

FirstName	
LastName	
BirthDate	
Bio	
Insert Cancel	

Figure 3-16

The markup code for the `DetailsView`'s `SqlDataSource` is very similar to the code of the first Data Source listed above, with an important difference:

```
<asp:SqlDataSource ID="sqlCustomerDetails" runat="server"
   ConnectionString="<%$ ConnectionStrings:SiteDB %>"
   SelectCommand="SELECT [ID], [FirstName], [LastName], [BirthDate], [Bio] FROM ⊃
   [Customers] WHERE ([ID] = @ID)" ...other commands like before...>


   <SelectParameters>
```

```
        <asp:ControlParameter ControlID="GridView1" Name="ID"
            PropertyName="SelectedValue" Type="Int32" />
    </SelectParameters>
    ...parameters for inserting, deleting and updating a record like before...
</asp:SqlDataSource>
```

The difference is in the `<SelectParameters>` collection, where instead of a general `Parameter` element a `ControlParameter` is used instead. This specifies that the `ID` parameter will be filled with the value of the `GridView` control's `SelectedValue` property, as stated above. There could have been other parameter configurations if you had selected one of the other options, such as `QueryStringParameter`, for the other parameter sources.

The declaration of the `DetailsView` control is similar to the declaration of the `GridView`. In fact, the most significant difference is that there is a `<Fields>` section instead of `<Columns>`, but their content is quite similar:

```
<asp:DetailsView ID="DetailsView1" runat="server" AllowPaging="True"
    AutoGenerateRows="False" CellPadding="4" DataKeyNames="ID"
    DataSourceID="sqlCustomerDetails" ForeColor="#333333" GridLines="None"
    Height="50px" Width="500px">

    <FooterStyle BackColor="#990000" Font-Bold="True" ForeColor="White" />
    <CommandRowStyle BackColor="#FFFFC0" Font-Bold="True" />
    <RowStyle BackColor="#FFFBD6" ForeColor="#333333" />
    <PagerStyle BackColor="#FFCC66" ForeColor="#333333" HorizontalAlign="Center" />
    <FieldHeaderStyle BackColor="#FFFF99" Font-Bold="True" />
    <HeaderStyle BackColor="#990000" Font-Bold="True" ForeColor="White" />
    <AlternatingRowStyle BackColor="White" />
    <EditRowStyle Width="100%" />

    <Fields>
        <asp:BoundField DataField="ID" HeaderText="ID"
            InsertVisible="False" ReadOnly="True" />
        <asp:BoundField DataField="FirstName" HeaderText="FirstName" />
        <asp:BoundField DataField="LastName" HeaderText="LastName" />
        <asp:BoundField DataField="BirthDate" HeaderText="BirthDate" />
        <asp:BoundField DataField="Bio" HeaderText="Bio" />
        <asp:CommandField ShowEditButton="True" ShowInsertButton="True" />
    </Fields>
</asp:DetailsView>
```

Using the FormsView Control

The `FormsView` control is meant to do exactly what the `DetailsView` control does, but it has no built-in tabular layout, and you're completely in charge of defining it yourself. Although it takes more work to use this control, it gives you much more control over the appearance, which can be a big advantage. As a demonstration, I'll show you how to use it in place of the `DetailsView` control already on the page. Drag and drop a `FormDetails` control onto your page, and choose the `SqlDataSource` created earlier for the `DetailsView` as its Data Source (`sqlCustomerDetails`). Its Smart Tasks editor is less powerful than those shown earlier because it doesn't have options to apply a style, or to change the order and position of the fields — these must be done manually by editing one of the available templates. There are templates to control the appearance for when the control is in display, insert or edit mode, for the header, the footer, and the pagination bar, and for when the control is in display mode but is not bound to any item (which happens when the Master control has no record selected, for example). Figure 3-17 is a screenshot of the control's Smart Tasks pop-up, showing the drop-down list from which you choose the template to edit.

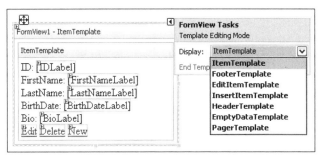

Figure 3-17

I'll edit the `ItemTemplate`, to show the `FirstName`, `LastName`, and `BirthDate` all on a single line, with the customer's bio a line below. Figure 3-18 shows the template after I make my changes.

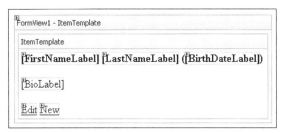

Figure 3-18

Figure 3-19 shows the result at runtime.

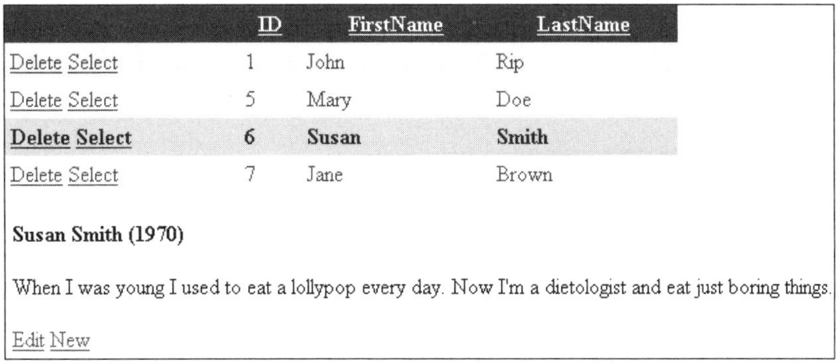

		ID	FirstName	LastName
Delete	Select	1	John	Rip
Delete	Select	5	Mary	Doe
Delete	**Select**	**6**	**Susan**	**Smith**
Delete	Select	7	Jane	Brown

Susan Smith (1970)

When I was young I used to eat a lollypop every day. Now I'm a dietologist and eat just boring things.

Edit New

Figure 3-19

When the control is in edit or insert mode it will be similar to the DetailsView, with one label and input control per line, but without all those colors and the alignment created with the table. You can, however, edit the EditItemTemplate and InsertItemTemplate to control how the input controls are displayed. The control's markup is similar to what you would write when you define a Repeater's ItemTemplate, only this template won't be repeated a number of times, but rather processed and rendered for a single record:

```
<asp:FormView ID="FormView1" runat="server" AllowPaging="True" DataKeyNames="ID"
    DataSourceID="sqlCustomerDetails">
    <EditItemTemplate>
        ID: <asp:Label ID="IDLabel1" runat="server"
            Text='<%# Eval("ID") %>' /><br />
        FirstName: <asp:TextBox ID="FirstNameTextBox" runat="server"
            Text='<%# Bind("FirstName") %>' /><br />
        LastName: <asp:TextBox ID="LastNameTextBox" runat="server"
            Text='<%# Bind("LastName") %>' /><br />
        BirthDate: <asp:TextBox ID="BirthDateTextBox" runat="server"
            Text='<%# Bind("BirthDate") %>' /><br />
        Bio: <asp:TextBox ID="BioTextBox" runat="server" Text='<%# Bind("Bio") %>' />
        <br />
        <asp:LinkButton ID="UpdateButton" runat="server" CausesValidation="True"
            CommandName="Update" Text="Update" />
        <asp:LinkButton ID="UpdateCancelButton" runat="server"
            CausesValidation="False" CommandName="Cancel" Text="Cancel" />
    </EditItemTemplate>
    <InsertItemTemplate>
        FirstName: <asp:TextBox ID="FirstNameTextBox" runat="server"
            Text='<%# Bind("FirstName") %>' /><br />
        LastName: <asp:TextBox ID="LastNameTextBox" runat="server"
            Text='<%# Bind("LastName") %>' /><br />
        BirthDate: <asp:TextBox ID="BirthDateTextBox" runat="server"
            Text='<%# Bind("BirthDate") %>' /><br />
        Bio: <asp:TextBox ID="BioTextBox" runat="server" Text='<%# Bind("Bio") %>' />
        <br />
        <asp:LinkButton ID="InsertButton" runat="server" CausesValidation="True"
            CommandName="Insert" Text="Insert" />
        <asp:LinkButton ID="InsertCancelButton" runat="server"
            CausesValidation="False" CommandName="Cancel" Text="Cancel" />
    </InsertItemTemplate>
    <ItemTemplate>
        <asp:Label ID="FirstNameLabel" runat="server"
            Text='<%# Bind("FirstName") %>' Font-Bold="True" />
        <asp:Label ID="LastNameLabel" runat="server"
            Text='<%# Bind("LastName") %>' Font-Bold="True" />
        (<asp:Label ID="BirthDateLabel" runat="server"
            Text='<%# Bind("BirthDate", "{0:yyyy}") %>' Font-Bold="True" />)<br />
        <br />
        <asp:Label ID="BioLabel" runat="server" Text='<%# Bind("Bio") %>' /><br />
        <br />
        <asp:LinkButton ID="EditButton" runat="server" CausesValidation="False"
            CommandName="Edit" Text="Edit" />
        <asp:LinkButton ID="NewButton" runat="server" CausesValidation="False"
            CommandName="New" Text="New" />
    </ItemTemplate>
</asp:FormView>
```

Note another new feature of ASP.NET 2.0 in the preceding code snippet: the Eval and Bind methods use a new shorter notation in the data-binding expressions. Instead of writing something like DataBinder.Eval (Container.DataItem, "FieldName"), now you can just write Bind("FieldName") or Eval("Field Name"). The difference between the two is that Eval should be used for a read-only ASP.NET control, or for one-way binding. Bind is used instead of Eval when you use input controls and want two-way binding. If you want the control to support the Data Source control's insert and update statement, you must use Bind to make it read the new values from the controls.

> In this section I've shown how to use template fields only in the FormView control. However, you can also use them in the GridView and DetailsView controls, which is very handy because you will typically want to add validation controls for the input fields, and you must use templates to do this. In the upcoming chapters you'll see many example of template usage in such controls.

The ObjectDataSource Control

You've seen how easy it is to work with the SqlDataSource. It's easy to use it to connect controls with a database, and it makes sense for use in very small applications, but for anything of medium complexity, or more, you shouldn't even consider it because it means you would be mixing UI and data access together, and there would be no business logic at all — this flies in the face of the best practices for multi-tier designs, and in fact it would not be a multi-tier design. It's not acceptable in most modern applications to make SQL calls directly from the UI, and cut out both the DAL and BLL. The ASP.NET team knows this very well, but they had to consider the needs of small companies with very limited staffs and budgets. It does make sense in that scenario in that they can crank out small applications quickly using the SqlDataSource, but even then there may be a time in the future when they may regret using this control extensively, especially if their small systems scale up into medium or large systems someday.

The ObjectDataSource is the new DataSource control that fits properly into the multi-tier methodology. This can bind the GridView and other visual controls to your BLL domain objects. Let's first create a sample class that wraps the Customer table's data, and provides methods for retrieving and deleting records. The class will be later used as data source by the GridView defined above. The test class we'll use here is something between a DAL and a BLL class, as it exposes the data in an object-oriented way, but is directly bound to the database. This is only being done here to keep this test fairly simple — the code in the following chapters will have a strong separation between the DAL and the BLL. Here's the code of the Customer class we'll test with (which will be hooked to the ObjectDataSource):

```
public class Customer
{
    private int _id = 0;
    public int ID
    {
        get { return _id; }
        private set { _id = value; }
    }

    private string _firstName = "";
    public string FirstName
    {
        get { return _firstName; }
        set { _firstName = value; }
```

```
      }

      private string _lastName = "";
      public string LastName
      {
         get { return _lastName; }
         set { _lastName = value; }
      }

      private DateTime _birthDate = DateTime.MinValue;
      public DateTime BirthDate
      {
         get { return _birthDate; }
         set { _birthDate = value; }
      }

      private string _bio = "";
      public string Bio
      {
         get { return _bio; }
         set { _bio = value; }
      }

      public Customer(int id, string firstName, string lastName,
         DateTime birthDate, string bio)
      {
         this.ID = id;
         this.FirstName = firstName;
         this.LastName = lastName;
         this.BirthDate = birthDate;
         this.Bio = bio;
      }

      public static List<Customer> GetCustomers()
      {
         using (SqlConnection cn = new SqlConnection(
            WebConfigurationManager.ConnectionStrings["SiteDB"].ConnectionString))
         {
            SqlCommand cmd = new SqlCommand(
               "SELECT ID, FirstName, LastName, BirthDate, Bio FROM Customers", cn);
            cn.Open();
            SqlDataReader reader = cmd.ExecuteReader();

            List<Customer> customers = new List<Customer>();
            while (reader.Read())
            {
               Customer cust = new Customer(
                  (int)reader["ID"],
                  reader["FirstName"].ToString(),
                  reader["LastName"].ToString(),
                  (DateTime)reader["BirthDate"],
                  reader["Bio"].ToString());
               customers.Add(cust);
            }
            return customers;
```

```
        }
    }

    public static bool DeleteCustomer(int id)
    {
        // delete the customer record with the specified ID
        ...
    }
}
```

The `GetCustomers` method takes no parameters, and returns all customers as a .NET 2.0 generic list collection (generic collections will be covered in more detail in the following chapters). If you enable pagination using the `ObjectDataSource.EnablePaging` property, the `ObjectDataSource` will expect to find two parameters named `startRowIndex` and `maximumRows` (the names are configurable). You'll see a concrete example of this in Chapter 5.

The BLL object's methods may be either static or instance-based. If they are instance methods, the class must have a parameterless constructor (it can have overloaded constructors, but one of them must be a "default" style constructor with no parameters).

Once you have this class, drag and drop an `ObjectDataSource` control over the form, and follow its configuration wizard. In the first step, shown in Figure 3-20, you select the Customer business object to use as a Data Source.

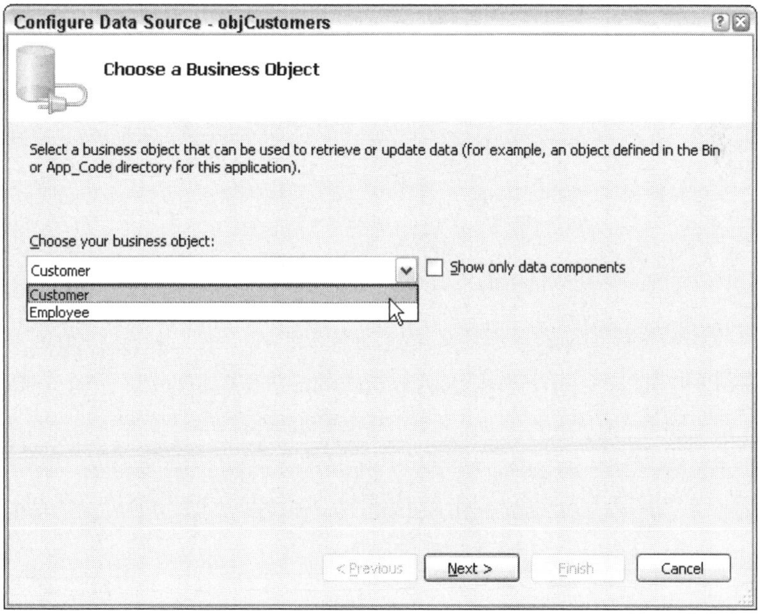

Figure 3-20

In the second step, shown in Figure 3-21, you choose the methods for retrieving, editing, inserting, and deleting data. In this particular case only the `SelectMethod` and the `DeleteMethod` are required.

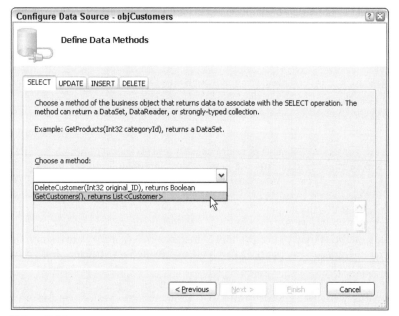

Figure 3-21

Finish the wizard and set your `GridView` control's `DataSourceID` property to the `ObjectDataSource` just created, and you're done; you don't need to modify anything else, and the grid's output and behavior will be absolutely identical to when it used a `SqlDataSource`. This is the beauty of the `DataSource` design model! The markup code is as follows:

```
<asp:ObjectDataSource ID="objCustomers" runat="server"
    DeleteMethod="DeleteCustomer"
    SelectMethod="GetCustomers" TypeName="Customer">
    <DeleteParameters>
        <asp:Parameter Name="id" Type="Int32" />
    </DeleteParameters>
</asp:ObjectDataSource>
```

If you wanted to define methods for inserting or updating data, you could write them in one of the following ways:

```
public int InsertCustomer(
    int id, string firstName, string lastName, DateTime birthDate, string bio)
{...}

public int InsertCustomer(Customer cust)
{...}
```

In the first case the method would be similar to the `DeleteCustomer` method implemented above. In the second case you use a `Customer` instance to pass all values with a single parameter. To support this approach, the `Customer` class must also be referenced in the `ObjectDataSource`'s `DataObjectTypeName` property.

This section provided you with just enough information for a quick start with these controls, and to understand the code in the upcoming chapter with no problems. However, the new data-bound and Data Source controls are much more complex and feature rich than what you've seen here. In the following chapters you will learn more details while working with them, as a sort of on-the-job training. However, if you want a complete reference on these new controls, you should refer to books such as Wrox's *Professional ASP.NET 2.0*. There's also a good article by Scott Mitchell about GridViews on MSDN entitled "GridView Examples for ASP.NET 2.0," completely devoted to this topic and spanning 122 pages! Find it on the MSDN web site at http://msdn.microsoft.com/asp.net/community/authors/scottmitchell/default.aspx?pull=/library/en-us/dnaspp/html/gridviewex.asp.

Solution

The "Solution" section of this chapter is thinner than those found in most of the other chapters. In fact, in this chapter you've been presented with some new controls and features that won't be part of a common custom framework, but will be used in most of the upcoming chapters as parts of other classes to be developed. Other features, such as exception handling and logging, and the transaction management, are already built in and are so easy to use that they don't need to be encapsulated within custom business classes. The discussion about the DAL and BLL design will be extremely useful for the next chapters, because they follow the design outlined here. Understand that ASP.NET 2.0 already has a number of built-in common services to handle many of your general framework-level needs, which allows you to focus more of your time and efforts on your specific business problems. The rest of the chapter shows the code for the small base classes for the DAL and the BLL, the custom configuration section, and the code for raising and handling web events.

TheBeerHouse Configuration Section

Following is the code (located in the /App_Code/ConfigSection.cs file) for the classes that map the <theBeerHouse> custom configuration section, and the inner <contactForm> element, whose meaning and properties were already described earlier:

```
namespace MB.TheBeerHouse
{
    public class TheBeerHouseSection : ConfigurationSection
    {
        [ConfigurationProperty("defaultConnectionStringName",
            DefaultValue = "LocalSqlServer")]
        public string DefaultConnectionStringName
        {
            get { return (string)base["defaultConnectionStringName"]; }
            set { base["defaultConnectionStringName"] = value; }
        }

        [ConfigurationProperty("defaultCacheDuration", DefaultValue = "600")]
        public int DefaultCacheDuration
        {
            get { return (int)base["defaultCacheDuration"]; }
            set { base["defaultCacheDuration"] = value; }
        }

        [ConfigurationProperty("contactForm", IsRequired=true)]
        public ContactFormElement ContactForm
        {
```

```
            get { return (ContactFormElement) base["contactForm"]; }
        }

    }

    public class ContactFormElement : ConfigurationElement
    {
        [ConfigurationProperty("mailSubject",
            DefaultValue="Mail from TheBeerHouse: {0}")]
        public string MailSubject
        {
            get { return (string)base["mailSubject"]; }
            set { base["mailSubject"] = value; }
        }

        [ConfigurationProperty("mailTo", IsRequired=true)]
        public string MailTo
        {
            get { return (string)base["mailTo"];  }
            set { base["mailTo"] = value;  }
        }

        [ConfigurationProperty("mailCC")]
        public string MailCC
        {
            get { return (string)base["mailCC"]; }
            set { base["mailCC"] = value; }
        }
    }
}
```

The TheBeerHouseSection class must be mapped to the <theBeerHouse> section through a new element under the web.config file's <configSections> section. Once you've defined the mapping you can write the custom settings, as follows:

```
<configuration xmlns="http://schemas.microsoft.com/.NetConfiguration/v2.0">
    <configSections>
        <section name="theBeerHouse"
            type="MB.TheBeerHouse.TheBeerHouseSection, __code"/>
    </configSections>

    <theBeerHouse defaultConnectionStringName="LocalSqlServer">
        <contactForm mailTo="thebeerhouse@wrox.com"/>
    </theBeerHouse>
    <!-- other configuration sections... -->
</configuration>
```

To make the settings easily readable from any part of the site, we will add a public field of type TheBeerHouseSection in the Globals class that was added to the project in the previous chapter, and set it as follows:

```
namespace MB.TheBeerHouse
{
    public static class Globals
    {
```

```
public readonly static TheBeerHouseSection Settings =
    (TheBeerHouseSection)WebConfigurationManager.GetSection("theBeerHouse");

public static string ThemesSelectorID = "";
    }
}
```

To see how these settings are actually used, let's create the `Contact.aspx` page, which enables users to send mail to the site administrator by filling in a form online. Figure 3-22 is a screenshot of the page at runtime.

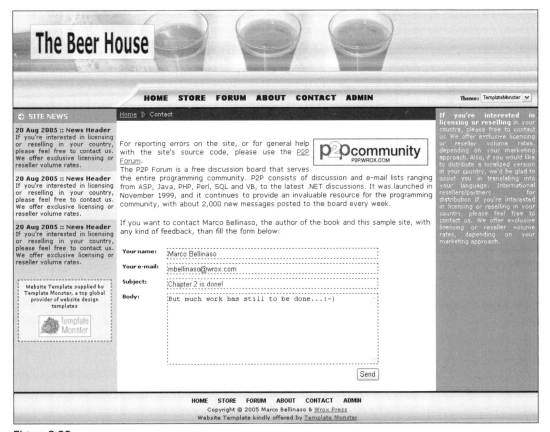

Figure 3-22

The following code is the markup for the page, with the layout structure removed to make it easier to follow:

```
Your name: <asp:TextBox runat="server" ID="txtName" Width="100%" />
<asp:RequiredFieldValidator runat="server" Display="dynamic" ID="valRequireName"
    SetFocusOnError="true" ControlToValidate="txtName"
    ErrorMessage="Your name is required">*</asp:RequiredFieldValidator>

Your e-mail: <asp:TextBox runat="server" ID="txtEmail" Width="100%" />
```

```
<asp:RequiredFieldValidator runat="server" Display="dynamic" ID="valRequireEmail"
    SetFocusOnError="true" ControlToValidate="txtEmail"
    ErrorMessage="Your e-mail address is required">*</asp:RequiredFieldValidator>
<asp:RegularExpressionValidator runat="server" Display="dynamic"
    ID="valEmailPattern"  SetFocusOnError="true" ControlToValidate="txtEmail"
    ValidationExpression="\w+([-+.']\w+)*@\w+([-.]\w+)*\.\w+([-.]\w+)*"
    ErrorMessage="The e-mail address you specified is not well-formed">*
</asp:RegularExpressionValidator>

Subject: <asp:TextBox runat="server" ID="txtSubject" Width="100%" />
<asp:RequiredFieldValidator runat="server" Display="dynamic" ID="valRequireSubject"
    SetFocusOnError="true" ControlToValidate="txtSubject"
    ErrorMessage="The subject is required">*</asp:RequiredFieldValidator>

Body: <asp:TextBox runat="server" ID="txtBody" Width="100%"
    TextMode="MultiLine" Rows="8" />
<asp:RequiredFieldValidator runat="server" Display="dynamic" ID="valRequireBody"
    SetFocusOnError="true" ControlToValidate="txtBody"
    ErrorMessage="The body is required">*</asp:RequiredFieldValidator>

<asp:Label runat="server" ID="lblFeedbackOK" Visible="false"
    Text="Your message has been successfully sent." SkinID="FeedbackOK" />
<asp:Label runat="server" ID="lblFeedbackKO" Visible="false"
    Text="Sorry, there was a problem sending your message." SkinID="FeedbackKO" />

<asp:Button runat="server" ID="btnSubmit" Text="Send" OnClick="btnSubmit_Click" />
<asp:ValidationSummary runat="server" ID="valSummary"
    ShowSummary="false" ShowMessageBox="true" />
```

When the Send button is clicked, a new `System.Net.Mail.MailMessage` is created, with its To, CC and Subject properties set from the values read from the site's configuration; the From and Body are set with the user input values, and then the mail is sent:

```
protected void btnSubmit_Click(object sender, EventArgs e)
{
    try
    {
        // send the mail
        MailMessage msg = new MailMessage();
        msg.IsBodyHtml = false;
        msg.From = new MailAddress(txtEmail.Text, txtName.Text);
        msg.To.Add(new MailAddress(Globals.Settings.ContactForm.MailTo));
        if (!string.IsNullOrEmpty(Globals.Settings.ContactForm.MailCC))
            msg.CC.Add(new MailAddress(Globals.Settings.ContactForm.MailCC));
        msg.Subject = string.Format(
            Globals.Settings.ContactForm.MailSubject, txtSubject.Text);
        msg.Body = txtBody.Text;
        new SmtpClient().Send(msg);
        // show a confirmation message, and reset the fields
        lblFeedbackOK.Visible = true;
        lblFeedbackKO.Visible = false;
        txtName.Text = "";
        txtEmail.Text = "";
        txtSubject.Text = "";
```

```
        txtBody.Text = "";
    }
    catch (Exception)
    {
        lblFeedbackOK.Visible = false;
        lblFeedbackKO.Visible = true;
    }
}
```

The SMTP settings used to send the message must be defined in the web.config file, in the <mailSettings> section, as shown here:

```
<configuration xmlns="http://schemas.microsoft.com/.NetConfiguration/v2.0">
    <system.web> <!-- some settings here...--> </system.web>
    <system.net>
        <mailSettings>
            <smtp deliveryMethod=" Network " from="thebeerhouse@wrox.com">
                <network defaultCredentials="true" host="(localhost)" port="25" />
            </smtp>
        </mailSettings>
    </system.net> </configuration>
```

The DataAccess Base DAL Class

The DataAccess class (located in /App_Code/DAL/DataAccess.cs) contains just a few properties, such as ConnectionString, EnableCaching, CachingDuration and Cache, and the ExecuteReader, ExecuteScalar and ExecuteNonQuery wrapper methods discussed in this chapter. Note that, except for the Cache property that just returns a reference to the current context's Cache object, the properties are not set directly in the class itself because they may have different values for different DAL classes. I don't plan to use the cache from the DAL because, as I said earlier, I prefer to implement caching in the BLL so it works regardless of which DAL provider is being used. However, I've put the caching-related properties in the DAL's base class also, in case there may be a need for some very provider-specific caching someday. Here's the complete code:

```
namespace MB.TheBeerHouse.DAL
{
    public abstract class DataAccess
    {
        private string _connectionString = "";
        protected string ConnectionString
        {
            get { return _connectionString; }
            set { _connectionString = value; }
        }

        private bool _enableCaching = true;
        protected bool EnableCaching
        {
            get { return _enableCaching; }
            set { _enableCaching = value; }
        }

        private int _cacheDuration = 0;
```

```
protected int CacheDuration
{
    get { return _cacheDuration; }
    set { _cacheDuration = value; }
}

protected Cache Cache
{
    get { return HttpContext.Current.Cache; }
}

protected int ExecuteNonQuery(DbCommand cmd)
{
    if (HttpContext.Current.User.Identity.Name.ToLower() == "sampleeditor")
    {
        foreach (DbParameter param in cmd.Parameters)
        {
            if (param.Direction == ParameterDirection.Output ||
                param.Direction == ParameterDirection.ReturnValue)
            {
                switch (param.DbType)
                {
                    case DbType.AnsiString:
                    case DbType.AnsiStringFixedLength:
                    case DbType.String:
                    case DbType.StringFixedLength:
                    case DbType.Xml:
                        param.Value = "";
                        break;
                    case DbType.Boolean:
                        param.Value = false;
                        break;
                    case DbType.Byte:
                        param.Value = byte.MinValue;
                        break;
                    case DbType.Date:
                    case DbType.DateTime:
                        param.Value = DateTime.MinValue;
                        break;
                    case DbType.Currency:
                    case DbType.Decimal:
                        param.Value = decimal.MinValue;
                        break;
                    case DbType.Guid:
                        param.Value = Guid.Empty;
                        break;
                    case DbType.Double:
                    case DbType.Int16:
                    case DbType.Int32:
                    case DbType.Int64:
                        param.Value = 0;
                        break;
                    default:
                        param.Value = null;
                        break;
                }
            }
```

```
                }
            }
            return 1;
        }
        else
            return cmd.ExecuteNonQuery();
    }
    protected IDataReader ExecuteReader(DbCommand cmd)
    {
        return ExecuteReader(cmd, CommandBehavior.Default);
    }

    protected IDataReader ExecuteReader(DbCommand cmd, CommandBehavior behavior)
    {
        return cmd.ExecuteReader(behavior);
    }

    protected object ExecuteScalar(DbCommand cmd)
    {
        return cmd.ExecuteScalar();
    }
    }
}
```

The only unusual aspect of this code is the ExecuteNonQuery method, which actually calls the ExecuteNonQuery method of the command object passed to it as an input, but only if the current context's user name is not "sampleeditor". If the user's name is "sampleeditor", then none of their inserts/updates/deletes will actually be processed; the method always returns 1, and sets all output parameters to a default value, according to their type. SampleEditor is a special account name for test purposes — this user can go into almost all protected areas, but cannot actually persist changes to the database, which is just what we want for demo purposes, as discussed earlier in this chapter.

The BizObject BLL Base Class

This class (found in /App_Data/BLL/BizObject.cs) defines a number of properties that can be useful for many of the module-specific BLL classes. For example, it returns the name and IP of the current user, the current context's Cache reference, and more. It also contains some methods to encode HTML strings, convert a null string to an empty string, and purge items from the cache:

```
namespace MB.TheBeerHouse.BLL
{
    public abstract class BizObject
    {
        protected const int MAXROWS = int.MaxValue;

        protected static Cache Cache
        {
            get { return HttpContext.Current.Cache; }
        }

        protected static IPrincipal CurrentUser
        {
            get { return HttpContext.Current.User; }
```

```csharp
        }

        protected static string CurrentUserName
        {
            get
            {
                string userName = "";
                if (HttpContext.Current.User.Identity.IsAuthenticated)
                    userName = HttpContext.Current.User.Identity.Name;
                return userName;
            }
        }

        protected static string CurrentUserIP
        {
            get { return HttpContext.Current.Request.UserHostAddress; }
        }

        protected static int GetPageIndex(int startRowIndex, int maximumRows)
        {
            if (maximumRows <= 0)
                return 0;
            else
                return (int)Math.Floor((double)startRowIndex / (double)maximumRows);
        }

        protected static string EncodeText(string content)
        {
            content = HttpUtility.HtmlEncode(content);
            content = content.Replace(" ", "  ").Replace("\n", "<br>");
            return content;
        }

        protected static string ConvertNullToEmptyString(string input)
        {
            return (input == null ? "" : input);
        }

        protected static void PurgeCacheItems(string prefix)
        {
            prefix = prefix.ToLower();
            List<string> itemsToRemove = new List<string>();

            IDictionaryEnumerator enumerator = BizObject.Cache.GetEnumerator();
            while (enumerator.MoveNext())
            {
                if (enumerator.Key.ToString().ToLower().StartsWith(prefix))
                    itemsToRemove.Add(enumerator.Key.ToString());
            }

            foreach (string itemToRemove in itemsToRemove)
                BizObject.Cache.Remove(itemToRemove);
        }
    }
}
```

The most interesting method is `PurgeCacheItems`, which takes as input a string, and cycles through the cached items and collects a list of all items whose key starts with the input prefix, and finally deletes all those items.

Configuring the Health Monitoring System

We need a custom event class to log when a record of any type is deleted by an administrator or an editor, through the site's administrative area. The `RecordDeletedEvent` defined here could have inherited directly from the framework's `WebBaseEvent` base class, but instead, I've created a custom `WebCustomEvent` class that inherits from `WebBaseEvent` and adds nothing to it; then I created the `RecordDeletedEvent`, making it inherit from `WebCustomEvent`, and with a new constructor that takes the name of the entity deleted (e.g., a category, a product, an article, etc.) and its ID. Here's the code:

```
namespace MB.TheBeerHouse
{
    public abstract class WebCustomEvent : WebBaseEvent
    {
        public WebCustomEvent(string message, object eventSource, int eventCode)
            : base(message, eventSource, eventCode) { }
    }

    public class RecordDeletedEvent : WebCustomEvent
    {
        private const int eventCode = WebEventCodes.WebExtendedBase + 10;
        private const string message =
            "The {0} with ID = {1} was deleted by user {2}.";

        public RecordDeletedEvent(string entity, int id, object eventSource)
            : base(string.Format(message, entity, id,
                HttpContext.Current.User.Identity.Name), eventSource, eventCode)
        { }
    }
}
```

> Note that for custom events to be dynamically loaded correctly when the application starts, they must be placed in their own pre-compiled assembly. This is because the ASP.NET runtimes try to load them before the `App_Code` files are dynamically compiled, so the custom event type wouldn't be found if you placed the source code there. Because of this, you must create a separate secondary project for the source code, and reference the compiled .dll file (named `MB.TheBeerHouse.Custom Events.dll`) from the main web project. If you add the Library Project to the solution containing the web project, you'll be able to reference the project instead of the compiled file, so that an updated version of the DLL will be generated and copied into the web project's bin folder every time you compile the solution.

The reason for using a custom base class is so we can add a rule to the `web.config` file's `<health Monitoring>` section to log all events that inherit from this `WebCustomEvent` class, instead of registering them all individually — a big time saver if you have many of them, and this frees us from worrying about the possibility that we might forget to register some of them:

```
<healthMonitoring heartbeatInterval="10800" >
   <providers>
      <remove name="SqlWebEventProvider" />
      <add name="SqlWebEventProvider" connectionStringName="LocalSqlServer"
         buffer="false" bufferMode="Notification"
         maxEventDetailsLength="1073741823"
         type="System.Web.Management.SqlWebEventProvider,System.Web,
            Version=2.0.0.0,Culture=neutral,PublicKeyToken=b03f5f7f11d50a3a" />
   </providers>
   <eventMappings>
      <add name="TBH Events"
         type="MB.TheBeerHouse.WebCustomEvent, MB.TheBeerHouse.CustomEvents" />
   </eventMappings>
   <rules>
      <clear />
      <add name="TBH Events" eventName="TBH Events"
         provider="SqlWebEventProvider" profile="Critical" />
      <add name="All Errors" eventName="All Errors"
         provider="SqlWebEventProvider" profile="Critical" />
      <add name="Failure Audits" eventName="Failure Audits"
         provider="SqlWebEventProvider" profile="Critical" />
      <add name="Heartbeats" eventName="Heartbeats"
         provider="SqlWebEventProvider" profile="Critical" />
   </rules>
</healthMonitoring>
```

This is an example of how you can record a delete event from methods of your business classes to be developed in the upcoming chapters (this example assumes we deleted an article with ID = 4):

```
new RecordDeletedEvent("article", 4, null).Raise();
```

Summary

This chapter provided several guidelines for building a flexible, easily configurable and instrumented site. First of all, we discussed the data access layer, which will be built using the provider model design pattern to support any type of data store (but we'll only be implementing a DAL for SQL Server). Next we covered a business logic layer built on the top of the DAL, which exposes the data in an object-oriented way, with the required validation logic, transaction management, event logging, and caching. Finally, we examined the User Interface presentation layer, which takes advantage of the new GridView, DetailsView, and FormView controls, and the companion ObjectDataSource, to quickly generate complex and feature-rich data-enabled UI controls. In the "Solution" section, we developed base class functionality that builds upon the built-in services of the new version of the framework. You should be very excited about all the new features and controls presented in this chapter, as they greatly reduce the time needed to build core services such as transaction management and exception handling, and enable you to focus on solving problems specific to your particular application requirements.

You now have a good foundation to start building the site upon! In the next chapter you'll discover the new ASP.NET 2.0's Membership system to manage user's account subscriptions and profiles, and will build a complete administration area for managing users, profiles, preferences, roles, and security settings.

Membership and User Profiling

The sample web site developed in this book contains dynamic content such as news, events, newsletters, polls, forum posts, and more. It can be considered a content-based site, where significant parts of the site can be easily changed or updated by privileged users (this functionality is sometimes called a *content management system*), although it differs from many content-based sites because we've also added an important e-commerce section that enables our investors to earn a healthy return on their investment. Here's a secret (although not a well-kept one) for any content-based site that wants to be successful: build a vigorous and thriving community of users! If you have a lot of loyal users, you can be sure that the site will increase its user base, and thus its size, its popularity, and your revenues. You want to encourage users to register for a free account on the site so you can enable them to customize their view, participate in message forums, and even order merchandise from e-commerce pages. Once they obtain a free account they will be a member of the site. Membership is a form of empowerment — they will feel special because they are a member, and you want to reward their loyalty by enabling them to customize certain visual aspects, and to remember their settings on their return visits. In order to track members, it is necessary to have some sort of *identity* to describe and distinguish them from other members and, more important, against anonymous users who have not logged in. This chapter will explain how to develop user registration functionality and user profiles. The user account will also be used to grant or deny access to special restricted pages of the site. The profile will be used by modules developed later in this book to customize content and give users a public "virtual face," visible to other members and users.

Problem

In reality, a membership system is a requirement for most web sites — not only for community and content-based sites. Sites typically have a number of administration pages that visitors should not have access to. The administration section can be as complete as an application in itself, or just a couple of simple pages to allow people to change some settings. However, you always need to identify each user who tries to access those restricted pages, and check whether they are authorized to do so. The means of identifying a user is called *authentication,* and the means of determining what access a user has is called *authorization.* Unfortunately, it's easy to confuse these terms, so it helps to think of the root words: authenticate (who are you?) and authorize (now that I know you, what are you allowed to do?). The authentication and authorization processes are part of the site's membership system, which includes the creation of new user accounts, the management of the user's credentials (including protection mechanisms such as encryption and password recovery in case passwords are lost or forgotten), and roles associated with an account. For the sample site, the membership system must be complete, as it will be used by administrators and editors to access protected areas, and by users who want to have their own identity within the community, post messages to the forums, and be recognized by other members. It must enable users to create their account interactively without administrator intervention, and to update their profile information on demand.

Administrators must also be able to see a list of registered users, and to control them. For example, if there is a user who regularly posts spam or offending messages to the forum, a good administrator (or forum moderator) will want to temporarily or permanently disable this user's account. Conversely, if a user always behaves well and respects the site's policies, an administrator may decide to promote him to the status of moderator, or even editor. In other words, modifying user account settings and their roles should be an easy thing to do, because the administrator may need to do it frequently. Thus, we require an easy-to-use administration section to manage user accounts.

To make it easier to manage security permissions, we'll create roles that are basically a group of users who have special permission in addition to the normal user permissions. For example, the Administrators role will be used to designate certain individuals who will have the capability to manage user accounts and site content.

Although a membership system is necessary for common security-related tasks, other things are needed in order to build an effective community of happy users. The users expect to have some benefits from their registration. For example, they could receive newsletters with useful information (with links back to the web site), and they could customize the home page so that it highlights the type of content they are most interested in. Furthermore, their preferred site template could be saved and restored between sessions. All this information makes up what's called a *user profile.* Implementing a system for profiling the user is a good thing not just for the end user, but also for the site administrators. Among the information stored in the profile is the user's age, gender, and full address. A savvy administrator could later make use of such data in a variety of ways:

❑ **To customize the user appearance for registered and profiled users:** For example, the news and events modules developed in the next chapter will use the details stored in the user's profile to highlight the news and events that happen in the user's country, state, or city with different colors, to identify the items closer to home. This rather simple feature can improve the user experience, and gives users an incentive to provide such personal details in their profile.

❑ **To implement targeted marketing:** For example, you could send a newsletter about a concert or some other event to all users that reside in a particular country, state, or city. You can do the same with banners or text notices on the site. Multiple criteria could be used for targeting the sponsored news, other than the user's location: It could be according to age, gender, or a combination of multiple conditions. The more details you have about your users, the more chances you have to sell advertisement spaces on your site(s) to external companies, or to effectively use the ad possibilities yourself.

The site administrator will need an intuitive console from which she can see and edit the profile of any user — to remove an offending signature or avatar image (an avatar image is a small picture of a user, or a "cool" signature picture a user wants to display next to their name) used in the forums.

Design

To recap, the "virtual client" has commissioned a membership system that handles the following operations and features:

❏ Users must be able to create new accounts independently, by filling out an online registration form.

❏ Users must be able to later change their own credentials, or recover them if they forget them.

❏ The administrator must be able to grant or deny access to specific sections or individual pages by certain users. The permissions should be editable even after deploying the site, without requiring the intervention of a developer to change complex code or settings.

❏ The administrator must be able to temporarily or permanently suspend a user account, such as when a user does not respect the site's policy of conduct.

❏ The administrator should be able to see summary and statistical data such as the number of total registered users and how many of them are online at a particular time. The administrator may also want to know when specific users registered, and the last time they logged in.

❏ A profiling system should enable each registered user to save data such as site preferences and personal details in a data store (such as a database), so that their information will be remembered on future visits. The administrator must be able to view and edit the profile of each user.

ASP.NET 2.0 introduces some great new features that help to develop the membership subsystem.

Password Storage Mechanisms

There are basically three methods for storing passwords, with each one offering different trade-offs between security and the convenience of developers, administrators, and users.

1. The most convenient method of password storage for developers and administrators is to store the password as plain text in a database field. This is also convenient for users because you can easily e-mail a user's password to them in case they forget it. However, this is the least secure option because all of the passwords are stored as plain text — if your database were compromised by a hacker, he'd have easy access to everyone's password. You need to be extremely careful about locking down your database and ensuring that you secure your database backup files.

2. To enhance the security of password storage you can encrypt the passwords before storing them in a database. There are many ways to encrypt passwords but the most common type is *symmetric encryption,* which uses a guarded system password to encrypt all user passwords. This is two-way encryption: You can encrypt a password and also decrypt it later. This offers medium convenience for developers, but still offers a lot of convenience for users because you can still e-mail them a forgotten password.

3. The highest level of security requires a form of encryption that prevents administrators and developers from gaining access to any user's password. This uses a one-way type of encryption known as *hashing*. You can always encrypt a password by hashing the password with a proven algorithm but you can never decrypt it. Therefore, you store the hashed version of the password, and later, when you want to verify a user's password when he logs in again, you can perform the same hashing algorithm on whatever he types in as his password. You can then compare this hash against the hash you stored in the database — if the two match then you know the user entered his password correctly. This offers a low amount of convenience to developers, administrators, and users because it's not possible to e-mail forgotten passwords. Instead, if a user forgets his password, your only choice is to change the user's password to a known value, and then save the hash for his new password.

Hashing (method 3) was used in the first edition of this book, but it caused a lot of confusion for administrators and frustration for users because people generally prefer having the option of "recovering" a lost password without requiring a new one. We will use symmetric encryption (method 2) in this edition, but please keep in mind that password hashes should always be used to protect web sites containing financial data or other very sensitive data (such as medical records, test scores, etc.). Most users would *not* like to see their super-secret banking password mailed to them in an e-mail message, and most don't even want bank employees to have access to passwords. A bank employee who is trusted today might become a disgruntled former employee tomorrow, and it's nice to know that he won't be taking your password with him!

Authentication Modes: Windows Security or Custom Login Form?

The first thing you have to decide when you set up a security mechanism for a web site is whether you want to use Windows or forms authentication. Windows authentication is the easiest to set up and use, while forms authentication requires you to create a custom database and a login form. Windows security is usually the best choice when you are developing an intranet site for which all users who have access to the site are also users of a company's internal network (where they have domain user accounts). With Windows security, users enjoy the capability to use restricted web pages without having to formally log in to the web site, the page is executed under the context of the user requesting it, and security restrictions are automatically enforced on all resources that the code tries to access and use (typically files and database objects). Another advantage is that Windows will securely store and encrypt user credentials so you don't have to. However, the requirement to have a local network account is a huge disadvantage that makes it a bad choice for Internet sites. If you use Windows security for users located outside of a company's network, the company would be required to create a network user account for each web site user, which makes it slow for users to gain access and expensive for companies to administer. While you could conceivably write some code to automate the creation of Windows network accounts, and could write a login page that uses Windows impersonation behind the scenes, it just doesn't make sense to employ Windows security with those nasty workarounds in our context (a public web site with possibly thousands of users). Instead, it makes more sense for us to use forms authentication, and store user account credentials and related profile data in a custom database.

A great new feature introduced in ASP.NET 2.0 is support for cookieless clients in forms authentication. ASP.NET 1.x supported the cookieless mode only for `Session` variables, but not for authentication, and you had to use dirty workarounds to make it work for cookieless authentication. Now, however, you only have to set the `<forms>` element's cookieless attribute in `web.config` to true or to AutoDetect. With AutoDetect, ASP.NET checks whether the user's browser supports cookies, and if so, uses a cookie to store a Session ID. If a user's browser doesn't support cookies, then ASP.NET will pass the Session ID in the URL. Only users who do not support cookies have to see a long and ugly Session ID in the URL.

The "Let's Do Everything on Our Own" Approach

Designing a module for handling user membership and profiling is not easy. It may not seem particularly difficult at first: You can easily devise some database tables for storing the required data (roles, account credentials and details, the associations between roles and accounts, and account profiles) and an API that allows the developer to request, create, and modify this data. However, things are rarely as easy as they appear at first! You must not downplay the significance of these modules because they are very crucial to the operation of the web site, and properly designing these modules is important because all other site modules rely on them. If you design and implement the news module poorly, you can go back and fix it without affecting all the other site's modules (forum, e-commerce, newsletter, polls, etc.). However, if you decide to change the design of the membership module after you have developed other modules that use it, chances are good that you will need to modify something in those modules as well. The membership module must be complete but also simple to use, and developers should be able to use its classes and methods when they design administration pages. They should also be able to create and edit user accounts by writing just a few lines of code or, better yet, no code at all. ASP.NET 1.1 provided a partial security framework that allowed you to specify roles that could or could not access specific pages or folders by specifying role restrictions in `web.config`. It also took care of creating an encrypted authentication cookie for the user, once the user logged in. However, the developer was completely responsible for all the work of writing the login and registration pages, authenticating the user against a database of credentials, assigning the proper roles, and administering accounts. In the first edition of this book we did everything ourselves, with custom code. The solution worked fine, but still suffered from a couple of problems:

1. The developer had to perform all security checks programmatically, typically in the `Page_Load` event, before doing anything else. If you later wanted to add roles or users to the ACL (access control list) of a page or site area, you had to edit the code, recompile, and re-deploy the assembly.

2. The membership system also included user profiling. The database table had columns for the user's first and last name, address, birth date and other related data. However, the table schema was fixed, so if you wanted to add more information to the profile later, you had to change the database, the related stored procedures, and many API methods, in addition to the user interface to insert the data.

Things could have been made more flexible, but it would have been more difficult to develop. You have to weigh the advantages of design extensibility against the time and effort to implement it. Fortunately, ASP.NET 2.0 has full-featured membership and profiling systems out of the box! Yes, that's right, you don't have to write a single line of code to register users, protect administrative pages, and associate a profile to the users, unless you want to customize the way they work (for example, to change the format in which the data is stored, or the storage medium itself).

This section first introduces the built-in security and profiling framework of ASP.NET 2.0; after that, you will learn how to profitably use it in your own project instead of "rolling your own" solution.

The Membership and MembershipUser Classes

The principal class of the ASP.NET 2.0's security framework is `System.Web.Security.Membership`, which exposes a number of static methods to create, delete, update, and retrieve registered users. The following table describes the most important methods.

Method	Description
CreateUser	Creates a new user account
DeleteUser	Deletes the specified user
FindUsersByEmail	Returns an array of users with the specified e-mail address. If SQL Server is used to store accounts, the input e-mail can contain any wildcard characters supported by SQL Server in LIKE clauses, such as % for any string of zero or more characters, or _ for a single character.
FindUsersByName	Returns an array of users with the specified name. Wildcard characters are supported.
GeneratePassword	Generates a new password with the specified length, and the specified number of non-alphanumeric characters
GetAllUsers	Returns an array with all the registered users
GetNumberOfUsersOnline	Returns an integer value indicating how many registered users are currently online
GetUser	Retrieves a specific user by name
GetUserNameByEmail	Returns the username of a user with the given e-mail address
UpdateUser	Updates a user
ValidateUser	Returns a Boolean value indicating whether the input credentials correspond to a registered user

Some of these methods (`CreateUser`, `GetAllUsers`, `GetUser`, `FindUsersByName`, `FindUsersByEmail` and `UpdateUser`) accept or return instances of the `System.Web.Security.MembershipUser` class, which represents a single user, and provides quite a lot of details about it. The following table describes the instance properties and methods exposed by this class.

Property	Description
Comment	A comment (typically entered by the administrator) associated with a given user
CreationDate	The date when the user registered
Email	The user's e-mail address
IsApproved	Indicates whether the account is enabled, and whether the user can log in
IsLockedOut	Indicates whether the user account was disabled after a number of invalid logins. This property is read-only, and the administrator can only indirectly set it back to false, by calling the UnlockUser method described below.
IsOnline	Indicates whether the user is currently online
LastActivityDate	The date when the user logged-in or was last authenticated. If the last login was persistent, this will not necessarily be the date of the login, but it may be the date when the user accessed the site and was automatically authenticated through the cookie.
LastLockoutDate	The date when the user was automatically locked-out by the membership system, after a (configurable) number of invalid logins
LastLoginDate	The date of the last login
LastPasswordChangedDate	When the user last changed his or her password
PasswordQuestion	The question asked of users who forget their password — used to prove it's really them
UserName	The user's username

Method	Description
ChangePassword	Changes the user's password. The current password must be provided.
ChangePasswordQuestionAndAnswer	Changes the question and answer asked of a user who forgets his or her password. Requires the current password as input (so someone can't change this for somebody else).
GetPassword	Returns the current password. Depending on how the membership system is set up, it may require the answer to the user's password question as input and will not work if only a password hash is stored in the database.

Table continued on following page

Method	Description
ResetPassword	Creates a new password for the user. This is the only function to change the password if the membership system was set up to hash the password.
UnlockUser	Unlocks the user if she was previously locked out by the system because of too many invalid attempts to log in.

When you change a user property, the new value is not immediately persisted to the data store; you have to call the UpdateUser method of the Membership class for that. This is done so that with a single call you can save multiple updated properties, and thus improve performance.

By using these two classes together, you can completely manage the accounts' data in a very intuitive and straightforward way. It's outside the scope of this book to provide a more exhaustive coverage of every method and overload, but I can show you a few examples about their usage in practice — please consult MSDN for all the details on these classes. Following is some code for registering a new account and handling the exception that may be raised if an account with the specified username or e-mail address already exists:

```
string msg = "User created successfully!";
try
{
    MembershipUser newUser = Membership.CreateUser(
        "Marco", "secret", "mbellinaso@wrox.com");
}
catch (MembershipCreateUserException exc)
{
    msg = "Unable to create the user. ";
    switch (exc.StatusCode)
    {
        case MembershipCreateStatus.DuplicateEmail:
            msg += "An account with the specified e-mail already exists.";
            break;
        case MembershipCreateStatus.DuplicateUserName:
            msg += "An account with the specified username already exists.";
            break;
        case MembershipCreateStatus.InvalidEmail:
            msg += "The specified e-mail is not valid.";
            break;
        case MembershipCreateStatus.InvalidPassword:
            msg += "The specified password is not valid.";
            break;
        default:
            msg += exc.Message;
            break;
    }
}

lblResult.Text = msg;
```

If you want to change some of the user's information, you first retrieve a MembershipUser instance that represents that user, change some properties as desired, and then update the user, as shown below:

```
MembershipUser user = Membership.GetUser("Marco");
if (DateTime.Now.Subtract(user.LastActivityDate).TotalHours < 2)
    user.Comment = "very knowledgeable user; strong forum participation!";
Membership.UpdateUser(user);
```

Validating user credentials from a custom login form requires only a single line of code (and not even that, as you'll see shortly):

```
bool isValid = Membership.ValidateUser("Marco", "secret");
```

In the "Solution" section of this chapter, you will use these classes to implement the following features in the site's Administration area:

❏   Retrieve the total number of users and determine how many of them are currently online.

❏   Find users by partial username or e-mail address.

❏   Display some information about the users returned by the search, listed in a grid, such as the date of the user's last activity and whether they are active or not. In another page we will display all the details of a specific user and will allow the administrator to change some details.

The Provider Model Design Pattern

I use the term "data store" to refer to any physical means of persisting (saving) data — this usually means saving data in a database or in Active Directory, but .NET abstracts the actual data storage mechanism from the classes that manipulate the data. The provider class is the one that stores the data on behalf of other classes that manipulate data. This *provider model design pattern,* introduced in Chapter 3, is pervasive in .NET 2.0 — you can frequently "plug in" a different back-end provider to change the mechanism used to save and retrieve data. The Membership class uses a secondary class (called a *membership provider*) that actually knows the details of a particular data store and implements all the supporting logic to read and write data to/from it. You can almost think of the Membership class as a business layer class (in that it only manipulates data), and the provider class as the data access class which provides the details of persistence (even though a pure architect might argue the semantics). Two built-in providers are available for the Membership system, and you can choose one by writing some settings in the web.config file. The built-in providers are the ones for SQL Server 2000/2005 (SqlMembershipProvider) and for Active Directory (ActiveDirectoryMembershipProvider), but you can also write your own or find one from a third party (for use with Oracle, MySQL, DB2, etc., or perhaps XML files). Figure 4-1 provides a visual representation of the provider model design pattern.

I find that the use of the provider model provides tremendous flexibility, because you can change the provider used by the Membership API under the hood without affecting the rest of the code, because you just access the Membership "business" class from the pages and the other business classes, and not the providers directly. Actually, you may even ignore which provider is used, and where and how the data is stored (this is the idea behind abstraction of the data store). Abstraction is obviously provided to users in the sense that they don't need to know exactly how their data will be stored, but now we also have abstraction for developers because they, too, don't always need to know how the data is stored!

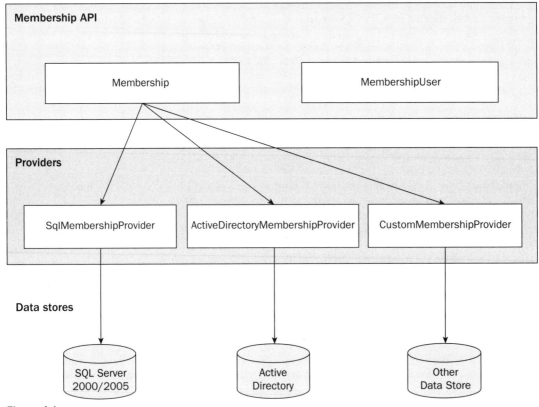

Membership API

Membership

MembershipUser

Providers

SqlMembershipProvider

ActiveDirectoryMembershipProvider

CustomMembershipProvider

Data stores

SQL Server 2000/2005

Active Directory

Other Data Store

Figure 4-1

To create a new provider you can either start from scratch by building a completely new provider that inherits directly from `System.Web.Security.MembershipProvider` (which in turn inherits from `System.Configuration.Provider.ProviderBase`) or you can just customize the way some methods of an existing provider work. For example, let's assume you want to modify the `SqlMembershipProvider` so it validates a user's password to make sure that it's not equal to his username. You simply need to define your own class, which inherits from `SqlMembershipProvider`, and you can just override the `CreateUser` method like this:

```
class SqlMembershipProviderEx : SqlMembershipProvider
{
    public override MembershipUser CreateUser(
        string username, string password, string email,
        string passwordQuestion, string passwordAnswer, bool isApproved,
        object providerUserKey, out MembershipCreateStatus status)
    {
        if (username.ToLower() == password.ToLower())
        {
            status = MembershipCreateStatus.InvalidPassword;
            return null;
        }
```

```
        else
        {
            return base.CreateUser(username, password, email,
                passwordQuestion, passwordAnswer, isApproved,
                providerUserKey, out status);
        }
    }
}
```

> The provider model design pattern is also very useful in the migration of legacy systems that already use their own custom tables and stored procedures. Your legacy database may already contain thousands of records of user information, and you want to avoid losing them, but now you want to modify your site to take advantage of the new `Membership` class. Instead of creating a custom application to migrate data to a new data store (or using SQL Server DTS to copy the data from your tables to the new tables used by the standard `SqlMembershipProvider`), you can just create your own custom provider that directly utilizes your existing tables and stored procedures. If you're already using a business class to access your account's data from the ASP.NET pages, then creating a compliant provider class may be just a matter of changing the name and signature of some methods. Alternately, you can follow this approach: Keep your current business class intact, but make it private, and then move it inside a new provider class that delegates the implementation of all its methods and properties to that newly private legacy business class. The advantage of doing this instead of just using your current business class "as is" is that you can change to a different data store later by just plugging it into the membership infrastructure — you wouldn't have to change anything in the ASP.NET pages that call the built-in `Membership` class.

Once you have the provider you want (either one of the default providers, a custom one you developed on your own, or a third-party offering) you have to tell ASP.NET which one you want to use when you call the `Membership` class' methods.

The `web.config` file is used to specify and configure the provider for the Membership system. Many of the default configuration settings are hard-coded in the ASP.NET runtime instead of being saved into the `Machine.Config` file. This is done to improve performance by reading and parsing a smaller XML file when the application starts, but you can still modify these settings for each application by assigning your own values in `web.config` to override the defaults. You can read the default settings by looking at the `Machine.config.default` file found in the following folder (the "*xxxxx*" part should be replaced with the build number of your installation):

```
C:\<Windows Folder>\Microsoft.NET\Framework\v2.0.xxxxx\CONFIG
```

What follows is the definition of the `<membership>` section of the file, where the `SqlMembershipProvider` is specified and configured:

```
<system.web>
    <membership>
        <providers>
            <add name="AspNetSqlMembershipProvider"
```

```
        type="System.Web.Security.SqlMembershipProvider, System.Web,
            Version=2.0.0.0, Culture=neutral, PublicKeyToken=b03f5f7f11d50a3a"
        connectionStringName="LocalSqlServer"
        enablePasswordRetrieval="false"
        enablePasswordReset="true"
        requiresQuestionAndAnswer="true"
        applicationName="/"
        requiresUniqueEmail="false"
        passwordFormat="Hashed"
        maxInvalidPasswordAttempts="5"
        passwordAttemptWindow="10"
        passwordStrengthRegularExpression=""
      />
    </providers>
  </membership>

  <!-- other settings... -->
</system.web>
```

You can register more providers inside the `<providers>` section, and choose which one you want to use by specifying its name in the `defaultProvider` attribute of the `<membership>` element (not shown above). Another attribute of `<membership>` is `userIsOnlineTimeWindow`, which specifies how many minutes after the last activity a user is still considered online. That is, if a user logs in, brings up one page, but then closes her browser immediately, she will be counted as being online for this number of minutes. We need this kind of parameter because we have no definite way to know when a user has left the site or closed down their browser. You can test this by checking the value returned by `Membership.GetNumberOfUsersOnline` as users come to your site and then leave.

For our site we will use SQL Server 2005 Express Edition, the free edition of SQL Server 2005, to store the accounts' credentials, and this database will also be used for all the dynamic content of the site. In the "Solution" section of this chapter, you'll see in practice how to add and configure the provider for this data store. Although this database edition is adequate for use on a developer's computer, it would be wise to use a more feature-laden edition of SQL Server 2005 for production deployment to get better development and analysis tools, and to get the best performance from high-end server computers.

More Details About SqlMembershipProvider

In the last code snippet, you saw the default settings used to register the `SqlMembershipProvider`. The following table lists the attributes you can specify when you register the provider, in the `<provider>` element.

Attribute	Description
applicationName	The name of the web application; used if you want to store data on user account's for multiple web sites in a single database
connectionStringName	The name of the connection string, registered in the <connectionStrings> section of web.config, that points to the SQL Server database used to store the data.
	Important: This is not the actual connection string! This is only a name that refers to web.config, where the actual connection string is stored.

Attribute	Description
description	A description for the provider
enablePasswordReset	Indicates whether you want to enable the methods and controls for resetting a password to a new, auto-generated one
enablePasswordRetrieval	Indicates whether you want to enable the methods and controls that allow a user to retrieve her forgotten password
maxInvalidPasswordAttempts	The maximum number of invalid login attempts. If the user fails to log in after this number of times, within the number of minutes specified by the passwordAttemptWindow attribute, the user account is "locked out" until the administrator explicitly calls the UnlockUser method of a MembershipUser instance representing the specific user.
minRequiredNonalphanumeric Characters	The minimum number of non-alphanumeric characters a password must have to be valid
minRequiredPasswordLength	The minimum number of characters for a valid password
name	The name used to register the provider. This is used to choose the provider by setting the defaultProvider attribute of the <membership> element.
passwordAttemptWindow	The number of minutes used to time invalid login attempts. See the description for maxInvalidPasswordAttempts.
passwordFormat	Specifies how the password is stored in the data store. Possible values are Clear, Encrypted, and Hashed.
passwordStrengthRegular Expression	The regular expression that a password must match to be considered valid
requiresQuestionAndAnswer	Indicates whether the user must respond to a personal secret question before retrieving or resetting her password. Questions and answers are chosen by users at registration time.
requiresUniqueEmail	Indicates whether the same e-mail address can be used to create multiple user accounts

By default, minRequiredPasswordLength is set to 7 and minRequiredNonalphanumericCharacters is set to 1, meaning that you must register with a password that is at least seven characters long and contains at least one non-alphanumeric character. Whether you leave these at their default settings or change them to suit your needs, remember to list these values on your registration page to let users know your password requirements.

These attributes let you fine-tune the membership system. For example, the ability to specify a regular expression that the password must match gives you great flexibility to meet stringent requirements. But one of the most important properties is certainly `passwordFormat`, used to specify whether you want passwords to be encrypted, or whether you just want a hash of them saved. Passwords are hashed or encrypted using the key information supplied in the `<machineKey>` element of the configuration file (you should remember to synchronize this machine key between servers if you will deploy to a server farm). The default algorithm used to calculate the password's hash is `SHA1`, but you can change it through the `validation` attribute of the `machineKey` element. Storing passwords in clear text offers the best performance when saving and retrieving the passwords, but it's the least secure solution. Encrypting a password adds some processing overhead, but it can greatly improve security. Hashing passwords provides the best security because the hashing algorithm is one way, which means the passwords cannot be retrieved in any way, even by an administrator. If a user forgets her password, she can only reset it to a new auto-generated one (typically sent by e-mail to the user). The best option always depends on the needs of each particular web site: If I were saving passwords for an e-commerce site on which I might also save user credit card information, I would surely hash the password and use a SSL connection in order to have the strongest security. For our content-based web site, however, I find that encrypting passwords is a good compromise. It's true that we're also building a small e-commerce store, but we're not going to store very critical information (credit cards numbers or other sensitive data) on our site.

> **Never store passwords in clear text. The small processing overhead necessary to encrypt and decrypt passwords is definitely worth the increased security, and thus the confidence that the users and investors have in the site.**

Exploring the Default SQL Server Data Store

Even though the ASP.NET 2.0 membership system is pre-built and ready to go, this is not a good reason to ignore its design and data structures. You should be familiar with this system to help you diagnose any problems that might arise during development or deployment. Figure 4-2 shows the tables used by the `SqlMembershipProvider` class to store credentials and other user data. Of course, the data store's design of other providers may be completely different (especially if they are not based on relational databases).

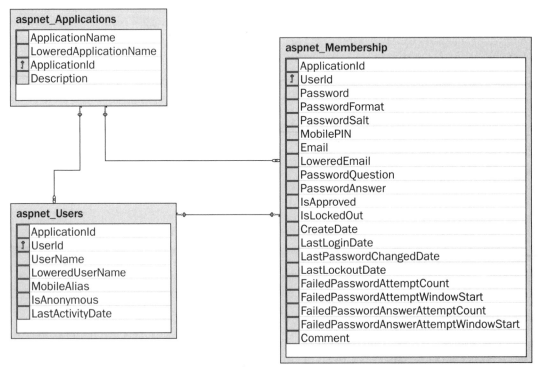

Figure 4-2

The interesting thing you can see from Figure 4-2 is the presence of the `aspnet_Applications` table, which contains a reference to multiple applications (web sites). Both the `aspnet_Users` table and the `aspnet_Membership` table contain a reference to a record in `aspnet_Applications` through the `ApplicationId` foreign key. This design enables you to use the same database to store user accounts for multiple sites, which can be very helpful if you have several sites using the same database server (commonly done with corporate web sites or with commercial low-cost shared hosting). In a situation where you have a critical application that requires the maximum security, you'll want to store the membership data in a dedicated database that only the site administrator can access. In our case, however, we're only using a SQL Server 2005 Express Edition database, and this requires us to use our own private database, deployed as a simple file under the `App_Data` special folder. In addition to these tables, there are also a couple of views related to membership (`vw_aspnet_MembershipUsers` and `vw_aspnet_Users`) and a number of stored procedures (`aspnet_membership_xxx`) for the CRUD (`Create`, `Read`, `Update`, and `Delete`) operations used for authorization. You can explore all these objects by using the Server Explorer window integrated within the Visual Studio's IDE, as shown in Figure 4-3.

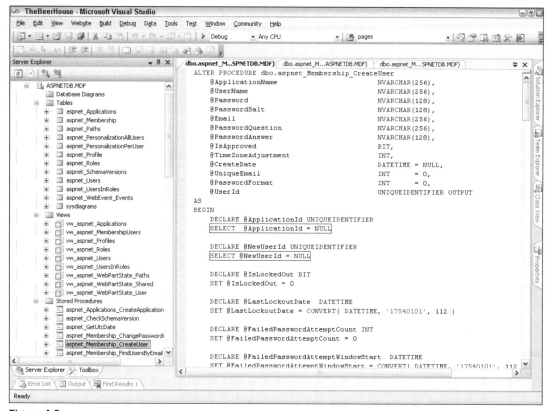

Figure 4-3

If you configure the provider so that it uses the default SQL Server Express database named `ASPNETDB` located under the `App_Data` folder, the ASP.NET runtime will automatically create all these database objects when the application is run for the first time! Because we are using this database for our site, we don't need to do anything else to set up the data store. However, if you're using SQL Server 2000 or a full edition of SQL Server 2005, you'll need to set up the tables manually by running the `aspnet_regsql.exe` tool from the Visual Studio 2005 command prompt. This little program lets you to choose an existing database on a specified server, and it creates all the required objects to support membership, along with caching, profiles, personalization, and more. Figure 4-4 displays a couple of screens generated by this tool.

Figure 4-4

The Graphical Login Controls

As you saw earlier, creating, validating, and managing users programmatically requires only a few lines of code. But what about writing no code at all? That's actually possible now, thanks to the new `Login` family of controls introduced with ASP.NET 2.0. These controls provide a pre-made user interface for the most common operations dealing with membership and security, such as creating a new account, logging in and out, retrieving or resetting a forgotten password, or showing different output according to the authenticated status of the current user. In Figure 4-5 you see a screenshot of the Visual Studio 2005 IDE, which shows the section of the Toolbox with the `Login` controls. It also shows a `CreateUserWizard` control dropped on a form, and its Smart Tasks pop-up window.

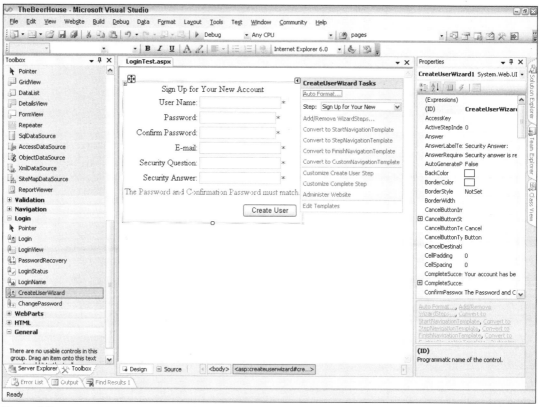

Figure 4-5

The Smart Tasks window is a new feature of Visual Studio 2005's Web Form Designer. It contains links to the given control's most common customizable settings and configuration options. It is usually opened automatically as soon as you drop the control on the form, but you can also open and close it later, by clicking on the small arrow icon that shows up on the top-right corner when the control is selected.

The CreateUserWizard Control

A wizard is a new feature in ASP.NET 2.0 used to create a visual interface for a process that involves multiple steps. Each step has a separate visual panel or frame containing its own group of controls. After the user fills in values for controls of each step, he can press a link to advance to the next step in the wizard.

The `CreateUserWizard` control creates a user interface for a user to register, by providing the username, password, and e-mail address. The secret question and answer are also requested, but only if the current membership provider has the `requiresQuestionAndAnswer` attribute set to `true`; otherwise, these two last textboxes are hidden. When the Submit button is clicked, the control calls `Membership.CreateUser` under the hood on your behalf. By default, the code produced by the designer (and visible in the Source View) is as follows:

```
<asp:CreateUserWizard ID="CreateUserWizard1" runat="server">
   <WizardSteps>
      <asp:CreateUserWizardStep runat="server">
      </asp:CreateUserWizardStep>
      <asp:CompleteWizardStep runat="server">
      </asp:CompleteWizardStep>
   </WizardSteps>
</asp:CreateUserWizard>
```

It contains no appearance attributes, and the control will look plain and simple, with the default font, background, and foreground colors. However, you can specify values for all the attributes used to control the appearance. An easy way to do that is by clicking Auto Format from the Smart Tasks window and selecting one of the pre-made styles. For example, if you select the Elegant style, the control will look as shown in Figure 4-6.

Figure 4-6

The corresponding source code was automatically updated as follows:

```
<asp:CreateUserWizard ID="CreateUserWizard1" runat="server"
   BackColor="#F7F7DE" BorderColor="#CCCC99" BorderStyle="Solid"
   BorderWidth="1px" Font-Names="Verdana" Font-Size="10pt">
   <WizardSteps>
      <asp:CreateUserWizardStep runat="server">
      </asp:CreateUserWizardStep>
      <asp:CompleteWizardStep runat="server">
      </asp:CompleteWizardStep>
   </WizardSteps>
   <SideBarStyle BackColor="#7C6F57" BorderWidth="0px"
      Font-Size="0.9em" VerticalAlign="Top" />
   <SideBarButtonStyle BorderWidth="0px" Font-Names="Verdana"
      ForeColor="#FFFFFF" />
   <NavigationButtonStyle BackColor="#FFFBFF" BorderColor="#CCCCCC"
      BorderStyle="Solid" BorderWidth="1px" Font-Names="Verdana"
      ForeColor="#284775" />
   <HeaderStyle BackColor="#F7F7DE" BorderStyle="Solid" Font-Bold="True"
      Font-Size="0.9em" ForeColor="#FFFFFF" HorizontalAlign="Left" />
   <CreateUserButtonStyle BackColor="#FFFBFF" BorderColor="#CCCCCC"
      BorderStyle="Solid" BorderWidth="1px" Font-Names="Verdana"
      ForeColor="#284775" />
   <ContinueButtonStyle BackColor="#FFFBFF" BorderColor="#CCCCCC"
```

```
        BorderStyle="Solid" BorderWidth="1px" Font-Names="Verdana"
        ForeColor="#284775" />
    <StepStyle BorderWidth="0px" />
    <TitleTextStyle BackColor="#6B696B" Font-Bold="True" ForeColor="#FFFFFF" />
</asp:CreateUserWizard>
```

Back in Chapter 2, we discussed the disadvantages of having the appearance properties set in the .aspx source files, in comparison to having them defined in a separate skin file as part of an ASP.NET 2.0 Theme. Therefore, I strongly suggest that you *not* leave the auto-generated appearance attributes in the page's source code, but instead cut-and-paste it into a skin file. You can paste everything except for the ID property and the <WizardSteps> section, as they are not part of the control's appearance.

The <WizardSteps> section lists all the steps of the wizard. By default it includes the step with the registration form, and a second one with the confirmation message. You can add other steps between these two, and in our implementation we'll add a step immediately after the registration form, where the user can associate a profile to the new account. The wizard will automatically provide the buttons for moving to the next or previous step, or to finish the wizard, and raise a number of events to notify your program of what is happening, such as ActiveStepChanged, CancelButtonClick, ContinueButtonClick, FinishButtonClick, NextButtonClick, and PreviousButtonClick.

If the available style properties are not enough for you, and you want to change the structure of the control, i.e., how the controls are laid down on the form, you can do that by defining your own template for the CreateUserWizardStep (or for the CompleteWizardStep). As long as you create the textboxes with the IDs the control expects to find, the control will continue to work without requiring you to write code to perform the registration manually. The best and easiest way to find which ID to use for each control is to have Visual Studio .NET convert the step's default view to a template (click the Customize Create User Step link in the control's Smart Tasks window), and then modify the generated code as needed. The code that follows is the result of Visual Studio's conversion and the deletion of the HTML layout tables:

```
<WizardSteps>
    <asp:CreateUserWizardStep runat="server">
        <ContentTemplate>
        <b>Sign Up for Your New Account</b><p></p>
        User Name: <asp:TextBox ID="UserName" runat="server" />
        <asp:RequiredFieldValidator ID="UserNameRequired" runat="server"
            ControlToValidate="UserName" ErrorMessage="User Name is required."
            ValidationGroup="CreateUserWizard1">*</asp:RequiredFieldValidator>
        <br />
        Password: <asp:TextBox ID="Password" runat="server" TextMode="Password" />
        <asp:RequiredFieldValidator ID="PasswordRequired" runat="server"
            ControlToValidate="Password" ErrorMessage="Password is required."
            ValidationGroup="CreateUserWizard1">*</asp:RequiredFieldValidator>
        <br />
        Confirm Password: <asp:TextBox ID="ConfirmPassword" runat="server"
            TextMode="Password" />
        <asp:RequiredFieldValidator ID="ConfirmPasswordRequired" runat="server"
            ControlToValidate="ConfirmPassword"
            ErrorMessage="Confirm Password is required."
            ValidationGroup="CreateUserWizard1">*</asp:RequiredFieldValidator>
        <asp:CompareValidator ID="PasswordCompare" runat="server"
            ControlToCompare="Password" ControlToValidate="ConfirmPassword"
            ErrorMessage="The Password and Confirmation Password must match."
```

```
                ValidationGroup="CreateUserWizard1"></asp:CompareValidator>
            <br />
            E-mail: <asp:TextBox ID="Email" runat="server" />
            <asp:RequiredFieldValidator ID="EmailRequired" runat="server"
                ControlToValidate="Email" ErrorMessage="E-mail is required."
                ValidationGroup="CreateUserWizard1">*</asp:RequiredFieldValidator>
            <br />
            Security Question: <asp:TextBox ID="Question" runat="server" />
            <asp:RequiredFieldValidator ID="QuestionRequired" runat="server"
                ControlToValidate="Question" ErrorMessage="Security question is required."
                ValidationGroup="CreateUserWizard1">*</asp:RequiredFieldValidator>
            <br />
            Security Answer: <asp:TextBox ID="Answer" runat="server" />
            <asp:RequiredFieldValidator ID="AnswerRequired" runat="server"
                ControlToValidate="Answer" ErrorMessage="Security answer is required."
                ValidationGroup="CreateUserWizard1">*</asp:RequiredFieldValidator>
            <br />
            <asp:Literal ID="ErrorMessage" runat="server" EnableViewState="False" />
            </ContentTemplate>
        </asp:CreateUserWizardStep>
        <asp:CompleteWizardStep runat="server">
        </asp:CompleteWizardStep>
    </WizardSteps>
```

> **If you pay attention to the declaration of the various validation controls, you will
> note that all of them have a** ValidationGroup **property set to the control's name,
> i.e.,** CreateUserWizard1. **The** CreateUserWizard **creates a Submit button with the
> same property, set to the same value. When that button is clicked, only those valida-
> tors that have the** ValidationGroup **property set to the same value will be consid-
> ered. This is a powerful new feature of ASP.NET 2.0 that you can use anywhere to
> create different logical forms for which the validation is run separately, according to
> which button is clicked.**

*Note that for the custom-made Create User step of the wizard, the Question and Password fields are not
automatically hidden if the current membership provider has the requiresQuestionAndAnswer attribute
set to false, as would happen otherwise.*

You can also set up the control so that it automatically sends a confirmation e-mail to users when they
complete the registration process successfully. The setup is defined by the CreateUserWizard's
<MailDefinition> subsection, and consists of the sender's e-mail address, the mail subject, and a ref-
erence to the text file that contains the e-mail's body. The following code shows an example:

```
<asp:CreateUserWizard runat="server" ID="CreateUserWizard1">
    <WizardSteps>
        ...
    </WizardSteps>
    <MailDefinition
        BodyFileName="~/RegistrationMail.txt"
        From="yourname@yourserver.com"
        Subject="Mail subject here">
    </MailDefinition>
</asp:CreateUserWizard>
```

The `RegistrationMail.txt` file can contain the `<% UserName %>` and `<% Password %>` special placeholders, which at runtime will be replaced with the values taken from the new registration's data. To send the mail, you must have configured the SMTP server settings in the `web.config file`, through the `<mailSettings>` element and its sub-elements, as shown in the following code:

```
<configuration xmlns="http://schemas.microsoft.com/.NetConfiguration/v2.0">
    <system.web> <!-- some settings here...--> </system.web>
    <system.net>
        <mailSettings>
            <smtp deliveryMethod=" Network " from="thebeerhouse@wrox.com">
                <network defaultCredentials="true" host="(localhost)" port="25" />
            </smtp>
        </mailSettings>
    </system.net> </configuration>
```

The Login Control

The `Login` control does exactly what its name suggests: It allows the user to log in. It provides the user interface for typing the username and password, and choosing whether the login will be persistent (saved across different sessions) or not. For the default simple appearance, you just need to declare the control as follows:

```
<asp:Login ID="Login1" runat="server" />
```

However, if you apply the Elegant pre-built style to it, it will look as represented in Figure 4-7.

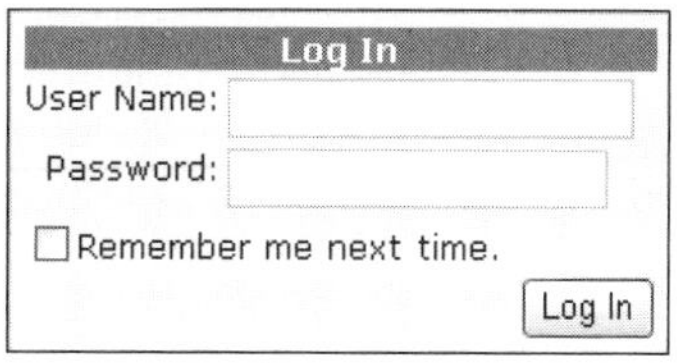

Figure 4-7

Under the covers, this control calls the `Membership.ValidateUser` method to check whether the provided credentials are found in the data store, and if so, it calls `FormsAuthentication`
`.RedirectFormLoginPage` to create the encrypted authentication ticket, saves it into a client cookie, and redirects to the page that the user originally tried to access before being redirected to the login page. The control exposes a lot of properties: Many are for changing its appearance (colors, fonts, etc.), and others enable you to specify whether you want to show a link to the registration page (`CreateUserText` and `CreateUserUrl` properties), a link to the page to recover a forgotten password (`PasswordRecoveryText` and `PasswordRecoveryUrl` properties), and whether the control should be hidden when the user is already logged in (the `VisibleWhenLoggedIn` property). Of course, as for the `CreateUserWizard` control, you can completely customize the way the control looks, by defining a template. Here's an example:

```
<asp:Login ID="Login1" runat="server">
    <LayoutTemplate>
        Username: <asp:TextBox ID="UserName" runat="server" />
        <asp:RequiredFieldValidator ID="UserNameRequired" runat="server"
            ControlToValidate="UserName" ErrorMessage="User Name is required."
```

```
                ValidationGroup="Login1">*</asp:RequiredFieldValidator>
        Password: <asp:TextBox ID="Password" runat="server" TextMode="Password" />
        <asp:RequiredFieldValidator ID="PasswordRequired" runat="server"
            ControlToValidate="Password" ErrorMessage="Password is required."
            ValidationGroup="Login1">*</asp:RequiredFieldValidator>
        <asp:CheckBox ID="RememberMe" runat="server" Text="Remember me next time." />
        <asp:Literal ID="FailureText" runat="server" EnableViewState="False" />
        <asp:Button ID="LoginButton" runat="server" CommandName="Login"
        Text="Log In" ValidationGroup="Login1" />
    </LayoutTemplate>
</asp:Login>
```

Remember that the only important thing is that you give textboxes, buttons, labels, and other controls the specific IDs that the parent control expects to find. If you start defining the template from the default template created by VS2005, this will be very easy.

The ChangePassword Control

The ChangePassword control allows users to change their current password, through the user interface shown in Figure 4-8.

Figure 4-8

This control is completely customizable in appearance, by means of either properties or a new template. As with the `CreateUserWizard` control, its declaration can contain a `<MailDefinition>` section where you can configure the control to send a confirmation e-mail to the user with her new credentials.

The PasswordRecovery Control

The `ChangePassword` control enables users to recover or reset their password, in case they forgot it. The first step, represented in Figure 4-9, is to provide the username.

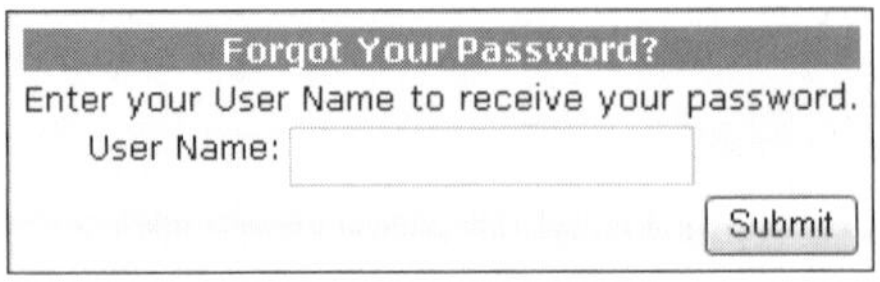

Figure 4-9

For the next step, the user will be asked the question he or she chose at registration time. If the answer is correct, the control sends the user an e-mail message. As expected, there must be the usual `MailDefinition`, along with the current password, or a newly generated one if the membership provider's `enable PasswordRetrieval` attribute is set to `false`, or if the provider's `passwordFormat` is hashed.

The LoginStatus, LoginName, and LoginView Controls

These last three controls are the simplest ones, and are often used together. The `LoginName` control shows the name of the current user. It has a `FormatString` property that can be used to show the username as part of a longer string, such as `"Welcome {0}!"`, where the username will replace the `{0}` placeholder. If the current user is not authenticated, the control shows nothing, regardless of the `FormatString` value.

The `LoginStatus` control shows a link to log out or log in, according to whether the current user is or is not authenticated. The text of the links can be changed by means of the `LoginText` and `LogoutText` properties, or you can use graphical images instead of plain text, by means of the `LoginImageUrl` and `LogoutImageUrl` properties. When the Login link is clicked, it redirects to the login page specified in the `web.config` file's `<forms>` element, or to the `Login.aspx` page if the setting is not present. When the Logout link is clicked, the control calls `FormsAuthentication.SignOut` to remove the client's authentication ticket, and then can either refresh the current page or redirect to a different one according to the values of the `LogoutAction` and `LogoutPageUrl` properties.

The `LoginView` allows you to show different output according to whether the current user is authenticated. Its declaration contains two subsections, `<AnonymousTemplate>` and `<LoggedInTemplate>`, where you place the HTML or ASP.NET controls that you want to display when the user is anonymous (not logged in) or logged in, respectively. The code that follows shows how to display the `login` control if the user is not authenticated yet, or a welcome message and a link to log out otherwise:

```
<asp:LoginView ID="LoginView1" runat="server">
   <AnonymousTemplate>
      <asp:Login runat="server" ID="Login1" />
   </AnonymousTemplate>
   <LoggedInTemplate>
      <asp:LoginName ID="LoginName1" runat="server" FormatString="Welcome {0}" />
      <br />
      <asp:LoginStatus ID="LoginStatus1" runat="server" />
   </LoggedInTemplate>
</asp:LoginView>
```

Setting Up and Using Roles

An authentication/authorization system is not complete without support for roles. Roles are used to group users together for the purpose of assigning a set of permissions, or authorizations. You could decide to control authorizations separately for each user, but that would be an administrative nightmare! Instead, it's helpful to assign a user to a predetermined role and give him the permissions that accompany the role. For example, you can define an Administrator's role to control access to the restricted pages used to add, edit, and delete the site's content, and only users who belong to the Administrators role will be able to post new articles and news. It is also possible to assign more than one role to a given user. In ASP.NET 1.x, there wasn't any built-in support for roles in forms authentication — roles were only supported with Windows security. You could have added role support manually (as shown in the first edition of this book), but that required you to create your own database tables and write code to retrieve the roles when the user logged in. You could have written the code so that the roles were retrieved at runtime — and then encrypted together by the authentication ticket on a client's cookie — so that they were not retrieved separately from the database with each request. Besides taking a considerable amount of development time that you could have spent adding value to your site, it was also a crucial task: Any design or implementation bugs could impact performance, or even worse, introduce serious security holes. The good news is that ASP.NET 2.0 has built-in support for roles, and it does it the right way with regard to performance, security, and flexibility. In fact, as is true in many other pieces of ASP.NET 2.0 (membership, sessions, profiles, personalization), it is built on the provider model design pattern: A provider for SQL Server is provided, but if you don't like some aspect of how it works, or you want to use a different data store, you can write your own custom provider or acquire one from a third party.

The role management is disabled by default to improve performance for sites that don't need roles—role support requires the execution of database queries, and consequent network traffic between the database server and the web server. You can enable it by means of the `<roleManager>` element in the web.config file, as shown here:

```
<roleManager enabled="true" cacheRolesInCookie="true" cookieName="TBHROLES" />
```

This element allows you to enable roles and configure some options. For example, the preceding code enables role caching in the client's cookie (instead of retrieving them from the database on each web request), which is a suggested best practice. Unless specified otherwise, the default provider will be used, with a connection string to the default local SQL Server Express database (the ASPNETDB file under the App_Data folder). If you want to use a different database, just register a new provider within the `<roleManager>` element, and choose it by setting the roleManager's defaultProvider attribute.

System.Web.Security.Roles is the class that allows you to access and manage role information programmatically. It exposes several static methods, the most important of which are listed in the following table.

Method	Description
AddUserToRole, AddUserToRoles, AddUsersToRole, AddUsersToRoles	Adds one or more users to one or more roles
CreateRole	Creates a new role with the specified name
DeleteRole	Deletes an existing role
FindUsersInRole	Finds all users who belong to the specified role, and who have a username that matches the input string. If the default provider for SQL server is used, the username can contain any wildcard characters supported by SQL Server in LIKE clauses, such as % for any string of zero or more characters, or _ for a single character.
GetAllRoles	Returns an array with all the roles
GetRolesForUser	Returns an array with all the roles to which the specified user belongs
GetUsersInRole	Returns the array of usernames (not MembershipUser instances) of users who belong to the specified role
IsUserInRole	Indicates whether the specified user is a member of the specified role

Method	Description
RemoveUserFromRole, RemoveUserFromRoles, RemoveUsersFromRole, RemoveUsersFromRoles	Removes one or more users from one or more roles
RoleExists	Indicates whether a role with the specified name already exists

Using these methods is straightforward, and you will see some practical examples in the "Solution" section of this chapter, where we implement the administration console to add/remove users to and from roles.

> The roles system integrates perfectly with the standard `IPrincipal` security interface, which is implemented by the object returned by the page's `User` property. Therefore, you can use the `User` object's `IsInRole` method to check whether the current user belongs to the specified role.

The SQL Server provider retrieves and stores the data from/to tables `aspnet_Roles` and `aspnet_UsersInRoles`. The latter links a user of the `aspnet_Users` table (or another user table, if you're using a custom membership provider for a custom database) to a role of the `aspnet_Roles` table. Figure 4-10 shows the database diagram again, updated with the addition of these two tables.

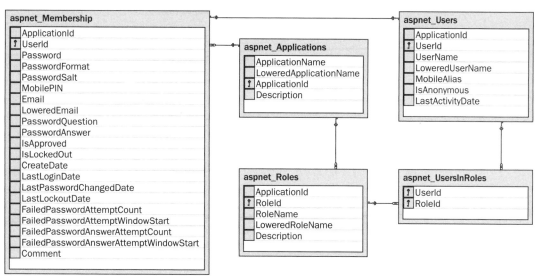

Figure 4-10

Using Roles to Protect Pages and Functions Against Unauthorized Access

Basically, you have two ways to control and protect access to sensitive pages: You can do it either imperatively (programmatically) or declaratively (using a `config` file). If you want to do it by code, in the page's Load event you would write something like the following snippet:

```
if (!Roles.IsUserInRole("Administrators"))
{
    throw new System.Security.SecurityException(
        "Sorry, this is a restricted function you are not authorized to perform");
}
```

When you don't pass the username to the `Roles.IsUserInRole` method, it takes the name of the current user, and then "forwards" the call to the `IsInRole` method of the current user's `IPrincipal` interface. Therefore, you can call it directly and save some overhead using the following code:

```
if (!this.User.IsInRole("Administrators"))
{
    throw new System.Security.SecurityException(
        "Sorry, this is a restricted function you are not authorized to perform");
}
```

> *When Roles.IsUserInRole is called with the overload that takes in the username (which is not necessarily equal to the current user's username), the check is done by the selected role's provider. In the case of the built-in SqlRoleProvider, a call to the aspnet_UsersInRoles_IsUserInRole stored procedure is made.*

The biggest disadvantage of imperative (programmatic) security is that in order to secure an entire folder, you have to copy and paste this code in multiple pages (or use a common base class for them). Even worse, when you want to change the ACL (access control list) for a page or folder (because, for example, you want to allow access to a newly created role), you will need to change the code in all those files! Declarative security makes this job much easier: you define an `<authorization>` section in a `web.config` (either for the overall site or for a subfolder), which specifies the users and roles who are allowed to access a certain folder or page. The following snippet of `web.config` gives access to members of the Administrators role, while everyone else (*) is denied access to the current folder's pages:

```
<configuration xmlns="http://schemas.microsoft.com/.NetConfiguration/v2.0">
    <system.web>
        <authorization>
            <allow roles="Administrators" />
            <deny users="*" />
        </authorization>
        <!-- other settings... -->
    </system.web>
</configuration>
```

Authorization conditions are evaluated from top to bottom, and the first one that matches the user or role stops the validation process. This means that if you switched the two conditions above, the `<deny>` condition would match for any user, and the second condition would never be considered; as a result, nobody could access the pages. This next example allows everybody except anonymous users (those who have not logged in and who are identified by the ? character):

```
<authorization>
    <deny users="?" />
    <allow users="*" />
</authorization>
```

If you want to have different ACLs for different folders, you can have a different `<authorization>` section in each folder's `web.config` file. As an alternative, you can place all ACLs in the root `web.config`, within different `<location>` sections, such as in this code:

```
<configuration xmlns="http://schemas.microsoft.com/.NetConfiguration/v2.0">
  <system.web>
    <!-- settings for the current folder -->
    <authorization>
      <allow users="*" />
    </authorization>
  </system.web>

  <location path="Admin">
    <!-- settings for the Admin sub-folder -->
    <system.web>
      <authorization>
        <allow roles="Administrators" />
        <deny users="*" />
      </authorization>
    </system.web>
  </location>

  <location path="Members">
    <!-- settings for the Members sub-folder -->
    <system.web>
      <authorization>
        <deny users="?" />
        <allow users="*" />
      </authorization>
    </system.web>
  </location>
</configuration>
```

The path attribute of the `<location>` section can be the name of a subfolder (as shown above) or the virtual path of a single page. Using the `<location>` section is the only way to declaratively assign a different ACL to specific individual pages, since you can't have page-level `web.config` files. Although it's possible to restrict individual pages, it's more common to restrict entire subfolders.

Programmatic security checks are still useful and necessary in some cases, though, such as when you want to allow everybody to load a page, but control the visibility of some visual controls (e.g., buttons to delete a record, or a link to the administration section) of that page to specific users. In these cases you can use the code presented earlier to show, or hide, some server-side controls or containers (such as `Panel`) according to the result of a call to `User.IsInRole`. Alternatively, you can use a `LoginView` control that, in addition to its sections for anonymous and logged-in users, can also define template sections visible only to users who belong to specific roles. The next snippet produces different output according to whether the current user is anonymous, is logged in as a regular member, or is logged in and belongs to the Administrators role:

```
<asp:LoginView ID="LoginView1" runat="server">
  <AnonymousTemplate>anonymous user</AnonymousTemplate>
  <LoggedInTemplate>member</LoggedInTemplate>
```

```
        <RoleGroups>
          <asp:RoleGroup Roles="Administrators">
            <ContentTemplate>administrator</ContentTemplate>
          </asp:RoleGroup>
        </RoleGroups>
      </asp:LoginView>
```

Note that in cases where the currently logged-in user is also in the Administrators role, the `LoginView` control only outputs the content of the `<Administrators>` section, not that of the more general `<LoggedInTemplate>` section.

Finally, roles are also integrated with the site map, which lets you specify which roles will be able to see a particular link in the `Menu` or `TreeView` control that consumes the site map. This is a very powerful feature that makes it easy to show a user only the menu options he is actually allowed to access! For example, if you want the Admin link to be visible only to Administrators, here's how you define the map's node:

```
<siteMapNode title="Admin" url="~/Admin/Default.aspx" roles="Administrators">
```

However, to enable this to work you must also register a new provider for the SiteMap system (in the `<siteMap>` section of the `web.config` file), and set its `securityTrimmingEnabled` attribute to `true`. Registering the provider for the site map is very similar to registering a provider for the membership or roles system; in the "Solution" section you will see code examples to illustrate this.

Setting Up and Using User Profiles

In the ASP.NET 1.x days, if you wanted to associate a profile to a registered user, you typically added a custom table to your database, or stored them together with the user credentials, in the same table. You also had to write quite a lot of code for the business and data access layers, to store, retrieve, and update that data from your web pages. ASP.NET 2.0 provides a built-in mechanism to manage user profiles, in an easy, yet very complete and flexible, way. This new feature can save you hours or even days of work! The Profile module takes care of everything — you just need to configure what the profile will contain, i.e., define the property name, type, and default value. This configuration is done in the root `web .config` file, within the `<profile>` section. The following snippet shows how to declare two properties, `FavoriteTheme` of type `String`, and `BirthDate` of type `DateTime`:

```
<configuration xmlns="http://schemas.microsoft.com/.NetConfiguration/v2.0">
  <system.web>
    <profile>
      <properties>
        <add name="FavoriteTheme" type="String" />
        <add name="BirthDate" type="DateTime" />
      </properties>
    </profile>
    <!-- other settings... -->
  </system.web>
</configuration>
```

Amazingly, this is all you need to do to set up a profile structure! When the application is run, the ASP.NET runtime dynamically adds a `Profile` property to the `Page` class, which means you will not find such a property in the Object Browser at design time. The object returned is of type `ProfileCommon` (inherited from `System.Web.Profile.ProfileBase`); you will not find this class in the Object Browser either, or on the documentation, because this class is generated and compiled on-the-fly, according to the properties defined in the `web.config` file. The result is that you can just access the page's `Profile` property and read/write its subproperties. The following code demonstrates how to read the values of the current user's profile to show them on the page when it loads, and then updates them when a Submit button is clicked:

```
protected void Page_Load(object sender, EventArgs e)
{
    if (!this.IsPostBack)
    {
        ddlThemes.SelectedValue = this.Profile.FavoriteTheme;
        txtBirthDate.Text = this.Profile.BirthDate.ToShortDateString();
    }
}


protected void btnSubmit_Click(object sender, EventArgs e)
{
    this.Profile.FavoriteTheme = ddlThemes.SelectedValue;
    this.Profile.BirthDate = DateTime.Parse(txtBirthDate.Text);
}
```

Even though you can't see these properties in the Object Browser, Visual Studio .NET is smart enough to compile this class in the background when the `web.config` file is modified, so you get full IntelliSense in the IDE, just as if the `Profile` properties were built-in properties of the `Page` class, like all the others. Figure 4-11 is a screenshot of the IDE with the IntelliSense in action.

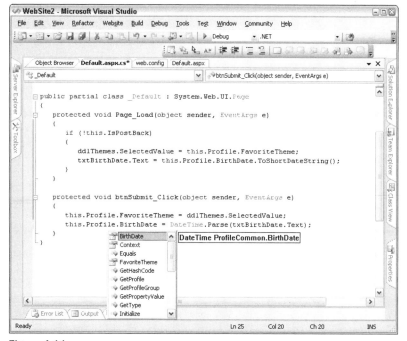

Figure 4-11

> Having a class dynamically generated by Visual Studio 2005 with all the custom profile properties (and the IntelliSense for them) doesn't just speed up development, but also helps developers reduce inadvertent coding errors. In fact, this class provides strongly typed access to the user's profile, so if you try to assign a string or an integer to a property that expects a date, you'll get a compile-time error so you can correct the problem immediately!

When you define a profile property, you can also assign a default value to it, by means of the `defaultValue` attribute:

```
<add name="FavoriteTheme" type="String" defaultValue="Colorful" />
```

The default value for strings is an empty string, not null, as you may have thought. This makes it easier to read string properties, because you don't have to check whether they are null before using the value somewhere. The other data types have the same default values that a variable of the same type would have (e.g., zero for integers).

When you declare profile properties, you can also group them into subsections, as shown below:

```
<profile>
    <properties>
        <add name="FavoriteTheme" type="String" />
        <add name="BirthDate" type="DateTime" />
        <group name="Address">
            <add name="Street" type="String" />
            <add name="City" type="String" />
        </group>
    </properties>
</profile>
```

The `Street` property will be accessible as `Profile.Address.Street`. Note, however, that you can't define nested groups under each other, but can only have a single level of groups. If this limitation is not acceptable to you, you can define your own custom class with subcollections and properties, and reference it in the `type` attribute of a new property. In fact, you are not limited to base types for profile properties; you can also reference more complex classes (such as `ArrayList` or `Color`), and your own enumerations, structures, and classes, as long as they are serializable into a binary or XML format (the format is dictated by the property's `serializeAs` attribute).

The Profile system is built upon the provider model design pattern. ASP.NET 2.0 comes with a single built-in profile provider that uses a SQL Server database as a backing store. However, as usual, you can build your own providers or find them from third parties.

Accessing Profiles from Business Classes

Sometimes you may need to access the user's profile from a business class, or from a page base class. The `Profile` property is dynamically added only to the aspx pages' code-behind classes, so you can't use it in those situations. However, you can still access it through the `Profile` property exposed by the current `HttpContext`. The `HttpContext` class is the container for the current web request — it's used to pass around objects that are part of the request: forms, properties, `ViewState`, etc. Anytime you process a page, you will have this `HttpContext` information, so you can always pull a `Profile` class instance out of the `HttpContext` class. The returned type is `ProfileBase`, though, not the `ProfileCommon` object generated on-the-fly that enabled you to use IntelliSense and access properties in a strongly typed manner. Therefore, the resulting `Profile` class instance read from the `HttpContext.Current` `.Profile` will not be strongly typed. No problem — just do the cast and you are ready to use the profile as usual. Individual properties of the profile will be strongly typed, as expected. The following snippet shows a practical example:

```
ProfileCommon profile = HttpContext.Current.Profile as ProfileCommon;
profile.BirthDate = new DateTime(1980, 09, 28);
```

Accessing the Profile for Users Other Than the Current User

So far, all the examples have shown how to read and write the profile for the current user. However, you can also access other users' profiles — very useful if you want to implement an administration page to read and modify the profiles of your registered members. Your administrator must be able to read and edit the profile properties for any user. The `ProfileCommon` class exposes a `GetProfile` method that returns the profile for any specified user, and once you obtain this profile instance you can read and edit the profile properties just as you can do for the current user's profile. The only difference is that after changing some values of the retrieved profile, you must explicitly call its `Save` method, which is not required when you modify the profile for the current user (in the case of the current user, `Save` is called automatically by the runtime when the page unloads). Here's an example of getting a profile for a specified user, and then modifying a property value in that profile:

```
ProfileCommon profile = Profile.GetProfile("Marco");
profile.BirthDate = new DateTime(1980, 09, 28);
profile.Save();
```

Adding Support for Anonymous Users

The code shown above works only for registered users who are logged in. Sometimes, however, you want to be able to store profile values for users who are not logged in. You can explicitly enable the anonymous identification support by adding the following line to `web.config`:

```
<anonymousIdentification enabled="true"/>
```

After that, you must indicate what properties are available to anonymous users. By default, a property is only accessible for logged-in users, but you can change this by setting the property's `allowAnonymous` attribute to `true`, as follows:

```
<add name="FavoriteTheme" type="String"
    allowAnonymous="true" defaultValue="Colorful" />
```

This is useful to allow an anonymous user to select a theme for his current session. This would not be saved after his session terminates because we don't have an actual user identity to allow us to persist the settings. Another important concern regarding profiles for anonymous users is the migration from anonymous to authenticated status. Consider the following situation: A registered user comes to the site and browses it without logging in. He or she then changes some profile properties available to anonymous users, such as the name of the favorite theme. At some point he or she wants to access a restricted page and needs to log in. Now, because the favorite theme was selected while the user was anonymous, it was stored into a profile linked to an anonymous user ID. After the user logs in, he or she then becomes an authenticated user with a different user ID. Therefore, that user's previous profile settings are loaded, and the user will get a site with the theme selected during a previous session, or the default one. What you wanted to do, however, was to migrate the anonymous user's profile to the authenticated user's profile at the time he logged in. This can be done by means of the `Profile_MigrateAnonymous` global event, which you can handle in the `Global.asax` file. Once this event is raised, the `HttpContext.Profile` property will already have returned the authenticated user's profile, so it's too late for us to save the anonymous profile values. You can, however, get a reference to the anonymous profile previously used by the user, and then copy values from it to the new profile. In the "Solution" section you will see how to implement this event to avoid losing the user's preferences.

The Web Administration Tool

As you've seen thus far, the preferred method of setting up and configuring all the membership and profiling services introduced by ASP.NET 2.0 is to configure XML tags in the `web.config` file, which is the declarative coding method. To make your job even easier, you now have IntelliSense when you edit `web.config` in Visual Studio 2005, which wasn't supported in earlier versions, as you can see in Figure 4-12.

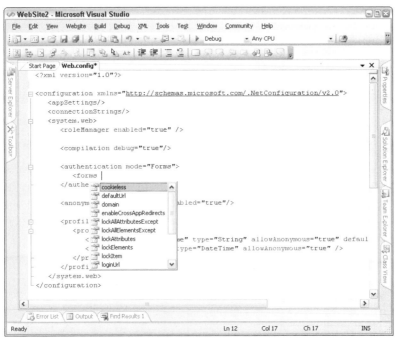

Figure 4-12

However, the ASP.NET and VS2005 teams made things even simpler still by providing a web-based administration tool that you can launch by clicking the ASP.NET Configuration item from Visual Studio's Web Site Tool. This application provides help in the following areas:

❑ **Security:** It enables you to set up the authentication mode (you can choose between the Intranet/Windows and the Internet/form-based model), create and manage users, create and manage roles, and create access rules for folders (you select a subfolder and declare which roles are granted or denied access to it). Figure 4-13 shows a couple of screenshots of these pages.

❑ **Application:** It enables you to create and manage application settings (those inside the `<appSettings>` section), and configure the SMTP e-mail settings, debugging and tracing sections, and the default error page.

❑ **Provider:** It enables you to select a provider for the Membership and the Roles systems. However, the providers must already be registered in `web.config`.

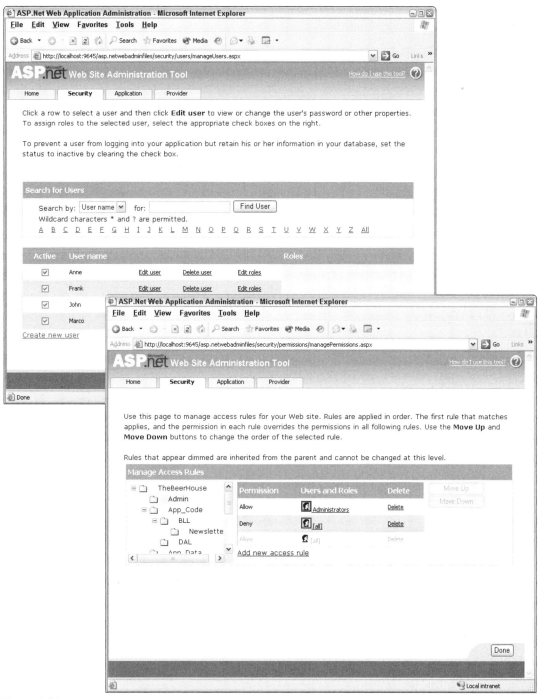

Figure 4-13

These pages use the new configuration API to read and write sections and elements to and from the `web.config` file. This tool, however, is only intended to be used on the local server, not a remote site. If you want to administer these kinds of settings for a remote site (as we want to do for our site), you will need to modify the web pages for this tool, or design your own pages. Fortunately, the complete source code for the ASP.NET Administration Tool is available under `C:\<Windows Folder>\Microsoft.NET\Framework\v2.0.xxxxx\ASP.NETWebAdminFiles`. You can go look at these pages to see how Microsoft implemented the features, and then you can do something similar for your own custom administration console.

Designing Our Solution

So far we have described the general features of the new membership and profile services introduced in ASP.NET 2.0, but we can now build upon this knowledge and design exactly how we can implement these features in our particular web site. Here's the summary of our design objectives regarding membership and profile features, and a description of the corresponding web pages:

❑ A login box will be visible in the top-right corner of each page whenever the user is anonymous. After the user logs in, the login box will be hidden. Instead, we'll show a greeting message and links for Logout and Edit Profile.

❑ A `Register.aspx` page will allow new users to register (create their own account), and we'll populate some profile settings upon registration. The profile will have the following first-level properties: `FirstName` (`String`), `LastName` (`String`), `Gender` (`String`), `BirthDate` (`DateTime`), `Occupation` (`String`), and `Website` (`String`). A profile group named `Address` will have the following subproperties: `Street`, `PostCode`, `City`, `State`, and `Country`, all of type `String`. Another group named `Contacts` will have the following string sub-properties: `Phone` and `Fax`. A final group named `Preferences` will have the `Theme`, `Culture`, and `Newsletter` properties. The `Theme` property is the only one that will be made available to anonymous users.

❑ Our `PasswordRecovery.aspx` page will allow users to recover forgotten passwords; it can e-mail the password to the user's e-mail address that we have on file. This is possible because we'll configure the membership module to encrypt the password, instead of storing it as a hash (a hashed password is a one-way encryption that is not reversible). We had to decide whether we wanted the best possible security (hashing) or a more user-friendly encryption method that enables us to recover the user's password. In our scenario we've determined that the user-friendly option is the best choice.

❑ Our `EditProfile.aspx` page will only be accessible to registered members, and it will allow them to change their account's password and the profile information they set up at registration time.

❑ We'll create some administration pages to allow the administrator to read and edit all the information about registered users (members). A `ManageUsers.aspx` page will help the administrator look up records for members either by their username or e-mail address (searches by partial text will also be supported). Among the data returned will be their username, e-mail address, when they registered or last accessed the site, and whether they are active or not. A second page, `EditUser.aspx`, will show additional details about a single user, and will allow the administrator to enable or disable the account, assign new roles to the user, remove roles from the user, and edit the user's personal profile.

Solution

We'll get right into the implementation because we've already covered the basic material and our objectives in the "Design" section of this chapter. Now we'll put all the pieces together to create the pages and the supporting code to make them work. These are the steps used to tackle our solution:

1. Define all the settings required for membership, roles, and profiles in `web.config`.

2. Create the login box on the master page, and the "access denied" page. To test the login process before creating the registration page, we can easily create a user account from the ASP.NET Web Administration Tool.

3. Create the registration and profiling page.

4. Create the password recovery page.

5. Create the page to change the current password and all the profile information.

6. Design profiles to save the user's favorite theme, and handle the migration from an anonymous user to an authenticated user so we won't lose his theme preference.

7. Create the administration pages to display all users, as well as edit and delete them.

The Configuration File

Following is a partial snippet of the `web.config` file (located in the site's root folder) used to configure the authentication type, membership, role manager, profile, and sitemap provider (in this order):

```
<configuration xmlns="http://schemas.microsoft.com/.NetConfiguration/v2.0">
    <!-- other settings... -->
    <system.web>
        <authentication mode="Forms">
            <forms cookieless="AutoDetect"
                loginUrl="~/AccessDenied.aspx" name="TBHFORMAUTH" />
        </authentication>

        <membership defaultProvider="TBH_MembershipProvider"
            userIsOnlineTimeWindow="15">
            <providers>
                <add name="TBH_MembershipProvider"
                    connectionStringName="LocalSqlServer"
                    applicationName="/"
                    enablePasswordRetrieval="true"
                    enablePasswordReset="true"
                    requiresQuestionAndAnswer="true"
                    requiresUniqueEmail="true"
                    passwordFormat="Encrypted"
                    maxInvalidPasswordAttempts="5"
                    passwordAttemptWindow="10"
                    minRequiredPasswordLength="5"
                    minRequiredNonalphanumericCharacters="0"
                    type="System.Web.Security.SqlMembershipProvider, System.Web,
    Version=2.0.0.0, Culture=neutral, PublicKeyToken=b03f5f7f11d50a3a"
                />
```

```
            </providers>
        </membership>

        <roleManager enabled="true" cacheRolesInCookie="true"
            cookieName="TBHROLES" defaultProvider="TBH_RoleProvider">
            <providers>
                <add name="TBH_RoleProvider"
                    connectionStringName="LocalSqlServer"
                    applicationName="/"
                    type="System.Web.Security.SqlRoleProvider, System.Web,
Version=2.0.0.0, Culture=neutral, PublicKeyToken=b03f5f7f11d50a3a"
                    />
            </providers>
        </roleManager>

        <anonymousIdentification cookieless="AutoDetect"  enabled="true"/>

        <profile defaultProvider="TBH_ProfileProvider">
            <providers>
                <add name="TBH_ProfileProvider"
                    connectionStringName="LocalSqlServer"
                    applicationName="/"
                    type="System.Web.Profile.SqlProfileProvider, System.Web,
Version=2.0.0.0, Culture=neutral, PublicKeyToken=b03f5f7f11d50a3a"
                    />
            </providers>
            <properties>
                <add name="FirstName" type="String" />
                <add name="LastName" type="String" />
                <add name="Gender" type="String" />
                <add name="BirthDate" type="DateTime" />
                <add name="Occupation" type="String" />
                <add name="Website" type="String" />
                <group name="Address">
                    <add name="Street" type="String" />
                    <add name="PostalCode" type="String" />
                    <add name="City" type="String" />
                    <add name="State" type="String" />
                    <add name="Country" type="String" />
                </group>
                <group name="Contacts">
                    <add name="Phone" type="String" />
                    <add name="Fax" type="String" />
                </group>
                <group name="Preferences">
                    <add name="Theme" type="String" allowAnonymous="true" />
                    <add name="Culture" type="String" defaultValue="en-US" />
                    <add name="Newsletter"
type="MB.TheBeerHouse.BLL.Newsletters.SubscriptionType" />
                </group>
            </properties>
        </profile>

        <machineKey
validationKey="287C5D125D6B7E7223E1F719E3D58D17BB967703017E1BBE28618FAC6C4501E910C7
E59800B5D4C2EDD5B0ED98874A3E952D60BAF260D9D374A74C76CB741803"
```

```
                decryptionKey="5C1D8BD9DF3E1B4E1D01132F234266616E0D5EF772FE80AB"
                validation="SHA1"/>

        <siteMap defaultProvider="TBH_SiteMapProvider" enabled="true">
            <providers>
                <add name="TBH_SiteMapProvider"
                    type="System.Web.XmlSiteMapProvider"
                    securityTrimmingEnabled="true"
                    siteMapFile="web.sitemap"
                />
            </providers>
        </siteMap>
    </system.web>

    <location path="EditProfile.aspx">
        <system.web>
            <authorization>
                <deny users="?" />
                <allow users="*" />
            </authorization>
        </system.web>
    </location>

    <system.net>
        <mailSettings>
            <smtp deliveryMethod="Network">
                <network defaultCredentials="true" host="vsnetbeta2" port="25"
                    from="mbellinaso@wrox.com"></network>
            </smtp>
        </mailSettings>
    </system.net>
</configuration>
```

As you can see, a provider is defined and configured for all modules that support this pattern. I specified the provider settings even though they are often the same as the default providers found in `machine.config.default`, because I can't be sure whether the defaults will always be the same in future ASP.NET releases, and I like to have this information handy in case I might want to make further changes someday. To create these settings I copied them from `machine.config.default`, and then I made a few tweaks as needed.

I defined a Newsletter profile property as type `MB.TheBeerHouse.BLL.Newsletters.Subscription Type`, which is an enumeration defined in the `Enum.cs` file located under `App_Code/BLL/Newsletter`:

```
namespace MB.TheBeerHouse.BLL.Newsletters
{
    public enum SubscriptionType : int
    {
        None = 0,
        PlainText = 1,
        Html
    }
}
```

In order to configure the cryptographic keys, we need to set the `validationKey` and `decryptionKey` attributes of the `machineKey` element. Because we are configuring the membership module to encrypt passwords, we can't leave them set at `AutoGenerate`, which is the default. You can find some handy utilities on the Internet that will help you set these values. You can check the following Microsoft Knowledge Base article for more information: `http://support.microsoft.com/kb/313091/`. This article shows how to implement a class that makes use of the cryptographic classes and services to create values for these keys. Alternately, if you want an easier way to create these keys, check out this online tool: `www.aspnetresources.com/tools/keycreator.aspx`.

I want to reiterate a point I made earlier in this chapter: If you'll be deploying your application to a web farm (more than one web server configured to distribute the load between the servers), then you need to specify the same machine keys for each server. In addition to password encryption, these keys are also used for session state. By synchronizing these keys with all your servers, you ensure that the same encryption will be used on each server. This is essential if there's a chance that a different server might be used to process the next posting of a page.

Creating the Login Box

In Chapter 2, when we created the master page (the `template.master` file), we defined a `<div>` container on the top-right corner that we left blank for future use. A `<div>` declares an area on a web page called a *division* — it's typically used as a container for other content. Now it's time to fill that `<div>` with the code for the login box. ASP.NET typically uses customizable templates to control the visual rendering of standard controls, and this template concept has been expanded in version 2.0 to include most of the new controls. In this section we will customize the default user interface of the login controls by providing our own template. Using custom templates offers the following advantages:

1. You have full control over the appearance of the produced output, and you can change many aspects of the behavior. For example, our custom template can be used with validator controls, and you can set their `SetFocusOnError` property to `true` (this defaults to `false` in the default template). This property is new to ASP.NET 2.0 and specifies whether the validator will give the focus to the control it validates if the client-side validation fails. This is desirable in our case because we want the focus to go to the first invalid control after the user clicks the Submit button if some controls have invalid input values.

2. If you don't redefine the `TextBox` controls, the `SetInputControlsHighlight` method we developed in Chapter 2 will not find them, and thus the textboxes will not get the special highlight behavior that gives users a visual cue as to which `TextBox` currently has the focus.

Here's the complete code that uses a `LoginView` to display a login box. This login box contains links to register a new account or to recover a forgotten password when the user is anonymous, or it will contain a welcome message, a logout link, and a link to the `EditProfile` page if the user is currently logged in:

```
<div id="loginbox">
<asp:LoginView ID="LoginView1" runat="server">
    <AnonymousTemplate>
        <asp:Login ID="Login" runat="server" Width="100%"
            FailureAction="RedirectToLoginPage">
            <LayoutTemplate>
                <table border="0" cellpadding="0" cellspacing="0" width="100%">
                    <tr>
                        <td width="60px">Username:</td>
                        <td><asp:TextBox id="UserName" runat="server" Width="95%" /></td>
```

```
                            <td width="5px" align="right">
                                <asp:RequiredFieldValidator ID="valRequireUserName"
                                    runat="server" SetFocusOnError="true" Text="*"
                                    ControlToValidate="UserName" ValidationGroup="Login" />
                            </td>
                        </tr>
                        <tr>
                            <td>Password:</td>
                            <td><asp:TextBox ID="Password" runat="server"
                                TextMode="Password"  Width="95%" /></td>
                            <td width="5px" align="right">
                                <asp:RequiredFieldValidator ID="valRequirePassword"
                                    runat="server" SetFocusOnError="true" Text="*"
                                    ControlToValidate="Password" ValidationGroup="Login" />
                            </td>
                        </tr>
                    </table>
                    <table border="0" cellpadding="0" cellspacing="0" width="100%">
                        <tr>
                            <td><asp:CheckBox ID="RememberMe" runat="server"
                                Text="Remember me"></asp:Checkbox></td>
                            <td align="right">
                                <asp:ImageButton ID="Submit" runat="server"
                                    CommandName="Login" ImageUrl="~/images/go.gif"
                                    ValidationGroup="Login" />
                            </td>
                            <td width="5px" align="right"> </td>
                        </tr>
                    </table>
                    <div style="border-top: solid 1px black; margin-top: 2px">
                        <asp:HyperLink ID="lnkRegister" runat="server"
                            NavigateUrl="~/Register.aspx">Create new account
                        </asp:HyperLink><br />
                        <asp:HyperLink ID="lnkPasswordRecovery" runat="server"
                            NavigateUrl="~/PasswordRecovery.aspx">I forgot my password
                        </asp:HyperLink>
                    </div>
                </LayoutTemplate>
            </asp:Login>
        </AnonymousTemplate>
        <LoggedInTemplate>
            <div id="welcomebox">
                <asp:LoginName ID="LoginName1" runat="server"
                    FormatString="Hello  {0}!" /><br />
                <small>
                <font face="Webdings">4</font>
                <asp:HyperLink ID="lnkProfile" runat="server" Text="Edit Profile"
                    NavigateUrl="~/EditProfile.aspx" />
                <font face="Webdings">3</font><br />
                <font face="Webdings">4</font>
                <asp:LoginStatus ID="LoginStatus1" Runat="server" />
                <font face="Webdings">3</font>
                </small>
            </div>
        </LoggedInTemplate>
    </asp:LoginView>
</div>
```

Absolutely no code is needed in the master page's code-behind files. In fact, because we used the right IDs for the textboxes and other controls in the template sections of the `Login` control, it will continue working autonomously as if it were using the default UI. To test the control, first create a new user through the ASP.NET Web Site Configuration Tool described earlier, and then try to log in. In Figure 4-14 you can see what the home page looks like from an anonymous user's and an authenticated user's point of view.

Figure 4-14

Observe the login box in the first window (only displayed for anonymous users), and the new greeting message and links in the second window that are displayed after the user logs in. Also, note that an Admin link is visible on the second browser's menu bar. That Admin link only appears for users who have been assigned the Administrators role. The `web.sitemap` file is used to generate the menu, and the item representing the Admin link was modified by adding the `roles` attribute, which was set to `Administrators`:

```
<siteMap xmlns="http://schemas.microsoft.com/AspNet/SiteMap-File-1.0" >
    <siteMapNode title="Home" url="~/Default.aspx">
        <!-- other items -->
        <siteMapNode title="Admin" url="~/Admin/Default.aspx"
            roles="Administrators" />
    </siteMapNode>
</siteMap>
```

Of course, you can test the sitemap-controlled menu by assigning the Administrators role to your sample user. You can even do this role assignment from the online configuration application!

The AccessDenied.aspx Page

If you look a few pages back, you'll see that the `loginUrl` attribute of the `web.config`'s `<forms>` is set to `AccessDenied.aspx`. As its name clearly suggests, this is the URL of the page we want to redirect control to when the user tries to access a protected page to which he doesn't have permission. In many cases you would place the login box in this page, hence the attribute name (`loginUrl`). In our case, however, we have a site that lets anonymous users access many different pages, and we only require the user to log in to gain access to a small number of pages, so we want to make sure the login box is visible from any page when the user is anonymous. The login box invites the user to log in if they already have an account, or to register if they don't have one. This `AccessDenied` page is also loaded when a user tries to log in but gives invalid credentials, or when they are already logged in but they don't have a role required by the page they requested. Therefore, the page has three possible messages, and the following code uses three labels for them:

```
<%@ Page Language="C#" AutoEventWireup="true" CodeFile="AccessDenied.aspx.cs"
    Inherits="AccessDenied" Title="The Beer House - Access Denied"
    MasterPageFile="~/Template.master" %>

<asp:Content ID="MainContent" ContentPlaceHolderID="MainContent" Runat="Server">
<asp:Image ID="imgLock" runat="server"
    ImageUrl="~/images/lock.gif" ImageAlign="left" />

<asp:Label runat="server" ID="lblLoginRequired" Font-Bold="true">
You must be a registered user to access this page. If you already have an account,
please login with your credentials in the box on the upper-right corner. Otherwise
<a href="Register.aspx">click here</a> to register now for free.
</asp:Label>
<asp:Label runat="server" ID="lblInsufficientPermissions" Font-Bold="true">
Sorry, the account you are logged with does not have the permissions required to
access this page.
</asp:Label>
<asp:Label runat="server" ID="lblInvalidCredentials" Font-Bold="true">
The submitted credentials are not valid. Please check they are correct and try
again.
If you forgot your password, <a href="PasswordRecovery.aspx">click here</a> to
recover it.
</asp:Label>
</asp:Content>
```

The `Page_Load` event handler in the code-behind file contains the logic for showing the proper label and hiding the other two. You need to do some tests to determine which of the three cases applies:

❑ If the querystring contains a `loginfailure` parameter set to `1`, it means that the user tried to log in but the submitted credentials were not recognized.

❑ If the user is not authenticated and there is no `loginfailure` parameter on the querystring, it means that the user tried to access a page that is not available to anonymous users.

❑ If the current user is already authenticated and this page is loaded anyway, it means the user does not have sufficient permission (read "does not belong to a required role") to access the requested page.

Here is how to translate this description to code:

```
public partial class AccessDenied : BasePage
{
    protected void Page_Load(object sender, EventArgs e)
    {
        lblInsufficientPermissions.Visible = this.User.Identity.IsAuthenticated;
        lblLoginRequired.Visible = (!this.User.Identity.IsAuthenticated &&
            string.IsNullOrEmpty(this.Request.QueryString["loginfailure"]));
        lblInvalidCredentials.Visible = (
            this.Request.QueryString["loginfailure"] != null &&
            this.Request.QueryString["loginfailure"] == "1");
    }
}
```

Figure 4-15 is a screenshot of the first situation — note the message by the image of the padlock.

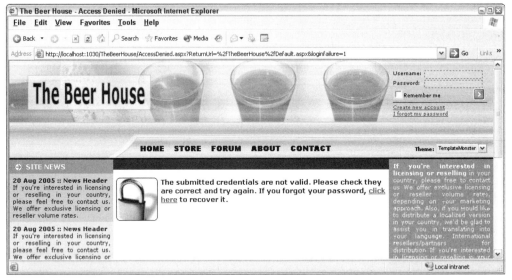

Figure 4-15

The UserProfile Control

The user interface and the logic required to show and update a user's profile is contained in a user control named `UserProfile.ascx` and placed under the `Controls` folder. Profile properties can be edited in both the registration page and in the page users access to change their profile, so it makes sense to put this code in a user control that can easily be reused in multiple places. The user interface part consists of simple HTML code to layout a number of server-side controls (textboxes and drop-down lists) that will show users their profile properties and let them edit those properties:

```
<%@ Control Language="C#" AutoEventWireup="true" CodeFile="UserProfile.ascx.cs"
Inherits="UserProfile" %>
<div class="sectionsubtitle">Site preferences</div>
<p></p>
<table cellpadding="2">
    <tr>
        <td width="130" class="fieldname">Newsletter:</td>
        <td width="300">
            <asp:DropDownList runat="server" ID="ddlSubscriptions">
                <asp:ListItem Text="No subscription" Value="None" Selected="true" />
                <asp:ListItem Text="Subscribe to plain-text version"
                    Value="PlainText" />
                <asp:ListItem Text="Subscribe to HTML version" Value="Html" />
            </asp:DropDownList>
        </td>
    </tr>
    <tr>
        <td class="fieldname">Language:</td>
        <td>
            <asp:DropDownList runat="server" ID="ddlLanguages">
                <asp:ListItem Text="English" Value="en-US" Selected="true" />
                <asp:ListItem Text="Italian" Value="it-IT" />
            </asp:DropDownList>
        </td>
    </tr>
</table>
<p></p>
<div class="sectionsubtitle">Personal details</div>
<p></p>
<table cellpadding="2">
    <tr>
        <td width="130" class="fieldname">First name:</td>
        <td width="300">
            <asp:TextBox ID="txtFirstName" runat="server" Width="99%"></asp:TextBox>
        </td>
    </tr>
    <tr>
        <td class="fieldname">Last name:</td>
        <td>
            <asp:TextBox ID="txtLastName" runat="server" Width="99%" />
        </td>
    </tr>
    <tr>
        <td class="fieldname">Gender:</td>
        <td>
            <asp:DropDownList runat="server" ID="ddlGenders">
                <asp:ListItem Text="Please select one..." Value="" Selected="True" />
                <asp:ListItem Text="Male" Value="M" />
                <asp:ListItem Text="Female" Value="F" />
            </asp:DropDownList>
        </td>
```

```
            </tr>
            <tr>
                <td class="fieldname">Birth date:</td>
                <td>
                    <asp:TextBox ID="txtBirthDate" runat="server" Width="99%"></asp:TextBox>
                    <asp:CompareValidator runat="server" ID="valBirthDateFormat"
                        ControlToValidate="txtBirthDate"
                        SetFocusOnError="true" Display="Dynamic" Operator="DataTypeCheck"
                        Type="Date" ErrorMessage="The format of the birth date is not valid."
                        ValidationGroup="EditProfile">
                        <br />The format of the birth date is not valid.
                    </asp:CompareValidator>
                </td>
            </tr>
            <tr>
                <td class="fieldname">Occupation:</td>
                <td>
                    <asp:DropDownList ID="ddlOccupations" runat="server" Width="99%">
                        <asp:ListItem Text="Please select one..." Value="" Selected="True" />
                        <asp:ListItem Text="Academic" />
                        <asp:ListItem Text="Accountant" />
                        <asp:ListItem Text="Actor" />
                        <asp:ListItem Text="Architect" />
                        <asp:ListItem Text="Artist" />
                        <asp:ListItem Text="Business Manager" />
                        <%-- other options... --%>
                        <asp:ListItem Text="Other" />
                    </asp:DropDownList>
                </td>
            </tr>
            <tr>
                <td class="fieldname">Website:</td>
                <td>
                    <asp:TextBox ID="txtWebsite" runat="server" Width="99%" />
                </td>
            </tr>
        </table>
        <p></p>
        <div class="sectionsubtitle">Address</div>
        <p></p>
        <table cellpadding="2">
            <tr>
                <td width="130" class="fieldname">Street:</td>
                <td width="300">
                    <asp:TextBox runat="server" ID="txtStreet" Width="99%" />
                </td>
            </tr>
            <tr>
                <td class="fieldname">City:</td>
                <td><asp:TextBox runat="server" ID="txtCity" Width="99%" /></td>
            </tr>
            <tr>
                <td class="fieldname">Zip / Postal code:</td>
                <td><asp:TextBox runat="server" ID="txtPostalCode" Width="99%" /></td>
            </tr>
```

```
<tr>
    <td class="fieldname">State / Region:</td>
    <td><asp:TextBox runat="server" ID="txtState" Width="99%" /></td>
</tr>
<tr>
    <td class="fieldname">Country:</td>
    <td>
        <asp:DropDownList ID="ddlCountries" runat="server"
            AppendDataBoundItems="True" Width="99%">
            <asp:ListItem Text="Please select one..." Value="" Selected="True" />
        </asp:DropDownList>
    </td>
</tr>
</table>
<p></p>
<div class="sectionsubtitle">Other contacts</div>
<p></p>
<table cellpadding="2">
    <tr>
        <td width="130" class="fieldname">Phone:</td>
        <td width="300"><asp:TextBox runat="server" ID="txtPhone" Width="99%" /></td>
    </tr>
    <tr>
        <td class="fieldname">Fax:</td>
        <td><asp:TextBox runat="server" ID="txtFax" Width="99%" /></td>
    </tr>
</table>
```

As you see, there is a `DropDownList` control that enables users to select their country. The Select an Option item is selected by default and it serves to give users instructions about what they need to do. You may need that country list in other places, and also inside business components, so instead of hard-coding it into this control, the countries are passed as a string array by a helper method. This way, it can easily bind the country list to the drop-down lists, but it can also be used in other ways. Here's the code for the helper method:

```
public static class Helpers
{
    private static string[] _countries = new string[] {
        "Afghanistan", "Albania", "Algeria", "American Samoa", "Andorra",
        "Angola", "Anguilla", "Antarctica", "Antigua And Barbuda", "Argentina",
        "Armenia", "Aruba", "Australia", "Austria", "Azerbaijan",
        "Bahamas", "Bahrain", "Bangladesh", "Barbados", "Belarus",
        "Belgium", "Belize", "Benin", "Bermuda", "Bhutan",
        /* add here all the other countries */
    };

    /// <summary>
    /// Returns an array with all countries
    /// </summary>
    public static StringCollection GetCountries()
    {
        StringCollection countries = new StringCollection();
        countries.AddRange(_countries);
        return countries;
```

```
        }

        // other methods...
    }
```

The `DropDownList` control has the `AppendDataBoundItems` property set to `true`. This is a new property of ASP.NET 2.0 that allows you to specify whether the values added to the control via data-binding will be added to those defined at design time, or will overwrite them as is done with ASP.NET 1.x. Also note that the user control has no Submit button, as this will be provided by the hosting page.

Persisting Properties Through the New Control State

Because this control will be used in the administration area to read and edit the profile for any user, it needs a public property that stores the name of the user for whom you are querying. In ASP.NET 1.x, the typical way to make a property value persistent across postbacks is to save it into the control's `ViewState` collection, so that it is serialized into a blob of base-64 encoded text, together with all the other property values, and saved into the __VIEWSTATE HTML hidden field. This is better than session state because it doesn't use server resources to save temporary values because the values are saved as part of the overall page. The user won't see the hidden values, but they are there in the user's browser and he'll post them back to the server along with the other form data each time he does a postback. The problem with view state is that it can be disabled, by setting the page's or control's `EnableViewState` property to `False`. Disabling this feature is a common way to minimize the volume of data passed back and forth across the network. Unfortunately, controls that use view state to store values will not work correctly if view state is disabled on any particular host page. To solve this issue, ASP.NET 2.0 introduces a new type of state called *control state*, which is a similar to view state, except that it's only related to a particular control and it can't be disabled. Values that a control wants to save across postbacks can be saved in the control state, while values that are not strictly necessary can go into the view state. In reality, both categories of values will be serialized and saved into the same single __VIEWSTATE field, but the internal structure makes a difference between them. With the view state, you would just read and write the property value from and to the control's `ViewState` object from inside the property's accessor functions. In order to use control state you need to do the following things:

1. Define the property so that it uses a private field to store the value.

2. Call the parent page's `RegisterRequiresControlState` method, from the control's `Init` event handler. This notifies the page that the control needs to store some control state information.

3. Override the control's `SaveControlState` method to create and return an array of objects you want to save in the control state. The array values consist of the property values you need to be persisted, plus the base class' control state (this always goes into the array's first slot).

4. Override the `LoadControlState` method to unpack the input array of objects and initialize your properties' private fields with the values read from the array.

Following is the complete code needed to define and persist a control's `UserName` property:

```csharp
public partial class UserProfile : System.Web.UI.UserControl
{
    private string _userName = "";
    public string UserName
    {
        get { return _userName; }
```

```
        set { _userName = value; }
    }

    protected void Page_Init(object sender, EventArgs e)
    {
        this.Page.RegisterRequiresControlState(this);
    }

    protected override void LoadControlState(object savedState)
    {
        object[] ctlState = (object[])savedState;
        base.LoadControlState(ctlState[0]);
        _userName = (string)ctlState[1];
    }

    protected override object SaveControlState()
    {
        object[] ctlState = new object[2];
        ctlState[0] = base.SaveControlState();
        ctlState[1] = _userName;
        return ctlState;
    }
}
```

This is somewhat more complicated than the older method of using the host page's view state, but you gain the advantage of independence from that page's configuration. You have to weigh the added complexity against the needs of your application. If you'll have a large application with many pages, it is probably wise to use control state because you can't be sure if one of the host pages might have view state disabled (in a large system it's almost guaranteed that some pages will have it disabled). Also, if your controls might be used by other applications within your company, or even other companies, you should definitely use control state to give you the added peace of mind to know that your controls will always work.

Loading and Editing a Profile

Now you can write some code for handling user profiles within a control. In the control's code-behind, you should handle the Load event to first bind the countries array to the proper DropDownList control, and then load the specified user's profile so you can populate the various input controls with profile values. If no username is specified, the current user's profile will be loaded:

```
protected void Page_Load(object sender, EventArgs e)
{
    if (!this.IsPostBack)
    {
        ddlCountries.DataSource = Helpers.GetCountries();
        ddlCountries.DataBind();

        // if the UserName property contains an emtpy string, retrieve the profile
        // for the current user, otherwise for the specified user
        ProfileCommon profile = this.Profile;
        if (this.UserName.Length > 0)
            profile = this.Profile.GetProfile(this.UserName);

        ddlSubscriptions.SelectedValue = profile.Preferences.Newsletter.ToString();
```

```
        ddlLanguages.SelectedValue = profile.Preferences.Culture;
        txtFirstName.Text = profile.FirstName;
        txtLastName.Text = profile.LastName;
        ddlGenders.SelectedValue = profile.Gender;
        if (profile.BirthDate != DateTime.MinValue)
            txtBirthDate.Text = profile.BirthDate.ToShortDateString();
        ddlOccupations.SelectedValue = profile.Occupation;
        txtWebsite.Text = profile.Website;
        txtStreet.Text = profile.Address.Street;
        txtCity.Text = profile.Address.City;
        txtPostalCode.Text = profile.Address.PostalCode;
        txtState.Text = profile.Address.State;
        ddlCountries.SelectedValue = profile.Address.Country;
        txtPhone.Text = profile.Contacts.Phone;
        txtFax.Text = profile.Contacts.Fax;
    }
}
```

This control doesn't have a Submit button to initiate saving profile values, so create a public method named `SaveProfile` that the host page will call when needed:

```
public void SaveProfile()
{
    // if the UserName property contains an emtpy string, save the current user's
    // profile, othwerwise save the profile for the specified user
    ProfileCommon profile = this.Profile;
    if (this.UserName.Length > 0)
        profile = this.Profile.GetProfile(this.UserName);

    profile.Preferences.Newsletter = (SubscriptionType)Enum.Parse(
        typeof(SubscriptionType), ddlSubscriptions.SelectedValue);
    profile.Preferences.Culture = ddlLanguages.SelectedValue;
    profile.FirstName = txtFirstName.Text;
    profile.LastName = txtLastName.Text;
    profile.Gender = ddlGenders.SelectedValue;
    if (txtBirthDate.Text.Trim().Length > 0)
        profile.BirthDate = DateTime.Parse(txtBirthDate.Text);
    profile.Occupation = ddlOccupations.SelectedValue;
    profile.Website = txtWebsite.Text;
    profile.Address.Street = txtStreet.Text;
    profile.Address.City = txtCity.Text;
    profile.Address.PostalCode = txtPostalCode.Text;
    profile.Address.State = txtState.Text;
    profile.Address.Country = ddlCountries.SelectedValue;
    profile.Contacts.Phone = txtPhone.Text;
    profile.Contacts.Fax = txtFax.Text;
    profile.Save();
}
```

The Register Page

Users can create an account for themselves through the `Register.aspx` page that is linked just below the login box. This page uses the `CreateUserWizard` control described earlier. The first step is to create the account; the user interface for this is implemented by our custom template. The second step allows the user to fill in some profile settings, and uses the `UserProfile` control just developed above. The registration code that follows is pretty long, but it should be easy to follow without further comments:

```
<%@ Page Language="C#" MasterPageFile="~/Template.master"
    AutoEventWireup="true" CodeFile="Register.aspx.cs" Inherits="Register"
    Title="The Beer House - Register" %>
<%@ Register Src="Controls/UserProfile.ascx"
    TagName="UserProfile" TagPrefix="mb" %>

<asp:Content ID="MainContent" ContentPlaceHolderID="MainContent" runat="Server">
<asp:CreateUserWizard runat="server" ID="CreateUserWizard1"
    AutoGeneratePassword="False" ContinueDestinationPageUrl="~/Default.aspx"
    FinishDestinationPageUrl="~/Default.aspx"
    OnFinishButtonClick="CreateUserWizard1_FinishButtonClick">
    <WizardSteps>
        <asp:CreateUserWizardStep runat="server">
            <ContentTemplate>
            <div class="sectiontitle">Create your new account</div>
            <p></p>
            <table cellpadding="2">
                <tr>
                    <td width="120" class="fieldname">Username:</td>
                    <td width="300">
                        <asp:TextBox runat="server" ID="UserName" Width="100%" />
                    </td>
                    <td>
                        <asp:RequiredFieldValidator ID="valRequireUserName"
                            runat="server" ControlToValidate="UserName"
                            SetFocusOnError="true" Display="Dynamic"
                            ErrorMessage="Username is required."
                            ValidationGroup="CreateUserWizard1">*
                        </asp:RequiredFieldValidator>
                    </td>
                </tr>
                <tr>
                    <td class="fieldname">Password:</td>
                    <td>
                        <asp:TextBox runat="server" ID="Password"
                            TextMode="Password" Width="100%" />
                    </td>
                    <td>
                        <asp:RequiredFieldValidator ID="valRequirePassword"
                            runat="server" ControlToValidate="Password"
                            SetFocusOnError="true" Display="Dynamic"
                            ErrorMessage="Password is required."
                            ValidationGroup="CreateUserWizard1">*
                        </asp:RequiredFieldValidator>
```

```
                   <asp:RegularExpressionValidator ID="valPasswordLength"
                      runat="server" ControlToValidate="Password"
                      SetFocusOnError="true" Display="Dynamic"
                      ValidationExpression="\w{5,}"
                      ErrorMessage="Password must be at least 5 characters long."
                      ValidationGroup="CreateUserWizard1">*
                   </asp:RegularExpressionValidator>
               </td>
           </tr>
           <tr>
               <td class="fieldname">Confirm password:</td>
               <td>
                   <asp:TextBox runat="server" ID="ConfirmPassword"
                      TextMode="Password" Width="100%" />
               </td>
               <td>
                   <asp:RequiredFieldValidator ID="valRequireConfirmPassword"
                      runat="server" ControlToValidate="ConfirmPassword"
                      SetFocusOnError="true" Display="Dynamic"
                      ErrorMessage="Confirm Password is required."
                      ValidationGroup="CreateUserWizard1">*
                   </asp:RequiredFieldValidator>
                   <asp:CompareValidator ID="valComparePasswords" runat="server"
                      ControlToCompare="Password" SetFocusOnError="true"
                      ControlToValidate="ConfirmPassword" Display="Dynamic"
                      ErrorMessage="Password and Confirmation Password must match."
                      ValidationGroup="CreateUserWizard1">*
                   </asp:CompareValidator>
               </td>
           </tr>
           <tr>
               <td class="fieldname">E-mail:</td>
               <td><asp:TextBox runat="server" ID="Email" Width="100%" /></td>
               <td>
                   <asp:RequiredFieldValidator ID="valRequireEmail" runat="server"
                      ControlToValidate="Email" SetFocusOnError="true"
                      Display="Dynamic" ErrorMessage="E-mail is required."
                      ValidationGroup="CreateUserWizard1">*
                   </asp:RequiredFieldValidator>
                   <asp:RegularExpressionValidator runat="server"
                      ID="valEmailPattern"  Display="Dynamic" SetFocusOnError="true"
                      ValidationGroup="CreateUserWizard1" ControlToValidate="Email"
                      ValidationExpression="\w+@\w+([-.]\w+)*\.\w+([-.]\w+)*"
                      ErrorMessage="The E-mail address is not well-formed.">*
                   </asp:RegularExpressionValidator>
               </td>
           </tr>
           <tr>
               <td class="fieldname">Security question:</td>
               <td><asp:TextBox runat="server" ID="Question" Width="100%" /></td>
               <td>
                   <asp:RequiredFieldValidator ID="valRequireQuestion"
                      runat="server" ControlToValidate="Question"
                      SetFocusOnError="true" Display="Dynamic"
```

```
                    ErrorMessage="Security question is required."
                    ValidationGroup="CreateUserWizard1">*
                </asp:RequiredFieldValidator>
            </td>
        </tr>
        <tr>
            <td class="fieldname">Security answer:</td>
            <td><asp:TextBox runat="server" ID="Answer" Width="100%" /></td>
            <td>
                <asp:RequiredFieldValidator ID="valRequireAnswer" runat="server"
                    ControlToValidate="Answer" SetFocusOnError="true"
                    Display="Dynamic"
                    ErrorMessage="Security answer is required."
                    ValidationGroup="CreateUserWizard1">*
                </asp:RequiredFieldValidator>
            </td>
        </tr>
        <tr>
            <td colspan="3" align="right">
                <asp:Label ID="ErrorMessage" SkinID="FeedbackKO" runat="server"
                    EnableViewState="False"></asp:Label>
            </td>
        </tr>
    </table>
    <asp:ValidationSummary ValidationGroup="CreateUserWizard1"
        ID="ValidationSummary1" runat="server" ShowMessageBox="True"
        ShowSummary="False" />
    </ContentTemplate>
</asp:CreateUserWizardStep>
<asp:WizardStep runat="server" Title="Set preferences">
    <div class="sectiontitle">Set-up your profile</div>
    <p></p>All settings in this section are required only if you want to order
    products from our e-store. However, we ask you to fill in these details in
    all cases, because they help us know our target audience, and improve the
    site and its contents accordingly. Thank you for your cooperation!
    <p></p>
    <mb:UserProfile ID="UserProfile1" runat="server" />
</asp:WizardStep>
<asp:CompleteWizardStep runat="server"></asp:CompleteWizardStep>
</WizardSteps>
<MailDefinition
    BodyFileName="~/RegistrationMail.txt"
    From="webmaster@effectivedotnet.com"
    Subject="The Beer House: your new account">
</MailDefinition>
</asp:CreateUserWizard>
</asp:Content>
```

The `CreateUserWizard`'s `<MailDefinition>` section contains all the settings needed for sending the confirmation mail. The most interesting property is `BodyFileName`, which references a disk file containing the mail's body text. In this file you will typically write a welcome message, and maybe the credentials used to register, so that users will be reminded of the username and password that they selected for your site Following is the content of `RegistrationMail.txt` that specifies the body text:

```
Thank you for registering to The Beer House web site! Following are your
credentials you selected for logging-in:

UserName: <% UserName %>
Password: <% Password %>

See you online!
- The Beer House Team
```

This example is e-mailing the username and password because this is a low-risk site and we chose user-friendliness over the tightest possible security. Besides, I wanted to demonstrate how to use placeholders in the body text file (<% UserName %> and <% Password %>). For serious e-commerce sites or in situations where your company (or your client) doesn't approve of e-mailing usernames and passwords, you should not follow this example!

The page's code-behind file is impressively short: You only need to handle the wizard's FinishButton Click event and have it call the UserProfile's SaveProfile method. The code that implements the registration it not placed here because it's handled by the user control:

```
protected void CreateUserWizard1_FinishButtonClick(
    object sender, WizardNavigationEventArgs e)
{
    UserProfile1.SaveProfile();
}
```

Figure 4-16 is a screenshot of the registration page on the first step of the wizard.

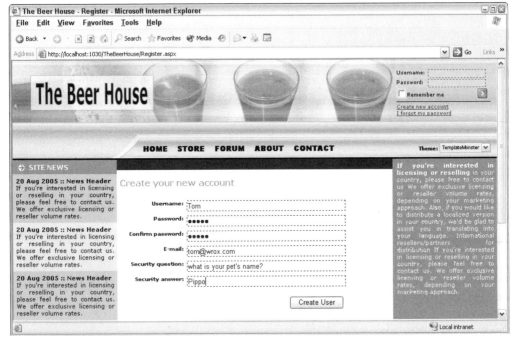

Figure 4-16

Figure 4-17 shows the second step, enabling users to set up their profile.

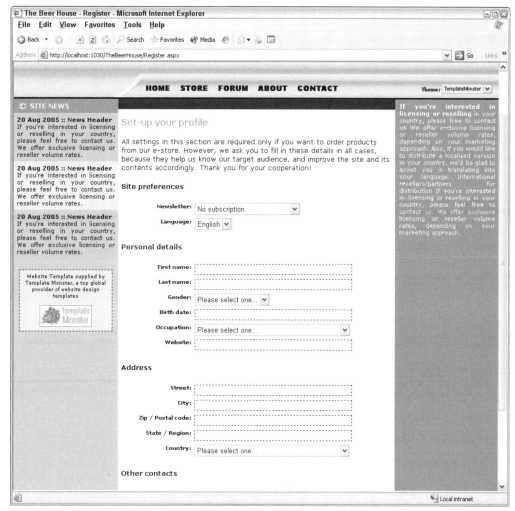

Figure 4-17

The PasswordRecovery Page

Under the login box is a link to `PasswordRecover.aspx`, which allows a user to recover a forgotten password, by sending an e-mail with the credentials. The page uses a `PasswordRecovery` control with a custom template for the two steps (entering the username and answering the secret question). The code follows:

```
<%@ Page Language="C#" MasterPageFile="~/Template.master" AutoEventWireup="true"
    CodeFile="PasswordRecovery.aspx.cs" Inherits="PasswordRecovery"
    Title="The Beer House - Password Recovery" %>
<asp:Content ID="MainContent" ContentPlaceHolderID="MainContent" Runat="Server">
<div class="sectiontitle">Recover your password</div>
<p></p>If you forgot your password, you can use this page to have it sent to you by
e-mail. <p></p>
<asp:PasswordRecovery ID="PasswordRecovery1" runat="server">
    <UserNameTemplate>
        <div class="sectionsubtitle">Step 1: enter your username</div>
        <p></p>
        <table cellpadding="2">
            <tr>
                <td width="80" class="fieldname">Username:</td>
                <td width="300">
                    <asp:TextBox ID="UserName" runat="server" Width="100%" />
                </td>
                <td>
                    <asp:RequiredFieldValidator ID="valRequireUserName" runat="server"
                        ControlToValidate="UserName" SetFocusOnError="true"
                        Display="Dynamic" ErrorMessage="Username is required."
                        ValidationGroup="PasswordRecovery1">*
                    </asp:RequiredFieldValidator>
                </td>
            </tr>
            <td colspan="3" align="right">
                <asp:Label ID="FailureText" runat="server" SkinID="FeedbackKO"
                    EnableViewState="False" />
                <asp:Button ID="SubmitButton" runat="server" CommandName="Submit"
                    Text="Submit" ValidationGroup="PasswordRecovery1" />
            </td>
        </table>
    </UserNameTemplate>
    <QuestionTemplate>
        <div class="sectionsubtitle">Step 2: answer the following question</div>
        <p></p>
        <table cellpadding="2">
            <tr>
                <td width="80" class="fieldname">Username:</td>
                <td width="300">
                    <asp:Literal ID="UserName" runat="server" />
                </td>
                <td></td>
            </tr>
            <tr>
                <td class="fieldname">Question:</td>
                <td><asp:Literal ID="Question" runat="server"></asp:Literal></td>
                <td></td>
```

```
            </tr>
            <tr>
                <td class="fieldname">Answer:</td>
                <td><asp:TextBox ID="Answer" runat="server" Width="100%" />
                </td>
                <td>
                    <asp:RequiredFieldValidator ID="valRequireAnswer" runat="server"
                        ControlToValidate="Answer" SetFocusOnError="true"
                        Display="Dynamic" ErrorMessage="Answer is required."
                        ValidationGroup="PasswordRecovery1">*
                    </asp:RequiredFieldValidator>
                </td>
            </tr>
            <tr>
                <td colspan="3" align="right">
                    <asp:Label ID="FailureText" runat="server"
                        SkinID="FeedbackKO" EnableViewState="False" />
                    <asp:Button ID="SubmitButton" runat="server" CommandName="Submit"
                        Text="Submit" ValidationGroup="PasswordRecovery1" />
                </td>
            </tr>
        </table>
    </QuestionTemplate>
    <SuccessTemplate>
        <asp:Label runat="server" ID="lblSuccess" SkinID="FeedbackOK"
            Text="Your password has been sent to you." />
    </SuccessTemplate>
    <MailDefinition
        BodyFileName="~/PasswordRecoveryMail.txt"
        From="webmaster@effectivedotnet.com"
        Subject="The Beer House: your password">
    </MailDefinition>
</asp:PasswordRecovery>
</asp:Content>
```

The body of the mail sent with the credentials is almost the same as the previous one, so we won't show it again here. Figure 4-18 shows a couple of screenshots for the two-step password recovery process.

Figure 4-18

The EditProfile Page

Once users log in, they can go to the EditProfile.aspx page, linked in the top-right corner of any page, and change their password or other profile settings. The password-changing functionality is implemented by way of a custom ChangePassword control, and the profile settings functionality is handled by the UserProfile control we already developed. Following is the code for the EditProfile.aspx file (with some layout code removed for clarity and brevity):

```
<%@ Page Language="C#" MasterPageFile="~/Template.master" AutoEventWireup="true"
    CodeFile="EditProfile.aspx.cs" Inherits="EditProfile"
    Title="The Beer House - Edit Profile" %>
<%@ Register Src="Controls/UserProfile.ascx"
    TagName="UserProfile" TagPrefix="mb" %>

<asp:Content ID="MainContent" ContentPlaceHolderID="MainContent" Runat="Server">
<div class="sectiontitle">Change your password</div><p></p>
<asp:ChangePassword ID="ChangePassword1" runat="server">
    <ChangePasswordTemplate>

        Current password:
        <asp:TextBox ID="CurrentPassword" TextMode="Password" runat="server" />
        ...validators here...
        New password:
        <asp:TextBox ID="NewPassword" TextMode="Password" runat="server" />
        ...validators here...

        Confirm password:
        <asp:TextBox ID="ConfirmNewPassword" TextMode="Password" runat="server" />
        ...validators here...

        <asp:Label ID="FailureText" runat="server" SkinID="FeedbackKO" />
        <asp:Button ID="ChangePasswordPushButton" runat="server"
            CommandName="ChangePassword" Text="Change Password"
            ValidationGroup="ChangePassword1" />
        <asp:ValidationSummary runat="server" ID="valChangePasswordSummary"
            ValidationGroup="ChangePassword1" ShowMessageBox="true"
            ShowSummary="false" />
    </ChangePasswordTemplate>
    <SuccessTemplate>
        <asp:Label runat="server" ID="lblSuccess" SkinID="FeedbackOK"
            Text="Your password has been changed successfully." />
    </SuccessTemplate>
    <MailDefinition
        BodyFileName="~/ChangePasswordMail.txt"
        From="webmaster@effectivedotnet.com"
        Subject="The Beer House: password changed">
    </MailDefinition>
</asp:ChangePassword>
<p></p>
<hr width="100%" size="1" noshade />
<div class="sectiontitle">Change your profile</div>
<p></p>
```

```
Some settings in this section are only required if you want to order products from
our e-store. However, we ask you to fill in these details in all cases, because
they help us know our target audience, and improve the site and its contents
accordingly. Thank you for your cooperation!
<p></p>
<mb:UserProfile ID="UserProfile1" runat="server" />
<asp:Label runat="server" ID="lblFeedbackOK" SkinID="FeedbackOK"
    Text="Profile updated successfully" Visible="false" />
<asp:Button runat="server" ID="btnUpdate" ValidationGroup="EditProfile"
    Text="Update Profile" OnClick="btnUpdate_Click" />
</asp:Content>
```

In the code-behind you don't have to do anything except handle the Update Profile Submit button's
`Click` event, where you call the `UserProfile` control's `SaveProfile` method, and then show a confirmation message:

```
protected void btnUpdate_Click(object sender, EventArgs e)
{
    UserProfile1.SaveProfile();
    lblFeedbackOK.Visible = true;
}
```

Figure 4-19 shows part of this page at runtime.

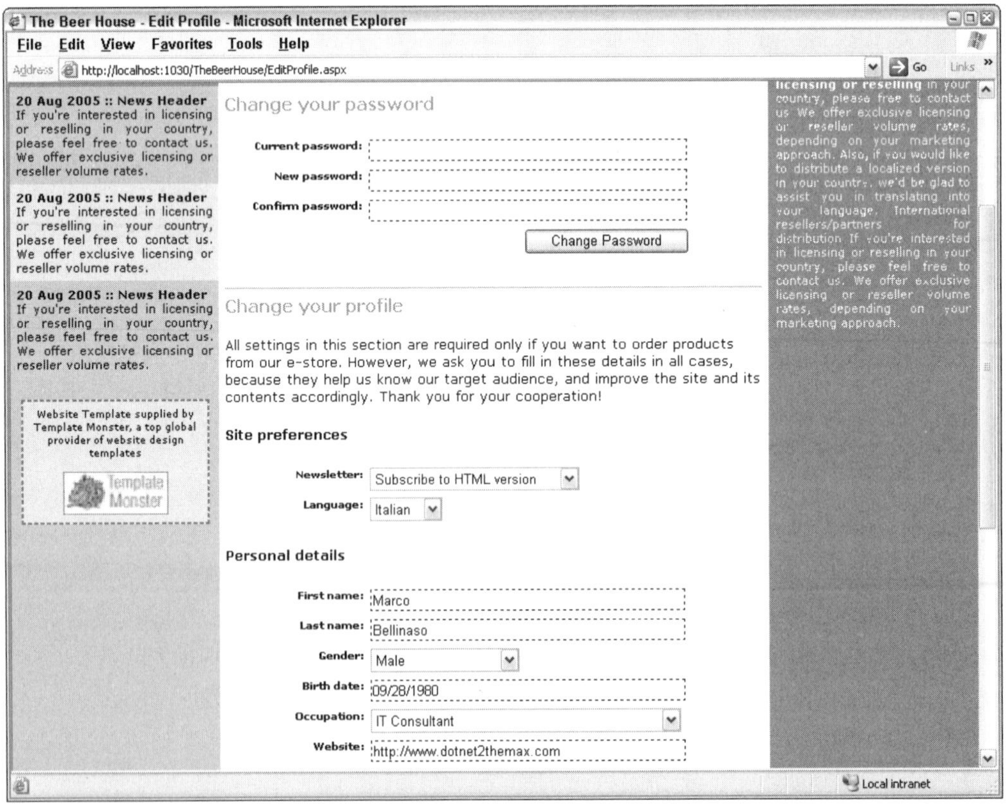

Figure 4-19

The last thing to do on this page is to ensure that anonymous users — who, of course, don't have a password or profile to change — cannot access this page. To do this you can create a `<location>` section for this page in the root `web.config`, and then write an `<authorization>` subsection that denies access to the anonymous user (identified by `"?"`) and grant access to everyone else. This is the code you should add to the `web.config` file:

```
<configuration xmlns="http://schemas.microsoft.com/.NetConfiguration/v2.0">
    <system.web> <!-- some settings here...--> </system.web>
    <location path="EditProfile.aspx">
        <system.web>
            <authorization>
                <deny users="?" />
                <allow users="*" />
            </authorization>
        </system.web>
    </location>
</configuration>
```

Persisting the Favorite Theme Between Sessions

In Chapter 2 we created a base page class from which all other pages inherit. One of the tasks of this class is to set the page's `Theme` property according to what is stored in a `Session` variable, which tells us what theme the user selected from the Themes drop-down list near the top-right corner. The problem with `Session` variables is that they only exist as long as the user's session is active, so we'll have to store this value in a persistent location. Thankfully, it turns out that we have a great place to store this — in the user profile. The following code highlights the changes done to the base page to allow us to save the `Profile.Preferences.Theme` property in the user's profile, and because we're putting it in the base page class we will not have to do this in all the other pages:

```
public class BasePage : System.Web.UI.Page
{
    protected override void OnPreInit(EventArgs e)
    {
        string id = Globals.ThemesSelectorID;
        if (id.Length > 0)
        {
            if (this.Request.Form["__EVENTTARGET"] == id &&
                !string.IsNullOrEmpty(this.Request.Form[id]))
            {
                this.Theme = this.Request.Form[id];
                (HttpContext.Current.Profile as ProfileCommon).Preferences.Theme =
                    this.Theme;
            }
            else
            {
                if (!string.IsNullOrEmpty(
                    (HttpContext.Current.Profile as ProfileCommon).Preferences.Theme))
                {
                    this.Theme =
                        (HttpContext.Current.Profile as ProfileCommon).Preferences.Theme;
                }
            }
        }
    }
```

```
        base.OnPreInit(e);
    }

    protected override void OnLoad(EventArgs e) { ... }
}
```

As mentioned before, we must also handle the `Profile_MigrateAnonymous` global event, so that when an anonymous user selects a theme and then logs in, his or her favorite theme will be migrated from the anonymous profile to the authenticated one. After this, the old profile can be deleted from the data store, and the anonymous ID can be deleted as well. Following is the complete code:

```
void Profile_MigrateAnonymous(object sender, ProfileMigrateEventArgs e)
{
    // get a reference to the previously anonymous user's profile
    ProfileCommon anonProfile = this.Profile.GetProfile(e.AnonymousID);
    // if set, copy its Theme to the current user's profile
    if (!string.IsNullOrEmpty(anonProfile.Preferences.Theme))
        this.Profile.Preferences.Theme = anonProfile.Preferences.Theme;
    // delete the anonymous profile
    ProfileManager.DeleteProfile(e.AnonymousID);
    AnonymousIdentificationModule.ClearAnonymousIdentifier();
}
```

The Administration Section

Now that the end-user part of the work is done, we only have the administration section to complete. The `~/Admin/Default.aspx` page linked by the Admin menu item is the administrator's home page, which contains links to all the administrative functions. First we will develop the page used to manage users and their profiles. To protect all the pages placed under the `Admin` folder against unauthorized access, you should add a `web.config` file under this `~/Admin` folder, and write an `<authorization>` section that grants access to the Administrators role and denies access to everyone else. In the "Design" section is a sample snippet to demonstrate this.

The ManageUsers Administrative Page

This page's user interface can be divided into three parts:

1. The first part tells the administrator the number of registered users, and how many of them are currently online.

2. The second part provides controls for finding and listing the users. There is an "alphabet bar" with all the letters of the alphabet; when one is clicked, a grid is filled with all the users having names starting with that letter. Additionally, an All link is present to show all users with a single click. The search functionality allows administrators to search for users by providing a partial username or e-mail address.

3. The third part of the page contains a grid that lists users and some of their properties.

The following code provides the user interface for the first two parts:

```
<%@ Page Language="C#" MasterPageFile="~/Template.master" AutoEventWireup="true"
    CodeFile="ManageUsers.aspx.cs" Inherits="ManageUsers"
    Title="The Beer House - Account management" %>
```

```
<asp:Content ID="MainContent" ContentPlaceHolderID="MainContent" Runat="Server">
<div class="sectiontitle">Account Management</div>
<p></p>
<b>- Total registered users: <asp:Literal runat="server" ID="lblTotUsers" /><br />
- Users online now: <asp:Literal runat="server" ID="lblOnlineUsers" /></b>
<p></p>
Click one of the following link to display all users whose name begins with that
letter:
<p></p>
<asp:Repeater runat="server" ID="rptAlphabet"
    OnItemCommand="rptAlphabet_ItemCommand">
    <ItemTemplate><asp:LinkButton runat="server" Text='<%# Container.DataItem %>'
        CommandArgument='<%# Container.DataItem %>' />  
    </ItemTemplate>
</asp:Repeater>
<p></p>
Otherwise use the controls below to search users by partial username or e-mail:
<p></p>
<asp:DropDownList runat="server" ID="ddlSearchTypes">
    <asp:ListItem Text="UserName" Selected="true" />
    <asp:ListItem Text="E-mail" />
</asp:DropDownList>
contains
<asp:TextBox runat="server" ID="txtSearchText" />
<asp:Button runat="server" ID="btnSearch" Text="Search"
    OnClick="btnSearch_Click" />
```

As you see, the alphabet bar is built by a `Repeater` control, not a fixed list of links. The `Repeater` will be bound to an array of characters, displayed as links. I used a `Repeater` instead of static links for a couple of reasons. First, this will make it much easier to change the bar's layout, if you want to do so later, because you need to change the template, not a series of links. Second, if you decide to add localization to this page later, the `Repeater`'s template could remain exactly the same, and it would be sufficient to bind it to a different array containing the selected language's alphabet.

The third part of the page that lists users and some of their properties contains a `GridView`, which is a powerful new grid added to ASP.NET 2.0 that has been already introduced in Chapter 3. `GridView` can automatically take care of sorting, paging, and editing, without requiring us to write a lot of code. In this particular instance, however, I am only using the basic functionality; we'll use other advanced features of the `GridView` in subsequent chapters. You need to define the number and types of columns for the grid within the control's `<Columns>` section. Following is a list of columns for the grid:

❑ Use `BoundField` columns (the `GridView`'s version of the old `DataGrid`'s `BoundColumn`) for the username, the creation date, and last access date. These values will be displayed as normal strings.

❑ Use a `CheckBoxField` column to show the user's `IsApproved` property by means of a read-only checkbox (this would have required a `TemplateColumn` in the old `DataGrid`, which would have been much harder to implement).

❑ Use a `HyperLinkField` to show the user's e-mail as an active link that uses the "mailto:" protocol to open the user's default mail client when the link is clicked.

❑ Use another `HyperLinkField` column to show an edit image that will redirect to a page called `EditUser.aspx` when clicked. This link will include the username on the querystring and will allow an administrator to edit a user's profile.

❑   Finally, use a `ButtonField` column to produce a graphical Delete button. If you set the column's `ButtonType` property to `"Image"`, you can also use its `ImageUrl` property to specify the URL of the image to display.

Following is the complete code used to define the grid:

```
<asp:GridView ID="gvwUsers" runat="server" AutoGenerateColumns="false"
DataKeyNames="UserName"
    OnRowCreated="gvwUsers_RowCreated" OnRowDeleting="gvwUsers_RowDeleting">
    <Columns>
        <asp:BoundField HeaderText="UserName" DataField="UserName" />
        <asp:HyperLinkField HeaderText="E-mail" DataTextField="Email"
            DataNavigateUrlFormatString="mailto:{0}" DataNavigateUrlFields="Email" />
        <asp:BoundField HeaderText="Created" DataField="CreationDate"
            DataFormatString="{0:MM/dd/yy h:mm tt}" />
        <asp:BoundField HeaderText="Last activity" DataField="LastActivityDate"
            DataFormatString="{0:MM/dd/yy h:mm tt}" />
        <asp:CheckBoxField HeaderText="Approved" DataField="IsApproved"
            HeaderStyle-HorizontalAlign="Center" ItemStyle-HorizontalAlign="Center" />
        <asp:HyperLinkField Text="<img src='../images/edit.gif' border='0' />"
            DataNavigateUrlFormatString="EditUser.aspx?UserName={0}"
            DataNavigateUrlFields="UserName" />
        <asp:ButtonField CommandName="Delete" ButtonType="Image"
            ImageUrl="~/images/delete.gif" />
    </Columns>
    <EmptyDataTemplate>No users found for the specified criteria</EmptyDataTemplate>
</asp:GridView>
</asp:Content>
```

Before looking at the code-behind file, I want to point out another small, but handy, new feature: The grid has a `<EmptyDataTemplate>` section that contains the HTML markup to show when the grid is bound to an empty data source. This is a very cool feature because you can use this template to show a message when a search produces no results. Under ASP.NET 1.x, you had to write some code to check for this situation, and then hide the grid and show a `Literal` or a `Label` instead. The 2.0 solution is much simpler and more elegant.

In the page's code-behind file there is a class-level `MemershipUserCollection` object that is initialized with all the user information returned by `Membership.GetAllUsers`. The `Count` property of this collection is used in the page's `Load` event to show the total number of registered users, together with the number of online users. In the same event, we also create the array of letters for the alphabet bar, and bind it to the `Repeater` control. The code is shown below:

```
public partial class ManageUsers : BasePage
{
    private MembershipUserCollection allUsers = Membership.GetAllUsers();

    protected void Page_Load(object sender, EventArgs e)
    {
        if (!this.IsPostBack)
        {
            lblTotUsers.Text = allUsers.Count.ToString();
            lblOnlineUsers.Text = Membership.GetNumberOfUsersOnline().ToString();
```

```
            string[] alphabet =
                "A;B;C;D;E;F;G;J;K;L;M;N;O;P;Q;R;S;T;U;V;W;X;Y;Z;All".Split(';');
            rptAlphabet.DataSource = alphabet;
            rptAlphabet.DataBind();
        }
    }

    // other methods and event handlers go here...
}
```

The grid is not populated when the page first loads, but rather after the user clicks a link on the alphabet bar or runs a search. This is done in order to avoid unnecessary processing and thus have a fast-loading page. When a letter link is clicked, the Repeater's ItemCommand event is raised. You handle this event to retrieve the clicked letter, and then run a search for all users whose name starts with that letter. If the All link is clicked, you'll simply show all users. Because this page also supports e-mail searches, a "SearchByEmail" attribute is added to the control and set to false, to indicate that the search is by username by default. This attribute is stored in the grid's Attributes collection so that it is persisted in the view state, and doesn't get lost during a postback. Here's the code:

```
protected void rptAlphabet_ItemCommand(object source, RepeaterCommandEventArgs e)
{
    gvwUsers.Attributes.Add("SearchByEmail", false.ToString());

    if (e.CommandArgument.ToString().Length == 1)
    {
        gvwUsers.Attributes.Add("SearchText", e.CommandArgument.ToString() + "%");
        BindUsers(false);
    }
    else
    {
        gvwUsers.Attributes.Add("SearchText", "");
        BindUsers(false);
    }
}
```

The code that actually runs the query and performs the binding is in the BindUsers method. It takes a Boolean value as an input parameter that indicates whether the allUsers collection must be repopulated (necessary just after a user is deleted). The text to search for and the search mode (e-mail or username) are not passed as parameters, but rather are stored in the grid's Attributes. Below is the code:

```
private void BindUsers(bool reloadAllUsers)
{
    if (reloadAllUsers)
        allUsers = Membership.GetAllUsers();

    MembershipUserCollection users = null;

    string searchText = "";
    if (!string.IsNullOrEmpty(gvwUsers.Attributes["SearchText"]))
        searchText = gvwUsers.Attributes["SearchText"];

    bool searchByEmail = false;
```

```
    if (!string.IsNullOrEmpty(gvwUsers.Attributes["SearchByEmail"]))
       searchByEmail = bool.Parse(gvwUsers.Attributes["SearchByEmail"]);

    if (searchText.Length > 0)
    {
       if (searchByEmail)
          users = Membership.FindUsersByEmail(searchText);
       else
          users = Membership.FindUsersByName(searchText);
    }
    else
    {
       users = allUsers;
    }

    gvwUsers.DataSource = users;
    gvwUsers.DataBind();
}
```

The `BindUsers` method is also called when the Search button is clicked. In this case, the `SeachByEmail` attribute will be set according to the value selected in the `ddlSearchTypes` drop-down list, and the `SearchText` will be equal to the entered search string with the addition of a leading and a trailing "`%`" character, so that a full `LIKE` query is performed:

```
protected void btnSearch_Click(object sender, EventArgs e)
{
    bool searchByEmail = (ddlSearchTypes.SelectedValue == "E-mail");
    gvwUsers.Attributes.Add("SearchText", "%" + txtSearchText.Text + "%");
    gvwUsers.Attributes.Add("SearchByEmail", searchByEmail.ToString());
    BindUsers(false);
}
```

When the trashcan icon is clicked, the `GridView` raises the `RowDeleting` event because the column's `CommandName` property is set to `Delete`. From inside this event handler you can use the static methods of the `Membership` and `ProfileManager` classes to delete the user account and its accompanying profile. After that, `BindUser` is called again with `true` as a parameter, so that the collection of all users is refreshed, and the label displaying the total number of users is also refreshed:

```
protected void gvwUsers_RowDeleting(object sender, GridViewDeleteEventArgs e)
{
    string userName = gvwUsers.DataKeys[e.RowIndex].Value.ToString();
    ProfileManager.DeleteProfile(userName);
    Membership.DeleteUser(userName);
    BindUsers(true);
    lblTotUsers.Text = allUsers.Count.ToString();
}
```

Deleting a user account is a serious action that can't be undone, so you should have the administrator confirm this action before proceeding! This can be done by adding a JavaScript "confirm" in the link's `onclick` client-side event, through the button's new `OnClientClick` property. Since the link is created dynamically, you must handle the grid's `RowCreated` event to get a reference to each link as soon as its parent row and all its contents are created. Here's the code:

```
protected void gvwUsers_RowCreated(object sender, GridViewRowEventArgs e)
{
    if (e.Row.RowType == DataControlRowType.DataRow)
    {
        ImageButton btn = e.Row.Cells[6].Controls[0] as ImageButton;
        btn.OnClientClick = "if (confirm('Are you sure you want to delete this user
account?') == false) return false;";
    }
}
```

Note that the script is added only for rows of type `DataRow`. This requires an explicit check before the `RowCreated` event is raised, and for the header, footer, and pagination bars (when present). Figure 4-20 is a screenshot of this page, listing all current users.

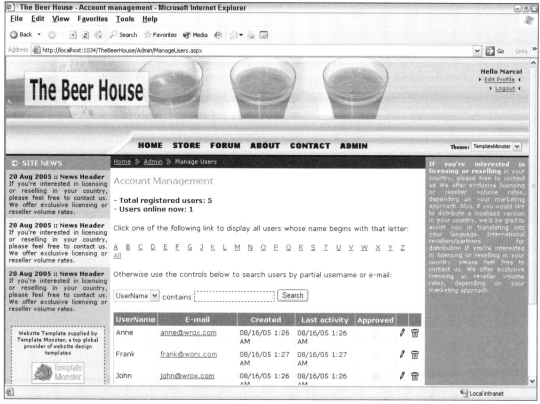

Figure 4-20

The EditUser Administrative Page

The `EditUser.aspx` page is linked from a row of the `ManagedUsers.aspx` grid. It takes a `username` parameter on the querystring, and allows an administrator to see all the membership details about that user (i.e., the properties of the `MembershipUser` object representing that user), and supports editing the user's personal profile. The user interface of the page is simple and is divided in three sections:

1. The first section shows the data read from `MembershipUser`. All controls are read-only, except for those that are bound to the `IsApproved` and `IsLockedOut` properties. For `IsLockedOut`, you can set it to `false` to unlock a user account, but you can't set it to `true` to lock a user account, as only the membership provider can lock out a user.

2. The second section contains a `CheckBoxList` that displays all the roles defined for the application, and allows the administrator to add or remove users to and from roles. There is also a `TextBox` control and a button to create a new role.

3. The third and last section displays a user's profile and allows edits to the profile, through the `UserProfile` user control developed earlier.

Following is the code for `EditUser.aspx`:

```
<%@ Page Language="C#" MasterPageFile="~/Template.master" AutoEventWireup="true"
    CodeFile="EditUser.aspx.cs" Inherits="EditUser"
    Title="The Beer House - Edit User" %>
<%@ Register Src="../Controls/UserProfile.ascx"
    TagName="UserProfile" TagPrefix="mb" %>

<asp:Content ID="MainContent" ContentPlaceHolderID="MainContent" Runat="Server">
<div class="sectiontitle">General user information</div>
<p></p>
<table cellpadding="2">
    <tr>
        <td width="130" class="fieldname">UserName:</td>
        <td width="300"><asp:Literal runat="server" ID="lblUserName" /></td>
    </tr>
    <tr>
        <td class="fieldname">E-mail:</td>
        <td><asp:HyperLink runat="server" ID="lnkEmail" /></td>
    </tr>
    <tr>
        <td class="fieldname">Registered:</td>
        <td><asp:Literal runat="server" ID="lblRegistered" /></td>
    </tr>
    <tr>
        <td class="fieldname">Last Login:</td>
        <td><asp:Literal runat="server" ID="lblLastLogin" /></td>
    </tr>
    <tr>
        <td class="fieldname">Last Activity:</td>
        <td><asp:Literal runat="server" ID="lblLastActivity" /></td>
    </tr>
    <tr>
        <td class="fieldname">Online Now:</td>
        <td><asp:CheckBox runat="server" ID="chkOnlineNow" Enabled="false" /></td>
    </tr>
    <tr>
        <td class="fieldname">Approved:</td>
        <td><asp:CheckBox runat="server" ID="chkApproved"
            AutoPostBack="true" OnCheckedChanged="chkApproved_CheckedChanged" /></td>
    </tr>
    <tr>
        <td class="fieldname">Locked Out:</td>
```

```
        <td><asp:CheckBox runat="server" ID="chkLockedOut"
            AutoPostBack="true" OnCheckedChanged="chkLockedOut_CheckedChanged" /></td>
    </tr>
</table>
<p></p>
<div class="sectiontitle">Edit user's roles</div>
<p></p>
<asp:CheckBoxList runat="server" ID="chklRoles" RepeatColumns="5" CellSpacing="4" />
<table cellpadding="2" width="450">
    <tr><td align="right">
        <asp:Label runat="server" ID="lblRolesFeedbackOK" SkinID="FeedbackOK"
            Text="Roles updated successfully" Visible="false" />
        <asp:Button runat="server" ID="btnUpdateRoles" Text="Update"
            OnClick="btnUpdateRoles_Click" />
    </td></tr>
    <tr><td align="right">
        <small>Create new role: </small>
        <asp:TextBox runat="server" ID="txtNewRole" />
        <asp:RequiredFieldValidator ID="valRequireNewRole" runat="server"
            ControlToValidate="txtNewRole" SetFocusOnError="true"
            ErrorMessage="Role name is required." ValidationGroup="CreateRole">*
        </asp:RequiredFieldValidator>
        <asp:Button runat="server" ID="btnCreateRole" Text="Create"
            ValidationGroup="CreateRole" OnClick="btnCreateRole_Click" />
    </td></tr>
</table>
<p></p>
<div class="sectiontitle">Edit user's profile</div>
<p></p>
<mb:UserProfile ID="UserProfile1" runat="server" />
    <table cellpadding="2" width="450">
    <tr><td align="right">
        <asp:Label runat="server" ID="lblProfileFeedbackOK" SkinID="FeedbackOK"
            Text="Profile updated successfully" Visible="false" />
        <asp:Button runat="server" ID="btnUpdateProfile"
            ValidationGroup="EditProfile" Text="Update"
            OnClick="btnUpdateProfile_Click" />
    </td></tr>
</table>
</asp:Content>
```

When the page loads, the username parameter is read from the querystring, a MembershipUser instance is retrieved for that user, and the values of its properties are shown by the first section's controls:

```
public partial class EditUser : BasePage
{
    string userName = "";

    protected void Page_Load(object sender, EventArgs e)
    {
        // retrieve the username from the querystring
        userName = this.Request.QueryString["UserName"];

        lblRolesFeedbackOK.Visible = false;
        lblProfileFeedbackOK.Visible = false;
```

```
        if (!this.IsPostBack)
        {
            UserProfile1.UserName = userName;

            // show the user's details
            MembershipUser user = Membership.GetUser(userName);
            lblUserName.Text = user.UserName;
            lnkEmail.Text = user.Email;
            lnkEmail.NavigateUrl = "mailto:" + user.Email;
            lblRegistered.Text = user.CreationDate.ToString("f");
            lblLastLogin.Text = user.LastLoginDate.ToString("f");
            lblLastActivity.Text = user.LastActivityDate.ToString("f");
            chkOnlineNow.Checked = user.IsOnline;
            chkApproved.Checked = user.IsApproved;
            chkLockedOut.Checked = user.IsLockedOut;
            chkLockedOut.Enabled = user.IsLockedOut;

            BindRoles();
        }
    }

    // other methods and event handlers go here...
}
```

In the `Page_Load` event handler you also call the `BindRoles` method, shown below, which fills a `CheckBoxList` with all the available roles and then retrieves the roles the user belongs to, and finally selects them in the `CheckBoxList`:

```
private void BindRoles()
{
    // fill the CheckBoxList with all the available roles, and then select
    // those that the user belongs to
    chklRoles.DataSource = Roles.GetAllRoles();
    chklRoles.DataBind();
    foreach (string role in Roles.GetRolesForUser(userName))
        chklRoles.Items.FindByText(role).Selected = true;
}
```

When the Update Roles button is pressed, the user is first removed from all her roles, and then is added to the selected ones. The first remove is necessary because a call to `Roles.AddUserToRole` will fail if the user is already a member of that role. As part of the following code, you use a new feature in C# 2.0 called a *generic list*. This is a list collection that enables you to specify the datatype you wish to support for objects stored in the list. When you declare an instance of this collection, you have to indicate which datatype you want to store in it by enclosing it in angle brackets. Therefore, if you say `"List<string>"` you are asking for a list collection that is strongly typed to accept strings. You could have also asked for a collection of any other datatype, including any custom class you might create to hold related data.

Here's the code for the `UpdateRoles` button-click event handler:

```
protected void btnUpdateRoles_Click(object sender, EventArgs e)
{
    // first remove the user from all roles...
    string[] currRoles = Roles.GetRolesForUser(userName);
```

```
        if (currRoles.Length > 0)
            Roles.RemoveUserFromRoles(userName, currRoles);
        // and then add the user to the selected roles
        List<string> newRoles = new List<string>();
        foreach (ListItem item in chklRoles.Items)
        {
            if (item.Selected)
                newRoles.Add(item.Text);
        }
        Roles.AddUserToRoles(userName, newRoles.ToArray());

        lblRolesFeedbackOK.Visible = true;
    }
```

As you see, you don't make individual calls to `Roles.AddUserToRole` for each selected role. Instead, you first fill a list of strings with the names of the selected roles, and then make a single call to `Roles.AddUser ToRoles`. When the Create Role button is pressed, you first check to see if a role with the same is already present, and if not you create it. Then, the `BindRoles` method is called to refresh the list of available roles:

```
    protected void btnCreateRole_Click(object sender, EventArgs e)
    {
        if (!Roles.RoleExists(txtNewRole.Text.Trim()))
        {
            Roles.CreateRole(txtNewRole.Text.Trim());
            BindRoles();
        }
    }
```

When the Approved checkbox is clicked, an auto-postback is made, and in its event handler you update the `MembershipUser` object's `IsApproved` property according to the checkbox's value, and then save the change:

```
    protected void chkApproved_CheckedChanged(object sender, EventArgs e)
    {
        MembershipUser user = Membership.GetUser(userName);
        user.IsApproved = chkApproved.Checked;
        Membership.UpdateUser(user);
    }
```

It works in a similar way for the Locked Out checkbox, except that the corresponding `MembershipUser` property is read-only, and the user is unlocked by calling the `UnlockUser` method. After this is done, the checkbox is made read-only because you can't lock out a user here (as mentioned previously). Take a look at the code:

```
    protected void chkLockedOut_CheckedChanged(object sender, EventArgs e)
    {
        if (!chkLockedOut.Checked)
        {
            MembershipUser user = Membership.GetUser(userName);
            user.UnlockUser();
            chkLockedOut.Enabled = false;
        }
    }
```

Finally, when the profile box's Update button is clicked, a call to the `UserProfile`'s `SaveProfile` is made, as you've done in other pages:

```
protected void btnUpdateProfile_Click(object sender, EventArgs e)
{
    UserProfile1.SaveProfile();
    lblProfileFeedbackOK.Visible = true;
}
```

Figure 4-21 shows a screenshot of this page in action.

Figure 4-21

Summary

This chapter covered a great deal of information regarding the new membership and profiling features introduced in ASP.NET 2.0. The "Solution" section contains surprisingly little code yet produces a complete membership system! We even managed to re-implement and extend the Security area of the ASP.NET Web Administration Tool. In addition, much of the code we've written is for HTML layout, which gives the pages a good appearance, but the code-behind code we've written is just over a hundred lines. I don't know about you, but I find this fact truly impressive! This was one of the primary goals of ASP.NET 2.0 — to dramatically reduce the amount of code developers need to write, and to add more functionality "out of the box."

One thing that can be improved upon is the fact that the membership module only supports users and roles, and not individual permissions as well. It might be useful in some cases to define a list of permissions, associate them to a role, add users to the role, and then check for the presence of a permission from code, instead of just checking whether the user belongs to a role. This would give a much finer granularity to the security settings and is something that we did in the custom security module developed in the first edition of this book. However, while that level of security control is almost always required in large browser-based applications, it is overkill for many small-to-medium size web sites and unnecessarily complicates the code. By sticking with simple built-in role security we are able to completely meet our requirements, and we can do so with simpler code that is easier to test and deploy. If you decide that your particular application requires a fine amount of control that can be enumerated in a list of permissions, you can extend the membership support by writing your own permissions module that links to the current users and roles.

5

News and Article Management

The example site is basically a container for content targeted to beer, food, and pub enthusiasts. Content can be in the form of news, articles, reports of special events, reviews, photo galleries, etc. This chapter describes the typical content-related problems that should be considered for a site of this type. You'll then design and develop an online article manager that allows the complete management of our site's content, in terms of acquiring articles; adding, activating, and removing articles; sharing articles with other parties, and so on.

Problem

Different sites use different methods of gathering news and information: Some site administrators hunt for news events and write their own articles, while others get news and articles directly from their users (a great example of this is the Add Your News link at www.aspwire.com) or they rely upon a company whose business is to gather and organize news to be sold to third-party sites. In the old days, some sites did *screen-scraping,* retrieving data from an external site's page and showing it on their pages with a custom appearance (of course, you must have the authorization from the external company and you must know the format they use to show the news on their pages). During the last few years we've seen an explosion in the use of RSS (Really Simple Syndication), a simple XML format for syndicating content, making it available to other clients. Atom is another XML-based syndication standard that was created to solve some problems of RSS — it is relatively new but already very popular. The basic idea with RSS and ATOM is for sites to provide an index of news items in the form of an XML document. A client program can fetch that XML document and provide users with a list of news items and hyperlinks that can direct them to the individual stories they are interested in. One site's XML index document is called a *newsfeed.* The client program is called a *news aggregator* (or *feed reader*) because it can extract newsfeeds from many sites and present them in one list, possibly arranged by categories. Users can subscribe to the XML feed and their aggregator program can periodically poll for new stories by fetching new XML documents automatically in the background. Because RSS and Atom are open standards, there are many web-based and fat-client desktop applications that can subscribe to any site that provides such feeds. Some popular open-source feed readers written in C# are RSS Bandit (`www.rssbandit.org`) and SharpReader (`www.sharpreader.com`). RSS and Atom are very convenient for users who want to keep up on the latest news and articles. You can advertise your new content via RSS and ATOM feeds, or you can even display a list of content from other sites by showing RSS links on one of your web pages. Your page can have an aggregator user control that makes it simple to display the content of specified RSS and ATOM feeds. This adds to any unique content you provide, and users will find value in returning to your site frequently to see your own updated content as well as a list of interesting links to updated news items on other sites.

It doesn't matter which methods you decide to use, but you must have fresh and updated content as often as possible for your site to be successful and entice users to return. Users will not return regularly to a site if they rarely find new content. You should use a variety of methods to acquire new content. You can't rely entirely on external content (retrieved as an RSS feed, by screen-scraping, or by inserting some JavaScript) because these methods often imply that you just publish a small extract of the external content on your site, and publish a link to the full article, thus driving traffic away from your site. It can be a solution for daily news about weather, stock exchanges, and the like, but not for providing real original content, which is why users surf the web. You must create and publish some content on your own, and possibly syndicate that content as RSS feeds, so that other sites can consume it, and bring new visitors to your site.

Once you have a source of articles, a second problem arises: how to add them to your site. You can immediately rule out manual updating of pages or adding new static HTML pages — if you have to add news several times a day, or even just every week, creating and uploading pages and editing all the links becomes an administrative nightmare. Additionally, the people who administer the site on a daily basis may not have the skills required to edit or create new HTML pages. You need a much more flexible system, one that allows the site administrators to easily publish fresh content without requiring special HTML code generator tools or knowledge of HTML. You want it to have many features, such as the capability to organize articles in categories and show abstracts, and even to allow some site users to post their own news items. You'll see the complete list of features you're going to implement in the "Design" section of this chapter. For now, suffice it to say that you must be able to manage the content of your site remotely over the web, without requiring any other tools. Think about what this implies: You can add or edit news as soon as it is available, in a few minutes, even if you're not in your office and even if you don't have access to your own computer; all you need is a connection to the Internet and a browser. And this can work the same way for your news contributors and partners. They won't have to e-mail the news to you and then wait for you to publish it. They can submit and publish content without your intervention (although in our case we will give administrators and editors the option to approve or edit the content before publication).

The last problem is the implementation of security. We want to give full control to one or more administrators and editors, allow a specific group of users (contributors) to submit news, and allow normal users to just read the news. You could even prevent them from reading the content if they have not registered with the site.

To summarize the problem, you need the following:

❑ An online tool for managing news content that allows specific users to add, update, and delete articles without knowing HTML or other publishing software

❏ A method of allowing other sites to use your content so that they publish an extract and link to your site for the entire articles, thus bringing more traffic

❏ A system that allows various users different levels of access to the site's content

Design

This section introduces the design of the solution and an online tool for acquiring, managing, and sharing the content of our site. Specifically we will do the following:

❏ Provide a full list of the features we want to implement

❏ Design the database tables for this module

❏ Create a list and a description of the stored procedures needed to provide access to the database

❏ Design the object models of the data and business layers

❏ Describe the user interface services needed for content management, such as the site pages and reusable user controls

❏ Explain how we will ensure security for the administration section and for other access-restricted pages

Features to Implement

Let's start our discussion by writing down a partial list of the features that the article manager module should provide in order to be flexible and powerful, but still easy to use:

❏ An article can be added to the database at any time, with an option to delay publication until a specified release date. Additionally, the person submitting the article must be able to specify an expiration date, after which the article will be automatically retired. If these dates are not specified, then the article should be immediately published and remain active indefinitely.

❏ Articles can have an approved status. If an administrator or editor submits the article, it should be approved immediately. If you allow other people, such as staff or users of the site (we will call them *contributors*), to post their own news and articles, then this content should be added to the database in a "pending" state. The site administrators or editors will then be able to control this content, apply any required modifications, and finally approve the articles for publishing once they are ready.

❏ The system must also track who originally submitted an article or news item. This is important because it provides information regarding whether a contributor is active, who is responsible for incorrect content, who to contact for further details if the article is particularly interesting, and so on.

❏ The administrator/editor must be able to decide whether an article can be read by all readers or only by registered users.

❏ There can be multiple categories, enabling articles to be organized in different virtual folders. Each category should have a description and an image that graphically represents it.

❑ There should be a page with the available categories as a menu. Each category should be linked to a page that shows a short abstract for each published article. By clicking on the article's title the user can read the whole text.

❑ Articles can be targeted to users from a specified location, e.g., country, state/province, or city. Consider the case where you might have stories about concerts, parties, and special events that will happen in a particular location. In Chapter 4, you implemented a registration and profiling system that includes the user's address. That will be used here to highlight events that are going to happen close to the user's location. This is a feature that can entice readers to provide that personal information, which you could use later for marketing purposes (ads can be geographically targeted also).

❑ Users can leave comments or ask questions about articles, and this feedback should be published at the end of the article itself, so that other readers can read it and create discussions around it (this greatly helps to increase traffic). You might recognize this approach as being common with *blogs*, which are web logs in which an individual publishes personal thoughts and opinions and other people add comments. As another form of feedback, users can rate articles to express how much they liked them.

❑ The module must count how many times an article is read. This information will also be shown to the reader, together with the abstract, the author name, the publication date, and other information. But it will be most important for the editors/administrators because it greatly helps them understand which topics the readers find most interesting, enabling administrators to direct energy, money, and time to adding new content on those topics.

❑ The new content must be available as an RSS feed to which a reader can subscribe, and read through his or her favorite RSS aggregator.

❑ Above all, the article manager and the viewer must be integrated with the existing site. In our case this means that the pages must tie in with the current layout, and that we must take advantage of the current authentication/authorization system to protect each section and to identify the author of the submitted content.

It's essential to have this list of features when designing the database tables, as we now know what information we need to store, and the information that we should retrieve from existing tables and modules (such as the user account data).

Designing the Database Tables

As described in Chapter 3 (where we looked at building the foundations for our site), we're going to use the tbh_ prefix for all our tables, so that we avoid the risk of naming a table such that it clashes with another table used by another part of the site (this may well be the case when you have multiple applications on the site that store their data on the same shared DB). We need three tables for this module: one for the categories, another one for the articles, and the last one for the user feedback. The diagram shown in Figure 5-1 illustrates how they are linked to each other.

Let's start by looking at these tables and their relationship in more detail.

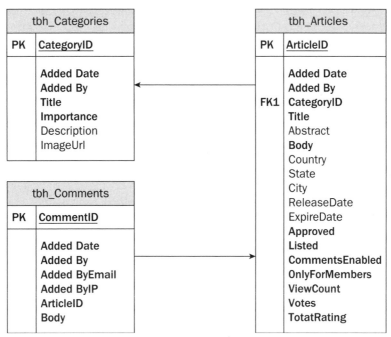

Figure 5-1

The tbh_Categories Table

Unsurprisingly, the tbh_Categories table stores some information about the article categories.

Column Name	Type	Size	Allow Null	Description
CategoryID	int - PK	4	No	Unique ID for the category
AddedDate	datetime	8	No	Category creation date/time
AddedBy	nvarchar	256	No	Name of the user who created the category
Title	nvarchar	256	No	Category's title
Importance	int	4	No	Category's importance. Used to sort the categories with a custom order, other than by name or by date.
Description	nvarchar	4000	Yes	Category's description
ImageUrl	nvarchar	256	Yes	URL of an image that represents the category graphically

This system supports a single-level category, meaning that we cannot have subcategories. This is plenty for small to mid-size sites that don't have huge numbers of new articles on a wide variety of topics. Having too many categories in sites of this size can even hinder the user's experience, because it makes it more difficult to locate desired content. Enhancing the system to support subcategories is left as an exercise if you really need it, but as a suggestion, the DB would only require an additional `ParentCategoryID` column containing the ID of the parent category.

`AddedDate` and `AddedBy` are two columns that you will find in all our tables—they record when a category/article/comment/product/message/newsletter was created, and by whom, to provide an audit trail. You may have thought that instead of having an `nvarchar` column for storing the username we could use an `integer` column that would contain a foreign key pointing to records of the `aspnet_Users` table introduced in Chapter 4. However, that would be a bad choice for a couple of reasons:

1.   The membership data may be stored in a separate database, and possibly on a different server.

2.   The membership module might use a provider other than the default one that targets SQL Server. In some cases the user account data will be stored in Active Directory or maybe an Oracle database, and thus there would be no SQL Server table to link to.

The tbh_Articles Table

This table contains the content and all further information for all the articles in all categories. It is structured as follows.

Column Name	Type	Size	Allow Null	Description
ArticleID	int – PK	4	No	Unique ID for the article
AddedDate	Datetime	8	No	Date/time the article was added
AddedBy	Nvarchar	256	No	Name of the user who created the article
CategoryID belongs	int – FK	4	No	ID of the category to which the news item
Title	Nvarchar	256	No	Article's title
Abstract	Nvarchar	4000	Yes	Article's abstract (short summary) to be shown in the page that lists the article, and in the RSS feed
Body	Ntext		No	Article's content (full version)
Country	Nvarchar	256	Yes	Country to which the article (concert/event) refers
State	nvarchar	256	Yes	State/province to which the article refers
City	nvarchar	256	Yes	City to which the article refers
ReleaseDate	datetime	8	Yes	Date/time the article will be publicly readable
ExpireDate	datetime	8	Yes	Date/time the article will be retired and no longer readable by the public

Column Name	Type	Size	Allow Null	Description
Approved	bit	1	No	Approved status of the article. If false, an administrator/editor has to approve the article before it is actually published and available to readers.
Listed	bit	1	No	Whether the article is listed in the articles page (indexed). If false, the article will not be listed, but will be still accessible if the user types the right URL, or if there is a direct link to it.
Comments Enabled	bit	1	No	Whether the user can leave public comments on the article
OnlyFor Members	bit	1	No	Whether the article is available to registered and authenticated users only, or to everyone
ViewCount	int	4	No	Number of times the article has been viewed
Votes	int	4	No	Number of votes the article has received
TotalRating	int	4	No	Total rating score the article has received. This is the sum of all the ratings posted by users.

The `ReleaseDate` and `ExpireDate` columns are useful because the site's staff can prepare content in advance and postpone its publication, and then let the site update itself at the specified date/time. In addition to the obvious benefit of spreading out the workload, this is also great during vacation periods, when the staff would not be in the office to write new articles but you still want the site to publish fresh content regularly.

The `Listed` column is also very important, because it enables you to add articles that will be hidden from the main article list page, and from the RSS feeds. Why would you want to do this? Suppose that you have a category called Photo Galleries (we'll actually create it later in the chapter) in which you publish the photos of a past event or meeting. In such photo gallery articles you would insert thumbnails of the photos with links to their full-size version. It would be nice if the reader could comment and rate each and every photo, not just the article listing them all, right? You can do that if instead of linking the big photo directly you link a secondary article that includes the photo. However, if you have many photos, and thus many short articles that contain each of them, you certainly don't want to fill the category's article listing with a myriad of links to the single photos. Instead, you will want to list only the parent gallery. To do this, you set the `Listed` property of all the photo articles to `false`, and leave it `true` only on the article with the thumbnails.

The `Country`, `State`, and `City` fields enable you to specify an accurate location for those articles that refer to an event (such as parties, concerts, beer contests, etc.). You may recall that we created the same properties in Chapter 2 for the user's profile. If the location for the article matches a specific user's location, even partially, then you could highlight the article with a particular color when it's listed on the web page. You may be wondering why it was necessary to define the `Country` and `State` fields as `varchar` fields, instead of an `int` foreign key pointing to corresponding records of the `tbh_Countries` and `tbh_States` lookup tables. The answer is that I want to use the `City` field to support not only U.S. states, but states and provinces for any other country, so I defined this as free text field. It's also good for performance if we de-normalize these fields. Using a lookup table is particularly useful when there is the possibility that some values may change; storing the information in one location minimizes the effort to update the data and makes it easier to ensure that we don't get out-of-sync. However, the list of countries will not realistically change, so this isn't much of a problem. In the remote case that this might happen, you will simply execute a manual update for all those records that have `Country="USA"` instead of `"United States"`, for example. This design decision can greatly improve the performance of the application.

You may be wondering why I decided to put the `Votes` and `TotalRating` columns into this table, instead of using a separate table to store all the single votes for all articles. That alternative has its advantages, surely: You could track the name and IP address of the user who submits the vote, and produce interesting statistics such as the number of votes for every level of rating (from one to 5 stars). However, retrieving the total number of votes, the total rating, and the number of votes for each rating level would require several `SUM` operations, in addition to the `SELECT` to the `tbh_Articles` table. I don't think the additional features are worth the additional processing time and traffic over the network, and thus I opted for this much lighter solution instead.

The tbh_Comments Table

This table contains the feedback (comments, questions, answers, etc.) for the published articles. The structure is very simple.

Column Name	Type	Size	Allow Null	Description
CommentID	int - PK	4	No	Unique ID for the comment
AddedDate	datetime	8	No	Date/time the comment was added
AddedBy	nvarchar	256	No	Name of the user who wrote the comment
AddedByEmail	nvarchar	256	No	User's e-mail address
AddedByIP	nchar	15	No	User's IP address
ArticleID	int	4	No	Article to which this comment refers
Body	ntext		No	Text of the comment

We will track the name of the user posting the comment, but she could even be an anonymous user, so this value will not necessarily be one of the registered usernames. We also store the user's e-mail address, so that the reader can be contacted with a private answer to her questions. Storing the IP address might be legally necessary in some cases, especially when you allow anonymous users to post content on a public site. In case of offensive or illegal content, it may be possible to geographically locate the user if you know her IP address and the time when the content was posted. In simpler cases, you may just block posts from that IP (not a useful option if it were a dynamically assigned IP, though).

Stored Procedures That Manage the Database

To manage the database, you will build a set of stored procedures that you'll use later in the data layer classes to do everything from the addition of categories, articles, and comments to the updating of single fields (such as the Approved status, or the `ViewCount` number). Procedures related to article management have the `tbh_Articles_` prefix, so that their name won't clash with procedures of other modules of this site.

> A common practice (and error) is to prefix stored procedure names with "sp". You should *not* do that, however, because "sp" is the prefix for system procedures, and if you use it for your custom user procedures, then SQL Server will first try to find them among the system procedures, it will fail, and then it will fall back and find it among custom procedures. This will slow down performance a bit.

The stored procedures you need, and their parameters, are listed in the following table (you'll be writing the code later in the chapter in the "Solution" section):

Procedure	Description
tbh_Articles_ApproveArticle	Sets the Approved field of the specified article to true
tbh_Articles_DeleteArticle	Deletes the article identified by the specified ID
tbh_Articles_DeleteCategory	Deletes the category identified by the specified ID
tbh_Articles_DeleteComment	Deletes the comment identified by the specified ID
tbh_Articles_GetArticleByID	Retrieves all details (the complete row) of the article identified by the specified ID
tbh_Articles_GetArticleCount	Returns the total number of articles in any categories
tbh_Articles_GetArticleCountByCategory	Returns the total number of articles in the specified category
tbh_Articles_GetArticles	Retrieves a partial list of articles located in any category. The list is partial because there are two parameters: to specify the index of the page of articles to retrieve, and the number of articles per page. This is used to implement a custom pagination system (because we can't fit all the articles on one page).
tbh_Articles_GetArticlesByCategory	Returns all details for a specified category
tbh_Articles_GetCategories	Returns all details about all categories
tbh_Articles_GetCategoryByID	Retrieves all details of the category identified by the specified ID
tbh_Articles_GetCommentByID	Retrieves all details of the comment identified by the specified ID

Table continued on following page

Procedure	Description
tbh_Articles_GetCommentCount	Returns the total number of comments for any article
tbh_Articles_GetCommentCountByArticle	Returns the total number of comments for the specified article
tbh_Articles_GetComments	Retrieves a partial list of comments for any article. The list is partial because there are two parameters: to specify the index of the page of comments to retrieve, and the number of comments per page. This is used to implement a custom pagination system.
tbh_Articles_GetCommentsByArticle	Retrieves comments for the specified article
tbh_Articles_GetPublishedArticleCount	Returns the total number of published articles in any category. A published article is an article that is approved, listed, and whose ReleaseDate-ExpireDate interval includes the specified current date.
tbh_Articles_ GetPublishedArticleCountByCategory	Returns the total number of published articles for the specified category
tbh_Articles_GetPublishedArticles	Retrieves a partial list of published articles located in any category. Similar to tbh_GetArticles, but gets only published articles, i.e., articles that are approved, listed, and are not expired (whose ReleaseDate-ExpireDate interval includes the specified current date).
tbh_Articles_ GetPublishedArticlesByCategory	Retrieves a partial list of published articles located in the specified category, and only the ones that did not expire
tbh_Articles_IncrementViewCount	Increments the ViewCount field of the specified article by one
tbh_Articles_InsertArticle	Creates a new article record, and returns its ID as an output parameter
tbh_Articles_InsertCategory	Creates a new category record, and returns its ID as an output parameter
tbh_Articles_InsertComment	Creates a new comment record, and returns its ID as an output parameter
tbh_Articles_InsertVote	Increases for the specified article the Votes field by one, and the TotalRating field by the specified value
tbh_Articles_UpdateArticle	Updates some fields of the specified article
tbh_Articles_UpdateCategory	Updates some fields of the specified category
tbh_Articles_UpdateComment	Updates some fields of the specified comment

Many of these stored procedures are pretty standard — procedures to insert, update, return, and delete rows. However, it's worth noting some design decisions that could have an impact on the performance of the site:

❑ All stored procedures that retrieve the list of articles and comments accept two input parameters: one that indicate the index of the page of records to retrieve, and one that indicates how many records there are per page. This is done to support a custom pagination mechanism in the administration and user pages where you will show the list of items. Potentially, there can be thousands of articles and comments, so implementing pagination is necessary both for performance and aesthetic reasons. On those occasions when you really want to retrieve all items (for example, when you want to show all comments for a specific article, below the article itself), you can just pass zero as the page index, and a large integer value as the page size.

❑ The tbh_Articles_GetArticleByID procedure returns all the details (fields) of the specified article. This includes the whole Body text, so the procedure is used when you need to display the entire article's content in its own dynamically filled page. If you only want summary data for use on an administration page, you can use the tbh_Articles_GetArticles, tbh_Articles_GetArticlesByCategory, tbh_Articles_GetPublishedArticles, and tbh_Articles_GetPublishedArticlesByCategory procedures. You should not return the Body field if it's not needed in order to keep performance high and network traffic low.

❑ The procedures that retrieve articles will be joined with the tbh_Categories table to retrieve the parent category's title, in addition to the ID stored in the tbh_Articles table. Similarly, the procedures that retrieve comments will be joined with the tbh_Comments table to retrieve the parent article's title. Returning this information together with the other data avoids running many separate queries when you have to list articles or comments on the page (an additional query would be needed for each article/comment otherwise).

❑ The tbh_Articles_UpdateXXX stored procedures do not update all the fields. Fields such as AddedDate, AddedBy, AddedByEmail, and AddedByIP cannot be changed, as they are there to track who originally created the record and when it was created. If it were possible to change that historical data, the tracking would be useless. Other fields such as ViewCount, Votes and TotalRating are also not directly updateable, as there are specific stored procedures to update them in the proper way.

Designing the Configuration Module

Chapter 3 introduced a custom configuration section named <theBeerHouse> that you must define in the root folder's web.config file, to specify some settings required in order for the site's modules to work. In that chapter we also developed a configuration class that would handle the <contact> sub-element of <theBeerHouse>, with settings for the Contact form in the Contact.aspx page. For the articles module of this chapter you'll need some new settings that will be grouped into a new configuration sub-element under <theBeerHouse>, called <articles>. This will be read by a class called ArticlesElement that will inherit from System.Configuration.ConfigurationElement, and that will have the public properties shown in the following table.

Property	Description
ProviderType	Full name (namespace plus class name) of the concrete provider class that implements the data access code for a specific data store
ConnectionStringName	Name of the entry in web.config's new <connectionStrings> section that contains the connection string to the module's database
PageSize	Default number of articles listed per page. The user will be able to change the page size from the user interface.
RssItems	Number of items returned by the module's RSS feeds
EnableCaching	Boolean value indicating whether the caching of data is enabled
CacheDuration	Number of seconds for which the data is cached

The settings in the web.config file will have the same name, but will follow the camelCase naming convention; therefore, you will use providerType, connectionStringName, pageSize, and so on, as shown in the following example:

```
<theBeerHouse>
    <contactForm mailTo="webmaster@effectivedotnet.com"/>
    <articles providerType="MB.TheBeerHouse.DAL.SqlClient.SqlArticlesProvider"
        connectionStringName="LocalSqlServer" pageSize="10" />
</theBeerHouse>
```

An instance of ArticlesElement is returned by the Articles property of the TheBeerHouseSection class, described in Chapter 3, that represents the <theBeerHouse> parent section. This class will also have a couple of other new properties, DefaultConnectionStringName and DefaultCacheDuration, to provide default values for the module-specific ConnectionStringName and CacheDuration settings. These settings will be available for each module, but you want to be able to set them differently for each module. For example, you may want to use one database for storing articles data, and a second database to store forums data, so that you can easily back them up independently and with a different frequency according to how critical the data is and how often it changes. The same goes for the cache duration. However, in case you want to assign the same settings to all modules (which is probably what you will do for small to mid-size sites), you can just assign the default values at the root section level, instead of copying and pasting them for every configuration sub-element.

In addition to the properties listed above, the ArticlesElement will have another property, ConnectionString. This is a calculated property, though, not one that is read from web.config. It uses the <articles>'s connectionStringName or the <theBeerHouse>'s defaultConnectionStringName and then looks up the corresponding connection string in the web.config file's <connectionStrings> section, so the caller will get the final connection string and not just the name of its entry.

Designing the Data Access Layer

Now that you have a clear picture in mind of the database tables and how to retrieve data through the stored procedures, you can now design the data services. As explained in Chapter 3, we'll be using a simplified version of the provider model design pattern for each module's data access layer (DAL). In practice, you will have an abstract class that implements some of the utility functions, and then a list of abstract methods having a signature, but no implementation. Then, you will have one or more provider classes that inherit from the abstract class and provide the concrete implementation of its abstract methods. The base class has also an `Instance` static property that uses reflection to create, and return, an instance of the provider class whose name is indicated in the `web.config` file. There is also a `DataAccess` class implemented in Chapter 3, which is the root of the inheritance tree and provides properties and methods useful to all data access classes, and a series of entity classes that encapsulate the data retrieved from the database. Generally, there is a one-to-one correspondence between the database tables and the DAL's entity classes. Figure 5-2 provides a graphical representation of these classes, with their inheritance relationships.

Chapter 3 showed how to implement the provider for SQL Server (having the name `MB.TheBeer House.DAL.SqlClient.SqlArtcilesProvider`), which wraps the calls to the stored procedures listed above. Some methods have a number of overloaded versions: for example, the `GetArticles` method has a version that takes the parent category's ID, the page index, and the page size, and another method that takes only the page index and size, and returns articles from any category. It's the same for `GetPublishedArticles`, and it's similar for `GetArticleCount` and `GetPublishedArticleCount` (two versions for each: one with the category ID and the other without it).

You won't use these classes directly from the presentation layer. Instead, we'll build a business layer that exposes a better object-oriented representation of the data, and the relationships between different entities (categories and articles, articles and comments). As I mentioned in Chapter 3, having a complete three-tier design improves maintainability and readability of code. These classes will be located under the `App_Code` folder of the main web project, and will be compiled together for use in the rest of the site. This is done for simplicity — not only does it enable us to avoid separately compiling and deploying multiple projects, but it also lets us take advantage of the new "edit and continue" compilation model that enables us to edit a class while the application is running, and have our changes be automatically compiled and utilized simply by refreshing the page in the browser! Alternatively, you could instead put it in a separate assembly if you prefer to have a physical separation between the layers to mirror the logical separation.

Designing the Business Layer

The data layer has a provider class with methods that call the stored procedures, but it doesn't represent an entity (or domain object) in a real object-oriented way. The entities are represented by the classes in the business layer, which use the data layer classes to access the database, representing the relationships between data elements. All the business classes indirectly descend from the `BizObject` class designed and implemented in Chapter 3, which provides information such as the name and IP of the current user and a reference to the current `HttpContext`'s cache; it also exposes utility functions to encode HTML text, calculate the index of the page for a record with the given index, and clear from the cache items that start with a given prefix. The business classes of the articles module directly descend from a `BaseArticle` class, which has some instance properties that wrap the common DB fields that all entities (category, article, and comment) have: `ID`, `AddedDate`, and `AddedBy`. This class also has a method for caching data: It is put here instead of in the `BizObject` class because it actually caches the data only if the articles module is configured to do so by a custom setting in the `web.config` file. Each module (articles, forums, newsletters, etc.) will have a separate configuration, and thus a separate `CacheData` method. The configuration is read by the `ArticlesElement` class described earlier and is used as the return type for the `BaseArticle`'s static and protected `Settings` property. Figure 5-3 is the UML diagram that describes the classes and their relationships.

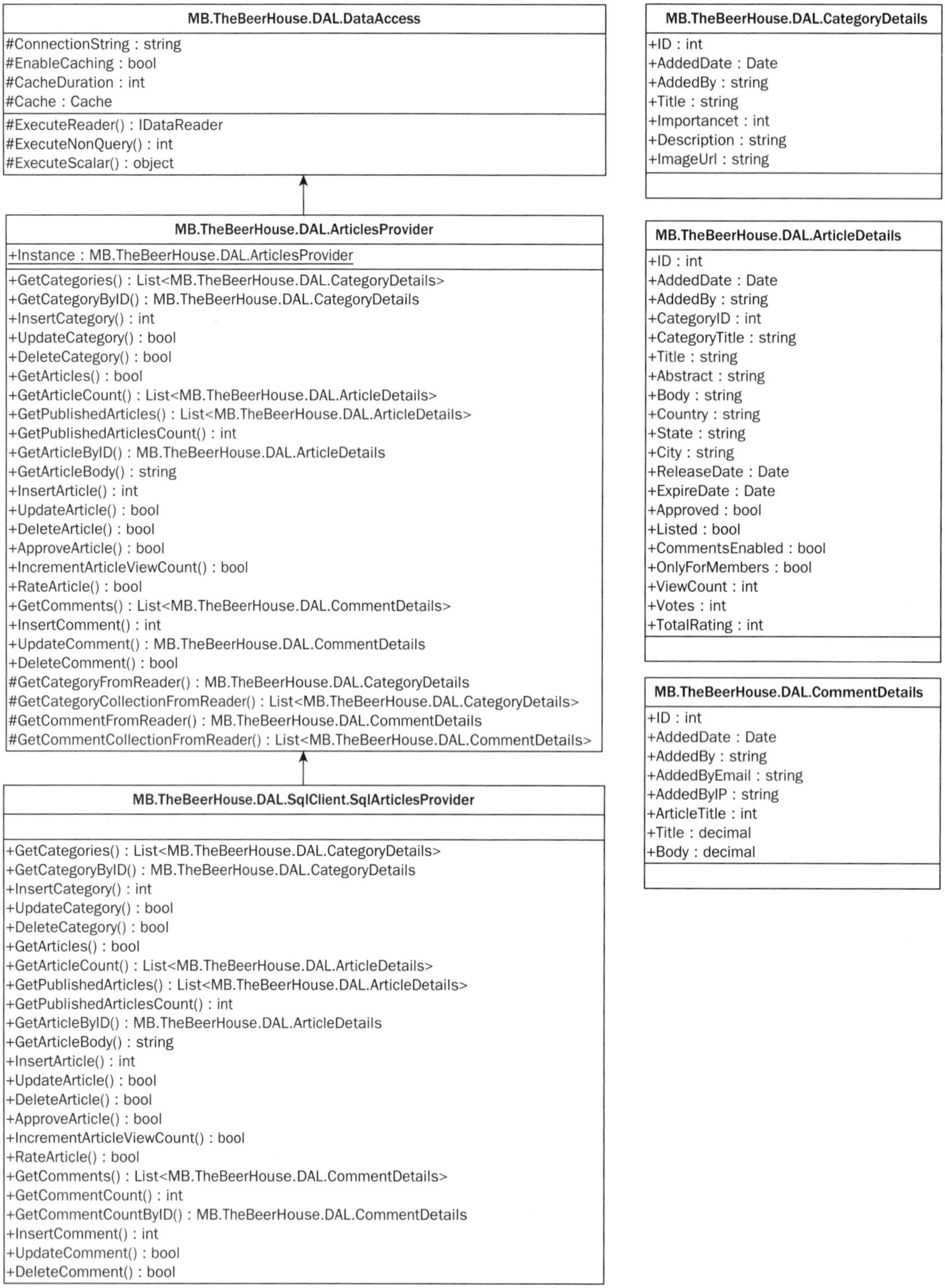

MB.TheBeerHouse.DAL.DataAccess

#ConnectionString : string
#EnableCaching : bool
#CacheDuration : int
#Cache : Cache

#ExecuteReader() : IDataReader
#ExecuteNonQuery() : int
#ExecuteScalar() : object

MB.TheBeerHouse.DAL.ArticlesProvider

+Instance : MB.TheBeerHouse.DAL.ArticlesProvider

+GetCategories() : List<MB.TheBeerHouse.DAL.CategoryDetails>
+GetCategoryByID() : MB.TheBeerHouse.DAL.CategoryDetails
+InsertCategory() : int
+UpdateCategory() : bool
+DeleteCategory() : bool
+GetArticles() : bool
+GetArticleCount() : List<MB.TheBeerHouse.DAL.ArticleDetails>
+GetPublishedArticles() : List<MB.TheBeerHouse.DAL.ArticleDetails>
+GetPublishedArticlesCount() : int
+GetArticleByID() : MB.TheBeerHouse.DAL.ArticleDetails
+GetArticleBody() : string
+InsertArticle() : int
+UpdateArticle() : bool
+DeleteArticle() : bool
+ApproveArticle() : bool
+IncrementArticleViewCount() : bool
+RateArticle() : bool
+GetComments() : List<MB.TheBeerHouse.DAL.CommentDetails>
+InsertComment() : int
+UpdateComment() : MB.TheBeerHouse.DAL.CommentDetails
+DeleteComment() : bool
#GetCategoryFromReader() : MB.TheBeerHouse.DAL.CategoryDetails
#GetCategoryCollectionFromReader() : List<MB.TheBeerHouse.DAL.CategoryDetails>
#GetCommentFromReader() : MB.TheBeerHouse.DAL.CommentDetails
#GetCommentCollectionFromReader() : List<MB.TheBeerHouse.DAL.CommentDetails>

MB.TheBeerHouse.DAL.SqlClient.SqlArticlesProvider

+GetCategories() : List<MB.TheBeerHouse.DAL.CategoryDetails>
+GetCategoryByID() : MB.TheBeerHouse.DAL.CategoryDetails
+InsertCategory() : int
+UpdateCategory() : bool
+DeleteCategory() : bool
+GetArticles() : bool
+GetArticleCount() : List<MB.TheBeerHouse.DAL.ArticleDetails>
+GetPublishedArticles() : List<MB.TheBeerHouse.DAL.ArticleDetails>
+GetPublishedArticlesCount() : int
+GetArticleByID() : MB.TheBeerHouse.DAL.ArticleDetails
+GetArticleBody() : string
+InsertArticle() : int
+UpdateArticle() : bool
+DeleteArticle() : bool
+ApproveArticle() : bool
+IncrementArticleViewCount() : bool
+RateArticle() : bool
+GetComments() : List<MB.TheBeerHouse.DAL.CommentDetails>
+GetCommentCount() : int
+GetCommentCountByID() : MB.TheBeerHouse.DAL.CommentDetails
+InsertComment() : int
+UpdateComment() : bool
+DeleteComment() : bool

MB.TheBeerHouse.DAL.CategoryDetails

+ID : int
+AddedDate : Date
+AddedBy : string
+Title : string
+Importancet : int
+Description : string
+ImageUrl : string

MB.TheBeerHouse.DAL.ArticleDetails

+ID : int
+AddedDate : Date
+AddedBy : string
+CategoryID : int
+CategoryTitle : string
+Title : string
+Abstract : string
+Body : string
+Country : string
+State : string
+City : string
+ReleaseDate : Date
+ExpireDate : Date
+Approved : bool
+Listed : bool
+CommentsEnabled : bool
+OnlyForMembers : bool
+ViewCount : int
+Votes : int
+TotalRating : int

MB.TheBeerHouse.DAL.CommentDetails

+ID : int
+AddedDate : Date
+AddedBy : string
+AddedByEmail : string
+AddedByIP : string
+ArticleTitle : int
+Title : decimal
+Body : decimal

Figure 5-2

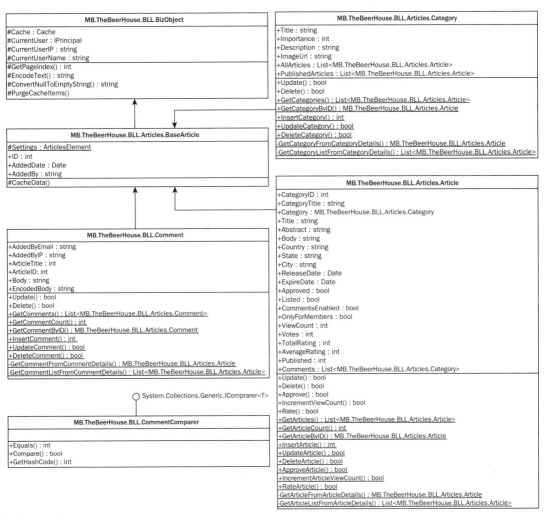

Figure 5-3

The `Article`, `Category`, and `Comment` classes have a series of instance public properties that fully describe a single element. They also have some instance methods, such as `Delete` and `Update`, which work with the instance properties representing the current object. Additionally, there are a number of static methods to retrieve a list of instances, create new records, update or delete existing records, etc. Since these are static methods, they cannot access any instance properties, and therefore all their data must be passed to them as parameters. One important aspect of the `Getxxx` methods is that they use `List<T>` as the return type, where `T` is article, category, or comment. This list type belongs to the `System.Collections.Generic.List` class, which is a new *generic* collection provided in C# 2.0. This provides a strongly typed and specialized version of a collection class. Therefore, when you declare

```
List<Article> articles = new List<Article>();
```

you're creating a collection that can only return and accept objects of the `Article` type — no casting, boxing, and unboxing are required because the internal type is being set as `Article` by this code, which instantiates the collection. The built-in collections in previous versions of C# had to store everything as type `System.Object`, which required casting because they didn't hold objects of a known type. Generics are one of the best new features in version 2.0 and I strongly recommend that you study this subject by reading articles on the MSDN web site or Wrox's *Professional C# 2005* (ISBN 0-7645-7534-1). The structure of the three main classes — `Article`, `Category`, and `Comment` — is very similar. Therefore, I'll only present the `Article` class in detail here, and just highlight the unique aspects of the others.

The Article Class

Some of the public properties of the `Article` class are just wrappers for the underlying DB fields, but others return calculated values. The following table lists all the properties.

Properties	Description
ID	Article's ID
AddedDate	Date/time the article was created
AddedBy	Name of the author
CategoryID	Parent category ID
CategoryTitle	Parent category title
Category	Reference to the article's parent Category object
Title	Title
Abstract	Abstract (short description)
Body	Body
Country	Country where the event described in the article will take place
State	State, region, or province where the event will take place
City	City where the event will take place
Location	Calculated read-only property that returns the full location of the event in the form: country, state, city
ReleaseDate	Date/time the article will be publicly readable by users
ExpireDate	Date/time the article will be retired and no longer readable by users
Approved	Whether the article is approved, or is waiting for approval
Listed	Whether the article is listed in the pages that list public articles
CommentsEnabled	Whether users can comment on this article
OnlyForMembers	Whether the article can only be read by registered and authenticated users, or by everyone
ViewCount	Number of times the article has been read

Properties	Description
Votes	Number of votes received by the article
TotalRating	Total rating received by the article, i.e., the sum of all votes
AverageRating	Average rating (as a double value), calculated as TotalRating/Votes
Published	Calculated value indicating whether the article is published (meaning the article is approved, and the current date is between the ReleaseDate and the ExpireDate)
Comments	List of comments submitted by users

The methods listed in the following table are instance methods, and use the object's `instance` property values to update, delete, or approve an article, and other operations with it.

Instance Method	Description
Update	Updates the current article
Delete	Deletes the current article
Approve	Approves the current article
IncrementViewCount	Increment the ViewCount of the current article by one
Rate	Rate the current article; the rating value is passed as a parameter

Besides these instance members, there are several static methods that allow the caller to retrieve a list of articles or a single article, create a new article, delete, approve, update, or rate an existing article, and more. As they are static, they don't use any instance properties, and they get all the data they need as input parameters.

Static Method	Description
GetArticles	Returns a list of Article instances, and has eight overloads to wrap all stored procedures that retrieve the list of articles described above (to retrieve all articles, only published articles, articles from a specific category, etc.)
	Note: the Article instances returned by these methods do not have the Body property filled with the real value, because it was not retrieved by the stored procedures called by the DAL class. As soon as the Body parameter is read, the missing value for the specific Article is retrieved and stored into the instance.
GetArticleCount	There are four overloads of this method that return the number of articles given no constraints (all articles), the parent category, the published status (but not the category), or the parent category plus the published status

Table continued on following page

Static Method	Description
GetArticleByID	Returns an Article instance that fully describes the article identified by the input ID
InsertArticle	Takes all the data for creating a new article, and returns its ID
UpdateArticle	Updates data for an existing article, and returns a Boolean value indicating whether the operation was successful
DeleteArticle	Deletes the article identified by an ID and returns a Boolean value indicating whether the operation was successful
ApproveArticle	Approves the article identified by an ID
IncrementArticle ViewCount	Increments the view count of the article identified by an ID
RateArticle	Rates the article identified by the ID, with a value from 1 to 5
GetArticleFrom ArticleDetails	Private method that takes an ArticleDetails object (from the DAL) and returns a new Article instance
GetArticleListFrom ArticleDetailsList	Private method that takes a list of ArticleDetails objects and returns a list of Article instances

This class uses the *lazy load* pattern, which means data is loaded only when requested and not when the object instance is created. There are quite a few variations on this pattern, and you should refer to a patterns book for complete coverage of the subject. For the `Article` class, you don't need the list of comments or the article's body unless you're inside the specific article page that shows all details of the article. In the page that lists the available articles, you don't need those details, so we won't waste time retrieving them from the DB. The `Article` class has the `CategoryID` and `CategoryTitle` instance properties, which are often all you need to know about the parent category. However, it also has a `Category` property that returns a full `Category` object with all the parent category's details. That object isn't retrieved when the `Article` object is created, but rather when that property is actually read. Also, once requested, we'll fetch the data and store it locally in case it is requested again from the same object instance. The implementation presented later in this chapter is very simple, but it can dramatically improve the performance of the application.

The `GetArticles` overloads that take parameters to specify the page of results do not expect the index of the page to retrieve. Rather, they take the number of the first row to retrieve, and the page size. I don't care for this personally, but it's a requirement of the `ObjectDataSource` (which will be used later in the user interface) to work with pagination. Because the DAL's `Select` methods expect the page index instead of the number of the first row to retrieve, we'll have to calculate the page index.

The Category Class

This class has instance properties that fully describe a category of articles, instance methods to delete and update an existing category, and static methods to create, update, or delete one category. I won't describe all of them here as they are pretty similar to the corresponding methods of the `Article` class. They're actually a little simpler because you don't need multiple overloads to support pagination and other filters. There are two properties, `Articles` and `PublishedArticles`, that use a couple of overloads of the `Article.GetArticles` static methods to return a list of `Article` objects. Like the `Article.Comments` property, these two properties also use the lazy load pattern, so articles are retrieved only once when the property is read for the first time.

The Comment Class

The `Comment` class has various overloads for the `GetComments` static method that, like `Article.Get Articles`, can take in input different parameters for the parent article ID and the pagination support. In addition to the data returned by the DAL it also exposes an `Article` property that uses the lazy load pattern to load all details of a comment's parent article as needed. Another property it exposes is `EncodedBody`, which returns the same text returned by the `Body` property, but first performs HTML encoding on it. This protects us against the so-called *script-injection* and *cross-site scripting* attacks. As a very simple example, consider a page on which you allow users to anonymously post a comment. If you don't validate the input, they may write something like the following:

```
<script>document.location = 'http://www.usersite.com';</script>
```

This text is sent to the server and you save it into the DB. Later, when you have to show the comments, you would retrieve the original comment text and send to the browser as is. However, when you output the preceding text, it won't be considered as text by the browser, but rather as a JavaScript routine that redirects the user to another web site, hijacking the user away from your web site! And this was just a basic attack — more complex scripts could be used to steal users' cookies, which could include authentication tickets and personal data, with potentially grave consequences. For our protection, ASP.NET automatically validates the user input sent to the server during a postback, and checks whether it matches a pattern of suspicious text. However, in that case it raises an exception and shows an error page. You should consider the case where a legitimate user tries to insert some simple HTML just to format the text, or maybe hasn't really typed HTML but only a < character. In that case, you don't want to show an error page, you only need to ensure that the HTML code isn't displayed in a browser (because you don't want users to put links or images on your site, or text with a font so big that it creates a mess with your layout). To do so you can disable ASP.NET's input validation (only for those pages on which the user is actually expected to insert text, not for all pages!), and save the text into the DB, but only show it on the page after HTML encoding, as follows:

```
&lt;script&gt; document.location = 'http://www.usersite.com'; &lt;/script&gt;
```

This way, text inserted by the user is actually shown on the page, instead of being considered HTML. The link will show as a link but it will not be a clickable link, and no JavaScript can be run this way. The `EncodedBody` property returns the HTML encoded text, but it can't completely replace the `Body` property, because the original comment text is still required in certain situations — for example, in the administration pages where you show the text into a textbox, and allow the administrator to edit it.

> *Scripting-based attacks must not be taken lightly, and you should ensure that your site is not vulnerable. One good reference on the web is www.technicalinfo.net/gunter/index.html, but you can easily find many others. Try searching for XSS using your favorite search engine.*

Sorting Comments

We will not implement sorting features for the categories and the articles. This is because categories will always be sorted by importance (the `Importance` field) and then by name, whereas articles will always be sorted by release date, from the newest to the oldest, which is the right kind of sorting for these features. However, comments should be sorted in two different ways according to the situation:

❑ From the oldest to the newest when they are listed on the user page, under the article itself, so that users will read them in chronological order so they can follow a discussion made up of questions and answers between the readers and the article's author, or between different readers.

❑ From the newest to the oldest in the administration page, so that the administration finds the new comments at the top of the list, and in the first page (remember that comments support pagination) so they can be immediately read, edited, and, if necessary, deleted if found offensive.

If you were to make a stored procedure that supports pagination of comments, it would become more complex than it needs to be. The alternative is to dynamically build the SQL SELECT statements, but you lose the advantages of stored procedures. I came to the following compromise: We can use the stored procedure to retrieve all the article's comments (instead of a stored procedure that uses pagination), and it can be sorted from the newest to the oldest; and we can invert the order on the client by reordering the collection programmatically. I came to this conclusion by considering that the pagination would only be used on the administration pages, a single article will not have more than a few dozen short comments, and it's acceptable to retrieve all of them together when the article must be displayed. You'll be using caching quite aggressively to minimize the overhead in collecting all the comments at once. You could have sorted the comments from the oldest to the newest directly from the stored procedure, but I prefer to do it from the client to make it consistent with the other stored procedure that uses pagination.

The List<T> generic collection class has a Sort instance method that takes an object implementing System.Collections.Generic.IComparer<T> as an input, and returns its collection of items with a different sort order. The logic to compare two objects (two Comment objects in this case) is put into the object that implements IComparer, and that, as you might expect, has to implement a method named Compare. This method takes as input two objects and returns -1, 0 or 1 according to whether the first parameter is less than the second, the two are equal, or the first is greater than the second. You can use any logic you want to compare the two objects, but in a simple case like ours it is sufficient to delegate the logic to the Compare method of the DataTime class, with the AddedDate value of the two comments as parameters. In the "Solution" section you will see how simple it is to implement this technique to obtain a flexible and dynamic sorting mechanism. You should always take advantage of functionality built into the Framework!

Designing the User Interface

The design of the ASP.NET pages in this module is not particularly special, so there's not much to discuss. We have a set of pages, some for the administrators and some for the end users, which allow us to manage articles, and navigate through categories and read articles, respectively. In the first edition of this book, the most important consideration for the UI section of the first chapters was the approach used to integrate the module-specific pages into the rest of the site. However, you're already seen from previous chapters that this is very straightforward in ASP.NET 2.0, thanks to master pages. Following is a list of pages we will code later:

❑ **~/Admin/ManageCategories.aspx:** This lists the current categories, and allows administrators to create new ones and delete and update existing ones.

❑ **~/Admin/ManageArticles.aspx:** This lists the current articles (with pagination support) and allows administrators to delete them. The creation of new articles and the editing of existing articles will be delegated to a secondary page.

❑ **~/Admin/AddEditArticle.aspx:** This allows administrators to create new articles and update existing articles.

❑   **~/Admin/ManageComments.aspx:** This lists the current comments for any article, has pagination support, and supports deletion and updates of existing comments.

❑   **~/ShowCategories.aspx:** This is an end-user page that lists all categories, with their title, description, and image.

❑   **~/BrowseArticles.aspx:** This end-user page allows users to browse published articles for a specific category, or for all categories. The page shows the title, abstract, author, release date, average rating, and location of the articles.

❑   **~/ShowArticle.aspx:** This end-user page shows the complete article, along with the current comments at the bottom, and a box to let users post new comments and rate the article.

❑   **~/GetArticlesRss.aspx:** This page does not return HTML, but rather the XML of the RSS feed for the "*n*" most recent articles of a specific category, or for any category. The "*n*" number is configurable with a setting in the `web.config` file. You don't want "n" to be too big because that would overwhelm users and could slow down your site because a lot of news aggregators download this feed list at regular intervals to determine whether you've published any new articles.

Writing Articles with a WYSIWYG Text Editor

The first and most important challenge you face is that the site must be easily updateable by the client herself, without requiring help from any technical support people. Some regular employees working in the pub must be able to write and publish new articles, and make them look good by applying various formatting, colors, pictures, tables, etc. All this must be possible without knowing any HTML, of course! This problem can be solved by using a WYSIWYG (the acronym for "what you see is what you get") text editor: These editors enable users to write and format text, and to insert graphical elements, much like a typical word processor (which most people are familiar with), and the content is saved in HTML format that can be later shown on the end-user page "as is." There are various editors available, some commercial and some free. Among the different options I picked up FCK Editor (www.fckeditor.net), mainly because it is open source and because it is compatible with most Internet browsers, including IE 5.5+, Firefox 1.0+, Mozilla 1.3+, and Netscape 7+. Figure 5-4 shows a screenshot of an online demo from the editor's web site.

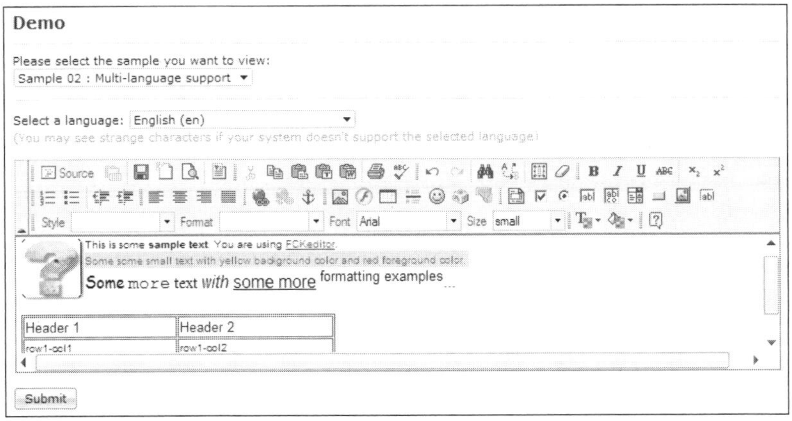

Figure 5-4

The editor is even localizable (language packs for many languages are already provided), and its user interface can be greatly customized, so you can easily decide what toolbars and what command buttons (and thus formatting and functions) you want to make available to users.

Uploading Files

The editor must be able to upload files, typically images for an article, or publish in a photo gallery, and maybe upload documents, screen savers, or other goodies that they want to distribute to their end users. An administrator of a site would be able to use an FTP program to upload files, but an editor typically does not have the expertise, or the credentials, needed to access the remote server and its file system. An online file manager might be very helpful in this situation. In the first edition of this book, an entire chapter was devoted to showing you how to build a full-featured online file manager that would enable users to browse and remove folders and files, upload new files, download, rename, copy and delete existing files, and even edit the content of text files. However, this would be overkill in most situations, as the administrator is the only one who needs to have full control over the files and folders and structure of the site, and the administrator will presumably use an FTP client for this purpose. Editors and contributors only need the capability to upload new files. To implement this functionality, we will develop a small user control that allows users to upload one file at a time, and when done, displays the full URL of the file saved on the server, so the user can easily link to it using the WYSIWYG editor. The control will be used in various pages: in the page to add and edit an article, and in the page to manage categories (as each category can have an image representing it); and later in book we'll use this in the pages that send newsletters and submit forum posts.

This user control, named `FileUploader.ascx`, will utilize the new ASP.NET 2.0 `FileUpload` control to select the file, submit it, and save it on the server. This control simply translates to an `<input type="file" />` control, with server-side methods to save the image. Under ASP.NET 1.x there was no such control; you had to add the `runat="server"` attribute to a plain HTML control declaration.

One important design decision we need to consider is how to avoid the possibility that different editors might upload files with the same name, overwriting previous files uploaded by someone else. A simple, but effective, solution is to save the file under `~/Uploads/{UserName}`, where the `{UserName}` placeholder is replaced by the actual user's name. This works because only registered and authenticated users will have access to pages where they can upload files. We do want to let users overwrite a file that they uploaded themselves, as they might want to change the file.

> **Remember that you will need to add NTFS write permission to the remote Uploads folder at deployment time, for the ASP.NET (Windows 2000 and XP) or Network Service user account (Windows Server 2003). It's easy to overlook this kind of thing, and you don't want to leave a bad impression with users when you set up a new site for them.**

Article List User Control

You will need a way to quickly add the list of articles (with title, author, abstract, and a few more details) to any page. It's not enough to have entirely new articles; you also need to show them on existing pages so users will know about them! You'll need to show the list on the `BrowseArticles.aspx` page for end users and on the `ManageArticles.aspx` page for administrators. You may also want to show the article list on the home page. If you've got a good understanding of user controls, you may have already guessed that a user control is the best solution for this list because it enables us to encapsulate this functionality into a single code unit (the .ascx file plus the cs code-behind file), which enables us to write the code once and then place that user control on any page using one line of code.

This user control will be named `ArticleListing.ascx`. It produces different output according to whether the user is a regular user, an administrator, or an editor. If they belong to one of the special roles, each article item will have buttons to delete, edit, or approve them. This way, we can have a single control that will behave differently according to its context. Besides this, when the control is placed into an administration page, it must show all articles, including those that are not yet published (approved), or those that have already been retired (based on the date). When the control is on an end-user page, it must show only the active and published articles. The control will expose the following public properties (all Boolean), so that it's content and its behavior can be changed in different pages:

Property	Description
EnableHighlighter	Indicates whether articles referring to events in the user's country, state/province, or city are highlighted with different colors
PublishedOnly	Indicates whether the control lists only articles that are approved, and whose ReleaseDate-ExpireDate interval includes the current date
RatingLockInterval	The number of days that must pass before a user can again rate the same article
ShowCategoryPicker	Indicates whether the control shows a drop-down list filled with all article categories, which lets the user filter articles by category. If the property is false the drop-down list will be hidden, and the control will filter the articles by category according to the CategoryID parameter passed on the querystring.
ShowPageSizePicker	Indicates whether the control shows a drop-down list representing the number of articles to be listed per page. If the property is true, the user will be able to change the page size to a value that best meets his desires and his connection speed (users with a slow connection may prefer to have fewer items per page so that it loads faster).
EnablePaging	Indicates whether the control will paginate the collection of articles resulting from the current filters (category and published status). When false, the control will have no paging bar and will only show the first "*n*" articles, where "*n*" is the page size. This allows us to use the control on the home page, for example, to list the "*n*" most recent additions. When true, it will show only the first "*n*" articles but will also show an indication of which page is displayed, and the user can switch between pages of articles.

Producing and Consuming RSS Feeds

You've already learned from the Introduction that we're going to implement a mechanism to provide the headlines of the site's new content as an RSS feed, so that external (online or desktop-based) aggregator programs can easily consume them, adding new content to their own site, but also driving new traffic to our site. This process of providing a list of articles via RSS is called *syndication*. The XML format used to contain RSS content is simple in nature (it's not an accident that the RSS acronym stands for "Really Simple Syndication"), and here's an example of one RSS feed that contains an entry for two different articles:

```
<rss version="2.0">
 <channel>
  <title>My RSS feed</title>
  <link>http://www.contoso.com</link>
  <description>A sample site with a sample RSS</description>
  <copyright>Copyright 2005 by myself</copyright>

  <item>
   <title>First article</title>
   <author>Marco</author>
   <description>Some abstract text here...</description>
   <link>http://www.contoso.com/article1.aspx</link>
   <pubDate>Sat, 03 Sep 2005 12:00:34 GMT</pubDate>
  </item>
  <item>
   <title>Second article</title>
   <author>Mary</author>
   <description>Some other abstract text here...</description>
   <link>http://www.contoso.com/article2.aspx</link>
   <pubDate>Mon, 05 Sep 2005 10:30:22 GMT</pubDate>
  </item>
 </channel>
</rss>
```

As you see, the root node indicates the version of RSS used in this file, and just below that is a `<channel>` section, which represents the feed. It contains several required sub-elements, `<title>`, `<link>`, and `<description>`, whose names are self-descriptive. There can also be a number of optional sub-elements, including `<copyright>`, `<webMaster>`, `<pubDate>`, `<image>`, and others. After all those feed-level elements is the list of actual posts/articles/stories, represented by `<item>` subsections. An item can have a number of optional elements, a few of which (`title`, `author`, `description`, `link`, `pubDate`) are shown in the preceding example. For details on the full list of elements supported by RSS you can check this link, `http://blogs.law.harvard.edu/tech/rss`, or just search for "RSS 2.0 Specification."

One important thing to remember is that this must be a valid XML format, and therefore you cannot insert HTML into the `<description>` element to provide a visual "look and feel" unless you ensure that it meets XML standards (XHTML is the name for tighter HTML that meets XML requirement). You must ensure that the HTML is well formed, so that all tags have their closing part (`<p>` has its `</p>`) or are self-closing (as in `<img.../>`), among other rules. If you don't want the hassle of making sure the HTML is XML-compliant, you can just wrap the text into a CDATA section, which can include any kind of data. Another small detail to observe is that the value for the `pubDate` elements must be in the exact format "ddd, dd MMM yyyy HH:mm:ss GMT", as in "Thu, 03 Jan 2002 10:20:30 GMT". If you aren't careful to meet these RSS requirements, your users may get errors when they try to view your RSS feed. Some feed readers are more tolerant than others so it's not sufficient to make sure it works in your own feed reader — you need to meet the RSS specifications.

The RSS feed will be returned by the `GetArticlesRss.aspx` page, and according to the querystring settings, it will return the "*n*" most recent entries for a specific category, or for any category ("*n*" is a value specified in `web.config`, as explained in the configuration module design). Per standard convention, we'll use the orange "RSS" image icon as a link to the `GetArticlesRss.aspx` page.

Once you have an RSS feed for your site, you can also consume the feed on this site itself, on the home page, to provide a list of articles! The `ArticleListing.ascx` user control we already discussed is good for a page whose only purpose is to list articles, but it's too heavy for the home page. On the home page you don't need details such as the location, the rating, and other information. The new article's title and the abstract is enough—when users click on the title, they will be redirected to the page with the whole article, according to the link entry for that article in the RSS feed. We'll build our own RSS reader user control to consume our own RSS feed. The control will be generic, so that it will be able to consume RSS feeds from other sources as well, such as the site forum's RSS, the products RSS, or some other external RSS feeds. Its public properties are listed in the following table:

Property	Description
RssUrl	Full URL of the RSS feed
Title	Title to be displayed
MoreUrl	URL of a page with the full listing of items (versus the last "n" items returned by the RSS items). In the case of the articles module, this will be the URL for the BrowseArticles.aspx page.
MoreText	Text used for the link pointing to MoreUrl

The only question left is how you can take the XML of the RSS feed and transform it into HTML to be shown on the page. Here are two possible solutions:

❑ Use an XSL stylesheet to apply to the XML content, and use an XSLT transform to write the templates that define how to extract the content from the XML and represent it with HTML.

❑ Dynamically build a `DataTable` with columns for the title, author, description, and the other `<item>`'s elements. Then fill the `DataTable` with the data read from the RSS feed, and use it as the data source for a `Repeater`, `DataList`, or other template-based control.

Personally, I strongly prefer the latter option, mostly because I find it much faster to change the template of a `Repeater` rather than to change the template in an XSL file. Additionally, with a `DataTable` I can easily add calculated columns, apply filters and sorting, and merge feeds coming from different sources (consider the case where you have multiple blogs or sources of articles and want to show their RSS feeds in a single box, with all items merged together and sorted by date). The `DataTable` approach is more flexible and easier to work with.

The Need for Security

The articles manager module is basically divided into two parts:

❑ The administration section allows the webmaster, or another designated individual, to add, delete, or edit the categories, publish articles, and moderate comments.

❑ The end-user section has pages to navigate through the categories, read the articles, rate an article or post feedback, and display the headlines on the home page.

Obviously, different pages may have different security constraints: An administration page should not be accessible by end users, and an article with the `OnlyForMembers` flag set should not be accessible by the anonymous users (users who aren't logged in). In the previous chapter, we developed a very flexible module that allows us to administer the registered users, read or edit their profile, and dynamically assign them to certain roles. For the articles manager module we will need the following roles:

- ❑ **Administrators and Editors:** These users have full control over the articles system. They can add, edit, or delete categories, approve and publish articles, and moderate comments. Only a very few people should belong to this role. (Note that Administrators also have full rights over the user management system, and all the other modules of the site, so it might be wise if only a single individual has this role.)

- ❑ **Contributors:** These users can submit their own articles, but they won't be published until an administrator or editor approves them. You could give this permission to many users if you want to gather as much content as possible, or just to a selected group of people otherwise.

Enforcing these security rules is a simple task, as you've learned in the previous chapter. In many cases it suffices to protect an entire page against unauthorized users by writing some settings in that page's folder's `web.config` file. Settings done in a configuration file are called *declarative coding*, and settings made with C# source code are called *imperative coding*. I favor declarative coding because it's easier to modify without recompiling source code, but in some more complex cases you have to perform some security checks directly from C# code. An example is the `AddEditArticle.aspx` page, which is used to post a new article or edit an existing one. The first action (post) is available to Contributors and upper roles, while the second (edit) is available only to Editors and Administrators. When the page loads you must understand in which mode the page is being loaded, according to some querystring settings, and check the user's roles accordingly.

Solution

In coding the solution, we'll follow the same path we used in the "Design" section: from database tables and stored procedure creation, to the implementation of security, passing through the DAL, BLL, and lastly the user interface.

The Database Solution

Creating the database tables is straightforward with Visual Studio's integrated Server Explorer and database manager, so we won't cover it here. You can refer to the tables in the "Design" section to see all the settings for each field. In the downloadable code file for this book, you will find the complete DB ready to go. Instead, here you'll create relationships between the tables and write some stored procedures.

Relationships Between the Tables

You create a new diagram from the Server Explorer: Drill down from Data Connections to your database (if you don't see your database you can add it as a new Data Connection), and then Database Diagrams. Right-click on Database Diagrams and select Add New Diagram. By following the wizard, you can add the `tbh_Categories`, `tbh_Articles`, and `tbh_Comments` tables to your diagram. As soon as the three tables are added to the underlying window, Server Explorer should recognize a relationship between `tbh_Categories` and `tbh_Articles`, and between `tbh_Articles` and `tbh_Comments`, and automatically create a parent-child relationship between them over the correct fields. However, if it does not, click on the `tbh_Articles'` `CategoryID` field and drag and drop the icons that appear over the `tbh_Categories` table. Once you release the button, a dialog with the relationship's properties appears, and you can ensure that the foreign key is the `tbh_Articles'` `CategoryID` field, while the primary key is `tbh_Categories'` `CategoryID`. Once the connection is set up, you also have to ensure that when a category record is deleted or updated, the action is cascaded to the child table too. To do this, select the connection, go to the Properties window (just press F4), and set the Delete Rule and Update Rule settings to Cascade, as shown in Figure 5-5.

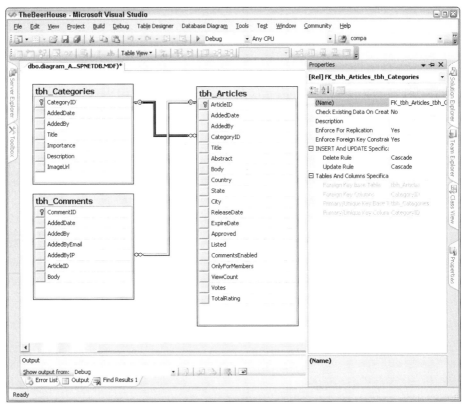

Figure 5-5

The `Update Rule = Cascade` option ensures that if you change the `CategoryID` primary key in the `tbh_Categories` table, this change is propagated to the foreign keys in the `tbh_Articles` table. The primary key should never be changed, as it is an identity and the administration pages won't allow you to change it. The `Delete Rule = Cascade` option ensures that if you delete a category, all the related articles are deleted as well. This means you won't have to delete the child articles from the stored procedure that deletes a category because they will be deleted automatically. This option is very important and must be checked, because if you forget it you'll end up with a database filled with unreachable articles because the parent category no longer exists!

Now you have to create a relationship between `tbh_Comments` and `tbh_Articles`, based on the `ArticleID` field of both tables. As before, click the `tbh_Comments'` `ArticleID` field, drag and drop the icon over the `tbh_Articles` table and complete the Properties dialog as before. When you're done with the diagram, go up to the tab, right-click on it, and save the diagram. Make sure you let it change your tables as specified in the diagram.

Creating the Stored Procedures

This section presents the code for some stored procedures. It covers a representative sample of the procedures, instead of every one, because the code is very similar whether you add, edit, or delete a category or article. The stored procedures that work with the articles are more complex than the respective procedures that manage the categories, because they have to join two tables, they have more parameters, and they support pagination, so these are the ones covered here.

tbh_Articles_InsertArticle

The following code inserts a new row in the `tbh_Articles` table and returns the ID of the added row through the `output` parameter:

```
CREATE PROCEDURE dbo.tbh_Articles_InsertArticle
(
    @AddedDate        datetime,
    @AddedBy          nvarchar(256),
    @CategoryID       int,
    @Title            nvarchar(256),
    @Abstract         nvarchar(4000),
    @Body             ntext,
    @Country          nvarchar(256),
    @State            nvarchar(256),
    @City             nvarchar(256),
    @ReleaseDate      datetime,
    @ExpireDate       datetime,
    @Approved         bit,
    @Listed           bit,
    @CommentsEnabled  bit,
    @OnlyForMembers   bit,
    @ArticleID        int OUTPUT
)
AS
SET NOCOUNT ON

INSERT INTO tbh_Articles
    (AddedDate, AddedBy, CategoryID, Title, Abstract, Body, Country, State, City,
        ReleaseDate, ExpireDate, Approved, Listed, CommentsEnabled, OnlyForMembers)
    VALUES (@AddedDate, @AddedBy, @CategoryID, @Title, @Abstract, @Body, @Country,
        @State, @City, @ReleaseDate, @ExpireDate, @Approved, @Listed,
        @CommentsEnabled, @OnlyForMembers)

SET @ArticleID = scope_identity()
```

The procedure is pretty simple, but a couple of details are worth underlining. The first is that I'm using the `scope_identity()` function to retrieve the last ID inserted into the table, instead of the `IDENTITY` system function. `IDENTITY` is probably more popular but it has a problem: It returns the last ID generated

210

in the current connection, but not necessarily in the current scope (where the scope is the stored procedure in this case). That is, it could return the ID of a record generated by a trigger that runs on the same connection, and this is *not* what we want! If we use `scope_identity`, we get the ID of the last record created in the current scope, which *is* what we want.

The other detail is the use of the SET NOCOUNT ON statement, to stop SQL Server from indicating the number of rows affected by the T-SQL statements as part of the result. When running INSERTs or SELECTs this value is typically not needed, so if you avoid retrieving it you'll improve performance a bit. However, the row count is useful when running UPDATE statements, because the code on the client computer (typically your C# program on the web server) can examine the number of rows affected to determine whether the stored procedure actually updated the proper number of rows you expected it to update.

tbh_Articles_UpdateArticle

This procedure updates many fields of a row, except for the ID, of course, and the count-related fields such as `ViewCount`, `Votes` and `TotalRating`, because they are not supposed to be updated directly by the editor from the Edit Article page:

```
CREATE PROCEDURE dbo.tbh_Articles_UpdateArticle
(
    @ArticleID          int,
    @CategoryID         int,
    @Title              nvarchar(256),
    @Abstract           nvarchar(4000),
    @Body               ntext,
    @Country            nvarchar(256),
    @State              nvarchar(256),
    @City               nvarchar(256),
    @ReleaseDate        datetime,
    @ExpireDate         datetime,
    @Approved           bit,
    @Listed             bit,
    @CommentsEnabled    bit,
    @OnlyForMembers     bit
)
AS

UPDATE tbh_Articles
    SET CategoryID = @CategoryID,
        Title = @Title,
        Abstract = @abstract,
        Body = @Body,
        Country = @Country,
        State = @State,
        City = @City,
        ReleaseDate = @ReleaseDate,
        ExpireDate = @ExpireDate,
        Approved = @Approved,
        Listed = @Listed,
        CommentsEnabled = @CommentsEnabled,
        OnlyForMembers = @OnlyForMembers
    WHERE ArticleID = @ArticleID
```

tbh_Articles_ApproveArticle

This procedure works exactly the same way as the last procedure, but the only field updated is the Approved field. This is useful when the administrator or editor only needs to approve an article, without having to supply the current values for all the other fields to the preceding procedure:

```
CREATE PROCEDURE dbo.tbh_Articles_ApproveArticle
(
 @ArticleID        int
)
AS


UPDATE tbh_Articles SET Approved = 1 WHERE ArticleID = @ArticleID
```

tbh_Articles_InsertVote

This procedure rates an article by incrementing the Votes field for the specified article, and at the same time it tallies the article's TotalRating field by adding in the new rating value:

```
CREATE PROCEDURE dbo.tbh_Articles_InsertVote
(
    @ArticleID  int,
    @Rating     smallint
)
AS


UPDATE tbh_Articles
    SET Votes = Votes + 1,
        TotalRating = TotalRating + @Rating
    WHERE ArticleID = @ArticleID
```

tbh_Articles_IncrementViewCount

This procedure increments the ViewCount field for the specified article:

```
CREATE PROCEDURE dbo.tbh_Articles_IncrementViewCount
(
    @ArticleID  int
)
AS


UPDATE tbh_Articles SET ViewCount = ViewCount + 1 WHERE ArticleID = @ArticleID
```

tbh_Articles_DeleteArticle

This is the easiest procedure: It just deletes the row with the specified ArticleID:

```
CREATE PROCEDURE dbo.tbh_Articles_DeleteArticle
(
 @ArticleID int
)
AS


DELETE tbh_Articles WHERE ArticleID = @ArticleID
```

tbh_Articles_GetArticleByID

This procedure returns all fields of the specified article. It joins the tbh_Articles and tbh_Categories tables so that it can also retrieve the title of the parent category:

```
CREATE PROCEDURE dbo.tbh_Articles_GetArticleByID
(
    @ArticleID  int
)
AS
SET NOCOUNT ON

SELECT tbh_Articles.ArticleID, tbh_Articles.AddedDate, tbh_Articles.AddedBy,
    tbh_Articles.CategoryID, tbh_Articles.Title, tbh_Articles.Abstract,
    tbh_Articles.Body, tbh_Articles.Country, tbh_Articles.State, tbh_Articles.City,
    tbh_Articles.ReleaseDate, tbh_Articles.ExpireDate, tbh_Articles.Approved,
    tbh_Articles.Listed, tbh_Articles.CommentsEnabled, tbh_Articles.OnlyForMembers,
    tbh_Articles.ViewCount, tbh_Articles.Votes, tbh_Articles.TotalRating,
    tbh_Categories.Title AS CategoryTitle
FROM tbh_Articles INNER JOIN
    tbh_Categories ON tbh_Articles.CategoryID = tbh_Categories.CategoryID
WHERE ArticleID = @ArticleID
```

tbh_Articles_GetArticles

The fun starts here! This procedure returns a "virtual page" of articles, from any category — the page index and page size values are input parameters. Before getting into the code for this procedure I want to explain the old way we implemented this type of functionality using SQL Server 2000. In the first edition of this book we used custom pagination for the forums module, and we implemented it by using one of the various techniques available at that time: temporary tables. You would first create a temporary table, with the ArticleID field from the tbh_Articles table, plus a new ID column that you would declare as IDENTITY, so that its value is automatically set with an auto-increment number for each record you add. Then you would insert into the temporary #TempArticles table the ArticleID values of all records from tbh_Articles. Finally, you would do a SELECT on the temporary table joined with the tbh_Articles table, making the filter on the temporary table's ID field. The #TempArticles table with the IDENTITY ID column was necessary because you needed a column whose IDs would go from 1 to the total number of records, without holes in the middle. You could not have used the ArticleID column directly to do this because you may have had some deleted records. Following is a sample implementation that we might have used following this approach:

```
CREATE PROCEDURE dbo.tbh_Articles_GetArticles
(
    @PageIndex  int,
    @PageSize   int
)
AS
SET NOCOUNT ON

-- create a temporary table
CREATE TABLE #TempArticles
(
    ID   int   IDENTITY(1,1),
    ArticleID   int
```

```
)

-- populate the temporary table
INSERT INTO #TempArticles (ArticleID)
    SELECT ArticleID FROM tbh_Articles ORDER BY ReleaseDate DESC

-- get a page of records from the temporary table,
-- and join them with the real table
SELECT ID, tbh_Articles.*
    FROM #TempArticles INNER JOIN tbh_Articles
        ON tbh_Articles.ArticleID = #TempArticles.ArticleID
    WHERE ID BETWEEN
        (@PageIndex*@PageSize+1) AND ((@PageIndex+1)*@PageSize)
```

This technique is still my favorite choice when working with SQL Server 2000 databases, but in SQL Server 2005 (including the free Express Edition) there is a much simpler solution that leverages the new ROW_NUMBER() function. As its name suggests, it returns a consecutive number sequence, starting from 1, which provides a unique number returned by each row of an ordered query. You can use it to add a calculated RowNum field to a SELECT statement, and then select all rows whose calculated RowNum is between the lower and upper bound of the specified page. Following is the complete stored procedure using this new ROW_NUMBER() function:

```
CREATE PROCEDURE dbo.tbh_Articles_GetArticles
(
    @PageIndex  int,
    @PageSize   int
)
AS
SET NOCOUNT ON

SELECT * FROM
(
    SELECT tbh_Articles.ArticleID, tbh_Articles.AddedDate, tbh_Articles.AddedBy,
        tbh_Articles.CategoryID, tbh_Articles.Title, tbh_Articles.Abstract,
        tbh_Articles.Body, tbh_Articles.Country, tbh_Articles.State,
        tbh_Articles.City, tbh_Articles.ReleaseDate, tbh_Articles.ExpireDate,
        tbh_Articles.Approved, tbh_Articles.Listed, tbh_Articles.CommentsEnabled,
        tbh_Articles.OnlyForMembers, tbh_Articles.ViewCount, tbh_Articles.Votes,
        tbh_Articles.TotalRating, tbh_Categories.Title AS CategoryTitle,
        ROW_NUMBER() OVER (ORDER BY ReleaseDate DESC) AS RowNum
    FROM tbh_Articles INNER JOIN
        tbh_Categories ON tbh_Articles.CategoryID = tbh_Categories.CategoryID
) Articles
    WHERE Articles.RowNum BETWEEN
        (@PageIndex*@PageSize+1) AND ((@PageIndex+1)*@PageSize)
    ORDER BY ReleaseDate DESC
```

You might not be familiar with the usage of a SELECT statement within the FROM clause of an outer SELECT statement — this is called an *in-line view* and it's a special kind of subquery; it can be thought of as being an automatically created temporary table named Articles. The ROW_NUMBER() function is being used in this inner query, and it is assigned a column alias named RowNum. This RowNum alias is then referenced in the outer query's WHERE clause. The ORDER BY specification in the ROW_NUMBER()

function's OVER clause specifies the sorting criteria for the inner query, and this must match the ORDER BY clause in the outer query. The rows in this case are always sorted by ReleaseDate in descending order (i.e., from the newest to the oldest). This syntax seems a little odd at first, but it's a very efficient way to handle paging, and it's much easier to implement than the older techniques.

tbh_Articles_GetArticleCount

This procedure simply returns the total number of rows in the tbh_Articles table. This count is needed by our pagination code because the grid control, which will be used in the user interface, must know how many items there are so it can correctly show the links to navigate through the pages of the resultset:

```
CREATE PROCEDURE dbo.tbh_Articles_GetArticleCount
AS
SET NOCOUNT ON

SELECT COUNT(*) FROM tbh_Articles
```

tbh_Articles_GetPublishedArticlesByCategory

This procedure returns a page of published articles from a specific category. The code for the pagination is the same as that just shown, but here we're adding filters to include only articles from a specific category: approved, listed, and those for which the current date is between the ReleaseDate and ExpireDate:

```
CREATE PROCEDURE dbo.tbh_Articles_GetPublishedArticlesByCategory
(
    @CategoryID    int,
    @CurrentDate   datetime,
    @PageIndex     int,
    @PageSize      int
)
AS
SET NOCOUNT ON

SELECT * FROM
(
    SELECT tbh_Articles.ArticleID, tbh_Articles.AddedDate, tbh_Articles.AddedBy,
        tbh_Articles.CategoryID, tbh_Articles.Title, tbh_Articles.Abstract,
        tbh_Articles.Body, tbh_Articles.Country, tbh_Articles.State,
        tbh_Articles.City, tbh_Articles.ReleaseDate, tbh_Articles.ExpireDate,
        tbh_Articles.Approved, tbh_Articles.Listed, tbh_Articles.CommentsEnabled,
        tbh_Articles.OnlyForMembers, tbh_Articles.ViewCount, tbh_Articles.Votes,
        tbh_Articles.TotalRating, tbh_Categories.Title AS CategoryTitle,
        ROW_NUMBER() OVER (ORDER BY ReleaseDate DESC) AS RowNum
        FROM tbh_Articles INNER JOIN
            tbh_Categories ON tbh_Articles.CategoryID = tbh_Categories.CategoryID
        WHERE Approved = 1 AND Listed = 1 AND
            ReleaseDate <= @CurrentDate AND ExpireDate > @CurrentDate
            AND tbh_Articles.CategoryID = @CategoryID
) Articles
    WHERE Articles.RowNum BETWEEN
        (@PageIndex*@PageSize+1) AND ((@PageIndex+1)*@PageSize)
    ORDER BY ReleaseDate DESC
```

This is the procedure with the most parameters, and thus is the most complex. We're passing the current date to the stored procedure as a parameter. You might think that this wouldn't be necessary, as you can easily get the current date using the T-SQL GETDATE() function. That's true, but the function would return the database server's current date, which may be different from the front-end's or the business logic server's date. We're interested in the current date of the server on which the application runs (typically the web server), and therefore it is safer to retrieve the date on that server and pass it as an input to the stored procedure. This is also handy in cases where an administrator or editor might want to use a future date as the current date to see how the site would look on that day (for example: Will the articles be published correctly on a specific date? Will other articles be retired after a specific date?). This will not be implemented in the proposed solution, but it can be a useful enhancement you might want to consider.

We also need the tbh_Articles_GetArticlesByCategory and tbh_Articles_GetPublished Articles procedures, but they are very similar to this procedure and tbh_Articles_GetArticles, so I won't show the code here. The full code is provided in the code download file for this book.

tbh_Articles_GetPublishedArticleCountByCategory

This procedure counts how many published articles exist in a specific category:

```
CREATE PROCEDURE dbo.tbh_Articles_GetPublishedArticleCountByCategory
(
    @CategoryID     int,
    @CurrentDate    datetime
)
AS
SET NOCOUNT ON

SELECT COUNT(*) FROM tbh_Articles
    WHERE CategoryID = @CategoryID AND Approved = 1 AND Listed = 1 AND
        ReleaseDate <= @CurrentDate AND ExpireDate > @CurrentDate
```

Implementing the Configuration Module

The ArticlesElement class is implemented in the ~/App_Code/ConfigSection.cs file. It descends from System.Configuration.ConfigurationElement and implements the properties that map the attributes of the <articles> element under the <theBeerHouse> custom section in the web.config file. The properties, listed and described in the "Design" section, are bound to the XML settings by means of the ConfigurationProperty attribute. Here's its code:

```
public class ArticlesElement : ConfigurationElement
{
    [ConfigurationProperty("connectionStringName")]
    public string ConnectionStringName
    {
        get { return (string)base["connectionStringName"]; }
        set { base["connectionStringName"] = value; }
    }

    public string ConnectionString
    {
```

```
        get
        {
            string connStringName = (string.IsNullOrEmpty(this.ConnectionStringName) ?
                Globals.Settings.DefaultConnectionStringName :
                this.ConnectionStringName );
            return WebConfigurationManager.ConnectionStrings[
                connStringName].ConnectionString;
        }
    }

    [ConfigurationProperty("providerType",
        DefaultValue = "MB.TheBeerHouse.DAL.SqlClient.SqlArticlesProvider")]
    public string ProviderType
    {
        get { return (string)base["providerType"]; }
        set { base["providerType"] = value; }
    }

    [ConfigurationProperty("pageSize", DefaultValue = "10")]
    public int PageSize
    {
        get { return (int)base["pageSize"]; }
        set { base["pageSize"] = value; }
    }

    [ConfigurationProperty("rssItems", DefaultValue = "5")]
    public int RssItems
    {
        get { return (int)base["rssItems"]; }
        set { base["rssItems"] = value; }
    }

    [ConfigurationProperty("enableCaching", DefaultValue = "true")]
    public bool EnableCaching
    {
        get { return (bool)base["enableCaching"]; }
        set { base["enableCaching"] = value; }
    }

    [ConfigurationProperty("cacheDuration")]
    public int CacheDuration
    {
        get
        {
            int duration = (int)base["cacheDuration"];
            return (duration > 0 ? duration : Globals.Settings.DefaultCacheDuration);
        }
        set { base["cacheDuration"] = value; }
    }
}
```

The ConnectionString property does not directly read/write a setting from/to the configuration file, but rather returns the value of the entry in the web.config's <connectionStrings> section identified by the name indicated in the <articles>'s connectionStringName attribute, or the <theBeerHouse>'s defaultConnectionStringName if the first setting is not present. The CacheDuration property returns the <articles>'s cacheDuration setting if it is greater than zero, or the <theBeerHouse>'s defaultCacheDuration setting otherwise.

DefaultConnectionStringName and DefaultCacheDuration are two new properties of the TheBeerHouseSection created in Chapter 3, now modified as shown here:

```
public class TheBeerHouseSection : ConfigurationSection
{
    [ConfigurationProperty("contactForm", IsRequired=true)]
    public ContactFormElement ContactForm
    {
        get { return (ContactFormElement) base["contactForm"]; }
    }

    [ConfigurationProperty("defaultConnectionStringName",
        DefaultValue = "LocalSqlServer")]
    public string DefaultConnectionStringName
    {
        get { return (string)base["defaultConnectionStringName"]; }
        set { base["connectionStdefaultConnectionStringNameringName"] = value; }
    }

    [ConfigurationProperty("defaultCacheDuration", DefaultValue = "600")]
    public int DefaultCacheDuration
    {
        get { return (int)base["defaultCacheDuration"]; }
        set { base["defaultCacheDuration"] = value; }
    }

    [ConfigurationProperty("articles", IsRequired = true)]
    public ArticlesElement Articles
    {
        get { return (ArticlesElement)base["articles"]; }
    }
}
```

The updated <theBeerHouse> section in web.config looks like this:

```
<theBeerHouse defaultConnectionStringName="LocalSqlServer">
    <articles providerType="MB.TheBeerHouse.DAL.SqlClient.SqlArticlesProvider"
        pageSize="10"
        rssItems="10"
        enableCaching="true"
        cacheDuration="300"
    />
    <contactForm mailTo="webmaster@effectivedotnet.com"/>
</theBeerHouse>
```

To read the settings from code you can do it this way: Globals.Settings.Articles.RssItems.

Implementing the Data Access Layer

Now that the DB is complete, we'll start writing the C# code for the data access layer. As mentioned earlier, we won't be putting this code in a separate assembly, as we did for the previous edition of the book. Instead, we'll be putting the C# files under the special App_Code folder so they will be compiled automatically when the application is run, thereby simplifying deployment and allowing us to take advantage of the new "Edit and Continue" functionality in Visual Studio 2005. For small to medium-size sites, this approach is very handy and practical. However, for larger enterprise-level sites it might be better to organize and compile this code separately so the UI developer can easily reference the separate assembly.

This section presents some classes of the DAL, but not all of them. The ArticleDetails, Category Details, and CommentDetails classes have the same structure, so there's no reason to show each one. The same goes for the methods to retrieve, insert, update, and delete records in the tbh_Articles, tbh_Categories and tbh_Comments tables. Therefore, as I did before for the stored procedure, I'll only show the code for the articles; you can refer to the code download for the rest of the code that deals with categories and comments.

The ArticleDetails Class

This class is implemented in the ~/App_Code/DAL/ArticleDetails.cs file. It wraps the article's entire data read from tbh_Articles. The constructor takes values as inputs, and saves them in the object's properties (the code that defines many properties is omitted for brevity's sake):

```csharp
namespace MB.TheBeerHouse.DAL
{
    public class ArticleDetails
    {
        public ArticleDetails() { }

        public ArticleDetails(int id, DateTime addedDate, string addedBy,
            int categoryID, string categoryTitle, string title, string artabstract,
            string body, string country, string state, string city,
            DateTime releaseDate, DateTime expireDate, bool approved,
            bool listed, bool commentsEnabled, bool onlyForMembers,
            int viewCount, int votes, int totalRating)
        {
            this.ID = id;
            this.AddedDate = addedDate;
            this.AddedBy = addedBy;
            this.CategoryID = categoryID;
            this.CategoryTitle = categoryTitle;
            this.Title = title;
            this.Abstract = artabstract;
            this.Body = body;
            this.Country = country;
            this.State = state;
            this.City = city;
            this.ReleaseDate = releaseDate;
            this.ExpireDate = expireDate;
            this.Approved = approved;
            this.Listed = listed;
```

```csharp
        this.CommentsEnabled = commentsEnabled;
        this.OnlyForMembers = onlyForMembers;
        this.ViewCount = viewCount;
        this.Votes = votes;
        this.TotalRating = totalRating;
    }

    private int _id = 0;
    public int ID
    {
        get { return _id;}
        set { _id = value;}
    }

    private DateTime _addedDate = DateTime.Now;
    public DateTime AddedDate
    {
        get { return _addedDate; }
        set { _addedDate = value; }
    }

    private string _addedBy = "";
    public string AddedBy
    {
        get { return _addedBy; }
        set { _addedBy = value; }
    }

    private int _categoryID = 0;
    public int CategoryID
    {
        get { return _categoryID; }
        set { _categoryID = value; }
    }

    private string _categoryTitle = "";
    public string CategoryTitle
    {
        get { return _categoryTitle; }
        set { _categoryTitle = value; }
    }

    private string _title = "";
    public string  Title
    {
        get { return _title; }
        set { _title = value; }
    }

    /* The code for all other properties would go here... */Country,
}
```

The ArticlesProvider Class

ArticlesProvider is an abstract class that defines a set of abstract CRUD (create, retrieve, update, delete) methods that will be implemented by a concrete class for a specific data store. We'll be using SQL Server as the data store, of course, but this abstract class has no knowledge of that. This class will be stored in the ~/App_Code/DAL/ArticlesProvider.cs file. It descends from the DataAccess class, and thus has ConnectionString, EnableCaching, and CacheDuration, which are set from within the constructor with the values read from the settings. Here's how it starts:

```
namespace MB.TheBeerHouse.DAL
{
    public abstract class ArticlesProvider : DataAccess
    {
        public ArticlesProvider()
        {
            this.ConnectionString = Globals.Settings.Articles.ConnectionString;
            this.EnableCaching = Globals.Settings.Articles.EnableCaching;
            this.CacheDuration = Globals.Settings.Articles.CacheDuration;
        }

        // methods that work with categories
        public abstract List<CategoryDetails> GetCategories();
        public abstract CategoryDetails GetCategoryByID(int categoryID);
        public abstract bool DeleteCategory(int categoryID);
        public abstract bool UpdateCategory(CategoryDetails category);
        public abstract int InsertCategory(CategoryDetails category);

        // methods that work with articles
        public abstract List<ArticleDetails> GetArticles(
            int pageIndex, int pageSize);
        public abstract List<ArticleDetails> GetArticles(
            int categoryID, int pageIndex, int pageSize);
        public abstract int GetArticleCount();
        public abstract int GetArticleCount(int categoryID);
        public abstract List<ArticleDetails> GetPublishedArticles(
            DateTime currentDate, int pageIndex, int pageSize);
        public abstract List<ArticleDetails> GetPublishedArticles(
            int categoryID, DateTime currentDate, int pageIndex, int pageSize);
        public abstract int GetPublishedArticleCount(DateTime currentDate);
        public abstract int GetPublishedArticleCount(
            int categoryID, DateTime currentDate);
        public abstract ArticleDetails GetArticleByID(int articleID);
        public abstract bool DeleteArticle(int articleID);
        public abstract bool UpdateArticle(ArticleDetails article);
        public abstract int InsertArticle(ArticleDetails article);
        public abstract bool ApproveArticle (int articleID);
        public abstract bool IncrementArticleViewCount(int articleID);
        public abstract bool RateArticle(int articleID, int rating);
        public abstract string GetArticleBody(int articleID);

        // methods that work with comments
        public abstract List<CommentDetails> GetComments(
            int pageIndex, int pageSize);
```

221

```
    public abstract List<CommentDetails> GetComments(
        int articleID, int pageIndex, int pageSize);
    public abstract int GetCommentCount();
    public abstract int GetCommentCount(int articleID);
    public abstract CommentDetails GetCommentByID(int commentID);
    public abstract bool DeleteComment(int commentID);
    public abstract bool UpdateComment(CommentDetails article);
    public abstract int InsertComment(CommentDetails article);
```

Besides the abstract methods, this `ArticlesProvider` class exposes some protected virtual methods that implement certain functionality that can be overridden in a subclass if the need arises. The `GetArticleFromReader` method reads the current record pointed to by the `DataReader` passed as an input, and uses its data to fill a new `ArticleDetails` object. An overloaded version allows us to specify whether the `tbh_Articles`' field must be read — remember that this field is not retrieved by the stored procedures that return multiple records (`GetArticles`, `GetArticlesByCategory`, etc.), so in those cases the method will be called with `false` as the second parameter:

```
    /// <summary>Returns a new ArticleDetails instance filled with the
    /// DataReader's current record data</summary>
    protected virtual ArticleDetails GetArticleFromReader(IDataReader reader)
    {
        return GetArticleFromReader(reader, true);
    }
    protected virtual ArticleDetails GetArticleFromReader(
        IDataReader reader, bool readBody)
    {
        ArticleDetails article = new ArticleDetails(
            (int)reader["ArticleID"],
            (DateTime)reader["AddedDate"],
            reader["AddedBy"].ToString(),
            (int)reader["CategoryID"],
            reader["CategoryTitle"].ToString(),
            reader["Title"].ToString(),
            reader["Abstract"].ToString(),
            null,
            reader["Country"].ToString(),
            reader["State"].ToString(),
            reader["City"].ToString(),
            (DateTime)reader["ReleaseDate"],
            (DateTime)reader["ExpireDate"],
            (bool)reader["Approved"],
            (bool)reader["Listed"],
            (bool)reader["CommentsEnabled"],
            (bool)reader["OnlyForMembers"],
            (int)reader["ViewCount"],
            (int)reader["Votes"],
            (int)reader["TotalRating"]);

        if (readBody)
            article.Body = reader["Body"].ToString();

        return article;
    }
```

Note that the first input parameter is of type `IDataReader`, a generalized interface that is implemented by `OleDbDataReader`, `SqlDataReader`, `OracleDataReader`, etc. This allows the concrete classes to pass their DB-specific `DataReader` objects to this method, which will operate with any of them because it knows that the specific reader object passed in will implement the methods of `IDataReader`. This style of coding is called *coding to an interface*. The second protected method, `GetArticleCollection FromReader`, returns a generic list collection of `ArticleDetails` objects filled with the data of all records in a `DataReader` — it does this by calling `GetArticleFromReader` until the `DataReader` has no more records:

```
/// <summary>Returns a collection of ArticleDetails objects with the
/// data read from the input DataReader</summary>
protected virtual List<ArticleDetails> GetArticleCollectionFromReader(
    IDataReader reader)
{
    return GetArticleCollectionFromReader(reader, true);
}
protected virtual List<ArticleDetails> GetArticleCollectionFromReader(
    IDataReader reader, bool readBody)
{
    List<ArticleDetails> articles = new List<ArticleDetails>();
    while (reader.Read())
        articles.Add(GetArticleFromReader(reader, readBody));
    return articles;
}
```

I won't show them here, but the code download has similar methods for filling `CategoryDetails` and `CommentDetails` objects from a `DataReader`. Finally, there is a static `Instance` property that uses reflection to create an instance of the concrete provider class indicated in the configuration file:

```
static private ArticlesProvider _instance = null;
/// <summary>
/// Returns an instance of the provider type specified in the config file
/// </summary>
static public ArticlesProvider Instance
{
    get
    {
        if (_instance == null)
            _instance = (ArticlesProvider)Activator.CreateInstance(
                Type.GetType(Globals.Settings.Articles.ProviderType));
        return _instance;
    }
}
```

Once the provider is created for the first time, it is saved in a static private property and won't be recreated again until the web application is shut down and restarted (for example, when IIS is stopped and restarted, or when the `web.config` file is changed).

The SqlArticlesProvider Class

This class, implemented in the file `~/App_Code/DAL/SqlClient/SqlArticlesProvider.cs`, provides the DAL code specific to SQL Server. Some of the stored procedures that will be called here use

SQL Server 2005–specific functions, such as the ROW_NUMBER() windowing function introduced earlier. However, you can change those procedures to use T-SQL code that is compatible with SQL Server 2000 if desired. One of the advantages of using stored procedures is that you can change their code later without touching the C#, which would require recompilation and redeployment of some DLLs.

All the code of this provider is pretty simple, as there is basically one method for each of the stored procedures designed and implemented earlier. I'll show you a few of the methods related to articles; you can study the downloadable code for the rest. The GetArticles method presented below illustrates the general pattern:

```
namespace MB.TheBeerHouse.DAL.SqlClient
{
    public class SqlArticlesProvider : ArticlesProvider
    {
        /// <summary>
        /// Retrieves all articles for the specified category
        /// </summary>
        public override List<ArticleDetails> GetArticles(
            int categoryID, int pageIndex, int pageSize)
        {
            using (SqlConnection cn = new SqlConnection(this.ConnectionString))
            {
                SqlCommand cmd = new SqlCommand(
                    "tbh_Articles_GetArticlesByCategory", cn);
                cmd.Parameters.Add("@CategoryID", SqlDbType.Int).Value = categoryID;
                cmd.Parameters.Add("@PageIndex", SqlDbType.Int).Value = pageIndex;
                cmd.Parameters.Add("@PageSize", SqlDbType.Int).Value = pageSize;
                cmd.CommandType = CommandType.StoredProcedure;
                cn.Open();
                return GetArticleCollectionFromReader(ExecuteReader(cmd), false);
            }
        }
    }
```

The SqlConnection class implements the IDisposable interface, which means that it provides the Dispose method that closes the connection if it is open. The connection object in this method is created within a using statement, so that it is automatically disposed when the block ends, avoiding the need to manually call Dispose. This ensures that Dispose will always be called, even when an exception is thrown, which prevents the possibility of leaving a connection open inadvertently. Inside the using block we create a SqlCommand object that references a stored procedure, fill its parameters, and execute it by using the DataAccess base class' ExecuteReader method. The resulting SqlDataReader is passed to the ArticlesProvider base class' GetArticleCollectionFromReader method implemented earlier, so that the records read by the DataReader are consumed to create a list of ArticleDetails to return to the caller; you pass false as second parameters, so that the article's body is not read.

> Remember to explicitly set the command's CommandType property to CommandType .StoredProcedure when you execute a stored procedure. If you don't, the code will work anyway, but the command text will first be interpreted as SQL text, that will fail, and then it will be re-executed as a stored procedure name. With the explicit setting, you avoid a wasted attempt to run it as a SQL statement, and therefore the execution speed will be a bit faster.

The method that returns a single `ArticleDetails` object is similar to the method returning a collection. The difference is that the `DataReader` returned by executing the command is passed to the base class' `GetArticleFromReader` method, instead of to `GetArticleCollectionFromReader`. It also moves the cursor ahead one position and confirms that the reader actually has a record; otherwise, it just returns null:

```
/// <summary>
/// Retrieves the article with the specified ID
/// </summary>
public override ArticleDetails GetArticleByID(int articleID)
{
    using (SqlConnection cn = new SqlConnection(this.ConnectionString))
    {
        SqlCommand cmd = new SqlCommand("tbh_Articles_GetArticleByID", cn);
        cmd.CommandType = CommandType.StoredProcedure;
        cmd.Parameters.Add("@ArticleID", SqlDbType.Int).Value = articleID;
        cn.Open();
        IDataReader reader = ExecuteReader(cmd, CommandBehavior.SingleRow);
        if (reader.Read())
            return GetArticleFromReader(reader, true);
        else
            return null;
    }
}
```

Methods that retrieve and return a single field have a similar structure, but use `ExecuteScalar` instead of `ExecuteReader`, and cast the returned object to the expected type. For example, here's how to execute the `tbh_Articles_GetArticleCount` stored procedure that returns an integer, and `tbh_Articles_GetArticleBody` that returns a string:

```
/// <summary>
/// Returns the total number of articles for the specified category
/// </summary>
public override int GetArticleCount(int categoryID)
{
    using (SqlConnection cn = new SqlConnection(this.ConnectionString))
    {
        SqlCommand cmd = new SqlCommand(
            "tbh_Articles_GetArticleCountByCategory", cn);
        cmd.CommandType = CommandType.StoredProcedure;
        cmd.Parameters.Add("@CategoryID", SqlDbType.Int).Value = categoryID;
        cn.Open();
        return (int)ExecuteScalar(cmd);
    }
}


/// <summary>
/// Retrieves the body for the article with the specified ID
/// </summary>
public override string GetArticleBody(int articleID)
{
    using (SqlConnection cn = new SqlConnection(this.ConnectionString))
    {
```

```
            SqlCommand cmd = new SqlCommand("tbh_Articles_GetArticleBody", cn);
            cmd.CommandType = CommandType.StoredProcedure;
            cmd.Parameters.Add("@ArticleID", SqlDbType.Int).Value = articleID;
            cn.Open();
            return (string)ExecuteScalar(cmd);
        }
    }
```

Methods that delete or update a record return a Boolean value indicating whether at least one record was actually affected by the operation. To do that, they check the value returned by the ExecuteNonQuery method. Here are a couple of examples, UpdateArticle and DeleteArticle, but similar code would be used for methods such as RateArticle, ApproveArticle, IncrementArticleViewCount, and others:

```
/// <summary>
/// Updates an article
/// </summary>
public override bool UpdateArticle(ArticleDetails article)
{
    using (SqlConnection cn = new SqlConnection(this.ConnectionString))
    {
        SqlCommand cmd = new SqlCommand("tbh_Articles_UpdateArticle", cn);
        cmd.CommandType = CommandType.StoredProcedure;
        cmd.Parameters.Add("@ArticleID", SqlDbType.Int).Value = article.ID;
        cmd.Parameters.Add("@CategoryID", SqlDbType.Int).Value =
            article.CategoryID;
        cmd.Parameters.Add("@Title", SqlDbType.NVarChar).Value = article.Title;
        cmd.Parameters.Add("@Abstract", SqlDbType.NVarChar).Value =
            article.Abstract;
        cmd.Parameters.Add("@Body", SqlDbType.NVarChar).Value = article.Body;
        cmd.Parameters.Add("@Country", SqlDbType.NVarChar).Value =
            article.Country;
        cmd.Parameters.Add("@State", SqlDbType.NVarChar).Value = article.State;
        cmd.Parameters.Add("@City", SqlDbType.NVarChar).Value = article.City;
        cmd.Parameters.Add("@ReleaseDate", SqlDbType.DateTime).Value =
            article.ReleaseDate;
        cmd.Parameters.Add("@ExpireDate", SqlDbType.DateTime).Value =
            article.ExpireDate;
        cmd.Parameters.Add("@Approved", SqlDbType.Bit).Value =
            article.Approved;
        cmd.Parameters.Add("@Listed", SqlDbType.Bit).Value = article.Listed;
        cmd.Parameters.Add("@CommentsEnabled", SqlDbType.Bit).Value =
            article.CommentsEnabled;
        cmd.Parameters.Add("@OnlyForMembers", SqlDbType.Bit).Value =
            article.OnlyForMembers;
        cn.Open();
        int ret = ExecuteNonQuery(cmd);
        return (ret == 1);
    }
}

/// <summary>
/// Deletes an article
/// </summary>
```

```
public override bool DeleteArticle(int articleID)
{
    using (SqlConnection cn = new SqlConnection(this.ConnectionString))
    {
        SqlCommand cmd = new SqlCommand("tbh_Articles_DeleteArticle", cn);
        cmd.CommandType = CommandType.StoredProcedure;
        cmd.Parameters.Add("@ArticleID", SqlDbType.Int).Value = articleID;
        cn.Open();
        int ret = ExecuteNonQuery(cmd);
        return (ret == 1);
    }
}
```

Finally, methods that insert a new record into the DB return the ID that was automatically created on the database server and returned by the stored procedure as an output parameter:

```
/// <summary>
/// Inserts a new article
/// </summary>
public override int InsertArticle(ArticleDetails article)
{
    using (SqlConnection cn = new SqlConnection(this.ConnectionString))
    {
        SqlCommand cmd = new SqlCommand("tbh_Articles_InsertArticle", cn);
        cmd.CommandType = CommandType.StoredProcedure;
        cmd.Parameters.Add("@AddedDate", SqlDbType.DateTime).Value =
            article.AddedDate;
        cmd.Parameters.Add("@AddedBy", SqlDbType.NVarChar).Value =
            article.AddedBy;
        cmd.Parameters.Add("@CategoryID", SqlDbType.Int).Value =
            article.CategoryID;
        cmd.Parameters.Add("@Title", SqlDbType.NVarChar).Value = article.Title;
        cmd.Parameters.Add("@Abstract", SqlDbType.NVarChar).Value =
            article.Abstract;
        cmd.Parameters.Add("@Body", SqlDbType.NVarChar).Value = article.Body;
        cmd.Parameters.Add("@Country", SqlDbType.NVarChar).Value =
            article.Country;
        cmd.Parameters.Add("@State", SqlDbType.NVarChar).Value = article.State;
        cmd.Parameters.Add("@City", SqlDbType.NVarChar).Value = article.City;
        cmd.Parameters.Add("@ReleaseDate", SqlDbType.DateTime).Value =
            article.ReleaseDate;
        cmd.Parameters.Add("@ExpireDate", SqlDbType.DateTime).Value =
            article.ExpireDate;
        cmd.Parameters.Add("@Approved", SqlDbType.Bit).Value =
            article.Approved;
        cmd.Parameters.Add("@Listed", SqlDbType.Bit).Value = article.Listed;
        cmd.Parameters.Add("@CommentsEnabled", SqlDbType.Bit).Value =
            article.CommentsEnabled;
        cmd.Parameters.Add("@OnlyForMembers", SqlDbType.Bit).Value =
            article.OnlyForMembers;
        cmd.Parameters.Add("@ArticleID", SqlDbType.Int).Direction =
            ParameterDirection.Output;
        cn.Open();
```

```
            int ret = ExecuteNonQuery(cmd);
            return (int)cmd.Parameters["@ArticleID"].Value;
        }
    }

    // other methods here...
    }
}
```

The SiteProvider Helper Class

To get a reference to the `Articles` provider indicated in the `web.config` file, you should specify `ArticlesProvider.Instance`. This is fine for one provider, but when you have other providers it would be better to have all of them grouped under a single "entry point." For this reason I've added a simple static helper class, implemented in `~/App_Code/DAL/SiteProvider.cs` and called `SiteProvider`, which exposes static methods to easily see and reference all current providers. Here's the code for this class:

```
namespace MB.TheBeerHouse.DAL
{
    public static class SiteProvider
    {
        public static ArticlesProvider Articles
        {
            get { return ArticlesProvider.Instance; }
        }
    }
}
```

It will be extended in subsequent chapters to support other providers, so that you'll be able to write `SiteProvider.Articles.{MethodName}`, `SiteProvider.Polls.{MethodName}`, and so on.

Implementing the Business Logic Layer

As we did for the data access classes, the business classes are created directly under the `~/App_Code` folder, in a BLL subfolder, so that they are automatically compiled at runtime, just like the pages. Business classes use the DAL classes to provide access to data and are mostly used to enforce validation rules, check constraints, and provide an object-oriented representation of the data and methods to work with it. Thus, the BLL serves as a mapping layer that makes the underlying relational database appear as objects to user interface code. Relational databases are inherently not object oriented, so this BLL provides a far more useful representation of data. Later you'll use the new `ObjectDataSource` to bind data from BLL classes to some template UI controls, such as the `GridView` and the `DataList`. This section presents the `Article` business class and describes some of the unique aspects of the other business classes.

The BaseArticle Class

The first business class we'll implement is `BaseArticle`, which is used as the base class for the `Article`, `Category`, and `Comment` classes. It descends from the `BizObject` class developed in Chapter 3, adding some article-specific properties. It starts by defining three properties, ID, AddedDate, and AddedBy, that are common to all business classes in the articles module:

```
namespace MB.TheBeerHouse.BLL.Articles
{
    public abstract class BaseArticle : BizObject
    {
        private int _id = 0;
        public int ID
        {
            get { return _id; }
            protected set { _id = value; }
        }
        private DateTime _addedDate = DateTime.Now;
        public DateTime AddedDate
        {
            get { return _addedDate; }
            protected set { _addedDate = value; }
        }

        private string _addedBy = "";
        public string AddedBy
        {
            get { return _addedBy; }
            protected set { _addedBy = value; }
        }
```

It then defines a Settings property that returns an instance of the ArticlesElement configuration class:

```
        protected static ArticlesElement Settings
        {
            get { return Globals.Settings.Articles; }
        }
```

Finally, it has a CacheData method that takes a key and a value, and if the value is not null it creates a new entry in the Cache object returned by the base class:

```
        protected static void CacheData(string key, object data)
        {
            if (Settings.EnableCaching && data != null)
            {
                BizObject.Cache.Insert(key, data, null,
                    DateTime.Now.AddSeconds(Settings.CacheDuration), TimeSpan.Zero);
            }
        }
    }
}
```

The CacheData method is located here instead of in the BizObject base class because it will cache the data only if caching is enabled, which is a module-specific setting (the forums module will have the EnableCaching setting as well, but it may have a different value).

The Article Class

This class is implemented in the ~/App_Code/BLL/Articles/Article.cs file. It starts with the declaration of the instance properties that wrap all data read from a record of the tbh_Articles table. The code that follows shows some of these properties (not all because they are very similar, and in most cases they just wrap a private field) and the constructor that initializes them:

```
namespace MB.TheBeerHouse.BLL.Articles
{
    public class Article : BaseArticle
    {
        public Article(int id, DateTime addedDate, string addedBy,
            int categoryID, string categoryTitle, string title, string artabstract,
            string body, string country, string state, string city,
            DateTime releaseDate, DateTime expireDate, bool approved,
            bool listed, bool commentsEnabled, bool onlyForMembers,
            int viewCount, int votes, int totalRating)
        {
            this.ID = id;
            this.AddedDate = addedDate;
            this.AddedBy = addedBy;
            this.CategoryID = categoryID;
            this.CategoryTitle = categoryTitle;
            this.Title = title;
            this.Abstract = artabstract;
            this.Body = body;
            this.Country = country;
            this.State = state;
            this.City = city;
            this.ReleaseDate = releaseDate;
            this.ExpireDate = expireDate;
            this.Approved = approved;
            this.Listed = listed;
            this.CommentsEnabled = commentsEnabled;
            this.OnlyForMembers = onlyForMembers;
            this.ViewCount = viewCount;
            this.Votes = votes;
            this.TotalRating = totalRating;
        }

        private int _categoryID = 0;
        public int CategoryID
        {
            get { return _categoryID; }
            set { _categoryID = value; }
        }

        private string _categoryTitle = "";
        public string CategoryTitle
        {
            get { return _categoryTitle; }
            private set { _categoryTitle = value; }
        }

        private string _title = "";
        public string Title
        {
            get { return _title; }
```

```
        set { _title = value; }
    }

    private string _abstract = "";
    public string Abstract
    {
        get { return _abstract; }
        set { _abstract = value; }
    }

    private string _body = null;
    public string Body
    {
        get
        {
            if (_body == null)
                _body = SiteProvider.Articles.GetArticleBody(this.ID);
            return _body;
        }
        set { _body = value; }
    }

    private DateTime _releaseDate = DateTime.Now;
    public DateTime ReleaseDate
    {
        get { return _releaseDate; }
        set { _releaseDate = value; }
    }

    private int _votes = 0;
    public int Votes
    {
        get { return _votes; }
        private set { _votes = value; }
    }

    private int _totalRating = 0;
    public int TotalRating
    {
        get { return _totalRating; }
        private set { _totalRating = value; }
    }
```

The Body property is interesting because it implements the lazy load pattern discussed earlier in this chapter. The Body field is retrieved by the getter function when the value of the Body property is requested by another class. Therefore, if the Body property is not accessed, this data will not be read from the database. Once it is requested and fetched, it will be held in memory in case it's requested again. If the private _body field is null it means that it wasn't loaded yet, so it's fetched by means of the DAL's GetArticleBody method and saved for possible use later. Thus, this Body property is providing lazy load and caching functionality, each of which enhance performance.

There are also a few calculated and read-only properties. The Location property returns a string with the full location of an event described in the article, consisting of the city, state/province, and country.

Remember that the `state` and `city` fields could include more names separated by a semicolon (typically variations and abbreviations of the state name, such as "New York", "NY", "New York", and so on). For this reason the fields are split, and the first token is used. Here's the complete code:

```csharp
public string Location
{
    get
    {
        string location = this.City.Split(';')[0];
        if (this.State.Length > 0)
        {
            if (location.Length > 0)
                location += ", ";
            location += this.State.Split(';')[0];
        }
        if (this.Country.Length > 0)
        {
            if (location.Length > 0)
                location += ", ";
            location += this.Country;
        }
        return location;
    }
}
```

The `AverageRating` calculated read-only property checks whether the total number of votes is 0; and the division is not done in that case to avoid a `DivideByZeroException`, and 0 is returned instead:

```csharp
public double AverageRating
{
    get
    {
        if (this.Votes >= 1)
            return ((double)this.TotalRating / (double)this.Votes);
        else
            return 0.0;
    }
}
```

The other calculated read-only property is `Published`, which returns `true` if the article is approved and the current date is between the specified `ReleaseDate` and `ExpireDate`:

```csharp
public bool Published
{
    get
    {
        return (this.Approved && this.ReleaseDate <= DateTime.Now &&
            this.ExpireDate > DateTime.Now);
    }
}
```

Other properties are `Category` and `Comments`, which also use the lazy load pattern to return, respectively, a full `Category` object representing the article's parent category, and the article's comments:

```
private Category _category = null;
public Category Category
{
   get
   {
      if (_category == null)
          _category = Category.GetCategoryByID(this.CategoryID);
      return _category;
   }
}

private List<Comment> _comments = null;
public List<Comment> Comments
{
   get
   {
      if (_comments==null)
          _comments = Comment.GetComments(this.ID, 0, Article.MAXROWS);
      return _comments;
   }
}
```

In addition to properties, the `Article` class also has a number of instance methods such as `Delete`, `Rate`, `Approve`, and so on, that delegate the work to the respective static methods (`DeleteArticle`, `RateArticle`, `ApproveArticle`, etc.) defined in the same class, which you'll see shortly. Here are a few examples:

```
public bool Delete()
{
   bool success = Article.DeleteArticle(this.ID);
   if (success) this.ID = 0;
   return success;
}

public bool Update()
{
   return Article.UpdateArticle(this.ID, this.CategoryID, this.Title,
       this.Abstract, this.Body, this.Country, this.State, this.City,
       this.ReleaseDate, this.ExpireDate, this.Approved, this.Listed,
       this.CommentsEnabled, this.OnlyForMembers);
}

public bool Approve()
{
   bool success = Article.ApproveArticle(this.ID);
   if (success) this.Approved = true;
   return success;
}

public bool IncrementViewCount()
{
   return Article.IncrementArticleViewCount(this.ID);
}
```

```
public bool Rate(int rating)
{
    return Article.RateArticle(this.ID, rating);
}
```

The rest of the code contains the static methods that use the DAL to retrieve, create, update, delete, rate, and approve an article. Let's first review a couple of overloads for the GetArticles method: one returns all articles for the specified category, and the other returns a page of articles for the specified category:

```
public static List<Article> GetArticles(int categoryID)
{
    return GetArticles(categoryID, 0, Article.MAXROWS);
}
public static List<Article> GetArticles(int categoryID,
    int startRowIndex, int maximumRows)
{
    if (categoryID <= 0)
        return GetArticles(startRowIndex, maximumRows);

    List<Article> articles = null;
    string key = "Articles_Articles_" + categoryID.ToString() +
        "_" + startRowIndex.ToString() + "_" + maximumRows.ToString();

    if (BaseArticle.Settings.EnableCaching && BizObject.Cache[key] != null)
    {
        articles = (List<Article>)BizObject.Cache[key];
    }
    else
    {
        List<ArticleDetails> recordset = SiteProvider.Articles.GetArticles(
            categoryID, GetPageIndex(startRowIndex, maximumRows), maximumRows);
        articles = GetArticleListFromArticleDetailsList(recordset);
        BaseArticle.CacheData(key, articles);
    }
    return articles;
}
```

The first version just forwards the call to the second version, passing 0 as the start index (business objects used by the ObjectDataSource are required to accept the start row index to support pagination, not the page index as the DAL and the stored procedures do), and a very large number (the maximum integer) as the page size. The second version actually contains the logic: If the input ID of the parent category is less than zero, then the call is forwarded to yet another version that takes no category ID and returns articles of any category. If caching is enabled and the pages of the article you are requesting are already in the cache, they are retrieved from there and returned. Otherwise, they are retrieved from the DB by means of a call to the DAL's GetArticles method, converted to a list of Article objects (the DAL method returns a list of ArticleDetails object), cached, and finally returned to the caller. Note that because the DAL method expects the page index, and not the index of the first record to retrieve, the BLL method's parameters are passed to the BizObject base class' GetPageIndex helper method for the conversion. Also note how the key for the cache entry is built: It is the sum of the module name (Articles), what you're going to retrieve (Articles), and all the input parameters—all joined with an underscore character. For example, the result may be something like Articles_Articles_4_30_10 (4 is the category ID, 30 is the starting row index, and 10 is the maximum rows, aka page size).

The conversion from a list of `ArticleDetails` to a list of `Article` objects is performed by the static private `GetArticleListFromArticleDetailsList` method, which in turn calls `GetArticleFrom ArticleDetails` for each object of the input `List`:

```
private static List<Article> GetArticleListFromArticleDetailsList(
   List<ArticleDetails> recordset)
{
   List<Article> articles = new List<Article>();
   foreach (ArticleDetails record in recordset)
      articles.Add(GetArticleFromArticleDetails(record));
   return articles;
}

private static Article GetArticleFromArticleDetails(ArticleDetails record)
{
   if (record == null)
      return null;
   else
   {
      return new Article(record.ID, record.AddedDate, record.AddedBy,
         record.CategoryID, record.CategoryTitle, record.Title,
         record.Abstract, record.Body, record.Country, record.State,
         record.City, record.ReleaseDate, record.ExpireDate,
         record.Approved, record.Listed, record.CommentsEnabled,
         record.OnlyForMembers, record.ViewCount, record.Votes,
         record.TotalRating);
   }
}
```

The `GetArticleCount` method returns the number of articles for a specific collection. Its structure is very similar to what you saw for `GetArticles`, including the use of caching:

```
public static int GetArticleCount(int categoryID)
{
   if (categoryID <= 0)
      return GetArticleCount();

   int articleCount = 0;
   string key = "Articles_ArticleCount_" + categoryID.ToString();

   if (BaseArticle.Settings.EnableCaching && BizObject.Cache[key] != null)
   {
      articleCount = (int)BizObject.Cache[key];
   }
   else
   {
      articleCount = SiteProvider.Articles.GetArticleCount(categoryID);
      BaseArticle.CacheData(key, articleCount);
   }
   return articleCount;
}
```

`GetArticleByID` is also very similar, but instead of calling `GetArticleListFromarticleDetailsList`, this time it calls `GetArticleFromArticleDetails` directly because there's a single object to convert:

```
public static Article GetArticleByID(int articleID)
{
    Article article = null;
    string key = "Articles_Article_" + articleID.ToString();

    if (BaseArticle.Settings.EnableCaching && BizObject.Cache[key] != null)
    {
        article = (Article)BizObject.Cache[key];
    }
    else
    {
        article = GetArticleFromArticleDetails(
            SiteProvider.Articles.GetArticleByID(articleID));
        BaseArticle.CacheData(key, article);
    }
    return article;
}
```

The InsertArticle method doesn't use caching because it doesn't retrieve and return data, but it has other peculiarities. First of all, it checks whether the current user belongs to the Administrators or Editors role, and if not it sets the Approved field to false. Then it checks whether the releaseDate and expireDate parameters are equal to the DateTime.MinValue, which would be the case if the respective textboxes in the administration user interface were left blank; in that case ReleaseDate is set to the current date, and ExpireDate is set to the DateTime's maximum value, so that in practice the article never expires (which is what the administrator intended when he left those fields blank). It then runs the DAL's InsertArticle method, and finally purges the Articles data from the cache, so that the next call to GetArticles will run a new query to fetch the record from the database. Here's the complete code:

```
public static int InsertArticle(int categoryID, string title,
    string Abstract, string body, string country, string state, string city,
    DateTime releaseDate, DateTime expireDate, bool approved, bool listed,
    bool commentsEnabled, bool onlyForMembers)
{
    // ensure that the "approved" option is false if the current user is not
    // an administrator or a editor (it may be a contributor for example)
    bool canApprove = (Article.CurrentUser.IsInRole("Administrators") ||
        Article.CurrentUser.IsInRole("Editors"));
    if (!canApprove)
        approved = false;

    title = BizObject.ConvertNullToEmptyString(title);
    Abstract = BizObject.ConvertNullToEmptyString(Abstract);
    body = BizObject.ConvertNullToEmptyString(body);
    country = BizObject.ConvertNullToEmptyString(country);
    state = BizObject.ConvertNullToEmptyString(state);
    city = BizObject.ConvertNullToEmptyString(city);

    if (releaseDate == DateTime.MinValue)
        releaseDate = DateTime.Now;
    if (expireDate == DateTime.MinValue)
        expireDate = DateTime.MaxValue;
```

```
        ArticleDetails record = new ArticleDetails(0, DateTime.Now,
            Article.CurrentUserName, categoryID, "", title, Abstract, body,
            country, state, city, releaseDate, expireDate,
            approved, listed, commentsEnabled, onlyForMembers, 0, 0, 0);
        int ret = SiteProvider.Articles.InsertArticle(record);

        BizObject.PurgeCacheItems("articles_article");
        return ret;
    }
```

Note that for string parameters the `BizObject`'s `ConvertNullToEmptyString` method is called, to ensure that they are converted to an empty string if they are `null` (otherwise the DAL method would fail). This could be done later from the user interface, by setting the `ConvertEmptyStringToNull` property of the `ObjectDataSource`'s insert parameter to `true`, so that an empty textbox will be read as an empty string and not `null`, as it is by default. However, I consider this to be more of a business rule, and I prefer to centralize it once in the business layer, instead of making sure that I set that parameter's property every time I use an `ObjectDataSource`.

The `UpdateArticle` method is similar, the only difference being that the DAL's `UpdateArticle` method is called instead of the `InsertArticle` method:

```
    public static bool UpdateArticle(int id, int categoryID,
        string title, string Abstract, string body, string country, string state,
        string city, DateTime releaseDate, DateTime expireDate, bool approved,
        bool listed, bool commentsEnabled, bool onlyForMembers)
    {
        title = BizObject.ConvertNullToEmptyString(title);
        Abstract = BizObject.ConvertNullToEmptyString(Abstract);
        body = BizObject.ConvertNullToEmptyString(body);
        country = BizObject.ConvertNullToEmptyString(country);
        state = BizObject.ConvertNullToEmptyString(state);
        city = BizObject.ConvertNullToEmptyString(city);

        if (releaseDate == DateTime.MinValue)
            releaseDate = DateTime.Now;
        if (expireDate == DateTime.MinValue)
            expireDate = DateTime.MaxValue;

        ArticleDetails record = new ArticleDetails(id, DateTime.Now, "",
            categoryID, "", title, Abstract, body, country, state, city,
            releaseDate, expireDate, approved, listed, commentsEnabled,
            onlyForMembers, 0, 0, 0);
        bool ret = SiteProvider.Articles.UpdateArticle(record);

        BizObject.PurgeCacheItems("articles_article_" + id.ToString());
        BizObject.PurgeCacheItems("articles_articles");              return ret;
    }
```

Other methods that update data in the `tbh_Articles` table are even simpler, as they just call their respective method in the DAL, and purge the current data from the cache. The cache is cleared to force a fetch of the newly updated data the next time it's requested. `DeleteArticle` and `ApproveArticle` do just that:

```
        public static bool DeleteArticle(int id)
        {
            bool ret = SiteProvider.Articles.DeleteArticle(id);
            new RecordDeletedEvent("article", id, null).Raise();
            BizObject.PurgeCacheItems("articles_article");
            return ret;
        }

        public static bool ApproveArticle(int id)
        {
            bool ret = SiteProvider.Articles.ApproveArticle(id);
            BizObject.PurgeCacheItems("articles_article_" + id.ToString());
            BizObject.PurgeCacheItems("articles_articles");
            return ret;
        }
```

Methods such as IncrementArticleViewCount and RateArticle call the DAL method to process the update, except that they don't clear the cache. It's only necessary to clear the cache when the underlying data held by the cache has changed:

```
        public static bool IncrementArticleViewCount(int id)
        {
            return SiteProvider.Articles.IncrementArticleViewCount(id);
        }

        public static bool RateArticle(int id, int rating)
        {
            return SiteProvider.Articles.RateArticle(id, rating);
        }

        // other static methods...
    }
}
```

The Category Class

The Category class (implemented in the file ~/App_Code/BLL/Articles/Category.cs) is not much different from the Article class, but it's shorter and simpler because it doesn't have as many wrapper properties and methods, no support for pagination (and thus fewer overloads), and nothing other than the basic CRUD methods. The most interesting properties are AllArticles and PublishedArticles, both of which use the lazy load pattern to retrieve the list of child articles. They use the Article's GetArticles static method, but they each use a different overload of it. PublishedArticles uses the overload that takes in a Boolean value indicating that you want to retrieve only published articles, and passes true:

```
    private List<Article> _allArticles = null;
    public List<Article> AllArticles
    {
        get
        {
            if (_allArticles == null)
                _allArticles = Article.GetArticles(this.ID, 0, Category.MAXROWS);
            return _allArticles;
        }
    }
```

```
private List<Article> _publishedArticles = null;
public List<Article> PublishedArticles
{
   get
   {
      if (_publishedArticles == null)
         _publishedArticles = Article.GetArticles(true, this.ID,
            0, Category.MAXROWS);
      return _publishedArticles;
   }
}
```

The Comment and CommentComparer Classes

The Comment class (implemented in the file ~/App_Code/BLL/Articles/Comment.cs) is quite simple so I won't show it here in its entirety. As for the properties, the only notable one is the calculated EncodedBody property, which encodes the HTML text returned by the plain Body property by means of the BizObject base class' EncodeText static method. Here they are:

```
private string _body = "";
public string Body
{
   get { return _body; }
   set { _body = value; }
}

public string EncodedBody
{
   get { return BizObject.EncodeText(this.Body); }
}
```

One of the overloaded GetComments methods that's called from the administration section returns the comments sorted from the newest to the oldest, and supports pagination. The UI code that lists comments below a particular article calls another GetComments overload that retrieves all comments for a specific article, and with no pagination support, and in that case they are sorted from oldest to newest. Let's look at the code for a couple of overloads that sort items from the newest to the oldest:

```
public static List<Comment> GetComments(int startRowIndex, int maximumRows)
{
   List<Comment> comments = null;
   string key = "Articles_Comments_" + startRowIndex.ToString() +
      "_" + maximumRows.ToString();

   if (BaseArticle.Settings.EnableCaching && BizObject.Cache[key] != null)
   {
      comments = (List<Comment>)BizObject.Cache[key];
   }
   else
   {
      List<CommentDetails> recordset = SiteProvider.Articles.GetComments(
      GetPageIndex(startRowIndex, maximumRows), maximumRows);
      comments = GetCommentListFromCommentDetailsList(recordset);
      BaseArticle.CacheData(key, comments);
   }
```

```
        return comments;
    }

    public static List<Comment> GetComments(int articleID,
        int startRowIndex, int maximumRows)
    {
        List<Comment> comments = null;
        string key = "Articles_Comments_" + articleID.ToString() + "_" +
            startRowIndex.ToString() + "_" + maximumRows.ToString();

        if (BaseArticle.Settings.EnableCaching && BizObject.Cache[key] != null)
        {
            comments = (List<Comment>)BizObject.Cache[key];
        }
        else
        {
            List<CommentDetails> recordset = SiteProvider.Articles.GetComments(articleID,
            GetPageIndex(startRowIndex, maximumRows), maximumRows);
            comments = GetCommentListFromCommentDetailsList(recordset);
            BaseArticle.CacheData(key, comments);
        }
        return comments;
    }
```

The final `GetComments` overload first retrieves the records from the second overload just shown, with 0 as start row index, and the maximum integer as page size, so that it retrieves all comments for an article. Next, it uses the `CommentComparer` class (that you'll see in a moment) to invert the order. Here's its code:

```
    public static List<Comment> GetComments(int articleID)
    {
        List<Comment> comments = GetComments(articleID, 0, Comment.MAXROWS);
        comments.Sort(new CommentComparer("AddedDate ASC"));
        return comments;
    }
```

The `CommentComparer` class takes the `sort` clause in the constructor method, and uses it later to determine which field it must compare two comments against. The code in the constructor method also checks whether the sort string ends with `"DESC"` and if so sets a `_reverse` field to `true`. Then, the `Compare` method compares two comments by delegating the comparison logic to `DateTime`'s or `String`'s `Compare` method (according to whether the comparison is being made against the `AddedDate` or `AddedBy` field), and if the `_reverse` field is `true` it inverts the result. The `Equals` method returns `true` if the two comments have the same ID. Here's the complete code:

```
    public class CommentComparer : IComparer<Comment>
    {
        private string _sortBy;
        private bool _reverse;

        public CommentComparer(string sortBy)
        {
            if (!string.IsNullOrEmpty(sortBy))
            {
```

```
                sortBy = sortBy.ToLower();
                _reverse = sortBy.EndsWith(" desc");
                _sortBy = sortBy.Replace(" desc", "").Replace(" asc", "");
        }
    }

    public int Compare(Comment x, Comment y)
    {
        int ret = 0;
        switch (_sortBy)
        {
            case "addeddate":
                ret = DateTime.Compare(x.AddedDate, y.AddedDate);
                break;
            case "addedby":
                ret = string.Compare(x.AddedBy, y.AddedBy,
                    StringComparison.InvariantCultureIgnoreCase);
                break;
        }
        return (ret * (_reverse ? -1 : 1));
    }

    public bool Equals(Comment x, Comment y)
    {
        return (x.ID == y.ID);
    }
}
```

Implementing the User Interface

The database design and the data access classes for the articles module are now complete, so it's time to code the user interface. We will use the business classes to retrieve and manage Article data from the DB. We'll start by developing the administration console, so that we can use it later to add and manage sample records when we code and test the UI for end users.

The ManageCategories.aspx Page

This page, located under the ~/Admin folder, allows the administrator and editors to add, delete, and edit article categories, as well as directly jump to the list of articles for a specific category. The screenshot of the page, shown in Figure 5-6, demonstrates what I'm talking about, and then you'll learn how to build it.

There's a GridView control that displays all the categories from the database (with the title, the description, and the graphical icon). Moreover, the icons on the very far right of the grid are, respectively, a HyperLink to the ManageArticles.aspx page, which lists the child articles of that category; a LinkButton to delete the category; and another one to edit it. When the pencil icon is clicked, the grid is not turned into edit mode as it was in the first edition of the book, but instead, the record is edited through the DetailsView box at the bottom of the page. This makes the page cleaner, and it doesn't mess with the layout if you need to edit more fields than those shown in Read mode. That is actually the case in this page, because the Importance field is not shown in the grid, but you can still edit it in the DetailsView.

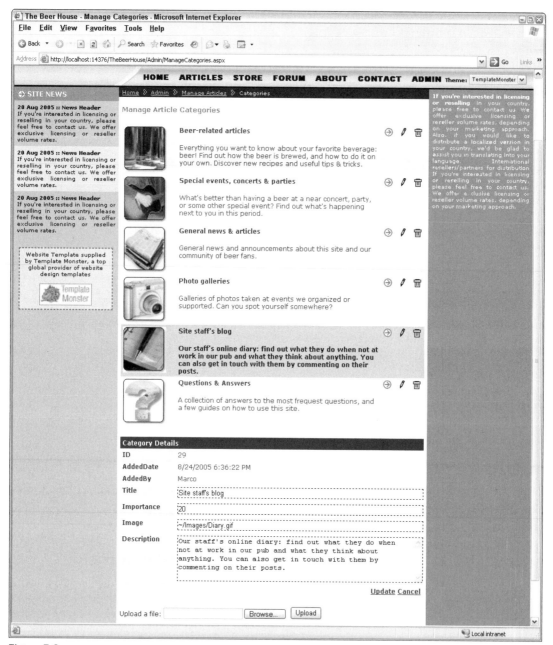

Figure 5-6

The DetailsView is also used to show additional fields, even if in read-only mode, such as ID, AddedDate, and AddedBy. Finally, it is also used to insert a new category — the insert mode is the default in this case, so it is used when the page loads, or if you click the Cancel command while you're editing a current category. At the very bottom of the page is a control used to upload a file, typically an image used to graphically represent a category.

Now we'll examine the page's source code piece-by-piece. The first step is to create the `ObjectDataSource` that will be the data source for the `GridView` control that displays the categories. You only need to define the `Select` and `Delete` methods, because the updates and the inserts will be done by the `DetailsView` control, which has a different `ObjectDataSource`:

```
<asp:ObjectDataSource ID="objAllCategories" runat="server"
    TypeName="MB.TheBeerHouse.BLL.Articles.Category"
    SelectMethod="GetCategories" DeleteMethod="DeleteCategory">
</asp:ObjectDataSource>
```

The declaration of the `GridView` is similar to what you might use for ASP.NET 1.1's `DataGrid`, in that it has a `<Columns>` section where you define its columns. In particular, it has the following fields:

❑ An `ImageField` to show the image whose URL is returned by the `Article`'s `ImageUrl`. This type of column is very convenient because you define everything in a single line. In ASP.NET 1.x you would have needed a `TemplateColumn` instead.

❑ A `TemplateField` to define a template column that shows the category's title and description.

❑ A `HyperLinkField` to create a link to `ManageArticles.aspx`, with the category's ID on the querystring, so that the page will retrieve it and display only that category's child articles.

❑ A `CommandField` of type `Select` that will be used to edit the category. We use the `Select` command instead of the `Edit` command because an `Edit` command would put that `GridView`'s row into edit mode, and that isn't what we want. Instead, we want to select (highlight) the row and have the `DetailsView` below enter the edit mode for the selected row.

❑ A `CommandField` of type `Delete`.

Of course, there are also some other `GridView` properties to set, the most important being the `DataSourceID` that hooks up the `ObjectDataSource` to the grid, and `DataKeyNames`, to specify that the `ID` field is the key field. Here is the `GridView`'s complete declaration:

```
<asp:GridView ID="gvwCategories" runat="server" AutoGenerateColumns="False"
    DataSourceID="objAllCategories" Width="100%" DataKeyNames="ID"
    OnRowDeleted="gvwCategories_RowDeleted" OnRowCreated="gvwCategories_RowCreated"
    OnSelectedIndexChanged="gvwCategories_SelectedIndexChanged" ShowHeader="false">
    <Columns>
        <asp:ImageField DataImageUrlField="ImageUrl">
            <ItemStyle Width="100px" />
        </asp:ImageField>
        <asp:TemplateField>
            <ItemTemplate>
                <div class="sectionsubtitle">
                <asp:Literal runat="server" ID="lblCatTitle"
                    Text='<%# Eval("Title") %>' />
                </div>
                <br />
                <asp:Literal runat="server" ID="lblDescription"
                    Text='<%# Eval("Description") %>' />
            </ItemTemplate>
        </asp:TemplateField>
        <asp:HyperLinkField
            Text="<img border='0' src='../Images/ArrowR.gif' alt='View articles' />"
```

```
            DataNavigateUrlFormatString="ManageArticles.aspx?ID={0}"
                DataNavigateUrlFields="ID">
            <ItemStyle HorizontalAlign="Center" Width="20px" />
        </asp:HyperLinkField>
        <asp:CommandField ButtonType="Image" SelectImageUrl="~/Images/Edit.gif"
            SelectText="Update category" ShowSelectButton="True">
            <ItemStyle HorizontalAlign="Center" Width="20px" />
        </asp:CommandField>
        <asp:CommandField ButtonType="Image" DeleteImageUrl="~/Images/Delete.gif"
            DeleteText="Delete category" ShowDeleteButton="True">
            <ItemStyle HorizontalAlign="Center" Width="20px" />
        </asp:CommandField>
    </Columns>
</asp:GridView>
```

There's a second `ObjectDataSource` used to handle the data retrieval, inserts, and updates from the bottom `DetailsView`. All parameters for the insert and update are automatically inferred from the `DetailsView`'s fields. The only specific parameter is the `category` ID for the `GetCategoryByID` `select` method, which is set to the `GridView`'s selected value (i.e., the key of the selected row):

```
<asp:ObjectDataSource ID="objCurrCategory" runat="server"
    TypeName="MB.TheBeerHouse.BLL.Articles.Category"
    InsertMethod="InsertCategory" SelectMethod="GetCategoryByID"
    UpdateMethod="UpdateCategory">
    <SelectParameters>
        <asp:ControlParameter ControlID="gvwCategories" Name="categoryID"
            PropertyName="SelectedValue" Type="Int32" />
    </SelectParameters>
</asp:ObjectDataSource>
```

The `DetailsView` control defines template fields for the `Title`, `Importance`, `ImageUrl`, and `Description` information, which are the fields that are not read-only. `TemplateFields` are usually better than an editable `BoundFields` because you typically need to validate input, and you can do that directly on the client side with some validators put into the `TemplateField`, which is better than doing the validation in the code-behind or in a business class:

```
<asp:DetailsView ID="dvwCategory" runat="server" AutoGenerateRows="False"
    DataSourceID="objCurrCategory" Height="50px" Width="50%"
    AutoGenerateEditButton="True" AutoGenerateInsertButton="True"
    HeaderText="Category Details" OnItemInserted="dvwCategory_ItemInserted"
    OnItemUpdated="dvwCategory_ItemUpdated" DataKeyNames="ID"
    OnItemCreated="dvwCategory_ItemCreated" DefaultMode="Insert"
    OnItemCommand="dvwCategory_ItemCommand">
    <FieldHeaderStyle Width="100px" />
    <Fields>
        <asp:BoundField DataField="ID" HeaderText="ID" ReadOnly="True"
            SortExpression="ID" InsertVisible="False" />
        <asp:BoundField DataField="AddedDate" HeaderText="AddedDate"
            InsertVisible="False" ReadOnly="True" SortExpression="AddedDate" />
        <asp:BoundField DataField="AddedBy" HeaderText="AddedBy"
            InsertVisible="False" ReadOnly="True" SortExpression="AddedBy" />
        <asp:TemplateField HeaderText="Title" SortExpression="Title">
            <ItemTemplate>
```

```
            <asp:Label ID="lblTitle" runat="server"
                Text='<%# Eval("Title") %>'></asp:Label>
        </ItemTemplate>
        <EditItemTemplate>
            <asp:TextBox ID="txtTitle" runat="server" Text='<%# Bind("Title") %>'
                MaxLength="256" Width="100%"></asp:TextBox>
            <asp:RequiredFieldValidator ID="valRequireTitle" runat="server"
                ControlToValidate="txtTitle" SetFocusOnError="true"
                Text="The Title field is required."
                ToolTip="The Title field is required." Display="Dynamic" />
        </EditItemTemplate>
    </asp:TemplateField>
    <asp:TemplateField HeaderText="Importance" SortExpression="Importance">
        <ItemTemplate>
            <asp:Label ID="lblImportance" runat="server"
                Text='<%# Eval("Importance") %>'></asp:Label>
        </ItemTemplate>
        <EditItemTemplate>
            <asp:TextBox ID="txtImportance" runat="server"
                Text='<%# Bind("Importance") %>' MaxLength="256"
                Width="100%"></asp:TextBox>
            <asp:RequiredFieldValidator ID="valRequireImportance" runat="server"
                ControlToValidate="txtImportance" SetFocusOnError="true"
                Text="The Importance field is required."
                ToolTip="The Importance field is required." Display="Dynamic" />
            <asp:CompareValidator ID="valInportanceType" runat="server"
                Operator="DataTypeCheck" Type="Integer"
                ControlToValidate="txtImportance"
                Text="The Importance must be an integer."
                ToolTip="The Importance must be an integer." Display="dynamic" />
        </EditItemTemplate>
    </asp:TemplateField>
    <asp:TemplateField HeaderText="Image" ConvertEmptyStringToNull="False">
        <ItemTemplate>
            <asp:Image ID="imgImage" runat="server"
                ImageUrl='<%# Eval("ImageUrl") %>'
                AlternateText='<%# Eval("Title") %>'
                Visible='<%# !string.IsNullOrEmpty(
                    DataBinder.Eval(Container.DataItem, "ImageUrl").ToString()) %>' />
        </ItemTemplate>
        <EditItemTemplate>
            <asp:TextBox ID="txtImageUrl" runat="server"
                Text='<%# Bind("ImageUrl") %>' MaxLength="256" Width="100%" />
        </EditItemTemplate>
    </asp:TemplateField>
    <asp:TemplateField HeaderText="Description" SortExpression="Description"
        ConvertEmptyStringToNull="False">
        <ItemTemplate>
            <asp:Label ID="lblDescription" runat="server"
                Text='<%# Eval("Description") %>' Width="100%"></asp:Label>
        </ItemTemplate>
        <EditItemTemplate>
            <asp:TextBox ID="txtDescription" runat="server"
                Text='<%# Bind("Description") %>' Rows="5" TextMode="MultiLine"
```

```
                MaxLength="4000" Width="100%"></asp:TextBox>
          </EditItemTemplate>
        </asp:TemplateField>
    </Fields>
</asp:DetailsView>
```

The page ends with the declaration of a control used to upload files on the server. This is done with a custom user control (which will be used in other pages as well) that will be covered soon.

The ManageCategories.aspx.cs Code-behind File

In the code-behind file there's absolutely no code to retrieve, update, insert, or delete data, because that's all done by the two `ObjectDataSource` controls on the page. There are, however, some event handlers for the `GridView` and the `DetailsView` controls. Let's see what they do, event by event. First, you handle the grid's `SelectedIndexChanged` event to switch the `DetailsView` to edit mode, so it lets the user edit the grid's selected category:

```
public partial class ManageCategories : BasePage
{
    protected void gvwCategories_SelectedIndexChanged(object sender, EventArgs e)
    {
        dvwCategory.ChangeMode(DetailsViewMode.Edit);
    }
```

Next it handles the grid's `RowDeleted` event, to deselect any row that may have been selected, and it rebinds the grid so that the deleted row is removed from the displayed grid, and then it switches the `DetailsView`'s mode back to insert (its default mode):

```
    protected void gvwCategories_RowDeleted(object sender,
        GridViewDeletedEventArgs e)
    {
        gvwCategories.SelectedIndex = -1;
        gvwCategories.DataBind();
        dvwCategory.ChangeMode(DetailsViewMode.Insert);
    }
```

Deleting a category is a critical operation because it will also delete the child articles (because of the cascaded delete we set up in the tables using the database diagram). Therefore, we must minimize the opportunities for a user to accidentally delete a category by clicking on a link by mistake. To ensure that the user really does want to delete an article, we'll ask for confirmation when the link is clicked. To do this we'll handle the `GridView`'s `RowCreated` event, and for each data row (i.e., rows that are not the header, footer, or pagination bar) we'll get a reference to the Delete `ImageButton` (the first and only control in the fifth column), and we'll insert a JavaScript Confirm dialog on its client-side `onclick` event. You've already done something similar for the User Management administration console developed in Chapter 2. Here's the event handler's code:

```
    protected void gvwCategories_RowCreated(object sender, GridViewRowEventArgs e)
    {
        if (e.Row.RowType == DataControlRowType.DataRow)
        {
            ImageButton btn = e.Row.Cells[4].Controls[0] as ImageButton;
            btn.OnClientClick =
```

```
                  " if (confirm('Are you sure you want to delete this category?') ==
    false) return false; ";
        }
    }
```

As for the `DetailsView`'s events, we'll intercept the creation and update of a record, and the `cancel` command, so that we can deselect any `GridView` row that may be currently selected, and rebind it to its data source to display the updated data:

```
    protected void dvwCategory_ItemInserted(object sender,
        DetailsViewInsertedEventArgs e)
    {
        gvwCategories.SelectedIndex = -1;
        gvwCategories.DataBind();
    }

    protected void dvwCategory_ItemUpdated(object sender,
        DetailsViewUpdatedEventArgs e)
    {
        gvwCategories.SelectedIndex = -1;
        gvwCategories.DataBind();
    }

    protected void dvwCategory_ItemCommand(object sender,
        DetailsViewCommandEventArgs e)
    {
        if (e.CommandName == "Cancel")
        {
            gvwCategories.SelectedIndex = -1;
            gvwCategories.DataBind();
        }
    }
```

Finally, we'll handle the control's `ItemCreated` event and, if the control is in insert mode, get a reference to the textbox for the `Importance` field, setting its default value to 0. Unfortunately, this is something you can't do with declarative properties, even though it's often necessary. Here's the workaround:

```
    protected void dvwCategory_ItemCreated(object sender, EventArgs e)
    {
        if (dvwCategory.CurrentMode == DetailsViewMode.Insert)
        {
            TextBox txtImportance = (TextBox)dvwCategory.FindControl("txtImportance");
            txtImportance.Text = "0";
        }
    }
```

The FileUploader.ascx User Control

This control, located under the `~/Controls` folder, allows administrators and editors to upload a file (normally an image file) to the server and save it into their own private user-specific folder. Once the file is saved, the control displays the URL so that the editor can easily copy and paste it into the `ImageUrl` field for a property, or reference the image file in the article's WYSIWYG editor. The markup code is simple — it just declares an instance of the `FileUpload` control, a Submit button, and a couple of `Label`s for the positive or negative feedback:

```
Upload a file:
<asp:FileUpload ID="filUpload" runat="server" /> 
<asp:Button ID="btnUpload" runat="server" OnClick="btnUpload_Click"
    Text="Upload" CausesValidation="false" /><br />
<asp:Label ID="lblFeedbackOK" SkinID="FeedbackOK" runat="server"></asp:Label>
<asp:Label ID="lblFeedbackKO" SkinID="FeedbackKO" runat="server"></asp:Label>
```

The file is saved in the code-behind's btnUpload_Click event handler, into a user-specific folder under
the ~/Uploads folder. The actual saving is done by calling the SaveAs method of the FileUpload's
PostedFile object property. If the folder doesn't already exist, it is created by means of the System.IO
.Directory.CreateDirectory static method:

```
protected void btnUpload_Click(object sender, EventArgs e)
{
    if (filUpload.PostedFile != null && filUpload.PostedFile.ContentLength > 0)
    {
        try
        {
            // if not already present, create a directory
            // named /Uploads/{CurrentUserName}
            string dirUrl = (this.Page as MB.TheBeerHouse.UI.BasePage).BaseUrl +
                "Uploads/" + this.Page.User.Identity.Name;
            string dirPath = Server.MapPath(dirUrl);
            if (!Directory.Exists(dirPath))
                Directory.CreateDirectory(dirPath);
            // save the file under the user's personal folder
            string fileUrl = dirUrl + "/" +
                Path.GetFileName(filUpload.PostedFile.FileName);
            filUpload.PostedFile.SaveAs(Server.MapPath(fileUrl));

            lblFeedbackOK.Visible = true;
            lblFeedbackOK.Text = "File successfully uploaded: " + fileUrl;
        }
        catch (Exception ex)
        {
            lblFeedbackKO.Visible = true;
            lblFeedbackKO.Text = ex.Message;
        }
    }
}
```

This control can only be used by editors and administrators, so when the control loads we need to determine which user is online and throw a SecurityException if the user isn't supposed to see this control:

```
protected void Page_Load(object sender, EventArgs e)
{
    // this control can only work for authenticated users
    if (!this.Page.User.Identity.IsAuthenticated)
        throw new SecurityException("Anonymous users cannot upload files.");

    lblFeedbackKO.Visible = false;
    lblFeedbackOK.Visible = false;
}
```

To register this control on a page, you write the following directive at the top of the page (for example, the `ManageCategories.aspx` page):

```
<%@ Register Src="~/Controls/FileUploader.ascx"
    TagName=" FileUploader" TagPrefix="mb" %>
```

And use this tag to create an instance of the control:

```
<mb:FileUploader ID="FileUploader1" runat="server" />
```

The ArticleListing.ascx User Control

As mentioned before, the code that lists articles in the administrative `ManageArticles.aspx` page, and the end-user `BrowseArticles.aspx` page, is located not in the pages themselves but in a separate user control called `~/Controls/ArticleListing.ascx`. This control displays a paginable list of articles for all categories or for a selected category, allows the user to change the page size, and can highlight articles referring to events that happen in the user's country, state, or city (if that information is present in the user's profile). In Figure 5-7, you can see what the control will look like once it's plugged into the `ManageArticles.aspx` page. Note that because the current user is an editor, each article row has buttons to edit or delete it (the pencil and trashcan icons). These won't be displayed if the control is put into an end-user page and the current user is not an editor or administrator.

The control starts with the declaration of an `ObjectDataSource` that uses the `Category`'s `GetCategory` method to retrieve the data, consumed by a `DropDownList` that serves as category picker to filter the articles:

```
<asp:ObjectDataSource ID="objAllCategories" runat="server"
    TypeName="MB.TheBeerHouse.BLL.Articles.Category"
    SelectMethod="GetCategories"></asp:ObjectDataSource>

<asp:Literal runat="server" ID="lblCategoryPicker">
    Filter by category:</asp:Literal>
<asp:DropDownList ID="ddlCategories" runat="server" AutoPostBack="True"
    DataSourceID="objAllCategories"
    DataTextField="Title" DataValueField="ID" AppendDataBoundItems="true"
    OnSelectedIndexChanged="ddlCategories_SelectedIndexChanged">
    <asp:ListItem Value="0">All categories</asp:ListItem>
</asp:DropDownList>
```

Note that an "All categories" `ListItem` is appended to those categories that were populated via databinding, so that the user can choose to have the articles of all categories displayed. To make this work, you also need to set the `DropDownList`'s `AppendDataBoundItems` to `true`; otherwise, the binding will first clear the `DropDownList` and then add the items. There's another `DropDownList` that lets the user select the page size from a preconfigured list of values:

```
<asp:Literal runat="server" ID="lblPageSizePicker">Articles per page:</asp:Literal>
<asp:DropDownList ID="ddlArticlesPerPage" runat="server" AutoPostBack="True"
    OnSelectedIndexChanged="ddlArticlesPerPage_SelectedIndexChanged">
    <asp:ListItem Value="5">5</asp:ListItem>
    <asp:ListItem Value="10" Selected="True">10</asp:ListItem>
    <asp:ListItem Value="25">25</asp:ListItem>
    <asp:ListItem Value="50">50</asp:ListItem>
    <asp:ListItem Value="100">100</asp:ListItem>
</asp:DropDownList>
```

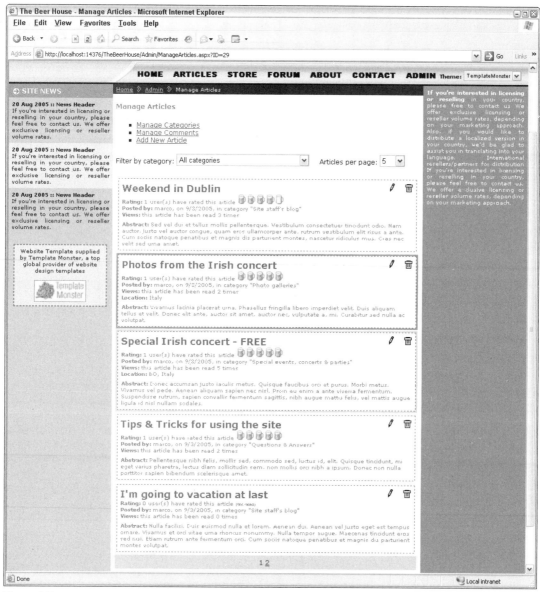

Figure 5-7

As you may remember from the "Design" section, the `<articles>` configuration element has a `pageSize` attribute that will be used as default for this `PageSize DropDownList`. If the value saved in the `config` file is not already present in the list, it will be appended and selected dynamically. This is handled in the code-behind file.

The remainder of the page contains a `GridView` for listing the articles. It needs an `ObjectDataSource` that uses the `Article` class as a business object, and its `GetArticles` and `DeleteArticle` methods are used to select and delete articles. Because it uses pagination, you must also specify the method that returns the total number of articles: `GetArticleCount`. The overload of `GetArticles` used in this situation is the one that takes a Boolean value indicating whether you want all the articles or only published ones, the ID of the parent category, the index of the first row to retrieve, and the page size. You don't have to specify the last two parameters explicitly — they are implicitly added and their value filled in when the control has the `EnablePaging` property set to `true`. The ID of the parent category is set to the selected value of the `ddlCategories` `DropDownList`. Finally, the `publishedOnly` parameter is set to `true` by default, but this can be changed from the code-behind according to a custom property added to the user control, which you'll see shortly. This is the code for the `ObjectDataSource`:

```
<asp:ObjectDataSource ID="objArticles" runat="server"
    TypeName="MB.TheBeerHouse.BLL.Articles.Article"
    DeleteMethod="DeleteArticle" SelectMethod="GetArticles"
    SelectCountMethod="GetArticleCount" EnablePaging="True" >
    <DeleteParameters>
        <asp:Parameter Name="id" Type="Int32" />
    </DeleteParameters>
    <SelectParameters>
        <asp:Parameter Name="publishedOnly" Type="Boolean" DefaultValue="true" />
        <asp:ControlParameter ControlID="ddlCategories" Name="categoryID"
            PropertyName="SelectedValue" Type="Int32" />
    </SelectParameters>
</asp:ObjectDataSource>
```

Next we'll cover the `GridView` that displays articles. Generally, a `GridView` is used to display data with a tabular format. In this case, however, we're building a single-column grid of type `TemplateField`, which shows the article's title, abstract, location, author, release date, and view count each on a separate line. We couldn't fit all these items on separate columns of the same line because some of them are very wide (title and abstract), so why not just use a `Repeater` or a `DataList` in this case? Because the `GridView` has built-in support for pagination, whereas the other two data-bound controls do not. The template also includes a `Panel` with `ImageButton` controls to delete and approve the article, and a link to `AddEditArticle.aspx` to edit the article. The `Panel`'s `Visible` property is bound to an expression that returns `true` (and thus makes the panel and its content visible) only if the current user is an administrator or an editor:

```
<asp:GridView SkinID="Articles" ID="gvwArticles" runat="server"  AllowPaging="True"
    AutoGenerateColumns="False" DataKeyNames="ID" DataSourceID="objArticles"
    PageSize="10" ShowHeader="False"
    EmptyDataText="<b>There is no article to show for the selected category</b>"
    OnRowDataBound="gvwArticles_RowDataBound" OnRowCommand="gvwArticles_RowCommand">
    <Columns>
        <asp:TemplateField
            HeaderText="Article List (including those not yet published)">
            <HeaderStyle HorizontalAlign="Left" />
            <ItemTemplate>
                <div class="articlebox">
                <table cellpadding="0" cellspacing="0" style="width: 100%;"><tr><td>
                    <div class="articletitle">
                    <asp:HyperLink runat="server" ID="lnkTitle" CssClass="articletitle"
                        Text='<%# Eval("Title") %>'
```

```
                              NavigateUrl='<%# "~/ShowArticle.aspx?ID=" + Eval("ID") %>'/>
                    <asp:Image runat="server" ID="imgKey" ImageUrl="~/Images/key.gif"
                        AlternateText="Requires login"
                        Visible='<%# (bool)Eval("OnlyForMembers") &&
                            !Page.User.Identity.IsAuthenticated %>' />
                    <asp:Label runat="server" ID="lblNotApproved" Text="Not approved"
                        SkinID="NotApproved" Visible='<%# !(bool)Eval("Approved") %>' />
                </div>
            </td>
            <td style="text-align: right;">
                <asp:Panel runat="server" ID="panEditArticle"
                    Visible='<%# UserCanEdit %>'>
                <asp:ImageButton runat="server" ID="btnApprove"
                    ImageUrl="~/Images/checkmark.gif" CommandName="Approve"
                    CommandArgument='<%# Eval("ID") %>'
                    AlternateText="Approve article"
                    Visible='<%# !(bool)Eval("Approved") %>'
                    OnClientClick=" if (confirm('Are you sure you want to approve
this article?') == false) return false; " />
                  
                <asp:HyperLink runat="server" ID="lnkEdit" ToolTip="Edit article"
                    NavigateUrl='<%# "~/Admin/AddEditArticle.aspx?ID=" +
                        Eval("ID") %>' ImageUrl="~/Images/Edit.gif" />
                  
                <asp:ImageButton runat="server" ID="btnDelete"
                    ImageUrl="~/Images/Delete.gif"
                    CommandName="Delete" AlternateText="Delete article"
                    OnClientClick=" if (confirm('Are you sure you want to delete this
article?') == false) return false; " />
                </asp:Panel>
            </td></tr></table>
            <b>Rating: </b>
            <asp:Literal runat="server" ID="lblRating"
                Text='<%# Eval("Votes") + " user(s) have rated this article " %>' />
            <mb:RatingDisplay runat="server" ID="ratDisplay"
                Value='<%# Eval("AverageRating") %>' />
            <br />

            <b>Posted by: </b> <asp:Literal runat="server" ID="lblAddedBy"
                Text='<%# Eval("AddedBy") %>' />, on
            <asp:Literal runat="server" ID="lblAddedDate"
                Text='<%# Eval("ReleaseDate", "{0:d}") %>' />, in category "
            <asp:Literal runat="server" ID="lblCategory"
                Text='<%# Eval("CategoryTitle") %>' />"
            <br />
            <b>Views: </b>
            <asp:Literal runat="server" ID="lblViews"
                Text='<%# "this article has been read " +
                    Eval("ViewCount") + " times" %>' />
            <asp:Literal runat="server" ID="lblLocation"
                Visible='<%# Eval("Location").ToString().Length > 0 %>'
                Text='<%# "<br /><b>Location: </b>" + Eval("Location") %>' />
            <br />
            <div class="articleabstract">
            <b>Abstract: </b>
```

```
            <asp:Literal runat="server" ID="lblAbstract"
                Text='<%# Eval("Abstract") %>' />
            </div>
            </div>
        </ItemTemplate>
    </asp:TemplateField>
</Columns>
</asp:GridView>
```

The two `ImageButton` controls use the `OnClientClick` property to specify a JavaScript Confirm dialog that will execute the postback only after an explicit user confirmation. This isn't done from the grid's `RowCreated` event as it is in the `ManageCategories.aspx` page because here the `ImageButton` controls are defined explicitly (and thus you can set their `OnClientClick` property directly from the markup code), while in the previous page the `ImageButton` was created dynamically by the `CommandField` column.

The code for the `Article` rating is defined here also, and it's in a `RatingDisplay` control, whose `Value` property is bound to the `Article`'s `AverageRating` property.

Finally, on the right side of the article's title there is an `Image` representing a key indicating that the article requires the user to login before viewing it. This image is only displayed when the article's `OnlyForMembers` property is `true` and the current user is anonymous.

The ArticleListing.ascx.cs Code-behind File

The `ArticleListing` code-behind classes define the properties described earlier in the "Design" section. They are just wrappers for private fields that are made persistent across postbacks by means of the `SaveControlState` and `LoadControlState` protected methods, which save and load the properties to and from the `ControlState` part of the control's `ViewState` (this is new functionality in ASP.NET 2.0):

```
public partial class ArticleListing : System.Web.UI.UserControl
{
    private bool _enableHighlighter = true;
    public bool EnableHighlighter
    {
        get { return _enableHighlighter; }
        set { _enableHighlighter = value; }
    }

    private bool _publishedOnly = true;
    public bool PublishedOnly
    {
        get { return _publishedOnly; }
        set
        {
            _publishedOnly = value;
            objArticles.SelectParameters[
                "publishedOnly"].DefaultValue = value.ToString();
        }
    }

    private bool _showCategoryPicker = true;
    public bool ShowCategoryPicker
    {
```

```
      get { return _showCategoryPicker; }
      set
      {
        _showCategoryPicker = value;
        ddlCategories.Visible = value;
        lblCategoryPicker.Visible = value;
        lblSeparator.Visible = value;
      }
    }

    private bool _showPageSizePicker = true;
    public bool ShowPageSizePicker
    {
      get { return _showPageSizePicker; }
      set
      {
        _showPageSizePicker = value;
        ddlArticlesPerPage.Visible = value;
        lblPageSizePicker.Visible = value;
      }
    }

    private bool _enablePaging = true;
    public bool EnablePaging
    {
      get { return _enablePaging; }
      set
      {
        _enablePaging = value;
        gvwArticles.PagerSettings.Visible = value;
      }
    }

    private bool _userCanEdit = false;
    protected bool UserCanEdit
    {
      get { return _userCanEdit; }
      set { _userCanEdit = value; }
    }

    private string _userCountry = "";
    private string _userState = "";
    private string _userCity = "";

    protected override void LoadControlState(object savedState)
    {
      object[] ctlState = (object[])savedState;
      base.LoadControlState(ctlState[0]);
      this.EnableHighlighter = (bool)ctlState[1];
      this.PublishedOnly = (bool)ctlState[2];
      this.ShowCategoryPicker = (bool)ctlState[3];
      this.ShowPageSizePicker = (bool)ctlState[4];
      this.EnablePaging = (bool)ctlState[5];
    }
```

```
    protected override object SaveControlState()
    {
        object[] ctlState = new object[6];
        ctlState[0] = base.SaveControlState();
        ctlState[1] = this.EnableHighlighter;
        ctlState[2] = this.PublishedOnly;
        ctlState[3] = this.ShowCategoryPicker;
        ctlState[4] = this.ShowPageSizePicker;
        ctlState[5] = this.EnablePaging;
        return ctlState;
    }

    // other event handlers here...
}
```

The `PublishedOnly` property in the preceding code has a setter that, in addition to setting the `_publishedOnly` private field, sets the default value of the `publishedOnly` parameter for the `objArticles` ObjectDataSource's `Select` method. The developer can plug the control into an end-user page and show only the published content by setting this property to `true`, or set it to `false` on an administrative page to show all the articles (published or not).

The class also has event handlers for a number of events of the `GridView` control and the two `DropDown Lists`. In the `Page_ Load` event handler, you can preselect the category for the category list, whose ID is passed on the querystring, if any. Then you do then same for the page size list, taking the value from the `Articles` configuration; if the specified value does not exist in the list you can add it to the list and then select it. Finally, you execute the `DataBind` with the current category filter and page size:

```
protected void Page_Load(object sender, EventArgs e)
{
    if (!this.IsPostBack)
    {
        // preselect the category whose ID is passed in the querystring
        if (!string.IsNullOrEmpty(this.Request.QueryString["CatID"]))
        {
            ddlCategories.DataBind();
            ddlCategories.SelectedValue = this.Request.QueryString["CatID"];
        }

        // Set the page size as indicated in the config file. If an option for that
        // size doesn't already exist, first create and then select it.
        int pageSize = Globals.Settings.Articles.PageSize;
        if (ddlArticlesPerPage.Items.FindByValue(pageSize.ToString()) == null)
        {
            ddlArticlesPerPage.Items.Add(new ListItem(pageSize.ToString(),
                pageSize.ToString()));
        }
        ddlArticlesPerPage.SelectedValue = pageSize.ToString();
        gvwArticles.PageSize = pageSize;

        gvwArticles.DataBind();
    }
}
```

If the user manually changes the page size, you need to change the `GridView`'s `PageSize` property and set the `PageIndex` to 0 so that the grid displays the first page (because the current page becomes invalid when the user selects a different page size) and rebind the data from the `DropDownList`'s `SelectedIndexChanged` event:

```
protected void ddlArticlesPerPage_SelectedIndexChanged(object sender, EventArgs e)
{
    gvwArticles.PageSize = int.Parse(ddlArticlesPerPage.SelectedValue);
    gvwArticles.PageIndex = 0;
    gvwArticles.DataBind();
}
```

When a category is selected from the `DropDownList` you don't have to do anything to set the new filter, because that's automatically done by the `GridView`'s `ObjectDataSource`. However, you must explicitly set the grid's page index to 0 because the current page index might be invalid with the new data (if, for example, there are no articles for the newly selected category, and you're on page 2). After setting the grid's page index you need to rebind the data:

```
protected void ddlCategories_SelectedIndexChanged(object sender, EventArgs e)
{
    gvwArticles.PageIndex = 0;
    gvwArticles.DataBind();
}
```

When the editor clicks the `Delete` command you don't need to do anything, because it's the grid's companion `ObjectDatasource` that calls the `Article.DeleteArticle` static method with the ID of the row's article. This doesn't happen for the `Approve` command, of course, because that's not a CRUD method supported by the `ObjectDataSource`, so you need to handle it manually. More specifically, you handle the `GridView`'s generic `RowCommand` event (raised for all types of commands, including `Delete`). First you verify that the event was raised because of a click on the `Approve` command, then you retrieve the ID of the article to approve from the event's `CommandArgument` parameter, execute the `Article.ApproveArticle` method, and lastly rebind the data to the control:

```
protected void gvwArticles_RowCommand(object sender, GridViewCommandEventArgs e)
{
    if (e.CommandName == "Approve")
    {
        int articleID = int.Parse(e.CommandArgument.ToString());
        Article.ApproveArticle(articleID);
        gvwArticles.DataBind();
    }
}
```

It is interesting to see how the articles that refer to events are highlighted to indicate that the article's location is close to the user's location. This is done in the grid's `RowDataBound` event, but only if the user is authenticated (otherwise her profile will not have the `Country`, `State`, and `City` properties) and if the control's `EnableHighlighter` property is `true`. The row is highlighted by applying a different CSS style class to the row itself. Remember that the article's `State` and `City` properties might contain multiple names separated by a semicolon—the value is therefore split on the semicolon character and the user's state and city are searched in the arrays resulting from the split:

```
protected void gvwArticles_RowDataBound(object sender, GridViewRowEventArgs e)
{
    if (e.Row.RowType == DataControlRowType.DataRow &&
        this.Page.User.Identity.IsAuthenticated && this.EnableHighlighter)
    {
        // hightlight the article row according to whether the current user's
        // city, state or country is found in the article's city, state or country
        Article article = (e.Row.DataItem as Article);
        if (article.Country.ToLower() == _userCountry)
        {
            e.Row.CssClass = "highlightcountry";

            if (Array.IndexOf<string>(
                article.State.ToLower().Split(';'), _userState) > -1)
            {
                e.Row.CssClass = "highlightstate";

                if (Array.IndexOf<string>(
                    article.City.ToLower().Split(';'), _userCity) > -1)
                {
                    e.Row.CssClass = "highlightcity";
                }
            }
        }
    }
}
```

The user's location is not retrieved directly from her profile in the preceding code because that would cause a read for each and every row. Instead, the user's country, state, and city are read only once from the profile, and saved in local variables. Page_Load cannot be used for this because the automatic binding done by the ObjectDataSource happens earlier, so we have to use the Page_Init event handler:

```
protected void Page_Init(object sender, EventArgs e)
{
    this.Page.RegisterRequiresControlState(this);

    this.UserCanEdit = (this.Page.User.Identity.IsAuthenticated &&
        (this.Page.User.IsInRole("Administrators") ||
         this.Page.User.IsInRole("Editors")));

    try
    {
        if (this.Page.User.Identity.IsAuthenticated)
        {
            _userCountry = this.Profile.Address.Country.ToLower();
            _userState = this.Profile.Address.State.ToLower();
            _userCity = this.Profile.Address.City.ToLower();
        }
    }
    catch (Exception) { }
}
```

The ArticleListing user control is now complete and ready to be plugged into the ASPX pages.

The RatingDisplay.ascx Control

The `ArticleListing` control uses a secondary user control that you haven't seen yet. It's the `Rating Display.ascx` user control, which shows an image representing the average rating of an article. Many sites use star icons for this, but TheBeerHouse, in keeping with its theme, uses glasses of beer for this rating! There are nine different images, representing one glass, one glass and a half, two glasses, two glasses and a half, and so on until we get to five full glasses. The proper image will be chosen according to the average rating passed in to the `Value` property's setter function. The markup code only defines an `Image` and a `Label`:

```
<asp:Image runat="server" ID="imgRating" AlternateText="Average rating" />
<asp:Label runat="server" ID="lblNotRated" Text="(Not rated)" />
```

All the code is in the code-behind's setter function, which determines which image to display based on the value:

```
private double _value = 0.0;
public double Value
{
    get {return _value; }
    set
    {
        _value = value;
        if (_value >= 1)
        {
            lblNotRated.Visible = false;
            imgRating.Visible = true;
            imgRating.AlternateText = "Average rating: " + _value.ToString("N1");
            string url = "~/images/stars{0}.gif";
            if (_value <= 1.3)
                url = string.Format(url, "10");
            else if (_value <= 1.8)
                url = string.Format(url, "15");
            else if (_value <= 2.3)
                url = string.Format(url, "20");
            else if (_value <= 2.8)
                url = string.Format(url, "25");
            else if (_value <= 3.3)
                url = string.Format(url, "30");
            else if (_value <= 3.8)
                url = string.Format(url, "35");
            else if (_value <= 4.3)
                url = string.Format(url, "40");
            else if (_value <= 4.8)
                url = string.Format(url, "45");
            else
                url = string.Format(url, "50");
            imgRating.ImageUrl = url;
        }
        else
        {
            lblNotRated.Visible = true;
            imgRating.Visible = false;
        }
    }
}
```

In addition to the graphical representation, a more accurate numerical value is shown in the image's alternate text (tooltip).

The ManageArticles.aspx Page

This page just has an instance of the `ArticlesListing` control, with the `PublishedOnly` property set to `false` so that it displays all articles:

```
<%@ Register Src="../Controls/ArticleListing.ascx"
    TagName="ArticleListing" TagPrefix="mb" %>
...
<mb:ArticleListing id="ArticleListing1" runat="server" PublishedOnly="False" />
```

The AddEditArticle.aspx Page

This page allows Administrators, Editors, and Contributors to add new articles or edit existing ones. It decides whether to use edit or insert mode according to whether an `ArticleID` parameter was passed on the querystring. If it was, then the page loads in edit mode for that article, but only if the user is an Administrator or Editor (the edit mode is only available to Administrators and Editors, while the insert mode is also available to Contributors as well). This security check must be done programmatically, instead of declaratively from the `web.config` file. Figure 5-8 is a screenshot of the page while in edit mode for an article.

As you might guess from studying this picture, it uses a `DetailsView` with a few read-only fields (`ID`, `AddedDate`, and `AddedBy` as usual, but also `ViewCount`, `Votes`, and `Rating`) and many other editable fields. The `Body` field uses the open-source FCKeditor described earlier. It is declared on the page as any other custom control, but it requires some configuration first. To set up FCK you must download two packages from www.fckeditor.net:

1. FCKeditor (which at the time of writing is in version 2.1) includes the set of HTML pages and JavaScript files that implement the control. The control can be used not only with ASP.NET, but also with ASP, JSP, PHP, and normal HTML pages. This first package includes the "host-independent" code, and some ASP/ASP.NET/JSP/PHP pages that implement an integrated file browser and file uploader.

2. FCKedit.Net is the .NET custom control that wraps the HTML and JavaScript code of the editor.

You unzip the first package into an FCKeditor folder, underneath the site's root folder. Then you unzip the second package and put the compiled dll underneath the site's bin folder. The .NET custom control class has a number of properties that let you customize the look and feel of the editor; some properties can only be set in the `fckconfig.js` file found under the FCKeditor folder. The global FCKConfig JavaScript editor enables you to configure many properties, such as whether the `File Browser` and `Image Upload` commands are enabled. Here's how to disable them in code (we already have our own file uploader so we don't want to use it here, and we don't want to use the file browser for security reasons):

```
FCKConfig.LinkBrowser = false;
FCKConfig.ImageBrowser = false;
FCKConfig.LinkUpload = false;
FCKConfig.ImageUpload = false;
```

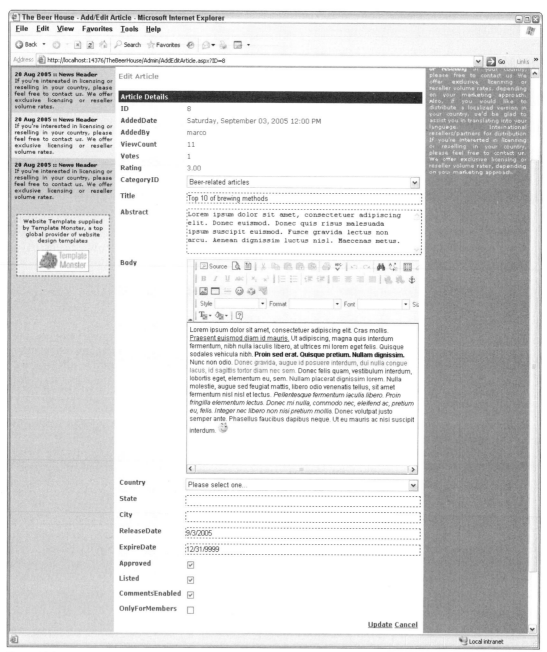

Figure 5-8

You can even create a customized editor toolbar by adding the commands that you want to implement. For example, this shows how you can define a toolbar named "TheBeerHouse" with commands to format the text, insert smileys and images, but not insert input controls or Flash animations:

```
FCKConfig.ToolbarSets["TheBeerHouse"] = [
  ['Source','Preview','Templates'],
  ['Cut','Copy','Paste','PasteText','PasteWord','-','Print','SpellCheck'],
  ['Undo','Redo','-','Find','Replace','-','SelectAll','RemoveFormat'],
  ['Bold','Italic','Underline','StrikeThrough','-','Subscript','Superscript'],
  ['OrderedList','UnorderedList','-','Outdent','Indent'],
  ['JustifyLeft','JustifyCenter','JustifyRight','JustifyFull'],
  ['Link','Unlink','Anchor'],
  ['Image','Table','Rule','Smiley','SpecialChar','UniversalKey'],
  ['Style','FontFormat','FontName','FontSize'],
  ['TextColor','BGColor'],
  ['About']
];
```

Many other configurations can be set directly from the ASP.NET page that hosts the control, as you'll see shortly.

The `AddEditArticle.aspx` page first declares the `ObjectDataSource`, as usual. Then it uses the `Article`'s `GetArticleByID`, `DeleteArticle`, `InsertArticle`, and `UpdateArticle` methods for the complete management of a single article:

```
<asp:ObjectDataSource ID="objCurrArticle" runat="server"
    TypeName="MB.TheBeerHouse.BLL.Articles.Article"
    DeleteMethod="DeleteArticle" InsertMethod="InsertArticle"
    SelectMethod="GetArticleByID" UpdateMethod="UpdateArticle">
    <SelectParameters>
        <asp:QueryStringParameter Name="articleID"
            QueryStringField="ID" Type="Int32" />
    </SelectParameters>
</asp:ObjectDataSource>
```

The only explicit parameter is the optional `articleID` value passed on the querystring. The parameters for the `Delete`, `Update`, and `Insert` methods are automatically inferred from the `DetailsView`'s fields and the method's signature. Two other `ObjectDataSource` controls are used on the page: one for the `DropDownList` with the available categories, and the other for the `DropDownList` with countries:

```
<asp:ObjectDataSource ID="objAllCategories" runat="server"
    TypeName="MB.TheBeerHouse.BLL.Articles.Category" SelectMethod="GetCategories">
</asp:ObjectDataSource>
<asp:ObjectDataSource ID="objAllCountries" runat="server"
    TypeName="MB.TheBeerHouse.UI.Helpers" SelectMethod="GetCountries">
    <SelectParameters>
        <asp:Parameter DefaultValue="true" Name="insertEmpty" Type="Boolean" />
    </SelectParameters>
</asp:ObjectDataSource>
```

The `DetailsView` control uses a `BoundField` for some read-only fields mentioned earlier, and uses `TemplateFields` for the editable fields. We don't use `DataBound` fields for the editable properties because that wouldn't support the use of validators. Many of the fields are edited by means of a textbox for text properties, a checkbox for Boolean properties (e.g., `OnlyForMembers`, `Listed`, `Approved`), or a `DropDownList` for lists of values (`Country` and `Category`). The following code shows some representative fields:

```
<asp:DetailsView ID="dvwArticle" runat="server" AutoGenerateDeleteButton="True"
    AutoGenerateEditButton="True" AutoGenerateInsertButton="True"
    AutoGenerateRows="False" DataKeyNames="ID" DataSourceID="objCurrArticle"
    DefaultMode="Insert" HeaderText="Article Details"
    OnItemCreated="dvwArticle_ItemCreated" OnDataBound="dvwArticle_DataBound"
    OnModeChanged="dvwArticle_ModeChanged">
    <FieldHeaderStyle Width="100px" />
    <Fields>
        <asp:BoundField DataField="ID" HeaderText="ID" InsertVisible="False"
            ReadOnly="True" />
        <asp:BoundField DataField="AddedDate" HeaderText="AddedDate"
            InsertVisible="False" ReadOnly="True" DataFormatString="{0:f}" />
        <!-- other read-only BoundFields... -->
        <asp:TemplateField HeaderText="CategoryID">
            <ItemTemplate>
                <asp:Label ID="lblCategory" runat="server"
                    Text='<%# Eval("CategoryTitle") %>'></asp:Label>
            </ItemTemplate>
            <EditItemTemplate>
                <asp:DropDownList ID="ddlCategories" runat="server"
                    DataSourceID="objAllCategories" DataTextField="Title"
                    DataValueField="ID"
                    SelectedValue='<%# Bind("CategoryID") %>' Width="100%" />
            </EditItemTemplate>
        </asp:TemplateField>
        <asp:TemplateField HeaderText="Title">
            <ItemTemplate>
                <asp:Label ID="lblTitle" runat="server"
                    Text='<%# Eval("Title") %>'></asp:Label>
            </ItemTemplate>
            <EditItemTemplate>
                <asp:TextBox ID="txtTitle" runat="server" Text='<%# Bind("Title") %>'
                    Width="100%" MaxLength="256"></asp:TextBox>
                <asp:RequiredFieldValidator ID="valRequireTitle" runat="server"
                    ControlToValidate="txtTitle" SetFocusOnError="true"
                    Text="The Title field is required."
                    ToolTip="The Title field is required."
                    Display="Dynamic"></asp:RequiredFieldValidator>
            </EditItemTemplate>
        </asp:TemplateField>
        <asp:TemplateField HeaderText="Abstract" SortExpression="Abstract">
            <ItemTemplate>
                <asp:Label ID="lblAbstract" runat="server"
                    Text='<%# Eval("Abstract") %>'></asp:Label>
            </ItemTemplate>
            <EditItemTemplate>
                <asp:TextBox ID="txtAbstract" runat="server"
                    Text='<%# Bind("Abstract") %>' Rows="5" TextMode="MultiLine"
                    Width="100%" MaxLength="4000"></asp:TextBox>
            </EditItemTemplate>
        </asp:TemplateField>
        <asp:TemplateField HeaderText="Body" SortExpression="Body">
            <ItemTemplate>
                <asp:Label ID="lblBody" runat="server"
```

```
                Text='<%# Eval("Body") %>'></asp:Label>
          </ItemTemplate>
          <EditItemTemplate>
            <fckeditorv2:fckeditor id="txtBody" runat="server"
                Value='<%# Bind("Body") %>'
                ToolbarSet="TheBeerHouse" Height="400px" Width="100%" />
          </EditItemTemplate>
      </asp:TemplateField>
      <asp:TemplateField HeaderText="Approved" SortExpression="Approved">
          <ItemTemplate>
            <asp:CheckBox ID="chkApproved" runat="server"
                Checked='<%# Eval("Approved") %>' Enabled="False" />
          </ItemTemplate>
          <EditItemTemplate>
            <asp:CheckBox ID="chkApproved" runat="server"
                Checked='<%# Bind("Approved") %>' />
          </EditItemTemplate>
      </asp:TemplateField>
      <!-- other editable TemplateFields... -->
    </Fields>
</asp:DetailsView>
<p></p>
<mb:FileUploader id="FileUploader1" runat="server">
</mb:FileUploader>
```

The declaration of the FCKeditor shows the use of the `ToolbarSet` property, which references the TheBeerHouse toolbar defined earlier in the JavaScript configuration file.

The AddEditArticle.aspx.cs Code-behind File

The `DetailsView`'s mode is set to insert mode by default, but if an `ID` parameter is found on the querystring when the page loads, then it is switched to edit mode if the current user is an Administrator or Editor, and not just a Contributor. If a user not belonging to one of those two roles tries to manually load the page with an ID on the querystring, the page will throw a `SecurityException`:

```
protected void Page_Load(object sender, EventArgs e)
{
    if (!this.IsPostBack)
    {
        if (!string.IsNullOrEmpty(this.Request.QueryString["ID"]))
        {
            if (this.User.Identity.IsAuthenticated &&
                (this.User.IsInRole("Administrators") ||
                 this.User.IsInRole("Editors")))
            {
                dvwArticle.ChangeMode(DetailsViewMode.Edit);
            }
            else
                throw new SecurityException(
                    "You are not allowed to edit existent articles!");
        }
    }
}
```

The FCKeditor requires another property, BasePath, that points to the URL of the FCKeditor folder that contains all its HTML, JavaScript, and image files. Because the BasePath property is not bindable, we have to handle the DetailsView's ItemCreated event (raised after all the fields' controls have been created); and, inside this event handler, we have to get a reference to the txtBody (FCKeditor) and set its BasePath property to the URL of the folder:

```
protected void dvwArticle_ItemCreated(object sender, EventArgs e)
{
    Control ctl = dvwArticle.FindControl("txtBody");
    if (ctl != null)
    {
        FCKeditor txtBody = ctl as FCKeditor;
        txtBody.BasePath = this.BaseUrl + "FCKeditor/";
    }
}
```

There's one last detail to cover here: You should preselect the checkboxes that make the article listed and to allow comments when the DetailsView is in insert mode. You should also select and enable the Approved checkbox, but only if the current user belongs to the Administrators or Editors roles. You might think you could do this by defining an InsertItemTemplate (in addition to the EditItemTemplate) for the Listed, Approved, and AllowComments fields and then setting their Checked property to true, but it must be set to a binding expression in order to support the ObjectDataSource's Insert method correctly. The only solution I've found is to handle the DetailsView's DataBound event, get a reference to the checkboxes, and programmatically set their Checked property from there:

```
protected void dvwArticle_DataBound(object sender, EventArgs e)
{
    if (dvwArticle.CurrentMode == DetailsViewMode.Insert)
    {
        CheckBox chkApproved = dvwArticle.FindControl("chkApproved") as CheckBox;
        CheckBox chkListed = dvwArticle.FindControl("chkListed") as CheckBox;
        CheckBox chkCommentsEnabled = dvwArticle.FindControl("chkCommentsEnabled")
            as CheckBox;

        chkListed.Checked = true;
        chkCommentsEnabled.Checked = true;

        bool canApprove = (this.User.IsInRole("Administrators") ||
            this.User.IsInRole("Editors"));
        chkApproved.Enabled = canApprove;
        chkApproved.Checked = canApprove;
    }
}
```

The ManageComments.aspx Page

This page is located under the ~/Admin/ folder and it displays all comments of all articles, from the newest to the oldest, and allows an administrator or an editor to moderate the feedback by editing or deleting comments that may not be considered suitable. The page uses a paginable GridView for displaying the comments and a separate DetailsView on the bottom of the page to edit the comment selected in the grid. Figure 5-9 shows a screenshot of this page.

Figure 5-9

I won't cover the code for this page in detail because it's similar to other code that's already been discussed. The pagination for the `GridView` is implemented the same way as the pagination in the `ArticleListing` user control, and the editable `DetailsView` connected to the `GridView`'s selected row is like the `DetailsView` in the page `ManageCategories.aspx`. You can refer to the downloadable code for the complete implementation.

The ShowCategories.aspx Page

This is the first end-user page of this module, located in the site's root folder. Its only purpose is to display the article categories in a nice format, so that the reader can easily and clearly understand what the various categories are about and quickly jump to their content by clicking on the category's title. Figure 5-10 shows this page.

Figure 5-10

The list of categories is implemented as a DataList with two columns (with repeatColumns set to 2). We don't need pagination, sorting, or editing features here, so a simple DataList with support for repeated columns is adequate. Following is the code for the DataList and its companion ObjectDataSource:

```
<asp:ObjectDataSource ID="objAllCategories" runat="server" SelectMethod="GetCategories"
    TypeName="MB.TheBeerHouse.BLL.Articles.Category">
</asp:ObjectDataSource>
```

```
<asp:DataList ID="dlstCategories" EnableTheming="false" runat="server"
    DataSourceID="objAllCategories" DataKeyField="ID"
    GridLines="None" Width="100%" RepeatColumns="2">
    <ItemTemplate>
        <table cellpadding="6" style="width: 100%;">
            <tr>
                <td style="width: 1px;">
                    <asp:HyperLink runat="server" ID="lnkCatImage"
                        NavigateUrl='<%# "BrowseArticles.aspx?CatID=" + Eval("ID") %>' >
                        <asp:Image runat="server" ID="imgCategory" BorderWidth="0px"
                            AlternateText='<%# Eval("Title") %>'
                            ImageUrl='<%# Eval("ImageUrl") %>' />
                    </asp:HyperLink>
                </td>
                <td>
                    <div class="sectionsubtitle">
                    <asp:HyperLink runat="server" ID="lnkCatRss"
                        NavigateUrl='<%# "GetArticlesRss.aspx?CatID=" + Eval("ID") %>'>
                        <img style="border-width: 0px;" src="Images/rss.gif"
                            alt="Get the RSS for this category" /></asp:HyperLink>
                    <asp:HyperLink runat="server" ID="lnkCatTitle"
                        Text='<%# Eval("Title") %>'
                        NavigateUrl='<%# "BrowseArticles.aspx?CatID=" + Eval("ID") %>' />
                    </div>
                    <br />
                    <asp:Literal runat="server" ID="lblDescription"
                        Text='<%# Eval("Description") %>' />
                </td>
            </tr>
        </table>
    </ItemTemplate>
</asp:DataList>
```

The category's image and the title both link to the BrowseArticle.aspx page, with a CatID parameter on the querystring equal to the ID of the clicked row. This is the page we'll cover next. The Show Categories.aspx has no code in the code-behind file because its data values are generated by the DataList and ObjectDataSource pair, and there are no actions or events we need to handle.

The BrowseArticles.aspx Page

This is the end-user version of the ManageArticles.aspx page presented earlier. It only shows published content instead of all content, but otherwise it's the same as it just declares an instance of the shared ArticleListing user control:

```
<mb:ArticleListing id="ArticleListing1" runat="server" PublishedOnly="True" />
```

Figure 5-11 represents a screenshot of the page. Note that the page is available to all users, but because the current user is anonymous and the two articles listed on the page have their OnlyForMembers property set to false, the key image is shown next to them. If the user clicks the article's title, she will be redirected to the login page.

Figure 5-11

The ShowArticle.aspx Page

This end-user page outputs the whole article's text, and all its other information (author, release date, average rating, number of views, etc.). At the bottom of the page it has input controls to let the user rate the article (from one to five glasses of beer) and to submit comments. All comments are listed in chronological order, on a single page, so that it's easy to follow the discussion. When the page is loaded by an editor or an administrator, some additional buttons to delete, approve, and edit the article are also visible, and this also applies to the comments. Figure 5-12 shows a screenshot of the page as seen by an end user.

The code that renders the title, rating, and other information in the upper box is very similar to the code used in the `ArticleListing` user control, so I won't list it here again. The article's content is displayed in a simple `Literal` control. Let's consider the controls that allow the user to rate the article and provide feedback. The possible rating values are listed in a `DropDownList`, and below that there's a `Label` that tells the user what rating she selected. The `Label` will be made visible only after the user rates the article, of course, and once that happens the `DropDownList` will be hidden. This will be true also for future loads of the same article by the same user, because the vote will be remembered in a cookie, as you'll see shortly in the code-behind file:

```
<div class="sectiontitle">How would you rate this article?</div>
<asp:DropDownList runat="server" ID="ddlRatings">
    <asp:ListItem Value="1" Text="1 beer" />
    <asp:ListItem Value="2" Text="2 beers" />
    <asp:ListItem Value="3" Text="3 beers" />
    <asp:ListItem Value="4" Text="4 beers" />
    <asp:ListItem Value="5" Text="5 beers" Selected="true" />
</asp:DropDownList>
<asp:Button runat="server" ID="btnRate" Text="Rate"
    OnClick="btnRate_Click" CausesValidation="false" />
<asp:Literal runat="server" ID="lblUserRating" Visible="False"
    Text="Your rated this article {0} beer(s). Thank you for your feedback." />
```

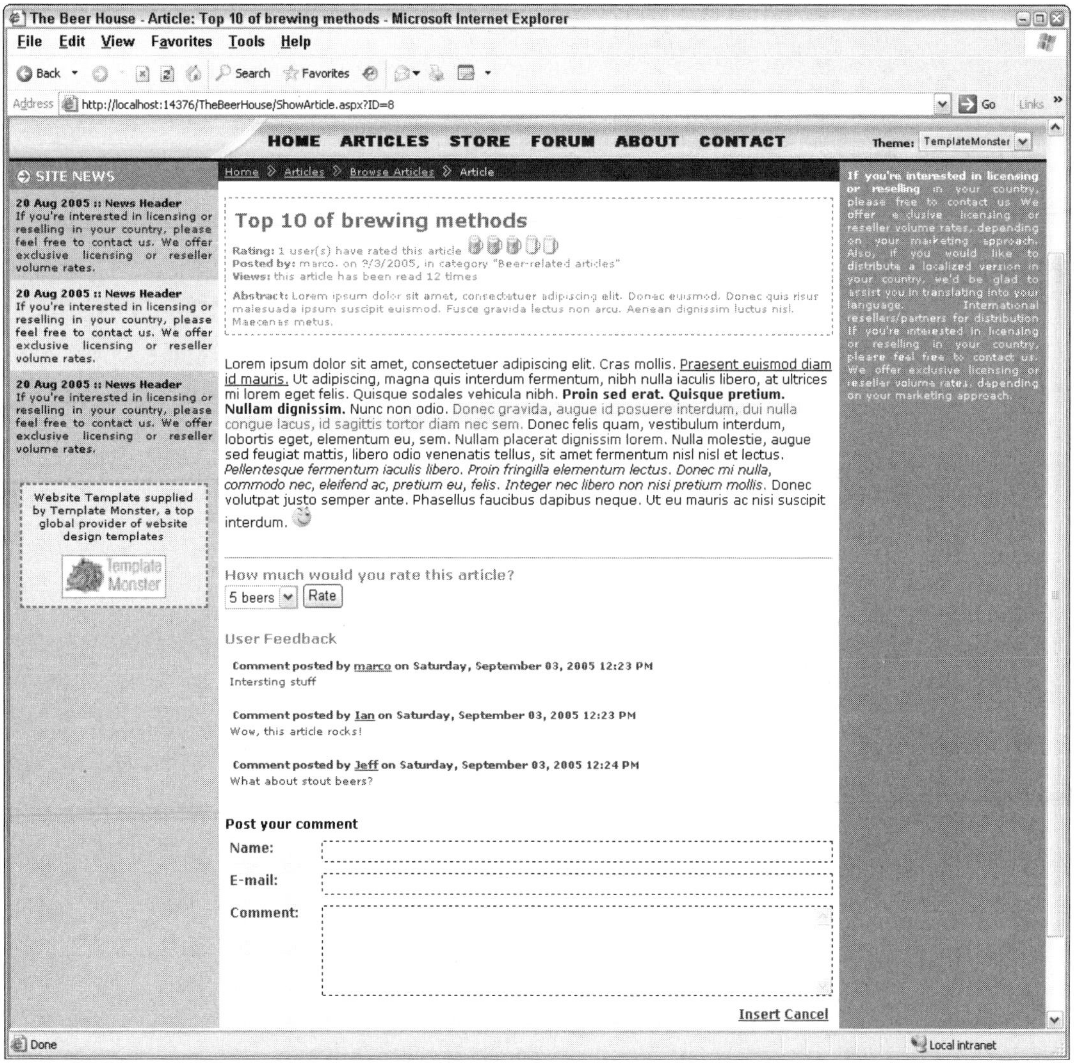

Figure 5-12

The rest of the page defines a `DataList` and an accompanying `ObjectDataSource` for listing the current comments. I won't show this piece because there's nothing new here. Instead, note the `DetailsView` at the bottom of the page, which is used to post a new comment and edit existing ones (when a comment in the `DataList` just shown is selected by an editor or administrator):

```
<asp:DetailsView id="dvwComment" runat="server" AutoGenerateInsertButton="True"
    AutoGenerateEditButton="true" AutoGenerateRows="False"
    DataSourceID="objCurrComment" DefaultMode="Insert"
    OnItemInserted="dvwComment_ItemInserted" OnItemCommand="dvwComment_ItemCommand"
    DataKeyNames="ID" OnItemUpdated="dvwComment_ItemUpdated"
    OnItemCreated="dvwComment_ItemCreated">
    <FieldHeaderStyle Width="80px" />
    <Fields>
        <asp:BoundField DataField="ID" HeaderText="ID:" ReadOnly="True"
            InsertVisible="False" />
        <asp:BoundField DataField="AddedDate" HeaderText="AddedDate:"
            InsertVisible="False" ReadOnly="True"/>
        <asp:BoundField DataField="AddedByIP" HeaderText="UserIP:" ReadOnly="True"
            InsertVisible="False" />
        <asp:TemplateField HeaderText="Name:">
            <ItemTemplate>
                <asp:Label ID="lblAddedBy" runat="server"
                    Text='<%# Eval("AddedBy") %>' />
            </ItemTemplate>
            <InsertItemTemplate>
                <asp:TextBox ID="txtAddedBy" runat="server"
                    Text='<%# Bind("AddedBy") %>' MaxLength="256" Width="100%" />
                <asp:RequiredFieldValidator ID="valRequireAddedBy" runat="server"
                    ControlToValidate="txtAddedBy" SetFocusOnError="true"
                    Text="Your name is required." Display="Dynamic" />
            </InsertItemTemplate>
        </asp:TemplateField>
        <asp:TemplateField HeaderText="E-mail:">
            <ItemTemplate>
                <asp:HyperLink ID="lnkAddedByEmail" runat="server"
                    Text='<%# Eval("AddedByEmail") %>'
                    NavigateUrl='<%# "mailto:" + Eval("AddedByEmail") %>' />
            </ItemTemplate>
            <InsertItemTemplate>
                <asp:TextBox ID="txtAddedByEmail" runat="server"
                    Text='<%# Bind("AddedByEmail") %>' MaxLength="256" Width="100%" />
                <asp:RequiredFieldValidator ID="valRequireAddedByEmail" runat="server"
                    ControlToValidate="txtAddedByEmail" SetFocusOnError="true"
                    Text="Your e-mail is required." Display="Dynamic" />
                <asp:RegularExpressionValidator runat="server" ID="valEmailPattern"
                    Display="Dynamic" SetFocusOnError="true"
                    ControlToValidate="txtAddedByEmail"
                    ValidationExpression="\w+([-+.']\w+)*@\w+([-.]\w+)*\.\w+([-.]\w+)*"
                    Text="The e-mail is not well-formed." />
            </InsertItemTemplate>
        </asp:TemplateField>
        <asp:TemplateField HeaderText="Comment:">
            <ItemTemplate>
                <asp:Label ID="lblBody" runat="server" Text='<%# Eval("Body") %>' />
            </ItemTemplate>
```

```
              <EditItemTemplate>
                <asp:TextBox ID="txtBody" runat="server" Text='<%# Bind("Body") %>'
                    TextMode="MultiLine" Rows="5" Width="100%"></asp:TextBox>
                <asp:RequiredFieldValidator ID="valRequireBody" runat="server"
                    ControlToValidate="txtBody" SetFocusOnError="true"
                    Text="The comment text is required." Display="Dynamic" />
              </EditItemTemplate>
          </asp:TemplateField>
      </Fields>
  </asp:DetailsView>
```

One unique aspect of the preceding code is that the AddedBy and AddedByEmail fields use the TemplateField's InsertItemTemplate instead of the EditItemTemplate that we used in the other DetailsView controls. This is because these fields must be editable only when adding new comments, whereas they are read-only when a comment is being edited. If we had used the EditItemTemplate, as we did for the Body field, that template would have been used for insert mode (unless you specify an InsertItemTemplate that's like the ItemTemplate, but that means replicating code without any advantage). The InsertItemTemplate is not used while the control is in edit mode instead; in that case the ItemTemplate is used, with the result that those fields cannot be changed.

The ShowArticle.aspx.cs Code-behind File

When the page loads, it reads the ID parameter from the querystring. The ID parameter must be specified; otherwise, the page will throw an exception because it doesn't know which article to load. After an Article object has been loaded for the specified article, you must also confirm that the article is currently published (it is not a future or retired article) and that the current user can read it (if the OnlyForMembers property is true, they have to be logged in). You must check these conditions because a cheating user might try to enter an ID in the URL manually, even if the article isn't listed in the BrowseArticles.aspx page. If everything is OK, the article's view count is incremented, and Labels and other controls on the page are filled with the article's data. Finally, you check whether the current user has already rated the article, in which case you show her rating and hide the ratings DropDownList to prevent her from recording a new vote. Here's the code for the Page_Load event handler where all this is done:

```
protected void Page_Load(object sender, EventArgs e)
{
    if (string.IsNullOrEmpty(this.Request.QueryString["ID"]))
        throw new ApplicationException("Missing parameter on the querystring.");
    else
        _articleID = int.Parse(this.Request.QueryString["ID"]);

    if (!this.IsPostBack)
    {
        // try to load the article with the specified ID, and raise an exception
        // if it doesn't exist
        Article article = Article.GetArticleByID(_articleID);
        if (article == null)
            throw new ApplicationException("No article found for the specified ID.");

        // Check if the article is published (approved + released + not yet expired).
        // If not, continue only if the current user is an Administrator or an Editor
        if (!article.Published)
        {
            if (!this.UserCanEdit)
```

271

```
            {
                throw new SecurityException(@"What are you trying to do???
                    You're not allowed to do view this article!");
            }
        }

        // if the article has the OnlyForMembers = true, and the current user
        // is anonymous, redirect to the login page
        if (article.OnlyForMembers && !this.User.Identity.IsAuthenticated)
            this.RequestLogin();

        article.IncrementViewCount();

        // if we get here, display all article's data on the page
        this.Title += article.Title;
        lblTitle.Text = article.Title;
        lblNotApproved.Visible = !article.Approved;
        lblAddedBy.Text = article.AddedBy;
        lblReleaseDate.Text = article.ReleaseDate.ToShortDateString();
        lblCategory.Text = article.CategoryTitle;
        lblLocation.Visible = (article.Location.Length > 0);
        if (lblLocation.Visible)
            lblLocation.Text = string.Format(lblLocation.Text, article.Location);
        lblRating.Text = string.Format(lblRating.Text, article.Votes);
        ratDisplay.Value = article.AverageRating;
        ratDisplay.Visible = (article.Votes > 0);
        lblViews.Text = string.Format(lblViews.Text, article.ViewCount);
        lblAbstract.Text = article.Abstract;
        lblBody.Text = article.Body;
        panComments.Visible = article.CommentsEnabled;
        panEditArticle.Visible = this.UserCanEdit;
        btnApprove.Visible = !article.Approved;
        lnkEditArticle.NavigateUrl = string.Format(
            lnkEditArticle.NavigateUrl, _articleID);

        // hide the rating box controls if the current user
        // has already voted for this article
        int userRating = GetUserRating();
        if (userRating > 0)
            ShowUserRating(userRating);
    }
}
```

The code for retrieving and displaying the user's vote will be shown in a moment, but first let's examine how the vote is remembered. When the Rate button is clicked, you retrieve the selected value from the Rating DropDownList and use it to call Article.RateArticle. Then you save the rating into a cookie named Rating_Article_{ArticleID}, and later you can retrieve it from the cookie:

```
protected void btnRate_Click(object sender, EventArgs e)
{
    // check whether the user has already rated this article
    int userRating = GetUserRating();
    if (userRating > 0)
    {
```

```
            ShowUserRating(userRating);
    }
    else
    {
        // rate the article, then create a cookie to remember this user's rating
        userRating = ddlRatings.SelectedIndex + 1;
        Article.RateArticle(_articleID, userRating);
        ShowUserRating(userRating);

        HttpCookie cookie = new HttpCookie(
            "Rating_Article" + _articleID.ToString(), userRating.ToString());
        cookie.Expires = DateTime.Now.AddDays(
            Globals.Settings.Articles.RatingLockInterval);
        this.Response.Cookies.Add(cookie);
    }
}
```

Notice that the cookie is set to have a lifetime of the number of days specified by the `RatingLockInterval` configuration setting. The default value is 15, but you can change it to a more suitable value according to a number of factors: For example, if your articles are not changed very often you will likely want to specify a much longer cookie lifetime. To determine whether a user has already voted, you simply need to check whether a cookie with that particular name exists. If it does, you read its value to get the rating:

```
protected int GetUserRating()
{
    int rating = 0;
    HttpCookie cookie = this.Request.Cookies[
        "Rating_Article" + _articleID.ToString()];
    if (cookie != null)
        rating = int.Parse(cookie.Value);
    return rating;
}
```

If the user has already voted on the article, you show their rating with the following method, which both hides the `DropDownList` and shows the `Label` with the message:

```
protected void ShowUserRating(int rating)
{
    lblUserRating.Text = string.Format(lblUserRating.Text, rating);
    ddlRatings.Visible = false;
    btnRate.Visible = false;
    lblUserRating.Visible = true;
}
```

One last detail: When the `DetailsView` is created in insert mode, you can prefill the `AddedBy` and `AddedByEmail` fields with the value retrieved from the user's membership account, if the user is authenticated:

```
protected void dvwComment_ItemCreated(object sender, EventArgs e)
{
    if (dvwComment.CurrentMode == DetailsViewMode.Insert &&
        this.User.Identity.IsAuthenticated)
    {
```

```
            MembershipUser user = Membership.GetUser();
            (dvwComment.FindControl("txtAddedBy") as TextBox).Text = user.UserName;
            (dvwComment.FindControl("txtAddedByEmail") as TextBox).Text = user.Email;
        }
    }
```

Figure 5-13 shows the `DataList` with all comments, and the `DetailsView` while editing one.

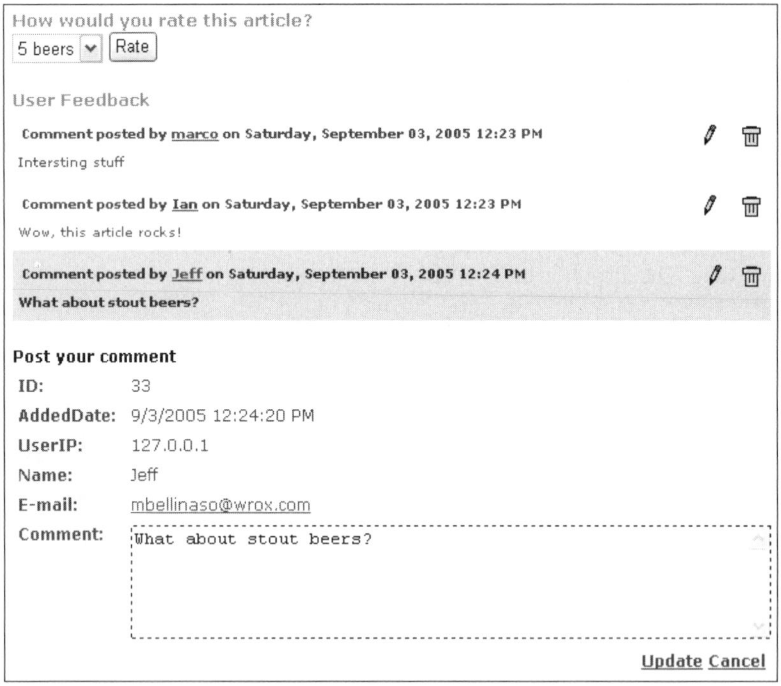

How would you rate this article?
5 beers ∨ [Rate]

User Feedback

Comment posted by marco on Saturday, September 03, 2005 12:23 PM

Intersting stuff

Comment posted by Ian on Saturday, September 03, 2005 12:23 PM

Wow, this article rocks!

Comment posted by Jeff on Saturday, September 03, 2005 12:24 PM

What about stout beers?

Post your comment

ID: 33
AddedDate: 9/3/2005 12:24:20 PM
UserIP: 127.0.0.1
Name: Jeff
E-mail: mbellinaso@wrox.com
Comment: What about stout beers?

                                                          Update Cancel

Figure 5-13

*Security warning: Never store a user's account number, or any sensitive data, in a cookie. In this appli-
cation the article rating is not sensitive in any way — you have already tallied the rating in the database
and the cookie is only used to display the rating made by that user. Using the cookie frees you from having to store each user's rating for each article in the database. You only need to store the total rating in
the database, which is far more efficient.*

The GetArticlesRss.aspx Page

This page returns the RSS feed for the "*n*" most recent articles (where "*n*" is specified in `web.config`)
of a specific category, or for any category, according to the `CatID` parameter on the querystring. In the
"Design" section of this chapter you saw the schema of a valid RSS 2.0 document. Here we apply that
structure to output a set of `Article` entries retrieved from the DB using a `Repeater` control. We don't
need a more advanced data control because the structure is simple and is completely format-free. Let's
examine the markup code of this page, and then I'll point out a few interesting details:

```
<%@ Page Language="C#" AutoEventWireup="true" ContentType="text/xml"
    EnableTheming="false"
    CodeFile="GetArticlesRss.aspx.cs" Inherits="GetArticlesRss" %>
<head runat="server" visible="false"></head>

<asp:Repeater id="rptRss" runat="server">
    <HeaderTemplate>
        <rss version="2.0">
            <channel>
                <title><![CDATA[The Beer House: <%# RssTitle %>]]></title>
                <link><%# FullBaseUrl %></link>
                <description>The Beer House: the site for beer fanatics</description>
                <copyright>Copyright 2005 by Marco Bellinaso</copyright>
    </HeaderTemplate>
    <ItemTemplate>
        <item>
            <title><![CDATA[<%# Eval("Title") %>]]></title>
            <author><![CDATA[<%# Eval("AddedBy") %>]]></author>
            <description><![CDATA[<%# Eval("Abstract") %>]]></description>
            <link><![CDATA[<%# FullBaseUrl + "ShowArticle.aspx?ID=" +
                Eval("ID") %>]]></link>
            <pubDate><%# string.Format("{0:R}", Eval("ReleaseDate")) %></pubDate>
        </item>
    </ItemTemplate>
    <FooterTemplate>
            </channel>
        </rss>
    </FooterTemplate>
</asp:Repeater>
```

Here are the interesting points about this code:

❑   The page's `ContentType` property is not set to `"text/html"` as usual, but to `"text/xml"`. This is necessary for the browser to correctly recognize the output as an XML document.

❑   There is a server-side `<head>` tag that has its `Visible` property set to `false`. The head tag is required if you've specified a theme in the `web.config` file, and even if you've explicitly disabled themes for this specific page, as we have done here (the page's `EnabledTheming` property is set to `false`). This is because ASP.NET has to dynamically create `<link>` tags for the CSS stylesheet files it finds under the `theme` folder when themes are enabled for the site. If the parent `<head>` tag is not found, it throws an exception. Having specified a `<head>` you can't leave it enabled because the output would not be a valid RSS document. Therefore, we specify a `<head>` but we make it invisible.

❑   All data retrieved from the DB is wrapped within an XML CDATA section so that it won't be considered to be XML text. As mentioned earlier, CDATA is a way of quoting literal data so that it will not be considered XML data. This is necessary in our case because we can't assume that all text stored in the DB will contain only characters that won't conflict with XML special characters (such as < and >).

❑   Our RSS feed will be consumed by desktop-based aggregators, or by other sites, so all the links you put into the feed (the link to the site's home page, and all the articles' links) must be complete links, and not relative to the site's root folder or to the current page. In other words, it must be something like `www.contoso.com/GetArticlesRss.aspx` instead of just `/GetArticlesRss.aspx`. For this reason, all links are prefixed by the value returned by `FullBaseUrl`, a custom property of the `BasePage` class that returns the site's base URL (e.g., `http://www.contoso.com/`).

The GetArticlesRss.aspx.cs Code-behind File

The code-behind file of this page is simple: It just loads the "*n*" most recent published articles and binds them to the `Repeater`. The overloaded version of `Article.GetArticles` we're using here is the one that takes a Boolean value indicating whether you want the published content only, the ID of a parent category (the `CatID` querystring parameter, or `0` if the parameter is not specified), the index of the first row to retrieve (`0` is used here), and the page size (read from the `Articles` configuration settings). Moreover, if the `CatID` parameter is passed on the querystring, the category with that ID is loaded, and its title is used to set the custom `RssTitle` property, to which the RSS's `<title>` element is bound. Here's the complete code:

```
public partial class GetArticlesRss : BasePage
{
    private string _rssTitle = "Recent Articles";
    public string RssTitle
    {
        get { return _rssTitle; }
        set { _rssTitle = value; }
    }

    protected void Page_Load(object sender, EventArgs e)
    {
        int categoryID = 0;
        if (!string.IsNullOrEmpty(this.Request.QueryString["CatID"]))
        {
            categoryID = int.Parse(this.Request.QueryString["CatID"]);
            Category category = Category.GetCategoryByID(categoryID);
            _rssTitle = category.Title;
        }

        List<Article> articles = Article.GetArticles(true, categoryID,
            0, Globals.Settings.Articles.RssItems);
        rptRss.DataSource = articles;
        rptRss.DataBind();
    }
}
```

The RssReader.ascx User Control

The final piece of code for this chapter's module is the `RssReader` user control. In the `ascx` file, you define a `DataList` that displays the title and description of the bound RSS items and makes the title a link pointing to the full article. It also has a header that will be set to the channel's title, a graphical link pointing to the source RSS file, and a link at the bottom that points to a page with more content:

```
<div class="sectiontitle">
<asp:Literal runat="server" ID="lblTitle"/>
<asp:HyperLink ID="lnkRss" runat="server" ToolTip="Get the RSS for this content">
    <asp:Image runat="server" ID="imgRss" ImageUrl="~/Images/rss.gif"
AlternateText="Get RSS feed" />
```

```
</asp:HyperLink>
</div>

<asp:DataList id="dlstRss" Runat="server" EnableViewState="False">
 <ItemTemplate>
    <small><%# Eval("PubDate", "{0:d}") %></small>
 <br>
 <div class="sectionsubtitle"><asp:HyperLink Runat="server" ID="lnkTitle"
    NavigateUrl='<%# Eval("Link") %>' Text='<%# Eval("Title") %>' /></div>
 <%# Eval("Description") %>
 </ItemTemplate>
</asp:DataList>
<p style="text-align: right;">
    <small><asp:HyperLink Runat="server" ID="lnkMore" /></small></p>
```

The RssReader.ascx.cs Code-behind File

The first part of the control's code-behind file defines all the custom properties defined in the "Design" section that are used to make this user control a generic RSS reader, and not specific to our site's content and settings:

```
public partial class RssReader : System.Web.UI.UserControl
{
    public string RssUrl
    {
        get { return lnkRss.NavigateUrl; }
        set
        {
            string url = value;
            if (value.StartsWith("/") || value.StartsWith("~/"))
            {
                url = (this.Page as BasePage).FullBaseUrl + value;
                url = url.Replace("~/", "");
            }
            lnkRss.NavigateUrl = url;
        }
    }

    public string Title
    {
        get { return lblTitle.Text; }
        set { lblTitle.Text = value; }
    }

    public int RepeatColumns
    {
        get { return dlstRss.RepeatColumns; }
        set { dlstRss.RepeatColumns = value; }
    }

    public string MoreUrl
    {
        get { return lnkMore.NavigateUrl; }
        set { lnkMore.NavigateUrl = value; }
    }
```

```
public string MoreText
{
    get { return lnkMore.Text; }
    set { lnkMore.Text = value; }
}
```

Note that you don't need to persist the property values in the `ControlState` here, as we did in previous controls, because all properties wrap a property of some other server-side control, and it will be that other control's job to take care of persisting the values. All the real work of loading and binding the data is done in `Page_Load`. First, you load the RSS document into a `System.Xml.XmlDataDocument`, a class that allows you to easily work with XML data. For each `<item>` element found in the document, you create a new row in a `DataTable` whose schema (the number and types of columns) is also generated from within this event handler. Finally, the `DataTable` is bound to the `DataList`:

```
protected void Page_Load(object sender, EventArgs e)
{
    try
    {
        if (this.RssUrl.Length == 0)
            throw new ApplicationException("The RssUrl cannot be null.");

        // create a DataTable and fill it with the RSS data,
        // then bind it to the Repeater control
        XmlDataDocument feed = new XmlDataDocument();
        feed.Load(this.RssUrl);
        XmlNodeList posts = feed.GetElementsByTagName("item");

        DataTable table = new DataTable("Feed");
        table.Columns.Add("Title", typeof(string));
        table.Columns.Add("Description", typeof(string));
        table.Columns.Add("Link", typeof(string));
        table.Columns.Add("PubDate", typeof(DateTime));

        foreach (XmlNode post in posts)
        {
            DataRow row = table.NewRow();
            row["Title"] = post["title"].InnerText;
            row["Description"] = post["description"].InnerText.Trim();
            row["Link"] = post["link"].InnerText;
            row["PubDate"] = DateTime.Parse(post["pubDate"].InnerText);
            table.Rows.Add(row);
        }

        dlstRss.DataSource = table;
        dlstRss.DataBind();
    }
    catch (Exception)
    {
        this.Visible = false;
    }
}
```

Note that everything is put into a `try...catch` block, and if something goes wrong the whole control will be hidden. To test the control you can plug it into the site's home page, with the following declaration:

```
<mb:RssReader id="RssReader1" runat="server" Title="Latest Articles"
    RssUrl="~/GetArticlesRss.aspx"
    MoreText="More articles..." MoreUrl="~/BrowseArticles.aspx" />
```

The output is shown in Figure 5-14.

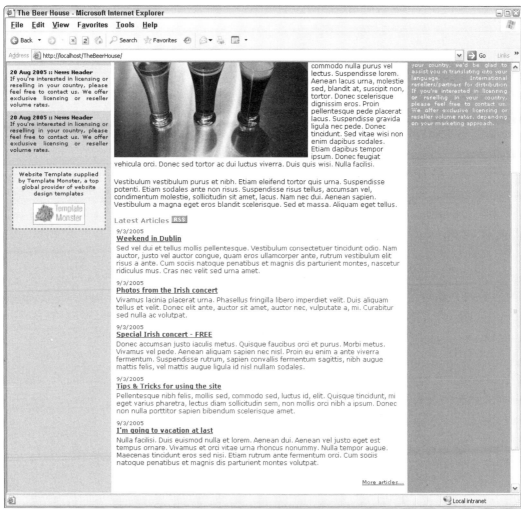

Figure 5-14

Configuring Security Settings

Many security checks have been implemented programmatically from the pages' code-behind. Now you need to edit the Admin folder's web.config file to add the Contributors role to the list of allowed roles for the AddEditArticle.aspx page:

```
<configuration xmlns="http://schemas.microsoft.com/.NetConfiguration/v2.0">
    <system.web>
        <authorization>
            <allow roles="Administrators,Editors" />
            <deny users="*" />
        </authorization>
    </system.web>

    <location path="AddEditArticle.aspx">
        <system.web>
            <authorization>
                <allow roles="Administrators,Editors,Contributors" />
                <deny users="*" />
            </authorization>
        </system.web>
    </location>

    <!-- ManageUsers.aspx and EditUser.aspx pages... -->
</configuration>
```

Final Touches — Friendly URLs with UrlMappings

The more meaningful and short a URL can be, the better. Those URLs are easier to communicate to people, and easier for them to remember. The current URLs that allow us to browse articles for a specific category are already pretty short, but it's not easy to remember all category IDs by heart . . . and thus to remember the URL. ASP.NET 2.0 introduces a new section in web.config that allows us to map a virtual URL to a real URL: This section's name is urlMapping, and it's located under <system.web>. When the user types the virtual URL, the page located at the corresponding real URL will be loaded. Here's what you can write in web.config to make your sample categories easier to reach:

```
<urlMappings>
    <add url="~/articles/beer.aspx" mappedUrl="~/BrowseArticles.aspx?CatID=28" />
    <add url="~/articles/events.aspx" mappedUrl="~/BrowseArticles.aspx?CatID=41" />
    <add url="~/articles/news.aspx" mappedUrl="~/BrowseArticles.aspx?CatID=31" />
    <add url="~/articles/photos.aspx" mappedUrl="~/BrowseArticles.aspx?CatID=40" />
    <add url="~/articles/blog.aspx" mappedUrl="~/BrowseArticles.aspx?CatID=29" />
    <add url="~/articles/faq.aspx" mappedUrl="~/BrowseArticles.aspx?CatID=42" />
</urlMappings>
```

Note that when the server receives a request for the virtual URL it doesn't make a normal redirect to the real URL. Before the page is loaded, ASP.NET rewrites the URL to the request's context. From that point on, the URL will be read from the context, and thus the correct URL will be retrieved. The bottom line is that the transition is done in memory on the server side, and users do not even see the real URL in their browser. Therefore, if a user maneuvers to ~/articles/beer.aspx she's really going to get ~/BrowseArticles.aspx?CatID=28. Furthermore, there is no physical page named ~/articles/beer.aspx.

This could have been done in ASP.NET 1.1, but you had to write your own custom HTTP module to do that, from which you would have used the current HttpContext's RewritePath method to do the in-memory redirect.

Summary

This chapter has shown you how to build a complex and articulate module to completely manage the site's articles, events, and possibly even photo galleries. It covered all of the following:

❑   An administrative section for managing the data in the database.

❑   Pages for browsing the published content.

❑   Integration with the built-in membership system to secure the module and track the authors of the articles.

❑   A syndication service that publishes a RSS feed of recent content for a specific category, or for every category, by means of an ASP.NET page.

❑   A generic user control that consumes any RSS feed. It has been used in this chapter to list the new articles on the home page, but you could also use it in the forums module, and in other situations.

By following along in this chapter you've seen some of the powerful things you can do with the `GridView` control, its accompanying `ObjectDataSource`, and a properly designed business logic layer (BLL). The provider-based data access layer (DAL) implemented in this chapter enables you to easily create new classes to support different data stores and plug them into the system without changing a single line of code in the BLL or the UI.

This system is flexible enough to be utilized in many real-world applications, but you can also consider making some of the following improvements:

❑   Support multi level categories (subcategories management).

❑   A search engine could be added to the public section of the modules. Currently, when users want to find a particular article, they have to go through all the content (which could fill several pages in the article list). You could add a Search box that searches for the specified words in the selected category, or in all the categories, and with further options.

❑   Extend the `ShowArticle.aspx` page, or create a separate page, that outputs a printer-friendly version of the article, i.e., the article without the site's layout (header, menus, footer, left- and right-hand columns). This could be done easily by adding a new stylesheet to the page (when the page is loaded with a `PrinterFriendly=1` parameter on the querystring) that makes some DIVs hidden (use the `visibility:hidden` style).

❑   Create a web service that allows other applications to retrieve the list of articles as an alternative to the RSS feed. This could also be used by Contributors to submit new articles, or even by Administrators and Editors to perform their duties. You could use the Microsoft Web Service Extensions (WSE) to make authentication much easier and even to support encryption — otherwise, you'd have to pass credentials in the SOAP headers, and encryption would only be possible by using SSL.

In the next chapter you'll work on a module for creating, managing, displaying, and archiving opinion polls, to implement a form of user-to-site communication.

6

Opinion Polls

Opinion polls consist of questions with a set of options from which users can select their response. Once a user votes in a poll it's customary to show them current statistics about how the poll is going at that particular time. This chapter explains why polls are useful and important for different web sites. Then you will learn how to design and implement a simple and maintainable voting module for our TheBeerHouse site.

Problem

There are basically two reasons why polls are used on a web site: because the site managers may be interested in what their users like (perhaps so they can modify their advertising or product offerings, or maybe in a more general sense to understand their users better) and to help users feel like they have some input to a site and make them feel like they are part of a community of users. Good polls always contain targeted questions that can help the site's managers to know who their users are and what they want to find on their site. This information can be used to identify which parts of the site to improve or modify. Polls are valuable for e-commerce sites too because they can indicate which products are of interest and in higher demand. Armed with this information, e-commerce businesses can highlight those products, provide more detailed descriptions or case studies, or offer discounts to convince users to buy from their site. Another use for the information is to attract advertising revenue. If you look on a typical medium to large-size site, you will frequently see an "Advertise with Us" link or something similar. If you were to inquire about the possibility of advertising on a particular site, that site's advertising department would likely give you some demographics regarding the typical users of that site, such as age, the region or country they live in, common interests, and so on. This information is often gathered by direct or indirect polls. The more details you provide about your typical audience, the more chance you have of finding a sponsor to advertise on your site.

The other major benefit is user-to-user communication. Users generally like to know what their peers think about a product or a subject of interest to them. I must admit that I'm usually curious when I see a poll on a web site. Even if I don't have a very clear opinion about the question being asked, I will often vote just so I can see the statistics of how the other users voted! This explains why polls are usually well accepted, and why users generally vote quite willingly. Another reason why users may desire to cast a vote is because they think their opinion may influence other users or the site managers. In addition, their votes really are important, as you've seen; and the results can definitely drive the future content of the site and perhaps even business decisions. For these reasons, you or your client may realize that you want the benefits of a poll feature, and thus you will implement some form of polling on the web site.

You should consider some design issues about web polls — namely, the problems that you must address to successfully run a poll system. First of all, as with the news and other content, the same poll shouldn't remain active for too long. If you left the same poll on the page for, say, two months, you might gather some more votes, but you would lose the interest of users who voted early. If you keep a poll up for just a couple of days, you may not achieve significant results because some of your users may not have visited your site within that time frame. The right duration depends mostly on the average number of visitors you have and how often they return to your site. As a rule-of-thumb, if you know that several thousands of users regularly come to visit the site each week, then that is a good duration for the active poll. Otherwise, if you have fewer visitors, you can leave the poll open for two or more weeks, but probably not longer than a month.

> *In case you're wondering how to get the information you need to make this decision, there are several services that enable you to easily retrieve statistics for your site, such as the frequency and number of visitors, and much more. Some of these services are commercial, but you can also find some good free ones. If you have a hosted web site through a hosting company, you probably have access to some statistics through your hosting company's control panel (these gather information by analyzing the IIS log files). Of course, you could implement your own hit counter by yourself — it would be pretty easy to track visitors and generate some basic statistics, but if you wanted to reproduce all the advanced features offered by specialized services it would be quite a lot of work, and it may be cheaper in the long run to subscribe to a professional service.*

When you change the active poll, a new question arises: What do you do with the old questions and their results? Should you throw them away? Certainly not! They might be very interesting for new users who didn't take part in the vote, and the information will probably remain valid for some time, so you should keep them available for viewing. Old polls can even be considered as part of the useful content of your site, and you should probably build an archive of past polls. If you allow a user to vote as many times as they want to, you'll end up with incorrect results. The overall results will be biased towards that user's personal opinion. Having false results is just as useless as having no results at all, because you can't base any serious decisions on them. Therefore, you want to prevent users from voting more than once for any given question. There are occasions when you might want to allow the user to vote several times, though. For example, during your own development and testing stage, you may need to post many votes to determine whether the voting module is working correctly. The administrator could just manually add some votes by entering them directly into the SQL table, or by directly calling the appropriate stored procedure, but that would not tell you if the polling front end is working right. If you enter votes using the polling user interface that you'll build in this chapter, it's more convenient and it thoroughly tests the module. There are reasons for wanting to allow multiple votes after deployment, too. Imagine that you are running a competition to select the best resource on any selected topic. The resources might be updated frequently, and if the poll lasts a month, then users may change their mind in the meantime, after voting. You may then decide to allow multiple votes, but no more than once per week (but you probably won't want to go to the trouble of letting a user eliminate their earlier vote).

This discussion talks about polls that only allow a single option to be selected (poll boxes with a series of radio buttons). However, another type of poll box enables users to vote for multiple options in a single step (the options are listed with checkboxes, and users can select more than one). This might be useful if you wanted to ask a question like "What do you usually eat at pubs?" and you wanted to allow multiple answers through multiple separate checkboxes. However, this type of poll is quite rare, and you could probably reword the question to ask what food they most like to eat at pubs if you only want to allow one answer. The design of a multiple-answer poll would needlessly complicate this module, so our example here won't use that kind of functionality.

To summarize what we've discussed here: You want to implement a poll facility on the site to gauge the opinions of your users and to generate a sense of community. You don't want users to lose interest by seeing the same poll for a long time, but you do want a meaningful number of users to vote, so you'll add new questions and change the current poll often. You also want to allow users to see old polls because that helps to add useful content to your page, but they won't be allowed to vote in the old polls. Finally, you want to be able to easily add the poll to any page, and you want the results to be as unbiased and accurate as possible. The next section describes the design in more detail, and considers how to meet these challenges.

Design

This section looks at how you can provide poll functionality for the site. This polling stores the data (questions, answers, votes, etc.) in the database shared by all modules of this book (although the configuration settings do allow each module to use a separate database, if there's a need to do that). To easily access the DB you'll need tables, stored procedures, a data access layer, and a business layer to keep the presentation layer separate from the DB and the details of its structure. Of course, some sort of user interface will allow administrators to see and manage the data using their favorite browser. We'll start with a list of features we want to implement, and then we'll design the database tables, stored procedures, data and business layers, user interface services, and security that we need for this module.

Features to Implement

Here's the list of features needed in the polls module:

- ❑ An access-protected administration console to easily change the current poll and add or remove questions. It should allow multiple polls and their response options to be added, edited, or deleted. The capability to have multiple polls is important because you might want to have different polls in different sections of your site. The administration pages should also show the current statistical results for each poll, and the total number of votes for each poll, as a quick general summary.

- ❑ A user control that builds the poll box that can be inserted into any page. The poll box should display the question text and the available options (usually rendered as radio buttons to allow only one choice). Each poll will be identified by a unique ID, which should be specified as a custom property for the user control, so that the webmaster can easily change the currently displayed question by setting the value for that property.

- ❑ You should prevent users from voting multiple times for the same poll. Or, even better, you should be able to dynamically decide if you want to allow users to vote more than once, or specify the period for which they will be prevented from voting again

❑ You can only have one poll question declared as the current default. When you set a poll question as being current, the previous current one should change its state. The current poll will be displayed in a poll box unless you specify a non-default poll ID. Of course, you can have different polls on the site at the same time depending on the section (perhaps one for the Beer-related article category, and one for party bookings), but it's useful to set a default poll question because you'll be able to add a poll box without specifying the ID of the question to display, and you can change the poll question through the administration console, without manually changing the page and re-deploying it.

❑ A poll should be archived when you decide that you no longer want to use it as an active poll. Once archived, if a poll box is still explicitly bound to that particular poll, the poll will only be shown in Display state (read-only), and it will show the recorded results.

❑ We need a page that displays all the archived polls and their results. A page for the results of the current poll is not necessary, as they will be shown directly by the poll box — instead of the list of response options — when it detects that the user has already voted. This way, users are forced to express their opinion if they want to see the poll's results (before the poll expires), which will bring in more votes than we would get if we made the current results freely available to users that have not yet voted. There must also be an option that specifies whether the archive page is accessible by everyone, or just by registered users. You may prefer the second option to give the user one more reason to register for the site.

Handling Multiple Votes

As discussed in the "Problem" section, we want to be able to control whether users can cast multiple votes, and allow them to vote again after a specified period. Therefore, you would probably like to give the administrator the capability to prevent multiple votes, or to allow multiple votes but with a specified lock duration (one week in the previous example). You still have to find a way to ensure that the user does not vote more times than is allowed. The simplest, and most common and reliable, solution is writing a cookie to the client's browser that stores the ID of the poll for which the user has voted. Then, when the poll box loads, it first tries to find a cookie matching the poll. If a cookie is not found, the poll box displays the options and lets the user vote. Otherwise, the poll box shows the latest results and does not allow the user to vote again. To allow multiple votes, the cookie will have an expiration date. If you set it to the current date plus seven days, it means that the cookie expires in seven days, after which the user will be allowed to vote again on that same question.

Writing and checking cookies is straightforward, and in most cases it is sufficient. The drawback of this method is that the user can easily turn off cookies through a browser option, or delete the cookies from their machine, and then be allowed to vote as many times as they want to. Only a very small percentage of users keep cookies turned off — except for company users where security is a major concern — because they are used on many sites and are sometimes actually required. Because of this, it shouldn't be much of an issue because most people won't bother to go to that much trouble to re-vote, and this is not a high security type of voting mechanism that would be suitable for something very important, such as a political election.

There's an additional method to prevent multiple votes: IP locking. When users vote, their computer's IP address can be retrieved and stored in the cache together with the other vote details. Later in the same user session, when the poll box loads or when the user tries to vote again, you can check whether the cache contains a vote for a specific poll, by a specified IP. To implement this, the Poll ID and user's IP may be part of the item's key if you use the `Cache` class; otherwise, the Poll ID is enough if you choose to store it in Session state storage, because that's already specific to one user. If a vote is found, the user has already voted and you can prevent further voting. This method only prevents re-voting within the same session — the same user can vote again the next day. We don't want to store the user's IP address in the database because it might be different tomorrow (because most users today have dynamically assigned IP addresses). Also, the user might share an IP with many other users if they are in a company using network address translation (NAT) addresses, and we don't want to prevent other users within the same company from voting. Therefore, the IP locking method is normally not my first choice.

There's yet another option. You could track the logged users through their username, instead of their computer's IP address. However, this will only work if the user is registered. In our case we don't want to limit the vote to registered users only, so we won't cover this method further.

In this module we'll provide the option to employ both methods (cookie and IP), only one of them, or neither. Employing neither of them means that you will allow multiple votes with no limitations, and this method should only be used during the testing stage. In a real scenario you might need to disable one of the methods — maybe your client doesn't want to use cookies for security reasons, or maybe your client is concerned about the dynamic IP issue and doesn't want to use that method. I personally prefer the cookie option in most cases.

In conclusion, the polls module will have the following options:

❑   Multiple votes per poll can be allowed or denied.

❑   Multiple votes per poll can be prevented with client cookies or IP locking.

❑   Limited multiple votes can be allowed, in which case the administrator can specify lock duration for either method (users can vote again in seven days, for example).

This way, the polls module will be simple and straightforward, but still flexible, and it can be used with the options that best suit the particular situation. Online administration of polls follows the general concept of allowing the site to be remotely controlled by managers and administrators using a web browser.

Designing the Database Tables

We will need two tables for this module: one to contain the poll questions and their attributes (such as whether a poll is current or archived) and another one to contain the polls' response options and the number of votes each received. The diagram in Figure 6-1 shows how they are linked to each other.

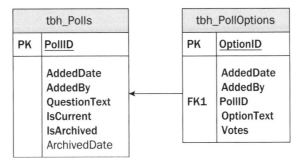

Figure 6-1

Here you see the primary and foreign keys, the usual AddedDate and AddedBy fields that are used in most tables for audit and recovery purposes, and a few extra fields that store the poll data. The tbh_Polls table has a QuestionText field that stores the poll's question, an IsArchived bit field to indicate whether that poll was archived and no longer available for voting, and an ArchivedDate field for the date/time when the poll was archived (this last column is the only one that is nullable). There is also an IsCurrent bit field, which can be set to 1 only for a single poll, which is the overall default poll. The other table, tbh_PollOptions, contains all the configurable options for each poll, and makes the link to the parent poll by means of the PollID foreign key. There is also a Votes integer field that contains the number of user votes received by the option. In the first edition of the book we had a separate Votes table, in addition to these two, that would store every vote in a separate row, with the date/time of the vote and the IP of the user who cast the vote. I changed the design in this new edition because that additional table made the implementation more difficult and had worse performance (caused by the aggregations you had to run to count the total number of votes for each option), without adding any real benefit.

The Stored Procedures That Manage the Database

The stored procedures in the following table will be needed by the poll administration pages.

Property	Description
tbh_Polls_InsertPoll	Inserts a new poll with the specified question text. If the new poll must become the new current one, this procedure first resets the IsCurrent field of all existing polls.
tbh_Polls_UpdatePoll	Updates an existing poll. If the poll being updated must become the new current one, the procedure first resets the IsCurrent field of all existing polls.
tbh_Polls_DeletePoll	Deletes a poll with the specified ID
tbh_Polls_ArchivePoll	Archives a poll with the specified ID, by setting its Is archived field to 1, and the ArchivedDate field to the current date and time
tbh_Polls_GetPolls	Retrieves all data for the rows of the tbh_Polls table, plus a calculated field that is the sum of all votes for the poll's child options. The procedure takes as input a couple of methods that enable you to specify whether you want to include the active (non-archived) polls in the results, and whether you want to include the archived polls in this poll box.
tbh_Polls_GetPollByID	Like tbh_Polls_GetPolls but for a single poll whose ID is specified in input
tbh_Polls_GetCurrentPollID	Returns the ID of the poll marked as current, or -1 if no current poll is found
tbh_Polls_InsertOption	Inserts a new response option for the specified poll
tbh_Polls_UpdateOption	Updates the text for the specified option
tbh_Polls_DeleteOption	Deletes an existing option

Property	Description
tbh_Polls_GetOptions	Retrieves all data for all options of a specified poll, plus a Percentage decimal calculated field, which is the percentage of each option's votes out of the total number of votes for the poll
tbh_Polls_GetOptionByID	Like tbh_Polls_GetOptions, but for a single option
tbh_Polls_InsertVote	Inserts a new vote for a specified option, by incrementing the option's Votes integer field

Most of these stored procedures are straightforward and shouldn't need any further explanation. In fact, they won't even be shown again in the "Solution" section, as they just include some very basic SQL code (their full text is available in the code download, of course). We'll only examine some of the most interesting procedures. Only two procedures are worth special attention: the one that retrieves the polls and vote sums for each child option, and the one that retrieves the options and calculates the percentage of votes for each single option. The two parameters of the tbh_Polls_GetPolls procedures are useful because they enable you to retrieve only the active polls to be shown in the management page, and only the archived page to be shown in the archive page. There's a single procedure instead of two separate procedures (such as tbh_Polls_GetActivePolls and tbh_Polls_GetArchivedPolls) because should you later want to show all polls in the management page instead of just the active one, you will just need to change a parameter when calling the procedure, instead of calling two procedures and doing additional work to merge the two resultsets.

Designing the Configuration Module

I've already mentioned that the polls module will need a number of configuration settings that enable or disable multiple votes, make the archive public to everyone, and more. In addition, there will be settings to specify which DAL provider to use (either the supplied one for SQL Server 2005 or one for some other data store) and the connection string for the database. Following is the list of properties for a new class, named PollsElement, which inherits from the framework's ConfigurationElement class, and will read the settings of a <polls> element under the <theBeerHouse> custom configuration section (this was introduced in Chapter 3, and then used again in Chapter 5).

Property	Description
ProviderType	The full name (namespace plus class name) of the concrete provider class that implements the data access code for a specific data store
ConnectionStringName	The name of the entry in web.config's new <connectionStrings> section that contains the connection string to the module's database
VotingLockInterval	An integer indicating when the cookie with the user's vote will expire (number of days to prevent re-voting)
VotingLockByCookie	A Boolean value indicating whether a cookie will be used to remember the user's vote

Table continued on following page

Property	Description
VotingLockByIP	A Boolean value indicating whether the vote's IP address is kept in memory to prevent duplicate votes from that IP in the current session
ArchiveIsPublic	A Boolean value indicating whether the poll's archive is accessible by everyone, or if it's restricted to registered members
EnableCaching	A Boolean value indicating whether the caching of data is enabled
CacheDuration	The number of seconds for which the data is cached if there aren't inserts, deletes, or updates that invalidate the cache

Designing the Data Access Layer

The DAL of this module is based on a simple form of the provider model design pattern, introduced in Chapter 3 and then implemented for the articles module in Chapter 5. You'll follow the same strategy here, to create a `PollsProvider` abstract class that defines the signature of data access methods, and some helper methods that copy data from a `DataReader` into a single custom entity class or a collection of objects, and then a concrete provider class, `SqlPollProvider`, that implements the abstract methods. The methods implemented by the SQL Server–specific provider will only be simple wrappers around the stored procedures listed above — there is a one-to-one relationship. There are also two custom entity classes, `PollDetails` and `PollOptionDetails`, which have wrapper properties for all fields of the `tbh_Polls` and `tbh_PollOptions` database tables, plus the additional `Votes` and `Percentage` fields added by the stored procedures. The diagram shown in Figure 6-2 represents all these classes and lists their methods and properties, which should be self-explanatory.

Designing the Business Layer

The BLL for this module is composed of a couple of classes, `Poll` and `Option`, which wrap the data of the `PollDetails` and `PollOptionDetails`, respectively, and add both instance and static methods to work with that data. These are the classes that you access from the UI layer (by means of the `ObjectDataSource` control, or manually) to retrieve the data to display on the page, and modify it. The UI layer must never call into the DAL directly — it only interacts with the BLL classes. The diagram in Figure 6-3 represents the business classes and their relationships.

As you see, the structure is the same as the structure employed in Chapter 5. There's a `BizObject` base class with a number of properties and methods that are shared among all business classes. Then there's a module-specific `BasePoll` class that defines the `ID`, `AddedBy`, and `AddedDate` properties (that both the polls and the poll options have), a reference to the `PollsElement` configuration element described above, and a `CacheData` method that caches the input data if the settings indicate that caching is active. In addition to the data read from a `PollDetails` object, the `Poll` class also has `CurrentPollID` and `CurrentPoll` static properties: the former returns the integer ID of the poll marked as current, and the latter returns an instance of `Poll` that completely represents the current poll.

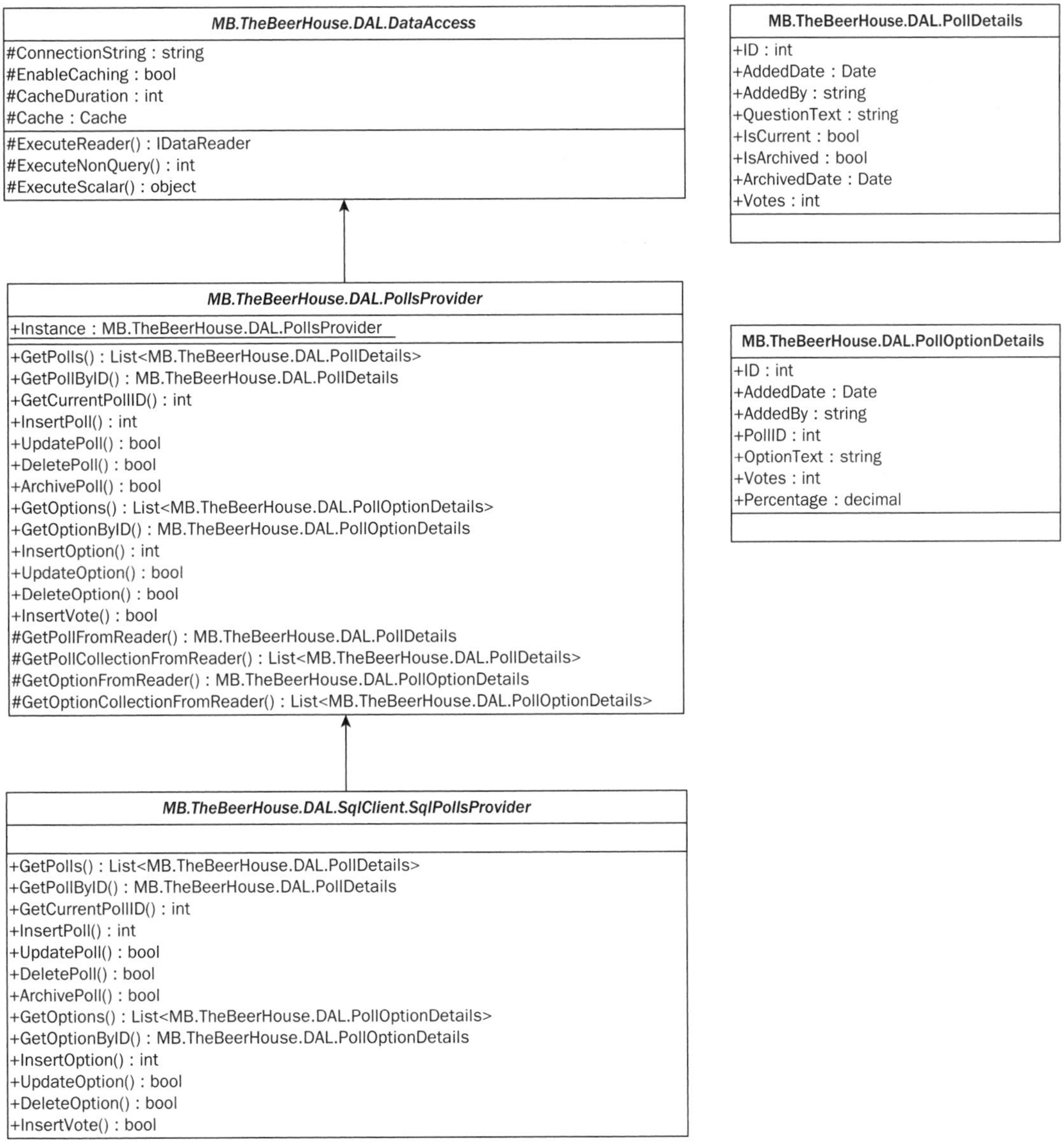

MB.TheBeerHouse.DAL.DataAccess
#ConnectionString : string
#EnableCaching : bool
#CacheDuration : int
#Cache : Cache
#ExecuteReader() : IDataReader
#ExecuteNonQuery() : int
#ExecuteScalar() : object

MB.TheBeerHouse.DAL.PollDetails
+ID : int
+AddedDate : Date
+AddedBy : string
+QuestionText : string
+IsCurrent : bool
+IsArchived : bool
+ArchivedDate : Date
+Votes : int

MB.TheBeerHouse.DAL.PollsProvider
+Instance : MB.TheBeerHouse.DAL.PollsProvider
+GetPolls() : List<MB.TheBeerHouse.DAL.PollDetails>
+GetPollByID() : MB.TheBeerHouse.DAL.PollDetails
+GetCurrentPollID() : int
+InsertPoll() : int
+UpdatePoll() : bool
+DeletePoll() : bool
+ArchivePoll() : bool
+GetOptions() : List<MB.TheBeerHouse.DAL.PollOptionDetails>
+GetOptionByID() : MB.TheBeerHouse.DAL.PollOptionDetails
+InsertOption() : int
+UpdateOption() : bool
+DeleteOption() : bool
+InsertVote() : bool
#GetPollFromReader() : MB.TheBeerHouse.DAL.PollDetails
#GetPollCollectionFromReader() : List<MB.TheBeerHouse.DAL.PollDetails>
#GetOptionFromReader() : MB.TheBeerHouse.DAL.PollOptionDetails
#GetOptionCollectionFromReader() : List<MB.TheBeerHouse.DAL.PollOptionDetails>

MB.TheBeerHouse.DAL.PollOptionDetails
+ID : int
+AddedDate : Date
+AddedBy : string
+PollID : int
+OptionText : string
+Votes : int
+Percentage : decimal

MB.TheBeerHouse.DAL.SqlClient.SqlPollsProvider
+GetPolls() : List<MB.TheBeerHouse.DAL.PollDetails>
+GetPollByID() : MB.TheBeerHouse.DAL.PollDetails
+GetCurrentPollID() : int
+InsertPoll() : int
+UpdatePoll() : bool
+DeletePoll() : bool
+ArchivePoll() : bool
+GetOptions() : List<MB.TheBeerHouse.DAL.PollOptionDetails>
+GetOptionByID() : MB.TheBeerHouse.DAL.PollOptionDetails
+InsertOption() : int
+UpdateOption() : bool
+DeleteOption() : bool
+InsertVote() : bool

Figure 6-2

291

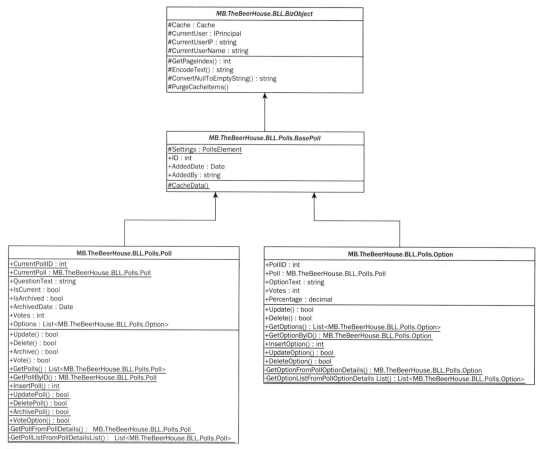

Figure 6-3

Designing the User Interface Services

This section describes the pages and controls that constitute the user interface layer of this module. In particular, there are two ASP.NET pages, and one user control:

❑   **~/Admin/ManagePolls.aspx:** This is the page through which an administrator or editor can manage polls: add, edit, archive and remove poll options, see current results, and set the current poll. This page only lists active polls, however: Once a poll is archived, it will be visible only in the archived polls page (you can't change history).

❑   **~/ArchivedPolls.aspx:** This page lists the archived polls and shows their results. If the user accessing it is an administrator or an editor, she will also see buttons for deleting polls. The archived polls are not editable; they can only be deleted if you don't want them to appear on the archive page.

❑   The **PollBox user control** will enable us to insert the poll box into any page, with only a couple of lines of code. This control is central to the poll module and is described in further detail in the following section.

The `ManagePoll.aspx` page will be accessible only to administrator and editors, and you only have to place this page under the `~/Admin` folder to protect it from unauthorized users, because that folder already has configuration settings in `web.config` to prevent access by anyone who is not an administrator or editor. The archive page may, or may not, be accessible to everyone, according to a custom configuration parameter, and therefore the security check will be done programmatically when the page loads.

The PollBox User Control

This control has two functions:

1. If it detects that the user has not voted for the question yet, the control will present a list of radio buttons with the various response options, and a Vote button.

2. If it detects that the current user has already voted, instead of displaying the radio buttons it displays the results. It will show the percentage of votes for each option, both as a number and graphically, as a colored bar. This will also happen if the poll being shown were archived.

In both cases the control can optionally show header text and a link at the bottom that points to the archive page. This method of changing behavior based on whether the user has already voted is elegant, doesn't need an additional window, and intelligently hides the radio buttons if the user can't vote. The control's properties, which enable us to customize its appearance and behavior, are shown in the following table.

Property	Description
PollID	The ID of the poll to display in the poll box. If no ID is specified, or if it is explicitly set to -1, the poll with the IsCurrent field set to 1 will be used.
HeaderText	The text for the control's header bar
ShowHeader	Specifies whether the control's header bar is visible
ShowQuestion	Specifies whether the poll's question is visible
ShowArchiveLink	Specifies whether the control shows a link at the bottom of the control pointing to the poll's Archive page

When you add this control to a page, you will normally configure it to show the header, the question, and the link to the archive page. If, however, you have multiple polls on the page, you may want to show the link to the archive in just one poll box, maybe the one with the poll marked as the current default. The control will also be used in the archive page itself, to show the results of the old polls (the second mode described previously): In this case the question text will be shown by some other control that lists the polls, and thus the `PollBox` control will have the `ShowHeader`, `ShowQuestion`, and `ShowArchiveLink` properties set to `false`.

Solution

Now that the design is complete, you should have a very clear idea about what is required, so now we can consider how we're going to implement this functionality. You'll follow the same order as the "Design" section, starting with the creation of database tables and stored procedures, the configuration, DAL and BLL classes, and finally the ASPX pages and the PollBox user control.

Working on the Database

The tables and stored procedures required for this module are added to the same sitewide SQL Server 2005 database (aspnetdb.mdf) shared by all modules, although the configuration settings enable you to have the data and the db objects separated into multiple databases if you prefer to do it that way. It's easy to create the required objects with Visual Studio 2005 using the integrated Server Explorer, which has been enhanced in the 2005 version so that it's almost like using SQL Server 2000's Enterprise Manager, but right from within the Visual Studio IDE. Figure 6-4 is a screenshot of the IDE when adding columns to the tbh_Polls tables, and setting the properties for the PollID primary key column.

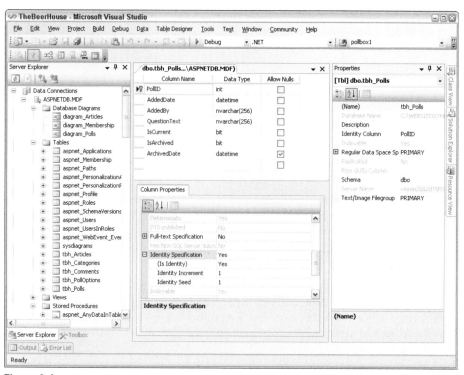

Figure 6-4

After creating the two tables with the columns indicated in Figure 6-1, you need to create a relationship between them over the PollID column, and set up cascade updates and deletes (Select Data ➪ Add New ➪ Diagram to bring up the interactive diagram that enables you to create the relationship — as explained in Chapter 5). Figure 6-5 is a screenshot of the relationship diagram.

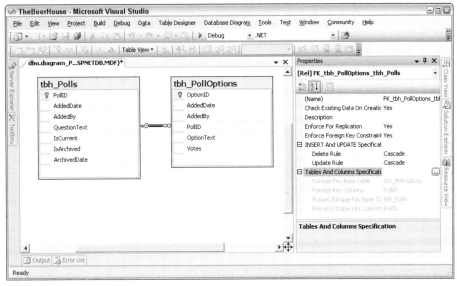

Figure 6-5

Now we'll cover the most interesting stored procedures (as mentioned earlier, the code for all stored procedures is in the code download for this book).

The tbh_Polls_InsertPoll Stored Procedure

This procedure inserts a new poll, in the form of a new row into the `tbh_Polls` table. It takes input values for all fields of this table, minus the `IsArchived` and `ArchivedDate` columns because archiving is not possible when creating a new poll. When adding a new poll you can pass `true` in `IsCurrent` if you want this new poll to be the default poll, in which case the procedure first resets the `IsCurrent` field of all existing rows to `0`:

```
ALTER PROCEDURE dbo.tbh_Polls_InsertPoll
(
    @AddedDate      datetime,
    @AddedBy        nvarchar(256),
    @QuestionText   nvarchar(256),
    @IsCurrent      bit,
    @PollID         int OUTPUT
)
AS
SET NOCOUNT ON

BEGIN TRANSACTION InsertPoll

IF @IsCurrent = 1
    BEGIN
    UPDATE tbh_Polls SET IsCurrent = 0
    END

INSERT INTO tbh_Polls
```

```
    (AddedDate, AddedBy, QuestionText, IsCurrent, IsArchived, ArchivedDate)
    VALUES (@AddedDate, @AddedBy, @QuestionText, @IsCurrent, 0, null)

SET @PollID = scope_identity()

IF @@ERROR > 0
    BEGIN
    RAISERROR('Insert of poll failed', 16, 1)
    ROLLBACK TRANSACTION InsertPoll
    RETURN 99
    END


COMMIT TRANSACTION InsertPoll
```

Because the stored procedure may run two separate statements (if the IsCurrent parameter is true), the code is wrapped into a TSQL transaction so that if the second statement fails for some reason, then the first statement running the UPDATE is rolled back as well. We're also using a transaction in the tbh_Polls_UpdatePoll procedure.

The tbh_Polls_ArchivePoll Stored Procedure

This procure is used to archive a poll. It only takes the ID of the poll to archive. The poll's ArchivedDate field is set to the current date/time, retrieved by the TSQL's getdate function:

```
ALTER PROCEDURE dbo.tbh_Polls_ArchivePoll
(
 @PollID          int
)
AS

UPDATE tbh_Polls
    SET IsCurrent = 0, IsArchived = 1, ArchivedDate = getdate()
    WHERE PollID = @PollID
```

The tbh_Polls_GetPolls Stored Procedure

The tbh_Polls_GetPolls procedure takes two parameters that specify whether the active and archived polls are included in the resultset to be returned, respectively. There are four possible combinations (active only, archived only, both archived and active, none), determined by the value of a single IsArchived field (of course, it makes no sense to call this stored procedure if you don't want either active or archived polls). Instead of writing three separate SELECTs, and choosing which one to execute according the input values, we'll run a single statement with two WHERE conditions to determine which rows to select (active or archived). The two conditions are defined once, in the single SELECT statement, but their values are stored in private variables according to the values of the procedure's input. This procedure also adds a calculated column named Votes to the resultset, whose value is the sum of the Votes field of all child response options. Following is the complete code:

```
ALTER PROCEDURE dbo.tbh_Polls_GetPolls
(
   @IncludeActive     bit,
   @IncludeArchived   bit
)
AS
```

```
SET NOCOUNT ON

DECLARE @IsArchived1  bit
DECLARE @IsArchived2  bit

SELECT @IsArchived1 = 1
SELECT @IsArchived2 = 0

IF @IncludeActive = 1 AND @IncludeArchived = 0
   BEGIN
     SELECT @IsArchived1 = 0
     SELECT @IsArchived2 = 0
   END

IF @IncludeActive = 0 AND @IncludeArchived = 1
   BEGIN
     SELECT @IsArchived1 = 1
     SELECT @IsArchived2 = 1
   END

SELECT PollID, AddedDate, AddedBy, QuestionText, IsCurrent, IsArchived,
ArchivedDate,
   (SELECT SUM(Votes) FROM tbh_PollOptions WHERE PollID = P.PollID) AS Votes
   FROM tbh_Polls P
   WHERE IsArchived = @IsArchived1 OR IsArchived = @IsArchived2
   ORDER BY IsArchived ASC, ArchivedDate DESC, AddedDate DESC
```

The tbh_Polls_GetPollByID Stored Procedure

This procedure returns all data, including the calculated Votes field, for a single poll, whose ID is passed as an input:

```
ALTER PROCEDURE dbo.tbh_Polls_GetPollByID
(
    @PollID  int
)
AS
SET NOCOUNT ON

SELECT PollID, AddedDate, AddedBy, QuestionText, IsCurrent, IsArchived,
ArchivedDate,
   (SELECT SUM(Votes) FROM tbh_PollOptions WHERE PollID = @PollID) AS Votes
   FROM tbh_Polls
   WHERE PollID = @PollID
```

The tbh_Polls_GetCurrentPollByID Stored Procedure

This procedure returns the ID of the poll row with the IsCurrent field set to true. If there is no such row, the SELECT would return NULL. In that case, -1 is returned instead, so that the client code will be able to safely cast the result to an integer and then give a special meaning to that value:

```
ALTER PROCEDURE dbo.tbh_Polls_GetCurrentPollID
(
    @PollID       int OUTPUT
)
```

```
AS
SET NOCOUNT ON

SELECT @PollID = PollID
   FROM tbh_Polls
   WHERE IsCurrent = 1 AND IsArchived = 0

IF @PollID IS NULL
   BEGIN
   SELECT @PollID = -1
   END
```

The tbh_Polls_GetOptions Stored Procedure

This procedure returns the options for the specified poll, including all their values and a new calculated column, Percentage, which indicates the percentage of votes received by each poll out of the total number of votes received by all poll response options. Here's the code:

```
ALTER PROCEDURE dbo.tbh_Polls_GetOptions
(
    @PollID  int
)
AS
SET NOCOUNT ON

DECLARE @TotVotes int
SELECT @TotVotes = SUM(Votes)
   FROM tbh_PollOptions
   WHERE PollID = @PollID

IF @TotVotes = 0
   BEGIN
   SELECT @TotVotes = 1
   END

SELECT OptionID, AddedDate, AddedBy, PollID, OptionText, Votes,
   (CAST(Votes as decimal) * 100 / @TotVotes) As Percentage
   FROM tbh_PollOptions
   WHERE PollID = @PollID
   ORDER BY AddedDate ASC
```

It first gets the total number of votes for all the options of this poll, and then saves this value in a local variable. If no votes are found, it sets the variable to 1, because otherwise the forthcoming division would produce an error. Finally, it executes the SELECT query and adds the Percentage column, with the following code:

```
(CAST(Votes as decimal) * 100 / @TotVotes) As Percentage
```

The number of votes for a response option is multiplied by 100 and then divided by the total number of votes for the poll. It's worth noting that the expression is CAST to Decimal, in order to achieve more accuracy than an integer percentage would provide.

The tbh_Polls_GetOptionByID Stored Procedure

The code for this procedure is similar to the code of the sp_Polls_GetOptions procedure, with two exceptions. First, it is restricted to a single record. Second, the parent poll's ID is not provided as a parameter but must be retrieved with a simple SELECT query that selects the PollID field of the specified response option:

```
ALTER PROCEDURE dbo.tbh_Polls_GetOptionByID
(
    @OptionID   int
)
AS
SET NOCOUNT ON

DECLARE @PollID   int
SELECT @PollID = PollID FROM tbh_PollOptions WHERE OptionID = @OptionID

DECLARE @TotVotes int
SELECT @TotVotes = SUM(Votes) FROM tbh_PollOptions WHERE PollID = @PollID

IF @TotVotes = 0
    BEGIN
    SELECT @TotVotes = 1
    END

SELECT OptionID, AddedDate, AddedBy, PollID, OptionText, Votes,
    (CAST(Votes As decimal) * 100 / @TotVotes) As Percentage
    FROM tbh_PollOptions
    WHERE OptionID = @OptionID
```

Implementing the Configuration Module

The custom configuration class must be developed before any other code because the custom settings are used in all other layers. This class is similar to the one seen in the previous chapter. It inherits from ConfigurationElement and has the properties previously defined:

```
public class PollsElement : ConfigurationElement
{
    [ConfigurationProperty("connectionStringName")]
    public string ConnectionStringName
    {
        get { return (string)base["connectionStringName"]; }
        set { base["connectionStringName"] = value; }
    }

    public string ConnectionString
    {
        get
        {
            string connStringName = (string.IsNullOrEmpty(this.ConnectionStringName) ?
                Globals.Settings.DefaultConnectionStringName :
                this.ConnectionStringName);
            return WebConfigurationManager.ConnectionStrings[
```

```
            connStringName].ConnectionString;
      }
   }

   [ConfigurationProperty("providerType",
      DefaultValue = "MB.TheBeerHouse.DAL.SqlClient.SqlPollsProvider")]
   public string ProviderType
   {
      get { return (string)base["providerType"]; }
      set { base["providerType"] = value; }
   }

   [ConfigurationProperty("votingLockInterval", DefaultValue = "15")]
   public int VotingLockInterval
   {
      get { return (int)base["votingLockInterval"]; }
      set { base["votingLockInterval"] = value; }
   }

   [ConfigurationProperty("votingLockByCookie", DefaultValue = "true")]
   public bool VotingLockByCookie
   {
      get { return (bool)base["votingLockByCookie"]; }
      set { base["votingLockByCookie"] = value; }
   }

   [ConfigurationProperty("votingLockByIP", DefaultValue = "true")]
   public bool VotingLockByIP
   {
      get { return (bool)base["votingLockByIP"]; }
      set { base["votingLockByIP"] = value; }
   }

   [ConfigurationProperty("archiveIsPublic", DefaultValue = "false")]
   public bool ArchiveIsPublic
   {
      get { return (bool)base["archiveIsPublic"]; }
      set { base["archiveIsPublic"] = value; }
   }

   [ConfigurationProperty("enableCaching", DefaultValue = "true")]
   public bool EnableCaching
   {
      get { return (bool)base["enableCaching"]; }
      set { base["enableCaching"] = value; }
   }

   [ConfigurationProperty("cacheDuration")]
   public int CacheDuration
   {
      get
      {
         int duration = (int)base["cacheDuration"];
         return (duration > 0 ? duration : Globals.Settings.DefaultCacheDuration);
      }
```

```
        set { base["cacheDuration"] = value; }
    }
}
```

To make this class map a `<polls>` element under the top-level `<theBeerHouse>` section, we add a property of type `PollsElement` to the `TheBeerHouseSection` class developed in the previous chapter and then use the `ConfigurationProperty` attribute to do the mapping:

```
public class TheBeerHouseSection : ConfigurationSection
{
    // other properties here...

    [ConfigurationProperty("polls", IsRequired = true)]
    public PollsElement Polls
    {
        get { return (PollsElement)base["polls"]; }
    }
}
```

If you want to make the archive available to everyone, and disable vote locking by the user's IP, you would use these settings in the `web.config` file:

```
<theBeerHouse defaultConnectionStringName="LocalSqlServer">
    <contactForm mailTo="mbellinaso@wrox.com"/>
    <articles pageSize="10" />
    <polls archiveIsPublic="true" votingLockByIP="false"  />
</theBeerHouse>
```

The default value will be used for all those settings not explicitly defined in the configuration file, such as `connectionStringName`, `providerType`, `votingLockByCookie`, `votingLockInterval`, and the others.

Implementing the Data Access Layer

The `PollsProvider` abstract class starts with the `Instance` static property that uses reflection to create, and return, an instance of the concrete provider class specified in the `web.config` section for data access methods. The constructor reads some other configuration settings (the connection string, whether the caching is enabled and for how long) and saves them in the `DataAccess`' common properties. We also have a list of data access methods, having only a signature without an implementation:

```
public abstract class PollsProvider : DataAccess
{
    static private PollsProvider _instance = null;
    /// <summary>
    /// Returns an instance of the provider type specified in the config file
    /// </summary>
    static public PollsProvider Instance
    {
        get
        {
            if (_instance == null)
                _instance = (PollsProvider)Activator.CreateInstance(
```

```
                 Type.GetType(Globals.Settings.Polls.ProviderType));
        return _instance;
    }
}

public PollsProvider()
{
    this.ConnectionString = Globals.Settings.Polls.ConnectionString;
    this.EnableCaching = Globals.Settings.Polls.EnableCaching;
    this.CacheDuration = Globals.Settings.Polls.CacheDuration;
}

// methods that work with polls
public abstract List<PollDetails> GetPolls(bool includeActive,
    bool includeArchived);
public abstract PollDetails GetPollByID(int pollID);
public abstract int GetCurrentPollID();
public abstract bool DeletePoll(int pollID);
public abstract bool ArchivePoll(int pollID);
public abstract bool UpdatePoll(PollDetails poll);
public abstract int InsertPoll(PollDetails poll);
public abstract bool InsertVote(int optionID);

// methods that work with poll options
public abstract List<PollOptionDetails> GetOptions(int pollID);
public abstract PollOptionDetails GetOptionByID(int optionID);
public abstract bool DeleteOption(int optionID);
public abstract bool UpdateOption(PollOptionDetails option);
public abstract int InsertOption(PollOptionDetails option);
```

Finally, the class has a few concrete protected methods, which populate single or multiple instances of the PollDetails and PollOptionDetails custom entity classes from the input IDataReader:

```
/// <summary>Returns a new PollDetails instance filled with the DataReader's
/// current record data </summary>
protected virtual PollDetails GetPollFromReader(IDataReader reader)
{
    return new PollDetails(
        (int)reader["PollID"],
        (DateTime)reader["AddedDate"],
        reader["AddedBy"].ToString(),
        reader["QuestionText"].ToString(),
        (bool)reader["IsCurrent"],
        (bool)reader["IsArchived"],
        (reader["ArchivedDate"] == DBNull.Value ?
            DateTime.MinValue : (DateTime)reader["ArchivedDate"]),
        (reader["Votes"] == DBNull.Value ? 0 : (int)reader["Votes"]));
}

/// <summary>Returns a collection of PollDetails objects with the data read from
/// the input DataReader</summary>
protected virtual List<PollDetails> GetPollCollectionFromReader(
    IDataReader reader)
{
    List<PollDetails> polls = new List<PollDetails>();
```

```
        while (reader.Read())
            polls.Add(GetPollFromReader(reader));
        return polls;
    }


    /// <summary>Returns a new PollOptionDetails instance filled with the
    /// DataReader's current record data</summary>
    protected virtual PollOptionDetails GetOptionFromReader(IDataReader reader)
    {
        PollOptionDetails option = new PollOptionDetails(
            (int)reader["OptionID"],
            (DateTime)reader["AddedDate"],
            reader["AddedBy"].ToString(),
            (int)reader["PollID"],
            reader["OptionText"].ToString(),
            (int)reader["Votes"],
            Convert.ToDouble(reader["Percentage"]));

        return option;
    }

    /// <summary>Returns a collection of PollOptionDetails objects with the data
    /// read from the input DataReader</summary>
    protected virtual List<PollOptionDetails> GetOptionCollectionFromReader(
        IDataReader reader)
    {
        List<PollOptionDetails> options = new List<PollOptionDetails>();
        while (reader.Read())
            options.Add(GetOptionFromReader(reader));
        return options;
    }
}
```

In this chapter I won't show the code for the entity classes, as they are just wrapper classes for all the retrieved database fields. The information in the diagram in Figure 6-2 is enough to completely define the class. I won't show the SQL Server provider either, as it is just a wrapper for the stored procedures listed and implemented earlier, and their structure is similar to the DAL code shown in the previous chapter. Consult the code download for this book to see all of the code.

Implementing the Business Logic Layer

This section describes one of the two BLL classes — namely, MB.TheBeerHouse.BLL.Polls.Poll, which is found in the ~/App_Code/BLL/Polls/Poll.cs file. The Option class won't be presented here because it is similar to Poll in structure, but shorter and simpler. The Poll class begins with the definition of the wrapper properties for the data that will come from the DAL in the form of a PollDetails instance, and with a constructor that takes all the values to initialize the properties:

```
public class Poll : BasePoll
{
    private string _questionText = "";
    public string QuestionText
    {
        get { return _questionText; }
        private set { _questionText = value; }
```

```
    }

    private bool _isCurrent = false;
    public bool IsCurrent
    {
        get { return _isCurrent; }
        private set { _isCurrent = value; }
    }

    private bool _isArchived = false;
    public bool IsArchived
    {
        get { return _isArchived; }
        private set { _isArchived = value; }
    }

    private DateTime _archivedDate = DateTime.MinValue;
    public DateTime ArchivedDate
    {
        get { return _archivedDate; }
        private set { _archivedDate = value; }
    }

    private int _votes = 0;
    public int Votes
    {
        get { return _votes; }
        private set { _votes = value; }
    }

    private List<Option> _options = null;
    public List<Option> Options
    {
        get
        {
            if (_options == null)
                _options = Option.GetOptions(this.ID);
            return _options;
        }
    }

    public Poll(int id, DateTime addedDate, string addedBy, string questionText,
        bool isCurrent, bool isArchived, DateTime archivedDate, int votes)
    {
        this.ID = id;
        this.AddedDate = addedDate;
        this.AddedBy = addedBy;
        this.QuestionText = questionText;
        this.IsCurrent = isCurrent;
        this.IsArchived = isArchived;
        this.ArchivedDate = archivedDate;
        this.Votes = votes;
    }
```

The only property that does more than just wrap a private field is `Options`, which returns the list of the poll's response options. It implements a simple form of the lazy load pattern, by actually retrieving the options only when they're required, and then it saves them in a local field in case they're requested again. The class has a number of instance methods (`Delete`, `Update`, `Archive`, and `Vote`) that forward the call to the corresponding static methods you'll see shortly, and pass the value of the instance properties as parameters:

```
public bool Delete()
{
    bool success = Poll.DeletePoll(this.ID);
    if (success)
        this.ID = 0;
    return success;
}

public bool Update()
{
    return Poll.UpdatePoll(this.ID, this.QuestionText, this.IsCurrent);
}

public bool Archive()
{
    bool success = Poll.ArchivePoll(this.ID);
    if (success)
    {
        this.IsCurrent = false;
        this.IsArchived = true;
        this.ArchivedDate = DateTime.Now;
    }
    return success;
}

public bool Vote(int optionID)
{
    bool success = Poll.VoteOption(this.ID, optionID);
    if (success)
        this.Votes += 1;
    return success;
}
```

A couple of static properties return the ID of the current poll, and a `Poll` instance represents it. The `CurrentPollID` property caches the ID after retrieving it so that it doesn't have to request it every time if the current poll doesn't change. The current poll will probably be shown on every page of the site (if you plug it into the master page's left- or right-hand column), and by using caching you will save a SQL query for every page hit. Consider that there may be many requests per second, and you'll see why using caching in this situation can improve performance considerably! Here's the code:

```
public static int CurrentPollID
{
    get
    {
        int pollID = -1;
```

```
            string key = "Polls_Poll_Current";

            if (BasePoll.Settings.EnableCaching && BizObject.Cache[key] != null)
            {
                pollID = (int)BizObject.Cache[key];
            }
            else
            {
                pollID = SiteProvider.Polls.GetCurrentPollID();
                BasePoll.CacheData(key, pollID);
            }

            return pollID;
        }
    }

    public static Poll CurrentPoll
    {
        get
        {
            return GetPollByID(CurrentPollID);
        }
    }
```

Now we'll cover the static methods, which forward the call to the corresponding DAL provider method to actually retrieve and modify the data, but these will also add caching and wrap the results in instances of the Poll class itself. The GetPolls method has a couple of overloaded versions: one takes two parameters to include or exclude the active and archived polls, and the other version has no parameters and just forwards the call to the first method by passing true for both parameters to include both current and archived polls. The structure of GetPolls and GetPollByID is quite similar to the CurrentPollID property just seen: They first check whether the request's data is already in the cache. If so, they retrieve it from there; otherwise, they make a call to the DAL to fetch the data, save it in the cache for later requests, and return it (following the same lazy load design pattern you've seen already):

```
/// <summary>
/// Returns a collection with all polls
/// </summary>
public static List<Poll> GetPolls()
{
    return GetPolls(true, true);
}
public static List<Poll> GetPolls(bool includeActive, bool includeArchived)
{
    List<Poll> polls = null;
    string key = "Polls_Polls_" + includeActive.ToString() + "_" +
        includeArchived.ToString();

    if (BasePoll.Settings.EnableCaching && BizObject.Cache[key] != null)
    {
        polls = (List<Poll>)BizObject.Cache[key];
    }
    else
    {
        List<PollDetails> recordset = SiteProvider.Polls.GetPolls(includeActive,
```

```
                    includeArchived);
            polls = GetPollListFromPollDetailsList(recordset);
            BasePoll.CacheData(key, polls);
        }
        return polls;
    }


    /// <summary>
    /// Returns a Poll object with the specified ID
    /// </summary>
    public static Poll GetPollByID(int pollID)
    {
        Poll poll = null;
        string key = "Polls_Poll_" + pollID.ToString();

        if (BasePoll.Settings.EnableCaching && BizObject.Cache[key] != null)
        {
            poll = (Poll)BizObject.Cache[key];
        }
        else
        {
            poll = GetPollFromPollDetails(SiteProvider.Polls.GetPollByID(pollID));
            BasePoll.CacheData(key, poll);
        }
        return poll;
    }
```

Note how the cache key is built because it will be important when you have to purge specific data. While the GetXXX methods cache their data, the methods that add, edit, or delete data will purge data from the cache, because it becomes stale at that time. In particular, the UpdatePoll method first performs the update for a specified poll, which causes that poll's cached data to become stale, and the list of active polls (you don't need to purge the archived polls because they are not editable). If the poll is also being set as the current one, the ID of the current poll is also removed from the cache. Following is the code:

```
    /// <summary>Updates an existing poll</summary>
    public static bool UpdatePoll(int id, string questionText, bool isCurrent)
    {
        PollDetails record = new PollDetails(id, DateTime.Now, "",
            questionText, isCurrent, false, DateTime.Now, 0);
        bool ret = SiteProvider.Polls.UpdatePoll(record);
        BizObject.PurgeCacheItems("polls_polls_true");
        BizObject.PurgeCacheItems("polls_poll_" + id.ToString());
        if (isCurrent)
            BizObject.PurgeCacheItems("polls_poll_current");
        return ret;
    }
```

When a poll is deleted, you have to purge all polls from the cache because you can't know whether the poll being deleted is an active or archived poll without executing a query to the database. As an alternative, you may want to run the query here and purge only the affected polls. This method also raises the RecordDeletedEvent developed in Chapter 3, so that this operation is logged by the provider specified in the web.config file (we're using the SqlWebEventProvider in this sample site, to log events to the site's SQL Server database):

```
/// <summary>Deletes an existing poll</summary>
public static bool DeletePoll(int id)
{
    bool ret = SiteProvider.Polls.DeletePoll(id);
    new RecordDeletedEvent("poll", id, null).Raise();
    BizObject.PurgeCacheItems("polls_polls");
    BizObject.PurgeCacheItems("polls_poll_" + id.ToString());
    BizObject.PurgeCacheItems("polls_poll_current");
    return ret;
}
```

When a poll is archived, the lists containing both the active and archived polls are purged from the cache, as they will both change (the poll being archived will no longer be part of the active polls and will become part of the archived polls):

```
/// <summary>Archive an existing poll</summary>
public static bool ArchivePoll(int id)
{
    bool ret = SiteProvider.Polls.ArchivePoll(id);
    BizObject.PurgeCacheItems("polls_polls");
    BizObject.PurgeCacheItems("polls_poll_" + id.ToString());
    BizObject.PurgeCacheItems("polls_poll_current");
    return ret;
}
```

When the user submits a vote for a response option, the poll receiving the vote and the list with active polls are both purged, because the poll's Votes field will change. The list containing poll response options is also removed, of course, as their Votes and Percentage fields will change:

```
/// <summary>Votes for a poll option</summary>
public static bool VoteOption(int pollID, int optionID)
{
    bool ret = SiteProvider.Polls.InsertVote(optionID);
    BizObject.PurgeCacheItems("polls_polls_true");
    BizObject.PurgeCacheItems("polls_poll_" + pollID.ToString());
    BizObject.PurgeCacheItems("polls_options_" + pollID.ToString());
    return ret;
}
```

When a new poll is inserted, the list containing active polls is removed from the cache, and the ID for the current poll if the new poll is being set as the current one:

```
/// <summary>Creates a new poll</summary>
public static int InsertPoll(string questionText, bool isCurrent)
{
    PollDetails record = new PollDetails(0, DateTime.Now,
        BizObject.CurrentUserName, questionText, isCurrent,
        false, DateTime.Now, 0);
    int ret = SiteProvider.Polls.InsertPoll(record);
    BizObject.PurgeCacheItems("polls_polls_true");
    if (isCurrent)
        BizObject.PurgeCacheItems("polls_poll_current");
    return ret;
}
```

The class ends with two private helper methods that take a single instance of `PollDetails` or a collection of them, and return an instance of `Poll`, or a collection of `Poll` objects, respectively:

```
/// <summary>Returns a Poll object filled with the data taken from
/// the input PollDetails</summary>
private static Poll GetPollFromPollDetails(PollDetails record)
{
    if (record == null)
        return null;
    else
    {
        return new Poll(record.ID, record.AddedDate, record.AddedBy,
            record.QuestionText, record.IsCurrent,
            record.IsArchived, record.ArchivedDate, record.Votes);
    }
}

/// <summary>Returns a list of Comment objects filled with the data taken from
/// the input list of CommentDetails</summary>
private static List<Poll> GetPollListFromPollDetailsList(
    List<PollDetails> recordset)
{
    List<Poll> polls = new List<Poll>();
    foreach (PollDetails record in recordset)
        polls.Add(GetPollFromPollDetails(record));
    return polls;
}
```

Implementing the User Interface

Now it's time to build the user interface: the administration page, the poll box user control, and the archive page.

The ManagePolls.aspx page

This page, located under the ~/Admin folder, allows the administrator and editors to add, delete, and edit any active poll and its response options, review their votes, and archive a poll when it is no longer wanted as active. Polls and options are all managed in a single page: There is a GridView that lists the active polls, and below it is a DetailsView for inserting new polls or editing the selected one; there's also another GridView that lists the options for the selected poll, and another DetailsView for inserting new options for the selected poll, or editing the selected option. Figure 6-6 is a screenshot of the page when editing an existing poll.

The two DetailsView controls are in insert mode by default. When a row in their respective master grid is selected, they switch to edit mode, so the selected item can be modified. To change back to insert mode the user can either click Update or Cancel, according to whether she actually wants to persist the changes or just end the edit mode. The GridView and DetailsView controls for the options will be visible only when a poll is selected, as an option can't exist without a parent poll. Figure 6-7 shows the page in design mode from inside the Visual Studio 2005's web designer. Note that all controls have a white background and back text (the default appearance) and don't show up with the color scheme of the controls of the picture above. This is because the colors and other appearance settings are stored in the theme's skin files (applied at runtime), used to create a consistent look and feel among all pages, and to make it easy to change the visual styles for the entire site by changing a single file.

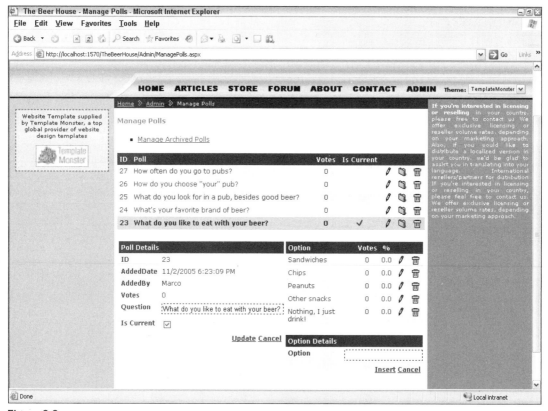

Figure 6-6

The screenshot should give you a good idea of how the page is composed and how the various controls are displayed on the form. In subsequent screenshots, I'll only show you the code taken from the Source View, instead of showing all the steps to visually create the interface. First, there's the ObjectDataSource for the GridView listing the active polls. It references the MB.TheBeerHouse.BLL.Polls.Poll class and uses the GetPolls method to retrieve the polls, and DeletePoll to delete one of them. The parameters for the GetPolls select method are set to true and false, to include active polls and exclude archived ones:

```
<asp:ObjectDataSource ID="objPolls" runat="server" SelectMethod="GetPolls"
    TypeName="MB.TheBeerHouse.BLL.Polls.Poll" DeleteMethod="DeletePoll">
    <DeleteParameters>
        <asp:Parameter Name="id" Type="Int32" />
    </DeleteParameters>
    <SelectParameters>
        <asp:Parameter DefaultValue="true" Name="includeActive" Type="Boolean" />
        <asp:Parameter DefaultValue="false" Name="includeArchived" Type="Boolean" />
    </SelectParameters>
</asp:ObjectDataSource>
```

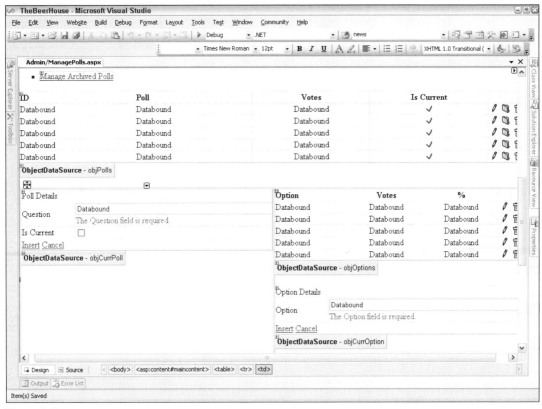

Figure 6-7

The `GridView` that follows it uses the `ObjectDataSource` above as data source, and defines a number of columns to show the poll's ID, question text, and number of votes; and a checkbox is shown if the poll is the current one. The checkbox is not automatically rendered by a `CheckBoxField` but is an image shown from inside a `TemplateField` whose `Visible` property is bound to the poll's `IsCurrent` property. On the right side of the grid are three columns with buttons to select, archive, and delete a poll. The image representing a pencil in the figures is used to change a row to edit mode, which is actually a `Select` command (they are selected in the `GridView` and edited in the `DetailsView`). The `Select` and `Edit` commands are rendered by two `CommandField` columns, according to the `ShowSelectButton` and `ShowDeleteButton` properties. The `Archive` command is a custom command instead, created with a `ButtonField` column whose events will be handled manually and not by the associated `ObjectDataSource`. Here's the complete code for the `GridView`:

```
<asp:GridView ID="gvwPolls" runat="server" AutoGenerateColumns="False"
    DataSourceID="objPolls" Width="100%" DataKeyNames="ID"
    OnRowCreated="gvwPolls_RowCreated" OnRowDeleted="gvwPolls_RowDeleted"
    OnSelectedIndexChanged="gvwPolls_SelectedIndexChanged"
    OnRowCommand="gvwPolls_RowCommand">
    <Columns>
```

```
    <asp:BoundField DataField="ID" HeaderText="ID"
        HeaderStyle-HorizontalAlign="Left" ReadOnly="True" />
    <asp:BoundField DataField="QuestionText" HeaderText="Poll"
        HeaderStyle-HorizontalAlign="Left" />
    <asp:BoundField DataField="Votes" ReadOnly="True"
        HeaderText="Votes" ItemStyle-HorizontalAlign="center" />
    <asp:TemplateField HeaderText="Is Current"
        ItemStyle-HorizontalAlign="center">
        <ItemTemplate>
            <asp:Image runat="server" ID="imgIsCurrent" ImageUrl="~/Images/OK.gif"
                Visible='<%# Eval("IsCurrent") %>' />
        </ItemTemplate>
    </asp:TemplateField>
    <asp:CommandField ButtonType="Image" SelectImageUrl="~/Images/Edit.gif"
        SelectText="Edit poll" ShowSelectButton="True">
        <ItemStyle HorizontalAlign="Center" Width="20px" />
    </asp:CommandField>
    <asp:ButtonField ButtonType="Image" ImageUrl="~/Images/Folder.gif"
        CommandName="Archive">
        <ItemStyle HorizontalAlign="Center" Width="20px" />
    </asp:ButtonField>
    <asp:CommandField ButtonType="Image" DeleteImageUrl="~/Images/Delete.gif"
        DeleteText="Delete poll" ShowDeleteButton="True">
        <ItemStyle HorizontalAlign="Center" Width="20px" />
    </asp:CommandField>
    </Columns>
    <EmptyDataTemplate><b>No polls to show</b></EmptyDataTemplate>
</asp:GridView>
```

Note that the grid also defines an `<EmptyDataTemplate>` section, with a message that will be displayed when the `GetPolls Select` method returns no polls to display.

Following is the `ObjectDataSource` used by the `DetailsView` under the grid to insert and update polls, by means of the `InsertPoll` and `UpdatePoll` static methods of the `Poll` business class. A `Select` command is also required to show the details of the row selected in the master `GridView`. `GetPollByID` is called by the `GridView`'s `Select` method:

```
<asp:ObjectDataSource ID="objCurrPoll" runat="server" InsertMethod="InsertPoll"
    SelectMethod="GetPollByID" UpdateMethod="UpdatePoll"
    TypeName="MB.TheBeerHouse.BLL.Polls.Poll">
    <SelectParameters>
        <asp:ControlParameter ControlID="gvwPolls" Name="pollID"
            PropertyName="SelectedValue" Type="Int32" />
    </SelectParameters>
    <UpdateParameters>
        <asp:Parameter Name="id" Type="Int32" />
        <asp:Parameter Name="questionText" Type="String" />
        <asp:Parameter Name="isCurrent" Type="Boolean" />
    </UpdateParameters>
    <InsertParameters>
        <asp:Parameter Name="questionText" Type="String" />
        <asp:Parameter Name="isCurrent" Type="Boolean" />
    </InsertParameters>
</asp:ObjectDataSource>
```

The `DetailsView` shows all fields of the poll, including `AddedDate` and `AddedBy`, which are not included in the `GridView` due to space constraints. However, only the `QuestionText` and the `IsCurrent` fields are editable; the other fields are read-only in edit mode, and not visible in insert mode. The `QuestionText` field is defined by means of a `TemplateField`, so it's possible to insert a `RequiredFieldValidator` in the `EditItemTemplate` section, to ensure that the textbox is populated by the user:

```
<asp:DetailsView ID="dvwPoll" runat="server" AutoGenerateRows="False"
    DataSourceID="objCurrPoll" Width="100%" AutoGenerateEditButton="True"
    AutoGenerateInsertButton="True" HeaderText="Poll Details" DataKeyNames="ID"
    DefaultMode="Insert" OnItemCommand="dvwPoll_ItemCommand"
    OnItemInserted="dvwPoll_ItemInserted" OnItemUpdated="dvwPoll_ItemUpdated"
    OnItemCreated="dvwPoll_ItemCreated">
    <FieldHeaderStyle Width="100px" />
    <Fields>
        <asp:BoundField DataField="ID" HeaderText="ID" ReadOnly="True"
            InsertVisible="False" />
        <asp:BoundField DataField="AddedDate" HeaderText="AddedDate"
            InsertVisible="False" ReadOnly="True" />
        <asp:BoundField DataField="AddedBy" HeaderText="AddedBy"
            InsertVisible="False" ReadOnly="True" />
        <asp:BoundField DataField="Votes" HeaderText="Votes" ReadOnly="True"
            InsertVisible="False" />
        <asp:TemplateField HeaderText="Question">
            <ItemTemplate>
                <asp:Label ID="lblQuestion" runat="server"
                    Text='<%# Eval("QuestionText") %>'></asp:Label>
            </ItemTemplate>
            <EditItemTemplate>
                <asp:TextBox ID="txtQuestion" runat="server"
                    Text='<%# Bind("QuestionText") %>' MaxLength="256" Width="100%" />
                <asp:RequiredFieldValidator ID="valRequireQuestion" runat="server"
                    ControlToValidate="txtQuestion" SetFocusOnError="true"
                    Text="The Question field is required." Display="Dynamic"
                    ValidationGroup="Poll"></asp:RequiredFieldValidator>
            </EditItemTemplate>
        </asp:TemplateField>
        <asp:CheckBoxField DataField="IsCurrent" HeaderText="Is Current" />
    </Fields>
</asp:DetailsView>
```

The page then declares another `GridView` and another `DetailsView` to list and edit response options for a poll. They are both declared within a `Panel` control, so that they can be easily shown or hidden when a parent is, or is not, selected. Their definition is similar to the code seen for the polls — the only difference is that `GridView`, displaying the options, is the master control for the `DetailsView` used to edit and insert options. But this `GridView` itself is a detail control for the polls `GridView`:

```
<asp:Panel runat="server" ID="panOptions" Visible="false" Width="100%">
<asp:GridView ID="gvwOptions" runat="server" AutoGenerateColumns="False"
    DataSourceID="objOptions" DataKeyNames="ID" Width="100%"
    OnRowCreated="gvwOptions_RowCreated" OnRowDeleted="gvwOptions_RowDeleted"
    OnSelectedIndexChanged="gvwOptions_SelectedIndexChanged">
    <Columns>
        <asp:BoundField DataField="OptionText" HeaderText="Option">
            <HeaderStyle HorizontalAlign="Left" />
        </asp:BoundField>
```

```
        <asp:BoundField DataField="Votes" HeaderText="Votes" ReadOnly="True">
            <ItemStyle HorizontalAlign="Center" />
        </asp:BoundField>
        <asp:BoundField DataField="Percentage" DataFormatString="{0:N1}"
            HtmlEncode="False" HeaderText="%" ReadOnly="True">
            <ItemStyle HorizontalAlign="Center" />
        </asp:BoundField>
        <asp:CommandField ButtonType="Image" SelectImageUrl="~/Images/Edit.gif"
            SelectText="Edit option" ShowSelectButton="True">
            <ItemStyle HorizontalAlign="Center" Width="20px" />
        </asp:CommandField>
        <asp:CommandField ButtonType="Image" DeleteImageUrl="~/Images/Delete.gif"
            DeleteText="Delete option" ShowDeleteButton="True">
            <ItemStyle HorizontalAlign="Center" Width="20px" />
        </asp:CommandField>
    </Columns>
    <EmptyDataTemplate>
        <b>No options to show for the selected poll</b></EmptyDataTemplate>
</asp:GridView>
<asp:ObjectDataSource ID="objOptions" runat="server" DeleteMethod="DeleteOption"
    SelectMethod="GetOptions" TypeName="MB.TheBeerHouse.BLL.Polls.Option">
    <DeleteParameters>
        <asp:Parameter Name="id" Type="Int32" />
    </DeleteParameters>
    <SelectParameters>
        <asp:ControlParameter ControlID="gvwPolls" Name="pollID"
            PropertyName="SelectedValue" Type="Int32" />
    </SelectParameters>
</asp:ObjectDataSource>
<p></p>
<asp:DetailsView ID="dvwOption" runat="server" AutoGenerateRows="False"
    DataSourceID="objCurrOption" Width="100%" AutoGenerateEditButton="True"
    AutoGenerateInsertButton="True" HeaderText="Option Details" DataKeyNames="ID"
    DefaultMode="Insert" OnItemCommand="dvwOption_ItemCommand"
    OnItemInserted="dvwOption_ItemInserted" OnItemUpdated="dvwOption_ItemUpdated"
    OnItemCreated="dvwOption_ItemCreated">
    <FieldHeaderStyle Width="100px" />
    <Fields>
        <asp:BoundField DataField="ID" HeaderText="ID" ReadOnly="True"
            InsertVisible="False" />
        <asp:BoundField DataField="AddedDate" HeaderText="AddedDate"
            InsertVisible="False" ReadOnly="True" />
        <asp:BoundField DataField="AddedBy" HeaderText="AddedBy"
            InsertVisible="False" ReadOnly="True" />
        <asp:BoundField DataField="Votes" HeaderText="Votes" ReadOnly="True"
            InsertVisible="False" />
        <asp:BoundField DataField="Percentage" DataFormatString="{0:N1}"
            HtmlEncode="False" HeaderText="Percentage" ReadOnly="True"
            InsertVisible="False" />
        <asp:TemplateField HeaderText="Option">
            <ItemTemplate>
                <asp:Label ID="lblOption" runat="server"
                    Text='<%# Eval("OptionText") %>'></asp:Label>
            </ItemTemplate>
            <EditItemTemplate>
```

```
            <asp:TextBox ID="txtOption" runat="server"
                Text='<%# Bind("OptionText") %>' MaxLength="256"
                Width="100%"></asp:TextBox>
            <asp:RequiredFieldValidator ID="valRequireOption" runat="server"
                ControlToValidate="txtOption" SetFocusOnError="true"
                Text="The Option field is required." Display="Dynamic"
                ValidationGroup="Option"></asp:RequiredFieldValidator>
        </EditItemTemplate>
      </asp:TemplateField>
    </Fields>
  </asp:DetailsView>
  <asp:ObjectDataSource ID="objCurrOption" runat="server" InsertMethod="InsertOption"
      SelectMethod="GetOptionByID" TypeName="MB.TheBeerHouse.BLL.Polls.Option"
      UpdateMethod="UpdateOption">
      <SelectParameters>
          <asp:ControlParameter ControlID="gvwOptions" Name="optionID"
              PropertyName="SelectedValue" Type="Int32" />
      </SelectParameters>
      <UpdateParameters>
          <asp:Parameter Name="id" Type="Int32" />
          <asp:Parameter Name="optionText" Type="String" />
      </UpdateParameters>
      <InsertParameters>
          <asp:ControlParameter ControlID="gvwPolls" Name="pollID"
              PropertyName="SelectedValue" Type="Int32" />
          <asp:Parameter Name="optionText" Type="String" />
      </InsertParameters>
  </asp:ObjectDataSource>
</asp:Panel>
```

The `RequiredFieldValidator` in this last block of code has the `ValidationGroup` property set to
`"Option"`, while the property was set to `"Poll"` in the block showing the code for the Poll
`DetailsView`. They have different values to define two separate "logical" forms, so the input controls of
the second form are not validated when you submit the page by clicking a button of the first logical
form, and vice versa. To make this work, however, you need to set the same properties to the same values for the Submit buttons of each logical form. This can't be done from the ASPX page itself, though,
because the `Button` or `LinkButton` controls are not declared explicitly, but rather are created dynamically at runtime by the `CommandField` columns. Because of this, the `ValidationGroup` property for
these buttons must be set programmatically from the code-behind, when the row and its controls are created, (i.e., from the `DetailsView`'s `ItemCreated` event). The next section explains the code in the
page's `.cs` code-behind file, which performs this operation, among other things.

The ManagePolls.aspx.cs Code-behind File

In the code-behind for this page you won't find any code to retrieve and bind data to the controls, or to edit
or delete polls and options, as these operations are all done automatically by the four `ObjectDataSource`
controls defined on the page. Instead, from this file you handle some events of the `GridView` and the
`DetailsView` controls to do the following things:

❑ Put the `DetailsView` for the polls into insert mode, and hide the controls that display and edit
the options when there's no poll selected or when the currently selected poll is deselected. This
happens when a new poll is inserted or an existing poll is deleted, archived, or updated, and
when the user clicks Cancel while editing a poll:

315

```
private void DeselectPoll()
{
    gvwPolls.SelectedIndex = -1;
    gvwPolls.DataBind();
    dvwPoll.ChangeMode(DetailsViewMode.Insert);
    panOptions.Visible = false;
}

protected void gvwPolls_RowDeleted(object sender, GridViewDeletedEventArgs e)
{
    DeselectPoll();
}

protected void dvwPoll_ItemInserted(object sender, DetailsViewInsertedEventArgs e)
{
    DeselectPoll();
}

protected void dvwPoll_ItemUpdated(object sender, DetailsViewUpdatedEventArgs e)
{
    DeselectPoll();
}

protected void dvwPoll_ItemCommand(object sender, DetailsViewCommandEventArgs e)
{
    if (e.CommandName == "Cancel")
        DeselectPoll();
}
```

❑   Put the DetailsView for the options into insert mode when a new option is inserted or an existing option is deleted or updated, and when the user clicks Cancel while editing an option:

```
private void DeselectOption()
{
    gvwOptions.SelectedIndex = -1;
    gvwOptions.DataBind();
    dvwOption.ChangeMode(DetailsViewMode.Insert);
}

protected void dvwOption_ItemInserted(object sender,
    DetailsViewInsertedEventArgs e)
{
    DeselectOption();
}

protected void dvwOption_ItemUpdated(object sender, DetailsViewUpdatedEventArgs e)
{
    DeselectOption();
}

protected void gvwOptions_RowDeleted(object sender, GridViewDeletedEventArgs e)
{
    DeselectOption();
}

protected void dvwOption_ItemCommand(object sender, DetailsViewCommandEventArgs e)
```

```
{
    if (e.CommandName == "Cancel")
        DeselectOption();
}
```

❑ Show the controls that display and edit the options when a poll is selected, which is processed from inside the gvwPolls GridView's SelectedIndexChanged event handler; and put the DetailsView for the selected poll into edit mode:

```
protected void gvwPolls_SelectedIndexChanged(object sender, EventArgs e)
{
    dvwPoll.ChangeMode(DetailsViewMode.Edit);
    panOptions.Visible = true;
}
```

❑ Put the DetailsView for the selected option into edit mode from inside the gvwOptions GridView's SelectedIndexChanged event handler:

```
protected void gvwOptions_SelectedIndexChanged(object sender, EventArgs e)
{
    dvwOption.ChangeMode(DetailsViewMode.Edit);
}
```

❑ Archive a poll when the respective image link is clicked, which is processed from inside the gvwPolls GridView's RowCommand event handler:

```
protected void gvwPolls_RowCommand(object sender, GridViewCommandEventArgs e)
{
    if (e.CommandName == "Archive")
    {
        int pollID = Convert.ToInt32(
            gvwPolls.DataKeys[Convert.ToInt32(e.CommandArgument)][0]);
        MB.TheBeerHouse.BLL.Polls.Poll.ArchivePoll(pollID);
        DeselectPoll();
    }
}
```

❑ Add a JavaScript confirmation pop-up when the user clicks the commands to delete or update a poll, or delete an option. This is done from the respective grid's RowCreated event handler, from which you get a reference to the LinkButton control found in a specified column, and then add the JavaScript by means of its OnClientClick property:

```
protected void gvwPolls_RowCreated(object sender, GridViewRowEventArgs e)
{
    if (e.Row.RowType == DataControlRowType.DataRow)
    {
        ImageButton btnArchive = e.Row.Cells[5].Controls[0] as ImageButton;
        btnArchive.OnClientClick =
            @"if (confirm('Are you sure you want to archive this poll?') == false)
                return false;";
        ImageButton btnDelete = e.Row.Cells[6].Controls[0] as ImageButton;
        btnDelete.OnClientClick =
            @"if (confirm('Are you sure you want to delete this poll?') == false)
                return false;";
    }
```

```
    }

    protected void gvwOptions_RowCreated(object sender, GridViewRowEventArgs e)
    {
        if (e.Row.RowType == DataControlRowType.DataRow)
        {
            ImageButton btn = e.Row.Cells[4].Controls[0] as ImageButton;
            btn.OnClientClick =
                @"if (confirm('Are you sure you want to delete this option?') == false)
                    return false;";
        }
    }
```

❑   Set the ValidationGroup property of the Update buttons of the two Poll and Option logical
    forms to the proper values (i.e., the values used for the RequiredFieldValidator in the .aspx
    file). This is done from the ItemCreated event handlers of the two DetailsView controls.
    Because the ID for those controls is created dynamically, you don't know it at design-time, and
    thus you can't use the FindControl method to easily reference them. Instead, you loop thor-
    ough all the controls in the last row of the DetailsView (i.e., the command bar row) and stop
    when you find a LinkButton with the CommandName property set to "Insert" or "Update":

```
protected void dvwPoll_ItemCreated(object sender, EventArgs e)
{
    foreach (Control ctl in
        dvwPoll.Rows[dvwPoll.Rows.Count - 1].Controls[0].Controls)
    {
        if (ctl is LinkButton)
        {
            LinkButton lnk = ctl as LinkButton;
            if (lnk.CommandName == "Insert" || lnk.CommandName == "Update")
                lnk.ValidationGroup = "Poll";
        }
    }
}

protected void dvwOption_ItemCreated(object sender, EventArgs e)
{
    foreach (Control ctl in
        dvwOption.Rows[dvwOption.Rows.Count - 1].Controls[0].Controls)
    {
        if (ctl is LinkButton)
        {
            LinkButton lnk = ctl as LinkButton;
            if (lnk.CommandName == "Insert" || lnk.CommandName == "Update")
                lnk.ValidationGroup = "Option";
        }
    }
}
```

Referring to Figure 6-6, you may have noticed that there's no way to cast a vote — this functionality
hasn't been developed yet. In order to be able to test the grid on the administration page, you would
need to set the votes for some options in the tbh_PollOptions table manually, using VS2005's Server
Explorer interface. The administration page is now complete, and we will cover the implementation of
the end-user part of the poll module.

The PollBox.ascx User Control

Now it's time to build the PollBox user control that you'll plug into the site's common layout (i.e., the master page). The PollBox.ascx user control is created under the ~/Controls folder, together with all other user controls.

This user control can be divided into four parts. The first defines a panel with an image and a label for the configurable header text. This content is placed into a Panel so that it can be hidden if the ShowHeader property is set to false. It also defines another label for the poll's question text:

```
<%@ Control Language="C#" AutoEventWireup="true" CodeFile="PollBox.ascx.cs"
Inherits="PollBox" %>
<div class="pollbox">
<asp:Panel runat="server" ID="panHeader">
<div class="sectiontitle">
<asp:Image ID="imgArrow" runat="server" ImageUrl="~/images/arrowr.gif"
    style="float: left; margin-left: 3px; margin-right: 3px;"/>
<asp:Label runat="server" ID="lblHeader"></asp:Label>
</div>
</asp:Panel>
<div class="pollcontent">
<asp:Label runat="server" ID="lblQuestion" CssClass="pollquestion"></asp:Label>
```

The second part is a Panel to show when the poll box allows the user to vote (i.e., when it detects that the poll being shown is not archived, and the user has not already voted for it). The Panel contains a RadioButtonList to list the options, a RequiredFieldValidator that ensures that at least one option is selected when the form is submitted, and the button to do the postback:

```
<asp:Panel runat="server" ID="panVote">
    <div class="polloptions">
    <asp:RadioButtonList runat="server" ID="optlOptions"
        DataTextField="OptionText" DataValueField="ID" />
    <asp:RequiredFieldValidator ID="valRequireOption" runat="server"
        ControlToValidate="optlOptions" SetFocusOnError="true"
        Text="You must select an option." ToolTip="You must select an option"
        Display="Dynamic" ValidationGroup="PollVote"></asp:RequiredFieldValidator>
    </div>
    <asp:Button runat="server" ID="btnVote" ValidationGroup="PollVote"
        Text="Vote" OnClick="btnVote_Click" />
</asp:Panel>
```

The third part defines the Panel to be displayed when the control detects that the user has already voted for the current poll. In this situation the control displays the results, which is done by means of a Repeater that outputs the option text and the number of votes it has received. It also creates a <div> element whose width style attribute is set to the option's Percentage value, so that the user will get a visual representation of the vote percentage, in addition to seeing the percentage as a number:

```
<asp:Panel runat="server" ID="panResults">
    <div class="polloptions">
    <asp:Repeater runat="server" ID="rptOptions">
        <ItemTemplate>
            <%# Eval("OptionText") %>
            <small>(<%# Eval("Votes") %> vote(s) -
                <%# Eval("Percentage", "{0:N1}") %>%)</small>
```

```
            <br />
            <div class="pollbar" style="width: <%# Eval("Percentage")%>%"> </div>
        </ItemTemplate>
    </asp:Repeater>
    <br />
    <b>Total votes: <asp:Label runat="server" ID="lblTotalVotes" /></b>
    </div>
</asp:Panel>
```

Finally, the last section of the control defines a link to the archive page, which can be hidden by means of the control's ShowArchiveLink custom property, plus a couple of closing tags for <div> elements opened earlier to associate some CSS styles to the various parts of the control:

```
<asp:HyperLink runat="server" ID="lnkArchive"
    NavigateUrl="~/ArchivedPolls.aspx" Text="Archived Polls" />
</div>
</div>
```

The PollBox.ascx.cs Code-behind File

The control's code-behind file begins by defining all those custom properties described in the "Design" section. Most of these properties are just wrappers for the Text or Visible properties of inner labels and panels, so they don't need their values persisted:

```
public partial class PollBox : System.Web.UI.UserControl
{
    public bool ShowArchiveLink
    {
        get { return lnkArchive.Visible; }
        set { lnkArchive.Visible = value; }
    }

    public bool ShowHeader
    {
        get { return panHeader.Visible; }
        set { panHeader.Visible = value; }
    }

    public string HeaderText
    {
        get { return lblHeader.Text; }
        set { lblHeader.Text = value; }
    }

    public bool ShowQuestion
    {
        get { return lblQuestion.Visible; }
        set { lblQuestion.Visible = value; }
    }
```

The PollID property, instead, does not wrap any other property, and therefore its value is manually stored and retrieved to and from the control's state, as part of the control's ViewState collection. As already shown in previous chapters, this is done by overriding the control's LoadControlState and SaveControlState methods and registering the control to specify that it requires the control state, from inside the Init event handler:

```
private int _pollID = -1;
public int PollID
{
    get { return _pollID; }
    set { _pollID = value; }
}

protected void Page_Init(object sender, EventArgs e)
{
    this.Page.RegisterRequiresControlState(this);
}

protected override void LoadControlState(object savedState)
{
    object[] ctlState = (object[])savedState;
    base.LoadControlState(ctlState[0]);
    this.PollID = (int)ctlState[1];
}

protected override object SaveControlState()
{
    object[] ctlState = new object[2];
    ctlState[0] = base.SaveControlState();
    ctlState[1] = this.PollID;
    return ctlState;
}
```

The control can be shown because it is explicitly defined on the page, or because it is dynamically created by some template-based control, such as Repeater, DataList, DataGrid, GridView, and DetailsView. In the first case, the code that loads and shows the response options (in either edit or display mode) will be run from the control's Load event handler. Otherwise, it will run from the control's DataBind method, which you can override. The code itself is placed in a separate method, DoBinding, and it's called from these two methods, as follows:

```
protected void Page_Load(object sender, EventArgs e)
{
    if (!this.IsPostBack)
        DoBinding();
}

public override void DataBind()
{
    base.DataBind();
    // with the PollID set, do the actual binding
    DoBinding();
}
```

Note that in the `DataBind` method, the base version of `DataBind` is called before executing the custom binding code of `DoBinding`. The call to the base version, in turn, makes a call to the control's standard `OnDataBinding` method, which parses and evaluates the control's expressions. This is necessary because when the control is placed into a template it will have the `PollID` property bound to some expression, and this binding expression must be evaluated before actually executing the `DoBinding` method, so that it will find the final `PollID` value.

The `DoBinding` method retrieves the data from the database (via the BLL), binds it to the proper `RadioButtonList` and the `Repeater` controls, and either shows or hides the options or results, depending on whether the user has already voted for the question being asked. However, before retrieving the poll and its options, it must check whether the `PollID` property is set to -1, in which case it must first retrieve the ID of the current poll:

```
protected void DoBinding()
{
    panResults.Visible = false;
    panVote.Visible = false;
    int pollID = (this.PollID == -1 ? Poll.CurrentPollID : this.PollID);

    if (pollID > -1)
    {
        Poll poll = Poll.GetPollByID(pollID);
        if (poll != null)
        {
            lblQuestion.Text = poll.QuestionText;
            lblTotalVotes.Text = poll.Votes.ToString();
            valRequireOption.ValidationGroup += poll.ID.ToString();
            btnVote.ValidationGroup = valRequireOption.ValidationGroup;
            optlOptions.DataSource = poll.Options;
            optlOptions.DataBind();
            rptOptions.DataSource = poll.Options;
            rptOptions.DataBind();
            if (poll.IsArchived || GetUserVote(pollID) > 0)
                panResults.Visible = true;
            else
                panVote.Visible = true;
        }
    }
}
```

To check whether the current user has already voted for the poll, a call to the `GetUserVote` method is made. If the method returns a value greater than `0`, it means that a vote for the specified poll was found. You'll see the code for this method in a moment, but first consider the code executed when the Vote button is clicked. The button's `Click` event handler calls the `Poll.VoteOption` business method to add a vote for the specified option (whose ID is read from the `RadioButtonList`'s `SelectedValue`), and then shows the results panel and hides the edit panel. In order to remember that the user has voted for this poll, you create a cookie named `Vote_Poll{x}`, where `{x}` is the ID of the poll. The cookie's value is the ID of the option the user has voted for. The cookie is created only if the `VotingLockByCookie` configuration property is set to `true` (the default) and the cookie's expiration is set to the current date plus the number of days also stored in the `<polls>` custom configuration element (15 by default). Finally, it saves the votes in the cache (unless the `VotingLockByIP` setting is set to `false`), to ensure that it will be remembered at least for the current user's session even if the client has his cookies turned off. The cache's key is defined as `{y}_Vote_Poll{x}`, where `{y}` is replaced by the client's IP address. This is necessary because the `Cache` is not user-specific like session state, and thus you need to create different keys for different users. Here's the code of the `Click` event handler:

```
protected void btnVote_Click(object sender, EventArgs e)
{
    int pollID = (this.PollID == -1 ? Poll.CurrentPollID : this.PollID);

    // check that the user has not already voted for this poll
    int userVote = GetUserVote(pollID);
    if (userVote == 0)
    {
        // post the vote and then create a cookie to remember this user's vote
        userVote = Convert.ToInt32(opt1Options.SelectedValue);
        Poll.VoteOption(pollID, userVote);
        // hide the panel with the radio buttons, and show the results
        DoBinding();
        panVote.Visible = false;
        panResults.Visible = true;

        DateTime expireDate = DateTime.Now.AddDays(
            Globals.Settings.Polls.VotingLockInterval);
        string key = "Vote_Poll" + pollID.ToString();

        // save the result to the cookie
        if (Globals.Settings.Polls.VotingLockByCookie)
        {
            HttpCookie cookie = new HttpCookie(key, userVote.ToString());
            cookie.Expires = expireDate;
            this.Response.Cookies.Add(cookie);
        }

        // save the vote also to the cache
        if (Globals.Settings.Polls.VotingLockByIP)
        {
            Cache.Insert(
                this.Request.UserHostAddress.ToString() + "_" + key,
                userVote);
        }
    }
}
```

The final piece of code is the `GetUserVote` method discussed earlier, which takes the ID of a poll, and checks whether it finds a vote in a client's cookie or in the cache, according to the `VotingLockByCookie` and `VotingLockByIP` settings, respectively. If no vote is found in either place, 0 is returned, indicating that the current user has not yet voted for the specified poll:

```
protected int GetUserVote(int pollID)
{
    string key = "Vote_Poll" + pollID.ToString();
    string key2 = this.Request.UserHostAddress.ToString() + "_" + key;

    // check if the vote is in the cache
    if (Globals.Settings.Polls.VotingLockByIP && Cache[key2] != null)
        return (int)Cache[key2];

    // if the vote is not in cache, check if there's a client-side cookie
    if (Globals.Settings.Polls.VotingLockByCookie)
    {
        HttpCookie cookie = this.Request.Cookies[key];
        if (cookie != null)
            return int.Parse(cookie.Value);
    }

    return 0;
}
}
```

Plugging the PollBox Control into the Site's Layout

The `PollBox` user control is now ready, and you can finally plug it into any page. For this sample site we'll put it into the site's master page, so that the polls will be visible in all pages. As an example of adding more, you can add two `PollBox` instances to the master page: The first will have no `PollID` specified, so that it will dynamically use the current poll; and the second one has the `PollID` property set to a specific value so it can reference a different poll and has the `ShowArchiveLink` property set to `false` to hide the link to the archive page, as it's already shown by the first poll box. Here's the code:

```
<%@ Register Src="Controls/PollBox.ascx" TagName="PollBox" TagPrefix="mb" %>
...
<mb:PollBox id="PollBox1" runat="server" HeaderText="Poll of the week" />
<mb:PollBox id="PollBox2" runat="server" HeaderText="More polls"
    PollID="18" ShowArchiveLink="False" />
```

Figure 6-8 shows the result: the home page with the two poll boxes displayed in the site's left-hand column. You can change the first poll simply by going to the administrative page and setting a different (existing or new) poll as the current one. If you want to change the second, you'll need to change the ID in the master page's source code file.

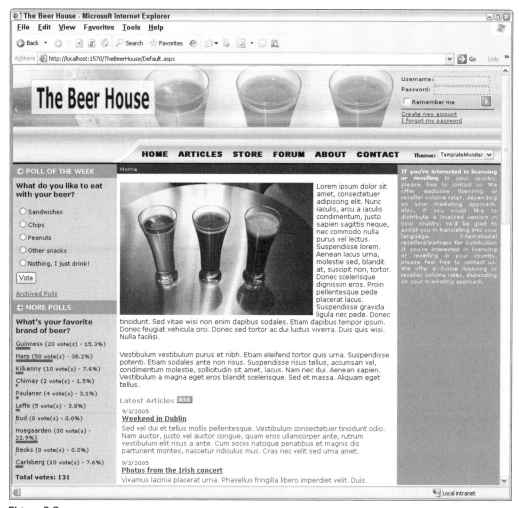

Figure 6-8

The ArchivedPolls.aspx Page

This is the last page that we'll develop for this module. It lists all archived polls, one per line, and when the user clicks one it has to expand and display its options and results. The page allows you to have multiple questions expanded at the same time if you prefer. It initially shows them in "collapsed" mode because you don't want to create a very long page, distracting users and making it hard for them to search for a particular question. Displaying the questions only when the page is first loaded produces a cleaner and more easily navigable page. If the current user is an administrator or an editor, she will also see command links on the right side of the listed polls to delete them. Figure 6-9 shows the page as seen by a normal anonymous user, which has expanded two of the three polls listed on the page.

Figure 6-9

If you compare the poll results on the page's central section with the results of the poll in the left-hand column, you'll notice that they look similar. Actually, they are nearly identical, except for the fact that in the former case the question text is shown as a link and not as bold text. As you can easily guess, the poll results rendered in the page's content section are created by `PollBox` controls, which have the `ShowHeader`, `ShowQuestion`, and `ShowArchiveLink` properties set to `false`. The link with the poll's text is created by a binding expression defined within a `TemplateField` column of a parent `GridView` control. The `PollBox` control itself is defined inside the sample template section and has its `PollID` property set to a binding expression that retrieves the `PollID` value from the `Poll` object being bound to every row, and is wrapped by a `<div>` that is hidden by default (it has the `display` style attribute set to `none`). When the user clicks the link, he doesn't navigate to another page, but executes a local JavaScript function that takes the name of a `<div>` (named after `poll{x}`, where `{x}` is the ID of a poll) and toggles its display state (if set to none, it sets it to an empty string to make it visible, and vice versa). Following is the code for the `GridView` and its templated column, the companion `ObjectDataSource` that references the `Poll` object's methods used to retrieve and delete the records, and the JavaScript function that hides and shows the `<div>` with the results:

```
<script type="text/javascript">
    function toggleDivState(divName)
    {
        var ctl = window.document.getElementById(divName);
        if (ctl.style.display == "none")
            ctl.style.display = "";
        else
            ctl.style.display = "none";
    }
</script>

<div class="sectiontitle">Archived Polls</div>
<p>Here is the complete list of archived polls run in the past. Click on the poll's
question to see its results.</p>
<asp:GridView ID="gvwPolls" runat="server" AutoGenerateColumns="False"
    DataSourceID="objPolls" Width="100%" DataKeyNames="ID"
    OnRowCreated="gvwPolls_RowCreated" ShowHeader="false">
    <Columns>
        <asp:TemplateField>
            <ItemTemplate>
                <img src="images/arrowr2.gif" />
                <a href="javascript:toggleDivState('poll<%# Eval("ID") %>');">
                <%# Eval("QuestionText") %></a>
                <small>(archived on <%# Eval("ArchivedDate", "{0:d}") %>)</small>
                <div style="display: none;" id="poll<%# Eval("ID") %>">
                <mb:PollBox id="PollBox1" runat="server" PollID='<%# Eval("ID") %>'
                    ShowHeader="False" ShowQuestion="False" ShowArchiveLink="False" />
                </div>
            </ItemTemplate>
        </asp:TemplateField>
        <asp:CommandField ButtonType="Image" DeleteImageUrl="~/Images/Delete.gif"
            DeleteText="Delete poll" ShowDeleteButton="True">
            <ItemStyle HorizontalAlign="Center" Width="20px" />
        </asp:CommandField>
    </Columns>
    <EmptyDataTemplate><b>No polls to show</b></EmptyDataTemplate>
</asp:GridView>
<asp:ObjectDataSource ID="objPolls" runat="server" SelectMethod="GetPolls"
    TypeName="MB.TheBeerHouse.BLL.Polls.Poll" DeleteMethod="DeletePoll">
    <DeleteParameters>
        <asp:Parameter Name="id" Type="Int32" />
    </DeleteParameters>
    <SelectParameters>
        <asp:Parameter DefaultValue="false" Name="includeActive" Type="Boolean" />
        <asp:Parameter DefaultValue="true" Name="includeArchived" Type="Boolean" />
    </SelectParameters>
</asp:ObjectDataSource>
```

The ArchivedPolls.aspx.cs Code-behind File

In the `GridView` defined above, a `CommandField` column is declared to create a `Delete` command for each of the listed polls. However, this command must be visible only to users who belong to the Editors and Administrators roles. When the page loads, if the user is not authorized to delete polls, then the `GridView`'s second column is hidden. Before doing this, however, you have to check whether the user is anonymous and, if so, whether the page is accessible to everyone or only to registered members. If the check fails, the `RequestLogin` method of the `BasePage` base class is called to redirect the user to the login page. Here's the code:

```
protected void Page_Load(object sender, EventArgs e)
{
    if (!this.User.Identity.IsAuthenticated &&
        !Globals.Settings.Polls.ArchiveIsPublic)
    {
        this.RequestLogin();
    }

    gvwPolls.Columns[1].Visible = (this.User.Identity.IsAuthenticated &&
        (this.User.IsInRole("Administrators") || this.User.IsInRole("Editors")));
}
```

The only other code in the code-behind file for this page is the event handler for the `GridView`'s `RowCreated` event, from which you add the JavaScript confirmation pop-up to the `Delete` command buttons:

```
protected void gvwPolls_RowCreated(object sender, GridViewRowEventArgs e)
{
    if (e.Row.RowType == DataControlRowType.DataRow)
    {
        ImageButton btn = e.Row.Cells[1].Controls[0] as ImageButton;
        btn.OnClientClick =
            @"if (confirm('Are you sure you want to delete this poll?') == false)
                return false;";
    }
}
```

Summary

This chapter has presented a working solution for handling multiple dynamic polls on your web site. The complete polls module is made up of an administration console for managing the polls through a web browser, integration with the membership system to secure the administration and archive pages, and a user control that enables us to show different polls on any page using only a couple of lines of code. This module can easily be employed in many real-world sites as it is now, but of course you can expand and enhance it as desired. Here are a few suggestions:

❑ Add the capability to remind users which option they voted for. Currently they can see the results, but the control does not indicate how they voted; the vote is stored in a cookie, which is easy to retrieve.

❑ Add a `ReleaseDate` and `ExpireDate` to the polls, so that you can schedule the current poll to change automatically. We do this type of thing with the articles module.

❑ Provide the option to allow only registered users to vote.

In the next chapter you're going to continue the development of the TheBeerHouse site through the addition of another module that integrates with the rest of the site's architecture. This new module will be used for creating and sending out newsletters to users who subscribed to the newsletter at registration time.

7

Newsletters

In this chapter we'll design and implement a complete newsletter mailing list system. This will allow users to subscribe to online newsletters, and administrators to manage the newsletter content. First, we'll look at what newsletters can offer to web sites like the one developed in this book, and we'll examine the various management aspects that must be addressed in order to make the mailing list administrator's life as easy as possible. By the end of the chapter, we'll have a powerful newsletter module fully developed and integrated into our site!

Problem

Throughout this book I've mentioned that the key to a successful site is having good content. This content also needs to be logically organized to ease navigability, have an attractive design, and offer some interaction with the user. The content not only has to be interesting and accurate, but must also be fresh and regularly updated to ensure that users keep coming back to visit the site. To help us achieve this for our TheBeerHouse web site, an article management module was developed in Chapter 5, to allow administrators and editors to easily manage and publish new content. Although you should try to publish new content on a regular basis, this is not always possible, especially if you can't afford a dedicated team to take care of this, or if your company has no news to pass on to users. Unfortunately, if users see a static page for too long, then chances are good that they won't come back very often, and they may end up forgetting about the site. But even when you frequently add fresh content to the site, not every user will be aware of it. They might not visit the site daily or weekly to see the latest updates, especially if the site is updated on a random basis with no public announcement.

A good way to inform users that some new content has been added to the site (for example, an article, a new product for sale, or a new layout design) is to send them an e-mail newsletter that lists all the new resources available on the site. Many sites offer the option of subscribing to a mailing list, which typically represents a group of users interested in a certain kind of news. A newsletter is created and sent to a mailing list to remind the community of users that the site is still worth visiting. However, many visitors don't like to submit their e-mail address just to be informed about changes to the web site, so to encourage people to maintain their subscriptions, and to encourage more people to sign up, a webmaster should offer something extra that is only available to the mailing list's subscribers, such as a short tip, article, or some kind of discount for one of the site's products (this is often called a *kicker* in marketing lingo).

The primary purpose of a mailing list system is to inform users that new material is available online, and to convince them to revisit the site again. It is also possible to make money from your mailing list. If you have several thousands of subscribers you could sell some space in your newsletters for advertisement spots. These shouldn't be anything too invasive, perhaps just a two- or three-line description of a partner site or company, or the manufacturer of a product you sell on your site. If you provide some valuable content in your newsletters, and the advertisement is short and preferably related to the theme of the site and the newsletter, the users won't complain about it. You can inform potential sponsors that this space in the newsletter is very valuable because it's only sent to users who have elected to receive it, so those users will likely read it thoroughly, and therefore the advertisement will get much more attention than it would receive through a common banner ad on a site. Research shows that the average click-through from spots in newsletters is around 4–5%, compared to around 1% or less for common banner ads.

However you decide to promote your web site to get more people to subscribe, you will face the problem of managing all the details of your clients, such as e-mail addresses, keeping track of the e-mail newsletter messages you send, and building a system to enable users to subscribe or unsubscribe easily (users must have the right to unsubscribe at any time). Some small sites manually collect the addresses from an HTML form, create a group of contacts in Outlook (or other messaging client), and use it to write a message to all their subscribers. This mostly applies to small, static sites, where ASP or other server-side code is not used. However, when the site grows and you get a significant number of subscribers, manually adding or removing users several times a week becomes a real chore, and if the number is on the order of thousands, it's almost impossible! Also, if you send out a newsletter to an Outlook group of contacts, you won't be able to personalize the newsletters in any way: they'll be exactly the same for every user. It would be much better to personalize every e-mail — for example, with the name of the subscriber if this information is available, because this will help to build a more personal relationship with subscribers. It's worth noting, however, that the most common way of subscribing to a list is for a user to enter her e-mail address in a form on the home page and press Submit. It's totally impersonal, and it will only enable you to personalize the newsletter with the user's e-mail address. In order to achieve a more extensive personalization, you have to ask the users to provide more details, such as their first and last name. Our newsletter module should support both a basic and extended subscription form, to accommodate both situations.

In summary, you may realize that you are losing traffic because you have no way of letting your users know that your content has been updated. Therefore, the aim of this chapter is to build a newsletter mailing list system. A secondary problem is that managing the system and personalizing newsletters is time-consuming, so we want to include a subscription and administration system that automates most of the tasks and enables the administrator to complete these tasks easily. Yet another problem is that you need to generate revenue, so you'll want to allow for the possibility of including advertising spots in the newsletters. Once you know what problems you want to solve, you can then move on to specifying the features you want it to have, i.e., the design stage. The next section provides a more detailed list of features we need to implement to have a fully functional mailing list module.

Design

The first thing we need to think about is how we will store the subscription data, such as the user's e-mail address, first and last names, and other information that can be used to personalize the newsletters. In the previous edition of the book, I created a new database table to store this information, and wrote code to retrieve it, save it, and modify it. This time around, things are much easier because of the rich support provided by the membership and profiling system we already developed in Chapter 4. As you may recall, the membership data includes the username and e-mail address, while the profile includes, among other things, the user's first and last name and the format of newsletter she would like to subscribe to (plain-text format, HTML format, or no newsletter at all). To make things simpler and prevent storing the same data in multiple places, we'll use those same fields. You may think that this would require the user to register for the site just to receive the newsletter, and this is not required by many other sites, so this may be a bad idea. Yes, it will require users to register for the site, but the only information strictly required by the registration system is just the username, e-mail address, and password; all the other profile information is optional. For that reason, I don't think that requiring users to choose a username and password, in addition to an e-mail address (needed anyway to send the newsletter), is much of a problem, or a valid reason for us to avoid using the membership system and create a whole new user-data system from scratch just for use by the newsletter module. My proposed solution is much better integrated with the site, and by registering, the user will also gain access to protected articles, the archived polls and newsletters (in case the administrator chooses not to allow everybody to see them), the forums, and more. This approach also makes it easy for a subscriber to change her registration type, or other information. For example, if she wants to switch from plain-text newsletters to HTML newsletters, she can do this from her password-protected profile, and no one else could do this on her behalf.

Besides the registration work, there are other parts of the module, and other features, to design. First, the administrator or editor needs a protected page from which she can send a newsletter to all subscribers, and to enter the body in both plain-text and HTML formats. We also need the option to send multi-part MIME messages, i.e., e-mails that contain both the plain-text and the HTML versions of the body, and leave it to the user's e-mail client program to decide which version to display. However, the reason why the user may wish to subscribe to the plain-text newsletter, instead of the HTML version, is not because the user's e-mail client software doesn't support HTML, but rather because the user doesn't want to download a large message, or for security reasons doesn't want (or cannot, as dictated by their company's policies) to download images and scripts with the e-mails. Because of this, I decided that it's better to send distinct versions of the newsletter according to each subscriber's preferences. In addition to the administrative send page, there must be an archive page that allows users to read past newsletters online. The administrator must also be able to specify whether this page can be accessed by everyone, or only by registered members. This is the same type of security restriction code we've already implemented in the previous chapter, for the polls module. The reason for protecting the page against anonymous access is to encourage users to register, thus enabling you to gather new data about your users — data that you may later use for a number of marketing purposes, as explained in Chapter 4 when we discussed membership.

Because the membership registration system was already implemented, the next thing to design and implement is the system that sends out the newsletters. Sending a single e-mail message is an easy task, but sending out a newsletter to a mailing list of thousands of subscribers is a much more complex job that requires some analysis and a good design. In the next section, I'll present the classes of the .NET Framework that you can use to send e-mail messages, and then discuss the issues to consider and solve when delivering mass e-mails. After introducing this background information, we'll draw together all the considerations and techniques discussed, and design the module.

A Word About Spam

Before going any further I want to clarify that this module is not intended to send unsolicited e-mail newsletters, or messages of any kind, to users who did not request them. Many countries have laws against this, but regardless of the legality of doing this, I strongly believe that it hurts a site's reputation considerably to undertake this kind of action, and it ends up damaging the favorable impression that you've worked so hard to create. This newsletter system is only intended to send e-mail messages to users who have specifically opted in. Furthermore, users must be allowed to easily change their mind and stop any further e-mails from the site.

Creating and Sending E-mails

The `System.Net.Mail` namespace defined in the `System.dll` assembly contains all the classes used to send e-mails. The older `System.Web.Mail` namespace, and its related classes, that were used with ASP.NET 1.x are still there, but its use has been deprecated now in favor of these new classes in ASP.NET 2.0 that provide more features. The principal classes are `MailMessage`, which represents an e-mail message, and the `SmtpClient` class, which provides the methods used to send a `MailMessage` by connecting to a configured SMTP server (SMTP is the Simple Mail Transfer Protocol, which is the low-level protocol used by Microsoft Exchange and other mail servers).

`MailMessage` fully describes an e-mail message, with its subject, body (in plain-text, HTML, or in both formats), the To, CC, and BCC addresses, and any attachments that might be used. The simplest way to create an e-mail is using the `MailMessage` constructor, which takes the sender's address, the recipient's address, the mail's subject, and the body, as shown below:

```
MailMessage mail = new MailMessage(
    "from@somewhere.com", "to@somewhere.com", "subject", "body");
```

However, this approach will be too limited in most cases, because you may want to specify the sender's display name in addition to his e-mail address (the display name is what is displayed by the mail client, if present, instead of the address, and makes the mail and its sender look more professional). You may also want to send to more than one recipient, use an HTML body (as an alternative, or in addition, to the plain-text version), include some attachments, use a different encoding, modify the mail's priority, and so on. All these settings, and more, are specified by means of a number of instance properties of the `MailMessage` class. Their names should be self-explanatory, and some examples include the following: `Subject`, `Body`, `IsBodyHtml`, `From`, `To`, `CC`, `Bcc`, `BodyEncoding`, `Attachments`, `AlternateViews`, `Headers`, `Priority`, and `ReplyTo`. The class' constructor enables you to specify a `From` property of type `MailAddress`, `Address`, and `UserName` properties. The `To`, `CC`, and `Bcc` properties are of type `MailAddressCollection` and thus can accept multiple `MailAddress` instances (you can add them by means of the collection's `Add` method). Similarly, the `MailMessage`'s `Attachments` property is of type `AttachmentCollection`, a collection of `Attachment` instances that point to files located on the server. The following example shows how to build an HTML-formatted e-mail message that will be sent to multiple recipients, with high priority, and that includes a couple of attachments:

```
// create the message
MailMessage mail = new MailMessage();
// set the sender's address and display name
mail.From = new MailAddress("mbellinaso@wrox.com", "Marco Bellinaso");
// add a first recipient by specifying only her address
mail.To.Add("john@wroxfans.com");
// add a second recipient by specifying her address and display name
mail.To.Add(new MailAddress("anne@wroxfans.com", "Anne Gentle"));
// add a third recipient, but to the CC field this time
mail.CC.Add("mike@wroxfans.com");
// set the mail's subject and HTML body
mail.Subject = "Sample Mail";
mail.Body = "Hello, <b>my friend</b>!<br />How are you?";
```

```
mail.IsBodyHtml = true;
// set the mail's priority to high
mail.Priority = MailPriority.High;
// add a couple of attachments
mail.Attachments.Add(
    new Attachment(@"c:\demo.zip", MediaTypeNames.Application.Octet));
mail.Attachments.Add(
    new Attachment(@"c:\report.xls", MediaTypeNames.Application.Octet));
```

If you also wanted to provide a plain-text version of the body in the same mail, so that the display format (plain text or HTML) would depend on the user's e-mail client settings, you would add the following lines:

```
string body = "Hello, my friend!\nHow are you?";
AlternateView plainView = new AlternateView(body, MediaTypeNames.Text.Plain);
mail.AlternateViews.Add(plainView);
```

Once a `MailMessage` object is ready, the e-mail message it describes can be sent out by means of the `Send` method of the `SmtpClient` class, as shown here:

```
SmtpClient smtpClient = new SmtpClient();
smtpClient.Send(mail);
```

Before calling the `Send` method, you may need to set some configuration settings, such as the SMTP server's address (the `SmtpClient`'s `Host` property), port (the `Port` property) and its credentials (the `Credentials` property), whether the connection in encrypted with SSL (the `EnableSsl` property), and the timeout in milliseconds for sending the mail (the `Timeout` property, which defaults to 100 seconds). An important property is `DeliveryMethod`, which defines how the mail message is delivered. It's of type `SmtpDeliveryMethod`, an enumeration with the following values:

❑ **Network:** The e-mail is sent through a direct connection to the specified SMTP server.

❑ **PickupDirectoryFromIis:** The e-mail message is prepared and the EML file is saved into the default directory from which IIS picks up queued e-mails to send. By default this is `<drive>:\Inetpub\mailroot\Queue`.

❑ **SpecifiedPickupDirectory:** The EML file with the mail being sent is saved into the location specified by the `PickupDirectoryLocation` property of the `smtpClient` object. This is useful when you have an external custom program that picks up e-mails from that folder and processes them.

The delivery method you choose can dramatically change the performance of your site when sending many e-mails and can produce different errors during the send operation. If you select the Network delivery method, the `SmtpClient` class takes care of sending the mail directly and raises an error if the destination e-mail address is not found or if there are other transmission problems. With the other two methods, instead of sending the message directly, an EML mail file is prepared and saved to the file system, where another application (IIS or something else) will pick them up later for the actual delivery (a queue accumulates the messages, which means the web application will not have to wait for each message to be sent over the Internet). However, when using the second and third delivery methods, your web application cannot be notified of any errors that may occur during transmission of the message, and it will be up to IIS (or another mail agent that might be used) to handle them. In general, the `Pickup DirectoryFromIis` method is the preferred one, unless your ASP.NET application is not given the right to write to IIS mail folders (check with your web hosting provider service if you don't use your own servers).

If you set all SmtpClient properties mentioned above directly in your C# code, you'll have to recompile the application or edit the source file every time you want to change any of these settings. This, of course, is not an option if you're selling a packaged application, or you want to let the administrator change these settings on his own without directly involving you. As an alternative to hard-coding the delivery method, you can set it declaratively in the web.config file, which now supports a new configuration section named <mailSettings>, located under <system.net>, which allows you to specify delivery settings. The SmtpClient class automatically loads those settings from web.config to configure itself at runtime, so you should generally not set your delivery and SMTP options directly in your C# code. Following is an extract of the configuration file that shows how to select PickupDirectoryFromIis as the delivery method, set up the sender's e-mail address and the SMTP server's name (or IP address) and port, and specify that you want to use the default credentials to connect to the server:

```
<configuration xmlns="http://schemas.microsoft.com/.NetConfiguration/v2.0">
    <system.net>
        <mailSettings>
            <smtp deliveryMethod="PickupDirectoryFromIis"
                from="mbellinaso@wrox.com">
                <network defaultCredentials="true"
                    host="vmwin2003" port="25"></network>
            </smtp>
        </mailSettings>
    </system.net>
    <!-- other configuration sections... -->
</configuration>
```

The SmtpClient's Send method used in the preceding code snippet sends the e-mail synchronously, which means that the task must complete before the execution of your application can resume. The term synchronous means "do what I asked, and I'll stop and wait for you to finish," and the term asynchronous means "do what I asked, but let me continue doing other work, and you should notify me when you're done." The SmtpClient class also has a SendAsync method to send the mail asynchronously. It returns immediately, and the e-mail is prepared and sent out on a separate thread. When the send task is complete, the SmtpClient's SendCompleted event is raised. This event is also raised in case of errors, and the Error and Cancelled properties of its second argument (of type AsyncCompletedEventArgs) tell you whether it was raised because the send was cancelled, because there was an error, or because the send completed successfully. Here's a sample snippet that shows how to send the mail asynchronously, and handle the resulting completion event:

```
SmtpClient smtpClient = new SmtpClient();
smtpClient.SendCompleted += new SendCompletedEventHandler(MailSendCompleted);
smtpClient.SendAsync(message, null);
...

public static void MailSendCompleted(object sender, AsyncCompletedEventArgs e)
{
    if (e.Cancelled)
        Trace.Write("Send canceled.");
    if (e.Error != null)
        Trace.Write(e.Error.ToString());
    else
        Trace.Write("Message sent.");
}
```

An asynchronous send operation can be cancelled before completion by calling the SmtpClient's SendAsyncCancel method. Note that you can't send a second e-mail while a SmtpClient has another send in progress; if you try to do so, you'll receive an InvalidOperationException.

Managing Long Operations on the Server

Because of the disconnected nature of the web, when you submit a form, you typically have to wait some time to get a response, and in the meantime you see nothing but a blank page. The browser can't check how the server-side processing is going, and it can't provide any feedback to the user. As long as the user only has to wait less than five seconds, that's normally fine. But if the application takes longer to produce a response, then you've got a problem because you can't leave users stranded without visual feedback for more than a few seconds, or they will start to think that the application got stuck, or had a serious problem, and they will close their browser and go away. If a user presses refresh to resend the data and restart the processing, that's bad as well, because that action actually requests the same operation a second time, and the server will do the same work twice, causing duplication and possibly data integrity problems. There are many situations where the server-side processing might take a long time to complete: you may execute long-running SQL queries, call an external web service, or forward a call to an external application (a payment processing application, for example) and wait for a response, and so on. In our case, you'll be sending potentially thousands of e-mails, and to do this you'll need to retrieve the profile for all registered members (that means multiple SQL queries), parse the newsletter's body and replace all the personalization placeholders, and insert the newsletter into the archive. This can possibly take many minutes, not just seconds! You can't expect your newsletter editor to look at a blank page for such a long period of time. In the previous edition of the book, we just set a much higher timeout for the page sending the newsletter, so that it wouldn't terminate with an error after the normal 90 seconds, but we didn't tackle the real problem: The page provided no feedback to the editor about the send progress, and this was a serious design flaw. In this new version we'll fix that flaw! Several techniques could be employed to solve this issue and provide some feedback to the user. Here is a list of some of the alternatives and their pros and cons:

❑   When users click the Submit button, you can redirect them to a second page that shows a wait message. When this wait page arrives on the client browser it uses some simple JavaScript, or the refresh metatag, to immediately post back to the server — either to itself or to another page. For example, the following metatag declared at the top of the page makes the current page redirect to processing.aspx after two seconds:

```
<meta http-equiv="refresh"

content="2; URL=http://www.contoso.com/processing.aspx">.
```

After this second postback, the long processing task will be executed. While the task is running on the server, the current wait page will remain visible on the client. You can provide an animated gif representing an incrementing progress bar, in addition to the wait message, so that users get the idea that processing is taking place behind the scenes. This simple approach doesn't provide any real feedback about the task's actual progress, but it would suffice for many situations.

❑   When the user clicks the Submit button, on the server side you can start a secondary thread that will process the long task in the background. The page will then immediately redirect to a wait page that shows the user a message, while the real action continues on the server on that separate thread. The code executing on the background thread will also update some server-side variables indicating the percentage of the task completed, and some other optional information.

The wait page will automatically refresh every "*n*" seconds, and every time it loads it will read the variables written by the second thread and display the progress status accordingly. To refresh itself, it can use some JavaScript that submits the form, or it can use the refresh metatag, but without the URL of the page to load, as shown in the following:

```
<meta http-equiv="refresh" content="2">
```

This approach can be quite effective, because it gives the user some real feedback about the background processing; however, with the page refreshing every few seconds, the user will continuously see the browser's content flickering. A better solution would be to load the wait/progress page into a small IFRAME, which would show only the progress bar and nothing else. When the processing completes, the wait page will not show the progress bar again, but will instead redirect the user to the page showing the confirmation and the results. Still, when the progress bar is updated, it will disappear for a short time when the page in the IFRAME refreshes, and this creates an ugly visual effect.

❑   The preceding option can be improved if, instead of refreshing the whole page or IFRAME, you just update the progress bar representing the processing status, and then use some JavaScript to call a server-side page that returns the required information, which uses this information to dynamically update some part of the page, such as the progress bar's width and the percentage text. The only disadvantage of this approach is that it requires JavaScript to be enabled on the client browser, but this shouldn't be a concern because all your users will likely have JavaScript enabled. Even if it were a problem, in our specific case the page requiring a real-time progress bar is only used in the administrative section, and thus it's not a problem to dictate some basic requirements (such as browser support for JavaScript) for your editors and administrators. Other than this small concern, this solution has everything you need: When the user submits the page, the page returns immediately and starts showing a progress bar that lets the user monitor how the long task is progressing in real time; in addition, you no longer have timeout problems because the page does almost nothing and completes instantaneously, while the background thread doing the real work can go on for a long time without problems.

Instead of showing you how to implement all three possible solutions, we will go straight to the best one, which is of course the third one. In the next section I'll provide you with some background information about multi-threaded programming and script programming for partial page updating, which you'll use in the "Solution" section to implement the newsletter delivery task.

Background Threads

Background, or secondary, threads can be used to execute long-running tasks without tying up the main UI task. Creating new threads in .NET is very easy, but you have to be careful about multiple threads trying to access the same memory at the same time. All the classes you need are under the System.Threading namespace, in the mscorlib.dll assembly. The basic steps required are as follows:

1.   Create a ThreadStart delegate that points to the method that will run in the secondary thread. The method must return void and can't accept any input parameters.

2.   Create a Thread object that takes the ThreadStart delegate in its constructor. You can also set a number of properties for this thread, such as its name (useful if you need to debug threads and identify them by name instead of by ID) and its priority. The Priority property, in particular, can be dangerous, because it can seriously affect the performance of the whole application. It's of type ThreadPriority, an enumeration, and by default it's set to ThreadPriority.Normal, which means that the primary thread and the secondary thread have the same priority, and the

CPU time given to the process is equally divided between them. Other values of the `ThreadPriority` enumeration are `AboveNormal`, `BelowNormal`, `Highest`, and `Lowest`. In general, you should never assign the `Priority` property an `AboveNormal` or `Highest` value for a background thread. Instead, it's usually a good idea to set the property to `BelowNormal`, so that the background thread doesn't slow down the primary thread any noticeable degree, and it won't interfere with ASP.NET.

3. Call the `Start` method of the `Thread` object. The thread starts, and you can control its lifetime from the thread that created it. For example, to affect the lifetime of the thread you can call the `Abort` method to start terminating the thread (in an asynchronous way), the `Join` method to make the primary thread wait until the secondary thread has completed, and the `IsAlive` property, which returns a Boolean value indicating whether the background thread is still running.

The following snippet shows how to start the `ExecuteTask` method, which can be used to perform a long task in a background thread:

```
// create and start a background thread
ThreadStart ts = new ThreadStart(Test);
Thread thread = new Thread(ts);
thread.Priority = ThreadPriority.BelowNormal;
thread.Name = "TestThread";
thread.Start();
// main thread goes ahead immediately
...


// the method run asynchronously by the background thread
void ExecuteTask()
{
    // execute time consuming processing here
    ...
}
```

One problem of multi-threaded programming in .NET 1.x was the difficulty in passing parameters to the secondary thread. The `ThreadStart` delegate cannot point to methods that accept parameters, so the developers had to find workarounds for this. The most common one was to create a class with some properties, and the main thread would create an instance of the class and use the object's properties as parameters for the method pointed to by `ThreadStart`. Thankfully, this becomes much easier in .NET 2.0, thanks to the new `ParameterizedThreadStart` delegate, which points to methods that take an object parameter. Because an object can be anything, you can pass a custom object with properties that you define as parameters, or simply pass an array of objects if you prefer. The following snippet shows how you can call the `ExecuteTask` method and pass an array of objects to it, where the first object is a string, the second is an integer (that is boxed into an object), and the last is a `DateTime`. The `ExecuteTask` method takes the object parameter and casts it to a reference of type `object` array, and then it extracts the single values and casts them to the proper type, and finally performs the actual processing:

```
// create and start a background thread with some input parameters
object[] parameters = new object[]{"val1", 10, DateTime.Now};
ParameterizedThreadStart pts = new ParameterizedThreadStart(ExecuteTask);
Thread thread = new Thread(pts);
thread.Priority = ThreadPriority.BelowNormal;
thread.Start(parameters);
// main thread goes ahead immediately
```

```
    ...

    // the method run asynchronously by the background thread
    void ExecuteTask(object data)
    {
        // extract the parameters from the input data object
        object[] parameters = (object[])data;
        string val1 = (string)parameters[0];
        int val2 = (int)parameters[1];
        DateTime val3 = (DateTime)parameters[2];

        // execute time consuming processing here
        ...
    }
```

The most serious issue with multi-threaded programming is synchronizing access to shared resources. That is, if you have two threads reading and writing to the same variable, you must find some way to synchronize these operations so that one thread cannot read or write a variable while another thread is also writing it. If you don't take this into account, your program may produce unpredictable results and have strange behaviors, it may lock up at unpredictable times, and possibly even cause data integrity problems. A shared resource is any variable or field within the scope of the current method, including class-level public and private fields and static variables. In C#, the simplest way to synchronize access to these resources is through the `lock` statement. It takes a non-null object (i.e., a reference type—value types are *not* accepted), which must be accessible by all threads, and is typically a class-level field. The type of this object is not important, so many developers just use an instance of the root `System.Object` type for this purpose. You can simply declare an object field at the class level, assign it a reference to a new object, and use it from the methods running in different threads. Once the code enters a lock block, the execution must exit the block before another thread can enter a lock block for the same locking variable. Here's an example:

```
    private object lockObj = new object();
    private int counter = 0;

    void MethodFromFirstThread()
    {
        lock(lockObj)
        {
            counter = counter + 1;
        }
        // some other work...
    }

    void MethodFromSecondThread()
    {
        lock(lockObj)
        {
            if (counter >= 10)
                DoSomething();
        }
    }
```

In many situations, however, you don't want to completely lock a shared resource against both read and write operations. That is, you normally allow multiple threads to read the same resource at the same time, but no write operation can be done from any thread while another thread is reading or writing the resource (multiple reads, but exclusive writes). To implement this type of lock, you use the ReaderWriterLock object, whose AcquireWriterLock method protects code following that method call against other reads or writes from other threads, until a call to ReleaseWriterLock is made. If you call AcquireReaderLock (not to be confused with AcquireWriterLock), another thread will be able to enter its own AcquireReaderLock block and read the same resources, but an AcquireWriterLock call would wait for all the other threads to call ReleaseReaderLock. Following is an example that shows how you can synchronize access to a shared field when you have two different threads that read it, and another one that writes it:

```
public static ReaderWriterLock Lock = new ReaderWriterLock();
private int counter = 0;

void MethodFromFirstThread()
{
    Lock.AcquireWriterLock(Timeout.Infinite);
    counter = counter + 1;
    Lock.ReleaseWriterLock();

    // some other work...
}

void MethodFromSecondThread()
{
    Lock.AcquireReaderLock(Timeout.Infinite);
    if (counter >= 10)
        DoSomething();
    Lock.ReleaseReaderLock();
}

void MethodFromThirdThread()
{
    Lock.AcquireReaderLock(Timeout.Infinite);
    if (counter != 50)
        DoSomethingElse();
    Lock.ReleaseReaderLock();
}
```

In our specific case, you'll have a business class that runs a background thread to asynchronously send out the newsletters; after sending each mail, it updates a number of server-side variables that indicate the total number of mails to send, the number of mails already sent, the percentage of mails already sent, and whether the task has completed. Then, an ASP.NET page from the presentation layer, and thus from a different thread, will read this information to update the status information on the client's screen. Because the information is shared between two threads, you'll need to synchronize the access, and the ReaderWriterLock will be used for this purpose.

> Multi-threaded programming is a very complex subject, and there are further considerations regarding the proper way to design code so that it performs well and doesn't cause deadlocks that may freeze the entire application. You should also avoid creating too many threads if it's not strictly required, because the operating system and the thread scheduler (the portion of the OS that distributes the CPU time among the existing threads) consume CPU time and memory for managing them. There are also other classes that I haven't discussed here (such as `Monitor`, `Semaphore`, `Interlocked`, `ThreadPoll`, etc.) because they will not be necessary for implementing the solution of this specific module. If you are interested in digging deeper into the subject of multi-threading, I recommend you get a book that covers this subject in greater depth, such as *Professional C# 2005* (Wiley, 2005).

Partial Page Updates with Script Callbacks

To update the progress bar and the other status information on the page that provides feedback about the newsletter being sent, you must find some way to refresh parts of the page without posting the whole page to the server, because that would take time and temporarily show blank pages (which would appear as nasty flashes, even with fast computers and a broadband connection). The solution is to use JavaScript plus DHTML to change the text of some container elements (DIVs or SPANs) and the width of the progress bar, but to do this you must still request the updated values from the server every few seconds. However, instead of making the request by posting the current page to the server, you can post the request programmatically with some client-side JavaScript code, thanks to the `XmlHttpRequest` object, which is available on both Internet Explorer (as an ActiveX control marked as safe) and Firefox/Netscape browsers (as an object built directly into the browser's document object model). You can post values to the page being called either as `POST` or `GET` parameters; the requested page will then do its normal work and the `XmlHttpRequest` object will retrieve the output from the server, as a string. The output can be anything, but it will usually be some plain-text or XML text containing the results of some server-side processing; it will be parsed using JavaScript in the browser, interpreted, and used to update some information on the current page. Therefore, you're actually making a request to the server from the browser without doing a page postback, and the user will not notice it; even if some information is updated, from the user's point of view everything looks like it happened on the client. I like to call this a *transparent server request*.

As a quick example, consider how to create a page that makes a transparent request to the server to multiply the number inserted into a textbox by two, when a button is clicked. When the button is clicked, it calls a client-side JavaScript function called `DoCalc` and passes the current value of the textbox (which is expected to be an integer number). The `DoCalc` function will then use the `XmlHttpRequest` object (instantiated as an ActiveX, or from the DOM, according to the browser's capabilities) to call the `multiply.aspx` page with its input value passed to the page on the querystring. When the request returns, the `DoCall` function takes the output produced and shows it to the user by means of an alert message box. Following is the code of the page making the request:

```
<%@ Page Language="C#" AutoEventWireup="true"
    CodeFile="Default.aspx.cs" Inherits="Default" %>

<html xmlns="http://www.w3.org/1999/xhtml" >
<head runat="server">
    <title>Test</title>

    <script type="text/javascript">
```

```
        function DoCalc(val)
        {
            var url = "multiply.aspx?val=" + val;
            var request = null;

            if (window.XMLHttpRequest)
            {
                request = new XMLHttpRequest();
                request.open("GET", url, false);
                request.send(null);
            }
            else if (window.ActiveXObject)
            {
                request = new ActiveXObject("Microsoft.XMLHTTP");
                request.open("GET", url, false);
                request.send();
            }

            if (request)
            {
                var result = request.responseText;
                alert(result);
            }
        }
    </script>
</head>
<body>
    <form id="form1" runat="server">
        <asp:TextBox ID="txtValue" runat="server" />
        <input id="btnSubmit" runat="server" type="button" value="Calc"
          onclick="javascript:DoCalc(document.getElementById('txtValue').value);"/>
    </form>
</body>
</html>
```

The multiply.aspx page takes the val parameter passed on the querystring, converts it to an integer (in a real-world situation you would need to validate the input, and handle possible conversion exceptions), multiplies it by two, and returns the result as a string. It also calls Response.End to ensure that nothing else is sent to the client. Here's the code of its Page_Load event handler:

```
protected void Page_Load(object sender, EventArgs e)
{
    int val = int.Parse(this.Request.QueryString["val"]);
    Response.Write((val*2).ToString());
    Response.Flush();
    Response.End();
}
```

The technique just described works in any version of ASP.NET, and it works basically the same in any other web programming platform, such as classic ASP, PHP, JSP, etc., because it's mostly based on platform-independent JavaScript that runs on the client. However, ASP.NET 2.0 introduces a new feature, called a *script callback*, that simplifies this task. It wraps all the plumbing related to XmlHttpResponse (preparing the request, sending it, and receiving the response) and lets the developer focus on the code that accepts the response and performs the partial page update. The following code presents a new and simplified version of the previous page, with the JavaScript block only containing a function that takes the result of the server-side processing, displaying it to the user:

```aspx
<%@ Page Language="C#" AutoEventWireup="true"
    CodeFile="Default.aspx.cs" Inherits="_Default" %>

<html xmlns="http://www.w3.org/1999/xhtml" >
<head runat="server">
    <title>Test</title>

    <script type="text/javascript">
      function ShowResult(result, context)
      {
          alert(result);
      }
    </script>
</head>
<body>
    <form id="form1" runat="server">
        <asp:TextBox ID="txtValue" runat="server" />
        <input id="btnSubmit" runat="server" type="button" value="Calc" />
    </form>
</body>
</html>
```

From the C# code-behind file you must get a reference to a JavaScript function that makes the transparent post and was automatically generated and added to the page by ASP.NET itself, and attach it to the button's `OnClickonclick` event. This is done by the `GetCallbackEventReference` of the page's `ClientScript` property. `ClientScript` is a new page property of type `ClientScriptManager`, which exposes all methods to work with scripts, such as registering scripts at the top of the page (`RegisterClientScriptBlock`) that run when the page finishes loading (`RegisterStartupMethod`), or just before it is submitted (`RegisterOnSubmitStatement`). The `GetCallbackReference` takes a reference to a page or control that implements the `ICallbackEventHander` (described in a moment), an argument passed from the client side to the server side (which may be a simple value or a script that returns a dynamically calculated value), the name of the client-side callback function that will consume the values returned from the server, and finally a value passed to the client-side callback function (just as for the second argument, this may be a client-side script that returns a value). In the example being written, the first argument is a reference to the page itself, the second argument a script that returns the value of the `txtValue` textbox, the third argument is a reference to a JavaScript function called `ShowResult`, and the last argument is just `null`. The string returned by the `GetCallbackReference` is the call to the ASP.NET-generated `WebForm_DoCallback` JavaScript function, which is assigned to the button's `OnClick` attribute, into the `Attributes` collection. This sounds complicated, but the actual code is pretty simple. Here's how the code-behind class begins, with the `Page_Load` event handler:

```csharp
public partial class _Default : System.Web.UI.Page, ICallbackEventHandler
{
    protected void Page_Load(object sender, EventArgs e)
    {
        string callbackRef = this.ClientScript.GetCallbackEventReference(this,
            "window.document.getElementById('txtValue').value",
            "ShowResult", null);

        btnSubmit.Attributes.Add("onclick", callbackRef);
    }
```

Now you have to implement the `ICallbackEventHandler` interface, which is composed of a couple of methods: `RaiseCallbackEvent` and `GetCallbackResult`. The first one is the server-side callback method that takes the parameters passed by the client, producing the result. The result is saved into a class-level field because it is returned to the client by `GetCallbackResult`. Here's the code:

```
string callbackResult = "";

public string GetCallbackResult()
{
    return callbackResult;
}

public void RaiseCallbackEvent(string eventArgument)
{
    callbackResult = (int.Parse(eventArgument) *2).ToString();
}
}
```

When you run the page, you can type a number into the textbox, click the button, and almost immediately you'll get the result in an alert message box, without the page flashing at all for a postback; the round-trip to the server happened transparently without any obvious signs from the user's perspective (which, of course, was our goal). If you take a look at the page's HTML source code, this is what you'll see for the button:

```
<input name="btnSubmit" type="button" id="btnSubmit" value="Calc"
    onclick="WebForm_DoCallback(
        '__Page',window.document.getElementById('txtValue').value,
        ShowResult,null,null,false)" />
```

You won't see the `WebForm_DoCallback` function in the page at design time; instead, there's a `<script>` block that links to the `WebResource.axd` resource, which supplies all the required JavaScript to the browser at runtime:

```
<script src="/ScripCallbackDemo/WebResource.axd?d=u8VFVkrxgbyFhFIpAniF-
Q2&amp;t=632671582519943712" type="text/javascript"></script>
```

If you want to examine how Microsoft implemented the client-side part of the script callback feature, just point your browser to the URL copied from the `<script>` tag, and download that output locally for your inspection.

WebResource.axd is a standard HTTP handler introduced in ASP.NET 2.0 to replace the aspnet_client folder used to contain JavaScript code sent down to browsers in ASP.NET 1.x. This handler extracts resources (scripts, images, and more) from ASP.NET's standard assemblies, according to its querystring parameters, and returns the stream to the caller. This makes deployment much easier because you don't have to worry about how the correct version of the client scripts will be provided to the browser — it just seems to happen "auto-magically."

On the server, the page calls the `ICallbackEventHandler`'s methods only when it finds some special arguments from the posted data; in that case it calls the methods discussed earlier, and then it terminates immediately, without proceeding with the rest of the page life cycle, and without producing any other output. This streamlined method of sending parameters to the server and getting data back is often called a *lightweight postback*, or an *out-of-band postback*.

The example of adding numbers together on the server side is not an efficient way to do math, since you could just add the numbers using JavaScript, with no need to do a lightweight postback to the server, but this was just a simple example of how the script callback feature works in ASP.NET 2.0. There are many better ways to use this feature in the real world, such as performing complex validations and operations that can only be done on the server (checking the existence of a record, or retrieving some child records from the database, according to the parent ID passed as an input), so you can imagine how useful the script callback feature can be! Later in this chapter, in the "Solution" section, we'll use this feature in a more complex scenario — to periodically ask for the updated progress information about the newsletter being sent. The server-side information is updated by the background thread doing the real work, and a JavaScript function will use the information to update a progress bar and show the number of e-mails already sent.

Asynchronous ASP.NET Pages

ASP.NET pages are normally processed in a synchronous manner, which means that when a request arrives to the ASP.NET engine, it takes a free thread from its own internal thread pool, and executes the page; the page completes its whole life cycle to produce the output for the client, and finally the thread is put back into the thread pool and made available for other requests. If no thread is free when a new request arrives, the request is queued until a thread becomes available. In some situations a page might take a long time to process, maybe three to five seconds, not because of the processing that generates the HTML output, but rather because of some I/O-bound operation, such as a long query run on a remote database, or a call to a web service. In such cases, ASP.NET is mostly sitting idle while it waits for the external work to be done. The side effect of this is that the thread given to that page is unproductive because it's just waiting most of the time, and because the threads in the thread pools are limited this has the effect of slowing down any other simultaneous requests while they wait for this thread to become available. Asynchronous page processing is meant to be a solution for this problem: When a request arrives, a thread is assigned to process it, and when the page calls an external web service, that request's thread is put back into the thread pool and the external request will proceed on another thread taken from a different thread pool (not from the main ASP.NET pool). Finally, when that external call completes, ASP.NET spins off another thread from the thread pool to complete the original page request. ASP.NET only uses its own threads when it has real work to do, and it releases them when they would just wait for external processing, assuming the page was designed for asynchronous processing.

Asynchronous page processing was technically possible in ASP.NET 1.x, by implementing the `IHttpAsyncHandler` interface in your page's code-behind file. However, this was quite complex and difficult to use. Now, however, with ASP.NET 2.0, things became much more straightforward, and implementing asynchronous page processing is much easier.

The first thing you do is set the `Async` attribute of the `@Page` directive to `true`, as follows:

```
<%@ Page Language="C#" AutoEventWireup="true" Async="true"
    CodeFile="AsyncDemo.aspx.cs" Inherits="AsyncDemo" %>
```

Then, from the `Page_Load` event handler in the code-behind file, you call the page's `AddOnPreRenderCompleteAsync` method to specify the method that will begin the asynchronous call (as a `BeginEventHandler` delegate), and the method that will complete it in the second thread taken from the ASP.NET's thread pool (as an `EndEventHandler` delegate):

```
public partial class AsyncDemo : System.Web.UI.Page
{
```

```
private ecomm.OrderProcessor orderProcessor = null;

protected void Page_Load(object sender, EventArgs e)
{
    this.AddOnPreRenderCompleteAsync(
        new BeginEventHandler(OnPageBeginMethod),
        new EndEventHandler(OnPageEndMethod));
}
```

The page follows its normal life cycle until just after the PreRender event, when it calls the method pointed to by the BeginEventHandler delegate. The code in this method just makes the asynchronous call and immediately returns an IAsyncResult object that will allow ASP.NET to determine when the secondary thread completes. As you may recall, an object of this type is returned by the BeginXXX method of a web service, for example (where XXX is the real method name, e.g., BeginProcessOrder). The same metaphor that was used for asynchronous web services in .NET 1.x has now been applied to ASP.NET 2.0 page processing! Here's the code that instantiates a web service called ecomm.OrderProcessor, and calls its ProcessOrder method in the asynchronous manner, thus using the Begin prefix:

```
IAsyncResult OnPageBeginMethod(object sender, EventArgs e,
    AsyncCallback cb, object state)
{
    orderProcessor = new ecomm.OrderProcessor();
    return orderProcessor.BeginProcessOrder("order123", cb, state);
}
```

After calling OnPageBeginMethod, the ASP.NET thread processing the page request is returned to its thread pool. When ASP.NET detects that the thread calling the web service has completed, it starts a new thread from its thread pool and calls the OnPageEndMethod method specified above, which just completes the call to the ProcessOrder — by calling EndProcessOrder — and shows the result in a Label control:

```
void OnPageEndMethod(IAsyncResult ar)
{
    string result = orderProcessor.EndProcessOrder(ar);
    lblResult.Text = result;
}
```

There are many other details concerning asynchronous pages, such as the possibility to call multiple external methods and make ASP.NET wait for all of them before starting the thread to complete the request, the timeout options, etc. However, in this section I just wanted to give you an idea of how simple asynchronous processing can be; you should refer to a reference book such as Wrox's Professional ASP.NET 2.0 by Bill Evjen (Wiley, 2005), or the article written by Jeff Prosise for the October 2005 issue of MSDN Magazine, titled "Asynchronous Pages in ASP.NET 2.0" and available online at http://msdn.microsoft.com/msdnmag/issues/05/10/WickedCode/.

In this chapter's "Solution" section you won't be using asynchronous pages, because although they are good for handling I/O-bound tasks that last longer than a few seconds, they don't fit into our model of providing some feedback to the user during the wait. I mentioned them here because they fit into the general discussion of multi-threaded web programming and can be very handy in some situations where you have heavily loaded servers that commonly wait on asynchronous external processing.

Designing the Database Tables

Now that we've covered all the background information, we can start the actual design for this module. As usual, we'll start by designing the database tables, then move on to design stored procedures and the data access and business logic layers, finishing with the presentation layer's ASP.NET pages and controls. The database design is very simple (see Figure 7-1). There's a single table to store newsletters that were sent out previously but were archived for future reference by online subscribers.

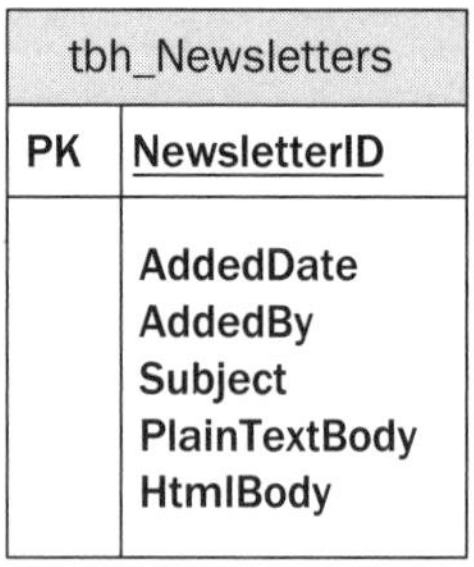

tbh_Newsletters	
PK	**NewsletterID**
	AddedDate AddedBy Subject PlainTextBody HtmlBody

Figure 7-1

All fields are self-explanatory, so I won't spend time describing them, except to point out that `Subject` is of type `nvarchar(256)`, while `PlainTextBody` and `HtmlBody` are of type `ntext`. The other fields, `AddedDate` and `AddedBy`, are common to all of the other tables, and we've discussed them in previous chapters.

The Stored Procedures

Because this module has only a single table, the stored procedures are simple as well. You just need the basic procedures for the CRUD (`Create`, `Retrieve`, `Update`, and `Delete`) operations:

Property	Description
Tbh_Newsletters_InsertNewsletter	Inserts a newsletter with the specified subject and body in plain-text and HTML
tbh_Newsletters_UpdateNewsletter	Updates an existing newsletter with the specified ID
tbh_Newsletters_DeleteNewsletter	Deletes a newsletter with the specified ID
tbh_Newsletters_GetNewsletters	Retrieves all data for the rows in the tbh_Newsletters table, except for the PlainTextBody and HtmlBody fields. It takes a datetime parameter, and it returns only those rows with AddedDate less than or equal to that date.
tbh_Newsletters_GetNewsletterByID	Retrieves all data for the specified newsletter

As an optimization, the `tbh_Newsletters_GetNewsletters` procedure doesn't include the body fields in the resultset, because the body won't be shown in the page that lists the archived newsletters; only the `AddedData` and `Subject` are required in that situation. When the user goes to the page showing the whole content of a specific newsletter, the `tbh_Newsletter_GetNewsletterByID` procedure will be used to retrieve all the details.

Designing the Configuration Module

Like any other module of this book, the newsletter module has its own configuration setting, which will be defined as attributes of the `<newsletter>` element under the `<theBeerHouse>` section in `web.config`. That element is mapped by a `NewsletterElement` class, which has the following properties:

Property	Description
ProviderType	The full name (namespace plus class name) of the concrete provider class that implements the data access code for a specific data store
ConnectionStringName	The name of the entry in web.config's new <connectionStrings> section that contains the connection string to the module's database
EnableCaching	A Boolean value indicating whether the caching of data is enabled
CacheDuration	The number of seconds for which the data is cached if there aren't any inserts, deletes, or updates that invalidate the cache
FromEmail	The newsletter sender's e-mail address, used also as a reply address
FromDisplayName	The newsletter sender's display name, which will be shown by the e-mail client program
HideFromArchiveInterval	The number of days before a newsletter appears in the archive.
ArchiveIsPublic	A Boolean value indicating whether the polls archive is accessible by everyone, or restricted to registered members

The first four settings are common to all modules. You may argue that the sender's e-mail address can be read from the built-in `<mailSettings>` section of web.config, as shown earlier. However, that is usually set to the postmaster's or administrator's e-mail address, which is used to send service e-mails such as the confirmation for a new registration, the lost password e-mail, and the like. In other situations you may want to differentiate the sender's e-mail address, and use one for someone on your staff, so that if the user replies to an e-mail, his reply will actually be read. In the case of a newsletter, you may have a specific e-mail account, such as newseditor@contoso.com, used by your newsletter editor.

The `ArchiveIsPublic` property has the same meaning as the similarly named property found in the poll module's configuration class — it enables the administrator to decide whether the archived newsletters can be read only by registered members; she may want to set this to `True` to give users another reason to subscribe. `HideFromArchiveInterval` is also very important, because it allows you to decide how many days must pass before the newsletter just sent is available from the archive. If you set this property to zero, some users may decide not to subscribe to the newsletter, and just go to the archive occasionally to see it. If you set this to 15 instead (which is the default value), they will have to subscribe to the newsletter if they want to read it without waiting 15 days to see it in the archives.

Designing the Data Access Layer

As usual, the DAL for this module is based on the provider model design pattern, and the SQL Server provider is included as an example, which is just a wrapper around the stored procedures described above. The DAL uses a `NewsletterDetails` custom entity class, which wraps the data of a single newsletter record. The diagram in Figure 7-2 describes the DAL classes and their relationships.

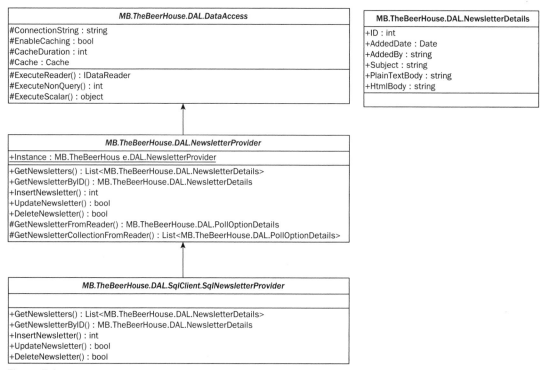

Figure 7-2

Designing the Business Layer

This is where things become interesting, because in addition to wrapping the data operations of the DAL in an object-oriented class, the `MB.TheBeerHouse.BLL.Newsletters.Newsletter` class also contains all the logic for sending out a newsletter asynchronously from a separate background thread, and for updating the progress status information. Figure 7-3 represents the UML diagram of this class (together with the usual `Bizobject` base class) and lists its public and private properties and methods.

When the user calls the `SendNewsletter` public static method, a new record is inserted into the `tbh_Newsletters` table, and the ID of the record is returned to the caller. Just before finishing the method, it spins off a new low-priority thread to asynchronously execute the `SendEmails` private static method. It's inside this method that the newsletter is actually sent to all subscribers, in plain text or HTML format according to their profile.

MB.TheBeerHouse.BLL.BizObject
#Cache : Cache #CurrentUser : IPrincipal #CurrentUserIP : string #CurrentUserName : string
#GetPageIndex() : int #EncodeText() : string #ConvertNullToEmptyString() : string #PurgeCacheItems()

MB.TheBeerHouse.BLL.Newsletters.Newsletter
-Settings : NewslettersElement +IsSending : bool +PercentageCompleted : double +TotalMails : int +SentMails : int +Lock : ReaderWriterLock +ID : int +AddedDate : Date +AddedBy : string +Subject : string +PlainTextBody : string +HtmlBody : string
+Update() : bool +Delete() : bool -FillBody() +GetNewsletters() : List<MB.TheBee rHouse.BLL.Newsletters.Newsletter> +GetNewsletterByID() : MB.TheBeerHouse.BLL.Newsletters.Newsletter +SendNewsletter() : int +UpdateNewsletter() : bool +DeleteNewsletter() : bool -SendEmails() -HasPersonalizationPlaceholders() : bool -ReplacePersonalizationP laceholders() : string -GetNewsletterFromNewsletterDetails() : MB.TheBeerHouse.BLL.Newsletters.Newsletter -GetNewsletterListFromNewsletterDetailsList() : List<MB.TheBeerHouse.BLL.Newsletters.Newsletter> -CacheData()

Figure 7-3

When the SendNewsletter method begins, it also sets the IsSending static property, so that the caller (from the administration page) can check whether another newsletter is currently being sent, to avoid calling SendNewsletter again before it has finished. As discussed previously, every time you access a property/field that's shared among multiple threads, you must synchronize this operation; and in this case it is done by means of the static field Lock, which is an instance of ReaderWriterLock. The Lock field is public because the caller will need to use the same ReaderWriterLock used by the business class in order for the synchronization to work properly. Note that the Common Language Runtime does not automatically handle locking, so if your code doesn't properly handle the synchronization, it could cause performance problems, occasionally lock-ups, and possibly even data corruption.

The TotalMails property is set from within the SendEmails method, before the first mail is set, and just after counting the number of site members having their Newsletter profile property set to a value other than SubscriptionType.None (this enumeration was defined in Chapter 4, when discussing membership and profiles). Every time SendEmails sends an e-mail, it also updates the SentMails and PercentageCompleted static properties, using the same synchronization approach based on the ReaderWriterLock.

Finally, as soon as SendEmails has sent the last e-mail, it sets IsSending back to false, so that the administrator can send another newsletter if desired. The SendEmails method uses the Has PersonalizationPlaceholders and ReplacePersonalizationPlaceholders methods, respectively, to check whether the newsletter's plain-text and HTML bodies contain personalization placeholders (the supported ones are <% username %>, <% email %>, <% firstname %>, and <% lastname %>, but you may add more if you wish), and to actually replace them for a given user. If HasPersonalization Placeholders returns false, the call to ReplacePersonalizationPlaceholders is completely skipped, to avoid running the replacement regular expression if you already know that no placeholders will be found. SendEmails calls HasPersonalizationPlaceholders just once for each of the two body formats, but it can save thousands of calls to ReplacePersonalizationPlaceholders, which is done separately for each user.

Designing the User Interface Services

The last part of the design phase is to design the pages and user controls that make up the module's presentation layer. Here is list of the user interface files that we'll develop later in the "Solution" section:

❑ **~/Admin/SendNewsletter.aspx:** This page lets the administrator or editor send a newsletter to current subscribers. If another newsletter is already being sent when this page is first loaded, an error message appears instead of the normal form showing the other newsletter's subject and body, and a link to the page that displays that newsletter's progress. The page must also take into account situations in which no newsletter is being sent when the page loads, but later when the user clicks the Submit button to send this newsletter another newsletter is found to be under way at that time, because another user may have sent it from another location while the first editor was completing the form on her browser. In this case, the current newsletter is not sent and a message explaining the situation is shown, but the form showing the current newsletter's data is kept visible so that the data is not lost and can be sent later when the other newsletter has completed transmission.

❑ **~/Admin/SendingNewsletter.aspx:** This page uses the script callback feature to update the statistics on the number of e-mails already sent (out of the total number of e-mails) and a progress bar representing the percentage of completed work. The lightweight postback will take place every couple of seconds, but you can change the update interval. The editor is automatically redirected to this page after she clicks the Submit button from SendNewsletter.

❑ **~/ArchivedNewsletters.aspx:** This page lists all past newsletters sent at least "x" days before the current date, where x is equal to the HideFromArchiveInterval custom configuration setting. Anonymous users will be able to access this page only if the ArchiveIsPublic setting is set to true in the `web.config` file's `<newsletters>` element, under the `<theBeerHouse>` section. The list of newsletters will show the date when each newsletter was sent and its subject. The subject is rendered as a link that points to another page showing the newsletter's entire content.

❑ **~/ShowNewsletter.aspx:** This page displays the full plain-text and HTML body of the newsletter whose ID is passed on the querystring.

❑ **~/Controls/NewsletterBox.ascx:** This user control determines whether the current site user is logged in; if not, it assumes she is not registered and not subscribed to the newsletter, and thus it displays a message inviting her to subscribe by typing her e-mail address into a textbox. When the user clicks the Submit button, the control redirects her to the `Register.aspx` page developed in Chapter 4, passing her e-mail on the querystring, so that `Register.aspx` will be able to read it and prefill its own e-mail textbox. If the user is already a member and is logged in, the control instead displays a message explaining that she can change her subscription type or cancel the subscription by going to the `EditProfile.aspx` page (also developed in Chapter 4) to which it links. In both cases, a link to the newsletter archive page is shown at the bottom of the control.

Solution

The design is complete, and you have all the information you need to start coding the solution. This module's database objects are simple (a single table, with no relationships and foreign keys, and only a few stored procedures for the basic CRUD operations) so I won't demonstrate how to create the table and the stored procedures' code. You can refer to previous chapters for general information about how you can work with these objects from Visual Studio 2005, and you can refer to the downloadable code to see the full implementation.

Implementing the Configuration Module

The code for the `NewslettersElement` custom configuration element is found in the `~/App_Code/ConfigSection.cs` file, together with the classes that map the other elements under the `<theBeerHouse>` section. Following is the whole class, which defines the properties listed in the design section, their default values, whether they are required or not, and their mapping to the respective attributes of the `<newsletters>` element:

```
public class NewslettersElement : ConfigurationElement
{
    [ConfigurationProperty("connectionStringName")]
    public string ConnectionStringName
    {
        get { return (string)base["connectionStringName"]; }
        set { base["connectionStringName"] = value; }
    }

    public string ConnectionString
    {
        get
        {
            string connStringName = (string.IsNullOrEmpty(this.ConnectionStringName) ?
                Globals.Settings.DefaultConnectionStringName :
```

```
            this.ConnectionStringName);
         return WebConfigurationManager.ConnectionStrings[
            connStringName].ConnectionString;
      }
   }

   [ConfigurationProperty("providerType",
      DefaultValue = "MB.TheBeerHouse.DAL.SqlClient.SqlNewslettersProvider")]
   public string ProviderType
   {
      get { return (string)base["providerType"]; }
      set { base["providerType"] = value; }
   }

   [ConfigurationProperty("fromEmail", IsRequired=true)]
   public string FromEmail
   {
      get { return (string)base["fromEmail"]; }
      set { base["fromEmail"] = value; }
   }

   [ConfigurationProperty("fromDisplayName", IsRequired = true)]
   public string FromDisplayName
   {
      get { return (string)base["fromDisplayName"]; }
      set { base["fromDisplayName"] = value; }
   }

   [ConfigurationProperty("hideFromArchiveInterval", DefaultValue = "15")]
   public int HideFromArchiveInterval
   {
      get { return (int)base["hideFromArchiveInterval"]; }
      set { base["hideFromArchiveInterval"] = value; }
   }

   [ConfigurationProperty("archiveIsPublic", DefaultValue = "false")]
   public bool ArchiveIsPublic
   {
      get { return (bool)base["archiveIsPublic"]; }
      set { base["archiveIsPublic"] = value; }
   }

   [ConfigurationProperty("enableCaching", DefaultValue = "true")]
   public bool EnableCaching
   {
      get { return (bool)base["enableCaching"]; }
      set { base["enableCaching"] = value; }
   }

   [ConfigurationProperty("cacheDuration")]
   public int CacheDuration
   {
      get
      {
         int duration = (int)base["cacheDuration"];
```

```
                return (duration > 0 ? duration : Globals.Settings.DefaultCacheDuration);
        }
        set { base["cacheDuration"] = value; }
    }
}
```

A property named `Newsletters` of type `NewslettersElement` is added to the `TheBeerHouseSection` (found in the same file), which maps the `<theBeerHouse>` section:

```
public class TheBeerHouseSection : ConfigurationSection
{
    // other properties...

    [ConfigurationProperty("newsletters", IsRequired = true)]
    public NewslettersElement Newsletters
    {
        get { return (NewslettersElement)base["newsletters"]; }
    }
}
```

Now you can go to the `web.config` file and configure the module with the attributes of the `<newsletters>` element. The `SenderEmail` and `SenderDisplayName` are required, the others are optional. The following extract shows how you can configure these two attributes, plus others that make the archive public (it is not by default) and specify that 10 days must pass before a sent newsletter appears in the archive:

```
<theBeerHouse defaultConnectionStringName="LocalSqlServer">
    <contactForm mailTo="mbellinaso@wrox.com"/>
    <articles pageSize="10" />
    <polls archiveIsPublic="true" votingLockByIP="false"  />
    <newsletters fromEmail="mbellinaso@wrox.com" fromDisplayName="TheBeerHouse"
        archiveIsPublic="true" hideFromArchiveInterval="10" />
</theBeerHouse>
```

Implementing the Data Access Layer

Create a file named `NewsletterProvider.cs` (located under ~/App_Code/) to define the base provider class (named `NewsletterProvider`) for the newsletter module. This class has an `instance` property that returns the instance of the concrete provider indicated in the configuration, and is almost identical to the similarly named property found in the previous modules' base provider class. It loads some other settings from the configuration in its constructor, and defines some abstract methods that specify the signature of the methods described earlier, and which will be given a concrete implementation in the DAL class specific to SQL Server (or any other data store you want to support):

```
public abstract class NewslettersProvider : DataAccess
{
    static private NewslettersProvider _instance = null;
    static public NewslettersProvider Instance
    {
        get
        {
            if (_instance == null)
                _instance = (NewslettersProvider)Activator.CreateInstance(
```

```
                    Type.GetType(Globals.Settings.Newsletters.ProviderType));
         return _instance;
      }
   }

   public NewslettersProvider()
   {
      this.ConnectionString = Globals.Settings.Newsletters.ConnectionString;
      this.EnableCaching = Globals.Settings.Newsletters.EnableCaching;
      this.CacheDuration = Globals.Settings.Newsletters.CacheDuration;
   }

   // methods that work with newsletters
   public abstract List<NewsletterDetails> GetNewsletters(DateTime toDate);
   public abstract NewsletterDetails GetNewsletterByID(int newsletterID);
   public abstract bool DeleteNewsletter(int newsletterID);
   public abstract bool UpdateNewsletter(NewsletterDetails newsletter);
   public abstract int InsertNewsletter(NewsletterDetails newsletter);

   /// <summary>Returns a new NewsletterDetails instance filled with the
   /// DataReader's current record data</summary>
   protected virtual NewsletterDetails GetNewsletterFromReader(IDataReader reader)
   {
      return GetNewsletterFromReader(reader, true);
   }
   protected virtual NewsletterDetails GetNewsletterFromReader(
      IDataReader reader, bool readBody)
   {
      NewsletterDetails newsletter = new NewsletterDetails(
         (int)reader["NewsletterID"],
         (DateTime)reader["AddedDate"],
         reader["AddedBy"].ToString(),
         reader["Subject"].ToString(),
         null, null);

      if (readBody)
      {
         newsletter.PlainTextBody = reader["PlainTextBody"].ToString();
         newsletter.HtmlBody = reader["HtmlBody"].ToString();
      }

      return newsletter;
   }

   /// <summary>Returns a collection of NewsletterDetails objects with
   /// the data read from the input DataReader</summary>
   protected virtual List<NewsletterDetails> GetNewsletterCollectionFromReader(
      IDataReader reader)
   {
      return GetNewsletterCollectionFromReader(reader, true);
   }
   protected virtual List<NewsletterDetails> GetNewsletterCollectionFromReader(
      IDataReader reader, bool readBody)
   {
      List<NewsletterDetails> newsletters = new List<NewsletterDetails>();
```

```
            while (reader.Read())
                newsletters.Add(GetNewsletterFromReader(reader, readBody));
            return newsletters;
        }
    }
```

The other methods of the class are `GetNewsletterFromReader` and
`GetNewsletterCollectionFromReader`, which, respectively, create a new instance of the
`NewsletterDetails` entity class (not shown here, but it's just a simple class that wraps the database
fields), or a collection of them. Note that in addition to the `IDataReader` parameter, both these methods
have an overloaded version that accepts a Boolean value indicating whether the newsletter's plain-text
and HTML body must be read—together, the `NewsletterID`, `AddedDate`, `AddedBy`, and `Subject`
fields. The SQL Server provider calls these methods specifying `false` for that parameter from within the
`GetNewsletters` method, while it calls them specifying `true` from within the `GetNewsletterByID`
method. This is because the body is only returned from the database when you retrieve a specific
newsletter, and not when you retrieve the list of newsletters.

Implementing the Business Logic Layer

The `Newsletter` class is found under `~/App_Code/BLL/Newsletters/Newsletter.cs`. It's the code that
wraps the newsletter's data with OOP instance properties, supports updating and deleting the newsletter
represented by a particular instance, implements the static methods for retrieving a single newsletter or all
newsletters before a specified date, and supports updating and deleting an existing newsletter:

```
public class Newsletter : BizObject
{
    private static NewslettersElement Settings
    {
        get { return Globals.Settings.Newsletters; }
    }

    private int _id = 0;
    public int ID
    {
        get { return _id; }
        private set { _id = value; }
    }

    private DateTime _addedDate = DateTime.Now;
    public DateTime AddedDate
    {
        get { return _addedDate; }
        private set { _addedDate = value; }
    }

    private string _addedBy = "";
    public string AddedBy
    {
        get { return _addedBy; }
        private set { _addedBy = value; }
    }

    private string _subject = "";
```

```csharp
public string Subject
{
    get { return _subject; }
    set { _subject = value; }
}

private string _plainTextBody = null;
public string PlainTextBody
{
    get
    {
        if (_plainTextBody == null)
            FillBody();
        return _plainTextBody;
    }
    set { _plainTextBody = value; }
}

private string _htmlBody = null;
public string HtmlBody
{
    get
    {
        if (_htmlBody == null)
            FillBody();
        return _htmlBody;
    }
    set { _htmlBody = value; }
}

public Newsletter(int id, DateTime addedDate, string addedBy,
    string subject, string plainTextBody, string htmlBody)
{
    this.ID = id;
    this.AddedDate = addedDate;
    this.AddedBy = addedBy;
    this.Subject = subject;
    this.PlainTextBody = plainTextBody;
    this.HtmlBody = htmlBody;
}

public bool Delete()
{
    bool success = Newsletter.DeleteNewsletter(this.ID);
    if (success)
        this.ID = 0;
    return success;
}

public bool Update()
{
    return Newsletter.UpdateNewsletter(this.ID, this.Subject,
    this.PlainTextBody, this.HtmlBody);
}

private void FillBody()
```

```
{
   NewsletterDetails record =
      SiteProvider.Newsletters.GetNewsletterByID(this.ID);
   this.PlainTextBody = record.PlainTextBody;
   this.HtmlBody = record.HtmlBody;
}

/************************************
 * Static methods
 ************************************/

/// <summary>Returns a collection with all newsletters sent before
/// the specified date</summary>
public static List<Newsletter> GetNewsletters()
{
   return GetNewsletters(DateTime.Now);
}
public static List<Newsletter> GetNewsletters(DateTime toDate)
{
   List<Newsletter> newsletters = null;
   string key = "Newsletters_Newsletters_" + toDate.ToShortDateString();

   if (Settings.EnableCaching && BizObject.Cache[key] != null)
   {
      newsletters = (List<Newsletter>)BizObject.Cache[key];
   }
   else
   {
      List<NewsletterDetails> recordset =
         SiteProvider.Newsletters.GetNewsletters(toDate);
      newsletters = GetNewsletterListFromNewsletterDetailsList(recordset);
      CacheData(key, newsletters);
   }
   return newsletters;
}

/// <summary>Returns a Newsletter object with the specified ID</summary>
public static Newsletter GetNewsletterByID(int newsletterID)
{
   Newsletter newsletter = null;
   string key = "Newsletters_Newsletter_" + newsletterID.ToString();

   if (Settings.EnableCaching && BizObject.Cache[key] != null)
   {
      newsletter = (Newsletter)BizObject.Cache[key];
   }
   else
   {
      newsletter = GetNewsletterFromNewsletterDetails(
         SiteProvider.Newsletters.GetNewsletterByID(newsletterID));
      CacheData(key, newsletter);
   }
   return newsletter;
}

/// <summary>Updates an existing newsletter</summary>
```

```
public static bool UpdateNewsletter(int id, string subject,
    string plainTextBody, string htmlBody)
{
    NewsletterDetails record = new NewsletterDetails(id, DateTime.Now, "",
        subject, plainTextBody, htmlBody);
    bool ret = SiteProvider.Newsletters.UpdateNewsletter(record);
    BizObject.PurgeCacheItems("newsletters_newsletter");
    return ret;
}

/// <summary>
/// Deletes an existing newsletter
/// </summary>
public static bool DeleteNewsletter(int id)
{
    bool ret = SiteProvider.Newsletters.DeleteNewsletter(id);
    new RecordDeletedEvent("newsletter", id, null).Raise();
    BizObject.PurgeCacheItems("newsletters_newsletter");
    return ret;
}

/// <summary>Returns a Newsletter object filled with the data taken
/// from the input NewsletterDetails</summary>
private static Newsletter GetNewsletterFromNewsletterDetails(
    NewsletterDetails record)
{
    if (record == null)
        return null;
    else
    {
        return new Newsletter(record.ID, record.AddedDate, record.AddedBy,
            record.Subject, record.PlainTextBody, record.HtmlBody);
    }
}

/// <summary>Returns a list of Newsletter objects filled with the data
/// taken from the input list of NewsletterDetails</summary>
private static List<Newsletter> GetNewsletterListFromNewsletterDetailsList(
    List<NewsletterDetails> recordset)
{
    List<Newsletter> newsletters = new List<Newsletter>();
    foreach (NewsletterDetails record in recordset)
        newsletters.Add(GetNewsletterFromNewsletterDetails(record));
    return newsletters;
}

/// <summary>
/// Cache the input data, if caching is enabled
/// </summary>
private static void CacheData(string key, object data)
{
    if (Settings.EnableCaching && data != null)
    {
        BizObject.Cache.Insert(key, data, null,
```

```
                DateTime.Now.AddSeconds(Settings.CacheDuration), TimeSpan.Zero);
        }
    }
}
```

All the preceding code is similar to other BLL code seen in the previous chapter, so I won't comment on it again, but it's worth noting that the default value for the `PlainTextBody` and `HtmlBody` properties is null, and not an empty string. The null value denotes that the body has not been populated from the DAL, typically because the current `Newsletter` instance was created as part of a collection of newsletters, and thus the body was not retrieved from the database. However, if the UI code accesses the property, the private `FillBody` method is called to retrieve another `Newsletter` instance with all the fields populated so that the body can be copied into the current object.

At this point you add code to send newsletters to the subscribers, starting from the static properties containing the progress information, and the companion `ReaderWriterLock` field to synchronize access to them:

```csharp
public static ReaderWriterLock Lock = new ReaderWriterLock();

private static bool _isSending = false;
public static bool IsSending
{
    get { return _isSending; }
    private set { _isSending = value; }
}

private static double _percentageCompleted = 0.0;
public static double PercentageCompleted
{
    get { return _percentageCompleted; }
    private set { _percentageCompleted = value; }
}

private static int _totalMails = -1;
public static int TotalMails
{
    get { return _totalMails; }
    private set { _totalMails = value; }
}

private static int _sentMails = 0;
public static int SentMails
{
    get { return _sentMails; }
    private set { _sentMails = value; }
}
```

Following is the `SendNewsletter` method, which first resets all the progress status properties and sets `IsSending` to true, inserts a newsletter record into the archive table through the DAL provider, and finally starts a new thread that will execute the `SendEmails` private method:

```csharp
/// <summary>Sends a newsletter</summary>
public static int SendNewsletter(string subject, string plainTextBody,
    string htmlBody)
{
```

```
Lock.AcquireWriterLock(Timeout.Infinite);
Newsletter.TotalMails = -1;
Newsletter.SentMails = 0;
Newsletter.PercentageCompleted = 0.0;
Newsletter.IsSending = true;
Lock.ReleaseWriterLock();

// if the HTML body is an empty string, use the plain-text body
// converted to HTML
if (htmlBody.Trim().Length == 0)
{
    htmlBody = HttpUtility.HtmlEncode(plainTextBody).Replace(
        " ", " ").Replace("\t", "   ").Replace("\n", "<br/>");
}

// create the record into the DB
NewsletterDetails record = new NewsletterDetails(0, DateTime.Now,
    BizObject.CurrentUserName, subject, plainTextBody, htmlBody);
int ret = SiteProvider.Newsletters.InsertNewsletter(record);
BizObject.PurgeCacheItems("newsletters_newsletters_" +
    DateTime.Now.ToShortDateString());

// send the newsletters asynchronously
object[] parameters = new object[]{subject, plainTextBody, htmlBody,
    HttpContext.Current};
ParameterizedThreadStart pts = new ParameterizedThreadStart(SendEmails);
Thread thread = new Thread(pts);
thread.Name = "SendEmails";
thread.Priority = ThreadPriority.BelowNormal;
thread.Start(parameters);

return ret;
}
```

Note that only the plain-text body is strictly required by this method. In fact, if the HTML body is an empty string, then the plain-text body will be used for HTML newsletters as well, after encoding it and manually replacing spaces, tabs, and carriage returns with " " and "<br />" strings. But it's the last few lines of the method that are the most important, because that's where the e-mail creation and delivery is started in the background thread. A `ParameterizedThreadStart` delegate is used instead of a simpler `ThreadStart` delegate, so you can pass input parameters to the `SendEmails` method. These parameters consist of an object array containing the newsletter's subject and body in both formats, plus a reference to the current `HttpContext`. The `HttpContext` will be required by `SendEmails` to retrieve the list of members and their profiles—this is required because the method does not run from inside the same thread that is processing the current ASP.NET request, so it won't have access to its context.

The `SendEmail` method starts by cycling through all the registered members, loads their profiles (refer to Chapter 4 to see how to load member profiles and registration information such as the e-mail) and finds those who are subscribed to the newsletter in either plain-text or HTML format. However, it doesn't send the e-mail to each subscriber immediately, because it must first count the subscribers and update the `TotalEmails` property, so this information can be updated in the administrator's feedback page. Therefore, upon finding a subscriber, it increments `TotalEmails` by one and saves the subscriber's information for later use in sending the newsletter. The required information includes the subscription format, the e-mail address, and the first and last names (required for personalization). This information is wrapped by a tailor-made `SubscriberInfo` structure defined as follows:

```
public struct SubscriberInfo
{
    public string UserName;
    public string Email;
    public string FirstName;
    public string LastName;
    public SubscriptionType SubscriptionType;

    public SubscriberInfo(string userName, string email,
        string firstName, string lastName, SubscriptionType subscriptionType)
    {
        this.UserName = userName;
        this.Email = email;
        this.FirstName = firstName;
        this.LastName = lastName;
        this.SubscriptionType = subscriptionType;
    }
}
```

SendMails uses a strongly typed collection of type `List<SubscriberInfo>` to store the information of all subscribers it finds. Then, for each `SubscriberInfo` object present in the collection it creates a new `MailMessage`, sets the sender's e-mail and display name with the values read from the configuration settings, sets its `IsBodyHtml` property according to the subscriber's `SubscriptionType` profile property, and sets the subject and body, after replacing the personalization placeholders, if any. When ready, the `MailMessage` is sent to subscribers by the synchronous `Send` method of a `SmtpClient` object, the `SentMails` property is incremented by one, and the `PercentageCompleted` value is recalculated. Finally, when the last subscriber has been sent her newsletter, the `IsSending` property is set to `false` and the method (and its dedicated background thread) ends. Following is the complete code, whose comments provide more details about the way it works:

```
private static void SendEmails(object data)
{
    object[] parameters = (object[])data;
    string subject = (string)parameters[0];
    string plainTextBody = (string)parameters[1];
    string htmlBody = (string)parameters[2];
    HttpContext context = (HttpContext)parameters[3];

    Lock.AcquireWriterLock(Timeout.Infinite);
    Newsletter.TotalMails = 0;
    Lock.ReleaseWriterLock();

    // check if the plain-text and the HTML bodies have personalization placeholders
    // that will need to be replaced on a per-mail basis. If not, the parsing will
    // be completely avoided later.
    bool plainTextIsPersonalized = HasPersonalizationPlaceholders(
        plainTextBody, false);
    bool htmlIsPersonalized = HasPersonalizationPlaceholders(htmlBody, true);

    // retrieve all subscribers to the plain-text and HTML newsletter,
    List<SubscriberInfo> subscribers = new List<SubscriberInfo>();
    ProfileCommon profile = context.Profile as ProfileCommon;

    foreach (MembershipUser user in Membership.GetAllUsers())
```

```
    {
        ProfileCommon userProfile = profile.GetProfile(user.UserName);
        if (userProfile.Preferences.Newsletter != SubscriptionType.None)
        {
            SubscriberInfo subscriber = new SubscriberInfo(
                user.UserName, user.Email, userProfile.FirstName, userProfile.LastName,
                userProfile.Preferences.Newsletter);
            subscribers.Add(subscriber);
            Lock.AcquireWriterLock(Timeout.Infinite);
            Newsletter.TotalMails += 1;
            Lock.ReleaseWriterLock();
        }
    }

    // send the newsletter
    SmtpClient smtpClient = new SmtpClient();
    foreach (SubscriberInfo subscriber in subscribers)
    {
        MailMessage mail = new MailMessage();
        mail.From = new MailAddress(Settings.FromEmail, Settings.FromDisplayName);
        mail.To.Add(subscriber.Email);
        mail.Subject = subject;
        if (subscriber.SubscriptionType == SubscriptionType.PlainText)
        {
            string body = plainTextBody;
            if (plainTextIsPersonalized)
                body = ReplacePersonalizationPlaceholders(body, subscriber, false);
            mail.Body = body;
            mail.IsBodyHtml = false;
        }
        else
        {
            string body = htmlBody;
            if (htmlIsPersonalized)
                body = ReplacePersonalizationPlaceholders(body, subscriber, true);
            mail.Body = body;
            mail.IsBodyHtml = true;
        }
        try
        {
            smtpClient.Send(mail);
        }
        catch { }

        Lock.AcquireWriterLock(Timeout.Infinite);
        Newsletter.SentMails += 1;
        Newsletter.PercentageCompleted =
            (double)Newsletter.SentMails * 100 / (double)Newsletter.TotalMails;
        Lock.ReleaseWriterLock();
    }

    Lock.AcquireWriterLock(Timeout.Infinite);
    Newsletter.IsSending = false;
    Lock.ReleaseWriterLock();
}
```

The `SendEmails` method uses the `HasPersonalizationPlaceholders` private method to check whether the plain-text and HTML bodies contain any personalization tags, and it is implemented as follows:

```
private static bool HasPersonalizationPlaceholders(string text, bool isHtml)
{
    if (isHtml)
    {
        if (Regex.IsMatch(text, @"&lt;%\s*username\s*%&gt;",
            RegexOptions.IgnoreCase | RegexOptions.Compiled)) return true;
        if (Regex.IsMatch(text, @"&lt;%\s*email\s*%&gt;",
            RegexOptions.IgnoreCase | RegexOptions.Compiled)) return true;
        if (Regex.IsMatch(text, @"&lt;%\s*firstname\s*%&gt;",
            RegexOptions.IgnoreCase | RegexOptions.Compiled)) return true;
        if (Regex.IsMatch(text, @"&lt;%\s*lastname\s*%&gt;",
            RegexOptions.IgnoreCase | RegexOptions.Compiled)) return true;
    }
    else
    {
        if (Regex.IsMatch(text, @"<%\s*username\s*%>",
            RegexOptions.IgnoreCase | RegexOptions.Compiled)) return true;
        if (Regex.IsMatch(text, @"<%\s*email\s*%>",
            RegexOptions.IgnoreCase | RegexOptions.Compiled)) return true;
        if (Regex.IsMatch(text, @"<%\s*firstname\s*%>",
            RegexOptions.IgnoreCase | RegexOptions.Compiled)) return true;
        if (Regex.IsMatch(text, @"<%\s*lastname\s*%>",
            RegexOptions.IgnoreCase | RegexOptions.Compiled)) return true;
    }
    return false;
}
```

In addition to the body text, it takes a Boolean parameter indicating whether the body is in plain-text or HTML format: If it is plain text, it will search for `<%placeholder_name_here%>` placeholders; otherwise, it searches for `&lt;%placeholder_name_here%&gt;`. This is because the HTML body will typically be written from the administrator's page, which uses the FCKeditor already covered in Chapter 5. When you enter special characters such as `<` and `>` in the default Design View, it will encode them to `&lt;` and `&gt;`. This method uses regular expressions to check whether a given pattern is found within the given input string. Please refer to the sidebar "A One-page Summary of Regular Expression Syntax" for more info about the syntax used. It just needs to check whether any placeholder is present. If so, it returns `true` as soon as it finds one.

If this method returns true, `SendEmails` will call `ReplacePersonalizationPlaceholders` on a per-subscriber basis, doing the real replacement of the placeholders with the values received as inputs. Following is the code for this method:

```
private static string ReplacePersonalizationPlaceholders(string text,
    SubscriberInfo subscriber, bool isHtml)
{
    if (isHtml)
    {
        text = Regex.Replace(text, @"&lt;%\s*username\s*%&gt;",
         subscriber.UserName, RegexOptions.IgnoreCase | RegexOptions.Compiled);
        text = Regex.Replace(text, @"&lt;%\s*email\s*%&gt;",
            subscriber.Email, RegexOptions.IgnoreCase | RegexOptions.Compiled);
        text = Regex.Replace(text, @"&lt;%\s*firstname\s*%&gt;",
```

```
            (subscriber.FirstName.Length > 0 ? subscriber.FirstName : "reader"),
            RegexOptions.IgnoreCase | RegexOptions.Compiled);
        text = Regex.Replace(text, @"&lt;%\s*lastname\s*%&gt;",
            subscriber.LastName, RegexOptions.IgnoreCase | RegexOptions.Compiled);
    }
    else
    {
        text = Regex.Replace(text, @"<%\s*username\s*%>",
            subscriber.UserName, RegexOptions.IgnoreCase | RegexOptions.Compiled);
        text = Regex.Replace(text, @"<%\s*email\s*%>",
            subscriber.Email, RegexOptions.IgnoreCase | RegexOptions.Compiled);
        text = Regex.Replace(text, @"<%\s*firstname\s*%>",
            (subscriber.FirstName.Length > 0 ? subscriber.FirstName : "reader"),
            RegexOptions.IgnoreCase | RegexOptions.Compiled);
        text = Regex.Replace(text, @"<%\s*lastname\s*%>",
            subscriber.LastName, RegexOptions.IgnoreCase | RegexOptions.Compiled);
    }
    return text;
}
```

Regular expressions are a very powerful tool to validate, and find/replace, substrings inside text. They enable you to define very complex patterns, and their processing can be much faster than working with the String class's Replace, Substring, IndexOf, and the other basic methods. Entire books have been written on the subject of regular expressions, such as *Beginning Regular Expressions* (Wrox Press, ISBN 0-7645-7489-2), or *Teach Yourself Regular Expressions in 24 Hours* (Sams Press, ISBN 0-672319-36-5).

A One-page Summary of Regular Expression Syntax

The following tables summarize the most frequently used syntax constructs for the regular expressions. In the first table, you can see how to express the characters that we want to match.

Character escapes	Description
Ordinary characters	Characters other than .$^{[(|)*+?\ match themselves
\b	Matches a backspace
\t	Matches a tab
\r	Matches a carriage return
\v	Matches a vertical tab
\f	Matches a form feed
\n	Matches a newline
\	If followed by a nonordinary character (one of those listed in the first row), matches that character — for example, \+ matches a + character

In addition to single characters, you can specify a class or a range of characters that can be matched in the expression. That is, you could allow any digit or any vowel in a position, and exclude all the other characters. The character classes in the following table enable you to do this.

Character class	Description
.	Matches any character except \n
[aeiou]	Matches any single character specified in the set
[^aeiou]	Matches any character not specified in the set
[3-7a-dA-D]	Matches any character specified in the specified ranges (in the example, the ranges are 3-7, a-d, A-D)
\w	Matches any word character — that is, any alphanumeric character or the underscore (_)
\W	Matches any nonword character
\s	Matches any whitespace character (space, tab, formfeed, new line, carriage return, or vertical feed)
\S	Matches any nonwhitespace character
\d	Matches any decimal character
\D	Matches any nondecimal character

You can also specify that a certain character or class of characters must be present at least once, or between two and six times, and so on. The quantifiers are put just after a character or a class of characters and enable you to specify how many times the preceding character/class must be matched, as the following table shows.

Quantifier	Description
*	Zero or more matches
+	One or more matches
?	Zero or one matches
{N}	N matches
{N,}	N or more matches
{N,M}	Between N and M matches

As an example, suppose that you have the expression [aeiou]{2,4}\+[1-5]*: This means that a string to correctly match this expression must start with two to four vowels, have a + sign, and terminate with zero or more digits between 1 and 5.

Implementing the User Interface

In this last part of the "Solution" section you'll implement the administration pages for sending out a newsletter and checking its progress, as well as the end-user pages that display the list of archived newsletters, and the content of a specific newsletter. Finally, there is the `NewsletterBox` user control that you will plug into the site's master page, which creates a subscription box and a link to the archive page.

The SendNewsletter.aspx Page

This page, located under the `~/Admin` folder, allows any editor or administrator to create and send a newsletter. It's composed of two panels. The first panel includes the simple textboxes and the FCKeditor that will contain the newsletter's subject, plain-text and HTML body, and the Submit button. The other panel includes a message saying that another newsletter is already being sent, and it shows a link to the `SendingNewsletter.aspx` page (to show which newsletter is being sent). Which of these two panels will be shown when the page loads is determined according to the value of the static `Newsletter.IsSending` property. Here's the page's markup code:

```
<asp:Panel runat="server" ID="panSend">
    <small><b>Subject:</b></small><br />
    <asp:TextBox ID="txtSubject" runat="server" Width="99%"
        MaxLength="256"></asp:TextBox>
    <asp:RequiredFieldValidator ID="valRequireSubject" runat="server"
        ControlToValidate="txtSubject" SetFocusOnError="true"
        Text="The Subject field is required."Display="Dynamic"
        ValidationGroup="Newsletter"></asp:RequiredFieldValidator>
    <p></p>

    <small><b>Plain-text Body:</b></small><br />
    <asp:TextBox ID="txtPlainTextBody" runat="server" Width="99%"
        TextMode="MultiLine" Rows="14"></asp:TextBox>
    <asp:RequiredFieldValidator ID="valRequirePlainTextBody" runat="server"
        ControlToValidate="txtPlainTextBody" SetFocusOnError="true"
        Text="The plain-text body is required." Display="Dynamic"
        ValidationGroup="Newsletter"></asp:RequiredFieldValidator>
    <p></p>

    <small><b>HTML Body:</b></small><br />
    <fckeditorv2:fckeditor id="txtHtmlBody" runat="server"
        ToolbarSet="TheBeerHouse" Height="400px" Width="99%" />
    <p></p>

    <asp:Button ID="btnSend" runat="server" Text="Send" ValidationGroup="Newsletter"
        OnClientClick="if (confirm(
            'Are you sure you want to send the newsletter?') == false) return false;"
        OnClick="btnSend_Click" />
</asp:Panel>

<asp:Panel ID="panWait" runat="server" Visible="false">
    <asp:Label runat="server" id="lblWait" SkinID="FeedbackKO">
    <p>Another newsletter is currently being sent. Please wait until it completes
    before compiling and sending a new one.</p><p>You can check the current
    newsletter's completion status from
```

```
        <a href="SendingNewsletter.aspx">this page</a>.</p>
        </asp:Label>
    </asp:Panel>
```

Note that there's no `RequiredFieldValidator` control for the HTML body editor; if HTML content is not specified, then the plain-text body will be used to create it. When the page loads, is shows or hides the two panels according to the value of `IsSending`, as shown below:

```
protected void Page_Load(object sender, EventArgs e)
{
    bool isSending = false;
    Newsletter.Lock.AcquireReaderLock(Timeout.Infinite);
    isSending = Newsletter.IsSending;
    Newsletter.Lock.ReleaseReaderLock();

    if (!this.IsPostBack && isSending)
    {
        panWait.Visible = true;
        panSend.Visible = false;
    }
    txtHtmlBody.BasePath = this.BaseUrl + "FCKeditor/";
}
```

Then, when the form is submitted, it checks the variable again, because another editor may have sent a newsletter in the meantime. In that case it shows the panel with the wait message, but it doesn't hide the panel with the form, so that users don't lose their own newsletter's text. If no newsletter is currently being sent, it sends this new one and redirects the user to the page showing the progress:

```
protected void btnSend_Click(object sender, EventArgs e)
{
    bool isSending = false;
    Newsletter.Lock.AcquireReaderLock(Timeout.Infinite);
    isSending = Newsletter.IsSending;
    Newsletter.Lock.ReleaseReaderLock();

    if (isSending)
    {
        panWait.Visible = true;
    }
    else
    {
        int id = Newsletter.SendNewsletter(txtSubject.Text,
            txtPlainTextBody.Text, txtHtmlBody.Value);
        this.Response.Redirect("SendingNewsletter.aspx");
    }
}
```

Note that the call to `Newsletter.SendNewsletter` is very simple — it's not obvious that the newsletter is sent asynchronously from looking at the preceding code. This is intentional: We're hiding the details of the complex code to free the UI developer from needing to know the underlying details. Figure 7-4 is a screenshot of the page with some plain-text and HTML content in the textboxes.

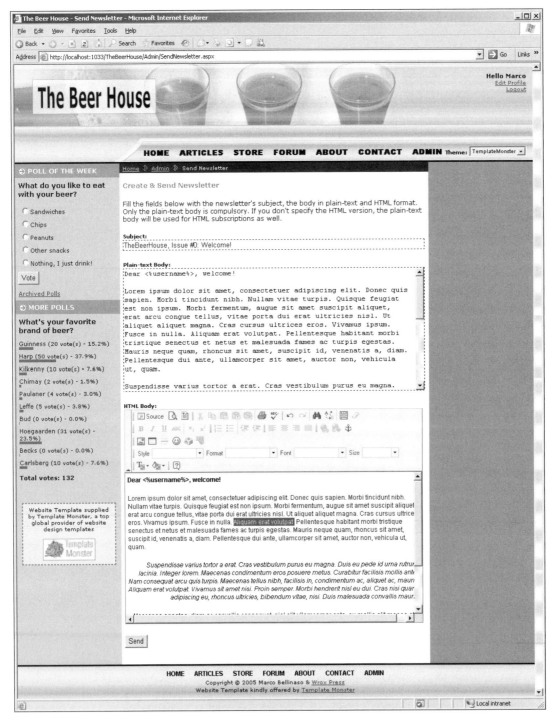

Figure 7-4

When the page loads, and another newsletter is already being sent, it will look like Figure 7-5.

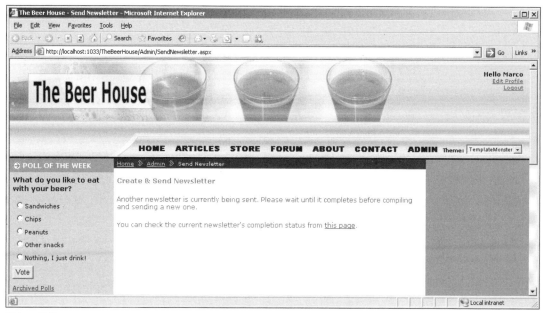

Figure 7-5

The SendingNewsletter.aspx Page

The markup of this page can be split up into two parts: The first includes the code for the progress bar and the status information (or a panel with a message if no newsletter is being sent), and the other has the JavaScript callback function called after ASP.NET performs the lightweight postback to the server, to retrieve information about the progress of the newsletter being sent. The progress bar is rendered as two nested DIVs: The outer DIV is as large as the page's content section, and the inner DIV's width will be set to the completed percentage retrieved from the server, and updated every couple of seconds. There's also another DIV that will contain the number of e-mails sent and the number of total subscribers, as textual information. Finally, there's another DIV that's initially hidden, containing an image representing an "OK hand"; this will be displayed when the completion percentage reaches 100%. All three DIVs are assigned a fixed ID, so that it will be easy to reference them from the JavaScript code by means of the `window.document.getElementById` DOM function. Here's the code for this first part:

```
<asp:Panel ID="panProgress" runat="server">
    <div class="progressbarcontainer">
        <div class="progressbar" id="progressbar"></div>
    </div>
    <br /><br />
    <div id="progressdescription"></div>
    <br /><br />
    <div style="text-align: center; display: none;" id="panelcomplete">
        <img src="../Images/100ok.gif" width="70px" /></div>
</asp:Panel>

<asp:Panel ID="panNoNewsletter" runat="server" Visible="false">
    <b>No newsletter is currently being sent.</b>
</asp:Panel>
```

The script of the second page contains an `UpdateProgress` function called by JavaScript after the lightweight postback. Its input parameter will be a string formatted like this: `"completed_percentage ;num_sent_mails;num_tot_mails"`. The function splits the string on the semicolon character and uses the three pieces of information to update the progress bar's width and a status message formatted as `"{completed_percentage}% completed - {num_sent_mails} out of {num_total_mails} have been sent."`.

At the end of the function, if the percentage is 100%, it shows the DIV containing the image; otherwise, it sets up a timer that will call the `CallUpdateProgress` function after two seconds. The `CallUpdate Progress` function performs another lightweight postback to retrieve updated progress information from the server; it does this by means of the ASP.NET-generated `WebForm_DoCallback` function. The call to `WebForm_DoCallback` is not here, but generated on the server through the `GetCallbackEvent Reference` method of the page's `ClientScript` object property. Therefore, in the `CallUpdate Progress` function there's just a `Literal` control, which will be populated at runtime with the JavaScript call created on the server. Here's the final part of the .aspx page:

```
<script type="text/javascript">
    function CallUpdateProgress()
    {
        <asp:Literal runat="server" ID="lblScriptName" />;
    }

    function UpdateProgress(result, context)
    {
        // result is a semicolon-separated list of values, so split it
        var params = result.split(";");
        var percentage = params[0];
        var sentMails = params[1];
        var totalMails = params[2];

        if (totalMails < 0)
            totalMails = '???';

        // update progressbar's width and description text
        var progBar = window.document.getElementById('progressbar');
        progBar.style.width = percentage + '%';
        var descr = window.document.getElementById('progressdescription');
        descr.innerHTML = '<b>' + percentage + '% completed</b> - ' +
            sentMails + ' out of ' + totalMails + ' e-mails have been sent.';

        // if the current percentage is less than 100%,
        // recall the server callback method in 2 seconds
        if (percentage == '100')
            window.document.getElementById('panelcomplete').style.display = '';
        else
            setTimeout('CallUpdateProgress()', 2000);
    }
</script>
```

When the page loads, in the `Page_Load` event handler you check whether there's actually a newsletter being sent. If not, you just show a panel with a message saying so. Otherwise, you get a reference to the `WebForm_DoCallback` JavaScript function that performs the lightweight callback and which calls `UpdateProgress` when it gets the response from the server. This reference is used as `Text` for the `Literal` control defined inside the `CallUpdateProgress` JavaScript function described above. This makes the server-side callback, and the `UpdateProgress` function will be called every two seconds once the cycle has started.

However, to make it start the very first time, you must also call `WebForm_DoCallback` automatically when the form loads (instead of from the `onclick` or `onchange` client-side events of some control): To do this you just create a script that calls `CallUpdateProgress` (which in turns calls `WebForm_DoCallback`), and register it at the bottom of the form, by means of the `ClientScriptManager`'s `RegisterStartupScript` method. Here's the code:

```
public partial class SendingNewsletter : BasePage, ICallbackEventHandler
{
    protected void Page_Load(object sender, EventArgs e)
    {
        bool isSending = false;
        Newsletter.Lock.AcquireReaderLock(Timeout.Infinite);
        isSending = Newsletter.IsSending;
        Newsletter.Lock.ReleaseReaderLock();

        if (!this.IsPostBack && !isSending)
        {
            panNoNewsletter.Visible = true;
            panProgress.Visible = false;
        }
        else
        {
            string callbackRef = this.ClientScript.GetCallbackEventReference(
                this, "", "UpdateProgress", "null");

            lblScriptName.Text = callbackRef;
            this.ClientScript.RegisterStartupScript(this.GetType(),
                "StartUpdateProgress",
                @"<script type=""text/javascript"">CallUpdateProgress();</script>");
        }
    }
}
```

The rest of the code-behind class is the implementation of the `ICallbackEventHandler` interface. In the `RaiseCallbackEvent` method, you create a semicolon-delimited string containing the three progress values needed to do the partial page update, and save it in a local field that is returned to the client by the `GetCallbackResult` method:

```
string callbackResult = "";

public string GetCallbackResult()
{
    return callbackResult;
}

public void RaiseCallbackEvent(string eventArgument)
{
    Newsletter.Lock.AcquireReaderLock(Timeout.Infinite);
    callbackResult = Newsletter.PercentageCompleted.ToString("N0") + ";" +
        Newsletter.SentMails.ToString() + ";" + Newsletter.TotalMails.ToString();
    Newsletter.Lock.ReleaseReaderLock();
}
```

Figure 7-6 shows the progress bar and the status information displayed on the page at runtime.

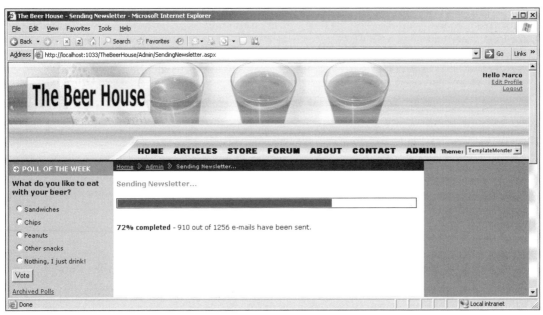

Figure 7-6

Figure 7-7 is a screenshot of the HTML newsletter represented in Figure 7-4 after it arrives in the subscriber's mailbox and is opened with Outlook Express.

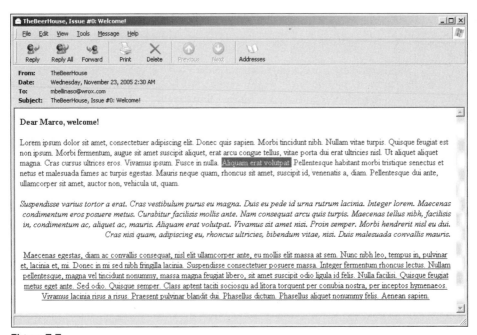

Figure 7-7

The ArchivedNewsletters.aspx Page

This page uses a `GridView` control to list archived newsletters retrieved by a companion `ObjectDataSource` control by means of the `Newsletter.GetNewsletters` BLL method. The grid displays the newsletter's subject and data in the first column, and a Delete button in a second column. The second column will be visible only to editors and administrators, of course. The subject in the first column is rendered as a link that points to the `ShowNewsletter.aspx` page, with the newsletter's ID passed on the querystring. Following is the page's markup code:

```
<asp:GridView ID="gvwNewsletters" runat="server" AutoGenerateColumns="False"
    DataSourceID="objNewsletters" Width="100%" DataKeyNames="ID"
    OnRowCreated="gvwNewsletters_RowCreated" ShowHeader="false">
    <Columns>
        <asp:TemplateField>
            <ItemTemplate>
                <img src="images/arrowr2.gif" alt=""
                    style="vertical-align: middle; border-width: 0px;" />
                <asp:HyperLink runat="server" ID="lnkNewsletter"
                    Text='<%# Eval("Subject") %>'
                    NavigateUrl='<%# "ShowNewsletter.aspx?ID=" + Eval("ID") %>' />
                <small>(sent on <%# Eval("AddedDate", "{0:d}") %>)</small>
            </ItemTemplate>
        </asp:TemplateField>
        <asp:CommandField ButtonType="Image" DeleteImageUrl="~/Images/Delete.gif"
            DeleteText="Delete newsletter" ShowDeleteButton="True">
            <ItemStyle HorizontalAlign="Center" Width="20px" />
        </asp:CommandField>
    </Columns>
    <EmptyDataTemplate><b>No newsletters to show</b></EmptyDataTemplate>
</asp:GridView>

<asp:ObjectDataSource ID="objNewsletters" runat="server"
    TypeName="MB.TheBeerHouse.BLL.Newsletters.Newsletter"
    SelectMethod="GetNewsletters"
    DeleteMethod="DeleteNewsletter">
    <DeleteParameters>
        <asp:Parameter Name="id" Type="Int32" />
    </DeleteParameters>
    <SelectParameters>
        <asp:Parameter Name="toDate" Type="DateTime" />
    </SelectParameters>
</asp:ObjectDataSource>
```

Remember that the `GetNewsletters` business method takes a `DateTime` parameter as an input and returns only those newsletters that were sent prior to that date. The value for this parameter must be set from the code-behind class, early in the page's life cycle, such as in the `Page_Init` event. It assumes different values according to the current user: If the user belongs to the Administrators or Editors roles, the parameter is set to the current date and time, because those users are always allowed to see all newsletters, even if one was just sent a minute ago. Otherwise, for all other users, the parameter is set to the current date and time minus the number of days indicated by the `hideFromArchiveInterval` attribute of the `<newsletters>` custom configuration element. Here's the code:

```
protected void Page_Init(object sender, EventArgs e)
{
    DateTime toDate = DateTime.Now;
```

```
    if (!this.User.Identity.IsAuthenticated ||
        (!this.User.IsInRole("Administrators") && !this.User.IsInRole("Editors"))))
    {
        toDate = toDate.Subtract(
            new TimeSpan(Globals.Settings.Newsletters.HideFromArchiveInterval,
            0, 0, 0));
    }
    objNewsletters.SelectParameters["toDate"].DefaultValue = toDate.ToString("f");
}
```

Note that the `DateTime` value is converted to `string` (all `ObjectDataSource` parameters are set as `string`, and they will be parsed internally into the proper type expected by the `SelectMethod` being called) with the `"f"` format, which includes full date and time information, instead of just the date. This is required because if you only include the date part, newsletters sent on that date but after 00:00 will not be included in the results.

In the `Page_Load` event handler, you check whether the user is anonymous, in which case it redirects the user to the `AccessDenied.aspx` page if the configuration `archiveIsPublic` setting is `false`. If the user can access the page, the execution goes ahead, and you check whether the user is an editor or an administrator. If not, the grid's second column with the Delete button is hidden:

```
protected void Page_Load(object sender, EventArgs e)
{
    if (!this.User.Identity.IsAuthenticated &&
        !Globals.Settings.Newsletters.ArchiveIsPublic) this.RequestLogin();

    gvwNewsletters.Columns[1].Visible = (this.User.Identity.IsAuthenticated &&
        (this.User.IsInRole("Administrators") || this.User.IsInRole("Editors")));
}
```

Figure 7-8 is a screenshot of this page as seen by an editor.

The ShowNewsletter.aspx Page

This is the last page of the module, and also the simplest one. It takes the ID of a newsletter on the querystring, loads that newsletter by means of the `Newsletter.GetNewsletterByID` method, and displays its subject, plain-text and HTML body, in three `Literal` controls. The bodies may be very long, though, and to avoid having a very long page that requires a lot of scrolling, the `Literals` for the two body versions are declared inside `<div>` containers with a fixed height and a vertical scrolling bar. Here's the simple markup body:

```
<small><b>Plain-text Body:</b></small>
<div style="border: dashed 1px black; overflow: auto; width: 98%; height: 300px;
padding: 5px;">
    <asp:Literal runat="server" ID="lblPlaintextBody" />
</div>
<p></p>
<small><b>HTML Body:</b></small>
<div style="border: dashed 1px black; overflow: auto; width: 98%; height: 300px;
padding: 5px;">
    <asp:Literal runat="server" ID="lblHtmlBody" />
</div>
```

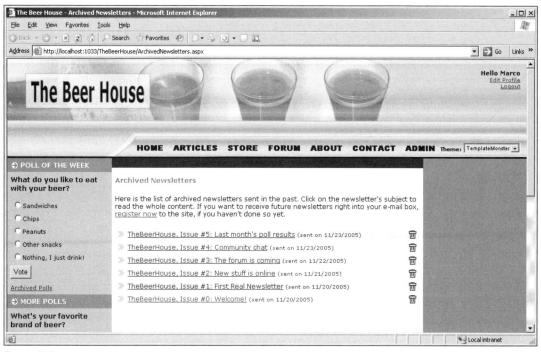

Figure 7-8

In the `Page_Load` event handler, you first confirm that the current user has the right to see this newsletter: You use the same constraints described for the `ArchivedNewsletter.aspx` page, and the date of the specific newsletter being sent must not be more recent than the current date minus the number of days specified in the configuration. Then you display the data on the page: Note that the plain-text body is encoded, so that if it contains special characters such as < and > they are not interpreted as HTML tags:

```
protected void Page_Load(object sender, EventArgs e)
{
    if (!this.User.Identity.IsAuthenticated &&
        !Globals.Settings.Newsletters.ArchiveIsPublic)
        this.RequestLogin();

    // load the newsletter with the ID passed on the querystring
    Newsletter newsletter = Newsletter.GetNewsletterByID(
        int.Parse(this.Request.QueryString["ID"]));

    // check that the newsletter can be viewed, according to the number of days
    // that must pass before it is published in the archive
    int days = ((TimeSpan)(DateTime.Now - newsletter.AddedDate)).Days;
    if (Globals.Settings.Newsletters.HideFromArchiveInterval > days &&
        (!this.User.Identity.IsAuthenticated ||
        (!this.User.IsInRole("Administrators") && !this.User.IsInRole("Editors"))))
        this.RequestLogin();

    // show the newsletter's data
```

```
      this.Title += newsletter.Subject;
      lblSubject.Text = newsletter.Subject;
      lblPlaintextBody.Text = HttpUtility.HtmlEncode(
         newsletter.PlainTextBody).Replace("  ", "  ").Replace(
         "\t", "   ").Replace("\n", "<br/>");;
      lblHtmlBody.Text = newsletter.HtmlBody;
   }
```

Figure 7-9 shows the newsletter sent earlier, and now archived.

Figure 7-9

The NewsletterBox User Control

The `NewsletterBox` control (located in `~/Controls/NewsletterBox.ascx`) displays a different output depending on whether the current user is anonymous. It uses a `LoginView` control, first introduced in Chapter 4, to do this through its `AnonymousTemplate` and `LoggedInTemplate` sections. In the first case, it invites the user to fill a textbox with her e-mail address and to press the OK button to subscribe. In the latter case it just shows a link to the `UserProfile.aspx` page where the existing member can change her subscription type. In both cases a link to the archive page is displayed also. When the anonymous user clicks the OK button, there is no postback; instead, the button's client-side `OnClick` event is handled, and the browser is redirected to the `Register.aspx` page, with the current content of the e-mail textbox passed on the querystring. Here's the whole markup code and the companion JavaScript code:

```
<asp:LoginView ID="LoginView1" runat="server">
    <AnonymousTemplate>
     <b>Register to the site for free</b>, and subscribe to the newsletter.
     Every month you will receive new articles and special content not available
     elsewhere on the site, right into your e-mail box!<br /><br />
     <input type="text" id="NewsletterEmail" value="E-mail here"
        onfocus="javascript:this.value = '';" style="width: 140px;" />
     <input type="button" value="OK" onclick="javascript:SubscribeToNewsletter();"/>
    </AnonymousTemplate>
    <LoggedInTemplate>
     You can change your subscription(plain-text, HTML or no newsletter) from your
     <asp:HyperLink runat="server" ID="lnkProfile"
        NavigateUrl="~/EditProfile.aspx" Text="profile" /> page.
     Click the link below to read the newsletters run in the past.
    </LoggedInTemplate>
</asp:LoginView>
<p></p>
<asp:HyperLink runat="server" ID="lnkArchive"
NavigateUrl="~/ArchivedNewsletters.aspx" Text="Archived Newsletters" />

<script type="text/javascript">
    function SubscribeToNewsletter()
    {
        var email = window.document.getElementById('NewsletterEmail').value;
        window.document.location.href='Register.aspx?Email=' + email;
    }
</script>
```

In the `Register.aspx` page you have to modify the declaration of the `Email` textbox so that its `Text` property is bound to a field declared in the code-behind class. This is the updated declaration:

```
<asp:TextBox runat="server" ID="Email" Width="100%" Text='<%# Email %>' />
```

In the `Page_Load` event handler you check whether an `Email` parameter was passed on the querystring (it's not there if the user reaches the page directly with the link at the top of the page's layout, and not through the `NewsletterBox` control). If it is found, the `Email` field is set to its value, and you call the `DataBind` method of the `CreateUserWizard` control. This will, in turn, call `DataBind` for all its child controls, including the `Email` textbox:

```
protected string Email = "";

protected void Page_Load(object sender, EventArgs e)
```

```
    {
        if (!this.IsPostBack &&
            !string.IsNullOrEmpty(this.Request.QueryString["Email"]))
        {
            Email = this.Request.QueryString["Email"];
            CreateUserWizard1.DataBind();
        }
    }
```

Note that you can't call the DataBind method of the Email textbox directly, because that control is declared inside a Template section, and as such will be dynamically created at runtime.

Now that the user control is complete, you reference it at the top of the master.template master page, and create a new instance of it in the right-hand column (see Figure 7-10):

```
<%@ Register Src="Controls/NewsletterBox.ascx" TagName="NewsletterBox"
TagPrefix="mb" %>

...

<mb:NewsletterBox id="NewsletterBox1" runat="server" />
```

Figure 7-10

Figure 7-11 shows just the NewsletterBox as shown by an authenticated member.

Figure 7-11

Summary

In this chapter you've implemented a complete module for sending out newsletters to members who registered to receive them, either at initial registration time or later. The module sends out the e-mails from a background thread instead of the main thread used to process the page request, so that you don't risk page timeouts, and, above all, so that you don't leave the editor with a blank page that may last several minutes or more. To provide some feedback to the editor about the newsletter being sent, there's a second page that updates a progress bar and shows the updated status information every couple of seconds. Finally, end users can look at past newsletters listed in an archive page.

To implement all this, you've used advanced features such as multi-threaded programming, script callbacks, and the `SmtpClient` and `MailMessage` classes to compose and send e-mail messages. You've also seen other new features of ASP.NET such as asynchronous pages, which is a useful feature in many situations.

However, although this module works fine, there's always room for enhancements. Here are some suggestions for improvements you may wish to make:

❑ Add the capability to send attachments with the newsletters. This can be very useful if you want to send HTML newsletters with images. Currently, you can only send e-mails with images, by referencing the full URL of the images on your server.

❑ Add support for setting the priority of the newsletter e-mails.

❑ Add the capability to have different mailing lists, for different topics, such as Parties, New Articles, or New Products in your store. This would require having more profile properties, and an expanded `SendNewsletter` page, so that you can choose the target mailing list.

❑ The personalization placeholder's list may be further expanded — to include placeholders for the subscriber's location, for example. You may also build a parser that manages custom tags defined into the newsletter's body, and includes or excludes their content according to the user's profile. For example, the content of a section `<profileProperty language="Italian">...</profile Property>` could be included only in the newsletters for subscribers who choose Italian for the `Language` property in their profile. Or `<profileProperty state="NY">...</profile Property>` could be used to include content only for subscribers living in New York state. This mechanism would not be difficult to implement, and it would allow editors to create very targeted newsletters, something that is especially important for commercial and marketing purposes.

Chapter 7

❑   When the messages are sent out, you won't get an error or exception if the e-mail doesn't reach its destination because the e-mail address isn't valid. The SMTP server does its work without letting you know about the results. However, messages sent to non-existent addresses usually come back to the sender with an error message saying that the message couldn't be successfully delivered because the address does not exist. These error messages are sent to the server's postmaster and then forwarded to the site's administrator. At this point, when you get such a message, you can manually set that account's Newsletter profile property to none. However, a much better and automated approach would be to write a program (probably as a Windows service) that parses the incoming messages to find the error messages, automatically performing the unsubscribe operation.

In the last few chapters we've developed modules to strengthen the site-to-user communications, such as the polls module and this newsletter manager. In the next chapter you're going to implement a module to manage forums, which is an important form of user-to-user communication.

8

Forums

Internet users like to feel part of a community of people with similar interests. A successful site should build a community of loyal visitors, a place where they can discuss their favorite subjects, ask questions, and reply to others. Community members return often to talk to other people with whom they've already shared messages, or to find comments and opinions about their interests. This chapter outlines some of the advantages of building such a virtual community, its goals, and the design and implementation of a new module for setting up and managing discussion boards.

Problem

User-to-user communication is important in many types of sites. For example, in a content site for pub enthusiasts, visitors to the site may want advice about the best way to brew their own beer, suggestions for good pubs in their area, to share comments on the last event they attended, and so on. Having contact with their peers is important so that they can ask questions and share their own knowledge. E-commerce sites have an added benefit of enabling users to review products online. Two ways to provide user-to-user communication are opinion polls and discussion boards. We've already looked at opinion polls in Chapter 6, and in this chapter we'll look at discussion boards, also known as forums. Visitors can browse the various messages in the forums, post their questions and topics, reply to other people's questions, and share ideas and tips. Forums act as a source of content, and provide an opportunity for users to participate and contribute. One reason why forums are especially attractive from a manager's perspective is because they require very little time and effort from employees because end users provide most of the content. However, a few minutes a day should be spent to ensure that nobody has posted any offensive messages, and that any problems that may be mentioned in a message receive some attention (maybe problems with the site, or questions about products, locations, etc.).

As for our TheBeerHouse site, we will offer discussion boards about brewing beers, pubs, concerts and parties, and more. These will be separate forums, used to group and categorize the threads by topic, so that it's easier for visitors to read what they are interested in. Early web-forum systems often threw up long lists of messages on a single page, which took ages to load. This can be avoided by displaying lists in pages, with each page containing a particular number of messages. The web site already has a way to identify users, and the forums will need to integrate with that membership system. Besides being identified by username in the forum module, users may like something "catchy" in order to be recognized by the community: something such as an avatar image (a small picture that represents the user on their messages) and a signature line. This information will be added to every post, and will help readers quickly identify the post's author. Of course, like any other module you've developed so far, the site's administrators and editors must be able to add, remove, or edit forums, topics, and replies.

Design

Before looking at the design, let's consider a more accurate list of features to be implemented:

❑   Support for multiple categories, or subforums, that are more or less specific to a single topic/argument. Subforums are identified by name and description, and optionally by an image.

❑   Forums must support moderation: When a forum is moderated (this is a forum-level option), all messages posted by anyone except power users (administrators, editors, and moderators) are not immediately visible on the forum, but must be approved by a member of one of the power user roles first. This is a useful option to ensure that posts are pertinent, non-offensive, and comply with the forum's policy. However, this also places a bigger burden on the power users because posts have to be approved often (at least several times a day, even on weekends), or users will lose interest. Because of the timeliness needed for moderation, most forums are not moderated, but they are checked at least once a day to ensure that the policy has not been violated (with no particular need to check on weekends).

❑   The list of threads for a subforum, and the list of posts for a thread, must be paginable. In addition, the list of threads must be sortable by the last posting date, or the number of replies or views, in ascending or descending order. Sort options are very helpful if there are a lot of messages.

❑   Posting is only permitted by registered members, whereas browsing is allowed by everybody. An extension of the forum implemented in this chapter may include more options to specify that browsing also requires login, or that posting is allowed by anonymous users.

❑   Users will be able to format their messages with a limited, and safe, set of HTML tags. This will be done by means of the FCKeditor control already used in Chapter 5, with a reduced toolbar.

❑   While creating a new thread, a user must be able to immediately close the thread so that other users cannot reply. If replies are allowed, they can later be disabled (and thus the thread closed) only by administrators, editors, and moderators.

❑   Users can modify their own posts anytime, but the operation must be logged in the message itself (a simple note in the message saying that it was edited will avoid confusion if another user remembers seeing something in a message but the next time they look it's gone).

❑   Users can have an avatar image associated with their account, which is displayed on every post they make. This helps them create a virtual, digital identity among other users of the forum. Users can also define a signature to be automatically added at the end of each post, so that it doesn't need to be copied and pasted every time. Signatures often includes a special greeting, motto, old saying, or any other quote taken from movies, from famous people, or coined by the member herself. Sometimes it will contain a URL of that person's own site—this is normally OK, but you probably don't want any kind of advertising in this manner (e.g., www.BuyMyProduct.com).

❏ The messages posted by users are counted, and the count is displayed together with the user's avatar, on each of the user's messages. This count is a form of recognition, and it lets other users know that this person might be more knowledgeable, or at least that they've hung around in the forums a lot (it tends to lend more credibility). In addition, the forum system supports three special user levels; these are descriptions tied to the number of posts each user has made. The number of posts needed to advance to the next level can be configured, just like the descriptions.

❏ Full support for RSS 2.0 feeds should allow users to track new messages in an RSS aggregator program (such as the free SharpReader, or RSS Bandit). There will be a flexible syndication system that provides distinct feeds to specific subforums, or all forums, and it will sort posts in different ways. This enables users to get a feed with the 10 newest threads posted into any forum, or with the 10 most popular threads (if sorted by number of replies). The feeds will be consumed by the generic RSS `Reader` control already developed in Chapter 5.

❏ Administrators, editors, and moderators can edit and delete any post. Additionally, they can move an entire thread to a different forum, which is helpful for ensuring that all threads are published in the appropriate place.

> Remember that you need some kind of policy statement somewhere in the forum pages that tells users what the rules are. This is usually needed for legal reasons in case a nasty, hateful, or untruthful message is posted and not caught quickly — just some kind of disclaimer to protect the site owners/administrators from lawsuits.

Designing the Database Tables

To help you understand the database design of this module, we'll compare it to the design that was implemented in the first edition of this book, examining the changes (but it's OK if you didn't read the first edition — you will still see some value in this comparison). Figure 8-1 represents the first edition's UML diagram of all the tables.

With six tables for a single module, this made the forums system the most complex module of the book. In this edition, we'll simplify the design significantly. We'll also add some new features, but without removing anything important. In Figure 8-1 you can see that we had a two-level organization for message threads: categories and then subforums. A simpler design with multiple subforums would be entirely adequate in most situations. We also had two separate tables for storing the first message of threads (the Forums_Threads table) and the replies (the Forums_Replies table): These two tables do not differ for many fields, as they both have a primary key field and the Message, MemberID, MemberIP, and AddedDate fields. The first message of a thread and its replies are all forum posts, and dividing them in two separate tables only complicates things, i.e., it leads to longer queries and is more difficult to read and maintain. In the new design there is just a single table for all messages; the few fields that only make sense for one type of message will simply have a default value for the other type. Additionally, we had threads and replies linked to a record of the Forums_Members table, which contained a profile of the user, with her signature, avatar, and other information, and this was linked to a record in the Accounts_Users table, which contained the membership information (username, password, etc., of all user accounts). Yes, we had two redundant places to hold user data, and it was confusing and caused problems when they became out of sync. In the new version we'll consolidate all membership and profile data, and it will be stored and managed automatically by the ASP.NET provider classes!

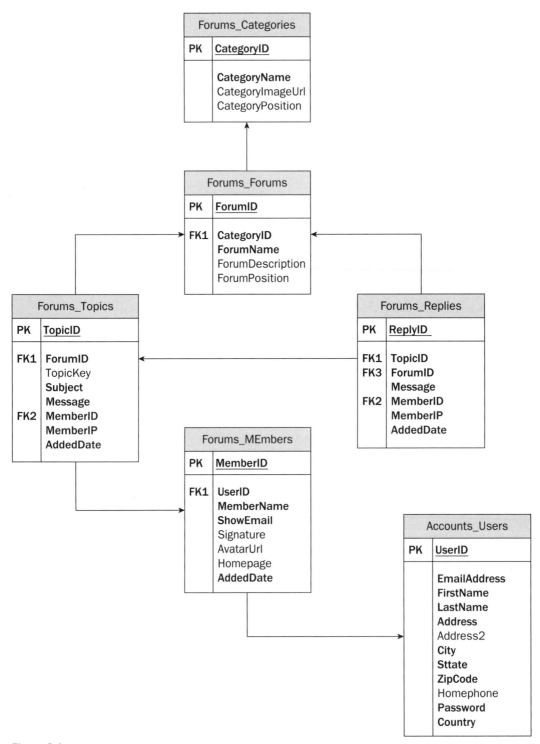

Figure 8-1

To recap, the new forums system will just have one table that stores subforum information, and another one that stores all messages. Figure 8-2 represents the tables as shown by the Database Diagram Editor window of VS 2005's Server Explorer tool (which is similar to what Enterprise Manager would show in SQL Server 2000 with VS 2003 — now you can stay inside VS most of the time).

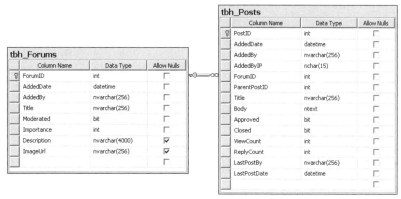

Figure 8-2

The tbh_Forums table is similar to the tbh_Categories table used in Chapter 5 for the articles module, with the addition of the Moderated column, which indicates whether the messages posted by normal users must be approved before they become visible in the forums' pages. The tbh_Posts table contains the following columns (the usual AddedDate and AddedBy fields aren't shown here):

❑   **PostID:** The primary key

❑   **AddedByIP:** The IP of the user who authored the message — used for auditing purposes. Remember that you may become partially responsible for what users write (this also depends on the laws of your country). You should try to log information about the user who posted a message (such as the date/time and IP address) so you can provide this to legal authorities in the unlikely event that it might be needed.

❑   **ForumID:** The foreign key to a parent forum

❑   **ParentPostID:** An integer referencing another record in the same table, which is the first message of a thread. When this field contains 0, it means that the post has no parent post; therefore, this is a thread post. Otherwise, this is a reply to an existent thread.

❑   **Title:** The title of the post. Reply posts also have a title; it will usually be "Re: {thread title here}", but it's not absolutely necessary and the user will be free to change it while posting a new reply.

❑   **Body:** The body of the post, in HTML format (only limited HTML tags are allowed)

❑   **Approved:** A Boolean value indicating whether the post has been approved by a power user (administrators, editors, and moderators), and visible on the end-user pages. If the parent forum is not moderated, this field is automatically set to 1 when the post is created.

❑   **Closed:** This field is only used for thread posts, and is a Boolean value indicating whether the thread is closed and no more replies can be added. The user will be able to specify this option only while creating the thread. Once a thread has been created, only power users can close the thread.

❏ **ViewCount:** An integer indicating the number of times a thread has been read. If the record represents a reply, this field will contain 0.

❏ **ReplyCount:** The number of replies for the thread post. If the record represents a reply, this field will contain 0.

❏ **LastPostBy:** The name of the member who submitted the last post to this thread. As long as there are no replies, the field contains the name of the member who created the thread, which is also the name stored in the record's AddedBy field.

❏ **LastPostDate:** The date and time of the last post to this thread. As long as there are no replies, the field contains the date and time when the thread was created, which is also the value stored in the record's AddedDate field.

In the case of ParentPostID, the replies will always link to the first post of the thread, and not to another reply. Therefore, the proposed structure does not support threaded discussions, such as those in Internet newsgroups. Instead, posts of non-threaded discussions will be shown to the reader, sorted by creation date, from the oldest to the newest, so that they are read in chronological order. Both of these two types of forum systems, threaded or not, have their pros and cons. Threaded discussions make it easier to follow replies to previous posts, but non-threaded discussions make it easier to follow the discussion with the correct temporal order (time-sequenced). To make it easier for the reader to follow the discussion, non-threaded discussions usually allow users to quote a previous reply, even if the referenced reply is a number of posts prior to that one. In my research, non-threaded discussions are more widely used, and easier to develop, so we'll use them for our sample site. If you want to modify the forum system to support threaded discussions, you'll be able to do that without modifying the DB; you just need to set the post's ParentPostID to the appropriate value.

Our first edition used SQL aggregate functions COUNT and MAX to dynamically compute the thread's message count values instead of storing them in the database. This was a serious problem in terms of performance because it took a long time to execute this SQL, and it ran often. It will save a lot of time if you store the values directly in the thread post's record, and update them when a new reply is added, as we'll do in this book.

The Stored Procedures

The following table contains the list of stored procedures for the typical CRUD operations on the two database tables, plus some special updates to handle approving posts, moving threads, incrementing the view count, and so on.

Property	Description
tbh_Forums_ApprovePost	Sets the Approved field to 1 for the specified post, indicating that the post will be visible to all users. It also increments the parent post's ReplyCount field by one, and sets the parent post's LastPostBy and LastPostDate fields to the corresponding values of the post being approved now.
tbh_Forums_CloseThread	Sets the Closed field of the specified thread to 1, meaning that the thread will not allow any further replies
tbh_Forums_DeleteForum	Deletes the specified forum, and all its child threads and posts

Property	Description
tbh_Forums_DeletePost	Deletes the specified post. If this post is the first message of a thread, this also deletes all its replies.
tbh_Forums_GetForumByID	Returns all details of the specified forum
tbh_Forums_GetForums	Returns all details of all forums
tbh_Forums_GetPostBody	Retrieves the body of the specified post
tbh_Forums_GetPostByID	Retrieves all details of the specified post
tbh_Forums_GetPostCount ByThread	Returns the number of posts for the specified thread
tbh_Forums_GetThreadByID	Returns all details for all posts in the specified thread
tbh_Forums_GetThreadCount	Returns the number of threads from all forums
tbh_Forums_GetThreadCount ByForum	Returns the number of threads from a specific forum
tbh_Forums_GetUnapproved Posts	Retrieves all details of all unapproved posts, sorted by type (thread posts first, and then reply posts) and then from the oldest to the newest. The logic behind these sorting options is that it's more important to approve new threads before new replies, and then it's more important to approve posts starting from the oldest because they have been waiting longer for approval.
tbh_Forums_Increment ViewCount	Increments the ViewCount field of the specified thread post by one
tbh_Forums_InsertForum	Creates a new forum with the specified details, and returns its auto-generated ID
tbh_Forums_InsertPost	Creates a new post and returns its auto-generated ID. If the post has its ParentPostID field set to 0, it means this is a thread post, and its LastPostBy and LastPostDate fields will be set equal to the AddedBy and AddedDate values specified. If the post represents a reply instead, and it is approved, then its AddedBy and AddedDate fields will be used to update its parent post's Last-PostBy and LastPostDate fields, and the parent post's Reply-Count field will be incremented by one.
tbh_Forums_MoveThread	Moves an entire thread to a different forum, by updating the ForumID field of the thread's posts to the specified destination forum's ID
tbh_Forums_UpdateForum	Updates some details of the specified forum
tbh_Forums_UpdatePost	Updates the title and body of the specified post. All other details are not editable by this procedure, but are editable by other stored procedures such as tbh_Forums_CloseThread, tbh_Forums_MoveThread, tbh_Forums_ApprovePost, tbh_Forums_IncrementViewCount, etc.

There are two notable queries missing from the preceding list. One is tbh_Forums_GetThreads, which returns the details of a page of threads. The other is tbh_Forums_GetThreadsByForum, which should return the details of a page of threads for a specific forum. These queries are not defined as stored procedures because the list of threads must support different ordering (LastPostDate, ReplyCount, and ViewCount), and unfortunately we can't parameterize the ORDER BY clause used in the stored procedure together with the ROW_NUMBER() ... OVER statement. The simplest solution to this problem is to dynamically build and execute these queries from the data access layer, according to the input parameters. As explained in Chapter 3, if you use parameters in the SQL query, SQL Server will be able to cache the execution plan and you'll be shielded against SQL injection attacks, even if you're not using a stored procedure.

Retrieving the list of threads present in all forums is only useful for sitewide RSS feeds that list the last "n" threads created, or the "n" most active threads (threads with the most replies).

Designing the Configuration Module

The configuration settings of the forums module are defined in a <forums> element within the <theBeerHouse> section of the web.config file. The class that maps the settings and exposes them is ForumsElement, which defines the following properties:

Property	Description
ProviderType	The full name (namespace plus class name) of the concrete provider class that implements the data access code for a specific data store
Connection StringName	The name of the entry in web.config's new <connectionStrings> section containing the connection string for this module's database
EnableCaching	A Boolean value indicating whether caching is enabled
CacheDuration	The number of seconds for which the data is cached if there aren't any inserts, deletes, or updates that invalidate the cache
ThreadsPageSize	The number of threads listed per page when browsing the threads of a subforum
PostsPageSize	The number of posts listed per page when reading a thread
RssItems	The number of threads included in the RSS feeds
HotThreadPosts	The number of posts that make a thread *hot*. Hot threads will be rendered with a special icon to be distinguished from the others.
BronzePosterPosts	The number of posts that the user must reach to earn the status description defined by BronzePosterDescription
BronzePoster Description	The title that the user earns after reaching the number of posts defined by BronzePosterPosts

Property	Description
SilverPosterPosts	The number of posts that the user must reach to earn the status description defined by SilverPosterDescription
SilverPoster Description	The title that the user earns after reaching the number of posts defined by SilverPosterPosts
GoldPosterPosts	The number of posts that the user must reach to earn the status description defined by GoldPosterDescription
GoldPoster Description	The title that the user earns after reaching the number of posts defined by GoldPosterPosts

Designing the Data Access Layer

As usual, the DAL consists of a number of entity classes that wrap data from the database tables (the ForumDetails and PostDetails classes), an abstract class defining a number of virtual methods to manipulate the data and a few helper methods (ForumsProvider), and finally a concrete class that inherits from the abstract class and implements its virtual methods with the code to call the respective stored procedures. Figure 8-3 shows the UML diagram of all these classes and their relationships.

Besides GetThreads, all other DAL methods simply wrap a stored procedure, so they don't require any further explanation. As explained earlier, GetThreads executes the dynamically constructed SQL queries in order to support different sorting options according to the input parameters.

Designing the Business Layer

Like the DAL, the BLL for this module is very similar to the other BLLs used in this book. There's a BaseForum class that contains the usual ID, AddedDate, and AddedBy properties common to both the tbh_Forums and the tbh_Posts tables, a Settings property, which returns an instance of the ForumsElement class, which wraps all forums' settings read from web.config, and finally a CacheData method that caches the input data according to the forums' settings. The derived classes are Forum and Post. Forum is almost identical to the Category class designed and implemented in Chapter 5, with the addition of the Moderated property. Post represents both threads (the first post of a thread) and replies, and it has properties that wrap all data coming from the PostDetails DAL class, plus instance methods such as Update, Delete, Approve, MoveThread, and CloseThread that manipulate the data contained in the current object. These instance methods simply forward the call to static methods that in turn call the respective DAL methods and add some logic to store and purge data from the cache, add data validation, and so on. The methods for retrieving a single post, the list of posts for a given thread, or the list of threads for a given forum are also implemented as static methods. Figure 8-4 shows the UML diagram of the BLL.

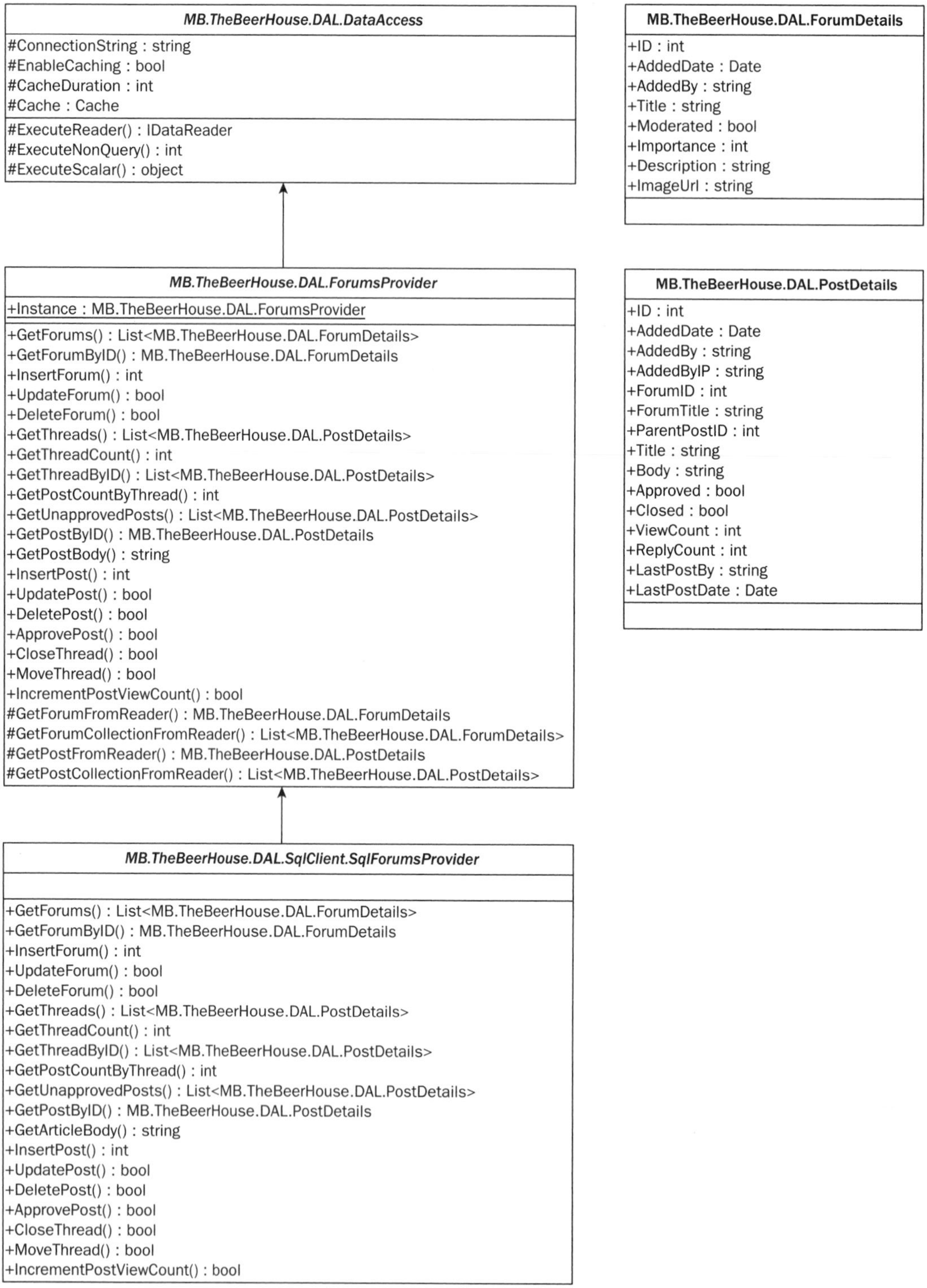

MB.TheBeerHouse.DAL.DataAccess
#ConnectionString : string
#EnableCaching : bool
#CacheDuration : int
#Cache : Cache
#ExecuteReader() : IDataReader
#ExecuteNonQuery() : int
#ExecuteScalar() : object

MB.TheBeerHouse.DAL.ForumDetails
+ID : int
+AddedDate : Date
+AddedBy : string
+Title : string
+Moderated : bool
+Importance : int
+Description : string
+ImageUrl : string

MB.TheBeerHouse.DAL.ForumsProvider
+Instance : MB.TheBeerHouse.DAL.ForumsProvider
+GetForums() : List<MB.TheBeerHouse.DAL.ForumDetails>
+GetForumByID() : MB.TheBeerHouse.DAL.ForumDetails
+InsertForum() : int
+UpdateForum() : bool
+DeleteForum() : bool
+GetThreads() : List<MB.TheBeerHouse.DAL.PostDetails>
+GetThreadCount() : int
+GetThreadByID() : List<MB.TheBeerHouse.DAL.PostDetails>
+GetPostCountByThread() : int
+GetUnapprovedPosts() : List<MB.TheBeerHouse.DAL.PostDetails>
+GetPostByID() : MB.TheBeerHouse.DAL.PostDetails
+GetPostBody() : string
+InsertPost() : int
+UpdatePost() : bool
+DeletePost() : bool
+ApprovePost() : bool
+CloseThread() : bool
+MoveThread() : bool
+IncrementPostViewCount() : bool
#GetForumFromReader() : MB.TheBeerHouse.DAL.ForumDetails
#GetForumCollectionFromReader() : List<MB.TheBeerHouse.DAL.ForumDetails>
#GetPostFromReader() : MB.TheBeerHouse.DAL.PostDetails
#GetPostCollectionFromReader() : List<MB.TheBeerHouse.DAL.PostDetails>

MB.TheBeerHouse.DAL.PostDetails
+ID : int
+AddedDate : Date
+AddedBy : string
+AddedByIP : string
+ForumID : int
+ForumTitle : string
+ParentPostID : int
+Title : string
+Body : string
+Approved : bool
+Closed : bool
+ViewCount : int
+ReplyCount : int
+LastPostBy : string
+LastPostDate : Date

MB.TheBeerHouse.DAL.SqlClient.SqlForumsProvider
+GetForums() : List<MB.TheBeerHouse.DAL.ForumDetails>
+GetForumByID() : MB.TheBeerHouse.DAL.ForumDetails
+InsertForum() : int
+UpdateForum() : bool
+DeleteForum() : bool
+GetThreads() : List<MB.TheBeerHouse.DAL.PostDetails>
+GetThreadCount() : int
+GetThreadByID() : List<MB.TheBeerHouse.DAL.PostDetails>
+GetPostCountByThread() : int
+GetUnapprovedPosts() : List<MB.TheBeerHouse.DAL.PostDetails>
+GetPostByID() : MB.TheBeerHouse.DAL.PostDetails
+GetArticleBody() : string
+InsertPost() : int
+UpdatePost() : bool
+DeletePost() : bool
+ApprovePost() : bool
+CloseThread() : bool
+MoveThread() : bool
+IncrementPostViewCount() : bool

Figure 8-3

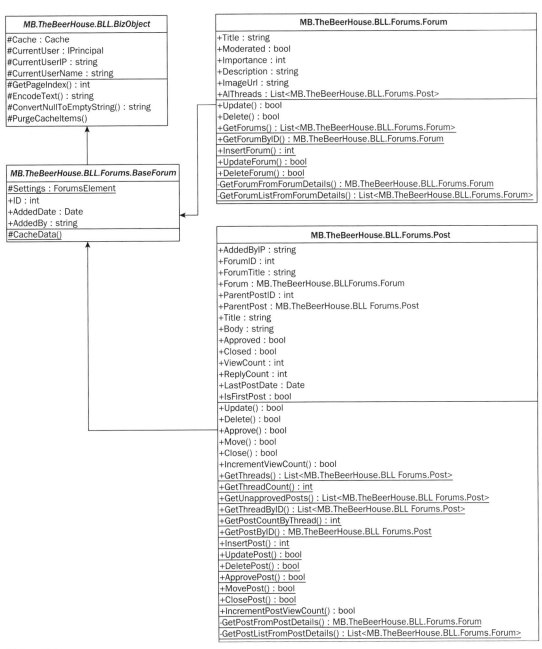

Figure 8-4

Designing the User Interface Services

The last thing we need to define are the UI pages and user controls that enable the user to browse forums and threads, post new messages, and administer the forum's content. Following is a list of the user interface pieces that we'll develop shortly in the "Solution" section:

❏   **~/Admin/ManageForums.aspx:** Adds, updates, and deletes forums

❏   **~/Admin/ManageUnapprovedPosts.aspx:** Lists all unapproved posts (first thread posts, and then replies, all sorted from the oldest to the newest), shows the entire content of a selected post, and approves or deletes it

❏   **~/Admin/MoveThread.aspx:** Moves a thread (i.e., the thread post and all its replies) to another forum

❏   **~/ShowForums.aspx:** Shows the list of all subforums, with their title, description, and image. Clicking on the forum's title will bring the user to another page showing the list of threads for that forum. For each forum, this also provides a link to its RSS feed, which returns the last "*n*" threads of that forum (where "*n*" is specified in `web.config`).

❏   **~/BrowseThreads.aspx:** Browses a forum's threads, page by page. The grid that lists the threads shows the thread's title, the number of times it was read, the number of replies, the author of the last post, and when the last post was created. Power users also see special links to delete, close, or move the thread. The results can be sorted by date, reply count, or view count.

❏   **~/ShowThread.aspx:** Shows all posts of a thread, in a paginated grid. For each post, it shows the title, body, author's signature, submission date and time, author's name, avatar image, and status description. Power users also see links to delete or edit any post, and a link to close the thread to stop replies. Normal members only see links to edit their own posts.

❏   **~/AddEditPost.aspx:** Creates a new thread, posts a new reply, or edits an existing message, according to the parameters on the querystring

❏   **~/GetThreadsRss.aspx:** Returns an RSS feed of the forum's content. According to the querystring parameters, it can return the feed for a specific subforum or include threads from any subforum, and supports various sorting options. This can retrieve a feed for the sitewide threads (if sorting by date) or for the most active threads (if sorting by reply count).

❏   **~/Controls/UserProfile.ascx:** This control already exists, as it was developed in Chapter 4 while implementing the membership and profiling system. However, you must extend it here to support the Avatar image and Signature profile properties.

Solution

In this section we'll cover the implementation of key parts of this module, as described in the "Design" section. But you won't find complete source code printed here, as many similar classes were discussed in other chapters. See the code download to get the complete source code.

Implementing the Database

The most interesting stored procedure is `tbh_Forums_InsertPost`. This inserts a new record into the `tbh_Posts table`, and if the new post being inserted is approved it must also update the `ReplyCount`,

`LastPostBy`, and `LastPostDate` fields of this post's parent post. Because there are multiple statements in this stored procedure, a transaction is used to ensure that they are both either committed successfully or rolled back:

```
ALTER PROCEDURE dbo.tbh_Forums_InsertPost
(
    @AddedDate          datetime,
    @AddedBy            nvarchar(256),
    @AddedByIP          nchar(15),
    @ForumID            int,
    @ParentPostID       int,
    @Title              nvarchar(256),
    @Body               ntext,
    @Approved           bit,
    @Closed             bit,
    @PostID             int OUTPUT
)
AS
SET NOCOUNT ON

BEGIN TRANSACTION InsertPost

INSERT INTO tbh_Posts
    (AddedDate, AddedBy, AddedByIP, ForumID, ParentPostID, Title, Body, Approved,
        Closed, LastPostDate, LastPostBy)
    VALUES (@AddedDate, @AddedBy, @AddedByIP, @ForumID, @ParentPostID, @Title,
        @Body, @Approved, @Closed, @AddedDate, @AddedBy)

SET @PostID = scope_identity()

-- if the post is approved, update the parent post's
-- ReplyCount and LastReplyDate fields
IF @Approved = 1 AND @ParentPostID > 0
    BEGIN
    UPDATE tbh_Posts SET ReplyCount = ReplyCount + 1, LastPostDate = @AddedDate,
        LastPostBy = @AddedBy
        WHERE PostID = @ParentPostID
    END

IF @@ERROR > 0
    BEGIN
    RAISERROR('Insert of post failed', 16, 1)
    ROLLBACK TRANSACTION InsertPost
    RETURN 99
    END

COMMIT TRANSACTION InsertPost
```

If the post being inserted must be reviewed before being approved, its parent posts won't be modified because we don't want to count posts that aren't visible. When it gets approved later, the `tbh_Forums_ApprovePost` stored procedure will set this post's `Approved` field to `1`, and then update its parent post's fields mentioned above. The `ReplyCount` field must also be incremented by one, but to update the parent post's `LastPostBy` and `LastPostDate` fields, the procedure needs the values of the `AddedBy` and

AddedDate fields of the post being approved, so it executes a fast query to retrieve this information and stores it in local variables, and then makes the parent post's update using those values, as shown below:

```
ALTER PROCEDURE dbo.tbh_Forums_ApprovePost
(
 @PostID   int
)
AS

BEGIN TRANSACTION ApprovePost

UPDATE tbh_Posts SET Approved = 1 WHERE PostID = @PostID

-- get the approved post's parent post and added date
DECLARE @ParentPostID    int
DECLARE @AddedDate       datetime
DECLARE @AddedBy         nvarchar(256)

SELECT @ParentPostID = ParentPostID, @AddedDate = AddedDate, @AddedBy = AddedBy
    FROM tbh_Posts
    WHERE PostID = @PostID

-- update the LastPostDate, LastPostBy and ReplyCount fields
-- of the approved post's parent post
IF @ParentPostID > 0
    BEGIN
    UPDATE tbh_Posts
        SET ReplyCount = ReplyCount + 1, LastPostDate = @AddedDate,
            LastPostBy = @AddedBy
        WHERE PostID = @ParentPostID
    END

IF @@ERROR > 0
    BEGIN
    RAISERROR('Approval of post failed', 16, 1)
    ROLLBACK TRANSACTION ApprovePost
    RETURN 99
    END

COMMIT TRANSACTION ApprovePost
```

Implementing the Data Access Layer

Most of the DAL methods are simply wrappers for stored procedures, so they won't be covered here. The GetThreads method is interesting: It returns the list of threads for a specified forum (a page of the results), and it is passed the page index and the page size. It also takes the sort expression used to order the threads. The method uses SQL Server 2005's new ROW_NUMBER function to provide a unique auto-incrementing number to all rows in the table, sorted as specified, and then selects those rows with an index number between the lower and the upper bound of the specified page. The SQL code is very similar to the tbh_Articles_GetArticlesByCategory stored procedure developed for the articles module in Chapter 5. The only difference (other than having the SQL code in a C# class instead of inside a stored procedure) is the fact that the sorting expression expected by the ORDER BY clause is dynamically added to the SQL string, as specified by an input parameter. Here's the method, which is implemented in the MB.TheBeerHouse.DAL.SqlClient.SqlForumsProvider class:

```
public override List<PostDetails> GetThreads(
    int forumID, string sortExpression, int pageIndex, int pageSize)
{
    using (SqlConnection cn = new SqlConnection(this.ConnectionString))
    {
        sortExpression = EnsureValidSortExpression(sortExpression);
        int lowerBound = pageIndex * pageSize + 1;
        int upperBound = (pageIndex + 1) * pageSize;
        string sql = string.Format(@"
SELECT * FROM
(
    SELECT tbh_Posts.PostID, tbh_Posts.AddedDate, tbh_Posts.AddedBy,
    tbh_Posts.AddedByIP, tbh_Posts.ForumID, tbh_Posts.ParentPostID, tbh_Posts.Title,
    tbh_Posts.Approved, tbh_Posts.Closed, tbh_Posts.ViewCount, tbh_Posts.ReplyCount,
    tbh_Posts.LastPostDate, tbh_Posts.LastPostBy, tbh_Forums.Title AS ForumTitle,
    ROW_NUMBER() OVER (ORDER BY {0}) AS RowNum
    FROM tbh_Posts INNER JOIN tbh_Forums ON tbh_Posts.ForumID = tbh_Forums.ForumID
    WHERE tbh_Posts.ForumID = {1} AND ParentPostID = 0 AND Approved = 1
) ForumThreads
WHERE ForumThreads.RowNum BETWEEN {2} AND {3} ORDER BY RowNum ASC",
            sortExpression, forumID, lowerBound, upperBound);

        SqlCommand cmd = new SqlCommand(sql, cn);
        cn.Open();
        return GetPostCollectionFromReader(ExecuteReader(cmd), false);
    }
}
```

At the beginning of the preceding method's body, the sortExpression string is passed to a method named EnsureValidSortExpression (shown below), and its result is assigned back to the sortExpression variable. EnsureValidSortExpression, as its name clearly suggests, ensures that the input string is a valid sort expression that references a field in the tbh_Posts table, and not some illegitimate SQL substring used to perform a SQL injection attack. You should always do this kind of validation when building a dynamic SQL query by concatenating multiple strings coming from different sources (this is not necessary when using parameters, but unfortunately the ORDER BY clause doesn't support the use of parameters). Following is the method's implementation:

```
protected virtual string EnsureValidSortExpression(string sortExpression)
{
    if (string.IsNullOrEmpty(sortExpression))
        return "LastPostDate DESC";

    string sortExpr = sortExpression.ToLower();
    if (!sortExpr.Equals("lastpostdate") && !sortExpr.Equals("lastpostdate asc") &&
        !sortExpr.Equals("lastpostdate desc") && !sortExpr.Equals("viewcount") &&
        !sortExpr.Equals("viewcount asc") && !sortExpr.Equals("viewcount desc") &&
        !sortExpr.Equals("replycount") && !sortExpr.Equals("replycount asc") &&
        !sortExpr.Equals("replycount desc") && !sortExpr.Equals("addeddate") &&
```

```
                !sortExpr.Equals("addeddate asc") && !sortExpr.Equals("addeddate desc") &&
                !sortExpr.Equals("addedby") && !sortExpr.Equals("addedby asc") &&
                !sortExpr.Equals("addedby desc") && !sortExpr.Equals("title") &&
                !sortExpr.Equals("title asc") && !sortExpr.Equals("title desc") &&
                !sortExpr.Equals("lastpostby") && !sortExpr.Equals("lastpostby asc") &&
                !sortExpr.Equals("lastpostby desc"))
        {
            return "LastPostDate DESC";
        }
        else
        {
            if (sortExpr.StartsWith("title"))
                sortExpr = sortExpr.Replace("title", "tbh_posts.title");
            if (!sortExpr.StartsWith("lastpostdate"))
                sortExpr += ", LastPostDate DESC";
            return sortExpr;
        }
    }
```

As you see, if the `sortExpression` is null or an empty string, or if it doesn't reference a valid field, the method returns `"LastPostDate DESC"` as the default, which will sort the threads from the newest to the oldest.

Implementing the Business Logic Layer

As for the DAL, the BLL of this module is similar to those used in other chapters — Chapter 5 in particular. It employs the same patterns for retrieving and managing data by delegating the work to the respective DAL methods, for caching and purging data, for loading expensive and heavy data (such as the post's body) only when required, and so on. Here's the `GetThreads` method of the `MB.TheBeerHouse` `.BLL.Forums.Post` class:

```
public static List<Post> GetThreads(int forumID)
{
    return GetThreads(forumID, "", 0, BizObject.MAXROWS);
}

public static List<Post> GetThreads(
    int forumID, string sortExpression, int startRowIndex, int maximumRows)
{
    if (forumID < 1)
        return GetThreads(sortExpression, startRowIndex, maximumRows);

    List<Post> posts = null;
    string key = "Forums_Threads_" + forumID.ToString() + "_" + sortExpression +
        "_" + startRowIndex.ToString() + "_" + maximumRows.ToString();

    if (BaseForum.Settings.EnableCaching && BizObject.Cache[key] != null)
    {
        posts = (List<Post>)BizObject.Cache[key];
    }
    else
    {
```

```
        List<PostDetails> recordset = SiteProvider.Forums.GetThreads(forumID,
            sortExpression, GetPageIndex(startRowIndex, maximumRows), maximumRows);
        posts = GetPostListFromPostDetailsList(recordset);
        BaseForum.CacheData(key, posts);
    }
    return posts;
}
```

This method has two overloads: The first takes the ID of the forum for which you want to retrieve the list of threads; and the other also takes a sort expression string, the index of the first row to retrieve, and the number of rows you want to retrieve in the page of results. The first overload simply calls the second one by passing default values for the last three parameters. If the forumID is less than 1, the call is forwarded to yet another overload of GetThreads (not shown here) that retrieves the threads without considering their parent forum.

Pagination of items is also supported by the page showing all the posts of a thread, which are retrieved by the Post.GetThreadByID method, which in turn calls the tbh_Forums_GetThreadByID stored procedure by means of the DAL. However, the stored procedure doesn't support pagination, and it returns all the records — this is done because a user will typically read all of the thread, or most of it, so it makes sense to retrieve, and cache, all posts in a single step. The BLL method adds some logic to return a sublist of Post objects, according to the startRowIndex and maximumRows input parameters. Here's how it works:

```
public static List<Post> GetThreadByID(int threadPostID)
{
    return GetThreadByID(threadPostID, 0, BizObject.MAXROWS);
}
public static List<Post> GetThreadByID(int threadPostID,
    int startRowIndex, int maximumRows)
{
    List<Post> posts = null;
    string key = "Forums_Thread_" + threadPostID.ToString();

    if (BaseForum.Settings.EnableCaching && BizObject.Cache[key] != null)
    {
        posts = (List<Post>)BizObject.Cache[key];
    }
    else
    {
        List<PostDetails> recordset = SiteProvider.Forums.GetThreadByID(
            threadPostID);
        posts = GetPostListFromPostDetailsList(recordset);
        BaseForum.CacheData(key, posts);
    }

    int count = (posts.Count < startRowIndex + maximumRows ?
        posts.Count - startRowIndex : maximumRows);
    Post[] array = new Post[count];
    posts.CopyTo(startRowIndex, array, 0, count);
    return new List<Post>(array); ;
}
```

Implementing the User Interface

Before you start coding the user interface pages, you should modify the web.config file to add the necessary profile properties to the <profile> section. The required properties are AvatarUrl and Signature, both of type string, and a Posts property, of type integer, used to store the number of posts submitted by the user. They are used by authenticated users, and are defined within a Forum group, as shown below:

```
<profile defaultProvider="TBH_ProfileProvider">
    <providers>...</providers>
    <properties>
        <add name="FirstName" type="String" />
        <add name="LastName" type="String" />
        <!-- ...other properties here... -->
        <group name="Forum">
            <add name="Posts" type="Int32" />
            <add name="AvatarUrl" type="String" />
            <add name="Signature" type="String" />
        </group>
        <group name="Address">...</group>
        <group name="Contacts">...</group>
        <group name="Preferences">...</group>
    </properties>
</profile>
```

You must also change the UserProfile.ascx user control accordingly, so that it sets the new AvatarUrl and Signature properties (but not the Posts property, because it can only be set programmatically). This modification just needs a few lines of markup code in the .ascx file, and a couple of lines of C# code to read and set the properties, so I won't show them here. Once this "background work" is done, you can start creating the pages.

Administering and Viewing Forums

The definition of a subforum is almost identical to article categories employed in Chapter 5, with the unique addition of the Moderated field. The DAL and BLL code is similar to that developed earlier, but the UI for adding, updating, deleting, and listing forums is also quite similar. Therefore, I won't cover those pages here, but Figure 8-5 shows how they should look. As usual, consult the code download for the complete code.

The AddEditPost.aspx Page

This page has a simple interface, with a textbox for the new post's title, a FCKeditor instance to create the post's body with a limited set of HTML formatting, and a checkbox to indicate that you won't allow replies to the post (the checkbox is only visible when a user creates a new thread and is not replying to an existing thread, or the user is editing an existing post). Figure 8-6 shows how it is presented to the user who wants to create a new thread.

Figure 8-5

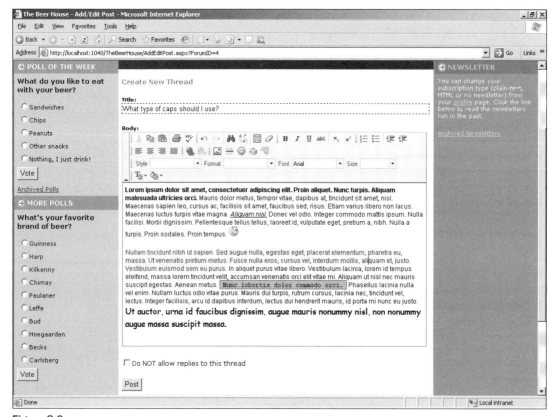

Figure 8-6

The page's markup is as simple, having only a few controls, so it's not shown here. The page's code-behind class defines a few private properties that store information retrieved from the querystring or calculate it:

```
private int forumID = 0;
private int threadID = 0;
private int postID = 0;
private int quotePostID = 0;
private bool isNewThread = false;
private bool isNewReply = false;
private bool isEditingPost = false;
```

Not all variables are used in every function of the page. The following list defines whether these variables are used, and how they are set for each function of the page:

❑   Creating a new thread:

  ❑   **forumID:** set with the ForumID querystring parameter

  ❑   **threadID:** not used

- ❏ **postID:** not used
- ❏ **quotePostID:** not used
- ❏ **isNewThread:** set to true
- ❏ **isNewReply:** set to false
- ❏ **isEditingPost:** set to false

❏ Posting a new reply to an existing thread:

- ❏ **forumID:** set with the ForumID querystring parameter
- ❏ **threadID:** set with the ThreadID querystring parameter, which is the ID of the target thread for the new reply
- ❏ **postID:** not used
- ❏ **quotePostID:** not used
- ❏ **isNewThread:** set to false
- ❏ **isNewReply:** set to true
- ❏ **isEditingPost:** set to false

❏ Quoting an existing post to be used as a base for a new reply to an existing thread:

- ❏ **forumID:** set with the ForumID querystring parameter
- ❏ **threadID:** set with the ThreadID querystring parameter
- ❏ **postID:** not used
- ❏ **quotePostID:** set with the QuotePostID querystring parameter, which is the ID of the post to quote
- ❏ **isNewThread:** set to false
- ❏ **isNewReply:** set to true
- ❏ **isEditingPost:** set to false

❏ Editing an existing post:

- ❏ **forumID:** set with the ForumID querystring parameter
- ❏ **threadID:** set with the ThreadID querystring parameter — necessary for linking back to the thread's page after submitting the change, or if the editor wants to cancel the editing and go back to the previous page
- ❏ **postID:** set with the PostID querystring parameter, which is the ID of the post to edit
- ❏ **quotePostID:** not used
- ❏ **isNewThread:** set to false
- ❏ **isNewReply:** set to false
- ❏ **isEditingPost:** set to true

The variables are set in the Page's Load event handler, which also has code that loads the body of the post to edit or quote, sets the link to go back to the previous page, and checks whether the current user is allowed to perform the requested function. Here's the code:

```csharp
protected void Page_Load(object sender, EventArgs e)
{
    // retrieve the querystring parameters
    forumID = int.Parse(this.Request.QueryString["ForumID"]);
    if (!string.IsNullOrEmpty(this.Request.QueryString["ThreadID"]))
    {
        threadID = int.Parse(this.Request.QueryString["ThreadID"]);
        if (!string.IsNullOrEmpty(this.Request.QueryString["QuotePostID"]))
        {
            quotePostID = int.Parse(this.Request.QueryString["QuotePostID"]);
        }
    }
    if (!string.IsNullOrEmpty(this.Request.QueryString["PostID"]))
    {
        postID = int.Parse(this.Request.QueryString["PostID"]);
    }

    isNewThread = (postID == 0 && threadID == 0);
    isEditingPost = (postID != 0);
    isNewReply = (!isNewThread && !isEditingPost);

    // show/hide controls, and load data according to the parameters above
    if (!this.IsPostBack)
    {
        bool isModerator = (this.User.IsInRole("Administrators") ||
            this.User.IsInRole("Editors") || this.User.IsInRole("Moderators"));

        lnkThreadList.NavigateUrl = string.Format(
          lnkThreadList.NavigateUrl, forumID);
        lnkThreadPage.NavigateUrl = string.Format(
            lnkThreadPage.NavigateUrl, threadID);
        txtBody.BasePath = this.BaseUrl + "FCKeditor/";
        chkClosed.Visible = isNewThread;

        if (isEditingPost)
        {
            // load the post to edit, and check that the current user has the
            // permission to do so
            Post post = Post.GetPostByID(postID);
            if (!isModerator &&
                !(this.User.Identity.IsAuthenticated &&
                this.User.Identity.Name.ToLower().Equals(post.AddedBy.ToLower()))))
                this.RequestLogin();

            lblEditPost.Visible = true;
            btnSubmit.Text = "Update";
            txtTitle.Text = post.Title;
            txtBody.Value = post.Body;
            panTitle.Visible = isModerator;
        }
        else if (isNewReply)
```

```
    {
        // check whether the thread the user is adding a reply to is still open
        Post post = Post.GetPostByID(threadID);
        if (post.Closed)
            throw new ApplicationException(
                "The thread you tried to reply to has been closed.");

        lblNewReply.Visible = true;
        txtTitle.Text = "Re: " + post.Title;
        lblNewReply.Text = string.Format(lblNewReply.Text, post.Title);
        // if the ID of a post to be quoted is passed on the querystring, load
        // that post and prefill the new reply's body with that post's body
        if (quotePostID > 0)
        {
            Post quotePost = Post.GetPostByID(quotePostID);
            txtBody.Value = string.Format(@"
<blockquote>
<hr noshade=""noshade"" size=""1"" />
<b>Originally posted by {0}</b><br /><br />
{1}
<hr noshade=""noshade"" size=""1"" />
</blockquote>", quotePost.AddedBy, quotePost.Body);
        }
    }
    else if (isNewThread)
    {
        lblNewThread.Visible = true;
        lnkThreadList.Visible = true;
        lnkThreadPage.Visible = false;
    }


    }
}
```

When the user clicks the Post button, the class fields discussed previously are used again to determine whether an `InsertPost` or an `UpdatePost` is required. When editing a post, a line is dynamically added at the end of the post's body to log the date and time of the update, and the editor's name. When the post is inserted, you must also check whether the target forum is moderated; and if it is, you can only pass `true` to the `InsertPost`'s `approved` parameter if the current user is a power user (administrator, editor, or moderator). After inserting the post, you also increment the author's `Posts` profile property. Here's the full code for the submit button's `OnClick` event handler:

```
protected void btnSubmit_Click(object sender, EventArgs e)
{
    if (isEditingPost)
    {
        // when editing a post, a line containing the current Date/Time and the
        // name of the user making the edit is added to the post's body so that
        // the operation gets logged
        string body = txtBody.Value;
        body += string.Format("<p>-- {0}: post edited by {1}.</p>",
            DateTime.Now.ToString(), this.User.Identity.Name);
        // edit an existing post
        Post.UpdatePost(postID, txtTitle.Text, body);
```

```
        panInput.Visible = false;
        panFeedback.Visible = true;
    }
    else
    {
        // insert the new post
        Post.InsertPost(forumID, threadID,
            txtTitle.Text, txtBody.Value, chkClosed.Checked);
        panInput.Visible = false;
        // increment the user's post counter
        this.Profile.Forum.Posts += 1;
        // show the confirmation message or the message saying that approval is
        // required, according to the target forum's Moderated property
        Forum forum = Forum.GetForumByID(forumID);
        if (forum.Moderated)
        {
            if (!this.User.IsInRole("Administrators") &&
                !this.User.IsInRole("Editors") &&
                !this.User.IsInRole("Moderators"))
                panApprovalRequired.Visible = true;
            else
                panFeedback.Visible = true;
        }
        else
        {
            panFeedback.Visible = true;
        }
    }
}
```

The ManageUnapprovedPosts.aspx Page

This page enables power users to see the list of messages waiting for approval for moderated forums, and allows them to review their content and then either approve or delete them. The page is pretty simple, as there's just a `GridView` that shows the title and a few other fields of the posts, without support for pagination or sorting. A screenshot is shown in Figure 8-7.

The code to manage this grid has a small peculiarity: When the editor clicks on the post's title to select the row and then load and review its full body, ideally we'd like to show the body along with the selected rows, instead of in a separate `DetailsView`, or even into a separate page. In more complex cases where you have to show a lot of details of the selected row, those are actually the best way to go, but in this case, we just have a single additional field to show when selecting the row, and I think that showing it in the row would make things easier and more intuitive for the editor. It would be great if the `GridView`'s `TemplateField` column had a `SelectedItemTemplate` section, like the `DataList` control, but unfortunately it doesn't. You could use a `DataList`, but then you'd have to replicate the grid's tabular structure by hand. The trick that enables us to use a custom template for the selected row in a `GridView` is to enable the edit mode for that row, and then use its `EditItemTemplate` to define its user interface for that mode. When the user clicks the post's title, this will put the row in edit mode (the `LinkButton`'s `CommandName` property will be set to `"Edit"`), and therefore the `EditItemTemplate` will be used. Of course, you are not forced to use input controls for the `EditItemTemplate`, and you can use other `Label` and read-only controls instead (exactly as you would do for a fictitious `SelectedItemTemplate` section, if it were supported). In practice, while the row will actually be in edit mode, it will look like it's in the selected mode. This is only possible when you don't need to support real editing for the row! The following code is an extract of the `GridView`'s definition, i.e., the declaration of the `TemplateField` column described here:

```
<asp:TemplateField HeaderText="Title" HeaderStyle-HorizontalAlign="Left">
    <ItemTemplate>
        <asp:LinkButton ID="lnkTitle" runat="server"
            Text='<%# Eval("Title") %>' CommandName="Edit" /><br />
        <small>by <asp:Label ID="lblAddedBy" runat="server"
            Text='<%# Eval("AddedBy") %>'></asp:Label></small>
    </ItemTemplate>
    <EditItemTemplate>
        <asp:Label ID="lblTitle" runat="server" Font-Bold="true"
            Text='<%# Eval("Title") %>' /><br />
        <small>by <asp:Label ID="lblAddedBy" runat="server"
            Text='<%# Eval("AddedBy") %>'></asp:Label><br /><br />
        <div style="border-top: dashed 1px;border-right: dashed 1px;">
            <asp:Label runat="server" ID="lblBody" Text='<%# Eval("Body") %>' />
        </div></small>
    </EditItemTemplate>
</asp:TemplateField>
```

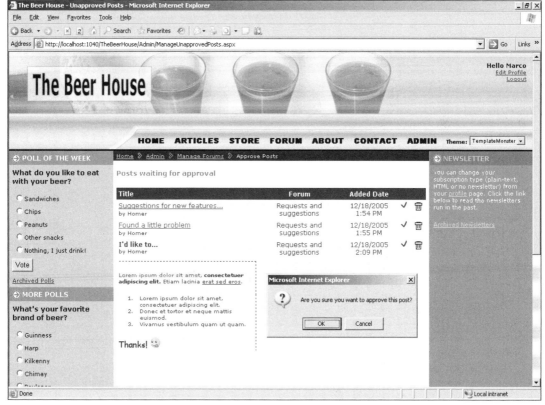

Figure 8-7

The BrowseThreads.aspx Page

This page takes a `ForumID` parameter on the querystring with the ID of the forum the user wants to browse, and fills a paginable `GridView` control with the thread list returned by the `Post.GetThreads` business method. Figure 8-8 shows a screenshot of this page.

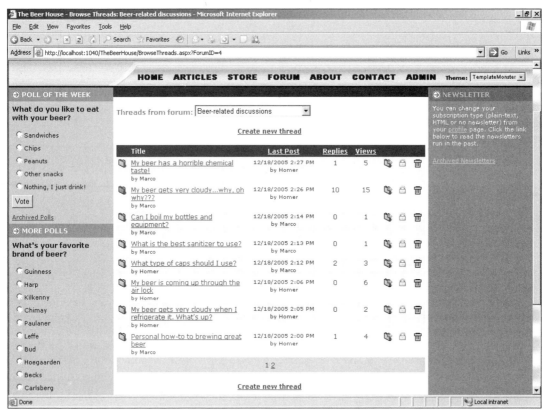

Figure 8-8

In addition to the `GridView` control with the threads, the page also features a `DropDownList` at the top of the page, which lists all available forums (retrieved by an `ObjectDataSource` that uses the `Forum.GetForums` business method) and allows users to quickly navigate to a forum by selecting one. The `DropDownList` `onchange` client-side (JavaScript) event redirects the user to the same `BrowseThreads.aspx` page, but with the newly selected forum's ID on the querystring:

```
<asp:DropDownList ID="ddlForums" runat="server" DataSourceID="objForums"
    DataTextField="Title" DataValueField="ID"
    onchange="javascript:document.location.href='BrowseThreads.aspx?ForumID=' +
this.value;" />
<asp:ObjectDataSource ID="objForums" runat="server" SelectMethod="GetForums"
    TypeName="MB.TheBeerHouse.BLL.Forums.Forum" />
```

The GridView is bound to another ObjectDataSource control, which specifies the methods to select and delete data. Because we want to support pagination, we use the GetThreadCount method to return the total thread count. To support sorting you must set SortParameterName to the name of the parameter that the SelectMethod (i.e., GetThreads) will use to receive the sort expression; in this case, as shown earlier, it's sortExpression. Here's the complete declaration of the ObjectDataSource:

```
<asp:ObjectDataSource ID="objThreads" runat="server"
    TypeName="MB.TheBeerHouse.BLL.Forums.Post"
    DeleteMethod="DeletePost" SelectMethod="GetThreads"
    SelectCountMethod="GetThreadCount"
    EnablePaging="true" SortParameterName="sortExpression">
    <DeleteParameters>
        <asp:Parameter Name="id" Type="Int32" />
    </DeleteParameters>
    <SelectParameters>
        <asp:QueryStringParameter Name="forumID"
            QueryStringField="ForumID" Type="Int32" />
    </SelectParameters>
</asp:ObjectDataSource>
```

The following GridView control has both the AllowPaging and AllowSorting properties set to true, and it defines the following columns:

❏ A TemplateColumn that displays an image representing a folder, which is used to identify a discussion thread. A templated column is used in place of a simpler ImageColumn, because the image being shown varies according to the number of posts in the thread. If the post count reaches a certain value (specified in the configuration), it will be considered a *hot thread,* and a red icon will be used to highlight it.

❏ A TemplateColumn defining a link to the ShowThread.aspx page on the first line, with the thread's title as the link's text, and the thread's author's name in smaller text on the second line. The link on the first line also includes the thread's ID on the querystring so that the page will load that specific thread's posts.

❏ A TemplateColumn that shows the date of the thread's last post on the first line, and the name of the author who entered the thread's last post on the second line. The column's SortExpression is LastPostDate.

❏ A BoundField column that shows the thread's ReplyCount, and has a header link that sorts threads on this column

❏ A BoundField column that shows the thread's ViewCount, and has a header link that sorts threads on this column

❏ A HyperLinkField column pointing to the MoveThread.aspx page, which takes the ID of the thread to move on the querystring. This column will not be shown if the current user is not a power user.

❏ A ButtonField column to close the thread and stop replies to it. This column will not be shown if the current user is not a power user.

❏ A ButtonField column to delete the thread with all its posts. This column will not be shown if the current user is not a power user.

Following is the complete markup code for the `GridView`:

```
<asp:GridView ID="gvwThreads" runat="server" AllowPaging="True"
   AutoGenerateColumns="False" DataSourceID="objThreads" PageSize="25"
   AllowSorting="True" DataKeyNames="ID" OnRowCommand="gvwThreads_RowCommand"
   OnRowCreated="gvwThreads_RowCreated">
   <Columns>
      <asp:TemplateField ItemStyle-Width="16px">
         <ItemTemplate>
            <asp:Image runat="server" ID="imgThread" ImageUrl="~/Images/Thread.gif"
               Visible='<%# (int)Eval("ReplyCount") <
                  Globals.Settings.Forums.HotThreadPosts %>'
               GenerateEmptyAlternateText="" />
            <asp:Image runat="server" ID="imgHotThread"
               ImageUrl="~/Images/ThreadHot.gif"
               Visible='<%# (int)Eval("ReplyCount") >=
                  Globals.Settings.Forums.HotThreadPosts %>'
               GenerateEmptyAlternateText="" />
         </ItemTemplate>
         <HeaderStyle HorizontalAlign="Left" />
      </asp:TemplateField>
      <asp:TemplateField HeaderText="Title">
         <ItemTemplate>
            <asp:HyperLink ID="lnkTitle" runat="server" Text='<%# Eval("Title") %>'
               NavigateUrl='<%# "ShowThread.aspx?ID=" + Eval("ID") %>' /><br />
            <small>by <asp:Label ID="lblAddedBy" runat="server"
               Text='<%# Eval("AddedBy") %>'></asp:Label></small>
         </ItemTemplate>
         <HeaderStyle HorizontalAlign="Left" />
      </asp:TemplateField>
      <asp:TemplateField HeaderText="Last Post" SortExpression="LastPostDate">
         <ItemTemplate>
            <small><asp:Label ID="lblLastPostDate" runat="server"
               Text='<%# Eval("LastPostDate", "{0:g}") %>'></asp:Label><br />
            by <asp:Label ID="lblLastPostBy" runat="server"
               Text='<%# Eval("LastPostBy") %>'></asp:Label></small>
         </ItemTemplate>
         <ItemStyle HorizontalAlign="Center" Width="130px" />
         <HeaderStyle HorizontalAlign="Center" />
      </asp:TemplateField>
      <asp:BoundField HeaderText="Replies" DataField="ReplyCount"
         SortExpression="ReplyCount" >
         <ItemStyle HorizontalAlign="Center" Width="50px" />
         <HeaderStyle HorizontalAlign="Center" />
      </asp:BoundField>
      <asp:BoundField HeaderText="Views" DataField="ViewCount"
         SortExpression="ViewCount" >
         <ItemStyle HorizontalAlign="Center" Width="50px" />
         <HeaderStyle HorizontalAlign="Center" />
      </asp:BoundField>
      <asp:HyperLinkField
         Text="<img border='0' src='Images/MoveThread.gif' alt='Move thread' />"
         DataNavigateUrlFormatString="~/Admin/MoveThread.aspx?ThreadID={0}"
         DataNavigateUrlFields="ID">
```

```
                <ItemStyle HorizontalAlign="Center" Width="20px" />
            </asp:HyperLinkField>
            <asp:ButtonField ButtonType="Image" ImageUrl="~/Images/LockSmall.gif"
                CommandName="Close">
                <ItemStyle HorizontalAlign="Center" Width="20px" />
            </asp:ButtonField>
            <asp:CommandField ButtonType="Image" DeleteImageUrl="~/Images/Delete.gif"
                DeleteText="Delete thread" ShowDeleteButton="True">
                <ItemStyle HorizontalAlign="Center" Width="20px" />
            </asp:CommandField>
        </Columns>
        <EmptyDataTemplate><b>No threads to show</b></EmptyDataTemplate>
    </asp:GridView>
```

There are just a few lines of code in the page's code-behind class. In the `Page_Init` event handler, you set the grid's `PageSize` to the value read from the configuration settings, overwriting the default hard-coded value used above:

```
protected void Page_Init(object sender, EventArgs e)
{
    gvwThreads.PageSize = Globals.Settings.Forums.ThreadsPageSize;
}
```

In the `Page_Load` event handler there's some simple code that uses the ID passed on the querystring to load a `Forum` object representing the forum: The forum's title read from the object is used to set the page's `Title`. Then the code preselects the current forum from the `DropDownList` at the top, sets the `ForumID` parameter on the hyperlinks that create a new thread, and hides the last three `GridView` columns if the current user is not a power user:

```
protected void Page_Load(object sender, EventArgs e)
{
    if (!this.IsPostBack)
    {
        string forumID = this.Request.QueryString["ForumID"];
        lnkNewThread1.NavigateUrl = string.Format(lnkNewThread1.NavigateUrl,
            forumID);
        lnkNewThread2.NavigateUrl = lnkNewThread1.NavigateUrl;

        Forum forum = Forum.GetForumByID(int.Parse(forumID));
        this.Title = string.Format(this.Title, forum.Title);
        ddlForums.SelectedValue = forumID;

        // if the user is not an admin, editor or moderator, hide the grid's column
        // with the commands to delete, close or move a thread
        bool canEdit = (this.User.Identity.IsAuthenticated &&
            (this.User.IsInRole("Administrators") || this.User.IsInRole("Editors") ||
             this.User.IsInRole("Moderators")));
        gvwThreads.Columns[5].Visible = canEdit;
        gvwThreads.Columns[6].Visible = canEdit;
        gvwThreads.Columns[7].Visible = canEdit;
    }
}
```

The click on the threads' Delete button is handled automatically by the GridView and its companion ObjectdataSource control. To make the Close button work, you have to manually handle the RowCommand event handler, and call the Post.CloseThread method, as shown here:

```
protected void gvwThreads_RowCommand(object sender, GridViewCommandEventArgs e)
{
    if (e.CommandName == "Close")
    {
        int threadPostID = Convert.ToInt32(
            gvwThreads.DataKeys[Convert.ToInt32(e.CommandArgument)][0]);
        MB.TheBeerHouse.BLL.Forums.Post.CloseThread(threadPostID);
    }
}
```

The MoveThread.aspx Page

This page contains a DropDownList with the list of available forums and allows power users to move the thread (whose ID is passed on the querystring) to one of the forums, after selecting it and clicking the OK button. Figure 8-9 shows this simple user interface.

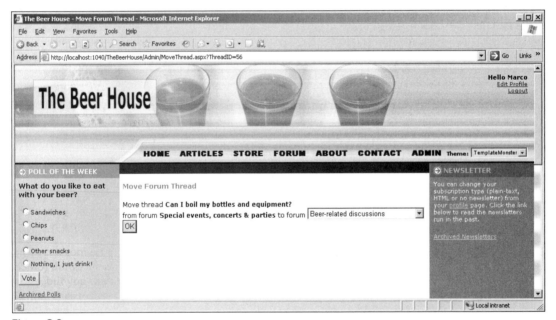

Figure 8-9

The code markup and C# code to fill the DropDownList and to preselect the current forum was already shown in the section describing BrowseThreads.aspx, which employs a very similar forum picker. When the OK button is clicked you just read the ID of the selected forum and call the Post.MoveThread method accordingly:

```
protected void btnSubmit_Click(object sender, EventArgs e)
{
    int forumID = int.Parse(ddlForums.SelectedValue);
    Post.MoveThread(threadID, forumID);
    this.Response.Redirect("~/BrowseThreads.aspx?ForumID=" + forumID.ToString());
}
```

The ShowThread.aspx Page

This page renders a paginable grid showing all posts of the thread, whose ID is passed on the querystring. Figure 8-10 shows this `GridView` in action.

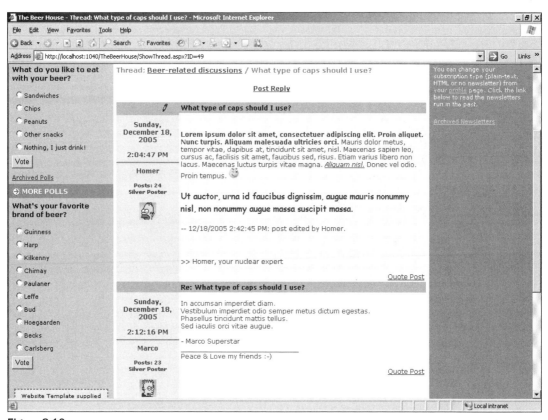

Figure 8-10

Some of the information (such as the post's title, body, author, and date/time) is retrieved from the bound data retrieved by the `GridView`'s companion `ObjectDataSource` (which uses `Post.GetThreadByID` as its `SelectMethod`, and `GetPostCountByThread` as its `SelectCountMethod` to support pagination). Some other data, such as the author's avatar, number of posts, and signature, are retrieved from the profile associated with the membership account named after the post author's name. The controls that show this profile data are bound to an expression that calls the `GetUserProfile` method, which takes the author's name and returns an instance of `ProfileCommon` for that user. Using the dynamically generated, strongly typed `ProfileCommon` object, you can easily reference the profile groups and subproperties. The following code declares the `GridView`'s first (of two) `TemplateField` column, which defines the links to edit and delete the post (these will be hidden by code in the code-behind if the current user should not see them), and then defines controls bound to the user's `Posts` and `AvatarUrl` profile properties:

```
<asp:TemplateField ItemStyle-Width="120px" ItemStyle-CssClass="postinfo">
    <ItemTemplate>
        <div class="posttitle" style="text-align:right;">
            <asp:HyperLink runat="server" ID="lnkEditPost"
                ImageUrl="~/Images/Edit.gif"
                NavigateUrl="~/AddEditPost.aspx?ForumID={0}&ThreadID={1}&PostID={2}" />
             
            <asp:ImageButton runat="server" ID="btnDeletePost"
                ImageUrl="~/Images/Delete.gif"
                OnClientClick="if (confirm('Are you sure you want to delete this {0}?')
== false) return false;"/>  
        </div>
        <asp:Literal ID="lblAddedDate" runat="server"
            Text='<%# Eval("AddedDate", "{0:D}<br/><br/>{0:T}") %>' /><hr />
        <asp:Literal ID="lblAddedBy" runat="server" Text='<%# Eval("AddedBy") %>' />
        <br /><br />
        <small><asp:Literal ID="lblPosts" runat="server"
            Text='<%# "Posts: " +
                GetUserProfile(Eval("AddedBy")).Forum.Posts.ToString() %>' />
        <asp:Literal ID="lblPosterDescription" runat="server"
            Text='<%# "<br />" +
                GetPosterDescription(GetUserProfile(Eval("AddedBy")).Forum.Posts) %>'
            Visible='<%# GetUserProfile(Eval("AddedBy")).Forum.Posts >=
                Globals.Settings.Forums.BronzePosterPosts %>'/></small><br /><br />
        <asp:Panel runat="server" ID="panAvatar" Visible='<%# GetUserProfile(
            Eval("AddedBy")).Forum.AvatarUrl.Length > 0 %>'>
        <asp:Image runat="server" ID="imgAvatar" ImageUrl='<%# GetUserProfile(
            Eval("AddedBy")).Forum.AvatarUrl %>' />
        </asp:Panel>
    </ItemTemplate>
</asp:TemplateField>
```

The second column renders the post's title, the body, and then the user's `Signature` profile property. Because the signature is in plain text, though, it first passes through a helper method named `ConvertToHtml`, which transforms the signature into simple HTML (it replaces carriage returns with `<br/>` tags, replaces multiple spaces and tabs with "` `", etc.). At the bottom it has a `HyperLink` to the `AddEditPost.aspx` page, which creates a new reply by quoting the current post's body:

```
<asp:TemplateField>
    <ItemTemplate>
        <div class="posttitle"><asp:Literal ID="lblTitle" runat="server"
            Text='<%# Eval("Title") %>' /></div>
        <div class="postbody">
            <asp:Literal ID="lblBody" runat="server" Text='<%# Eval("Body") %>' />
            <br /><br />
            <asp:Literal ID="lblSignature" runat="server"
                Text='<%# Helpers.ConvertToHtml(
```

```
                    GetUserProfile(Eval("AddedBy")).Forum.Signature) %>' /><br /><br />
          <div style="text-align: right;">
              <asp:HyperLink runat="server" ID="lnkQuotePost"
NavigateUrl="~/AddEditPost.aspx?ForumID={0}&ThreadID={1}&QuotePostID={2}">
Quote Post</asp:HyperLink>
          </div>
        </div>
    </ItemTemplate>
</asp:TemplateField>
```

There's some interesting code in the code-behind class: In the preceding code you can see that the GetUserProfile method is called six times for every single post. This can cause performance problems when you consider how many times this might execute in one page cycle. The same thread will likely have multiple posts by the same user: In a typical thread of 20 posts, four of them might be from the same user. This means we make 24 calls to GetUserProfile for the same user. This method uses ASP.NET's Profile.GetProfile method to retrieve a ProfileCommon object for the specified user, which unfortunately doesn't cache the result. This means that every time you call Profile.GetProfile, it will run a query to SQL Server to retrieve the user's profile, and then build the ProfileCommon object to be returned. In our situation, this would be an incredible waste of resources, because after the first query for a specific user, the next 23 queries for that user would produce the same result. To prevent this kind of waste, we'll use the GetUserProfile method to wrap the call to Profile.GetProfile by adding simple caching support that will last as long as the page's lifetime. It uses a Hashtable, which uses the username as a key, and the ProfileCommon object as the value; if the requested profile is not found in the Hashtable when the method is called, it forwards the call to Profile.GetProfile and then saves the result in the Hashtable for future needs. Here's how it's implemented:

```
Hashtable profiles = new Hashtable();

protected ProfileCommon GetUserProfile(object userName)
{
    string name = (string)userName;
    if (!profiles.Contains(name))
    {
        ProfileCommon profile = this.Profile.GetProfile(name);
        profiles.Add(name, profile);
        return profile;
    }
    else
        return profiles[userName] as ProfileCommon;
}
```

There's another helper method on the page, GetPosterDescription, which returns the user's status description according to the user's number of posts. It compares the number with the values of the GoldPosterPosts, SilverPosterPosts, and BronzePosterPosts configuration settings, and returns the appropriate description:

```
protected string GetPosterDescription(int posts)
{
    if (posts >= Globals.Settings.Forums.GoldPosterPosts)
        return Globals.Settings.Forums.GoldPosterDescription;
    else if (posts >= Globals.Settings.Forums.SilverPosterPosts)
        return Globals.Settings.Forums.SilverPosterDescription;
```

```
    if (posts >= Globals.Settings.Forums.BronzePosterPosts)
        return Globals.Settings.Forums.BronzePosterDescription;
    else
        return "";
}
```

The rest of the page's code-behind is pretty typical. For example, you handle the grid's RowDataBound event to show, or hide, the post's edit link according to whether the current user is the post's author or a power user, or just another user. It also sets the Delete button's CommandName property to DeleteThread or DeletePost, according to whether the post is the first post of the thread (and thus represents the whole thread) or not, and shows or hides the link to quote the post according to whether the thread is closed. The following code shows this:

```
protected void gvwPosts_RowDataBound(object sender, GridViewRowEventArgs e)
{
    if (e.Row.RowType == DataControlRowType.DataRow)
    {
        Post post = e.Row.DataItem as Post;
        int threadID = (post.IsFirstPost ? post.ID : post.ParentPostID);

        // the link for editing the post is visible to the post's author, and to
        // administrators, editors and moderators
        HyperLink lnkEditPost = e.Row.FindControl("lnkEditPost") as HyperLink;
        lnkEditPost.NavigateUrl = string.Format(lnkEditPost.NavigateUrl,
            post.ForumID, threadID, post.ID);
        lnkEditPost.Visible = (this.User.Identity.IsAuthenticated &&
            (this.User.Identity.Name.ToLower().Equals(post.AddedBy.ToLower()) ||
            (this.User.IsInRole("Administrators") || this.User.IsInRole("Editors") ||
            this.User.IsInRole("Moderators")))));

        // the link for deleting the thread/post is visible only to administrators,
        // editors and moderators
        ImageButton btnDeletePost = e.Row.FindControl(
            "btnDeletePost") as ImageButton;
        btnDeletePost.OnClientClick = string.Format(btnDeletePost.OnClientClick,
            post.IsFirstPost ? "entire thread" : "post");
        btnDeletePost.CommandName = (post.IsFirstPost ?
            "DeleteThread" : "DeletePost");
        btnDeletePost.CommandArgument = post.ID.ToString();
        btnDeletePost.Visible = (this.User.IsInRole("Administrators") ||
            this.User.IsInRole("Editors") || this.User.IsInRole("Moderators"));

        // if the thread is not closed, show the link to quote the post
        HyperLink lnkQuotePost = e.Row.FindControl("lnkQuotePost") as HyperLink;
        lnkQuotePost.NavigateUrl = string.Format(lnkQuotePost.NavigateUrl,
            post.ForumID, threadID, post.ID);
        lnkQuotePost.Visible = !(post.IsFirstPost ?
            post.Closed : post.ParentPost.Closed);
    }
}
```

You also handle the grid's RowCommand event to process the click action of the post's Delete button. You always call Post.DeletePost to delete a single post, or an entire thread (the situation is indicated by the CommandName property of the method's e parameter), but in the first case you just rebind the GridView to its data source, whereas in the second case you redirect to the page that browses the thread's parent forum's threads after deleting it:

```
protected void gvwPosts_RowCommand(object sender, GridViewCommandEventArgs e)
{
    if (e.CommandName == "DeleteThread")
    {
        int threadPostID = Convert.ToInt32(e.CommandArgument);
        int forumID = Post.GetPostByID(threadPostID).ID;
        Post.DeletePost(threadPostID);
        this.Response.Redirect("BrowseThreads.aspx?ForumID=" + forumID.ToString());
    }
    else if (e.CommandName == "DeletePost")
    {
        int postID = Convert.ToInt32(e.CommandArgument);
        Post.DeletePost(postID);
        gvwPosts.PageIndex = 0;
        gvwPosts.DataBind();
    }
}
```

Producing and Consuming RSS Feeds

The forums module includes the GetThreadsRss.aspx page, which returns an RSS feed of the forums' threads, either for a single subforum or for all subforums, depending on whether a ForumID parameter is passed on the querystring or not. It also supports a SortExpr parameter that specifies one of the supported sort expressions, such as "LastPostDate DESC" (the default), "ReplyCount DESC", etc. The page's markup uses a Repeater control to define the XML template of the RSS feed, and then binds to the thread list retrieved by calling the Post.GetThreads business method. This same technique has already been used for the GetArticlesRss.aspx page in Chapter 5. As usual, the code download for this book has the complete implementation for this page, and all the other pages.

Once you have the page working, you can use the generic RssReader.ascx user control (developed in Chapter 5) to consume some feeds, and therefore publish the list of threads (sorted in different ways) on various parts of the site. I've added two feeds on the ShowForums.aspx page, to show the list of "*n*" newest threads, and the "*n*" threads with the most replies (where "*n*" is specified in the web.config file), but you can also easily add them to the site's home page or to any other page you wish. Here's the code to consume the two feeds:

```
<table width="100%" cellpadding="4" cellspacing="0">
    <tr>
        <td width="50%">
            <div style="border-right: solid 1px;">
            <mb:RssReader id="rssLatestThreads" runat="server" Title="Latest Threads"
                RssUrl="~/GetThreadsRss.aspx?SortExpr=LastPostDate DESC" />
            </div>
        </td>
        <td width="50%">
            <mb:RssReader id="rssMostActiveThreads" runat="server"
                Title="Most Active Threads"
                RssUrl="~/GetThreadsRss.aspx?SortExpr=ReplyCount DESC" />
        </td>
    </tr>
</table>
```

Figure 8-11 shows a screenshot of the two lists.

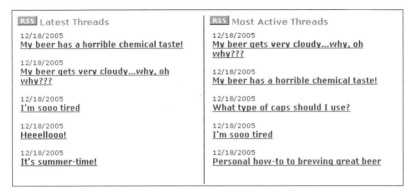

Figure 8-11

Securing the Forum Module

While developing the pages, we've already inserted many checks to ensure that only certain users can perform actions such as closing, moving, deleting, and editing posts. Programmatic security is required in some circumstances, but in other cases it suffices to use declarative security to allow or deny access to a resource by a given user or role. For example, the AddEditPost.aspx page must never be accessed by anonymous users in this implementation, and you can easily enforce this restriction by adding a declaration to the web.config file found in the site's root folder: You just need to add a new <location> section with a few <allow> and <deny> elements. There's one other aspect of the AddEditPost.aspx page that should be considered: If a member doesn't respect the site's policies, and repeatedly submits messages with spam or offensive language, then we'd like to be able to ban the member from adding any new posts. One way to do this is to block messages coming from that IP address, but it's even better to block that user account from accessing this page. However, we don't want to block that account completely; otherwise, that member would lose access to any other section of the site, which would be too restrictive for that particular crime! The easiest way to handle this is to add a new role called "Posters" to all new users at registration time, and then add a declarative restriction to web.config that ensures that only users who belong to the Administrators, Editors, Moderators, or Posters role can access the AddEditPost.aspx page, as shown below:

```
<location path="AddEditPost.aspx">
    <system.web>
        <authorization>
            <allow roles="Administrators,Editors,Moderators,Posters" />
            <deny users="*"/>
        </authorization>
    </system.web>
</location>
```

To automatically add a user to the Posters role immediately after the user has registered, you must modify the Register.aspx page developed in Chapter 4 to handle the CreateUserWizard's CreatedUser event (which is raised just after the user has been created), and then call the AddUserToRole method of ASP.NET's Roles class, as shown below:

```
protected void CreateUserWizard1_CreatedUser(object sender, EventArgs e)
{
    Roles.AddUserToRole(CreateUserWizard1.UserName, "Posters");
}
```

In the future, if you want to remove a given user's right to post new messages, you only need to remove the user from the `Posters` role, using the `EditUser.aspx` administration page developed in Chapter 4. This module's administration page also has some `<location>` section restrictions in the `web.config` file located under the `Admin` folder to ensure that only Administrators, Editors, and Moderators can access them.

Summary

In this chapter we've built a forums system from scratch, and we did it by leveraging much of the work done in earlier chapters, and many of the new features in ASP.NET 2.0. This was a further example showing how to integrate the built-in membership and profile systems into a custom module, as well as reusing other pages and controls (such as the `RssReader` control) developed previously. Our forums module supports multiple subforums, with optional moderation; it lists threads and replies through custom pagination (with different sorting options), offers support for publishing and consuming standard RSS feeds, and extends the user profiles with forum-specific properties. We also created administration features for deleting, editing, approving, moving, and closing threads and posts. This is a fairly complete forums module that should work well with many small to mid-size sites. However, the subject of user forums in general is a big area, and there are many possible options and features that you might want to consider adding to your forums module. Here are a few suggestions to get you started:

❑ Add support for some open forums, as a subforum-level option, which would be accessible by anonymous posters.

❑ Allow some subforums to have different moderators for more granular security control (especially useful for larger sites that may have multiple moderators who specialize in certain subforums).

❑ Add e-mail notification of new forum activity, or you can even send out e-mail message digests. E-mails could also be used by moderators to be notified about new messages waiting to be approved, and you might even allow the moderator to approve a message simply by clicking a link contained in the e-mail, after reviewing the post's body, also included in the e-mail.

❑ Support a list of banned words, and use regular expressions to replace them with acceptable alternatives, or maybe just a generic "###" pattern. Or, you can just tag offending messages for moderation, even if the forum is not a moderated forum (would require a little more work on the plumbing).

❑ Add private forums, whereby members can send each other messages, but each member can only read messages that were specifically addressed to them. This is a handy way to encourage people to communicate with each other, while allowing them to keep their own personal e-mail address hidden from other users (which is often desirable as a means of limiting spam). To make this easier to use, whenever you see the username of someone who posted a message in a forum, that username could have a link to another page that gives you the option to send that user a private message. To ensure that she will read your message, you could add an automatic check for private messages that would occur each time a registered user logs in.

❏ Implement a search feature to enable users to locate messages containing certain words or phrases.

❏ Let members upload their own attachments, which would be accessed from a link in a forum message (be sure to make this an option, because some site owners may not like this idea for security and bandwidth reasons). You could allow configurable filename extensions (disallowing .exe, .bat, .vbs, etc., but allowing .doc, .txt, etc.), and a configurable limit on allowable file size. You might also want to force any messages containing an attachment to be moderated so a power user can review the attachment before allowing it (this is especially important if you want to allow images to be uploaded).

There are numerous very complex and complete forums systems for ASP.NET, and many of them are free. You might want to use one of them if the simple forums module presented here doesn't meet your needs, or you might just want to study the others to get ideas for features you might want to add to your own forum module. One of the best, and most feature-rich, forums modules for ASP.NET is the Community Server, available at www.communityserver.org. This is 100% free for non-profit sites, and fairly inexpensive for use on commercial sites. This is the same forums module used by the famous www.asp.net site, Microsoft's official ASP.NET developer site. But don't be too quick to discard the forums module developed in this chapter, because even though it's missing some of the more advanced features, it still has several big benefits, including the fact that it's already integrated with the site's common layout and membership system (while others do not, unless you modify them, as they need to be installed on a separate virtual folder that makes it more difficult to share pieces of the parent site); it uses many of the new features in ASP.NET 2.0; and it is fairly easy to maintain and understand.

In the next chapter we'll implement another common requirement in a modern, full-featured web site: an e-commerce store with support for real-time electronic payments.

E-commerce Store

In this chapter we'll implement a working e-commerce store for TheBeerHouse, to enable users to shop for mugs, T-shirts, and other gadgets for beer-fanatics. This again gives us the opportunity to implement a good DAL and BLL that wraps and abstracts the database objects, a rich user interface that heavily leverages some new ASP.NET 2.0 controls such as `Wizard`, `MultiView`, and the `GridView` and `DetailsView` we've already used in other chapters. We'll also drill down into e-commerce-specific design and coding issues as we implement a persistent shopping cart, and we'll integrate a third-party payment processor service to support real-time credit card transactions. At the end of the chapter you'll have a complete e-commerce module that you can easily adapt to suit your own needs.

Problem

Let's assume the site's owner wants you to implement some features to help him turn the site into a profit-making enterprise. There are a number of ways to do this: Some sites gain revenue from renting advertising space (boxes and banners), some sell subscription-based access to their special content (articles, support forums, downloads, etc.), and some set up an e-commerce store for selling goods online. This chapter covers the design and implementation of an e-commerce store — this option was chosen for our demo web site because it's a good example of non-trivial design and coding, and it gives you a chance to examine some additional ASP.NET 2.0 technology in a real-world scenario. In addition, it is much more common for small sites to sell products, rather than ads and articles, unless they are extremely popular and active (ad revenue is small until your hit and click-through counts get pretty high). Building an e-commerce store from scratch is one of the most difficult jobs for a web developer, and it requires a good design up-front. It's not just a matter of building the site to handle the catalog, the orders, and the payments; a complete business analysis is required. You must identify your audience (potential customers), your competitors, a marketing strategy to promote your site, marketing offers to convince people to shop on your site rather than somewhere else, and plan for offers and other incentives to turn an occasional buyer into a repeat buyer. You also need to arrange a supplier for products that you can sell (in case the site's owner is not producing them herself), which involves the order management and shipping functions, and some consideration of local laws (licenses, tax collection, etc.). All of this could require a considerable amount of time, energy, and money, unless the site owner is already running some kind of physical store that they merely want to extend. In our case, we assume our sample site will be used by pubs that already have the business knowledge needed to answer the marketing-related questions, and we'll focus on the technical side of this project (a reasonable assumption because we are software developers and not marketing specialists).

For our sample project, let's say that the owner of TheBeerHouse wants to add an electronic store to the site — to sell beer glasses, T-shirts, key chains, and other gift items for beer enthusiasts. She needs the capability to create an online catalog that lists products divided into categories, one that provides a detailed and appealing description for each product, has pictures of products, and allows users to add them to an electronic shopping cart and pay for them online using a credit card (with a possible option of letting users phone in their orders in case they don't want to divulge their credit card information online). The owner needs the capability to run special promotions by setting up discounts for certain products, and to offer multiple shipping options at different prices. All this must be easily maintainable by the store keeper herself, without routine technical assistance, so we must also provide a very complete and intuitive administrative user interface. Finally, she also needs some kind of order reporting page that retrieves and lists the latest orders, the orders with a specific status (completed orders, orders that were confirmed but not yet processed, etc.) or orders for a specific customer. It should also enable her to change the order status, the shipment date, and the shipment tracking information, and, of course, see all order details, such as the customer's full address and contact information. In the next section you'll find a detailed list of requirements and features to be implemented.

Design

As you can gather from the "Problem" section above, implementing a custom e-commerce module can easily be a big challenge, and entire books have been devoted to this subject. With this in mind, and because of space constraints, this is the only chapter to cover this subject, so I've had to examine the feature set and select the basic and most common features that any such store must have. Although this module won't compete with sites like Amazon.com in terms of features, it will be complete enough to actually run a real, albeit small, e-store. As we've done in other chapters, we'll leverage much of the other functionality already developed, such as membership and profile management (Chapter 4), and our general DAL/BLL design, transaction management, and logging (Chapter 3). Therefore, the following list specifies the new functionality we'll implement in this chapter:

❑ Support for multiple store departments, used to categorize products so that they're easy to find if the catalog has a lot of items

❑ Products need a description with support for rich formatting, and images to graphically represent them. Because customers can't hold the product in their own hands, any written details and visual aids will help them understand the product, and may lead to a sale. A small thumbnail image will be shown in the products listing and on the product page, while a bigger image can be shown when the user clicks on the small image to zoom in.

❑ Products will support a discount percentage that the storekeeper will set when she wants to run a promotion for that item. The customer will still see the full price on the product page, along with the discount percentage (so that she can "appreciate" the sale, and feel compelled to order the product), and the final price that she will pay to buy the product.

❑   As we've already done for the articles and forums modules, this module will also expose an RSS feed for the products catalog, which can be consumed on the home page of the site itself, or by external RSS readers set up by customers who want to be notified about new products.

❑   Some simple stock availability management will be needed, such as the possibility to specify how many units of a particular item are in stock. This value will be decreased every time someone confirms an order for that product, and the storekeeper will be able to see which products need to be re-ordered (i.e., when there are only a few units left in stock).

❑   The storekeeper will be able to easily add, remove, and edit shipping methods, such as Standard Ground, Next Business Day, and Overnight, each with a different price. Customers will be able to specify a preferred shipping option when completing the order.

❑   The module needs a persistent shopping cart for items that the customer wants to purchase. Making it persistent means that the user can place some items in the shopping cart, close the browser and end her session, and come back to the site later and still find her shopping cart as she left it, so that she doesn't need to browse the entire catalog again to find the products she previously put in the cart. The customer may want time to consider the purchase before submitting it, she may want to compare your price with competitors first, or she may not have her credit card with her in that moment, so it's helpful for users to be able to put items in the cart and come back later to finalize the deal.

❑   The current content of the shopping cart (the names of the items that were put inside it, as well as their quantity and unit price) and the subtotal should be always visible on each page of the catalog, and possibly on the entire site, so that the user can easily keep it in mind (you want it to be easy for them to check out when they are ready, and you don't want them to forget to check out).

❑   A user account is required to complete the order, because you'll need some way to identify users when they come back to the site after submitting the order, to see the status of their order. However, a well-designed e-commerce module should not ask users to log in or create a user account until it actually requires it, to ease the shopping process. If a new user is asked to create an account (and thus fill up a long form, providing personal information, etc.) before even beginning to shop, this may be a bother and prevent visitors from even looking at your products. If, instead, you allow visitors to browse for products, add them to a shopping cart, and only ask them to log in or create a new account just before confirming the order, they'll consider this request as a normal step of the checkout process, and won't complain about it (and you've already hooked them into putting items in their cart).

❑   To make the checkout process as smooth as possible, the shipping address information should be pre-filled with the address stored in the user's profile, if found (remember that those details were optional at registration time). However, the shipping address may be different from the customer's address (possibly because the purchase is a gift for someone else), and thus the address may be edited for any order. The profile address should only be used as the default value. The billing address may be different also, but that will be collected by the payment processor service (more details later).

❑   The storekeeper must have a page that lists the orders of any specific interval of dates, using the last "n" days as a default interval ("n" is configurable in the default web.config file). She may also need to retrieve all orders for a specific customer, or jump directly to a particular order if she already knows its ID. The list will show a few order details, while a separate page will show the complete information, including the list of items ordered, the customer's contact information, and the shipping address. Besides this read-only history data, the storekeeper must be able to edit the order's status (the number and title of order statuses must also be customizable by the store's administrator), the shipping date, and optionally the transaction ID and tracking ID (if tracking is available by the shipping method chosen by the customer during checkout).

As anticipated, you may want, or need, to add many additional features. However, the features in the preceding list will give you a basic starting point with a working solution. In the following sections, you'll read more about some e-commerce-specific issues, such as choosing a service for real-time credit card processing, and then you'll create the typical design of the DAL, BLL, and UI parts of the module.

Choosing an Online Payment Solution

The user has visited your site, browsed the catalog, read the description of some products, and put them into the shopping cart. She finally decides that the prices and conditions are good, and wants to finalize the order. This means providing her personal information (name, contact details, and shipping address) and, of course, paying by credit card. You should plan for, and offer, as many payment solutions as you can, to satisfy all types of customers. Some prefer to send a check via snail mail, others prefer to provide the credit card information by fax or phone, and others are fine with paying via their credit card online. The best option for the storekeeper is, of course, the online transaction, as it is the most secure (information is encrypted and no physical person sees it), it gives immediate feedback to the user, and it doesn't require the storekeeper to do anything. Several third-party services, called *payment gateways,* provide this service. They receive some order details, perform a secure transaction for the customer, and keep a small fee for each order — typically a percentage of the transaction amount, but it may also be a fixed fee, or possibly a combination of the two. You can integrate your site with these services in one of two ways:

1. The customer clicks the button on your site to confirm the order and pays for it. At this point the user is redirected to the external site of the payment gateway. That site will ask your customer for her billing information (name, address, and credit card number) and will execute the transaction. The gateway's site resides on a secure server, i.e., a server where the SSL protocol is used to encrypt the data sent between the customer's browser and the server. After the payment, the customer is redirected back to your site. The process is depicted in Figure 9-1.

   The Secure Sockets Layer (SSL) is a secure web protocol that encrypts all data between a web server and a user's computer to prevent anyone else from knowing what information was sent over that connection. SSL certificates are used on web servers and are issued by third-party certificate authorities (CA), which guarantee to the customer that the site they're shopping at really has the identity they declare. A customer can identify the use of SSL by the presence of "https:" instead of "http:" in the URL, and by the padlock icon typically shown in the browser's status bar. To learn more about SSL, you can search on Google or visit the web sites of CAs such as VeriSign, Thawte, GeoTrust, or Comodo.

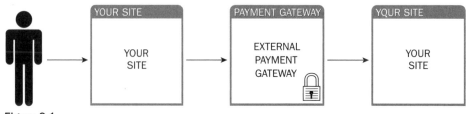

Figure 9-1

Our store's checkout page sends the payment gateway's page the amount to charge, the recipient account where it should place the money, the currency, and the URL where the customer will be redirected in case of a successful or cancelled order, using an HTML form that posts the data contained in a few hidden fields. The form below is an example:

```
<form method="post" action="https://payment_gateway_url_here">
    <input type="hidden" name="LoginName" value="THEBEERHOUSE">
    <input type="hidden" name="OrderAmount" value="46.50 ">
    <input type="hidden" name="OrderCurrency" value="USD">
    <input type="hidden" name="OrderID" value="#12345">
    <input type="hidden" name="OrderDescription" value="Beer Glass #2 (4 pieces)"
    <input type="hidden" name="ConfirmUrl"
        value="http://www.yoursite.com/order_ok.aspx">
    <input type="hidden" name="CancelUrl"
        value="http://www.yoursite.com/order_ko.aspx">
    <input type="submit" value="CLICK HERE TO PAY NOW!">
</form>
```

Every payment gateway has its own parameters, with different names, and accepts data following their own conventions, but the overall principle is the same for all of them. Many gateways also accept the expected parameters through a GET request instead of a POST, which means that parameters are passed on the querystring: In this case you can build the complete URL on your site, possibly from within the Click event handler of your ASP.NET form's Submit button, and then redirect the customer to it (but this method is less desirable because the query string is visible). Most of the information you pass to the gateway is also forwarded to the store site once the customer comes back to it, either in the "Order Confirmed" or the "Order Cancelled" page, so that the original order is recognized (by means of its ID) and the record representing it in your database is updated with the appropriate status code. Some payment gateway services encrypt the data they send to you and give you a private key used to decrypt the data, so that you can ensure that the customer did not manually jump directly to your order finalization page. Others use different mechanisms, but you always have some way to be notified whether payment was made (despite this automatic notification, it would be wise to validate that the payment was actually processed to ensure that a hacker has not tried to give us a false indication that a payment was made). The advantage of using an external payment service is its ease of integration and management. You only forward the user to the external gateway (to a URL built according the gateway's specifications guide), and handle the customer's return after she has paid for the order, or cancelled it. You don't have to deal with the actual money transaction, nor do you have to worry about the security of the transaction, which would at least imply setting up SSL on your site, and you don't have to worry about keeping the customer's credit card information stored in a safe manner and complying with privacy laws (if you only keep the customer's name and address you don't have to worry about the kinds of laws that protect account numbers). The disadvantage, however, is that the customer actually leaves your site for the payment process, which may be disorienting and inconvenient. While it's true that most payment gateway services allow the site's owner/developer to change their payment page's colors and insert the store's logo inside it, the customization often does not go much further, so the difference between the store's pages and the external payment page will be evident. This would not be a problem if you've just created and launched an e-commerce site that nobody knows and trusts. A customer may be more inclined to leave her credit card information on the site of a well-known payment gateway, instead of on your lesser known site. In that case, the visibility of the external payment service may actually help sales. For larger e-commerce sites that already have a strong reputation and are trusted by a large audience, this approach won't be as appealing, as it looks less professional than complete integration.

2. The second approach to handling online payments also relies on an external payment gateway, but instead of physically moving the user to the external site and then bringing her back to the our site, she never leaves our site in the first place: She enters all her billing and credit card information on our page, which we then pass to the external service behind the scenes (and we don't store it within our own system). The gateway will finally return a response code that indicates the transaction's success or failure (plus some additional information such as the transaction ID), and you can display some feedback to the user on your page. This approach is depicted in Figure 9-2.

The manner in which your page communicates and exchanges data with the gateway service may be a web service or some other simpler server-to-server technology, such as programmatically submitting a POST request with the System.Net.HttpWebRequest class of the .NET Framework, and handling the textual response (usually a simple string with some code indicating success or failure). The obvious advantage of this approach is that the customer stays at your site for the entire process, so that all the pages have the same look and feel, which you can customize as you prefer, and you don't need to worry about fake or customer-generated confirmation requests from the payment gateway, because everything happens from server-to-server during a single postback. The disadvantages of this approach are that you're in charge of securing the transmission of sensitive information from the customer's browser to your site (even though you don't store the info, it will still be transferred to and from your web server), by installing a SSL certificate on your server, and using https to access your own checkout pages. If credit card information is hijacked somehow during the transmission, or if you don't comply with all the necessary security standards, you may get into big legal troubles, and you may lose all your other customers if they hear about the problem. Another disadvantage is that if your site is small and unknown, then some customers may be reluctant to give you their credit card number, something they would feel comfortable doing with a large and well-known credit card processing service.

Figure 9-2

It should be clear by now which of the two approaches you may prefer, and this will be influenced by the size of the store, its transaction volume, its popularity among the customers, and how much money the store owner wants to invest. Implementing the second approach requires buying and installing a SSL certificate (or arranging to share one via your hosting company), it leaves more responsibilities to both you and the store's owner, and it requires longer development and implementation, so one might choose the first approach, which is simpler, more cost effective, and still very good for small sites. Conversely, if you're implementing a new e-commerce storefront for a large site that is already selling online and is very popular, then the complete integration of the payment process into the store is definitely the best and most professional option.

For the e-commerce store of TheBeerHouse, we'll follow the simpler approach and implement a payment solution that forwards the customer to the external payment service's page. As the store grows, you may wish to upgrade the site to use a fully integrated payment mechanism in the future.

There are many payment services to choose from, but some of them can only be used in one country, or may only accept a small variety of credit cards. Because I wanted to implement a solution that could work for as many readers as possible, and be simple to integrate with, I selected PayPal. PayPal is widely known as the main service used by eBay, and they accept many popular credit cards and work in many countries.

Using PayPal as the Payment Service

PayPal started as a service that enabled people to exchange money from one user's account to another, or to have payment sent to the user's home in the form of a check, but it has grown into a full-featured payment service that is used by a huge number of merchants worldwide as their favorite payment method, for a number of reasons:

❏ Competitive transaction fees, which are lower than most payment gateways.

❏ Great recognition among customers worldwide. At the time of writing, it reports more than 86 million registered users. Much of their popularity stems from their relationship with eBay, but PayPal is definitely not restricted to use within eBay.

❏ It is available to 56 countries, and it supports multiple languages and multiple currencies.

❏ It supports taking orders via phone, fax, or mail, and processes credit cards from a management console called Virtual Terminal (available to the U.S. only).

❏ Support for automated recurring payments, which is useful for sites that offer subscription-based access to their content, and need to bill their members regularly — on a monthly basis, for example.

❏ Easy integration. Just create an HTML form with the proper parameters to redirect the customer to the payment page, and specify the return URL for confirmed and cancelled payments.

❏ For businesses located in the U.S. that demand more flexibility and greater integration, PayPal also exposes web services for implementing hidden server-to-server communication (the second approach described above).

❏ Almost immediate setup. However, your store needs to use a validated PayPal account, which requires a simple process whereby they can send a small deposit to your linked bank account, and you verify the amount and date of the transfer. This validation step is simple, but necessary to prove that the electronic transfer works with your bank account, and it proves your identity.

❏ It has some good customization options, such as changing the payment pages' colors and logo, so that it integrates, at least partially, with your site's style.

❏ It offers complete control over which customers can make a purchase (for example, only U.S. customers with a verified address) and enables merchants to set up different tax and shipping amounts for different countries and states.

Choosing PayPal as the payment processor for TheBeerHouse allows us to start with its Website Payments Standard option (the HTML form that redirects the customer to the PayPal's pages) and later upgrade to Website Payments Pro if you want to completely integrate the payment process into your site, hiding PayPal from the customer's eyes. All in all, it offers a lot of options for flexibility, as well as support and detailed guides for merchants and developers who want to use it. I'll outline a few steps for setting up the PayPal integration here. See the official documentation at `www.paypal.com` and `http://developer.paypal.com` for further details and examples. Even without prior knowledge of PayPal, it's still trivial to set up, and it works well.

Of special interest for developers is the Sandbox, a complete replication of PayPal used for development and testing of systems that interact with PayPal (including all the administrative and management pages, where you configure all types of settings). This test environment doesn't make real transactions, but works with test credit card numbers and accounts. Developers can create an account for free (on `developer.paypal.com`), and then create PayPal test business accounts for use within the Sandbox. These test accounts can then be used as the recipient for sample transactions. You only need to know a few basic parameters, described in the following table:

Property	Description
cmd	Specifies in which mode you're using PayPal's pages. A value equal to _xclick specifies that you're using the Pay Now mode, whereby the customer lands on the PayPal's checkout page, types in her billing details, and completes the order. If the value is _cart, then you'll be using PayPal's integrated shopping cart, which allows users to keep going back and forth from your store site to PayPal to add multiple items to a cart managed by PayPal, until the customer wants to check out. In our case, we'll be implementing our own shopping cart, and only use PayPal only for the final processing, so the _xclick value will be used.
upload	A value of 1 indicates that we're using our own shopping cart.
currency_code	Specifies the currency in which the other amount parameters (see below) are denoted. If not specified, the default value is USD (United States Dollar). Other possible values are AUD (Australian Dollar), CAD (Canadian Dollar), EUR (Euro), GBP (Pound Sterling), and JPY (Japanese Yen). We'll allow our site administrator to configure this setting.
business	The e-mail address that identifies the PayPal business account that will be the recipient for the transaction. For example, I've created the account `thebeer house@wrox.com` through the Sandbox, to use for my tests. You should create a Sandbox account of your own for testing.
item_number	A number/string identifying the order
custom	A custom variable that can contain anything you want. This is called a pass-through parameter, because its value will be passed back to our store site when PayPal notifies us of the outcome of the transaction by calling our server-side page indicated by the notify_url page (see below).
item_name	A descriptive string for the order the customer is going to pay for, e.g., Order #25, or maybe "TheBeerHouse order 12345."
amount	The amount the user will pay, in the currency specified by currency_code. You must use the point (.) as the separator for the decimal part of the number, regardless of the currency and language being used, e.g., 33.80.
shipping	The cost of the shipping, specified in the same currency of the amount, and in the same format. This will be added to the amount parameter to calculate the total price the customer must pay. Example: 6.00

Property	Description
return	The URL the customer will be redirected to after completing the payment on PayPal's page, e.g., `www.yoursite.com/paypal/orderconfirmed.aspx`. In this page you'll typically provide some form of static feedback to your customer that gives further instructions to track the order status, and will mark the order as confirmed. The URL must be encoded, so the URL indicated above would become `http%3a%2f%2fwww.yoursite.com%2fPayPal%2fOrderCompleted.aspx`
cancel_return	The URL to which the customer will be redirected after canceling the payment on PayPal's page, e.g., `www.yoursite.com/paypal/ordercancelled.aspx`. In this page you'll typically provide your customer some information to make the payment later. This URL must be encoded as explained for the return parameter.
notify_url	The URL used by PayPal's Instant Payment Notification (IPN) to asynchronously notify you of the outcome of a transaction. This is done in addition to the redirection to the return URL, which happens just after the payment, and which you can't trust because a smart customer might manually type in the URL for your site's order confirmation page, once she has discovered its format (possibly from a previous regular order). IPN is a mechanism based on server-to-server communication: PayPal calls your page by passing some information that identifies the transaction (such as the order ID, the amount paid, etc.) and you interrogate PayPal to determine whether this notification is real, or was created by a malicious user. To verify the notification, you forward all the parameters received in the notification back to PayPal, making a programmatic asynchronous POST request (through the HttpWebRequest class), and see if PayPal responds with a "VERIFIED" string. If that's the case, you can finally mark the order as confirmed and verified.

Instead of creating a form making an HTTP POST (and thus passing the required parameters in the request's body), you can make a GET request and pass all parameters in the querystring, as in the example below:

```
https://www.sandbox.paypal.com/us/cgi-bin/webscr?cmd=_xclick&upload=1&rm=2&no_
shipping=1&no_note=1&currency_code=USD&business=thebeerhouse%40wrox.com&item_number
=25&custom=25&item_name=Order+%2325&amount=33.80&shipping=6.00&notify_url=http%3a%2
f%2fwww.yoursite.com%2fPayPal%2fNotify.aspx&return=http%3a%2f%2fwww.yoursite.com%2f
PayPal%2fOrderCompleted.aspx%3fID%3d25&cancel_return=http%3a%2f%2fwww.yoursite.com%
2fPayPal%2fOrderCancelled.aspx
```

The URL above would redirect the customer to the Sandbox test environment. To handle real payments later, all you need to do is replace the "https://www.sandbox.paypal.com/us/cgi-bin/webscr" part with "https://www.paypal.com/us/cgi-bin/webscr". Later in the chapter you'll see how to dynamically build URLs for order-specific checkout pages, and how to implement the return and verification pages. For now, however, you should have enough background information to get started! So let's proceed with the design of the database, and then the DAL, BLL, and UI.

Designing the Database Tables and Stored Procedures

The e-commerce store module uses six tables for the catalog of products and order management, as shown in Figure 9-3.

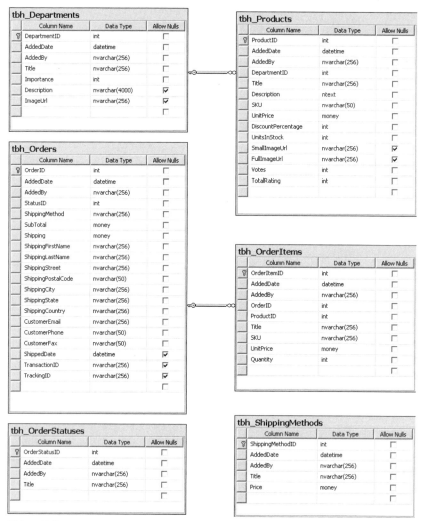

tbh_Departments

Column Name	Data Type	Allow Nulls
🔑 DepartmentID	int	☐
AddedDate	datetime	☐
AddedBy	nvarchar(256)	☐
Title	nvarchar(256)	☐
Importance	int	☐
Description	nvarchar(4000)	☑
ImageUrl	nvarchar(256)	☑
		☐

tbh_Products

Column Name	Data Type	Allow Nulls
🔑 ProductID	int	☐
AddedDate	datetime	☐
AddedBy	nvarchar(256)	☐
DepartmentID	int	☐
Title	nvarchar(256)	☐
Description	ntext	☐
SKU	nvarchar(50)	☐
UnitPrice	money	☐
DiscountPercentage	int	☐
UnitsInStock	int	☐
SmallImageUrl	nvarchar(256)	☑
FullImageUrl	nvarchar(256)	☑
Votes	int	☐
TotalRating	int	☐
		☐

tbh_Orders

Column Name	Data Type	Allow Nulls
🔑 OrderID	int	☐
AddedDate	datetime	☐
AddedBy	nvarchar(256)	☐
StatusID	int	☐
ShippingMethod	nvarchar(256)	☐
SubTotal	money	☐
Shipping	money	☐
ShippingFirstName	nvarchar(256)	☐
ShippingLastName	nvarchar(256)	☐
ShippingStreet	nvarchar(256)	☐
ShippingPostalCode	nvarchar(50)	☐
ShippingCity	nvarchar(256)	☐
ShippingState	nvarchar(256)	☐
ShippingCountry	nvarchar(256)	☐
CustomerEmail	nvarchar(256)	☐
CustomerPhone	nvarchar(50)	☐
CustomerFax	nvarchar(50)	☐
ShippedDate	datetime	☑
TransactionID	nvarchar(256)	☑
TrackingID	nvarchar(256)	☑
		☐

tbh_OrderItems

Column Name	Data Type	Allow Nulls
🔑 OrderItemID	int	☐
AddedDate	datetime	☐
AddedBy	nvarchar(256)	☐
OrderID	int	☐
ProductID	int	☐
Title	nvarchar(256)	☐
SKU	nvarchar(256)	☐
UnitPrice	money	☐
Quantity	int	☐
		☐

tbh_OrderStatuses

Column Name	Data Type	Allow Nulls
🔑 OrderStatusID	int	☐
AddedDate	datetime	☐
AddedBy	nvarchar(256)	☐
Title	nvarchar(256)	☐
		☐

tbh_ShippingMethods

Column Name	Data Type	Allow Nulls
🔑 ShippingMethodID	int	☐
AddedDate	datetime	☐
AddedBy	nvarchar(256)	☐
Title	nvarchar(256)	☐
Price	money	☐
		☐

Figure 9-3

All catalog data is stored in `tbh_Departments` (the categories of products, which is similar to `tbh_Categories` used by the articles module in Chapter 5) and `tbh_Products`, which contains the title, price, description, images, and other information about specific products. Note that it contains a `UnitPrice` field and a `DiscountPercentage` field, but the final price is not saved in the database, but will rather be dynamically calculated on the BLL. Similarly, there are the `Votes` and `TotalRating` fields (which have a similar usage to the `tbh_Articles` table), and the `AverageRating` information will be dynamically calculated later. The relationship between the two tables makes `tbh_Products.DepartmentID` a foreign key and establishes cascade updates and deletes, so that if a department is deleted, then all of its products are automatically deleted as well.

A similar relationship exists between `tbh_Orders` and `tbh_OrderItems`. The former stores information about the order, such as its subtotal and shipping amount, the complete customer's contact information and shipping address, shipping method, current order status, and transaction and tracking ID. The latter is the `Details` table of the master-detail relationship, and stores the order lines of the product, whereby a line describes each ordered product, with its title, ID, unit price, quantity, and stock-keeping unit (SKU) — a SKU is a marketing term designating a product; it's basically a model number (you will use the SKU to reorder more items of a given type). There are also two more support tables, which store shipping options and order status. You may be wondering why the `tbh_Orders` and `tbh_OrderItems` tables maintain a copy of many values that could be retrieved by joining two tables. Take for example the `tbh_Orders.ShippingMethod` and `tbh_Orders.Shipping` fields, which you may assume could be replaced with a single `ShippingMethodID` foreign key that references a record in `tbh_ShippingMethods`. As another example, consider that `tbh_OrderItems` contains the title, price, and SKU of the ordered product, even if it already has a reference to the product in the `tbh_Products` table through the `ProductID` foreign key. However, think about the situation when a shipping method is deleted or edited, which changes its title and price. If you only linked an order record to a record of `ShippedMethods`, this would result in a different total amount and a different shipping method after the change, which obviously can't be permitted after an order was submitted and confirmed (we can't modify data of a confirmed order because it would be too late). The same is true for products: You can delete or change the price of a product, but orders made before the change cannot be modified, and they must keep the price and all other information as they were at the time of the order. If a product is deleted, the storekeeper must still be able to determine the product's name, SKU, and price, to identify and ship it correctly. All this wouldn't be possible if you only stored the ID of the product because that would become useless once the product were deleted. The product ID is still kept in the `tbh_OrderItems` table, but only as optional information that would enable us to create a hyperlink to the product page if the product is still available. The `tbh_Orders` and `tbh_OrderItems` tables are self-contained history tables. The exception to this rule is the `tbh_Orders.StatusID` field, which actually references a record of `tbh_OrderStatuses`: there will be three built-in statuses in this table (for which you can customize at least the title), which identify an order waiting for payment, a confirmed order (PayPal redirected to the `OrderConfirmed.aspx` page), and a verified order (an order for which you've verified the payment's authenticity by means of PayPal's IPN notification). The `tbh_Orders` and `tbh_OrderItems` tables are also read-only for the most part, except for some information in the `tbh_Orders` table, such as the `StatusID`, `ShippedDate`, `TrackingID`, and `TransactionID` fields, which must be updateable to reflect the changes that happen to the order during its processing.

I won't list all the `tbh_Store_xxx` stored procedures here because, as in most previous chapters, they are the typical set of procedures that cover all the CRUD operations for the six tables mentioned above. The only exception is that there is only an `Insert` procedure for the `tbh_OrderItems` table, as all data stored here is read-only (not updateable once inserted). Orders can be retrieved by customer name by means of a stored procedure named `tbh_Store_GetOrdersByCustomer`, and by status by means of `tbh_Store_GetOrderByStatus`. Because there may be hundreds or thousands of orders in a certain status (according to how successful the store becomes), this second procedure also accepts two dates that define the interval of time in which to retrieve the orders in the given state. Lastly, products are not retrieved by stored procedures, but retrieved by dynamically constructed TSQL queries, because in addition to pagination you'll need to support sorting on different fields (such as `UnitPrice`, `Title`, etc.), which can't be done easily with a fixed stored procedure. This is the same approach taken for retrieving threads in the previous chapter, so please refer to it for more information.

Designing the Configuration Module

The configuration settings of the store module are defined in a `<store>` element within the `<theBeerHouse>` section of the `web.config` file. The class that maps the settings is `StoreElement`, which defines the following properties:

Property	Description
RatingLockInterval	Number of days that must pass before a customer can rate a product that she has already rated previously
PageSize	Default number of products listed per page. The user will be able to change the page size from the user interface.
RssItems	Number of products included in the RSS feeds
DefaultOrderListInterval	Number of days from the current date used to calculate the start date of the default date interval in which to retrieve the orders in a specific state (in the storekeeper's management console). The interval's start and end date can be changed in the administration page.
SandboxMode	Boolean value indicating whether the transactions will be run in PayPal's Sandbox test environment, or in the real PayPal
BusinessEmail	E-mail of the PayPal business account that will be the recipient for the money transfer executed on PayPal to pay for the order
CurrencyCode	String identifying the currency for the amounts that the customer will pay on PayPal. The default is USD. This currency code will also be used in the amounts shown in the end-user pages on the right side of the amounts (e.g., 12.50 USD).
LowAvailability	Lower threshold of units in stock that determines when a product should be re-ordered to replenish the stock. This condition will be displayed graphically on the page with special icons.

Designing the Data Access Layer

As usual, the DAL part of the module can be split into two virtual parts. The first part is a number of entity classes that wrap the data of the module's database tables and their fields with a one-to-one relationship, with some fields coming from the JOIN between two tables (such as `DepartmentTitle` in the `Product` entity class). Figure 9-4 is a graphical representation of these classes, generated by Visual Studio 2005's Class Designer.

Figure 9-4

The second part of the DAL consists of the base and concrete provider to perform the actual data access, i.e., calling the various stored procedures implemented at the database level. In this case there is a one-to-one relationship between the stored procedures and the methods of the provider, with the addition of some helper methods in the base `StoreProvider` class that accept an `IDataReader` object and can populate one or more instances of the entity classes. The `GetProducts` method, as mentioned earlier, is implemented by dynamically creating the SQL code necessary to retrieve products paginated and sorted according to one of the multiple available fields. The schema of these classes is represented in Figure 9-5.

Designing the Business Layer

As for other modules developed previously, the BLL has a base class named `BaseStore` that defines a number of properties that all domain objects have, such as `ID`, `AddedDate`, and `AddedBy`, plus a reference to the site's `StoreElement` configuration object, and the `CacheData` object, which works according to the cache settings specific to the store module. A number of BLL classes inherit from `BaseStore`, such as `Department`, `Product`, `Order`, `OrderItem`, `ShippingMethod`, and `OrderStatuses`, which are OOP abstractions of the DAL classes displayed above, with static methods that wrap the DAL methods, and a number of instance methods that simply call static methods, passing along the instance data. Figure 9-6 represents the classes that manage the store's catalog.

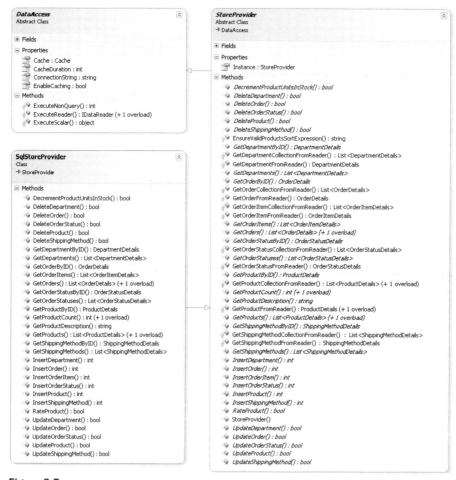

Figure 9-5

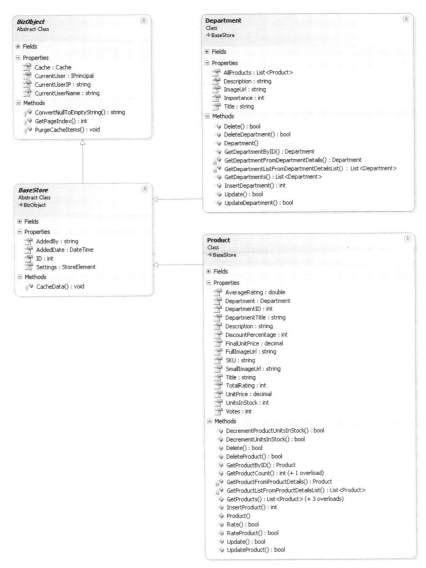

Figure 9-6

Figure 9-7 represents the classes needed for managing orders: the shopping cart, the shipping methods, the order statuses, and the actual order storage.

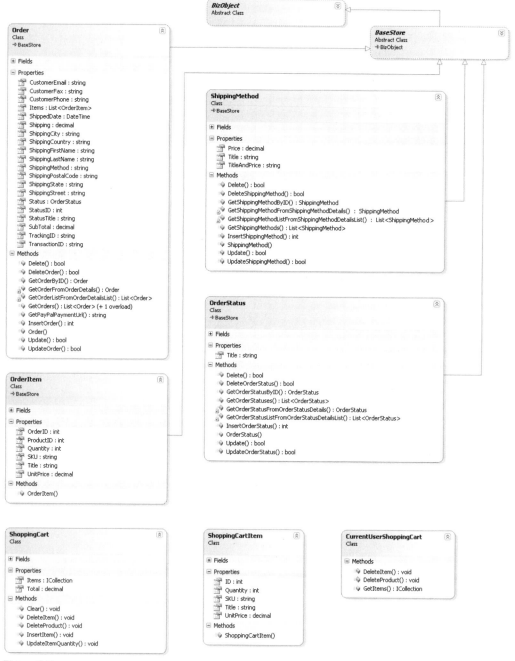

Figure 9-7

Most of the classes displayed in the figure don't require further explanation. However, the classes related to the shopping cart are not typical, and we'll examine these now. As mentioned earlier, we want to make the shopping cart persistent between different sessions of the same user. Prior to ASP.NET 2.0, projects like this would have required creating your own tables, stored procedures, and classes for saving the shopping cart data in a durable medium, instead of using `Session` variables that would only last a short time. Now, however, we can create a domain class that represents the cart, and, assuming the class is serializable, you can use it as a data type for a profile variable, and let ASP.NET's profile module persist and load it for the current user automatically, including anonymous users!

The `ShoppingCart` class displayed above is such a class: Its methods add, modify, and remove items (represented by `ShoppingCartItem` objects) to and from an internal `Dictionary` object (the generic version of `Dictionary` actually, which has been specialized for storing `ShoppingCartItem` objects, so that explicit casting is no longer necessary when retrieving an item from it), and its `Total` property dynamically calculates the shopping cart's total amount by multiplying the quantity by the unit price of each product, adding the result for each item. The other class, `CurrentUserShoppingCart`, provides static methods that just call the similarly named method of the `ShoppingCart` object for the current user; this class is used as the object referenced by an `ObjectDataSource` component, as it cannot directly reference a `profile` property in its `TypeName` property.

Finally, note in Figure 9-7 that the `Order.InsertOrder` method does not take a list of items, with all their details, to be copied into records of `thb_OrderItems`, but rather, takes an instance of the `ShoppingCart` class, which already contains all this data. Additionally, it also takes the customer's details and the shipping address, which is not contained in the `ShoppingCart`.

Designing the User Interface Services

This module is made up of many pages. As usual, there is a complete administration console that allows you to edit practically all the data it uses (other than the read-only fields such as those of the `tbh_Orders` and `tbh_OrderItems` tables, and a number of end-user pages that display departments, the product listings, and the specific products to the user, as well as manage the shopping cart and the checkout process, the order history page, and the generation of the products' RSS feed. In addition to the existing roles (Administrators, Editors, Contributors, and Posters) a new role named StoreKeepers should be created to designate which users will be allowed to administer the store. A new role, separate from the current Editors role, was necessary because people managing articles, polls, and newsletters are not necessarily the same people who will manage products and orders (and vice versa). However, there are a few sensitive functions that only an Administrator can perform, such as deleting orders. Below is a complete list of pages and user controls used by the module:

- ❑ **~/Admin/ManageDepartments.aspx:** Lets an administrator or store keeper add, edit, and delete store departments

- ❑ **~/Admin/ManageShippingMethods.aspx:** Lets an administrator or storekeeper add, edit, and delete shipping methods

- ❑ **~/Admin/ManageOrderStatuses.aspx:** Lets an administrator or storekeeper add, edit, and delete store order statuses

- ❑ **~/Admin/AddEditProduct.aspx:** Lets an administrator or storekeeper add a new product or edit an existing one

❑ **~/Admin/ManageProducts.aspx:** Lets an administrator or storekeeper view the list of products, with their title, unit price, average rating, availability, and other information. Also contains links and commands to edit and delete products.

❑ **~/Admin/ManageOrders.aspx:** Lets an administrator or storekeeper find and review orders by customer name, status, or ID. However, only administrators can delete orders.

❑ **~/Admin/EditOrder.aspx:** Lets an administrator or storekeeper manage a specific order, i.e., review all of its details and edit a few of its properties, such as the status, the shipping date, and the transaction and tracking ID

❑ **~/ShowDepartments.aspx:** This end-user page displays the list of store departments, with an image and a description for each of them, along with a link to browse their products.

❑ **~/BrowseProducts.aspx:** Renders a list of products with paging support, for a specific department or for all departments. Information such as the product's title, unit price, discount, average rating, availability, and a small image are displayed.

❑ **~/ShowProduct.aspx:** Shows all details about a specific product, allows a customer to rate the product, and allows them to add the product to their shopping cart, for later review or purchase

❑ **~/ShoppingCart.aspx:** Shows the current contents of the customer's shopping cart, allowing them to change the quantity of any item, remove an item, choose a shipping method, and then recalculate the subtotal, shipping, and total amounts. This page also provides a three-step wizard for checkout: The first step is the actual shopping cart just described; in the second step, the customers provide the shipping address (by default this is retrieved from the user's address, stored in their profile, if present), and in the final step customers can review all the order information, i.e., the list of items they're about to order (with unit price and quantity), the subtotal, the shipping method and its cost, the total amount, and the address to which the products will be shipped. After the last step is confirmed, the order is saved in the database, and the customer is sent to the PayPal site to pay for the order.

❑ **~/PayPal/OrderCompleted.aspx:** This is the page to which PayPal redirects customers after they pay for the order. The page provides some feedback to the user, and marks the order as confirmed.

❑ **~/PayPal/OrderCancelled.aspx:** This is the page to which PayPal redirects customers after they have cancelled the order. The page provides some feedback to the customer, explaining that the order was saved, and that it can be paid for later.

❑ **~/PayPal/Notify.aspx:** This is the page to which PayPal sends the transaction's result, as part of the Instant Payment Notification. It confirms that the notification is verified, and if so, marks it as such.

❑ **~/OrderHistory.aspx:** This lets customers review their past orders, to check their status, or if/when they were shipped, etc. For orders that were cancelled during payment, a link to return to PayPal and complete the payment is provided.

❑ **~/GetProductsRss.aspx:** This produces the RSS feed for the store catalog, returning a number of products (the number is specified by the `RssItems` configuration setting described earlier) sorted according to a querystring parameter. For example, it may return the 10 most recent products, the 10 least expensive products, or the 10 most discounted products (great for immediate syndication of special offers).

❑ **~/Controls/ShoppingCartBox.ascx:** This user control statically displays the current contents of the customer's shopping cart, with the name and quantity of the products. It doesn't support editing, but provides a link to the `ShoppingCart.aspx` page where this can be done. It also has a link to the `OrderHistory.aspx` page. The control will be plugged into the site's shared layout, so that these links and information are easily reachable from anywhere on the site.

❑ **~/Controls/AvailabilityDisplay.aspx:** This control represents the availability of a product with icons of different colors. A green icon means that the product is available, a yellow icon means that only a few units are in stock for that product (the limit for this icon is specified by the `LowAvailability` configuration property described earlier), and a red icon means no availability. This control will be used in the product listings and in the product-specific page.

Solution

We'll go very quickly through the implementation of the solution, as the structure of many classes and pages is similar to those developed for previous modules. In particular, creation of the database tables, the stored procedure, the configuration code, and the DAL classes is completely skipped in this chapter, due to space constraints. Of course, you'll find the complete details in the code download. Instead, I'll focus this space on the implementation of code containing new ASP.NET 2.0 features not already discussed, and code containing interesting logic, such as the shopping cart profile class and the companion classes, as well as the checkout process and the integration with PayPal.

Implementing the Business Logic Layer

First we'll examine the BLL classes related to the shopping cart, starting with the `ShoppingCartItem` class, which is an entity class that wraps data for an item in the cart, with its title, SKU, ID, unit price, and quantity. This class is decorated with the `[Serializable]` attribute, which is necessary to allow the ASP.NET profile system to persist the `ShoppingCartItem` objects. Here's the code:

```
[Serializable]
public class ShoppingCartItem
{
    private int _id = 0;
    public int ID
    {
        get { return _id; }
        private set { _id = value; }
    }

    private string _title = "";
    public string Title
    {
        get { return _title; }
        private set { _title = value; }
    }

    private string _sku = "";
    public string SKU
    {
```

```
      get { return _sku; }
      private set { _sku = value; }
   }

   private decimal _unitPrice;
   public decimal UnitPrice
   {
      get { return _unitPrice; }
      private set { _unitPrice = value; }
   }

   private int _quantity = 1;
   public int Quantity
   {
      get { return _quantity; }
      set { _quantity = value; }
   }

   public ShoppingCartItem(int id, string title, string sku, decimal unitPrice)
   {
      this.ID = id;
      this.Title = title;
      this.SKU = sku;
      this.UnitPrice = unitPrice;
   }
}
```

The ShoppingCart class exposes a number of methods for inserting, removing, and retrieving multiple ShoppingCartItem objects to and from an internal Dictionary object instantiated for that type. When an item is inserted, the class checks whether the Dictionary already contains an item with the same ID: If not, it adds it; otherwise, it increments the Quantity property of the existing item. The RemoveItem method works similarly, but it decrements the Quantity if the item is found; if the Quantity reaches 0, it completely removes the item from the shopping cart. RemoveProduct suggests the same action, but it's actually different, because it removes a product from the cart, regardless of its quantity. UpdateItemQuantity updates an item's quantity, and is used when the customer edits the quantities in the shopping cart page. Finally, the Clear method empties the shopping cart by clearing the internal Dictionary. Here's the complete code:

```
[Serializable]
public class ShoppingCart
{
   private Dictionary<int, ShoppingCartItem> _items =
      new Dictionary<int, ShoppingCartItem>();

   public ICollection Items
   {
      get { return _items.Values; }
   }

   /// <summary>
   /// Gets the sum total of the items' prices
   /// </summary>
   public decimal Total
```

```csharp
{
    get
    {
        decimal sum = 0.0m;
        foreach (ShoppingCartItem item in _items.Values)
            sum += item.UnitPrice * item.Quantity;
        return sum;
    }
}

/// <summary>
/// Adds a new item to the shopping cart
/// </summary>
public void InsertItem(int id, string title, string sku, decimal unitPrice)
{
    if (_items.ContainsKey(id))
        _items[id].Quantity += 1;
    else
        _items.Add(id, new ShoppingCartItem(id, title, sku, unitPrice));
}

/// <summary>
/// Removes an item from the shopping cart
/// </summary>
public void DeleteItem(int id)
{
    if (_items.ContainsKey(id))
    {
        ShoppingCartItem item = _items[id];
        item.Quantity -= 1;
        if (item.Quantity == 0)
            _items.Remove(id);
    }
}

/// <summary>
/// Removes all items of a specified product from the shopping cart
/// </summary>
public void DeleteProduct(int id)
{
    if (_items.ContainsKey(id))
    {
        _items.Remove(id);
    }
}

/// <summary>
/// Updates the quantity for an item
/// </summary>
public void UpdateItemQuantity(int id, int quantity)
{
    if (_items.ContainsKey(id))
    {
        ShoppingCartItem item = _items[id];
```

```
            item.Quantity = quantity;
            if (item.Quantity <= 0)
                _items.Remove(id);
        }
    }


    /// <summary>
    /// Clears the cart
    /// </summary>
    public void Clear()
    {
        _items.Clear();
    }
}
```

If you now go to the root's `web.config` file and change the `<profile>` section according to what is shown below, you'll have a fully working persistent shopping cart, also available to anonymous users:

```
<profile defaultProvider="TBH_ProfileProvider">
    <providers>...</providers>
    <properties>
        <add name="FirstName" type="String" />
        <add name="LastName" type="String" />
        ...
        <add name="ShoppingCart"
            type="MB.TheBeerHouse.BLL.Store.ShoppingCart"
            serializeAs="Binary" allowAnonymous="true" />
    </properties>
</profile>
```

> Note the class defined above is not serializable to XML, because a default constructor for the ShoppingCartItem is not present, and the ShoppingCart's Item property does not have a setter accessory. These requirements do not exist for binary serialization, though, and because of this I chose to use this serialization method and create more encapsulated classes.

With a few dozen lines of code we've accomplished something that previous versions of ASP.NET would have required hours of work to accomplish by creating database tables, stored procedures, and DAL classes. As explained earlier, we're also creating a helper `CurrentUserShoppingCart` that will be used to bind the current user's `ShoppingCart` profile property to a `GridView`, and other controls, by means of the `ObjectDataSource` component. Its implementation is very short, as its methods just reference the `ShoppingCart` profile property from the current context, and forward the call to its respective methods:

```
public class CurrentUserShoppingCart
{
    public static ICollection GetItems()
    {
        return (HttpContext.Current.Profile as
            ProfileCommon).ShoppingCart. Items;
```

```
        }

        public static void DeleteItem(int id)
        {
            (HttpContext.Current.Profile as ProfileCommon).ShoppingCart.DeleteItem(id);
        }

        public static void DeleteProduct(int id)
        {
            (HttpContext.Current.Profile as
                ProfileCommon).ShoppingCart.DeleteProduct(id);
        }
    }
```

Remember to update the `Profile_MigrateAnonymous` event handler in the `global.asax` file to migrate the `ShoppingCart` property from the anonymous user's profile to the profile of the member who just logged in. However, you must do it only if the anonymous customer's shopping cart is not empty, because otherwise you would always erase the registered customer's shopping cart:

```
void Profile_MigrateAnonymous(object sender, ProfileMigrateEventArgs e)
{
    // get a reference to the previously anonymous user's profile
    ProfileCommon anonProfile = this.Profile.GetProfile(e.AnonymousID);
    // if set, copy its Theme and ShoppingCart to the current user's profile
    if (anonProfile.ShoppingCart.Items.Count > 0)
        this.Profile.ShoppingCart = anonProfile.ShoppingCart;
    ...
}
```

Next we'll look at the `Order` class, for which `GetOrderByID` looks like all the `Get{xxx}ByID` methods of the other business classes in other modules:

```
public static Order GetOrderByID(int orderID)
{
    Order order = null;
    string key = "Store_Order_" + orderID.ToString();

    if (BaseStore.Settings.EnableCaching && BizObject.Cache[key] != null)
    {
        order = (Order)BizObject.Cache[key];
    }
    else
    {
        order = GetOrderFromOrderDetails(SiteProvider.Store.GetOrderByID(orderID));
        BaseStore.CacheData(key, order);
    }
    return order;
}
```

However, the `GetOrderFromOrderDetails` method of this class doesn't just wrap the data of a single DAL's entity class into a business class instance, it also retrieves all details for child `OrderItems`, wraps them into read-only `OrderItem` business objects, and set the order's `Items` property with them:

```csharp
private static Order GetOrderFromOrderDetails(OrderDetails record)
{
    if (record == null)
        return null;
    else
    {
        // create a list of OrderItems for the order
        List<OrderItem> orderItems = new List<OrderItem>();
        List<OrderItemDetails> recordset = SiteProvider.Store.GetOrderItems(
            record.ID);

        foreach (OrderItemDetails item in recordset)
        {
            orderItems.Add(new OrderItem(item.ID, item.AddedDate, item.AddedBy,
                item.OrderID, item.ProductID, item.Title, item.SKU,
                item.UnitPrice, item.Quantity));
        }

        // create new Order
        return new Order(record.ID, record.AddedDate, record.AddedBy,
            record.StatusID, record.StatusTitle, record.ShippingMethod,
            record.SubTotal, record.Shipping, record.ShippingFirstName,
            record.ShippingLastName, record.ShippingStreet, record.ShippingPostalCode,
            record.ShippingCity, record.ShippingState, record.ShippingCountry,
            record.CustomerEmail, record.CustomerPhone, record.CustomerFax,
            record.ShippedDate, record.TransactionID, record.TrackingID, orderItems);
    }
}
```

Another interesting method is `InsertOrder`, which accepts an instance of `ShoppingCart` with all the order items, and other parameters for the customer's contact information and the shipping address. Because it must insert multiple records (a record into `tbh_Orders`, and one or more records into `tbh_OrderDetails`), it must ensure that all these operations are executed in an atomic way so that all operations are committed or rolled back in case we get an exception. To ensure this, we're using the `System.Transactions.TransactionScope` class, new in .NET Framework 2.0. Refer to Chapter 3 to read about this class and its alternatives. The following code shows how it's used in a real situation:

```csharp
public static int InsertOrder(ShoppingCart shoppingCart,
    string shippingMethod, decimal shipping, string shippingFirstName,
    string shippingLastName, string shippingStreet, string shippingPostalCode,
    string shippingCity, string shippingState, string shippingCountry,
    string customerEmail, string customerPhone, string customerFax,
    string transactionID)
{
    using (TransactionScope scope = new TransactionScope())
    {
        string userName = BizObject.CurrentUserName;

        // insert the master order
        OrderDetails order = new OrderDetails(0, DateTime.Now,
            userName, 1, "", shippingMethod, shoppingCart.Total, shipping,
            shippingFirstName, shippingLastName, shippingStreet, shippingPostalCode,
            shippingCity, shippingState, shippingCountry, customerEmail,
            customerPhone, customerFax, DateTime.MinValue, transactionID, "");
```

```
            int orderID = SiteProvider.Store.InsertOrder(order);

            // insert the child order items
            foreach (ShoppingCartItem item in shoppingCart.Items)
            {
                OrderItemDetails orderItem = new OrderItemDetails(0, DateTime.Now,
                    userName, orderID, item.ID, item.Title, item.SKU,
                    item.UnitPrice, item.Quantity);
                SiteProvider.Store.InsertOrderItem(orderItem);
            }

            BizObject.PurgeCacheItems("store_order");
            scope.Complete();

            return orderID;
        }
    }
```

A transaction is also used in the `UpdateOrder` method. The detail records that are updated in this method relate to a single record of the `tbh_Orders` table (no order item is touched, however, as they are all read-only after an order is saved), and if the new order status is "confirmed" it also decreases the `UnitsInStock` value of all items purchased in the order, according to the ordered quantity:

```
public static bool UpdateOrder(int id, int statusID, DateTime shippedDate,
    string transactionID, string trackingID)
{
    using (TransactionScope scope = new TransactionScope())
    {
        transactionID = BizObject.ConvertNullToEmptyString(transactionID);
        trackingID = BizObject.ConvertNullToEmptyString(trackingID);

        // retrieve the order's current status ID
        Order order = Order.GetOrderByID(id);

        // update the order
        OrderDetails record = new OrderDetails(id, DateTime.Now, "", statusID, "",
            "", 0.0m, 0.0m, "", "", "", "", "", "", "", "", "", "", shippedDate,
            transactionID, trackingID);
        bool ret = SiteProvider.Store.UpdateOrder(record);

        // if the new status ID is "confirmed", than decrease the UnitsInStock
        // for the purchased products
        if (statusID == (int)StatusCode.Confirmed &&
            order.StatusID == (int)StatusCode.WaitingForPayment)
        {
            foreach (OrderItem item in order.Items)
                Product.DecrementProductUnitsInStock(item.ProductID, item.Quantity);
        }

        BizObject.PurgeCacheItems("store_order");
        scope.Complete();
        return ret;
    }
}
```

The `StatusCode` enumeration used in the preceding code includes the three built-in statuses required by the module: waiting for payment, confirmed, and verified, and is defined as follows:

```
public enum StatusCode : int
{
    WaitingForPayment = 1,
    Confirmed = 2,
    Verified = 3
}
```

Note, however, that because the `StatusID` property is an integer, an explicit cast to `int` is required. The `StatusID` type is `int` and not `StatusCode` because users can define their own additional status codes, and thus working with numeric IDs is more appropriate in most situations.

The last significant method in the `Order` class is `GetPayPalPaymentUrl`, which returns the URL to redirect the customer to PayPal to pay for the order. It dynamically builds the URL shown in the "Design" section with the amount, shipping, and order ID values taken from the current order, plus the recipient business e-mail and currency code taken from the configuration settings, and the return URLs that point to the `OrderCompleted.aspx`, `OrderCancelled.aspx`, and `Notify.aspx` pages described earlier:

```
public string GetPayPalPaymentUrl()
{
    string serverUrl = (Globals.Settings.Store.SandboxMode ?
        "https://www.sandbox.paypal.com/us/cgi-bin/webscr" :
        "https://www.paypal.com/us/cgi-bin/webscr");
    string amount = this.SubTotal.ToString("N2").Replace(',', '.');
    string shipping = this.Shipping.ToString("N2").Replace(',', '.');

    string baseUrl = HttpContext.Current.Request.Url.AbsoluteUri.Replace(
        HttpContext.Current.Request.Url.PathAndQuery, "") +
        HttpContext.Current.Request.ApplicationPath;
    if (!baseUrl.EndsWith("/"))
        baseUrl += "/";

    string notifyUrl = HttpUtility.UrlEncode(baseUrl + "PayPal/Notify.aspx");
    string returnUrl = HttpUtility.UrlEncode(
        baseUrl + "PayPal/OrderCompleted.aspx?ID=" + this.ID.ToString());
    string cancelUrl = HttpUtility.UrlEncode(
        baseUrl + "PayPal/OrderCancelled.aspx");
    string business = HttpUtility.UrlEncode(Globals.Settings.Store.BusinessEmail);
    string itemName = HttpUtility.UrlEncode("Order #" + this.ID.ToString());

    StringBuilder url = new StringBuilder();
    url.AppendFormat(
        "{0}?cmd=_xclick&upload=1&rm=2&no_shipping=1&no_note=1&currency_code={1}&
        business={2}&item_number={3}&custom={3}&item_name={4}&amount={5}&
        shipping={6}&notify_url={7}&return={8}&cancel_return={9}",
        serverUrl, Globals.Settings.Store.CurrencyCode, business, this.ID, itemName,
        amount, shipping, notifyUrl, returnUrl, cancelUrl);

    return url.ToString();
}
```

Note that the method uses a different base URL according to whether the store runs in real or test mode, as indicated by the Sandbox configuration setting. Also note that PayPal expects all amounts to use the period (.) as a separator for the amount's decimal parts, and only wants two decimal digits. You use `variable.ToString("N2")` to format the double or decimal variable as a string with two decimal digits. However, if the current locale settings are set to Italian or some other country's settings for which a comma is used, you'll get something like "33,50" instead of "33.50." For this reason you also do a `Replace` for "," with "." just in case.

Implementing the User Interface

Many administrative and end-user pages of this module are similar in structure of those in previous chapters, especially to those of the articles module described and implemented in Chapter 5. For example, in Figure 9-8 you can see how similar the page to manage departments is to the page to manage product categories.

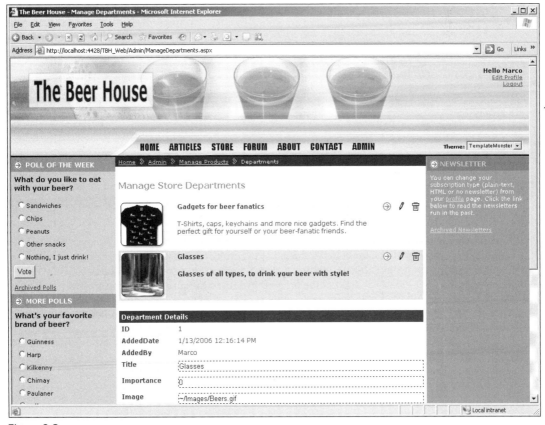

Figure 9-8

The page to manage shipping options, represented in Figure 9-9, is also similar: the `GridView` and `DetailsView` controls used to list and insert/modify records just define different fields, but the structure of the page is nearly identical.

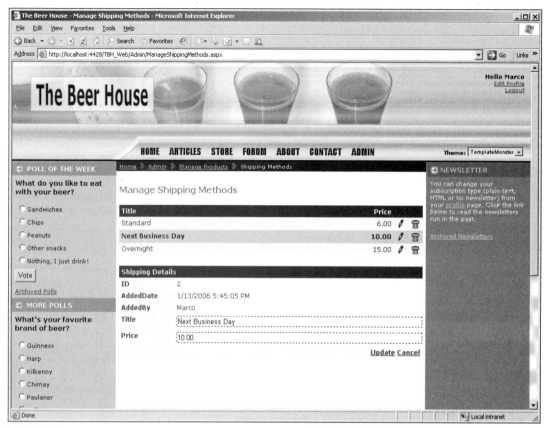

Figure 9-9

Note that in the page for managing order status, status records with IDs from 1 to 3 cannot be deleted, because they identify special, hard-coded values. For example, you've just seen in the implementation of the `Order` class that the `UpdateOrder` method checks whether the current order status is 2, in which case it decrements the `UnitsInStock` field of the ordered products. Because of this, you should handle the `RowCreated` event of the `GridView` displaying the records, and ensure that the Delete `LinkButton` is hidden for the first three records. Following is the code to place into this event handler, while Figure 9-10 shows the final result on the page:

```
protected void gvwOrderStatuses_RowCreated(object sender, GridViewRowEventArgs e)
{
    if (e.Row.RowType == DataControlRowType.DataRow)
    {
        ImageButton btn = e.Row.Cells[2].Controls[0] as ImageButton;

        int orderStatusID = Convert.ToInt32(
            gvwOrderStatuses.DataKeys[e.Row.RowIndex][0]);
```

```
    if (orderStatusID > 3)
        btn.OnClientClick = "if (confirm('Are you sure you want to delete this
order status?') == false) return false;";
    else
        btn.Visible = false;
    }
}
```

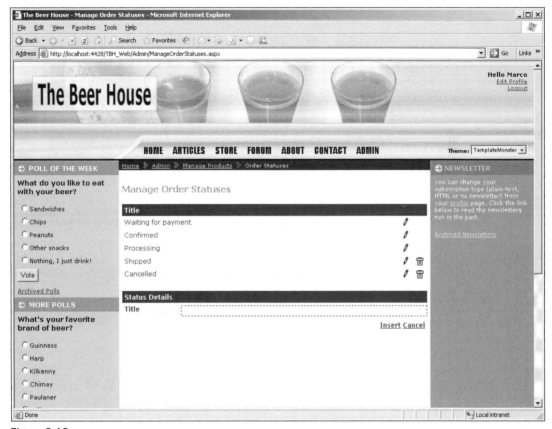

Figure 9-10

The AddEditProduct.aspx page uses a single DetailsView and a companion ObjectDataSource, and enables to you to edit an existing product or insert a new one according to the presence of an ID parameter on the querystring. The same thing was done (and shown in detail) in Chapter 5, so please refer to that chapter to see the implementation. Figure 9-11 shows how the resulting page looks.

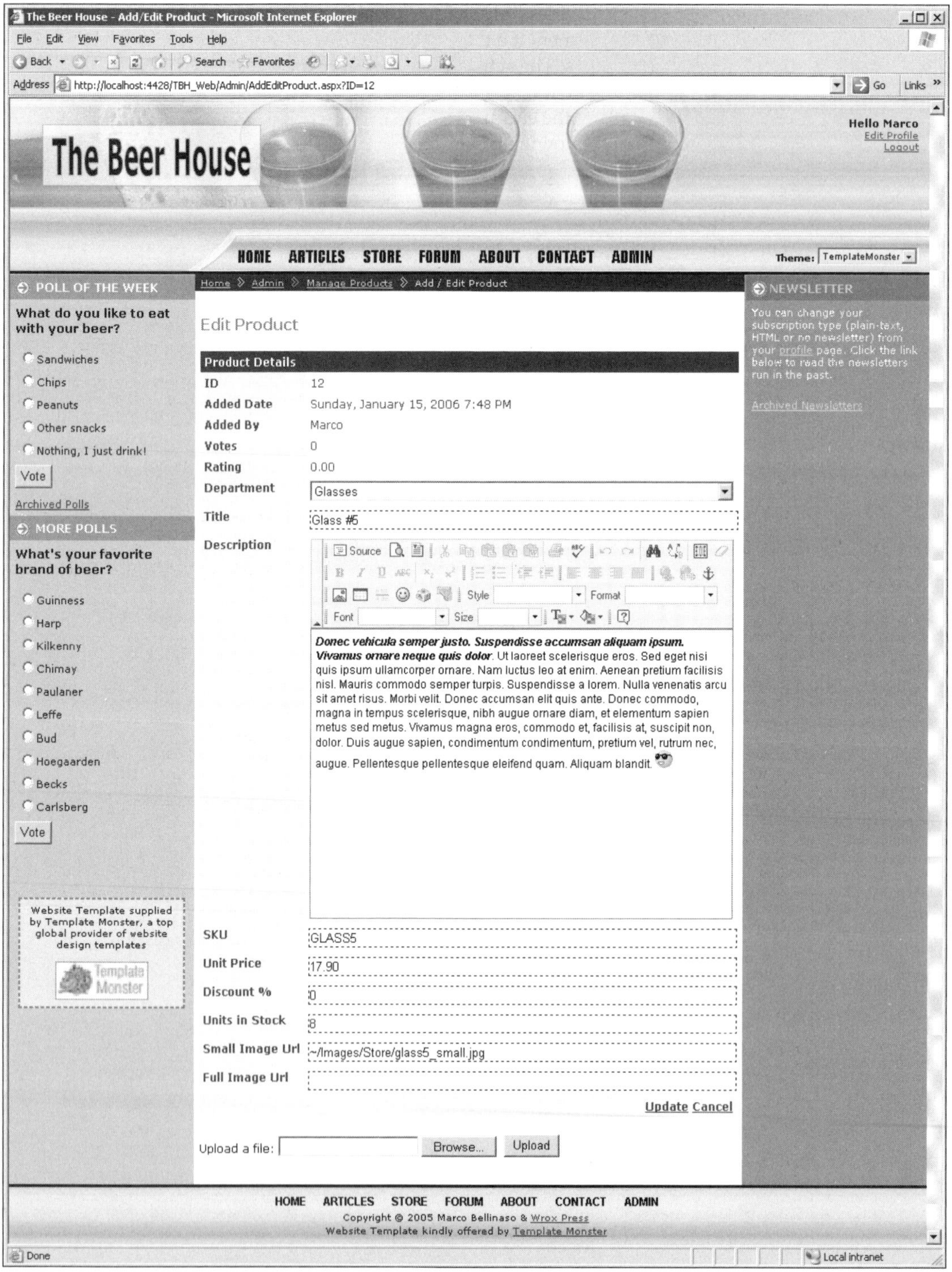
The Beer House - Add/Edit Product - Microsoft Internet Explorer
File Edit View Favorites Tools Help
Address http://localhost:4428/TBH_Web/Admin/AddEditProduct.aspx?ID=12
The Beer House
Hello Marco
Edit Profile
Logout
HOME ARTICLES STORE FORUM ABOUT CONTACT ADMIN
Theme: TemplateMonster
POLL OF THE WEEK
What do you like to eat with your beer?
Sandwiches
Chips
Peanuts
Other snacks
Nothing, I just drink!
Vote
Archived Polls
MORE POLLS
What's your favorite brand of beer?
Guinness
Harp
Kilkenny
Chimay
Paulaner
Leffe
Bud
Hoegaarden
Becks
Carlsberg
Vote
Website Template supplied by Template Monster, a top global provider of website design templates
Home » Admin » Manage Products » Add / Edit Product
Edit Product
Product Details
ID 12
Added Date Sunday, January 15, 2006 7:48 PM
Added By Marco
Votes 0
Rating 0.00
Department Glasses
Title Glass #5
Description
Donec vehicula semper justo. Suspendisse accumsan aliquam ipsum. Vivamus ornare neque quis dolor. Ut laoreet scelerisque eros. Sed eget nisi quis ipsum ullamcorper ornare. Nam luctus leo at enim. Aenean pretium facilisis nisl. Mauris commodo semper turpis. Suspendisse a lorem. Nulla venenatis arcu sit amet risus. Morbi velit. Donec accumsan elit quis ante. Donec commodo, magna in tempus scelerisque, nibh augue ornare diam, et elementum sapien metus sed metus. Vivamus magna eros, commodo et, facilisis at, suscipit non, dolor. Duis augue sapien, condimentum condimentum, pretium vel, rutrum nec, augue. Pellentesque pellentesque eleifend quam. Aliquam blandit.
SKU GLASS5
Unit Price 17.90
Discount % 0
Units in Stock 8
Small Image Url ~/Images/Store/glass5_small.jpg
Full Image Url
Update Cancel
Upload a file: Browse... Upload
NEWSLETTER
You can change your subscription type (plain-text, HTML or no newsletter) from your profile page. Click the link below to read the newsletters run in the past.
Archived Newsletters
HOME ARTICLES STORE FORUM ABOUT CONTACT ADMIN
Copyright © 2005 Marco Bellinaso & Wrox Press
Website Template kindly offered by Template Monster
Done
Local intranet

Figure 9-11

The `ManageProducts.aspx` page provides links to the other catalog management pages, and shows the list of the products of a specific department if a `DepID` parameter is found on the querystring; otherwise, it shows products from all departments. The actual listing is produced by the `ProductListing.ascx` user control, which is then plugged into `ManageProducts.aspx`: The code that creates the listing is placed there so that it can be reused in the end-user `BrowseProducts.aspx` page. The control contains a `GridView` control that defines the following columns:

❑ An `ImageField` that shows the product's small image, whose URL is stored in the `SmallImageUrl` field

❑ A `HyperLinkField` that creates a link that points to the product-specific page at ~/`Show Product.aspx`, with the product's ID passed on the querystring. The product's `Title` is used as the link's text.

❑ A `TemplateField` that shows the `RatingDisplay` user control developed in Chapter 5, bound to the product's `AverageRating` calculated property, to display the product's customer rating. However, this control is only displayed if there is at least one vote, and this is done by binding the control's `Visible` property to an expression.

❑ A `TemplateField` that shows the `AvailabilityDisplay` user control (implemented shortly) to represent the product's availability with icons of different colors. The control's `Value` property is bound to the `UnitsInStock` field of the product, which is the value used to select an icon. The same field is also used as `SortExpression` for the column, so that by clicking on this column's header, a customer, administrator, or storekeeper can see the products with the greatest or least availability first.

❑ A `TemplateField` to show the product's price. A `BoundField` bound to the `UnitPrice` field would not be enough, because if the product's `DiscountPercentage` value is greater than 0, then the `UnitPrice` amount must be displayed as crossed out, and the `DiscountPercentage` must be shown along with the calculated `FinalUnitPrice`.

❑ A `TemplateField` with a graphical hyperlink that links to the `AddEditProduct.aspx` page, passing the product's ID on the querystring, to edit the product. This column will be hidden from the `GridView`'s `RowCreated` event if the current user does not belong to the Administrators or StoreKeepers roles.

❑ A `CommandField` that raises the `Delete` command and thus deletes the product. This column will be hidden from the `GridView`'s `RowCreated` event if the current user does not belong to the Administrators or StoreKeepers roles.

Here's the code that defines the `GridView` just described:

```
<asp:GridView ID="gvwProducts" runat="server"  AllowPaging="True"
    AutoGenerateColumns="False" DataKeyNames="ID" DataSourceID="objProducts"
    PageSize="10" AllowSorting="True" OnRowCreated="gvwProducts_RowCreated">
    <Columns>
        <asp:ImageField DataImageUrlField="SmallImageUrl" ItemStyle-Width="110px" />
        <asp:HyperLinkField HeaderText="Product" SortExpression="Title"
            HeaderStyle-HorizontalAlign="Left" DataTextField="Title"
            DataNavigateUrlFormatString="~/ShowProduct.aspx?ID={0}"
            DataNavigateUrlFields="ID" />
```

```
        <asp:TemplateField HeaderText="Rating">
            <ItemTemplate>
                <div style="text-align: center">
                <mb:RatingDisplay runat="server" ID="ratDisplay"
                    Value='<%# Eval("AverageRating") %>'
                    Visible='<%# (int)Eval("Votes") > 0 %>' />
                </div>
            </ItemTemplate>
        </asp:TemplateField>
        <asp:TemplateField HeaderText="Available" SortExpression="UnitsInStock"
            ItemStyle-HorizontalAlign="Center">
            <ItemTemplate>
                <div style="text-align: center">
                    <mb:AvailabilityDisplay runat="server" ID="availDisplay"
                        Value='<%# Eval("UnitsInStock") %>' />
                </div>
            </ItemTemplate>
        </asp:TemplateField>
        <asp:TemplateField HeaderText="Price" SortExpression="UnitPrice"
            HeaderStyle-HorizontalAlign="Right">
            <ItemTemplate>
                <div style="text-align: right">
                    <asp:Panel runat="server"
                        Visible='<%# (int)Eval("DiscountPercentage") > 0 %>'>
                        <s><%# (this.Page as BasePage).FormatPrice(
                            Eval("UnitPrice")) %></s><br />
                        <b><%# Eval("DiscountPercentage") %>% Off</b><br />
                    </asp:Panel>
                    <%# (this.Page as BasePage).FormatPrice(Eval("FinalUnitPrice")) %>
                </div>
            </ItemTemplate>
        </asp:TemplateField>
        <asp:TemplateField ItemStyle-HorizontalAlign="Center" ItemStyle-Width="20px">
            <ItemTemplate>
                <asp:HyperLink runat="server" ID="lnkEdit" ToolTip="Edit product"
                    NavigateUrl='<%# "~/Admin/AddEditProduct.aspx?ID=" + Eval("ID") %>'
                    ImageUrl="~/Images/Edit.gif" />
            </ItemTemplate>
        </asp:TemplateField>
        <asp:CommandField ButtonType="Image" DeleteImageUrl="~/Images/Delete.gif"
            DeleteText="Delete product" ShowDeleteButton="True"
            ItemStyle-HorizontalAlign="Center" ItemStyle-Width="20px" />
    </Columns>
    <EmptyDataTemplate><b>No products to show</b></EmptyDataTemplate>
</asp:GridView>
```

There are other controls on the page, such as DropDownList controls to choose the parent department and the number of products to list on the page, but we've already created something almost identical for the ArticleListing.ascx control, so you can refer back to it for the code and the details. If you look closely at the column that displays the product's price, you'll see that it calls a method named FormatPrice to show the amount. This method is added to the `BasePage` class and it formats the input value as a number with two decimal digits, followed by the currency code defined in the configuration settings:

```
public string FormatPrice(object price)
{
    return Convert.ToDecimal(price).ToString("N2") + " " +
        Globals.Settings.Store.CurrencyCode;
}
```

Amounts are not displayed on the page with the default currency format (which would use the "C" format string) because you may be running the store in another country, such as Italy, which would display the euro symbol in the string; but you want to display USD regardless of the current locale settings. The other control used in the preceding code and not yet implemented is the `AvailabilityDisplay.ascx` user control. It just declares an `Image` control on the .ascx markup file, and then it defines a `Value` property in the code-behind class, which sets the image according to the input value:

```
public partial class AvailabilityDisplay : System.Web.UI.UserControl
{
    private int _value = 0;
    public int Value
    {
        get { return _value; }
        set
        {
            _value = value;
            if (_value <= 0)
            {
                imgAvailability.ImageUrl = "~/images/lightred.gif";
                imgAvailability.AlternateText = "Currently not available";
            }
            else if (_value <= Globals.Settings.Store.LowAvailability)
            {
                imgAvailability.ImageUrl = "~/images/lightyellow.gif";
                imgAvailability.AlternateText = "Few units available";
            }
            else
            {
                imgAvailability.ImageUrl = "~/images/lightgreen.gif";
                imgAvailability.AlternateText = "Available";
            }
        }
    }

    // the Page_Init event handler, and LoadControlState/SaveControlState
    // methods for the control's state management go here...
}
```

Figure 9-12 shows the page at runtime.

Figure 9-12

The ShowProduct.aspx Page

The BrowseProducts.aspx page only contains one line to reference the ProductListing user control, so we can jump straight to the product-specific ShowProduct.aspx page. This shows all the possible details about the product whose ID is passed on the querystring: the title, the average rating, the availability icon, the HTML long description, the small image (or a default "no image available" image if the SmallImageUrl field is empty), a link to the full-size image (displayed only if the FullImageUrl field is not empty), and the product's price. As for the product listing, the UnitPrice amount is shown if the DiscountPercentage is 0; otherwise, that amount is rendered as crossed out, and DiscountPercentage along with the FinalUnitPrice are displayed. Finally, there's a button on the page that will add the product to the customer's shopping cart and will redirect the customer to the ShoppingCart.aspx page. Following is the content of the .aspx markup page:

```
<table style="width: 100%;" cellpadding="0" cellspacing="0">
   <tr><td>
      <asp:Label runat="server" ID="lblTitle" CssClass="articletitle" />
   </td>
   <td style="text-align: right;">
      <asp:Panel runat="server" ID="panEditProduct">
      <asp:HyperLink runat="server" ID="lnkEditProduct"
         ImageUrl="~/Images/Edit.gif"
         ToolTip="Edit product" NavigateUrl="~/Admin/AddEditProduct.aspx?ID={0}" />
      <asp:ImageButton runat="server" ID="btnDelete"
         CausesValidation="false" AlternateText="Delete product"
            ImageUrl="~/Images/Delete.gif"
         OnClientClick="if (confirm('Are you sure you want to delete this
product?') == false) return false;" OnClick="btnDelete_Click" />
      </asp:Panel>
   </td></tr>
</table>
<p></p>
<b>Price: </b><asp:Literal runat="server" ID="lblDiscountedPrice">
   <s>{0}</s> {1}% Off = </asp:Literal>
<asp:Literal runat="server" ID="lblPrice" />
<p></p>
<b>Availability: </b>
   <mb:AvailabilityDisplay runat="server" ID="availDisplay" /><br />
<b>Rating: </b><asp:Literal runat="server" ID="lblRating"
   Text="{0} user(s) have rated this product " />
<mb:RatingDisplay runat="server" ID="ratDisplay" />
<p></p>
<div style="float: left; padding: 4px; text-align: center;">
   <asp:Image runat="Server" ID="imgProduct" ImageUrl="~/Images/noimage.gif"
      GenerateEmptyAlternateText="true" /><br />
   <asp:HyperLink runat="server" ID="lnkFullImage" Font-Size="XX-Small"
      Target="_blank">Full-size<br />image</asp:HyperLink>
</div>
<asp:Literal runat="server" ID="lblDescription" />
<p></p>
<asp:Button ID="btnAddToCart" runat="server"
   OnClick="btnAddToCart_Click" Text="Add to Shopping Cart" />
```

You can see that there's no binding expression in the preceding code, because everything is done from the `Page_Load` event handler, after loading a `Product` object according to the `ID` value read from the querystring. Once you have such an object, you can set all the `Text`, `Value`, and `Visible` properties of the various controls defined above, as follows:

```
protected void Page_Load(object sender, EventArgs e)
{
    if (string.IsNullOrEmpty(this.Request.QueryString["ID"]))
        throw new ApplicationException("Missing parameter on the querystring.");
    else
        _productID = int.Parse(this.Request.QueryString["ID"]);

    if (!this.IsPostBack)
    {
```

```
        // try to load the product with the specified ID, and raise
        // an exception if it doesn't exist
        Product product = Product.GetProductByID(_productID);
        if (product == null)
            throw new ApplicationException("No product found for the specified ID.");

        // display all article's data on the page
        this.Title = string.Format(this.Title, product.Title);
        lblTitle.Text = product.Title;
        lblRating.Text = string.Format(lblRating.Text, product.Votes);
        ratDisplay.Value = product.AverageRating;
        ratDisplay.Visible = (product.Votes > 0);
        availDisplay.Value = product.UnitsInStock;
        lblDescription.Text = product.Description;
        panEditProduct.Visible = this.UserCanEdit;
        lnkEditProduct.NavigateUrl = string.Format(
            lnkEditProduct.NavigateUrl, _productID);
        lblPrice.Text = this.FormatPrice(product.FinalUnitPrice);
        lblDiscountedPrice.Text = string.Format(lblDiscountedPrice.Text,
            this.FormatPrice(product.UnitPrice), product.DiscountPercentage);
        lblDiscountedPrice.Visible = (product.DiscountPercentage > 0);
        if (product.SmallImageUrl.Length > 0)
            imgProduct.ImageUrl = product.SmallImageUrl;
        if (product.FullImageUrl.Length > 0)
        {
            lnkFullImage.NavigateUrl = product.FullImageUrl;
            lnkFullImage.Visible = true;
        }
        else
            lnkFullImage.Visible = false;

        // hide the rating box controls if the current user has
        // already voted for this product...
    }
}
```

A screenshot of the result is shown in Figure 9-13.

When the customer clicks the Add to Shopping Cart button, we call the `InsertItem` method of the `ShoppingCart` object returned by the `profile` property, and pass in the product's data read from the `Product` object. Finally, we redirect the customer to the `ShoppingCart.aspx` page, where he can change the quantity of the products to order and proceed to the checkout process:

```
protected void btnAddToCart_Click(object sender, EventArgs e)
{
    Product product = Product.GetProductByID(_productID);
    this.Profile.ShoppingCart.InsertItem(
        product.ID, product.Title, product.SKU, product.FinalUnitPrice);
    this.Response.Redirect("ShoppingCart.aspx", false);
}
```

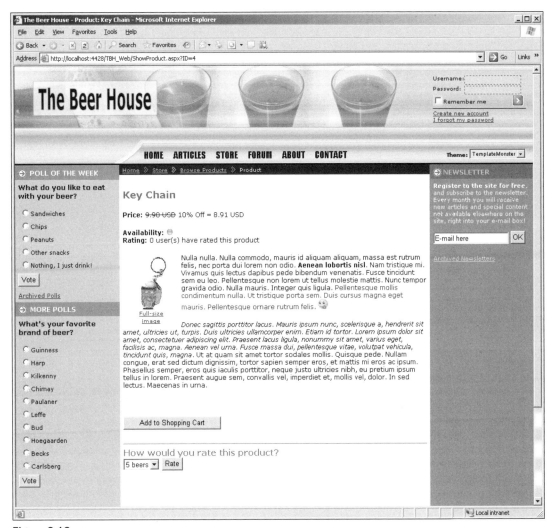

Figure 9-13

The ShoppingCart.aspx Page

As described earlier in the "Design" section for the user interface, this page is actually more complex than a page that just manages the shopping cart, as it includes a complete wizard for the checkout process, which includes steps to provide the contact information and the shipping address, and to review the order a last time before being redirected to PayPal for the payment. ASP.NET 2.0 introduces the new `Wizard` control, which allows us to define different views within it; and it automatically creates and manages the buttons/links at the bottom of the wizard to move backward and forward through the wizard's steps. The control's structure is outlined in the following code:

```
<asp:Wizard ID="wizSubmitOrder" runat="server" ActiveStepIndex="0"
    CancelButtonText="Continue Shopping" CancelButtonType="Link"
    CancelDestinationPageUrl="~/BrowseProducts.aspx" DisplayCancelButton="True"
    DisplaySideBar="False" FinishPreviousButtonType="Link"
    StartNextButtonText="Proceed with order" StartNextButtonType="Link" Width="100%"
    StepNextButtonText="Proceed with order" StepNextButtonType="Link"
    StepPreviousButtonText="Modify data in previous step"
    StepPreviousButtonType="Link" FinishCompleteButtonText="Submit Order"
    FinishCompleteButtonType="Link"
    FinishPreviousButtonText="Modify data in previous step"
    OnFinishButtonClick="wizSubmitOrder_FinishButtonClick"
    OnActiveStepChanged="wizSubmitOrder_ActiveStepChanged">

    <StepNextButtonStyle Font-Bold="True" />
    <StartNextButtonStyle Font-Bold="True" />
    <FinishCompleteButtonStyle Font-Bold="True" />
    <FinishPreviousButtonStyle Font-Bold="True" />

    <WizardSteps>
        <asp:WizardStep runat="server" Title="Shopping Cart">

        </asp:WizardStep>
        <asp:WizardStep runat="server" Title="Shipping Address">

        </asp:WizardStep>
        <asp:WizardStep runat="server" Title="Order Confirmation">

        </asp:WizardStep>
    </WizardSteps>
</asp:Wizard>
```

There's a `<WizardSteps>` section used to define one `<asp:WizardStep>` control for each step you want the wizard to have. The `WizardStep` is a template-based control used to declare the content of that step. The parent `Wizard` control has a number of properties that enable you to completely customize the visual appearance of the commands at the bottom, in addition to their text. The properties used in the preceding code are self-explanatory. The `Wizard` control also exposes a number of methods that a developer can handle to run code when the current step changes, or when the user clicks the button to complete the wizard. There will also be a `Cancel` command in each step that we'll use as the command to continue shopping, so it just redirects the user to the `BrowseProducts.aspx` page.

Let's start with the first step. It defines a `GridView` control with a companion `ObjectDataSource` that binds the grid to the list of `ShoppingCartItem` objects returned by `CurrentUserShoppingCart.GetItems`. The grid has a column for the item's title, a column that shows the item's price, a templated column that creates an editable textbox with the quantity for that product, and finally a column with a command link to completely remove that item from the shopping cart (which would be the same as manually setting the product's quantity to 0, and clicking the button to update the totals). Below the grid we define a `Label` that displays the shopping cart's subtotal amount, a `DropDownList` that lists the available shipping options and their price, and a final `Label` that displays the order's total amount. The `Labels` are updated when a button is clicked. Following is the code that goes into the first `WizardStep` control:

```
<asp:WizardStep runat="server" Title="Shopping Cart">
    <div class="sectiontitle">Shopping Cart</div>
    <p></p>Review and update the quantity of the products added to the cart before
    proceeding to checkout, or continue shopping.<p></p>
    <asp:GridView ID="gvwOrderItems" runat="server" AutoGenerateColumns="False"
        DataSourceID="objShoppingCart" Width="100%" DataKeyNames="ID"
        OnRowDeleted="gvwOrderItems_RowDeleted"
        OnRowCreated="gvwOrderItems_RowCreated">
        <Columns>
            <asp:HyperLinkField DataTextField="Title"
                HeaderStyle-HorizontalAlign="Left"
                DataNavigateUrlFormatString="~/ShowProduct.aspx?ID={0}"
                DataNavigateUrlFields="ID" HeaderText="Product" >
            </asp:HyperLinkField>
            <asp:TemplateField HeaderText="Price" HeaderStyle-HorizontalAlign="Right">
                <ItemTemplate>
                    <div style="text-align: right">
                        <%# FormatPrice(Eval("UnitPrice")) %>
                    </div>
                </ItemTemplate>
            </asp:TemplateField>
            <asp:TemplateField HeaderText="Quantity" ItemStyle-Width="60px">
                <ItemTemplate>
                    <div style="text-align: right;">
                        <asp:TextBox runat="server" ID="txtQuantity"
                            Text='<%# Bind("Quantity") %>' MaxLength="6" Width="30px" />
                        <asp:RequiredFieldValidator ID="valRequireQuantity"
                            runat="server" ControlToValidate="txtQuantity"
                            SetFocusOnError="true" ValidationGroup="ShippingAddress"
                            Text="The Quantity field is required."
                            ToolTip="The Quantity field is required." Display="Dynamic" />
                        <asp:CompareValidator ID="valQuantityType" runat="server"
                            Operator="DataTypeCheck" Type="Integer"
                            ControlToValidate="txtQuantity" Display="dynamic"
                            Text="The Quantity must be an integer."
                            ToolTip="The Quantity must be an integer." />
                    </div>
                </ItemTemplate>
            </asp:TemplateField>
            <asp:CommandField ButtonType="Image" DeleteImageUrl="~/Images/Delete.gif"
                DeleteText="Delete product" ShowDeleteButton="True" />
        </Columns>
        <EmptyDataTemplate><b>The shopping cart is empty</b></EmptyDataTemplate>
    </asp:GridView>
    <asp:ObjectDataSource ID="objShoppingCart" runat="server"
        SelectMethod="GetItems" DeleteMethod="DeleteProduct"
        TypeName="MB.TheBeerHouse.BLL.Store.CurrentUserShoppingCart" />
    <asp:Panel runat="server" ID="panTotals">
    <div style="text-align: right; font-weight: bold; padding-top: 4px;">
        Subtotal: <asp:Literal runat="server" ID="lblSubtotal" />
        <p>
        Shipping Method:
        <asp:DropDownList ID="ddlShippingMethods" runat="server"
            DataSourceID="objShippingMethods"
            DataTextField="TitleAndPrice" DataValueField="Price">
```

459

```
        </asp:DropDownList>
        <asp:ObjectDataSource ID="objShippingMethods" runat="server"
            SelectMethod="GetShippingMethods"
            TypeName="MB.TheBeerHouse.BLL.Store.ShippingMethod" />
        </p>
        <p>
        <u>Total:</u> <asp:Literal runat="server" ID="lblTotal" />
        </p>
        <asp:Button ID="btnUpdateTotals" runat="server"
            OnClick="btnUpdateTotals_Click" Text="Update totals" />
    </div>
    </asp:Panel>
</asp:WizardStep>
```

In the page's code-behind file is an `UpdateTotals` method that is called when a row is deleted from the `GridView` (a product was completely removed from the shopping cart) or when the customer clicks the Update button, typically after changing a product's quantity or selecting a shipping method. The `UpdateTotals` method loops through the rows of the `GridView` control, and for each row it finds the textbox control with the product's quantity, reads its value, and uses it to update the quantity of the product stored in the shopping cart, by means of the `ShoppingCart.UpdateItemQuantity` method. Then it can display the order's subtotal and total amounts according to the updated quantities and the currently selected shipping method. Finally, it checks whether the shopping cart actually contains something, because if that's not the case it doesn't make sense for the customer to proceed to the next step of the checkout wizard. Curiously, the `Wizard` control has no properties to explicitly disable the `Next` and `Previous` commands, but you can do that by setting the command's text to an empty string, so that they won't be visible. The property to set in this case is `StartNextButtonText`, because we are in the Start step (i.e., the first one) and we want to disable the `Next` command. Here's the implementation for this first part of the wizard:

```
protected void gvwOrderItems_RowDeleted(object sender, GridViewDeletedEventArgs e)
{
    UpdateTotals();
}


protected void btnUpdateTotals_Click(object sender, EventArgs e)
{
    UpdateTotals();
}


protected void UpdateTotals()
{
    // update the quantities
    foreach (GridViewRow row in gvwOrderItems.Rows)
    {
        int id = Convert.ToInt32(gvwOrderItems.DataKeys[row.RowIndex][0]);
        int quantity = Convert.ToInt32(
            (row.FindControl("txtQuantity") as TextBox).Text);
        this.Profile.ShoppingCart.UpdateItemQuantity(id, quantity);
    }

    // display the subtotal and the total amounts
    lblSubtotal.Text = this.FormatPrice(this.Profile.ShoppingCart.Total);
    lblTotal.Text = this.FormatPrice(this.Profile.ShoppingCart.Total +
```

```
            Convert.ToDecimal(ddlShippingMethods.SelectedValue));

    // if the shopping cart is empty, hide the link to proceed
    if (this.Profile.ShoppingCart.Items.Count == 0)
    {
        wizSubmitOrder.StartNextButtonText = "";
        panTotals.Visible = false;
    }

    gvwOrderItems.DataBind();
}
```

Figure 9-14 shows a sample screenshot of this first step at runtime.

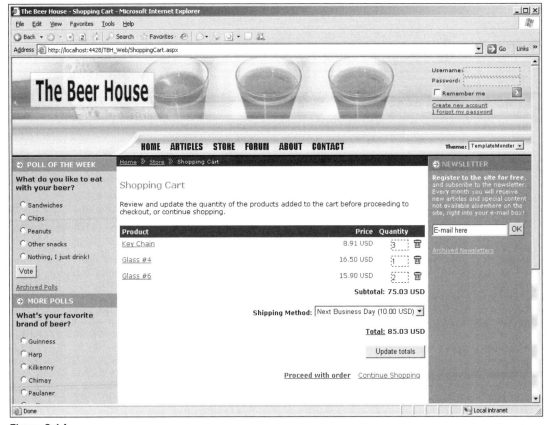

Figure 9-14

The second step is simpler than the first one; it's just a form that asks for contact information and the shipping address. This information is pre-filled with the information stored in the customer's profile, if provided, but customers can change everything in this form if they're buying a gift for someone and want the product(s) to be shipped directly to that person. Also, at this point a user account is required to proceed, so if the current user is anonymous, then she will be asked to log in or create a new user account, instead of displaying the input form. To do this, a `MultiView` control with two views is used, and the index of the desired view will be dynamically set when the page loads if the index of the wizard's current step is 1 (second step), according to whether the user is authenticated. A more traditional approach would have been to create two `Panels` and show/hide them according to that condition, but the `MultiView` control was intended to be a more elegant alternative to that solution. In practice, it's just a wizard control under the hood without the automatically created buttons to move forward and backward. Here's the markup code:

```
<asp:WizardStep runat="server" Title="Shipping Address">
    <div class="sectiontitle">Shipping Address</div>
    <p></p>
    <asp:MultiView ID="mvwShipping" runat="server">
        <asp:View ID="vwLoginRequired" runat="server">
            An account is required to proceed with the order submission. If you
            already have an account please login now, otherwise
            <a href="Register.aspx">create a new account</a> for free.
        </asp:View>
        <asp:View ID="vwShipping" runat="server">
            Fill the form below with the shipping address for your order...
            <p></p>
            <table cellpadding="2" width="410">
                <tr>
                    <td width="110" class="fieldname">
                        <asp:Label runat="server" ID="lblFirstName"
                            AssociatedControlID="txtFirstName" Text="First name:" />
                    </td>
                    <td width="300">
                        <asp:TextBox ID="txtFirstName" runat="server" Width="100%" />
                        <asp:RequiredFieldValidator ID="valRequireFirstName"
                            runat="server" ControlToValidate="txtFirstName"
                            SetFocusOnError="true" ValidationGroup="ShippingAddress"
                            Text="The First Name field is required." Display="Dynamic"
                            ToolTip="The First Name field is required." />
                    </td>
                </tr>
                <tr>
                    <td class="fieldname">
                        <asp:Label runat="server" ID="lblLastName"
                            AssociatedControlID="txtLastName" Text="Last name:" />
                    </td>
                    <td>
                        <asp:TextBox ID="txtLastName" runat="server" Width="100%" />
                        <asp:RequiredFieldValidator ID="valRequireLastName"
                            runat="server" ControlToValidate="txtLastName"
                            SetFocusOnError="true" ValidationGroup="ShippingAddress"
                            Text="The Last Name field is required." Display="Dynamic"
                            ToolTip="The Last Name field is required." />
                    </td>
                </tr>
                <!-- more rows for more shipping information here... -->
            </table>
        </asp:View>
    </asp:MultiView>
</asp:WizardStep>
```

Following is the code-behind that pre-fills the various textboxes if the current user is logged in. Also note that `UpdateTotals` is called in this event so that the totals are updated correctly even when the customer changed some quantities and proceeded to the next step without clicking the Update Total button:

```
protected void Page_Load(object sender, EventArgs e)
{
    if (!Page.IsPostBack)
    {...}
    else
    {
        bool isAuthenticated = this.User.Identity.IsAuthenticated;
        mvwShipping.ActiveViewIndex = (isAuthenticated ? 1 : 0);
        wizSubmitOrder.StepNextButtonText = (isAuthenticated ?
            wizSubmitOrder.StartNextButtonText : "");
    }
}

protected void wizSubmitOrder_ActiveStepChanged(object sender, EventArgs e)
{
    if (wizSubmitOrder.ActiveStepIndex == 1)
    {
    UpdateTotals();

    if (this.User.Identity.IsAuthenticated)
    {
        if (ddlCountries.Items.Count == 1)
        {
            ddlCountries.DataSource = Helpers.GetCountries();
            ddlCountries.DataBind();
        }

        if (txtFirstName.Text.Trim().Length == 0)
            txtFirstName.Text = this.Profile.FirstName;
        if (txtLastName.Text.Trim().Length == 0)
            txtLastName.Text = this.Profile.LastName;
        if (txtEmail.Text.Trim().Length == 0)
            txtEmail.Text = Membership.GetUser().Email;
        if (txtStreet.Text.Trim().Length == 0)
            txtStreet.Text = this.Profile.Address.Street;
        if (txtPostalCode.Text.Trim().Length == 0)
            txtPostalCode.Text = this.Profile.Address.PostalCode;
        if (txtCity.Text.Trim().Length == 0)
            txtCity.Text = this.Profile.Address.City;
        if (txtState.Text.Trim().Length == 0)
            txtState.Text = this.Profile.Address.State;
        if (ddlCountries.SelectedIndex == 0)
            ddlCountries.SelectedValue = this.Profile.Address.Country;
        if (txtPhone.Text.Trim().Length == 0)
            txtPhone.Text = this.Profile.Contacts.Phone;
        if (txtFax.Text.Trim().Length == 0)
            txtFax.Text = this.Profile.Contacts.Fax;
    }
    }
}
```

Figure 9-15 shows what this step looks like on the page at runtime.

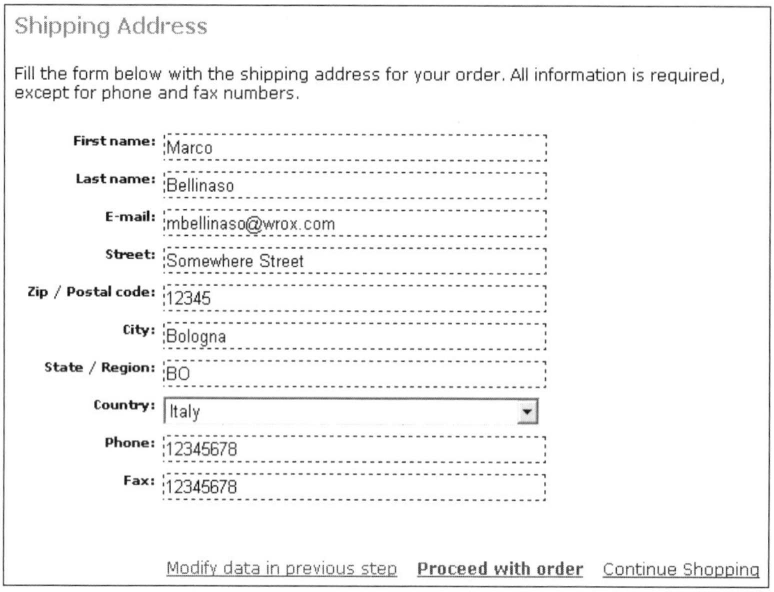

Shipping Address

Fill the form below with the shipping address for your order. All information is required, except for phone and fax numbers.

First name:	Marco
Last name:	Bellinaso
E-mail:	mbellinaso@wrox.com
Street:	Somewhere Street
Zip / Postal code:	12345
City:	Bologna
State / Region:	BO
Country:	Italy
Phone:	12345678
Fax:	12345678

Modify data in previous step   **Proceed with order**   Continue Shopping

Figure 9-15

The last step allows the customer to review all data inserted so far: the name, price, and quantity of the products she's about to order, the subtotal amount, the shipping method and its price, the total amount, as well as her personal contact information and the shipping address. The `WizardStep` template defines a number of `Labels` for most of this information, and a `Repeater` control bound to the same `ObjectDataSource` used for the first step's `GridView` to show the items in the shopping cart:

```
<asp:WizardStep runat="server" Title="Order Confirmation">
    <div class="sectiontitle">Order Summary</div>
    <p></p>
    Please carefully review the order information below...
    <p></p>
    <img src="Images/paypal.gif" style="float: right" />
    <b>Order Details</b>
    <p></p>
    <asp:Repeater runat="server" ID="repOrderItems" DataSourceID="objShoppingCart">
        <ItemTemplate>
            <img src="Images/ArrowR3.gif" border="0" />
            <%# Eval("Title") %> - <%# FormatPrice(Eval("UnitPrice")) %>
            <small>(Quantity = <%# Eval("Quantity") %>)</small>
            <br />
        </ItemTemplate>
    </asp:Repeater>
```

```
    <br />
    Subtotal = <asp:Literal runat="server" ID="lblReviewSubtotal" />
    <p></p>
    Shipping Method = <asp:Literal runat="server" ID="lblReviewShippingMethod" />
    <p></p>
    <u>Total</u> = <asp:Literal runat="server" ID="lblReviewTotal" />
    <p></p>
    <b>Shipping Details</b>
    <p></p>
    <asp:Literal runat="server" ID="lblReviewFirstName" />
    <asp:Literal runat="server" ID="lblReviewLastName" /><br />
    <asp:Literal runat="server" ID="lblReviewStreet" /><br />
    <asp:Literal runat="server" ID="lblReviewCity" />,
    <asp:Literal runat="server" ID="lblReviewState" />
    <asp:Literal runat="server" ID="lblReviewPostalCode" /><br />
    <asp:Literal runat="server" ID="lblReviewCountry" />
</asp:WizardStep>
```

When this step loads, we confirm that the wizard's `ActiveStepIndex` is 2, and then show all the information in the controls:

```
protected void wizSubmitOrder_ActiveStepChanged(object sender, EventArgs e)
{
    if (wizSubmitOrder.ActiveStepIndex == 1)
    { ... }
    else if (wizSubmitOrder.ActiveStepIndex == 2)
    {
        lblReviewFirstName.Text = txtFirstName.Text;
        lblReviewLastName.Text = txtLastName.Text;
        lblReviewStreet.Text = txtStreet.Text;
        lblReviewCity.Text = txtCity.Text;
        lblReviewState.Text = txtState.Text;
        lblReviewPostalCode.Text = txtPostalCode.Text;
        lblReviewCountry.Text = ddlCountries.SelectedValue;

        lblReviewSubtotal.Text = this.FormatPrice(this.Profile.ShoppingCart.Total);
        lblReviewShippingMethod.Text = ddlShippingMethods.SelectedItem.Text;
        lblReviewTotal.Text = this.FormatPrice(this.Profile.ShoppingCart.Total +
            Convert.ToDecimal(ddlShippingMethods.SelectedValue));
    }
}
```

The step is displayed as shown in Figure 9-16.

Figure 9-16

If the Finish button is clicked, the wizard's `FinishButtonClick` event handler will save the shopping cart's content as a new order in the database, clear the shopping cart, and use the `GetPayPalPaymentUrl` of the new `Order` instance to get the PayPal URL; and then we'll redirect the customer to pay for the ordered products. However, before doing all this we must determine whether the customer is still authenticated. In fact, consider the situation when the customer gets to this last step, and then goes away from the computer, maybe to find her credit card. When she comes back, her authentication cookie may have expired in the meantime, in which case we'd get an empty shopping cart for an anonymous user when accessing `Profile.ShoppingCart`. Therefore, if the current user is not authenticated at this point, then we'll redirect her to the page that requests the login; otherwise, we'll go ahead and send her to the PayPal site:

```
protected void wizSubmitOrder_FinishButtonClick(object sender,
    WizardNavigationEventArgs e)
{

    if (this.User.Identity.IsAuthenticated)
    {
        string shippingMethod = ddlShippingMethods.SelectedItem.Text;
        shippingMethod = shippingMethod.Substring(0,
            shippingMethod.LastIndexOf('('));

        // saves the order into the DB, and clear the shopping cart in the profile
        int orderID = Order.InsertOrder(this.Profile.ShoppingCart, shippingMethod,
            Convert.ToDecimal(ddlShippingMethods.SelectedValue),
            txtFirstName.Text, txtLastName.Text, txtStreet.Text, txtPostalCode.Text,
            txtCity.Text, txtState.Text, ddlCountries.SelectedValue, txtEmail.Text,
```

```
        txtPhone.Text, txtFax.Text, "");

    this.Profile.ShoppingCart.Clear();

    // redirect to PayPal for the credit-card payment
    Order order = Order.GetOrderByID(orderID);
    this.Response.Redirect(order.GetPayPalPaymentUrl(), false);
    }
    else
        this.RequestLogin();
}
```

Figure 9-17 is a screenshot of the PayPal payment page, run from inside the Sandbox test environment. Note that the subtotal, shipping, and total amounts are exactly the same as those shown in the previous figures.

Figure 9-17

Handing the Customer's Return from PayPal

When the customer cancels the order while she's on PayPal's page, she is redirected to the Order
Cancelled.aspx page, which has just a couple of lines of static feedback instructions explaining how
she can pay at a later time. If she completes the payment, then she'll be directed to the OrderCompleted
.aspx page instead: It expects the ID of the order paid by the customer on the querystring, so that it can
load an Order object for it, and then it updates its StatusID property from "waiting for payment" to
"confirmed," but not yet "verified":

```
protected void Page_Load(object sender, EventArgs e)
{
    Order order = Order.GetOrderByID(Convert.ToInt32(
        this.Request.QueryString["ID"]));
    if (order.StatusID == (int)StatusCode.WaitingForPayment)
    {
        order.StatusID = (int)StatusCode.Confirmed;
        order.Update();
    }
}
```

Figure 9-18 shows screenshots for both pages.

The Notify.aspx page is the one that receives the IPN notification. As explained earlier, the first thing
you do in this page is verify that the notification is real and was not faked by a dishonest user. To do this,
you send the notification data back to PayPal using HttpWebRequest, and see if PayPal responds with a
VERIFIED string:

```
private bool IsVerifiedNotification()
{
    string response = "";
    string post = Request.Form.ToString() + "&cmd=_notify-validate";
    string serverUrl = (Globals.Settings.Store.SandboxMode ?
        "https://www.sandbox.paypal.com/us/cgi-bin/webscr" :
        "https://www.paypal.com/us/cgi-bin/webscr");

    HttpWebRequest req = (HttpWebRequest)WebRequest.Create(serverUrl);
    req.Method = "POST";
    req.ContentType = "application/x-www-form-urlencoded";
    req.ContentLength = post.Length;

    StreamWriter writer = new StreamWriter(req.GetRequestStream(),
        System.Text.Encoding.ASCII);
    writer.Write(post);
    writer.Close();

    StreamReader reader = new StreamReader(req.GetResponse().GetResponseStream());
    response = reader.ReadToEnd();
    reader.Close();

    return (response == "VERIFIED");
}
```

Figure 9-18

This method is called from inside the `Page_Load` handler, and if the check succeeds, we extract some data from the request's parameters, such as `custom` (the order ID), `payment_status` (a string describing the current status for the order transaction) and `mc_gross` (the order's total amount). Then we get a reference to the `Order` object according to the order ID obtained from the notification, and we check whether the total amount stored in the database matches the amount indicated by the PayPal notification. If so, we update the order status to "verified." Here's the code:

```
protected void Page_Load(object sender, EventArgs e)
{
    if (IsVerifiedNotification())
    {
        int orderID = Convert.ToInt32(this.Request.Params["custom"]);
        string status = this.Request.Params["payment_status"];
        decimal amount = Convert.ToDecimal(this.Request.Params["mc_gross"],
            CultureInfo.CreateSpecificCulture("en-US"));

        // get the Order object corresponding to the input orderID,
        // and check that its total matches the input total
        Order order = Order.GetOrderByID(orderID);
        decimal origAmount = (order.SubTotal + order.Shipping);
        if (amount >= origAmount)
        {
            order.StatusID = (int)StatusCode.Verified;
            order.Update();
        }
    }
}
```

In the preceding code, when parsing the mc_gross string to a decimal value, a CultureInfo object for en-US (English for U.S.) is passed to the Convert.ToDecimal call. This is because PayPal always uses a period (.) as separator for the decimal part of the number, but if the current thread's locale is set to some other culture that uses a comma for the separator, the string would have been parsed incorrectly without this code.

> Note that there can be many more parameters that PayPal passes to your page in the IPN notifications than those used here. I strongly suggest you to refer to PayPal's documentation for the full coverage of these parameters, and for the guide on how to activate and set up the IPN notifications from your PayPal's account settings, which is not covered here.

The ShoppingCart.ascx User Control

So far I haven't shown any links to the ShoppingCart.aspx page, but we want the cart to be visible on any page. The shopping cart's current content should always be visible as well, so that the customer does not need to go to ShoppingCart.aspx just to see whether she's already put a product into the cart. We also want customers to see the subtotal so they won't get any surprises when they proceed to checkout. All this information can easily be shown on a user control that will be plugged into the site's master page, so it will always be present. The ShoppingCart.ascx control defines a Repeater control that's similar to the one used earlier in the last step of the ShoppingCart.aspx page, which shows the current list of shopping cart items with their name, unit price, and quantity. Below that is a label for displaying the shopping cart's total amount, and a hyperlink to the full ShoppingCart.aspx page, where the customer can change quantities and proceed with the checkout. If also defines a link to the OrderHistory.aspx page, which we'll create next:

```
<asp:Repeater runat="server" ID="repOrderItems">
   <ItemTemplate>
      <small>
      <asp:Image runat="Server" ID="imgProduct"
         ImageUrl="~/Images/ArrowR3.gif" GenerateEmptyAlternateText="true" />
      <%# Eval("Title") %> -
      <%# (this.Page as BasePage).FormatPrice(Eval("UnitPrice")) %>
      <small>(<%# Eval("Quantity") %>)</small><br />
   </ItemTemplate>
</asp:Repeater>
<br />
<b><asp:Literal runat="server" ID="lblSubtotalHeader" Text="Subtotal = " />
<asp:Literal runat="server" ID="lblSubtotal" /></b>
<asp:Literal runat="server" ID="lblCartIsEmpty" Text="Your cart is currently
empty." />
<p></p>
<asp:Panel runat="server" ID="panLinkShoppingCart">
   <asp:HyperLink runat="server" ID="lnkShoppingCart"
      NavigateUrl="~/ShoppingCart.aspx">Detailed Shopping Cart</asp:HyperLink>
</asp:Panel>
<asp:HyperLink runat="server" ID="lnkOrderHistory"
   NavigateUrl="~/OrderHistory.aspx" >Order History</asp:HyperLink>
```

In the control's code-behind class, we just handle the Load event to bind the Repeater with the data returned by the Items property of the Profile.ShoppingCart object, show the total amount in the label, and hide the panel with the link to ShoppingCart.aspx if the cart is empty:

```
protected void Page_Load(object sender, EventArgs e)
{
   if (!this.IsPostBack)
   {
      if (this.Profile.ShoppingCart.Items.Count > 0)
      {
         repOrderItems.DataSource = this.Profile.ShoppingCart.Items;
         repOrderItems.DataBind();

         lblSubtotal.Text = (this.Page as BasePage).FormatPrice(
            this.Profile.ShoppingCart.Total);
         lblSubtotal.Visible = true;
         lblSubtotalHeader.Visible = true;
         panLinkShoppingCart.Visible = true;
         lblCartIsEmpty.Visible = false;
      }
      else
      {
         lblSubtotal.Visible = false;
         lblSubtotalHeader.Visible = false;
         panLinkShoppingCart.Visible = false;
         lblCartIsEmpty.Visible = true;
      }
   }
}
```

Figure 9-19 shows how the control looks—both empty and not empty.

Figure 9-19

The OrderHistory.aspx Page

This page contains a `DataList` that lists all past orders for the current authenticated user. The `DataList`'s template section shows the order's title, the total amount, and the title of the current status, plus the detailed list of all order items, rendered by a `Repeater` similar to those used earlier. If the order's `StatusID` is 1 (waiting for payment), it also renders a link to the PayPal payment page, retrieved by means of the order's `GetPayPalPaymentUrl` method, already used in the last step of the `ShoppingCart.aspx` page's checkout wizard. At the end of the template it also displays the subtotal amount, and the shipping method's title and cost:

```
<asp:DataList runat="server" ID="dlstOrders">
    <ItemTemplate>
        <div class="sectionsubtitle">
            Order #<%# Eval("ID") %> - <%# Eval("AddedDate", "{0:g}") %></div>
        <br />
        <img src="Images/ArrowR4.gif" border="0" /> <u>Total</u> =
        <%# FormatPrice((decimal)Eval("SubTotal") + (decimal)Eval("Shipping")) %>
        <img src="Images/ArrowR4.gif" border="0" /> <u>Status</u> =
            <%# Eval("StatusTitle") %>
        <asp:HyperLink runat="server" ID="lnkPay" Font-Bold="true" Text="Pay Now"
            NavigateUrl='<%# (Container.DataItem as Order).GetPayPalPaymentUrl() %>'
            Visible = '<%# ((int)Eval("StatusID")) == 1 %>' /><p></p>
        <small>
        <b>Details</b><br />
        <asp:Repeater runat="server" ID="repOrderItems"
            DataSource='<%# Eval("Items") %>'>
            <ItemTemplate>
                <img src="Images/ArrowR3.gif" border="0" />
                <%# Eval("Title") %> - <%# FormatPrice(Eval("UnitPrice")) %>
                    <small>(Quantity = <%# Eval("Quantity") %>)</small><br />
            </ItemTemplate>
        </asp:Repeater>
        <br />
        Subtotal = <%# FormatPrice(Eval("SubTotal")) %><br />
        Shipping Method = <%# Eval("ShippingMethod") %>
            (<%# FormatPrice(Eval("Shipping")) %>)
        </small>
    </ItemTemplate>
```

```
      <SeparatorTemplate>
          <hr style="width: 99%; noshade: noshade;" />
      </SeparatorTemplate>
  </asp:DataList>
```

The page's code-behind contains only a couple of lines that bind the `DataList` with the list of orders returned by the `Order.GetOrders` overloaded method, which accepts the name of the current user:

```
  dlstOrders.DataSource = Order.GetOrders(this.User.Identity.Name);
  dlstOrders.DataBind();
```

Figure 9-20 is a screenshot of the page.

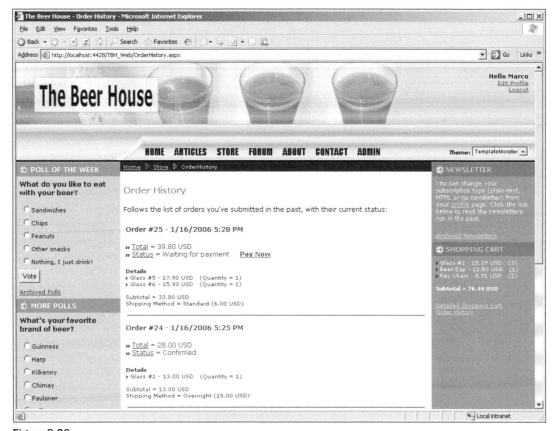

Figure 9-20

The ManageOrders.aspx and EditOrder.aspx Pages

This administrative page is used by storekeepers to retrieve the list of orders in a certain status created in a specified date interval, or to retrieve the list of all orders made by a given customer. If the storekeeper already knows the ID of a specific order and wants to update it, there's a form that lets her enter the ID and click the button to jump to the edit page. The following markup code defines the input forms to filter the data as described, as well as the `GridView` that actually displays the found orders, with their title, list of order items (through the usual `Repeater` already used, which shows the `SKU` field in addition to the others, as this is useful information for storekeepers), the subtotal amount, and the shipping amount. On the right side of each order row there's also a button to delete the order, but that will only be shown to Administrators, and not to StoreKeepers, as it's a sensitive operation that should only be performed rarely, and never by accident:

```
Status: <asp:DropDownList ID="ddlOrderStatuses" runat="server"
    DataSourceID="objAllStatuses" DataTextField="Title" DataValueField="ID" />
<asp:ObjectDataSource ID="objAllStatuses" runat="server"
    SelectMethod="GetOrderStatuses"
    TypeName="MB.TheBeerHouse.BLL.Store.OrderStatus" />
from: <asp:TextBox ID="txtFromDate" runat="server" Width="80px" />
to: <asp:TextBox ID="txtToDate" runat="server" Width="80px" />
<asp:Button ID="btnListByStatus" runat="server" Text="Load"
    OnClick="btnListByStatus_Click" ValidationGroup="ListByStatus" />
<!-- validator controls here ... -->

<div class="sectionsubtitle">Orders by customer</div>
Name: <asp:TextBox ID="txtCustomerName" runat="server" />
<asp:Button ID="btnListByCustomer" runat="server" Text="Load"
    OnClick="btnListByCustomer_Click" ValidationGroup="ListByCustomer" />

<div class="sectionsubtitle">Order Lookup</div>
ID: <asp:TextBox ID="txtOrderID" runat="server" />
<asp:Button ID="btnOrderLookup" runat="server" Text="Find"
    OnClick="btnOrderLookup_Click" ValidationGroup="OrderLookup" />
<asp:Label runat="server" ID="lblOrderNotFound" SkinID="FeedbackKO"
    Text="Order not found!" Visible="false" />

<asp:GridView ID="gvwOrders" runat="server" AutoGenerateColumns="False"
    Width="100%" DataKeyNames="ID" OnRowDeleting="gvwOrders_RowDeleting"
    OnRowCreated="gvwOrders_RowCreated">
    <Columns>
        <asp:BoundField HeaderText="Date" DataField="AddedDate"
            HeaderStyle-HorizontalAlign="Left" DataFormatString="{0:d}<br />{0:t}"
            HtmlEncode="False" />
        <asp:BoundField HeaderText="Customer" DataField="AddedBy"
            HeaderStyle-HorizontalAlign="Left" />
        <asp:TemplateField HeaderText="Items" HeaderStyle-HorizontalAlign="Left">
            <ItemTemplate>
                <small>
                <asp:Repeater runat="server" ID="repOrderItems"
                    DataSource='<%# Eval("Items") %>'>
                    <ItemTemplate>
                        <img src="../Images/ArrowR3.gif" border="0" />
                        [<%# Eval("SKU") %>]
                        <asp:HyperLink runat="server" ID="lnkProduct"
                            Text='<%# Eval("Title") %>'
```

```
                    NavigateUrl='<%# "~/ShowProduct.aspx?ID=" +
                        Eval("ProductID") %>' />
                    - (<%# Eval("Quantity") %>)
                    <br />
                </ItemTemplate>
            </asp:Repeater>
            </small>
        </ItemTemplate>
    </asp:TemplateField>
    <asp:BoundField HeaderText="Subtotal" DataField="SubTotal"
        HeaderStyle-HorizontalAlign="Right" ItemStyle-HorizontalAlign="Right"
        DataFormatString="{0:N2}" HtmlEncode="False" />
    <asp:BoundField HeaderText="Shipping" DataField="Shipping"
        HeaderStyle-HorizontalAlign="Right" ItemStyle-HorizontalAlign="Right"
        DataFormatString="{0:N2}" HtmlEncode="False" />
    <asp:HyperLinkField Text="<img border='0' src='../Images/ArrowR.gif' />"
        DataNavigateUrlFormatString="EditOrder.aspx?ID={0}"
        DataNavigateUrlFields="ID"
        ItemStyle-HorizontalAlign="Center" ItemStyle-Width="20px" />
    <asp:CommandField ButtonType="Image" DeleteImageUrl="~/Images/Delete.gif"
        DeleteText="Delete order" ShowDeleteButton="True"
        ItemStyle-HorizontalAlign="Center" ItemStyle-Width="20px" />
    </Columns>
    <EmptyDataTemplate><b>No orders to show</b></EmptyDataTemplate>
</asp:GridView>
```

When the page loads, the textbox for the end date of the date interval is pre-filled with the current date, while the textbox for the start date is pre-filled with the current date minus the number of days specified in the `DefaultOrderListInterval` configuration setting:

```
protected void Page_Load(object sender, EventArgs e)
{
    if (!this.IsPostBack)
    {
        txtToDate.Text = DateTime.Now.ToShortDateString();
        txtFromDate.Text = DateTime.Now.Subtract(
            new TimeSpan(Globals.Settings.Store.DefaultOrderListInterval,
            0, 0, 0)).ToShortDateString();
    }

    lblOrderNotFound.Visible = false;
    // if the user is not an admin, hide the grid's column with the delete button
    gvwOrders.Columns[6].Visible = (this.User.IsInRole("Administrators"));
}
```

When the user types an ID into the `txtOrderID` textbox and clicks the Lookup Order button, we need to determine whether an order with that ID exists: If so, then we redirect her to the `EditOrder.aspx` page (that you'll see shortly), passing the order's ID on the querystring; otherwise, we show a `Label` with an error message:

```
protected void btnOrderLookup_Click(object sender, EventArgs e)
{
    // if the order with the specified ID is not found, show the error label,
    // otherwise redirect to EditOrder.aspx with the ID on the querystring
    Order order = Order.GetOrderByID(Convert.ToInt32(txtOrderID.Text));
    if (order == null)
        lblOrderNotFound.Visible = true;
    else
        this.Response.Redirect("EditOrder.aspx?ID=" + txtOrderID.Text);
}
```

When the other two buttons are clicked, we'll set a GridView's attribute indicating the filter mode, and call the DoBinding method to load the orders, by means of one of the two overloads for the Order.GetOrders method:

```
protected void btnListByCustomer_Click(object sender, EventArgs e)
{
    gvwOrders.Attributes.Add("ListByCustomers", true.ToString());
    DoBinding();
}

protected void btnListByStatus_Click(object sender, EventArgs e)
{
    gvwOrders.Attributes.Add("ListByCustomers", false.ToString());
    DoBinding();
}

protected void DoBinding()
{
    bool listByCustomers = false;
    if (!string.IsNullOrEmpty(gvwOrders.Attributes["ListByCustomers"]))
        listByCustomers = bool.Parse(gvwOrders.Attributes["ListByCustomers"]);

    List<Order> orders = null;
    if (listByCustomers)
    {
        orders = Order.GetOrders(txtCustomerName.Text);
    }
    else
    {
        orders = Order.GetOrders(Convert.ToInt32(ddlOrderStatuses.SelectedValue),
            Convert.ToDateTime(txtFromDate.Text), Convert.ToDateTime(txtToDate.Text));
    }

    gvwOrders.DataSource = orders;
    gvwOrders.DataBind();
}
```

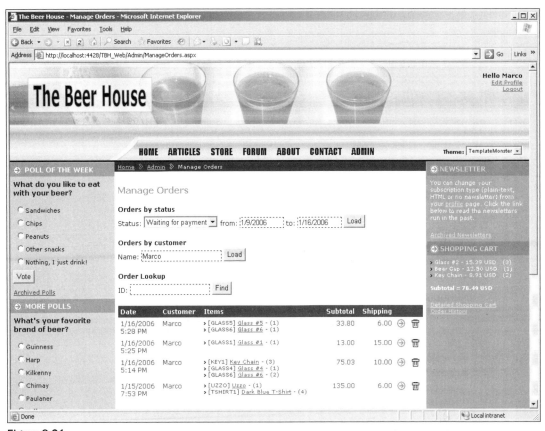

Figure 9-21

The `EditOrder.aspx` page defines a `DetailsView` control that allows users to edit a few fields of the order whose ID is passed on the querystring. The code is not presented here because it's similar to the other `AddEdit{xxx}.aspx` pages developed for this module (but actually simpler because most of the data is read-only, and the `DetailsView`'s insert mode is not supported), and other modules. Figure 9-22 shows a screenshot of it, however, so that you can get an idea of what it looks like and what it can do.

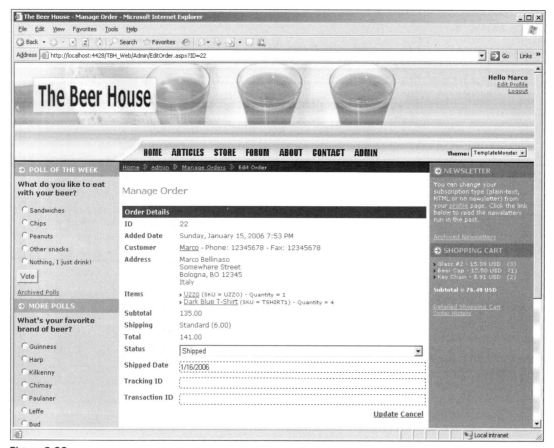

Figure 9-22

Summary

An e-commerce module is a big challenge for any site developer, and there are a lot of features we couldn't implement in this chapter that you may find useful, especially for larger sites. In fact, you can find many commercial modules for managing electronic stores among third-party vendors, and sometimes it can be cheaper to buy one than to develop one yourself: You need to consider the features that you want, and weigh the cost of commercial solutions against the cost of doing it yourself. The module in this chapter may be entirely adequate for small sites, or for a small store of a larger site, but you might also want to add some advanced features such as the capability to list a product under multiple categories, handle tax calculations on the store itself instead of leaving it to PayPal, support products with variations (color, size, etc.) that could also affect their price, support customer-level discounts (so that loyal customers get a better discount percentage, for example), support bundle offers and discounts based on the quantity of ordered products and the total price reached, integrating the shipment tracking offered by some shipping companies such as FedEx and UPS, and much more.

Nevertheless, in this chapter we've implemented a fully working e-commerce store with most of the basic features, including complete catalog and order management, a persistent shopping cart, integrated online payment via credit card, product rating, and more. All this required a fairly short amount of time to design and implement, and this was due in no small part to the powerful new features in ASP.NET 2.0 such as profiles (which enable us to implement persistent shopping carts in minutes instead of several hours or days) and UI controls such as the `GridView`, `DetailsView`, `Wizard`, and `MultiView` controls.

In the next chapter you'll discover another great feature of ASP.NET 2.0: Web Parts, which enable end users to personalize their pages by dynamically adding, removing, and moving around content boxes, and enable editors and administrators to change the home page's content and its disposition without actually changing the code of the page and uploading it every time.

10

Personalization and Web Parts

One of the major new features of ASP.NET 2.0 is Web Parts, which are controls and islands of content that users can move around the page and place where they prefer, enabling users to build a page according to their interests and tastes. Web Parts can be dynamically added and removed by users, customized, closed, minimized, and restored, so that pages can be fully personalized. In this chapter, you'll see how to extend the current site with the addition of new home page customization options thanks to ASP.NET 2.0 Web Parts.

Problem

So far you've built a pretty complete web site with membership, content management system, and e-commerce features. You've also added a few personalization features, such as theme selection and the highlighting of events located in the user's city, state, or country. These personalizations are related to appearance — the way that content is presented to the user. Sites such as Windows Live, My MSN, and My Yahoo push this idea further, enabling users to personalize their pages by choosing the actual content they want to have on the page, together with its position and appearance. By default, the home page may contain the weather forecasts on the top, the economics news on the bottom-left corner, and the currency/stock exchange values on the bottom-right corner. However, a user interested in both economics and technology may prefer to move the economics news to the top, and add a new content box on the home page just below that, with technology news; the stock exchange box may be shifted to the bottom-left corner, with the weather forecasts on the bottom-right corner. Another user may not be interested at all in weather forecasts, and may prefer to have that box of content hidden, so that the page results are cleaner and easier to read, with less distractions, and are quicker to load. These are just a few examples of how users can greatly improve their own user experience by having their favorite content at their fingertips, in the place they find most appropriate and easiest to view.

Many portal frameworks, such as Microsoft's Windows SharePoint Services and the open-source DotNetNuke project, enable you to create sites with support and home page personalization, by means of Web Parts. In this chapter, we want to add the same feature to TheBeerHouse site because, besides making it a much cooler site, it's another reason for users to register (because personalization is only available to authenticated users) and provide their personal details (which are precious for marketing purposes). If your users find a place that can be tailor-made on a per-user basis, according to their needs, they'll recognize the advantages of the site and want to visit frequently.

Web Parts and home page personalization are good not only from the end-user's perspective, but also for site administrators and editors. In fact, while ASP.NET's Web Part Framework allows normal registered end users to personalize their own personal view, it also allows users with the proper rights to edit a shared view of the page as seen by all users. Do you see the great opportunity here? An editor can add, move, or remove content from the home page without modifying the page's source code and uploading the edited page. This makes edits more immediate and easier to perform, because an editor is not required to have the technical knowledge that would otherwise be needed, and a developer will no longer be asked to make simple changes (which is more costly). Additionally, these types of changes can be performed while on the go, from a mobile device such as a PDA with an Internet browser that supports advanced JavaScript, without having the site's source code and a FTP client to download and upload it. The bottom line is that the introduction of Web Parts will be greatly appreciated by end users and administrators/editors.

Design

In this section we aren't going to develop a heavy infrastructure, as ASP.NET 2.0 already provides that for us! You can think of a Web Part as being similar to a user or custom control, with the addition of a title bar and a border (both of which are optional), and a drop-down menu with options to minimize and restore the Web Part, close it, delete it, and edit it. These commands are not always available and visible in the context menu, as this depends on the *display mode* in which the host page was loaded. The available display modes are as follows:

- ❑ **Browse:** In this mode the Web Part's context menu lists commands to minimize the Web Part so that only the title part will be visible, to restore it (if minimized), and to close it so it completely disappears from the page.

- ❑ **Design:** In this mode you can move Web Parts around, from one Web Part zone to another, by dragging and dropping them visually. Web Part zones are rectangular areas on the page where a Web Part can be dropped — only content in these areas can be personalized. A zone can be thought of as being a parking place on the page where Web Parts can reside: You can have a number of zones on one page. The Web Part's context menu also has a command to completely delete the Web Part from the page. The Delete command is different from Close, because Close just hides the Web Part from the page, but doesn't really remove it, so that you can re-open it later.

- ❑ **Edit:** In this mode an Edit command appears in the Web Part's context menu. When clicked, it shows editor boxes used to change the Web Part's standard and custom properties.

- ❑ **Catalog:** In this mode the page displays a catalog of available Web Parts that can be added to the page. There is a *page catalog*, and a more general catalog. The former lists Web Parts that are already present on the page, but are not visible because they have been closed by the user. The latter is a catalog that generally includes all Web Parts available for the entire site.

❑ **Connect:** In this mode the Web Part's context menu has a `Connect` item that allows the user to create a relationship between two Web Parts that implement the proper interfaces and use the proper attributes (a Web Part must be explicitly designed to support connection to another Web Part), so that they exchange information between each other. This allows users to configure master/detail views, where, for example, a Web Part listing categories is connected to another one that lists the products of the selected category. The Web Part listing products (which is a detail view under Categories) may itself be a master to another Web Part showing more details about the selected product. The Web Part listing products would be a *consumer* of categories in the first case and a *producer* of part details in the second case.

> All modes except the Browse mode are only available to registered and authenticated users. You can then specify which users or roles can design and edit the shared view, in addition to their own personal view.

ASP.NET's Web Part Framework is very easy and intuitive to work with, and provides a collection of controls to create Web Part zones, the Web Part catalogs, and the editor boxes, with just a few lines of code. A Web Part is written as a traditional user or a custom control, with just a few additional attributes; you can quickly turn an existing control into a Web Part once you add personalization to a site. In the first part of the "Design" section, you'll learn more about the various controls of this framework and how to put all the pieces to work together, and later you'll learn how to actually use Web Parts in our sample site.

Developing Web Parts

As mentioned earlier, a Web Part can be developed as a user control (which is like a partial page, with markup code and a code-behind) or a custom control (which is a class written in C# for which you create the output 100% programmatically). The choice between the two depends on your needs and requirements, and it's much like the choice between writing user and custom controls in general. If you want to compile everything into an assembly — so that the source code is protected and the output cannot be modified by an external developer and shared among multiple web sites by installing it in the GAC — then you'll want to go with custom controls. If, instead, you don't care much about those aspects, but prefer simplicity and speed of development, and the ease of changing the appearance of the Web Part by working with markup code instead of with C# code, then user controls will be your best bet. In this section, I'll provide a quick overview of both approaches.

Building a Web Part as a User Control

For our first example we'll build a simple online calculator, with two textboxes for the operands, a button to submit the form and do the calculation, and a label to show the result. You define the UI with the usual markup code, in the .ascx file (typical of user controls):

```
<%@ Control Language="C#" AutoEventWireup="true" CodeFile="Calculator.ascx.cs"
    Inherits=" Calculator" %>
Op1: <asp:TextBox ID="txtOp1" runat="server" /><br />
Op2: <asp:TextBox ID="txtOp2" runat="server" /><br />
<asp:Button ID="btnCalc" runat="server" Text="Calculate"
    OnClick="btnCalc_Click" /><br />
<asp:Label ID="lblResult" runat="server" />
```

The code-behind needs a property that specifies the type of operation to perform: addition, subtraction, division, or multiplication. The property is named `Operation`, and is of type `OperationType`, an enumeration that contains the values indicated above. Then, when the button is clicked, you simply retrieve the input strings, convert them to integers, perform the specified operation, and show the result (I'm not showing the type checks and other validations in order to keep this simple):

```
public enum OperationType : int
{
    Addition,
    Subtraction,
    Division,
    Multiplication
}

public partial class Calculator : System.Web.UI.UserControl
{
    private OperationType _operation = OperationType.Addition;
    public OperationType Operation
    {
        get { return _operation; }
        set { _operation = value; }
    }

    protected void btnCalc_Click(object sender, EventArgs e)
    {
        int op1 = Convert.ToInt32(txtOp1.Text);
        int op2 = Convert.ToInt32(txtOp2.Text);

        if (this.Operation == OperationType.Addition)
            lblResult.Text = (op1 + op2).ToString();
        else if (this.Operation == OperationType.Subtraction)
            lblResult.Text = (op1 - op2).ToString();
        if (this.Operation == OperationType.Division)
            lblResult.Text = ((double)op1 / (double)op2).ToString();
        else
            lblResult.Text = (op1 * op2).ToString();
    }
}
```

So far this is a 100% standard user control. Even so, it can be used as a Web Part on a page. Actually, any control can be used as a Web Part: ASP.NET will take care of wrapping it into a `GenericWebPart` at runtime. However, to enable users to personalize it by setting the properties, you need to add some attributes to the public properties that you want to make editable at runtime. In particular, the `WebBrowsable` attribute specifies that the property will be visible in the Web Part's Editor box; the `Personalizable` attribute specifies whether the property is editable (either for the shared view or also at the user level in the personal view); the `WebDisplayName` specifies the property title in the editor box, so that it's more understandable and user friendly; and the `WebDescription` attribute is a longer description of the property. In this example, you would decorate the `Operation` property with attributes as follows:

```
private OperationType _operation = OperationType.Addition;
[Personalizable(PersonalizationScope.User),
WebBrowsable,
WebDisplayName("Operation Type"),
WebDescription("The type of operation performed when submit is clicked.")]
```

```
public OperationType Operation
{
    get { return _operation; }
    set { _operation = value; }
}
```

Because this is just a normal user control that ASP.NET will wrap with `GenericWebPart`, it doesn't specify Web Part–specific attributes such as the title that should be listed on the Web Parts catalog, or an icon. You can add those attributes to a user control by implementing the `IWebPart` interface, which defines properties with self-descriptive names such as `Title`, `Description`, `TitleIconImageUrl`, `CatalogIconImage`, and `TitleUrl`. You implement these properties as simple wrappers for private fields, as follows:

```
public partial class Controls_Calculator : System.Web.UI.UserControl, IWebPart
{
    private string _catalogIconImageUrl = "";
    public string CatalogIconImageUrl
    {
        get { return _catalogIconImageUrl; }
        set { _catalogIconImageUrl = value; }
    }

    private string _description = "";
    public string Description
    {
        get { return _description; }
        set { _description = value; }
    }

    protected string _subTitle = "";
    public string Subtitle
    {
        get { return _subTitle; }
        set { _subTitle = value; }
    }

    protected string _title = "Online Calculator";
    public string Title
    {
        get { return _title; }
        set { _title = value; }
    }

    private string _titleIconImageUrl = "";
    public string TitleIconImageUrl
    {
        get { return _titleIconImageUrl; }
        set { _titleIconImageUrl = value; }
    }
    private string _titleUrl = "";
    public string TitleUrl
    {
        get { return _titleUrl; }
        set { _titleUrl = value; }
```

```
        }

        // ...the rest of the class as shown earlier...
    }
```

Note that the `_title` field is initialized with `"Online Calculator"`, which is the string that will be shown in the Web Part catalog to refer to this Web Part, and on the title bar of the Web Part itself when added on the page. You'll learn how to build and use the catalog shortly.

Building a Web Part as a Custom Control

Creating Web Parts as user controls is fine in many situations, and especially when the Web Part is very specific to your site and you don't plan to reuse it on other projects and redistribute it. As you should already know, custom controls (as opposed to user controls) are better when you want to have everything (both the UI and the logic behind it) compiled into a single assembly that's easier to move around and install into the GAC, so that you can reutilize the Web Part in multiple sites on the same server. However, even if the Web Part is site-specific, and you don't need to protect its UI against modifications by other developers, there's still another reason why you might prefer a custom control over a user control: When writing a Web Part as a custom control, you can make the class inherit from the `System.Web.UI.WebControls.WebParts.WebPart` base class, which enables you to initialize all the `IWebPart` interface's properties mentioned above, plus many others that specify whether the Web Part can by minimized, closed, moved around, edited, and so on: `AllowMinimize`, `AllowClose`, `AllowZoneChange`, `AllowEdit`, and `ChromeType` (border and title bar). `ExportMode` indicates whether the Web Part's settings can be saved to a local file (serialized) by the user (to be restored later in case the Web Part is reset), `AuthorizationFilter` specifies which users and roles can see it on the page, `Verbs` specifies the list of items in the Web Part's drop-down menu, and more. I won't show you all these possibilities here, but the following example shows a Web Part that displays the current date, whose format the user can change by means of the `Format` property (which is decorated with the same attributes described earlier in the section about user controls). The Web Part's output is rendered from inside the override of the `RenderContents` method, as you would do with any custom control. The `Verbs` property is also overridden to add a new item on the Web Part's menu, which when clicked executes some client-side JavaScript code that calculates and displays the time elapsed since 01/01/1970:

```
public class WhatTimeIsIt : WebPart
{
    public WhatTimeIsIt()
    {
        this.Title = "What Time Is It?";
    }

    private string _format = "T";
    [Personalizable(PersonalizationScope.User),
    WebBrowsable,
    WebDisplayName("Date/Time Format"),
    WebDescription("The format of the current date & time.")]
    public string Format
    {
        get { return _format; }
        set { _format = value; }
    }
```

```
    protected override void RenderContents(HtmlTextWriter writer)
    {
        writer.Write(DateTime.Now.ToString(this.Format));
    }

    public override WebPartVerbCollection Verbs
    {
        get
        {
            // We're specifying JavaScript to calculate the no. of days
            WebPartVerb popupDaysItem = new WebPartVerb("popupDaysItem",
@"var d, s, t;
var MinMilli = 1000 * 60;
var HrMilli = MinMilli * 60;
var DyMilli = HrMilli * 24;
d = new Date();
t = d.getTime();
s = 'It has been '
s += Math.round(t / DyMilli) + ' days since 01/01/1970';
alert(s);");
            popupDaysItem.Text = "Popup days since 1970";
            popupDaysItem.ImageUrl = "~/Images/Clock.gif";
            WebPartVerb[] verbs = new WebPartVerb[] { popupDaysItem };
            return new WebPartVerbCollection(verbs);
        }
    }
}
```

The `WebPartVerb` class also has a `ServerClick` event that allows you to process the click on the new menu item on the server, if that function can't be done on the client. You can also customize its appearance with an icon on the left of the caption, by means of the `ImageUrl` property. You'll see how this Web Part appears on the page in the next section.

The Built-in Controls of the Web Part Framework

Now that you have a couple of Web Parts, you can build a simple page that supports most of the basic features of the Web Part Framework. The built-in controls provided by ASP.NET used in this section are those listed under the WebParts tab of Visual Studio's Toolbox:

❑ **WebPartManager:** This control manages the current display mode, i.e., it allows you to switch between browse mode, design mode, edit mode, etc. It also allows you to change the current scope from user to shared view. The control does not provide any user interface per se; you have to build the UI yourself, and then call the `WebPartManager`'s method to change the display mode, or to programmatically add Web Parts on the page. There must be one and only one `WebPartManager` on the page, and it must be declared before any other control listed here; otherwise, you will get a runtime exception.

❑ **WebPartZone:** This control defines an area where Web Parts can be added programmatically, or dragged and dropped at runtime by the user. They are generally put inside table cells or `<div>` containers, which define the page's layout.

❑ **CatalogZone:** This control defines a region that will contain particular Web Parts (listed below) that create the catalog of Web Parts, declared on the page or already present on the page. This area is invisible until the page enters the catalog display mode.

❑ **DeclarativeCatalogPart:** This Web Part must be placed within the `CatalogZone`, and when the page is in catalog mode it shows a list of Web Parts declared at design time, and allows the user to insert one or more of them into a selected Web Part zone.

❑ **PageCatalogPart:** This Web Part must be placed within the `CatalogZone`, and when the page is in catalog mode it displays a list of Web Parts already present on the page but closed, and therefore not currently visible.

❑ **ImportCatalogPart:** This Web Part allows you to import a Web Part from a configuration file saved on the user's local computer, which is uploaded to the server. The file contains the URL of the Web Part to insert on the page, and the values for its properties. The file is generated by the `Export` command of the Web Part's menu. Note that the export is disabled by default, and must be explicitly enabled (covered later).

❑ **EditorZone:** This control defines a region that will contain particular Web Parts (listed below) that create the editor of Web Parts. This area is invisible until the page enters the edit display mode, and the `Edit` command for a specific Web Part is clicked.

❑ **AppearanceEditorPart:** This Web Part must be placed within the `EditorZone`, and allows you to edit the Web Part's properties related to its appearance, such as its title, the chrome type, and the size.

❑ **BehaviorEditorPart:** This Web Part must be placed within the `EditorZone`, and allows you to edit the Web Part's properties related to its behavior, such as whether the Web Part can be closed, minimized, or moved from one Web Part zone to another, and the URL to which users are redirected when they click the Web Part's title bar.

❑ **LayoutEditorPart:** This Web Part must be placed within the `EditorZone`, and allows you to edit the Web Part's properties related to its layout, such as its state (minimized or opened) and the zone where it is located.

❑ **PropertyGridEditorPart:** This Web Part must be placed within the `EditorZone`, and allows you to edit all the custom properties that have the `WebBrowsable` attribute. A default user interface is automatically built according to the type of the property. For example, Boolean properties are rendered as a checkbox, enumerations are displayed in a `DropDownList`, and other types are edited by means of a textbox. If you don't like the standard UI for a particular property, however, you could build your own editor and associate it to the property. A custom editor is just a custom control that inherits from `EditorPart`. On the Web Part, you must override the `WebBrowsableObject` property and the `CreateEditorParts` method, which returns the collection of custom editor parts to show in the `EditorZone`.

❑ **ConnectionsZone:** This Web Part creates the UI for connecting two Web Parts; one acts as a provider and the other as a consumer for the value being exchanged. The UI is displayed only when the page's display mode is correct.

It only takes a few minutes to build a sample page to test the appearance and behavior of the Web Part examples we made earlier. You can do everything from the visual designer: Draw a table with a first row that has a single cell spanning two columns, and put a `WebPartZone` inside it. Split a second row into two cells and insert a `WebPartZone` inside each of them. Then, on the first row, create two more columns that span two rows: Insert an `EditorZone` inside the first one, and drop all available `EditorParts` inside its surface; then do the same with the `CatalogZone` and the catalog parts on the last column. At the top of the page add a `WebPartManager` control, and a few `LinkButton` controls to activate the various display modes on the page. Finally, spice up the appearance of the page a bit, by applying one of the pre-built styles to the controls, from the controls' Smart Tasks Auto Format dialog window. Figure 10-1 shows the final page as displayed by the graphical designer.

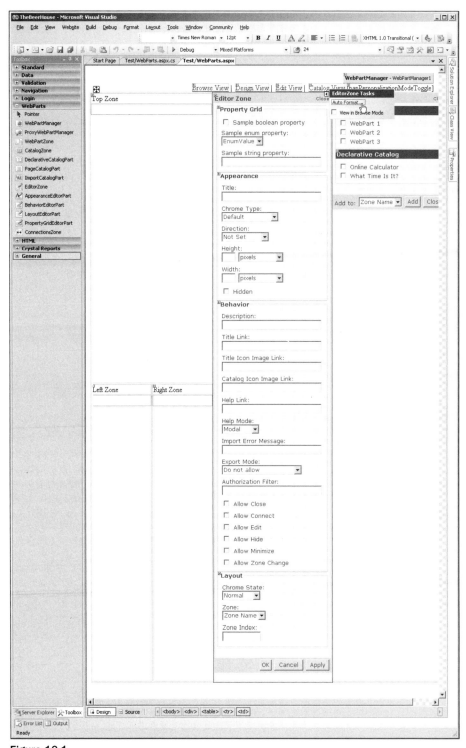

Figure 10-1

In order to add the Web Parts to the `DeclarativeCatalogPart`, you can just drag and drop them on its surface. You can do that with a user control by taking it directly from the Solution Explorer. For custom controls, you should compile them and add them to the Toolbox. Otherwise, you will need to declare them manually from the page's source code.

> **You can add Web Parts directly to `WebPartZone` controls, so they are created by default in the shared view, without the need for an editor to put them in place at runtime.**

Following is the page's source without the various appearance attributes added to the Web Part controls after using the Auto Format command on them (the code that references the Web Parts and then registers them in the catalog is marked in bold):

```
<%@ Page Language="C#" AutoEventWireup="true" CodeFile="WebParts.aspx.cs"
    Inherits="Test_WebParts" %>

<%@ Register Src="Calculator.ascx" TagName="Calculator" TagPrefix="mb" %>
<%@ Register Namespace="MB.TheBeerHouse.UI.Controls" TagPrefix="mb" %>

<!DOCTYPE html PUBLIC "-//W3C//DTD XHTML 1.0 Transitional//EN"
"http://www.w3.org/TR/xhtml1/DTD/xhtml1-transitional.dtd">

<html xmlns="http://www.w3.org/1999/xhtml" >
<head runat="server">
    <title>Web Parts Test</title>
</head>
<body>
    <form id="form1" runat="server">
    <div>
        <div style="text-align: right;">
            <asp:WebPartManager ID="WebPartManager1" runat="server" />
            <asp:LinkButton ID="btnBrowseView" runat="server"
                OnClick="btnBrowseView_Click">Browse View</asp:LinkButton> | 
            <asp:LinkButton ID="btnDesignView" runat="server"
                OnClick="btnDesignView_Click">Design View</asp:LinkButton> | 
            <asp:LinkButton ID="btnEditView" runat="server"
                OnClick="btnEditView_Click">Edit View</asp:LinkButton> | 
            <asp:LinkButton ID="btnCatalogView" runat="server"
                OnClick="btnCatalogView_Click">Catalog View</asp:LinkButton>
            <asp:Label runat="server" ID="panPersonalizationModeToggle">
                 | 
                <asp:LinkButton ID="btnPersonalizationModeToggle" runat="server"
                    OnClick="btnPersonalizationModeToggle_Click">Switch Scope (current =
                        <%= WebPartManager1.Personalization.Scope.ToString() %>)
                </asp:LinkButton>
            </asp:Label>
        </div>
        <table width="100%">
            <tr>
                <td colspan="2" valign="top">
                    <asp:WebPartZone ID="TopZone" runat="server" Width="100%"
                        HeaderText="Top Zone" Height="100%">
```

```
            </asp:WebPartZone>
        </td>
        <td rowspan="2" valign="top">
            <asp:EditorZone ID="EditorZone1" runat="server" Width="100%">
                <ZoneTemplate>
                    <asp:PropertyGridEditorPart ID="PropertyGridEditorPart1"
                        runat="server" />
                    <asp:AppearanceEditorPart ID="AppearanceEditorPart1"
                        runat="server" />
                    <asp:BehaviorEditorPart ID="BehaviorEditorPart1"
                        runat="server" />
                    <asp:LayoutEditorPart ID="LayoutEditorPart1"
                        runat="server" />
                </ZoneTemplate>
            </asp:EditorZone>
            <asp:CatalogZone ID="CatalogZone1" runat="server">
                <ZoneTemplate>
                    <asp:PageCatalogPart ID="PageCatalogPart1" runat="server" />
                    <asp:DeclarativeCatalogPart ID="DeclarativeCatalogPart1"
                        runat="server">
                    <WebPartsTemplate>
                        <mb:calculator id="Calculator1" runat="server" />
                        <mb:WhatTimeIsIt id="currDateTime" runat="server" />
                    </WebPartsTemplate>
                    </asp:DeclarativeCatalogPart>
                </ZoneTemplate>
            </asp:CatalogZone>
        </td>
    </tr>
    <tr>
        <td width="50%" valign="top">
            <asp:WebPartZone ID="LeftZone" runat="server" Width="100%"
                HeaderText="Left Zone" Height="100%">
            </asp:WebPartZone>
        </td>
        <td width="50%" valign="top">
          <asp:WebPartZone ID="RightZone" runat="server" Width="100%"
              HeaderText="Right Zone" Height="100%">
          </asp:WebPartZone>
        </td>
    </tr>
  </table>
 </div>
 </form>
</body>
</html>
```

The code-behind is very simple: You just handle the `Click` event of the `LinkButton` controls declared above, and call the methods of the `WebPartManager` control to switch to one of the available display modes. Every time the page loads you also check whether the modes are actually available (they might not be, depending on the current user's permissions), by checking for their existence in the `WebPartManager`'s `SupportedDisplayModes` collection, and then hide them if they are not:

```
public partial class Test_WebParts : System.Web.UI.Page
{
    protected void Page_Load(object sender, EventArgs e)
    {
        if (!this.IsPostBack)
            UpdateUI();
    }

    protected void UpdateUI()
    {
        btnBrowseView.Enabled = WebPartManager1.SupportedDisplayModes.Contains(
            WebPartManager.BrowseDisplayMode);
        btnDesignView.Enabled = WebPartManager1.SupportedDisplayModes.Contains(
            WebPartManager.DesignDisplayMode);
        btnEditView.Enabled = WebPartManager1.SupportedDisplayModes.Contains(
            WebPartManager.EditDisplayMode);
        btnCatalogView.Visible = WebPartManager1.SupportedDisplayModes.Contains(
            WebPartManager.CatalogDisplayMode);
        panPersonalizationModeToggle.Visible =
            WebPartManager1.Personalization.CanEnterSharedScope;
    }

    protected void btnBrowseView_Click(object sender, EventArgs e)
    {
        WebPartManager1.DisplayMode = WebPartManager.BrowseDisplayMode;
        UpdateUI();
    }

    protected void btnDesignView_Click(object sender, EventArgs e)
    {
        WebPartManager1.DisplayMode = WebPartManager.DesignDisplayMode;
        UpdateUI();
    }

    protected void btnEditView_Click(object sender, EventArgs e)
    {
        WebPartManager1.DisplayMode = WebPartManager.EditDisplayMode;
        UpdateUI();
    }

    protected void btnCatalogView_Click(object sender, EventArgs e)
    {
        WebPartManager1.DisplayMode = WebPartManager.CatalogDisplayMode;
        UpdateUI();
    }

    protected void btnPersonalizationModeToggle_Click(object sender, EventArgs e)
    {
        WebPartManager1.Personalization.ToggleScope();
        UpdateUI();
    }
}
```

Figure 10-2 shows how the page will look like at runtime, when in catalog mode.

Figure 10-2

Figure 10-3 shows the page in browse mode after adding both Web Parts. It also shows the drop-down menu of the `WhatTimeIsIt` Web Part, with its custom-made option that uses client-side JavaScript to pop up a message.

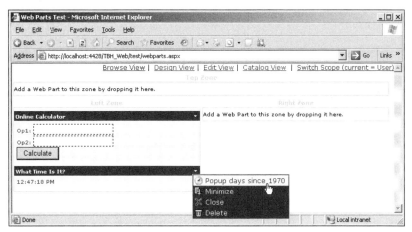

Figure 10-3

If you click the `Minimize` command (which is available in any display mode), the Web Part will show only the title bar, as shown in Figure 10-4 (the `WhatTimeIsIt` control is minimized). When in that state, the Web Part's menu will replace the `Minimize` command, and the `Restore` command will re-open the Web Part's box.

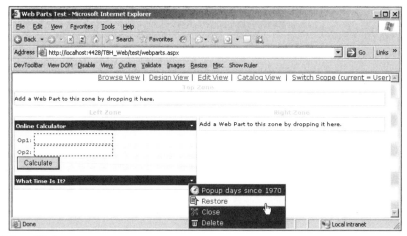

Figure 10-4

Figure 10-5 is the most spectacular because it shows the page in design mode as I was dragging a Web Part from one zone to another (don't confuse the Web Part design mode with Visual Studio's design mode — Web Parts have a runtime design mode to enable users to edit their configuration). The Web Part being dragged shows as a semi-transparent floating layer, which gives you clear feedback about what you're dragging and what space it is going to occupy after the drop.

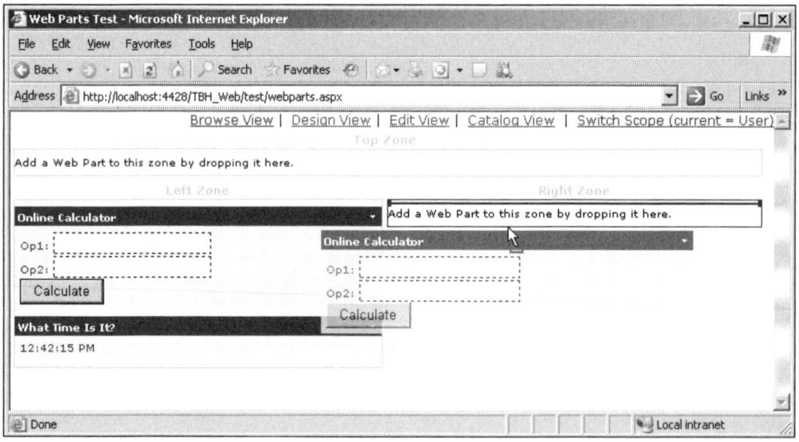

Figure 10-5

The drag and drop feature is not supported by non-IE browsers. It doesn't work with Firefox, and if you want to move a Web Part you must activate the edit mode for it and select the destination zone from the Layout editor (see Figure 10-7).

To edit a Web Part you must first enter the respective mode by clicking the link at the top of the page, and then click the Edit option from the drop-down menu of the specific Web Part, as shown in Figure 10-6.

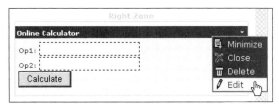

Figure 10-6

Figure 10-7 shows the page while editing the Online Calculator Web Part. Note how the `Operation` custom property is editable by means of a `DropDownList` control created by the `PropertygridEditorPart` control.

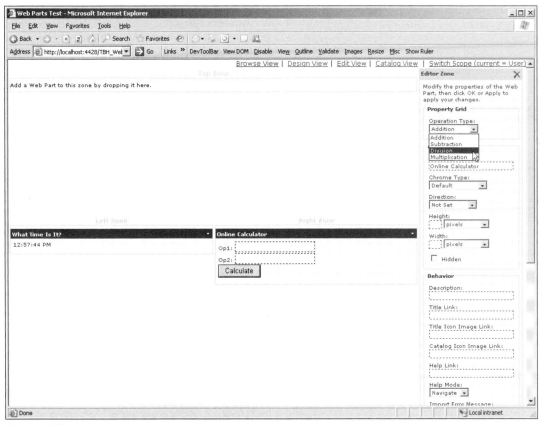

Figure 10-7

Configuring the Web Part Framework

When a user adds a Web Part on the page, for herself or for the shared view, and when she edits the properties of a Web Part, these personalizations of the page are stored persistently, so that the user will find the same configuration she left after her last visit, even if she closes the browser and returns a week later. Where this information is stored depends on the data access provider, because the Web Part Framework is based on the same provider model design pattern used by the membership and roles system, the logging framework, the profile module, and so on. The framework includes a single built-in provider for Web Parts management that targets SQL Server, but you could, of course, implement your own provider to save personalization information in XML files, an Oracle database, or somewhere else. As for all other ASP.NET modules and subframeworks, the configuration is located in the web.config file, and in this case the section is <webParts>. It has an enableExport attribute that enables users to export the configuration of a single Web Part to a local XML file, so that they can later restore it in case they reset or change the page during some tests to find the perfect configuration. This feature is disabled by default. There is then an inner section called <personalization> that specifies which provider to use to save/load information from those registered under the <providers> subsection. Under the <personalization> section there's also the <authorization> section, which defines which user roles are allowed to enter the shared scope, and thus modify the page and its Web Parts for all users. Here's a sample configuration, showing how to set up the Web Part Framework in TheBeerHouse site:

```
<webParts enableExport="true">
    <personalization defaultProvider="TBH_PersonalizationProvider">
        <providers>
            <add name="TBH_PersonalizationProvider"
                connectionStringName="LocalSqlServer"
                type="System.Web.UI.WebControls.WebParts.SqlPersonalizationProvider,
                    System.Web, Version=2.0.0.0, Culture=neutral,
                    azxmPublicKeyToken=b03f5f7f11d50a3a" />
        </providers>

        <authorization>
            <allow roles="Administrators,Editors" verbs="enterSharedScope" />
        </authorization>
    </personalization>
</webParts>
```

For your reference, Figure 10-8 shows which tables are used to store personalizations on the SQL Server database, and the relationships between them.

Personalization is always at the page level, which means that even if you put all the Web Part zones and the WebPartManager on a master page, different pages that use that same master page will have a different configuration, because the data is saved in different records according to the specific content page's URL. Personalization for the shared views and for the per-user views are saved in two separate tables, but in both cases there's a PageSettings image field that stores all the information in binary format.

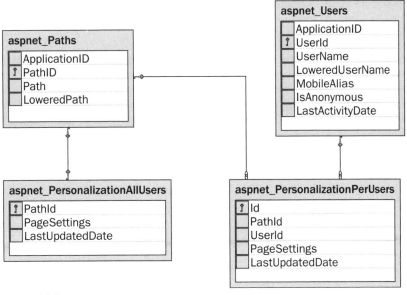

Figure 10-8

Summing Up: Designing Our Solution

Now that we've explored the Web Part Framework in general and looked at some examples, we can design the Web Parts for TheBeerHouse. This task is simple because, as you've seen, the framework does practically everything for you. First of all, you must decide which content you want to make personalizable, i.e., which controls will be turned into Web Parts. The perfect candidates are the `PollBox` control (developed in Chapter 6), which displays a poll with the given ID or the poll marked as the current one, and the `RssReader` control (developed in Chapter 5), which can render the RSS feed read from any URL. The `RssReader` has been used already more than once to read our own feeds for the latest articles, for the latest forum threads, and for the most active threads, but you could use it to display the feed offered by any other external site (maybe friendly sites you've partnered with to exchange information). Finally, the welcome text and graphics of the home page will also be put into a separate user control (`WelcomeBox`), so users will be able to close, minimize, or completely remove it from the page, and perhaps place the RSS feeds in a more visible position. All properties of the `RssReader` will be made personalizable by the user, but properties of the `PollBox` Web Part will be made accessible only for the shared view, so that only editors and administrators can set them. Both controls were implemented as user controls, so you can just "upgrade" them to a Web Part by adding the `WebBrowsable`, `Personalizable`, `WebDisplayName`, and `WebDescription` attributes to their properties. You also need to implement the `IWebPart` interface, so that you can set the Web Part's caption shown in the title bar and the catalog box. Instead of implementing `IWebPart` separately for each of the three Web Parts, you can just implement it in a common base class that inherits from `System.Web.UI.UserControl`, and then make the user controls' code-behind class inherit from this custom base class instead of from `UserControl` directly. This way you'll only implement `IWebPart` once.

The other important thing is deciding where, and how, to place all the necessary Web Part–related controls on the pages to which you want to add personalization support. Personalization is not something you'll want to add everywhere because it doesn't make much sense to move and change content in the page showing an article or a forum thread. However, you may want to support it in a few other pages in addition to the home page—for example, in the pages listing article categories (ShowCategories.aspx) and subforums (ShowForums.aspx). Instead of placing the WebPartManager, the WebPartZone controls, the editors, and the catalog controls on every page, you'll add all them just once, in the template .master page shared by all pages of the site. Figure 10-9 graphically represents where you'll declare all controls and zones. As you can see, there are parts with fixed content, with Web Part zones placed above and below them, in each of the three columns; in the larger central column there are also two sections where the available space is split into two columns, with a Web Part zone in each of them, so that you can put two or more Web Parts side by side.

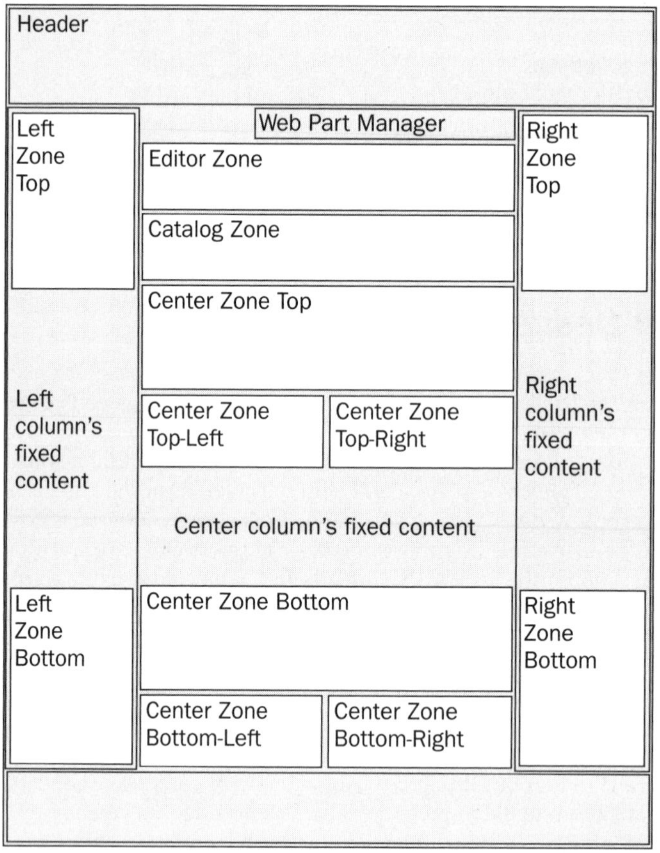

Header		
Left Zone Top	**Web Part Manager** Editor Zone Catalog Zone	Right Zone Top
Left column's fixed content	Center Zone Top Center Zone Top-Left / Center Zone Top-Right Center column's fixed content	Right column's fixed content
Left Zone Bottom	Center Zone Bottom Center Zone Bottom-Left / Center Zone Bottom-Right	Right Zone Bottom

Figure 10-9

The master page will have a custom EnablePersonalization property, which will be set to true only on those content pages that should support personalization: By doing this the controls used to switch the display mode will become visible; otherwise, they will be hidden. You've already seen in the previous section how to restrict the permissions for entering the shared scope and modifying the page from all users to users who belong to the Administrators or Editors roles.

Solution

In this last section you'll learn how to integrate most of what you've learned about Web Parts into the existing site. You'll follow the same order of the examples proposed in the "Design" section, i.e., starting from implementing the Web Parts, and then ending with modifying the current master page by adding Web Part zones, the `WebPartManager`, the editors, and the catalogs.

Creating the Web Parts

Because you already have the user controls that you want to insert into the Web Part catalog, all you need to do here is add the proper attributes to the controls' properties, and implement the `IWebPart` interface. You start from this second point: Implement the interface in a new class called `BaseWebPart` (found in `~/App_Code/BaseWebPart.cs`) that also inherits from `UserControl`:

```csharp
public class BaseWebPart : UserControl, IWebPart
{
    private string _catalogIconImageUrl = "";
    public string CatalogIconImageUrl
    {
        get { return _catalogIconImageUrl; }
        set { _catalogIconImageUrl = value; }
    }

    private string _description = "";
    public string Description
    {
        get { return _description; }
        set { _description = value; }
    }

    protected string _subTitle = "";
    public string Subtitle
    {
        get { return _subTitle; }
        set { _subTitle = value; }
    }

    protected string _title = "";
    public string Title
    {
        get { return _title; }
        set { _title = value; }
    }

    private string _titleIconImageUrl = "";
    public string TitleIconImageUrl
    {
        get { return _titleIconImageUrl; }
        set { _titleIconImageUrl = value; }
    }

    private string _titleUrl = "";
```

```
        public string TitleUrl
        {
            get { return _titleUrl; }
            set { _titleUrl = value; }
        }
    }
```

Then, you modify the user controls' code-behind class so that they inherit from this class, and then you add the property attributes. Following is the code for the `RssReader` control; the code for the `PollBox` control has been omitted because it would be very similar (except for the fact that the properties are editable only in the shared scope):

```
public partial class RssReader : BaseWebPart
{
    public RssReader()
    {
        this.Title = "RSS Reader";
    }

    [Personalizable(PersonalizationScope.User),
    WebBrowsable,
    WebDisplayName("Rss Url"),
    WebDescription("The Url of the RSS feed")]
    public string RssUrl
    {
        ...
    }

    [Personalizable(PersonalizationScope.User),
    WebBrowsable,
    WebDisplayName("Header Text"),
    WebDescription("The header's text")]
    public string HeaderText
    {
        ...
    }

    [Personalizable(PersonalizationScope.User),
    WebBrowsable,
    WebDisplayName("Number of columns"),
    WebDescription("The grid's number of columns")]
    public int RepeatColumns
    {
        ...
    }

    [Personalizable(PersonalizationScope.User),
    WebBrowsable,
    WebDisplayName("Moree Url"),
    WebDescription("The Url of the link pointing to more content")]
    public string MoreUrl
    {
        ...
    }
```

```
    [Personalizable(PersonalizationScope.User),
    WebBrowsable,
    WebDisplayName("More Url"),
    WebDescription("The text of the link pointing to more content")]
    public string MoreText
    {
        ...
    }

    // the control's event handlers and rest of the class goes here...
}
```

Note how the `Title` property of the `IWebPart` interface is set with a default value in the control's constructor. You may want do the same with the properties that specify the Web Part's icon for the title bar and the catalog.

Modifying the Master Page

Referring to Figure 10-9, you can edit the `Template.Master` file by adding the various Web Part zone controls inside the `<div>` containers (remember that we haven't used tables to define the site layout), and the editor and catalog zones and controls at the top of the layout's center content. For clarity, you can isolate the `LinkButton` controls that activate one of the available display modes in separate user controls, so that you have less code to add to the master page. The `PersonalizationManager` control is located under the `~/Controls` folder with all the others: Its code is not shown in this section because it's exactly the same code shown earlier in the test page, just copied and pasted into the .ascx file, and the same is true for the companion .cs code-behind file. Following is the code added to the master page:

```
<html>
<body>
<form id="Main" runat="server">
    ...
  <div id="container">
      <div id="container2">
          <div id="centercol">
              <div id="breadcrumb">
                  <mb:PersonalizationManager ID="PersonalizationManager1"
                      runat="server" Visible="false" />
                  <asp:SiteMapPath ID="SiteMapPath1" runat="server" />
              </div>

              <asp:EditorZone ID="EditorZone1" runat="server" Width="100%">
                  <ZoneTemplate>
                      <asp:AppearanceEditorPart ID="AppearanceEditorPart1"
                          runat="server" />
                      <asp:BehaviorEditorPart ID="BehaviorEditorPart1"
                          runat="server" />
                      <asp:LayoutEditorPart ID="LayoutEditorPart1" runat="server" />
                      <asp:PropertyGridEditorPart ID="PropertyGridEditorPart1"
                          runat="server" Title="Custom Properties" />
                  </ZoneTemplate>
              </asp:EditorZone>
              <asp:CatalogZone ID="CatalogZone1" runat="server" >
```

```
        <ZoneTemplate>
            <asp:DeclarativeCatalogPart ID="DeclarativeCatalogPart1"
                runat="server" Title="Site Catalog">
            <WebPartsTemplate>
                <mb:WelcomeBox ID="WelcomeBox1" runat="server" />
                <mb:RssReader id="rssReaderGeneric" runat="server"
                    Title="RSS Reader" />
                <mb:RssReader id="rssLatestArticles" runat="server"
                    Title="Latest Articles"
                    RssUrl="~/GetArticlesRss.aspx"
                    MoreText="More articles..."
                    MoreUrl="~/BrowseArticles.aspx" />
                <mb:RssReader id="rssLatestThreads" runat="server"
                    Title="Latest Threads"
                    RssUrl="~/GetThreadsRss.aspx?SortExpr=LastPostDate DESC"
                />
                <mb:RssReader id="rssMostActiveThreads" runat="server"
                    Title="Most Active Threads"
                    RssUrl="~/GetThreadsRss.aspx?SortExpr=ReplyCount DESC"
                />
                <mb:PollBox id="pollGeneric" runat="server"
                    ShowArchiveLink="False" ShowHeader="False" />
            </WebPartsTemplate>
            </asp:DeclarativeCatalogPart>
            <asp:PageCatalogPart ID="PageCatalogPart1" runat="server"
                Title="Local Page Catalog" />
        </ZoneTemplate>
    </asp:CatalogZone>

    <div id="centercolcontent">
        <div style="clear: both; margin-bottom: 5px;">
            <asp:WebPartZone ID="CenterZoneTop" Runat="server"
                HeaderText="Center Zone Top" Width="100%" />
            <table border="0" cellpadding="2" cellspacing="0" width="100%">
                <tr>
                    <td width="50%">
                        <asp:WebPartZone ID="CenterZoneTopLeft" Runat="server"
                            HeaderText="Center Zone Top-Left" Width="100%" />
                    </td>
                    <td width="50%">
                        <asp:WebPartZone ID="CenterZoneTopRight" Runat="server"
                            HeaderText="Center Zone Top-Right" Width="100%" />
                    </td>
                </tr>
            </table>
        </div>
        <asp:ContentPlaceHolder ID="MainContent" runat="server" />
        <div style="clear: both; margin-top: 5px;">
            <asp:WebPartZone ID="CenterZoneBottom" Runat="server"
                HeaderText="Center Zone Bottom" Width="100%" />
            <table border="0" cellpadding="2" cellspacing="0" width="100%">
                <tr>
                    <td width="50%">
                        <asp:WebPartZone ID="CenterZoneBottomLeft" Width="100%"
```

```
                                  Runat="server" HeaderText="Center Zone Bottom-Left"
                         />
                    </td>
                    <td width="50%">
                        <asp:WebPartZone ID="CenterZoneBottomRight Width="100%"
                                  Runat="server" HeaderText="Center Zone Bottom-Right"
                         />
                    </td>
                </tr>
            </table>
        </div>
      </div>
    </div>
    <div id="rightcol">
        <asp:WebPartZone ID="RightZoneTop" Runat="server"
            HeaderText="Right Zone Top" Width="100%" />
        <mb:NewsletterBox id="NewsletterBox1" runat="server" />
        <asp:ContentPlaceHolder ID="RightContent" runat="server" />
        <asp:WebPartZone ID="RightZoneBottom" Runat="server"
            HeaderText="Right Zone Bottom" Width="100%" />
    </div>
  </div>
  <div id="leftcol">
      <asp:WebPartZone ID="LeftZoneTop" Runat="server"
          HeaderText="Left Zone Top" Width="100%" />
      <mb:PollBox id="PollBox1" runat="server" HeaderText="Poll of the week" />
      <mb:PollBox id="PollBox2" runat="server" HeaderText="More polls"
          PollID="24" ShowArchiveLink="False" />
      <p></p>
      <asp:ContentPlaceHolder ID="LeftContent" runat="server" />
      <asp:WebPartZone ID="LeftZoneBottom" Runat="server"
          HeaderText="Left Zone Bottom" Width="100%" />
      ...
  </div>
 </div>
...
</form>
</body>
</html>
```

Note that the `RssReader` control has been added four times to the `DeclarativeCatalogPart:` One is a generic instance that the user will use to consume third-party feeds, while the other three have predefined values for the `RssUrl` property that refer to some of the feeds created in previous chapters. Also note that no appearance styles are present in the preceding markup code. This is because all those attributes are defined in the `Controls.skin` file located under each theme folder, as we have already done for the `GridView`, `DetailsView`, `DataList`, and many other controls. Following is the style declaration of the `WebPartZone` control, which defines the appearance of the Web Part zone, title bar, border, and drop-down menu of each Web Part:

```
<asp:WebPartZone runat="server" BorderColor="#CCCCCC" Font-Names="Verdana"
Padding="0" PartChromeType="TitleOnly">
    <PartTitleStyle CssClass="sectiontitle" />
    <MenuLabelHoverStyle ForeColor="#FFCC66" />
```

```
        <EmptyZoneTextStyle Font-Size="0.8em" />
        <MenuLabelStyle ForeColor="White" />
        <MenuVerbHoverStyle BackColor="#FFFBD6" BorderColor="#CCCCCC"
            BorderStyle="Solid" BorderWidth="1px" ForeColor="#333333" />
        <HeaderStyle Font-Bold="true" Font-Size="8pt" />
        <MenuVerbStyle BorderColor="#990000" BorderStyle="Solid"
            BorderWidth="1px" ForeColor="White" />
        <TitleBarVerbStyle Font-Size="0.6em" Font-Underline="False" ForeColor="White" />
        <MenuPopupStyle BackColor="#990000" BorderColor="#CCCCCC" BorderWidth="1px"
            Font-Names="Verdana" Font-Size="0.6em" />
        <MinimizeVerb ImageUrl="~/Images/GoDown.gif"></MinimizeVerb>
        <RestoreVerb ImageUrl="~/Images/GoUp.gif"></RestoreVerb>
        <EditVerb ImageUrl="~/Images/Edit.gif"></EditVerb>
        <CloseVerb ImageUrl="~/Images/Close.gif"></CloseVerb>
        <DeleteVerb ImageUrl="~/Images/Delete.gif" />
    </asp:WebPartZone>
```

In the master page's code-behind you define the `EnablePersonalization` Boolean property, which makes the `PersonalizationManager` visible if set to `true`, but only if the current user is authenticated; otherwise, it will have no effect:

```
public partial class TemplateMaster : System.Web.UI.MasterPage
{
    private bool _enablePersonalization = false;
    public bool EnablePersonalization
    {
        get { return _enablePersonalization; }
        set
        {
            _enablePersonalization = value;
            PersonalizationManager1.Visible = (
                this.Page.User.Identity.IsAuthenticated && value);
        }
    }

    protected void Page_Load(object sender, EventArgs e)
    {
        if (!this.Page.User.Identity.IsAuthenticated)
            PersonalizationManager1.Visible = false;
    }
}
```

Enabling Personalization at the Page Level

To enable personalization on a page, e.g., the `default.aspx` home page, you merely have to reference the master page by means of the `@MasterPage` directive at the top of the `.aspx` page, so that a strongly typed `Master` property will be built at runtime that exposes all the master page's custom properties:

```
<%@ MasterType VirtualPath="~/Template.master" %>
```

Then, you handle the `Page_Load` event and set to `true` the `EnablePersonalization` property of the master page:

```
protected void Page_Load(object sender, EventArgs e)
{
    this.Master.EnablePersonalization = true;
}
```

Figure 10-10 represents the home page while in design mode, with the Welcome Box in minimized state, and three instances of the `RssReader` control placed on three different Web Part zones in the site's central column.

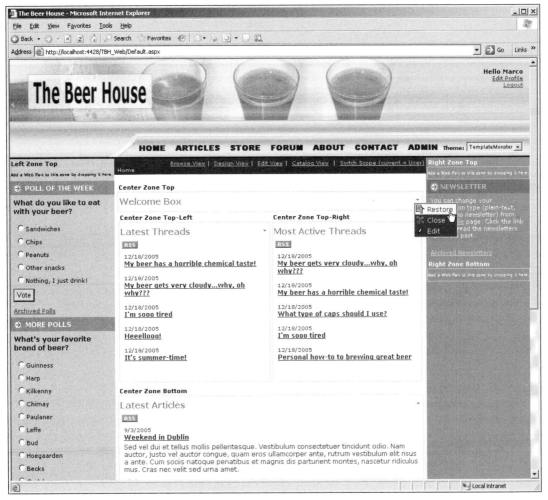

Figure 10-10

Summary

In this chapter, you've had an overview of the cool Web Part Framework introduced in ASP.NET 2.0. You can probably reproduce everything built here in only minutes, especially the visual drag and drop, whereas if you used custom DHTML and personalization storage, it would have taken several weeks or more (if you factor in debugging and testing time). Because of this, ASP.NET's personalization framework is truly something to appreciate, not only because of the spectacular appeal to users, but also because most of the difficult code needed to make this work right was already written by Microsoft! A small amount of developer time will multiply the value of your site to end users. The ASP.NET controls wrap the complex JavaScript code needed to give us the awesome client-side effects, and you can reuse your previous work to turn any control into a dragable and user-customizable piece of content.

Some of the more advanced features such as connections and custom editor parts weren't covered here, but if you're interested in going deeper you can find entire books dedicated to the subject, such as Wrox's *Professional Web Parts and Custom Controls with ASP.NET 2.0,* by Peter Vogel.

In the next chapter, you'll build the last part of the site: localization support, i.e., dynamically translating the site to different languages, according to the favorite language selected by the user in his profile.

11

Localizing the Site

We live in a global community consisting of people from many countries. The term *localizing* refers to the capability to present a site in the language of the local user, and to use the correct symbols for currency, decimals, dates, and so on. ASP.NET 2.0 adds some new features to its arsenal for localizing a site that make it easier than ever before. The developer is freed from writing clumsy code for managing multiple languages and locale settings, and translated strings and other resources can be compiled into independent files that can be easily plugged into the site, even after deployment, to add support for a new language that wasn't even considered when the site was designed. In this chapter, you'll look at the importance of localization and learn how the new ASP.NET features can help you localize your site with little effort.

Problem

These days, it seems that the word globalization is used everywhere. The beauty of the Internet and the World Wide Web is that you can reach anyone who has a computer and a phone line or some other sort of Internet connection, be it for fun, passion, business, and so on. Nevertheless, if you want to be able to communicate with people, you must speak (or write) a language the people can understand. Due to the great proliferation of English as a primary or secondary language, many sites use English as their base language, even if they are not run by people for which this language is the main tongue. However, offering a site in the user's first language is often a great advantage over competitors that don't, because all users find it easier and more comfortable reading their primary language even when they can understand others. This is true not only for text but also for the format used to display and parse numbers, dates, and currency names. In fact, an Italian reader, like me, would interpret 07/02/2006 as the February 2, whereas an American would interpret it to be July 2. And while this may cause misunderstandings when reading the date, it may cause errors when users insert data in one format while the system expects a different one. For this reason, any modern site that wants to target a worldwide audience must be multi-language, displaying numbers and dates according to the user's local settings, and translating the full site's text (or at least the most important parts) into the user's primary language.

Fully localizing a site based on dynamic content (articles, products, forums, polls, etc.) is an extremely difficult task, and there are a number of ways to approach it. The difficulty varies considerably depending on whether you intend to localize everything or just static content (text on the page layouts, menus, links, and page, section and field titles and descriptions, and so forth). ASP.NET 2.0 introduces some new features that significantly simplify localizing static parts of a site, and this is what I'll cover in this chapter. Conversely, localizing the dynamic content would be much harder and would require quite a lot of rework on the database, the UI structure, and the object model. If that's what you really need to achieve, it's usually better to create separate language-specific sites with their own content.

Design

The first thing you need to decide when localizing a site is whether you want to localize only static content (menus, links, copyright notices, usage agreement, titles and descriptions for pages, tables, fields, buttons, and other controls) or whether you want to provide a translation for everything, including articles, poll questions, product listings, and so on. Let me state up front that adding support for complete localization would be very difficult at this stage of development, as it would require a complete rework of the database design, the DAL, the BLL, and the UI. It's something that should be planned very early, during the initial site design and the foundations development. Complete localization in a single web site is not a common requirement: You normally wouldn't translate every article on the site, forums, polls, and newsletters, but rather, only those that have a special appeal to one country or language-specific audience. You may also want to present information differently for different languages — changing something in the site's layout, for example. Because of this, most sites that want to be fully localized "simply" provide multiple copies of their pages under different subdomains or folders, one copy for each language. For example, there could be www.contoso.com/en and www.contoso.com/it or http://en.contoso.com/ and http://it.contoso.com/. Each copy of the site would target an independent database that only contains data for that specific language. If you take this approach, you'll only need to make static content localizable, and then install the site multiple times for multiple languages. Another advantage of this strategy is that with completely separate web sites you can have different people managing them independently, who would be able to create content that best suits the audience for that particular language. In this chapter we'll localize the site's static content, and we'll support the different locale settings for dates and numbers in different languages.

Our sample site will only be installed once, and the language for which the site is localized will be specified by each user at registration time, or later from the Edit Profile page. This setting is mapped to the Preferences.Culture profile property, which was described and implemented in Chapter 4. An alternative would be to detect the user's favorite language from her browser's settings, which is sent to the web server with the request's header. However, many nontechnical users don't understand how to set this, and it would be difficult to explain it on your site and answer support questions from people who don't understand this. Therefore, it's better to directly ask users which language they'd like to use, so they understand what it's for, and how to change it. The next section provides an overview of the new features introduced by ASP.NET 2.0 regarding localization of static content.

A Recap of Localization in ASP.NET 1.x

ASP.NET (and the .NET Framework in general) has always supported localization to some extent. Displaying and parsing dates and numbers according to a specific culture, for example, only requires you to create a System.Globalization.CultureInfo instance for that culture (e.g., "en-US" for American English, or "it-IT" for Italian of Italy), and use it as the value for the CurrentCulture property of the current executing thread (`System.Threading.Thread.CurrentThread`). For example, after executing the following statement, all dates and numbers displayed to the user would follow the Italian format by default:

```
System.Threading.Thread.CurrentThread.CurrentCulture =
    System.Globalization.CultureInfo.CreateSpecificCulture("it-IT");
```

The preceding code would have been typically placed into the page's `Init` or `Load` event handlers, or even better in the `Application_BeginRequest` event handler accessible from the `Global.asax` file, so that it would execute for all pages of the site without replicating the code in each of them. Putting it into a custom base class from which all pages' code-behind class would inherit was another great solution.

Localizing static content by dynamically setting the properties of the various controls on a page (such as `Text`, `ToolTip`, etc.) with values translated to a specific language was much less easy in ASP.NET 1.x, though. You needed to create one or more resource files for each language you wanted to support (such as `Messages.resx` for the generic default culture, `Messages.it-IT.resx` for Italian, `Messages.fr-FR.resx` for French, and so on) and write key-value pairs into these files (they are XML files, but Visual Studio has an editor that allows editing them in a grid), where the *value* was some string translated into the language of the resource file. Then, from the code-behind class of every page that you wanted to localize, you had to manually write something like this:

```
using System.Resources;
using System.Reflection;

ResourceManager rm = new ResourceManager(
    "WebProjectName.Messages", Assembly.GetExecutingAssembly());
lblTitle.Text = rm.GetString("Title");
```

This would instantiate a `ResourceManager` object for the resources stored in a class called `WebProjectName.Messages` (created from the .resx file). Then, it would load the string resource with a key equal to `"Title"`, and use it for the `Text` property of a label control. `ResourceManager` automatically loads the resource class from the current assembly, or from one of the satellite resource-only assemblies, according to the culture specified by the `CurrentUICulture` property of the current thread. If the resource for the current UI culture is not found, the `ResourceManager` will fallback to the resources for the default neutral culture.

> Note that the property used by ResourceManager to load the correct satellite assemblies is CurrentUI Culture and not CurrentCulture, which is instead used to display and parse numbers and dates. The two properties are often set to the same culture, but not necessarily.

New Localization Features of ASP.NET 2.0

Although the previous framework had technology for localizing sites, the solution outlined in the preceding section had a number of problems that made the process unwieldy and prone to error. The most significant issues were as follows:

❑   You had to create the resource files manually, in a folder of your choice. However, the final name of the resource class would change because of the inclusion of the folder name, and many developers didn't realize this. This often resulted in errors whereby resources could not be found.

Chapter 11

❑ You had to specify the resource key as a string, and if you misspelled this string it resulted in errors whereby resources could not be found. If this were an enumeration it could avoid the possibility of misspelling it.

❑ You had to invent your own naming convention to choose key names that would identify the same resource but for different pages, such as `Page1_Title` and `Page2_Title`. This is because there were only site-wide global resources, and not page-specific resources. You could also create different .resx files, one for each page and thus simulate page specific resources. This was merely a way to physically separate resources as they were still accessible by any other page.

❑ Above all, you had to manually write the code to set the `Text` property (or any other localizable property) to the proper string loaded by means of a `ResourceManager`, as there wasn't a declarative way to do it from the .aspx markup file.

With ASP.NET 2.0 all this changes considerably, and even though under the cover things work pretty much the same, from the developer's viewpoint things are much easier and more intuitive now. Here's a list of improvements, which are described in detail in the following subsections:

❑ **Strongly typed global resources:** Once you create a global resource file (like the ones you may have used under ASP.NET 1.x), it is dynamically compiled into a class, and you can immediately see and access the class listed under the `Resources` namespace. Each resource of the file is accessible as a property, and IntelliSense is provided by Visual Studio to make it easier to select the right one. No more mistyped resource names!

❑ **Page-level resources:** In addition to global resource files, you also have page-specific resource files, so that you can place the resource strings only in the page that uses them. This enables you to have a resource called `Title` for every page, with different values, as they are stored in separate files. You no longer have to come up with a naming convention such as using the page name as the prefix for the resource keys.

❑ **New localization expressions:** Similar to data binding expressions, these enable a developer to associate an expression to the properties to localize directly in the .aspx markup file, so you don't need any C# code. A special declarative syntax is also available to bind all localizable properties to resources in a single step. Programmatic localization is still possible, of course, and has been improved as mentioned before for the global resources.

❑ **Improved Visual Studio designer support:** This enables you to graphically associate a localization expression to a resource string from a dialog box, without requiring the developer to write any code. There's also a command to automatically generate the neutral language page-level resource file for the current page, which you can copy, rename, or translate to another language.

❑ **Auto detection of the Accept-Language HTTP header:** This is used to automatically set the page's `UICulture` and `Culture` properties, which correspond to the current thread's `CurrentUICulture` and `CurrentCulture` properties.

❑ **Custom providers:** Should you want to store localized resources in a data store other than .resx files, such as a database, you can do that by writing your own custom provider. This enables you to build some sort of online UI for managing existing resources, and create new ones for additional languages, without the need to create and upload new resource files to the server.

Using Global Resources

Global resources are shared among all pages, controls, and classes, and are best suited to store localized data used in different places. When I say "data," I don't just mean strings, but also images, icons, sounds, and any other binary content. Although this was already possible in ASP.NET 1.x, VS.NET 2003 had worse graphical support for resource files. Now you access a resource file item (from the Add Item dialog box) under a folder named `App_GlobalResources`, which is a special folder, handled by the ASP.NET runtime and VS2005; and you can insert data into the grid-style editor represented in Figure 11-1.

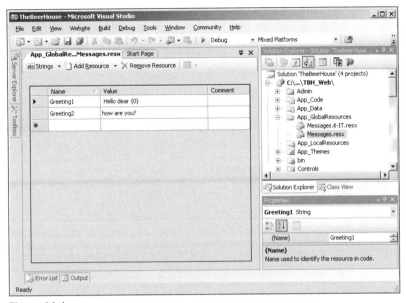

Figure 11-1

If you click the arrow on the right side of the editor's Add Resource toolbar button, you will be able to create an image or icon, or insert any other file. Figure 11-2 shows the window after choosing Images from the drop-down menu of the first toolbar icon (where Strings was selected in Figure 11-1) and after adding a few image files.

After adding a few strings and a few images, you can go to a `.cs` file in the editor and type **Resources:** IntelliSense will pop up a drop-down list with the names of the resource files added to the project, i.e., Messages in the example shown in Figure 11-1. Then, when you type Resources.Messages, it will list the string and image resources added earlier; and if you look closely at Figure 11-3, you'll also note that image resources are returned with the proper type of `System.Drawing.Bitmap`.

This results in less manual typing, less probability of mistyping a resource or key name, and less casting.

Programmatic access of resources is necessary in some cases, particularly when you need to retrieve them from business or helper classes, and in this case you'll be happy to know that IntelliSense for dynamically compiled resources works also! However, when the resource will be used as the value for a property of a control on a page, there's an even easier approach: Just select the control in the page's graphical designer and click the ellipses button on the right side of the "(Expressions)" item in the Properties window. From the dialog box that pops up you can select the property you want to localize, select Resources as the expression type, and select then the resource class name and key, as shown in Figure 11-4. Note that you just select the resource you want from a pre-filled drop-down list, so you don't need to type that yourself.

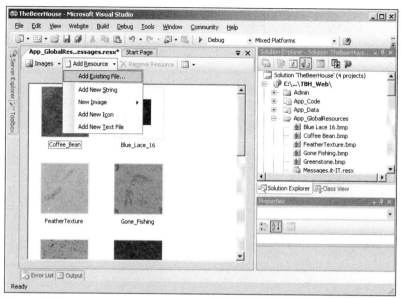

Figure 11-2

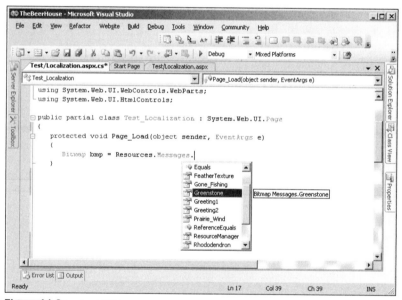

Figure 11-3

After using this dialog box on an ASP control, if you go to the Source View, the declaration of the localized `Label` control will look like this:

```
<asp:Label ID="lblGreeting2" runat="server"
    Text='<%$ Resources:Messages, Greeting2 %>' / >
```

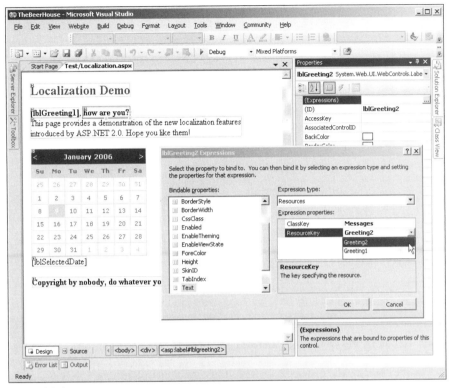

Figure 11-4

The `Text` property is set to a new localization expression (also called *dollar-expression,* because of the leading $ character), which at runtime will return the resource string from the `Greeting2` item of the `Messages` class. You can also write these expressions yourself if you prefer coding your pages directly in the Source View (as I do). In either case, these expressions in the `.aspx` code are much better than manually writing C# code in the code-behind file, as you had to do with ASP.NET 1.x.

Using Page-level Resources

You can create page-level resources by creating resource files just as you do for global resources, but placing them under a folder named `App_LocalResources` (as opposed to `App_GlobalResources` used for global resources) located at the same level of the page to localize. For example, if the page is in the root folder, then you'll create the `App_LocalResources` under the root folder, but if the page is under `/Test`, then you'll create a `/Test/App_LocalResources` folder. This means you can have multiple `App_LocalResources` folders, whereas you can only have one `App_GlobalResources` folder for the whole site. The name of the resource filename is also fundamental, as it must be named after the page or control file for which it contains the localized resources, plus the part with the culture name: For example, a culture-neutral resource file for `Localization.aspx` would be named `Localization .aspx.resx`, whereas it would be named `Localization.aspx.it-IT.resx` for the Italian resources. In Figure 11-5, you can see the organization of files in the Solution Explorer, and the resource file being edited in the grid editor.

513

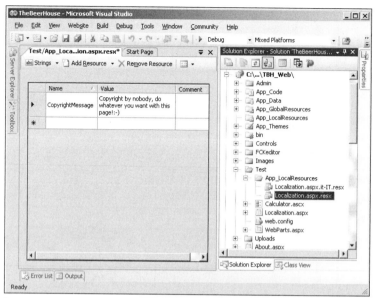

Figure 11-5

You can still use the Expressions dialog shown in Figure 11-4 to bind a control's property to an expression pointing to a localized resource: When you point to a page-specific resource you just leave the ClassKey textbox empty. The code below shows the generated expression:

```
<asp:Label ID="lblCopyright" runat="server"
    Text="<%$ Resources:CopyrightMessage %>" / >
```

It differs from the expression shown in the previous section, as it doesn't include the class name; it just specifies the resource key. If you want to access local resources programmatically, you use the page's GetLocalResourceObject method, which takes the resource key name and returns an Object that you must cast to string or to the proper destination type (such as Bitmap if you stored an image):

```
string copyrightMsg = (string)this.GetLocalResourceObject("CopyrightMessage");
```

Even with localization expressions and local resources, localizing full pages will be a slow task if you need to create the expressions for dozens of controls, and things get worse if you need to localize multiple properties for the same control, such as Text, ToolTip, ImageUrl, NavigateUrl, and so on, which is often the case. To speed things up, Visual Studio offers the Tools ➪ Generate Local Resource command, which generates a local resource file for the current page, and creates entries for all localizable properties of all controls on the page, following the ControlName.PropertyName naming convention for the names of the resources. Resource items are also automatically set with the value extracted from the page's markup; if a property is not used in the control's declaration, a resource item for it is generated anyway and left empty.

Localizable properties are those that are decorated with a [Localizable(true)] attribute, which you can add to the properties of your custom controls. However, even when you add it to properties of user controls, resources for those properties will not be automatically generated by the Generate Local Resource command. You can create the local resources for those properties yourself, and write the localization expressions to make the association: Everything will work perfectly at runtime, so this is only a design-time limitation. In addition, you'll have to write the localization expressions manually, because the (Expressions) item is not available from the Properties window when a user control is selected.

Figure 11-6 shows the resource editor for the `Localization.aspx.resx` local resource file after executing this Generate Local Resource command on the test page.

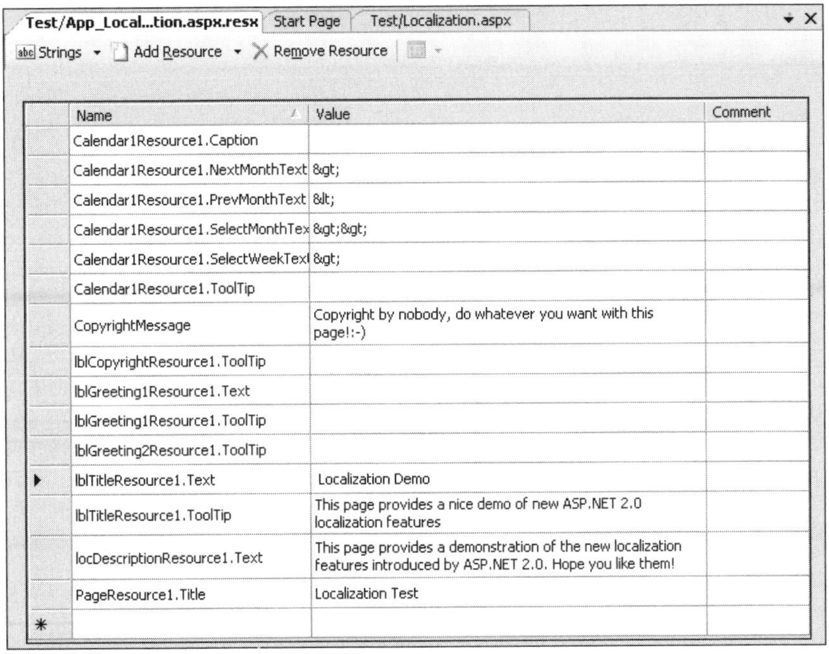

Name	Value	Comment
Calendar1Resource1.Caption		
Calendar1Resource1.NextMonthText	&gt;	
Calendar1Resource1.PrevMonthText	&lt;	
Calendar1Resource1.SelectMonthTex	>>	
Calendar1Resource1.SelectWeekText	&gt;	
Calendar1Resource1.ToolTip		
CopyrightMessage	Copyright by nobody, do whatever you want with this page!:-)	
lblCopyrightResource1.ToolTip		
lblGreeting1Resource1.Text		
lblGreeting1Resource1.ToolTip		
lblGreeting2Resource1.ToolTip		
lblTitleResource1.Text	Localization Demo	
lblTitleResource1.ToolTip	This page provides a nice demo of new ASP.NET 2.0 localization features	
locDescriptionResource1.Text	This page provides a demonstration of the new localization features introduced by ASP.NET 2.0. Hope you like them!	
PageResource1.Title	Localization Test	

Figure 11-6

Besides the automatic generation of the resource file (or the addition of the resource items, if a resource file for that page was already present in the proper folder), what's even more interesting is that each control's declaration is modified as follows (note the code in bold):

```
<asp:Label ID="lblTitle" runat="server" Font-Size="X-Large" ForeColor="#C00000"
    meta:resourcekey="lblTitleResource1" Text="Localization Demo"
    Text="This page provides a nice demo of new ASP.NET 2.0 localization features"
/>
```

A meta:resourcekey attribute is added to the declaration and is set to the prefix used in the local resource file to identify all localized properties of that control, such as lblTitleResource1.Text and lblTitleResource1.ToolTip. These are called *implicit localization expressions* (expressions used earlier are considered *explicit*). At runtime, the framework parses all resources and applies them to the properties of the corresponding controls, making the mapping of the first part of the key with the value of meta:resourcename. This means that the control's declaration is decorated with just a single new attribute, but may make multiple properties localizable. Later, if you want to localize a property that you didn't take into account originally, you just need to go to the resource editor and add an item following the naming schema described above, or edit its value if it already exists.

> Note that the controls retain their original property declarations after running the Generate Local Resource command. These declarations are no longer necessary, though, as the property's value will be replaced at runtime with the values saved in the resource file; therefore, you can completely remove the definition of the `Text`, `ToolTip`, and the other localized properties from the `.aspx` files to avoid confusion.

This behavior works with the page's title as well, originally defined in the `@Page` directive, which is modified as follows:

```
<%@ Page Language="C#" meta:resourcekey="PageResource1" ...other attributes... %>
```

Localizing More Static Content

All content that you want to localize must be displayed by some sort of server-side control, such as the `Label` or `Literal` controls. You'll typically want to use a `Literal` over a `Label` if you don't need the appearance properties of a `Label`, either because you don't need to format the text or because the formatting is done through raw HTML tags present directly within the text, which is frequently the case for static text such as section and field titles, descriptions, copyright notices, and so on. An alternative to `Literal` is the new `Localize` control, listed in the last position under the Toolbox's Standard tab. If you declare it manually from the Source View, it's identical to a `Literal`. If, however, you work in the graphical designer, you'll notice that it doesn't have any properties listed in the Properties window beside the ID, not even a `Text` property. The way you fill it with text in the designer is to place the caret inside it and type the text directly. In Figure 11-7, you can see the test page with the description text under the title placed inside a `Localize` control: Note the caret symbol in the current insert position.

The declaration produced, after executing the Generate Local Resource command, is the following:

```
<asp:Localize ID="locDescription" runat="server"
    meta:resourcekey="locDescriptionResource1" Text="The page provides a demo... "
/>
```

As mentioned earlier, you can completely remove the `Text` property from the declaration, as it will be set from the localized resources at runtime.

> When wrapping static content into a `Localize` or `Literal` control, it's advisable that you don't include HTML formatting tags in the control's `Text`, because that would go into the resource when the page is localized. If you were to pass that resource file to a nontechnical translator, she may not understand what those HTML tags are, and may modify them in some undesirable way. Because of this, if you have static content with HTML tags in the middle, then it may be wise to split it into multiple `Localize` controls, leaving the HTML formatting outside.

Setting the Current Culture

Once you've modified your page with localization expressions for the various controls displaying static content, and you've created local or global resource files for the different languages you want to support, it's time to implement some way to enable users to change the page's language. One method is to read the Accept-Language HTTP header sent by the client to the server, which contains the array of cultures set in the browser's preferences, as shown in the dialog box in Figure 11-8.

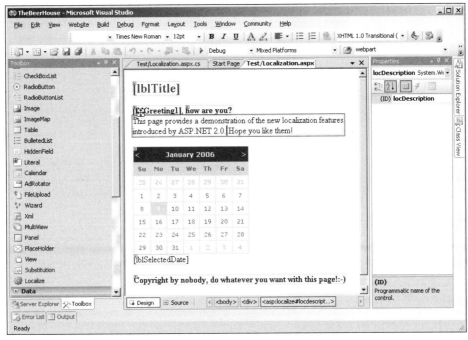

Figure 11-7

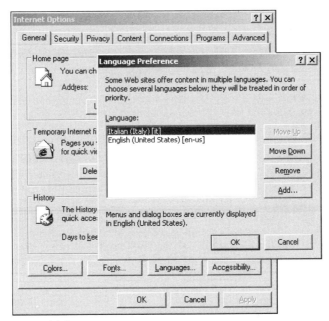

Figure 11-8

In ASP.NET 1.x, you would set the current thread's `CurrentCulture` and `CurrentUICulture` properties to the first item of the `UserLanguage` array of the `Request` object, which would contain the first language in the list. You would execute this code in the `Init` or `Load` event of a page (typically a `BasePage` class, so that all others would inherit the same behavior), or from the Application's `BeginRequest` event, as shown below:

```
void Application_BeginRequest (Object sender, EventArgs e)
{
    if (Request.UserLanguages.Length > 0)
    {
      CultureInfo culture = CultureInfo.CreateSpecificCulture(
          Request.UserLanguages[0]);
      Thread.CurrentThread.CurrentCulture = culture;
      Thread.CurrentThread.CurrentUICulture = culture;
    }
}
```

In ASP.NET 2.0, however, you only need to set the `culture` and `uiCulture` attributes of the `web.config` file's `<globalization>` element to `"auto"`, so that the user's favorite language will be retrieved and used automatically:

```
<configuration>
    <system.web>
        <globalization culture="auto" uiCulture="auto" />
        ...
    </system.web>
</configuration>
```

You can also specify these setting at the page-level, with the `Culture` and `UICulture` attributes of the `@Page` directive:

```
<%@ Page Culture="auto" UICulture="auto" ... %>
```

Figure 11-9 shows what the same page looks like when loaded for the American English or Italian language selected in the browser.

The `"auto"` setting only saves a few lines of code, but it's nice to have. In many situations, however, you'll prefer to set the culture by yourself anyway, because you'll need to extract the current culture from the user's profile, a session variable, or according to some other logic (I mentioned earlier that it's a good idea to let users specify their language of choice). If that's the case, the preceding code showing how to handle the application's `BeginRequest` is still valid, but you may actually prefer handling the application's `PostAcquireRequestState` event, so that the profile and session variables have been initialized already with the proper values. An even better solution is to override the page's new `InitializeCulture` method, to programmatically set the page's `Culture` and `UICulture` properties to the culture string (and not to a `CultureInfo` object as you do with the `Thread` properties). Here's an example:

```
protected override void InitializeCulture()
{
    string culture = Helpers.GetCurrentCulture();
    this.Culture = culture;
    this.UICulture = culture;
}
```

Figure 11-9

`Helpers.GetCurrentCulture` is a custom function that would return something like "en-US" or "it-IT" after reading the desired current culture from somewhere. In the "Solution" section, we'll read the culture from the user's profile, and override this method in the custom `BasePage` class, so that all pages inherit this behavior without the need to replicate the code more than once.

> **The Generate Local Resource command automatically sets the** `Culture` **and** `UICulture` **attributes of the** `@Page` **directive to** `auto`**. If you use one of the application's events in the** `Global.asax` **file to programmatically set the current culture, you must remember to remove those attributes from the** `@Page` **directive after running the command on** `.aspx` **pages; otherwise, the automatic settings will override what you do by hand, because the page is parsed after the** `global.asax` **events you would typically use. (There is no such problem when generating localization resources for user controls, though, because the** `@Control` **directive doesn't have those page-level attributes, of course.) If you follow the approach of overriding the page's** `InitializeCulture` **event this isn't important, because this method is raised after the page is parsed, so your code will override the culture set by the framework, as desired.**

Solution

As a sample implementation for this chapter, I fully localized the command layout stored in the `template.master` file, and most of the user controls, especially those that are part of the site's common structure, such as `NewsletterBox`, `PollBox`, `ShoppingCartBox`, `ThemeSelector`, `WelcomeBox`, and `PersonalizationManager`. To do this, you start by editing the `template.master` file and wrapping the static text you want to localize (such as the copyright notices, or the acknowledgments to Template Monster for providing the sample layout) into `Localize` controls. Then, from the Design View, you execute the Generate Local Resource command for the master page, thus creating a `Template.master.resx` file under the root `App_LocalResources` special folder. You copy this file into the same folder, rename it to `Template.master.it-IT.resx` (for Italian), open it in Visual Studio's resource editor, and translate all string values to the destination language. Figure 11-10 is a screenshot of the resource file for Italian opened in the editor.

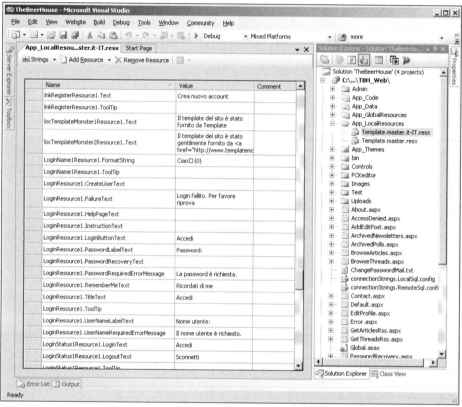

Figure 11-10

Then you follow the exact same process for the controls mentioned above, which will produce a number of resource files under `/Controls/App_LocalResources`, as shown in Figure 11-11.

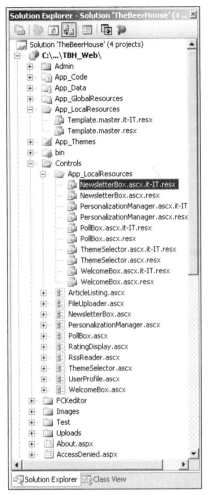

Figure 11-11

Yet another thing you want to localize is the `Web.sitemap` file. There isn't a command that localizes this automatically for you, however, so you must manually create global resource files for it, named `SiteMap.resx` and `SiteMap.it-IT.resx`, and located under the root `App_GlobalResources` folder. You create a key-value pair for each link defined in the site map, and translate them to the other language. At this point, the Solution Explorer and the resource file for the localized site map look like what is shown in Figure 11-12.

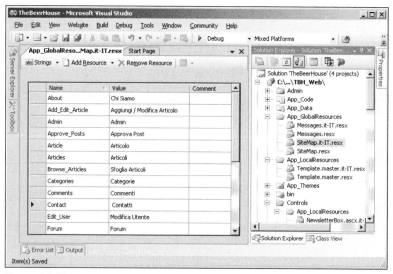

Figure 11-12

You then modify the original Web.sitemap file, by replacing the value of the title attribute with a localization expression referencing the proper key in the shared SiteMap resource file. Here is partial content of the modified file:

```
<siteMap xmlns="http://schemas.microsoft.com/AspNet/SiteMap-File-1.0"
    enableLocalization="true" >

    <siteMapNode title="$Resources: SiteMap, Home" url="~/Default.aspx">
        <siteMapNode title="$Resources: SiteMap, Articles"
            url="~/ShowCategories.aspx">
            <siteMapNode title="$Resources: SiteMap, Browse_Articles"
                url="~/BrowseArticles.aspx">
                <siteMapNode title="$Resources: SiteMap, Article"
                    url="~/ShowArticle.aspx" />
            </siteMapNode>
        </siteMapNode>
        <!-- more nodes here... -->
    </siteMapNode>
</siteMap>
```

Finally, you override the InitializeCulture method in the custom BasePage class, from which all your pages inherit, and set the page's Culture and UICulture properties to the Preferences.Culture profile property:

```
public class BasePage : System.Web.UI.Page
{
    protected override void InitializeCulture()
    {
        string culture =
            (HttpContext.Current.Profile as ProfileCommon).Preferences.Culture;
```

```
        this.Culture = culture;
        this.UICulture = culture;
    }

    // the rest of the class here...
}
```

Recall that in Chapter 4, this `profile` property was made accessible for anonymous users also, with a default value of `"en-US"`, so you don't need to verify that the current user is authenticated to safely read this property. You're now ready to test the localized home page: Run the site and log in with your test user, go to your profile page, switch the language to Italian (or to whatever language you've added support for) and return to the home page to see how it is translated. Figure 11-13 shows the home page fully translated to Italian, except for the dynamic data stored in the database, of course (such as poll questions and options, and forum thread and article titles).

Figure 11-13

If you intend to fully localize all the pages of the site, you'll find some hard-coded strings in a few .cs code-behind files. To localize them you can add resource strings into the `Messages.resx` and `Messages.it-IT.resx` global resource files created earlier as a test in the "Design" section, and replace the hard-coded strings with something like `Resources.Messages.ResourceKeyName`, as described earlier.

Summary

This chapter described the new localization features of ASP.NET 2.0. Automatic resource generation, implicit and explicit localization expressions, strongly typed, dynamically compiled global resources, and good Visual Studio designer support can all greatly speed up the implementation of localization support in your web site. The "Solution" section of this chapter was fairly short because you only need to follow a few simple steps, repeating them for all the pages you want to localize. It only took me a couple of hours to fully localize the site's common layout and the home page. I know from personal experience that this would have taken much longer with the previous version of ASP.NET and, of course, infinitely longer with even older technologies. If this power and flexibility still isn't enough for your needs, I invite you to go deeper and study the provider model for localization, which enables you to store and retrieve resources to and from any data store you prefer.

Now that the site is 100% feature complete, you can start thinking about its packing, distribution, and publication to the Internet for global usage. The next chapter shows you how to deploy the site to both a shared hosted server and a dedicated server under your control, and how to create redistributable installers for packaged applications.

12

Deploying the Site

You've come to the end of the development: Your site is ready, you've tested it locally and it all works fine, and now you have to publish it online. If you've ever had any experience with older legacy ASP/COM applications, and later with ASP.NET 1.x applications, you already know that .NET made deployment much easier: You no longer had any COM components to register, or shared components that might overwrite an existing version and thus break other applications. For pure ASP.NET applications it may suffice to do an XCOPY of all your deployment-related files (such as .aspx, .dll, .config, and image files) to the remote server, and then deploy the database. However, in the real world, things usually tend to get a little more complex than that because you have constraints and company policies to respect regarding the deployment of your application. Database deployment and configuration are also nontrivial, and you should consider this carefully before you start rolling out the site. In this final chapter, I will guide you through all of the different options to successfully deploy your web site's files and the database, explaining why and when some techniques are more suitable than another.

Problem

The problem described and solved here was a real problem that I faced while completing the sample site. I wanted to put the site online somewhere so that potential readers could browse it and consider whether it was worth the purchase, and so that I could show it to clients and colleagues during presentations about ASP.NET 2.0.

Not having a private dedicated server connected to the Internet available for this project, I chose to deploy the site to a typical shared web hosting service that uses servers running Windows Server 2003 and supports ASP.NET 2.0 and SQL Server 2005. Most of these Microsoft-centric web hosting companies now support this platform, and several of them offer plans that cost as little as $10 per month. When evaluating hosting service companies, you need to ensure that they offer you enough disk space and bandwidth, and that you factor in the cost of SQL Server 2005 (some companies charge extra for this). Of course, your specific hosting requirements may vary according to the type of project you're working on. For high-usage sites, or large-size sites, or just sites that require high availability, you'll want dedicated servers configured as a web farm (whereby a number of servers are running the same applications and load-balancing is used to determine which server will process a specific web request). Also consider that our sample web site is 100% pure ASP.NET 2.0, with no legacy COM components, COM+ services, or Windows services: These things would require special installation and are usually not allowed by basic low-cost hosting plans. In our case we don't need the benefits of a dedicated server or web farm, so a shared hosting plan is fine. For the situation just described, the problem statements are pretty simple to formulate:

- ❏ What files do I need to deploy?
- ❏ How do I deploy those files?
- ❏ How can I protect my source code against prying eyes, once the web site has been published on a shared remote server?
- ❏ How do I move my local SQL Server Express database into a full SQL Server 2005 database (when SQL Server Express has been used to develop the site)?
- ❏ How do I create an installer that automates the whole site's setup, which would be useful if I sold the web site as a product, or if I wish to deploy to a dedicated web server?

In the following pages you'll find answers for all of these questions.

Design

The complete deployment is basically split into two parts: deploying the database and deploying the site's files. If your web server supports SQL Server Express (only recommended for small workgroups), deploying the database is as simple as copying the contents of the App_Data folder to the remote server's App_Data folder, and the .mdf and .ldf files will automatically be attached to the remote SQL Server Express that is installed on the web server! However, production deployment normally requires a full-featured SQL Server 2005 (not the Express edition), for security, performance, and scalability reasons. Because of this, you need to find some way to turn the current SQL Server Express database into a SQL Server 2005 database. As for the site's files, you have different options here, as you'll see shortly.

One important point to consider is the fact that we did all our development using the VS2005's integrated web server (ASP.NET Development Server, based on Cassini) and not IIS. The integrated web server is fine for local testing but your site must be tested on IIS before deploying to a production server. Therefore, before deploying the site to the remote server you'll first test it on a local installation under IIS, replicating the configuration you have on the production server as much as possible. This will be a test of your deployment procedures and configuration, in addition to the obvious test of your code and pages. The following sections provide a detailed tutorial of the steps to take for a complete local deployment of the database and the application, and later you can follow the same steps for production deployment.

Deploying the Database to SQL Server 2005

When using a shared hosting service, you will typically have an empty database on a shared SQL Server 2005 database which you can access remotely through the SQL Server Management Studio (SSMS) desktop application (the new replacement for both Enterprise Manager and Query Analyzer), or with an online web front-end provided by the hoster. However, they usually don't give you the access rights to upload an .MDF file and attach it by running the `sp_attach_db` stored procedure (which was introduced in Chapter 3), because that would require administrative rights, and nor do you have permission to restore a database from backup files generated on your local server. Your hosting company's support staff may do this for you if you make a special request, but they may not. However, most hosting companies have some kind of web application that lets you run queries and SQL scripts on your remote database; and as mentioned earlier, they do allow you to connect remotely with SSMS (SSMS is usually better than the hosting company's web application).

When deploying to a particular server under your control (as opposed to a shared hosting company server), you can just create a new database on the server, and then create a new login and give that login permissions in your new database. This is *not* an end-user account; it's the account that our web site will use to access the database. The following SQL commands will do this (please select a good password in place of 'password'):

```
USE Master
GO
CREATE DATABASE TheBeerHouse
GO
USE TheBeerHouse
GO
EXEC sp_addlogin 'BeerHouseUser', 'password', 'TheBeerHouse'
EXEC sp_grantdbaccess 'BeerHouseUser', 'BeerHouseUser'
EXEC sp_addrolemember 'db_owner', 'BeerHouseUser'
EXEC sp_addrolemember 'db_datareader', 'BeerHouseUser'
EXEC sp_addrolemember 'db_datawriter', 'BeerHouseUser'
GO
```

To set up a remote database just like your local database, you need to create all its objects: tables, stored procedures, views, triggers, indexes, constraints, roles, etc. In addition to your own objects, you also have to re-create all the objects required by the SQL Server providers used by ASP.NET for features such as membership, profiling, personalization, and web events.

There are many ways to create all the database objects in a new remote database, but the following are among the best options (only the first option is covered in detail due to space constraints):

1. Make SQL scripts from your development server and execute those scripts on the new server (the code download for this book has SQL scripts, or you can make them yourself).

2. Use SQL Server Management Studio (SSMS) to copy the whole database from your local development database directly to the new server.

3. Copy your .mdf (database file) and .ldf (log file) from your local computer to the remote computer, and attach them to the remote instance of SQL Server.

4. Use SSMS or SQL commands to create a backup of your local database to a file, and restore from the file on the new server.

5. Use the new SQL Server Integration Services, which is a powerful and flexible replacement for the older DTS services.

6. Write your own data migration program using the SQL Server Management Objects (SMO), which is a new set of classes that enable you to manipulate SQL objects from a .NET program (SMO replaces the older SQL-DMO COM objects).

Option 2 is the easiest, but it requires you to have administrator access on both computers (not possible for a shared hosting deployment). In fact, options 2, 3, and 4 are normally not available for shared hosted sites, and options 5 and 6 may not be available in some shared hosting environments. This leaves option 1 as the most portable option that will always work for every situation. The only problem with option 1 is that you can't script data for image columns (used in the `aspnet_profile` table), so you need an alternate way to populate the data once the objects have been created.

Most of the aforementioned options are easiest to implement using SQL Server Management Studio (SSMS) on your local development computer, where both the local and remote databases are registered in the configuration. Many people using Visual Studio 2005 only have the Express edition of SQL Server 2005 on their own computer, and SSMS doesn't come with this edition. Fortunately, Microsoft does have a free version of SSMS for use with the Express edition: search the MSDN web site for the newest version of SQL Server Management Studio Express. Either edition of SSMS (full or express) can be used for this purpose. Due to space constraints here, I can't cover SSMS in detail, but I'll walk you through some of its most useful features that are helpful for deployment.

Create the Standard ASP.NET Objects

There's a convenient shortcut for creating the ASP.NET required objects (for profiles, membership, etc.): If you remember from Chapter 3, all those objects can be created by executing the `aspnet_regsql` command-line tool and specifying the target server and database. Of course, this requires that you can access the remote SQL Server over the Internet (i.e., you can connect to it from your desktop and not only from the web server running your site). This is the syntax you can use to install the ASP.NET 2.0 tables on a remote server at a specified IP address:

> aspnet_regsql.exe -U username -P password -S 111.222.333.444 -d DBname –A all

An alternative, in case you can't access your remote database this way, is to use the hoster's database manager (or SSMS) to manually run a set of SQL scripts to create those objects. Microsoft has provided these scripts under the `C:\WINDOWS\Microsoft.NET\Framework\v2.0.50727` folder. These script files must be run in the following order:

- ❏ InstallCommon.sql
- ❏ InstallMembership.sql
- ❏ InstallPersonalization.sql
- ❏ InstallProfile.sql
- ❏ InstallRoles.sql
- ❏ InstallWebEventSqlProvider.sql

> **Important! All of these scripts reference a database named** `aspnedb`. **Your database is probably named differently, so you'll need to edit the scripts to specify the name of your database (you should make copies and only edit the copies, of course).**

As you can see, it's very easy to create the standard objects, but you normally don't have to do this as a separate step. Instead, you can just script these objects along with your own objects, as you'll see in the following section.

Script All Your Database Objects

You can generate SQL CREATE scripts from your local development database, and then execute them on the remote database server.

Although Visual Studio 2005 is not quite as good as SSMS when it comes to generating scripts, it can be used for this. Using Visual Studio 2005, you can add a Database Project to your solution (select File ⇨ Add ⇨ New Project and then select Other Project Types ⇨ Database ⇨ Database Project) and then script objects one by one by browsing the local database on Visual Studio's Server Explorer window and clicking the Generate Create Script to Project command from the object's context menu (see Figure 12-1).

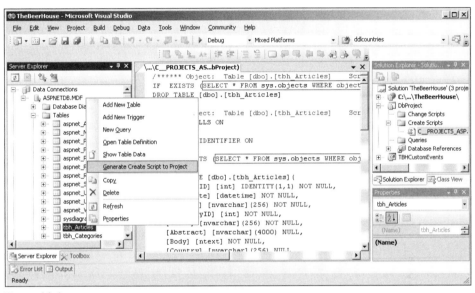

Figure 12-1

Although this method of creating SQL scripts works fine, it's not the most convenient approach because you have to generate scripts one object at a time, into separate files, and then merge everything together.

It's easier to generate one script that contains all the objects using SSMS. If you loaded the .MDF data file on your computer but haven't attached it to the local database yet, you can do this by means of the Attach... command from the Databases item's context menu (see Figure 12-2).

From the dialog box that pops up you select the .MDF file to attach and the name you want to give it in the SQL Server 2005 instance. For example, in Figure 12-3 the ASPNETDB.MDF file is being named after TheBeerHouse.

If you receive an error when attaching the file from SQL Server 2005's dialog box, ensure that it is not being used by some other process, and is not already attached to Visual Studio's Server Explorer tool. In the former case, just stop the guilty process; in the latter case, simply detach the file by means of the Detach comment, reachable from the database file's context menu.

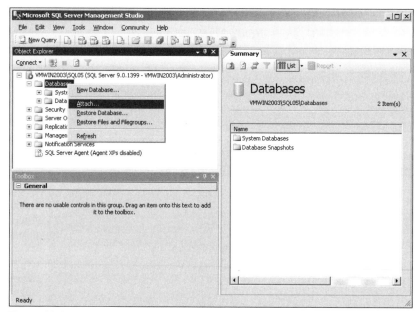

Figure 12-2

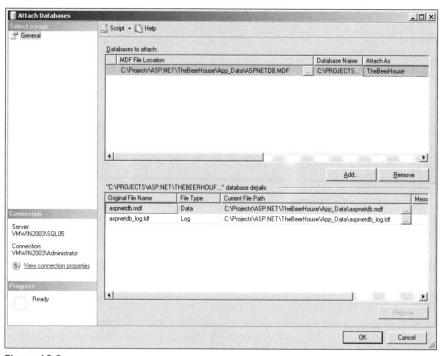

Figure 12-3

Once the database is attached to your local database, you can launch the Script Wizard by selecting the database from the Explorer window, and then clicking Tasks ➪ Generate Scripts... from the context menu (see Figure 12-4).

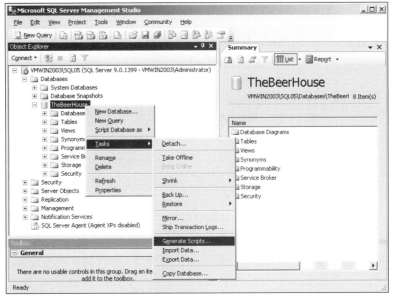

Figure 12-4

In a single step you can choose to script all tables, stored procedures, user-defined functions, roles, and views, and you have many more options to optionally script primary and foreign keys, check constraints, triggers, indexes, and so on (see Figure 12-5). This includes all the objects required by the ASP.NET features and providers, so if you follow this approach there will be no need to execute the individual scripts previously listed.

Once you have generated the script to create all the objects, you can execute the script on your new database to recreate the whole schema. This can be done with SSMS, or any other tool that lets you execute SQL commands on your new database. First, you have to register your remote database in SSMS (select View ⇨ Registered Servers, and then right-click in that window to add a new registered server). Then do a File ⇨ Open on your creation script, and have it connect to the remote server (make sure your database is selected in the drop-down list in the toolbar area), and run your creation script by pressing Execute or using the F5 shortcut key (see Figure 12-6).

Importing Existing Data

The script we created and executed created the objects but didn't populate the tables with data. While developing the site on your local computer, you created quite a lot of data to define article categories, forums, polls, products, users, and so on, and you'll want to import all that information into the new database instead of recreating it from scratch. You might think that you could generate a script with INSERT statements for all the records from all your tables, and then execute it on the new database. However, neither Visual Studio's Server Explorer, nor your local installation of SSMS have the ability to create SQL INSERT scripts for your data, and you may end up coding the statements manually. If you only need to script a few dozen records, writing statements by hand may be feasible, but if you have to generate hundreds or thousands of INSERT statements for any table, then you will want to look at one of the many third-party tools that can automatically generate the script for you.

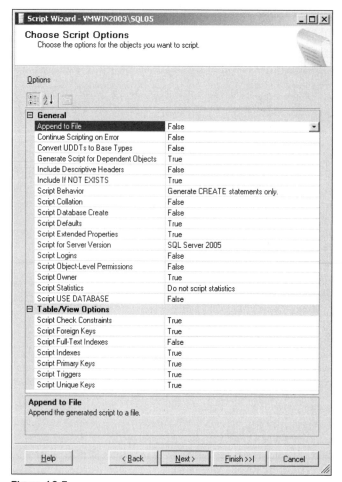

Figure 12-5

If you can connect to both the local and remote database by means of SQL Server Management Studio (SSMS) things are much easier. When you use the tool's Import Data feature, it allows you to choose all tables, but you can't select the order in which they will be imported, and you'll get many import errors if the tool tries to insert data into a detail table that has a foreign key to a master table for which the data hasn't been imported yet. To solve the problem, you need to temporarily disable the referential integrity checks during the import, so that the tool can insert data into a table even if the records reference other records that are not present in the master table yet. To do this you use the ALTER TABLE <tablename> NOCHECK CONSTRAINT ALL statement for every table, as follows:

```
ALTER TABLE tbh_Articles NOCHECK CONSTRAINT ALL
ALTER TABLE tbh_Categories NOCHECK CONSTRAINT ALL
ALTER TABLE tbh_Comments NOCHECK CONSTRAINT ALL
...do the same for all other tables required by ASP.NET and your application
```

After disabling constraints, select the target database in which you want to import the data (this may be a local database or a database on the remote server) in the Object Explorer, and select Tasks ➪ Import Data... from its context menu (see Figure 12-7) to open the Import and Export Wizard.

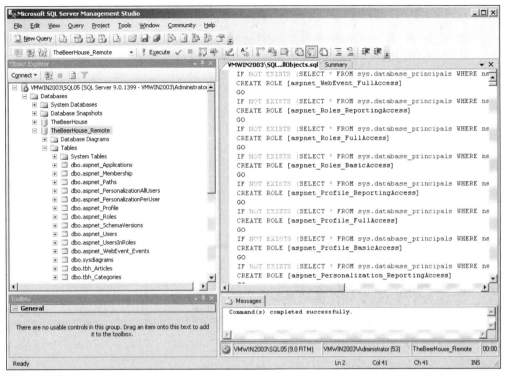

Figure 12-6

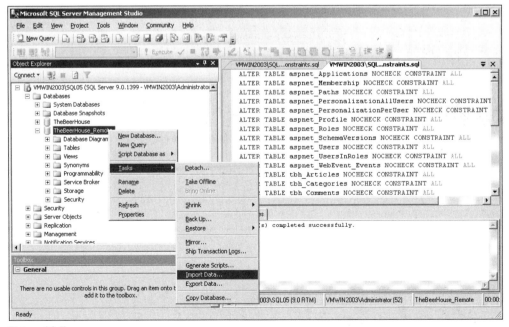

Figure 12-7

In the first wizard step you select the source database, which will be the TheBeerHouse database attached to the .MDF SQL Server Express file (see Figure 12-8).

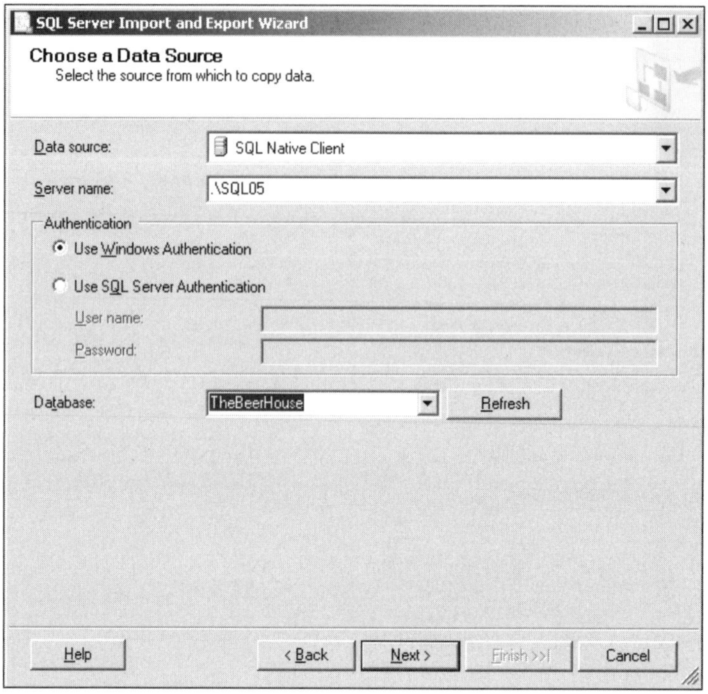

Figure 12-8

In the second step you choose the destination database, which will already be selected. If you're targeting a remote database (not on your own computer), you probably also need to modify the options to choose SQL Server Authentication, and your credentials to connect to it. In the next step you select all the tables you want to import, which will be all tables starting with aspnet_ and tbh_ (see Figure 12-9).

You could omit the following tables if you prefer: sysdiagrams and aspnet_WebEventEvents. Also, make sure you do not select the objects beginning with vw_aspnet, as these are views that don't contain their own data in reality. Before proceeding to the next step you must go into the import options of each selected table, by clicking the Edit... button on the right side of the grid listing the objects. Select the Enable Identity Insert option (see Figure 12-10) to ensure that records are imported with their original identity values (for columns such as ApplicationID, CategoryID, ArticleID, PollID, etc.). This is necessary so inserted rows will respect the referential integrity (other tables have foreign keys that reference the specific values in these identity columns, so we have to insert the original values instead of letting it assign new values). You might think it's a good idea to select Delete Rows in Destination Table so that you won't get duplicate key errors if you're re-importing the data. This won't work, however, because it will try to use truncate statements that don't work on any table that has foreign keys (even if the constraints are off). So you need to use a script to delete all rows first if you want to re-import data, rather than use this checkbox.

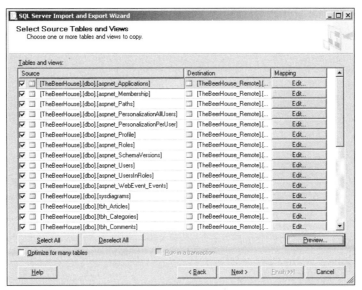

Figure 12-9

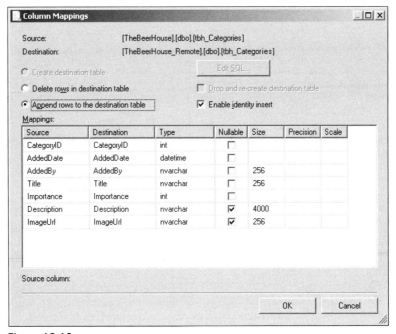

Figure 12-10

Complete the wizard and check the box that lets you save the SSIS package, and check File System. When you see the Package Protection dialog, select "Encrypt all data with password" and specify a password. Select a filename for this package and run the actual process; it will import all rows as specified.

Save the SSIS package in a file so you can easily rerun this import in the future without having to do all the setup steps again (just double-click on that file). However, be careful because you have to empty your tables before doing this and you don't want to do this once you have real users in a production environment! Figure 12-11 shows the screen providing feedback about the process, with the number of rows successfully imported for each table.

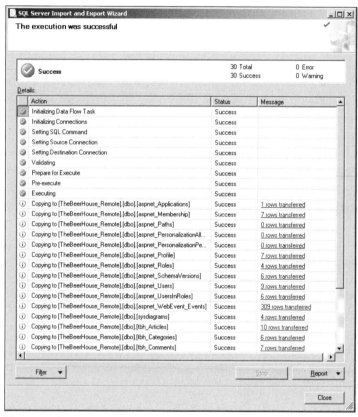

Figure 12-11

The last thing to do is re-enable the constraints we previously disabled, by running the following statements on the remote database, from a Query window:

```
ALTER TABLE tbh_Articles CHECK CONSTRAINT ALL
ALTER TABLE tbh_Categories CHECK CONSTRAINT ALL
ALTER TABLE tbh_Comments CHECK CONSTRAINT ALL
...do the same for all other tables required by ASP.NET and custom features
```

The entire import takes a couple of minutes to complete, and you end up with a perfect replication of the local SQL Server database.

When you're done, remember to detach the original SQL Server Express .MDF file used as a source; otherwise, you will no longer be able to open it from Visual Studio and run the site against it. This is not a concern if you used a full edition of SQL Server 2005 on your development computer.

Pointing the Providers to the SQL Server 2005 Database

Now you can change the connection string used by all ASP.NET providers, and by our own custom modules, so that it no longer points to the local SQL Server Express database file, but instead points to the remote database. The updated `web.config` file will then contain something similar to the following (the connection string has to be on one line; it had to be split for this book, but the provider name can be on the next line):

```
<connectionStrings>
   <remove name="LocalSqlServer"/>
   <add name="LocalSqlServer"
    connectionString="server=111.222.333.444;
Initial Catalog=DBname;uid=username;pwd=password"
      providerName="System.Data.SqlClient"/>
</connectionStrings>
```

Deploying the Site

There are three main methods to deploy the site's files:

❑ You can simply copy all files to the remote hosting space, including .aspx and .ascx files, .cs source code files, etc. Visual Studio 2005 includes a tool that allows you to copy the web project's file to another directory on the local machine, to a UNC path, to an IIS virtual application, or to a remote FTP site. This is the simplest option, but it's sometimes not desirable because your source code files will be copied as is, in "clear-text" format on the server, and many developers don't like this. As long as you deploy the site on your own in-house server that's fine, of course, but as soon as you need to deploy on a shared hosting space you'll probably want to pre-compile the source code so that you protect it (at least a bit, as it can always be decompiled if one really wants to see your code) from prying eyes.

Even if your source code files are deployed to the server, they still cannot be downloaded by users due to the IIS settings, but it's probably best not to have them on the server at all.

❑ In addition to pre-compiling the site's source code files (the .cs files), you can also pre-compile the files containing the markup code (such as .aspx and .ascx files). Then, you'll only deploy the compiler-generated .dll assemblies, plus the .aspx/.ascx files as usual. However, because you pre-compiled the markup files, their content was stripped out by the compilation process, and they now only contain a placeholder string. For the actual deployment you can use an FTP client to copy the pre-compiled files to the server. In addition to offering better protection of your code, you're also making it harder for anyone to change your site's UI: This is particularly important if you sell the site as a packaged product and you put copyright notices and logos on the pages, and you don't want your client to remove or change them. Another advantage is that your code won't have to be compiled the first time a user accesses the site (but there will still be a JIT compile to go from IL to native code), which leads to slightly better performance the first time your site is accessed after deployment, or after IIS recycles the application.

❑   You can generate an installer program that takes care of the complete setup of the web application, including extracting the site's files from CAB files, copying them to a folder selected by the user, creating a virtual directory/IIS application on the destination server, executing SQL scripts to create and pre-fill the database, and more. This option is particularly attractive to those of you who are developing a site that will be sold as a packaged application. In that case, it's standard to give users an installer program that takes care of the application's setup as much as possible. Note, however, that this approach isn't always useful because the user must have administrative rights on the destination server to install the site, and he needs to launch your installer program directly on the server itself. Therefore, this is not viable if you're targeting a shared hosting space. You can, however, create the installer anyway, so that clients will have the option to use it if they decide to deploy to their own server, or they can use FTP to deploy the site to a shared hosting service.

The following sections explore these options in more detail.

Copying the Site Locally or Remotely

One of the problems that developers need to be aware of when developing web sites with Visual Studio 2005 is that the built-in web server is not equivalent to IIS. It's normally very good, but you need to be aware that your web site may function differently in some ways when deployed to a real IIS server. For this reason you should always deploy your site to IIS and test it before deploying it to a production server. To demonstrate the new Visual Studio Copy Web Site built-in tool, I'll show you how to copy the site to an IIS application, so that you can test the site on a real web server. *Only professional and server versions of Windows have IIS*, and even then it's not installed by default. If you have a home version of Windows you'll have to deploy to a different system that has IIS installed. First create a virtual folder/IIS application from the IIS Administration console, as shown in Figure 12-12.

> *Note that I've created the application under a site named WroxServer because on my local machine the Default Web Site is taken by Windows SharePoint Server. Pro versions of windows only allow IIS to have the Default Web Site, but server versions allow multiple web sites to be defined.*

Ensure that ASP.NET version 2.0 is selected in the ASP.NET tab of the folder's Properties window: It is normally set to version 1.1 by default if the computer has both versions. Then, from Visual Studio 2005, click the Copy Web Site... item from the IDE's Website menu. First you must connect to the destination, which can be a normal folder, an IIS/HTTP site, or an FTP site. In Figure 12-13, I'm connecting to the TheBeerHouse application folder (created above) on my local IIS server.

The tool's user interface is simple: Once you select the destination, you can choose to copy everything from the source (the local copy of the site's files) to the destination, to copy everything from the destination back to the source (useful when someone else has updated the site and you want to download the latest version to your computer), or to synchronize the files on the source and destination according to their date. To deploy all your files, including source code, first make sure your `web.config` file has the connection string for your remote database. Then, connect to your remote site on the right side, and then select everything on the left, except for the `App_Data` folder, and copy it to the right side. Figure 12-14 illustrates the tool after a successful complete copy.

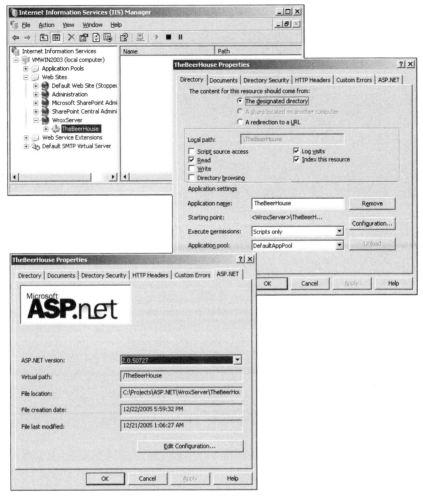

Figure 12-12

Although you can choose an FTP site as the destination for the copy, Visual Studio's Copy Web Site feature is slower than most third-party FTP clients, and it hung a few times while I was testing this feature. Because of this, I prefer using an external FTP client instead of the Copy Web Site feature when I am deploying to a remote site using FTP. Personally, I like the freeware FileZilla FTP client (http://filezilla.sourceforge.net/). However, the Copy Web Site feature works well when copying to a local folder or an IIS application.

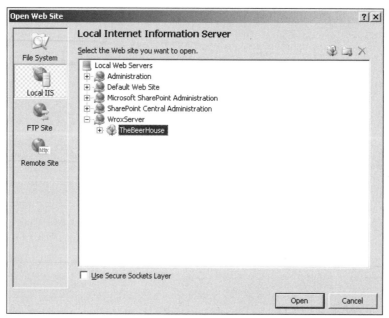

Figure 12-13

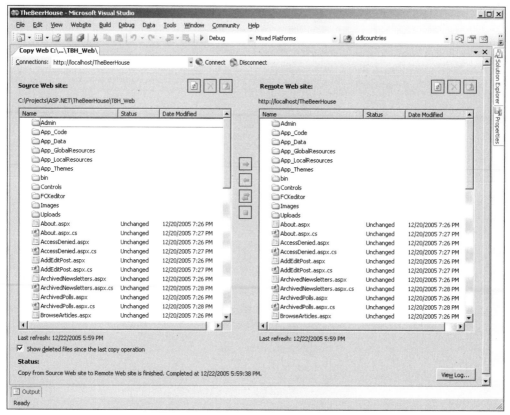

Figure 12-14

Pre-compiling the Site

If you deploy the site by copying all the files (including the source code), the pages and the source code files are compiled dynamically at runtime when they are first requested by a user. This is called *in-place compilation,* and the generated assemblies are compiled into a temporary folder. As an alternative, instead of deploying source files, you can use the `aspnet_compiler.exe` tool (located under `C:\WINDOWS\Microsoft.NET\Framework\v2.0.50727`) to pre-compile the source code files and (optionally) the markup files. This is the command you could use to pre-compile everything (this should all be entered on one line):

```
aspnet_compiler.exe -p c:\Projects\ASP.NET\TheBeerHouse\TBH_Web -v /TheBeerHouse
c:\Deployment\TheBeerHouse
```

The `-p` parameter specifies the source directory, and the `-v` parameter specifies the virtual directory used at runtime by the site. The path at the end of the command is the destination directory for the compiler output files. If you look under the `c:\Deployment\TheBeerHouse\bin` folder, you'll find multiple `.dll` assembly files, plus one `.compiled` XML file for each `.aspx` and `.ascx` file (see Figure 12-15).

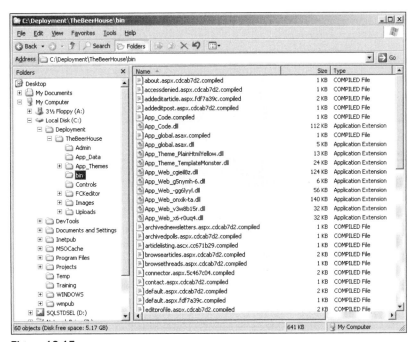

Figure 12-15

The files named with a `.compiled` extension contain XML text that shows the relationship between the virtual path of a page or user control and the corresponding type compiled into one of the assemblies. If you look into any of the .aspx files, you won't find any HTML/ASPX markup code, but rather the markup string printed below:

```
This is a marker file generated by the precompilation tool, and should not be
deleted!
```

After executing the `aspnet_compiler`, you take all the output generated by this tool and upload it to the remote server, typically via FTP. If you're deploying to a server within your network you might simply copy the files to a shared folder on that server. However, even local servers are often isolated behind a firewall, so FTP may be needed anyway.

Compiling the markup code may definitely be appealing in some circumstance, such as for packaged commercial products for which you don't want the client to change anything; however, if you're deploying to your own site this may not be particularly useful or necessary. Furthermore, it would complicate updates, because every time you need to change a line of markup you'd have to recompile everything and re-deploy the generated files. In the case of deploying to your own sites, it's simpler to pre-compile only the source code files but not the markup files. To do this, just add the -u switch (which stands for *updateable*) to the command line, as follows:

```
aspnet_compiler.exe -p c:\Projects\ASP.NET\TheBeerHouse\TBH_Web -v /TheBeerHouse -u
c:\Deployment\TheBeerHouse
```

With this command no `.compiled` files will be generated under the `/bin` folder, and the content of the `.aspx` and `.ascx` files won't be removed. However, the `CodeFile` attribute of the `@Page` and `@Control` directives will be removed, and the `Inherits` will be updated with a reference to the type compiled into one of the generated assemblies.

> **Note that all static files (images, .htm files, .css stylesheet files, etc.) are always copied "as is" to the target folder. These are never included as part of a pre-compile.**

However, there's a small deployment issue when using one of the two pre-compile commands described above: The assemblies they generate always have a different name, which makes it difficult to update the site locally and then replicate the changes remotely, because the assembly names will be different after each pre-compile. If you don't want to leave old and unused assemblies in the remote `/bin` folder, you need to delete them first and then upload all new `.dll` files. This is very annoying and time-consuming, so you can add the `-fixednames` compiler switch to cause the `aspnet_compiler` to create an assembly for each file it compiles, using a fixed name scheme. This is good because it allows you to update the site locally, recompile it, and then upload only the changed assembly file. This is the modified command line:

```
aspnet_compiler.exe -p c:\Projects\ASP.NET\TheBeerHouse\TBH_Web -v /TheBeerHouse -u
-fixednames c:\Deployment\TheBeerHouse
```

I covered the syntax of the command-line tool for completeness (and because many of you will want to script this procedure), but you don't have to remember all the various switches because Visual Studio provides a simple integrated UI for `aspnet_compiler`, which you can access by clicking Build ⇨ Publish Web Site. Figure 12-16 shows the graphical front-end that it provides, making it easy to select your options, and to select a local or remote IIS site, or an FTP site, as the destination for the operation, in addition to a local folder.

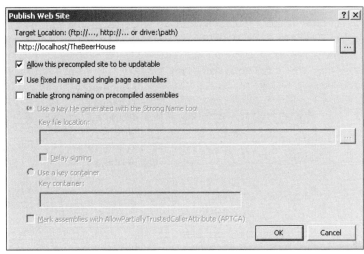

Figure 12-16

Some of you may be concerned about the large quantity of assemblies produced by the pre-compilation step. In large projects with hundreds of pages, the /bin folder will contain a lot of files, and it may be more convenient for deployment if you could combine all those .dll files into a single assembly file. There's no way to do this with the tools included in VS2005 and the standard installation of the .NET Framework 2.0, but Microsoft listened to its customers, and after releasing VS2005, they later released a free package called "Visual Studio 2005 Web Deployment Projects," which can be downloaded from http://msdn.microsoft.com/asp.net/reference/infrastructure/wdp/default.aspx. After installing the package, you'll find a new command-line tool called aspnet_merge.exe under the C:\Program Files\MSBuild\Microsoft\WebDeployment\v8.0 folder. As its name suggests, it enables you to merge the multiple assemblies generated by the aspnet_compiler tool into a single dll. When you run this program you only need to specify the path of the pre-compiled web site where it can find the assemblies you want to merge:

```
aspnet_merge.exe c:\Deployment\TheBeerHouse
```

The preceding command generates a dll for each of the web site's folders containing files that were pre-compiled by aspnet_compiler. This is useful when you have folders that include a sub-application supported by different developers (such as the administration console), and you want to have separate assemblies for separate sections so that you can update them independently on the production server. In other cases, however, you may prefer to merge everything into a single assembly: You can do so with the -o switch, which specifies the name of the assembly being generated:

```
aspnet_merge.exe c:\Deployment\TheBeerHouse -o MB.TheBeerHouse.dll
```

> Note that the tool can be used whether the aspnet_compiler.exe pre-compiled the markup code or not. But this tool never merges in any external libraries referenced by the web site's source files and pages, such as the MB.TheBeerHouse.CustomEvents.dll and the FredCK.FCKEditorV2.dll assemblies. It only merges assemblies generated by aspnet_compiler.exe.

As for `aspnet_compiler`, there's also a front-end UI for `aspnet_merge`. The Visual Studio 2005 Web Deployment Projects package is installed as an add-in for VS2005, and it adds a new project type called a "Deployment Project." You add a new deployment project to your solution by clicking the Add Web Deployment Project... option on the IDE's Build menu, or via the same option on the context menu of the web site in the Solution Explorer window. You create the project by choosing its name and location from the dialog box shown in Figure 12-17.

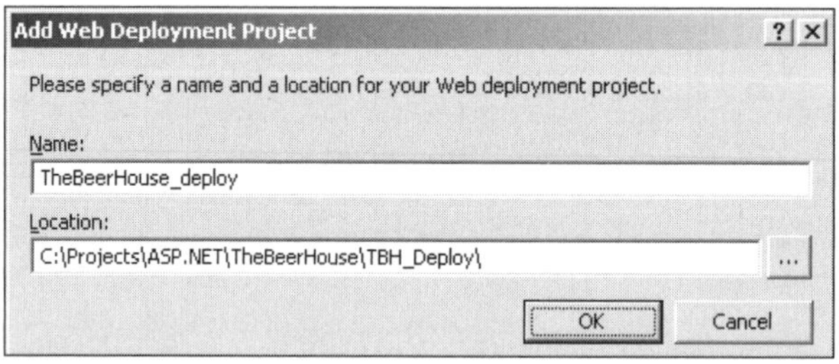

Figure 12-17

The project added to the Solution Explorer contains no files; you have to double click the project name to open its configuration dialog box, from which you can specify a number of options. Among other things, you can specify how you want the pre-compiler to work, and how you want the files merged. In the first field of the dialog box (see Figure 12-18), you specify the output folder and choose whether the user interface pages and controls should be pre-compiled (which is the updateable option, corresponding to the `-u` switch of the `aspnet_compiler.exe` tool).

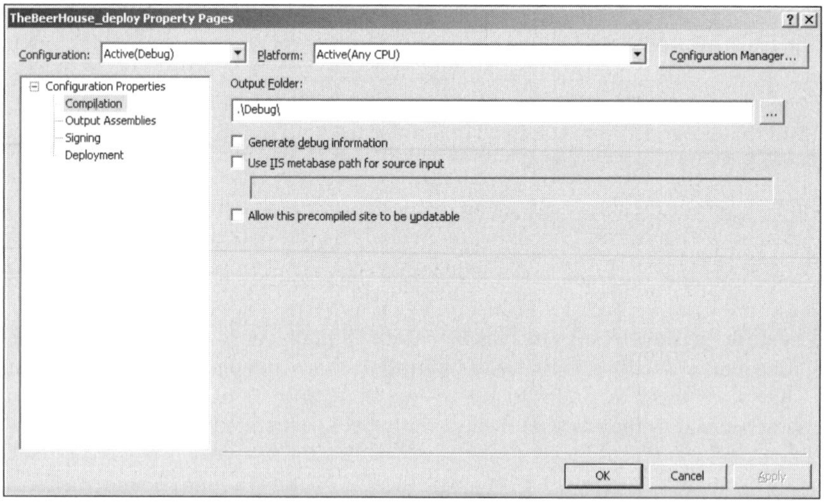

Figure 12-18

In the second tab, Output Assemblies (see Figure 12-19), you specify whether you want to compile everything into a single assembly, have an assembly for each folder, have an assembly for the user interface pages and controls, or have an assembly for each class and page being compiled (this last option means you don't want to use `aspnet_merge.exe`). From here you can also specify the version information of the generated assemblies. If this information is not provided, the settings specified in the `web.config` file located under the `/App_code` folder will be used instead (if the file is present, which is not a requirement).

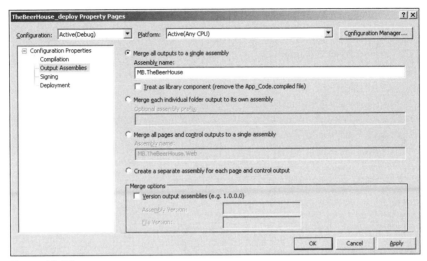

Figure 12-19

The third tab, Signing (not shown here), enables you to sign the generated assemblies with a key file generated by the `sn.exe` command-line tool, to give them a strong name. This isn't normally desired for your own sites, but may be useful when you're creating a packaged application and you want to ensure that your assemblies will not be tampered with. In the last tab, Deployment (see Figure 12-20), you can choose to replace one or more sections of the site's `web.config` file with the content from another file. For example, if you write `connectionStrings=connectionStrings.LocalSql.config`, the whole `<connectionStrings>` section will be replaced with the content of the `connectionStrings` `.LocalSql.config` file at the end of the build process. This enables you to have a connection string pointing the SQL Server Express database to be used while testing the site locally, and later have it automatically replaced with a connection string referencing a local or remote SQL Server 2005 database after building the project for deployment. You can specify additional sections to replace, one per line. You can also use this window to specify a virtual directory to be created during the build process, and whether the `App_Data` folder will be deleted from the files generated (useful when you will use a SQL Server 2005 database after the build, in which case you do not want to deploy your express files under `App_Data`).

Once you've completed the configuration, you can build the project. At the end of the build process you'll find a copy of the site with the pre-compiled and merged assemblies, plus all other files such as pages, controls, images, stylesheets, and so on in the output folder. You can then take this entire output and upload everything to the production server, typically via FTP.

Deployment projects simply consist of an XML file used to pass options to `MSBuild.exe`, the new Microsoft build tool capable of compiling and building complex projects and solutions. MSBuild is an extensible tool that uses configuration files that can contain many different options. And if an option or a task that you'd like doesn't exist yet, you can create it as a C# class, and have MSBuild call it. Many of the configuration settings described here were implemented as custom settings and tasks by the developers of the Web Deployment Projects add-in. There are many more available options in addition to those you can configure from the Properties window explored earlier, such as the option to exclude files from the build, create new folders, grant the ASP.NET account write access to a folder (only on your local machine, though — you'll still need to replicate these security settings on the remote production server), execute external programs, and much more. You can add more settings and tasks (i.e., operations to run before or after the build and the merge processes) directly from the XML configuration file, which can be opened by clicking the Open Project File option from the Web Deployment project's context menu. Covering MSBuild is beyond the scope of this book, but you can find a lot of good documentation about this on the web, and in the documents that come with the Web Deployment Projects package.

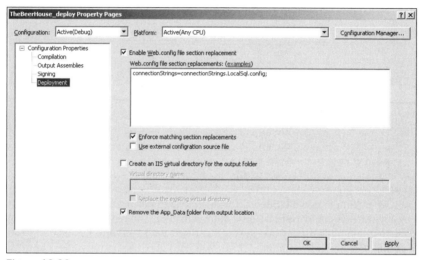

Figure 12-20

By default, all projects added to the solution are built in Visual Studio when you launch the primary project, i.e., the web site. Building the deployment project takes quite a lot of time, however, depending on the size of the site (on my machine it takes around 30 seconds to generate the pre-compiled site), and it is not something you want to do while testing the site locally. In order to avoid this waste of time, you can just exclude the project from the Debug Build from the Build ⇨ Configuration Manager... dialog box.

Creating an Installer for a Packaged Application

Creating an installer package that you can give to your clients, and that completely installs and sets up your site automatically, may be simpler than you think. In the old days, the setup programs were typically created with tools such as InstallShield or Wise Installation System, but starting with VS.NET 2003 they can be created with VS itself, thanks to the Web Setup Project types you find by selecting Other Project Types ⇨ Setup and Deployment, from the Add New Project dialog box (see Figure 12-21).

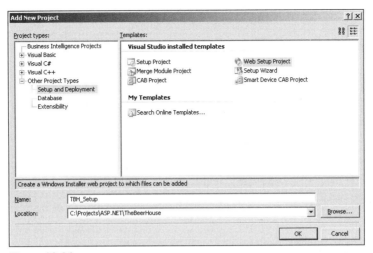

Figure 12-21

The Web Setup Project is tailor-made for creating installers for web-based applications. You add one such project to your current solution, and then you must tell it which files you want to include in the package. You could choose files one by one, but there may be thousands of files (including images and all static content files), so instead you can add the output of another project to the package (see Figure 12-22), and, in particular, the output of the Web Deployment project created earlier (see Figure 12-23). This includes everything you need (pages, controls, pre-compiled assemblies, and static content), so you shouldn't need to add anything else. If you do, however, then you could still add individual files from other sources — for example, if you wanted to include a manual that isn't among the web site's deployment-related files.

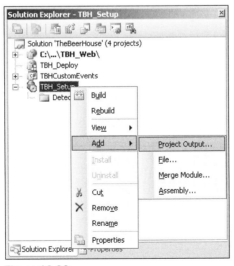

Figure 12-22

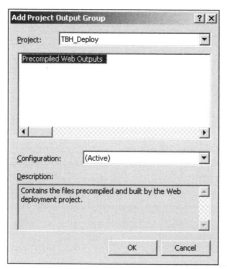

Figure 12-23

After you create the project, it pre-configures the creation of a Web Folder in the File System editor, as the destination for the installation process (see Figure 12-24): You can change its default name, the default page, application mappings, and related options that you would have manually configured from the virtual directory's Properties window in the IIS Administration console.

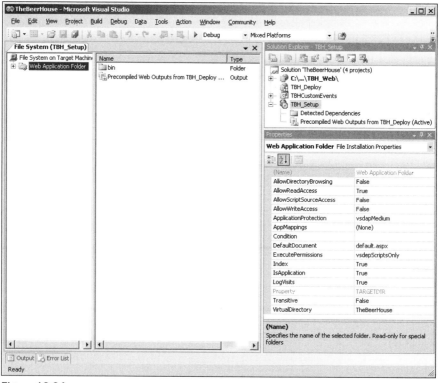

Figure 12-24

The default user interface includes steps for choosing the destination server and the folder name, and default options for the execution of the installation process. You can, however, open the User Interface editor (click the sixth icon from the left in Server Explorer's toolbar, after ensuring that the Setup project is selected) and add, remove, or modify steps. For example, you can put an image banner on them to customize their default appearance. Or, as shown in Figure 12-25, you can add a step that shows a license file, which users must agree to before proceeding.

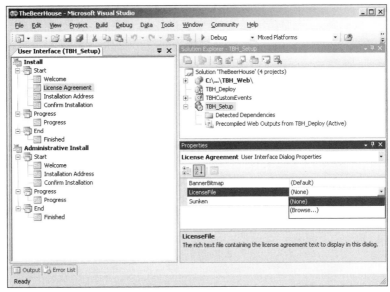

Figure 12-25

After you've configured everything, you can build the project, and you'll end up with a `setup.exe` file that launches an `.MSI` file. Figure 12-26 shows the installer at runtime, demonstrating the step where you choose the destination server and folder, and the classic progress bar.

Creating a setup program in a matter of minutes is very cool! This basic setup does quite a lot of things (it creates a destination folder, turns it into an IIS virtual application with the proper settings, and copies all the necessary files into it), but it could be further extended with custom steps and actions. For example, you could create an additional step that enables users to choose whether they want to use a SQL Server Express database or a SQL Server 2005 database; and in the latter case it could execute `.SQL` scripts to automatically create the database and the required objects. Covering these advanced topics is beyond the scope of this book, as it pertains to the Installer projects and desktop programming in general, but I wanted you to know that you can create some useful setup programs using only Visual Studio. However, in some situations where you have advanced needs, there is still some benefit to be obtained from third-party installation builders such as InstallShield and Wise.

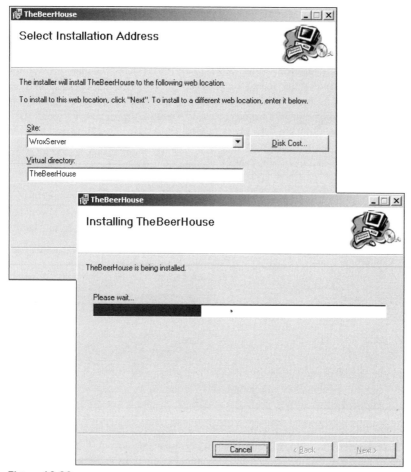

Figure 12-26

Solution

The "Solution" section of this chapter was actually merged with the "Design" section when I demonstrated how to solve the deployment problems while introducing some new ASP.NET 2.0 features, and I provided the background knowledge necessary to deploy the site. The solution I actually implemented for deploying the sample site consisted of using a Web Deployment Project to create a local pre-compiled copy of the site in an IIS virtual application, which I later deployed to the production server by means of an FTP client. I also switched from using SQL Server Express on my development computer to using the full SQL Server 2005 as my deployed target. To see my result, you can browse the sample site online by going to www.dotnet2themax.com/thebeerhouse. I also created a web installer so that I could easily redistribute the site to colleagues, friends, and other people.

Summary

In this chapter you've looked at all the options for deploying an ASP.NET 2.0 site, either on a local IIS server or to a remote production site. The new ASP.NET compilation model enables you do use a simple XCOPY deployment that includes everything but lacks protection of source code and takes a little time to compile upon the first page request. If that's a problem for you, you can use the command-line tools and the Visual Studio wizards to pre-compile the site and generate one or more assemblies to deploy. Different options for different needs: This new model is very flexible, and everyone will find something they like! This brings us to the end of our journey. I hope you like what you have read, and I wish you happy coding!

Index

Index

SYMBOLS AND NUMERICS

A

Form Maximizer.NET

Form Maximizer.NET is an innovative component library that extends standard Windows Forms controls with 35 new design-time properties and enables you to enhance existing applications **without replacing any existing control or writing a single line of code**. Here's a partial list of what Form Maximizer .NET enables you to do:

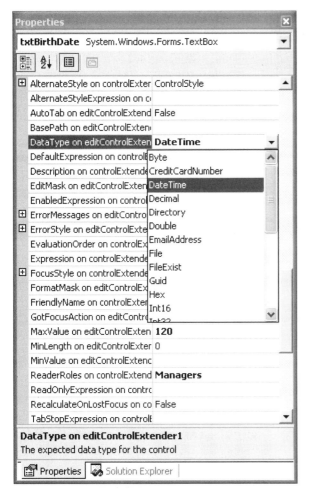

Validate user input: Force a specific data type, a valid range, a validation regex; or specify a custom expression that references other controls, form variables, and methods.

Define the state of a control: Decide when a control becomes visible, enabled, or read-only, depending on the value of other fields or the user's role.

Create calculated fields: Enter an expression in the Properties window and have the field automatically recalculated when other fields on the form change.

Change field appearance: Change the appearance of fields when they receive the input focus, fail to validate, or meet custom condition (e.g., negative numbers, empty fields).

Format data: Automatically format numbers and dates when the focus leaves the control.

Assign common tasks to buttons and menus: Load/save text files and images, show forms and common dialogs, launch applications without writing code.

...plus auto-tabbing, multiline tooltips, field descriptions, toolbar hotkeys, centralized events, nonrectangular forms, and more.

Form Maximizer.NET works with any .NET programming language. Full C# source code is available (in Form Maximizer .NET Enterprise Edition only).

Read more about Form Maximizer .NET and download a fully functional demo version at **www.dotnet2themax.com/formmaximizer.**

Form Maximizer.NET and CodeWall.NET have been developed and are distributed by Code Architects Srl, Italy (www.codearchitects.com), which gathers international experts such as Marco Bellinaso, Francesco Balena, and Giuseppe Dimauro.